Doing Business with
China

ContractStore now has more than 100 Legal documents online and a Chinese language website

Since ContractStore was launched in 2001, the business of the company has developed so that it now has over 100 contracts and legal documents available on its website. Sales have been made in more than 40 countries around the world and ContractStore's customer base now ranges from individuals to public companies, including many SMEs and some major law firms.

All the documents are written in clear language and the concise terms concentrate on the key commercial issues, while avoiding unnecessary 'legalese'. The contracts, which come with helpful and practical explanatory notes, can be downloaded by the purchaser on to his pc immediately after payment is cleared through the secure online system.

"I was quoted £700 by a lawyer for the same document I bought here for £50" said one customer in the UK recently. Another, in the United States, remarked "I am very happy with the contracts I've downloaded and so happy I found you!"

The extensive range of commercial and construction documents are written by English, Chinese, American and South African lawyers. A number of contracts, including the appointment of an agent, licence to manufacture goods and others intended for cross-border business, are available in a dual language - Chinese and English - version.

Last year a Chinese language website was set up which is linked to the English site and ContractStore documents can be purchased and downloaded from either the English website at –

 **www.contractstore.com** or from the Chinese language site – **www.contractstore.com.cn**

Xie Rong, a Chinese lawyer who is a member of the team based in the UK, also offers support to foreign companies wanting to do business in China as well as co-operating with Chinese lawyers to assist Chinese companies doing businesses internationally including in the UK and Europe.

合同商店网站内已有一百多份可供选择的法律文件，同时开通了中文网站

合同商店 2001 年开通以来，网上销售业务持续发展。如今网站内已有一百多份可供选择的法律文件。这些文件销售到世界四十多个国家，客户群从个人到公司到大型的律师事务所，也有许多是中小型企业。

合同商店所有的文件均使用清晰的英语，条款简明准确地阐述主要的商业要点，尽量免除使用不必要的生涩的法律词汇。购买人在支付购买款后，所购买的合同及附带的极有帮助的解释要点均可以直接下载。付款系统安全保密。

"同样的合同，一位律师给我的价格是七百英镑，我仅用了 50 英镑从你们的网上买到了"。一位英国客户如是说。另一位来自美国的客户则说"我对买到的文件十分满意，很高兴我找到了你们"。

合同商店网站中内容广泛的法律文件和合同均出自英国，中国，美国和南非的专业律师之手。其中一部分，如指定代理人合同，商品生产许可证协议等其他主要用于国际间商务的法律文件可提供双语—英文和中文文本。

合同商店的中文网站去年已经开通，与英文网站互通。购买与下载文件既可从中文网站也可从英文网站上实施。

网址：www.contractstore.com.cn   www.contractstore.com

居住在英国的中国律师谢蓉，是我们团队的一员，她可以提供协助英国公司到中国发展，同时与中国律师合作，提供中国公司到英国和欧洲国家开拓业务的支持。

Doing Business with
China

FIFTH EDITION

Consultant editors:

Jonathan Reuvid and Li Yong

Preface by:
Lord Brittan
Vice-Chairman, UBS Warburg

Forewords by:
Sir Digby Jones
Director General, Confederation of British Industry (CBI)

Shen Jueren
Honorary Chairman, China Association of International Trade,
Former Vice Minister of MOFTEC (now MOFCOM)

Published in association with:

HSBC ◆X◆
The world's local bank

GMB

First edition published in 1994 by Kogan Page Limited.
This fifth edition published in Great Britain and in the USA in 2005 by GMB Publishing Limited.

GMB Publishing Ltd
120 Pentonville Road
London N1 9JN
UK
www.globalmarketbriefings.com

Distributed by Kogan Page Ltd
120 Pentonville Road
London N1 9JN
UK

22883 Quicksilver Drive
Sterling VA 20166–2012
USA

© GMB Publishing and Contributors 2005

ISBN 1–905050–08–9

Library of Congress Cataloging-in-Publication Data

Doing business with China / consultant editors, Jonathan Reuvid and Li Yong.--
5th ed.
    p. cm.
Includes bibliographical references and index.
  ISBN 1-905050-08-9
  1. China--Economic conditions--2000- 2. China--Commercial policy. 3.China--
Foreign economic relations. 4. Business enterprises, Foreign--Government
policy--China. 5. Investments, Foreign--China. I.Reuvid, Jonathan. II. Li,
Yong.
  HC427.95.D65 2005
  658'.00951--dc22

2005017153

Typeset by Saxon Graphics Ltd, Derby
Printed and bound in Great Britain by Biddles Ltd, Kings Lynn, Norfolk

ADAMAS

Avocats Associés
Attorneys-at-Law

欧
洲
阿
達
姆
斯
聯
合
律
師
事
務
所

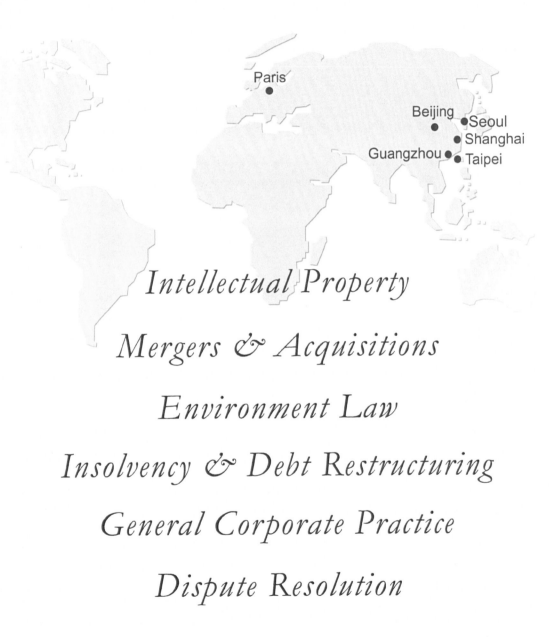

Paris

Beijing   Seoul
Shanghai
Guangzhou Taipei

Intellectual Property

Mergers & Acquisitions

Environment Law

Insolvency & Debt Restructuring

General Corporate Practice

Dispute Resolution

Beijing - Shanghai - Guangzhou - Seoul - Taipei - Paris

www.adamas.com.cn

Best Foreign Bank in China
Best Cash Management Bank in China
Best Trade Finance Bank

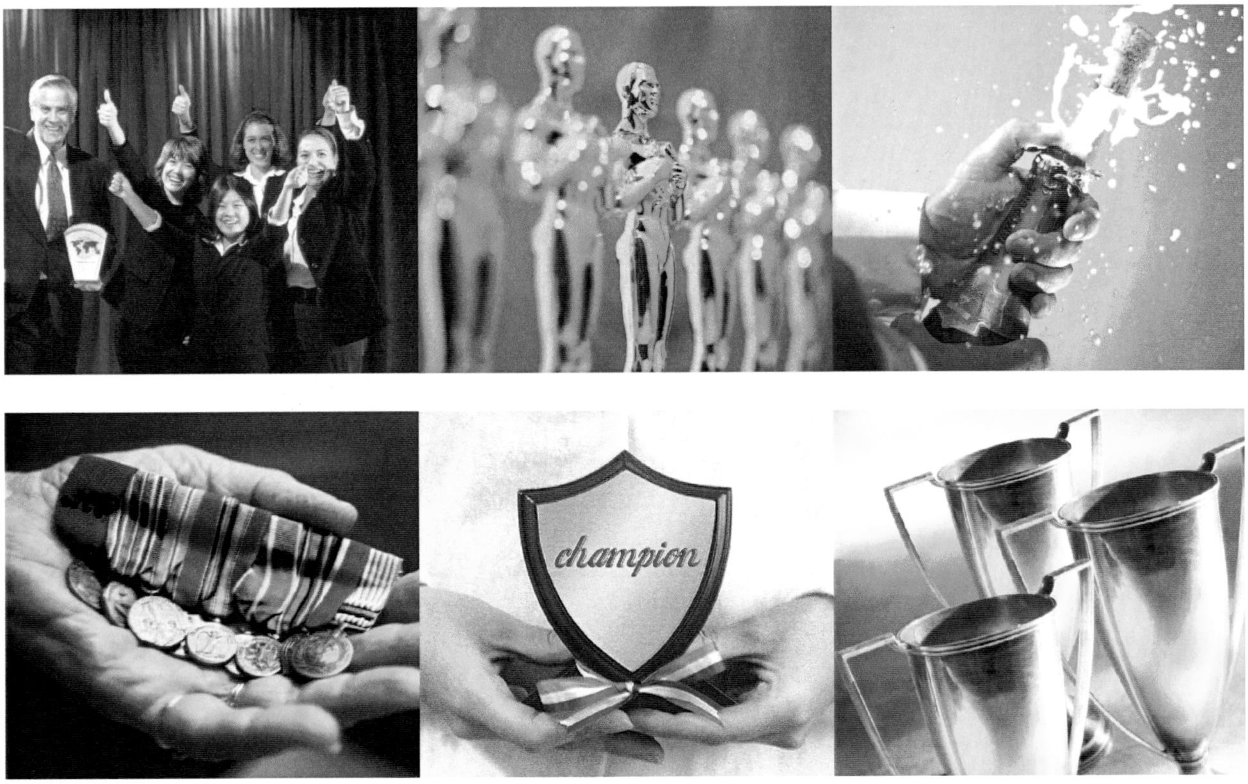
champion

No matter how many awards we win, we still strive to do better.

The recognition of our industry is vitally important to us. But we also realise that it is our hard work that forms the basis of our success in the future.

We value the many awards that we have won over the years - they remind us that the highly competitive global financial services industry demands extra efforts if we are to continue to succeed.

We always strive to do better.

FinanceAsia	**Best Foreign Bank in China, 2001-2004**
Asiamoney Poll	**Best Cash Management Bank in China, 2003-2004**
FinanceAsia	**Best Trade Finance Bank, 1997-2004**

▶ Enquiry Hotline: (86-21) 6841 1818 ▶ www.hsbc.com.cn

HSBC
The world's local bank

Contents

Preface   *Lord Brittan, Vice-Chairman, UBS Warburg*   xv

Forewords   *Sir Digby Jones, Director General, Confederation of British Industry (CBI)*   xvii

Shen Jueren, Honorary Chairman, China Association of International Trade and Former Vice Minister of MOFTEC (now MOFCOM)   xix

Introduction   *Jonathan Reuvid and Li Yong*   xxi

About the Editors   xxiv

Editorial Associates   xxv

Map   xxvi

PART ONE: CHINA'S ECONOMY AND ADMINISTRATION

1.1   **China's Economic Performance and Outlook**   3
Jonathan Reuvid

1.2   **China as a WTO Member: Systemic Issues**   10
Craig Pouncey and Lode van den Hende, Herbert Smith, Brussels

1.3   **The Chinese Government Structure**   16
Li Yong, Deputy Secretary General, China Association of International Trade

1.4   **China's Consumer Market**   26
Li Yong, Deputy Secretary General, China Association of International Trade, and Liu Baocheng, Professor, University of International Business and Economics, with updates by Jonathan Reuvid

1.5   **Developing Statistics in China**   43
Du Xishuang, Director, Senior Statistician, National Bureau of Statistics

PART TWO: CHINA WITHIN THE WTO

2.1   **The Opening up of the Chinese Market as a WTO Member**   53
Craig Pouncey and Lode van den Hende, Herbert Smith, Brussels

2.2	Foreign Trade Activity and its Administration	58

Li Yong, Deputy Secretary General, China Association of International Trade

2.3	China's Exchange Control System	65

Ma Shabo, Capital Account Administration Dept., State Administration of Foreign Exchange, and Li Yong, Deputy Secretary General, China Association of International Trade

2.4	Freight Forwarding in China	74

Liu Baocheng, Professor, University of International Business and Economics

PART THREE: LEGAL ASPECTS OF FOREIGN COMPANY OPERATIONS IN CHINA

3.1	Foreign-Invested Enterprises and Alternative Business Structures	81

Gary Lock and Brinton M Scott, Herbert Smith, Shanghai

3.2	Employment Law for Chinese and Foreign Nationals	90

Gary Lock and Brinton M Scott, Herbert Smith, Shanghai

3.3	Intellectual Property Rights in China	93

Franck Desevedavy, Adamas, China

3.4	Trademark and Patent Application and Protection in China	97

Fan Weimin, Patent Attorney, CCPIT Patent & Trademark Law Office

3.5	Environmental Due Diligence	109

Olivier Dubuis and Whui Min Chang, Attorney at Law, Adamas, China

3.6	Commercial Dispute Resolution	113

Gary Lock and Brinton M Scott, Herbert Smith, Shanghai

PART FOUR: ACCOUNTING, AUDITING AND TAXATION IN CHINA

4.1	Accounting and Auditing Requirements and Practices	119

Yvonne Kam, PricewaterhouseCoopers

4.2	Taxation Issues	123

Kelvin Lee, PricewaterhouseCoopers

4.3	Differences between the PRC Accounting Regulations and International Reporting Standards	129

Yvonne Kam, PricewaterhouseCoopers

PART FIVE: MARKET ENTRY AND BUSINESS DEVELOPMENT IN CHINA

5.1	Revisiting Chinese Cultural Roots	151

Liu Baocheng, Professor, University of International Business and Economics

5.2	Cultural Differences and Clashes in Communication	158

Li Yong, Deputy Secretary General, China Association of International Trade, and Liu Baocheng, Professor, University of International Business and Economics

5.3	Networking Practice in China	167

Wei-ping Wu, BA, MA, DPhil, MIEX, Assistant Professor, Department of Marketing and International Business, Lingnan University, Hong Kong, and Li Yong, Deputy Secretary General, China Association of International Trade

5.4   Due Diligence for Market Entrants   179
Li Yong, Deputy Secretary General, China Association of International Trade, and Jonathan Reuvid

5.5   Partner Selection and Negotiations   189
Jonathan Reuvid

5.6   Using Education and Training as a Strategic Marketing Tool in Winning International Business   198
Richard Hill, Rolls-Royce plc

5.7   Employing Staff in China   204
Li Yong, Deputy Secretary General, China Association of International Trade

5.8   Distribution in China   208
Liu Baocheng, Professor, University of International Business and Economics, with updates by Jonathan Reuvid

5.9   How the CBBC Operates   215
Humphrey Keenlyside, China Britain Business Council

PART SIX: MARKETING ISSUES IN CHINA

6.1   Industrial and Commercial Market Research   221
Li Yong, Deputy Secretary General, China Association of International Trade

6.2   Growing Consumerism Strategies for the China Market   227
T S Chan and Wei-ping Wu, Department of Marketing and International Business, Lingnan University, Hong Kong

6.3   Marketing Consumer Products in China   233
Li Yong, Deputy Secretary General, China Association of International Trade

6.4   Brand Management and Publicity   238
Li Yong, Deputy Secretary General, China Association of International Trade

6.5   Effective Public Relations   244
Li Yong, Deputy Secretary General, China Association of International Trade

PART SEVEN: BANKING, FOREIGN EXCHANGE TRANSACTIONS AND CORPORATE FINANCE

7.1   Banking Services for Foreign Invested Enterprises (FIEs)   255
HSBC

7.2   A Practical Guide to China's Currency and Payments System   260
HSBC

7.3   Import and Export Financing in China   264
Export-Import Bank of China

7.4   China's Securities Market   271
China Securities Regulatory Commission, with updates by Jonathan Reurid

7.5   Mergers and Acquisitions: Acquiring a Business in China   280
Olivier Dubuis and Whui Min Chang, Attorney at Law, Adamas, China

7.6   Mergers and Acquisitions Due Diligence   285
Olivier Dubuis and Whui Min Chang, Attorney at Law Adamas, China

7.7   Venture Capital Investment in China   290
Jonsson Yinya Li, Research Fellow of VCRC, Renmin University of China

PART EIGHT: KEY SECTOR REPORTS AND NOTES

8.1   China's Automotive Industry: Automobiles   303
Mark Norcliffe, Society of Motor Manufacturers and Traders (UK)

8.2   Automotive Components   312
Liu Baocheng, Professor, University of International Business and Economics, and Che Yanhua, Volkswagen, China, with updates by Jonathan Reuvid

8.3   China's Automotive Industry: Commercial Vehicles   322
Mark Norcliffe, Society of Motor Manufacturers and Traders (UK)

8.4   Banking: The Domestic Banks   327
Jonathan Reuvid

8.5   Banking: Foreign Bank Investment   332
Jonathan Reuvid

8.6   Computer Technology and IT   335
Jonathan Reuvid and Snapshots International

8.7   Consumables   338
Jonathan Reuvid and Snapshots International

8.8   Energy   341
Jonathan Reuvid and Snapshots International

8.9   China's Insurance Market   344
Liu Baocheng, University of International Business and Economics, with updates by Jonathan Reuvid

8.10   The Media Market   353
Jonathan Reuvid and Snapshots International

8.11   Oil and Gas   355
Jonathan Reuvid

8.12   The Petrochemical Industry   359
Li Yong, Deputy Secretary General, China Association of International Trade

8.13   Promotional Advertising   365
Li Yong, Deputy Secretary General, China Association of International Trade

8.14   Retailing   370
Li Yong, Deputy Secretary General, China Association of International Trade, and Chen Congcong, Guanghua Management School, Beijing University, with updates by Jonathan Reuvid

8.15   Steel Production and Core Minerals   377
Jonathan Reuvid

8.16   Telecommunications   380
Jonathan Reuvid and Snapshots International

8.17   Travel and Tourism   382
Jonathan Reuvid and Snapshots International

Appendices

I	Contributors Contact Details	387
II	Directory of Local Authorities of Commerce with Responsibilities for Foreign Trade and Economic Cooperation	391
III	Commercial Offices of PRC Embassies Worldwide	397

Index   411

A Sorbonne MBA@IFCM

Under the education co-operation agreement between Chinese and French governments, UIBE and FNEGE established *Sino-French School of International Management* (**IFCM**) in March, 1991. As the first Sino-foreign co-operative

MBA program in China, IFCM has received continuing support from French Ministry of Foreign Affairs, French Embassy in China, Chinese Ministry of Education, and the Degree Granting Committee of the State Council. IFCM is also

the first co-operative educational institution that was approved and recognized by Chinese Ministry of Education 13 years ago.

Situated on the campus of UIBE, IFCM has graduated more than 500 students. With knowledge in international management and a multi-cultural background, our students play a vital role in various professional fields and are favored by multinationals in their localization strategy.

[Features]

Intensiveness

Geared up to be adapted to the rapid rhythm of modern society, students are required to master fundamental management knowledge within one year and reach the equivalent level of their French counterparts. In addition to that, students who are not native speakers must participate in one-year intensive French language learning.

Comprehensiveness

Complete framework of management curriculum design that constitutes nine required courses, including internship paper.

Elitism

Enrolment examination includes

written test of English, and an interview conducted in English/French.

Internationalization

Most of the courses are taught in French with some in English for full-time students, and totally in English for part-time students; an effort to build multi-cultural capabilities.

Practicality

Management Education is all about bridging theory and practice. This is particularly true in a program such as Sorbonne MBA@IFCM where students alternate between the classroom and companies. While encouraging academic thinking and debating, IFCM focuses on

practical training. Students will apply what they have learned to their work situation. They will have the opportunity to work in a company for at least two months in order to obtain practical experiences of actual business operations and exposure to business problems. Often, these internships lead directly to jobs after graduation. A range of companies-large and small, new and well-established-visit the campus to recruit interns.

Tel: +86-10-64495806 (French Speaking)
64492036 (English Speaking)
Fax: +86-10-64492544 64494627
Website: http://www.ifcmbj.com
Email: info@ifcmbj.com
Address: 7th Fl., Chenxin Building, #12,
Huixin Dongjie, Beijing 100029, China

A Smith EMBA@SIM
http://www.sim-gbs.org

Executive MBA@SIM, *Beijing*
The Power-Engine for Success

The Sino-US School of International Management (SIM) is an institution of advanced management formed through a partnership between the University of Maryland, USA and the University of International Business and Economics (UIBE), China. SIM is officially recognized by the Ministry of Education and the Degree Granting Committee of the State Council. Upon graduation, students receive a *Master's degree in Business Administration* from the University of Maryland, as well as a formal certificate of program completion from UIBE. The Smith degree is accredited by the Degree Granting Committee of the Chinese State Council, by the Chinese Ministry of Education, and by the AACSB.

- **Leading American MBA program** delivered by Robert H. Smith School of Business professors at UIBE
- **Courses on weekends**
- **Same courses, same diploma**
  -Just as at the University of Maryland
- **A constellation of elite business people**
  -A class with highly experienced executives from different parts of the world
- **Action Learning Project**
  -Work on real-world business problem in 3-person teams
- **Tri-mentoring System**
  -One Smith and one UIBE professor, plus a corporate executive help each student with the action learning project
- **Academic session in the US**
  -All students will be invited for an academic session and participation of a graduation ceremony on the Maryland campus
- **Access to all online resources at the Smith School**

Robert **H. Smith School Of Business Recognition**	
#1 Best value among the top 25 US Business Schools	*Financial Times 2003*
#7 World Top Ten in faculty research	*Financial Times 2003*
#7 Alumni in the world	*Financial Times 2003*
#11 Part-time MBA program	*US News 2003*
#16 Full-time MBA program	*Wall Street Journal 2003*
World Top Ten Entrepreneurship Department	*(international surveys)*
World Top Ten Management Science Department	*(international surveys)*
World Top Ten Logistics Department	*(international surveys)*
World Top Ten Information Department	*(international surveys)*
#3 World Top Ten Entrepreneurial School by Alumni	*Entrepreneur Magazine 2003*
#7 US Top Ten Graduate Satisfaction	*Financial Times 2003*
#8 World Top Ten in Information Services	*US News 2003*
#5 World Top Ten in Information Technology	*Wall Street Journal 2002*
#7 World Top Ten in Communication	*Wall Street Journal 2002*

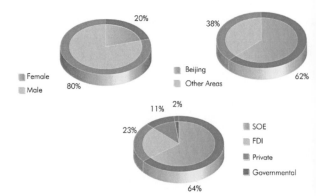

20% / 80%
- Female
- Male

38% / 62%
- Beijing
- Other Areas

2% / 11% / 23% / 64%
- SOE
- FDI
- Private
- Governmental

Robert H Smith School of Business

Tel: +86-10-64494625 64494628 64492036
Fax: +86-10-64494627
Website: http://www.sim-gbs.org
Email: simadmission@uibe.edu.cn
Address: 14th Fl., Chenxin Building, 12 Huixin Dongjie, Beijing 100029, China

Preface: China, the EU and the WTO after Chinese Accession

The Rt Hon The Lord Brittan of Spennithorne QC
Vice-Chairman of UBS Investment Bank and consultant to Herbert Smith
Former EU Commissioner for external trade relations and competition policy

Since the fourth edition of this publication was released, China has made significant progress in positioning itself at the forefront of the world economy. The economic statistics continue to chart the extraordinary rise of the Chinese economy, not least the relentless annual economic growth of nine per cent or more. With this growth, and both as a cause and effect of it, there have been significant investment opportunities for European companies. Most directly, these have resulted from the growing access to various Chinese product markets. The phased opening of the Chinese market, which originates from China's accession to the World Trade Organization (WTO) in 2001, is now almost complete, but the opportunities for European companies will continue to grow.

China's accession to the WTO and its impact on EU business has created a truly bilateral relationship, and the prophecies of a one-way relationship driven by Chinese exports only have proved to be false.

As far as China's access to the European market is concerned, it is important to stress the fact that the new rights that China has, whether vis-à-vis Europe or vis-à-vis other members of the WTO, are now legally enforceable rights within the world multilateral trading system. Whether talking about China's access to the EU's market or the EU's access to the Chinese market, there are bound to be disagreements in the future. This is not a reflection on a WTO member's good faith but of the fact that in any big agreement there are certain to be ambiguities and uncertainties. Those should be resolved as far as possible by discussion and negotiation but, if that is not possible, then I think both China and the EU should not feel in any way inhibited in going to a dispute settlement procedure. So far, however, disputes have been resolved amicably and in a timely

manner, and this is both a testament to the WTO, and the EU and China's respect for its rules.

In terms of the actual economic impact on the EU, the period of phasing in and opening up of the European market for China in many areas drew to a close at the start of 2005. The end of quotas is, of course, of particular significance, and European industry had ample time to prepare for it. However, the shock and awe inspired by Chinese manufacturing abilities has, I think, probably exceeded even the most seasoned observers' imaginations.

From a Chinese exporting perspective, the biggest immediate impact of China's WTO membership in terms of market access may well be the expiration of the WTO *Textiles Agreement*, which has now opened up the world's textile market to a country that is considered to be capable of providing over 50 per cent of its supply. The EU, the US and other major trading partners are currently seeking to review the access that is given to China and other developing countries in the textiles market. While there is a legal right in certain closely defined circumstances to protect domestic industry through the use of safeguards and anti-dumping measures, it should be remembered that the WTO is grounded in the theory of comparative advantage and not protectionism. For this reason other WTO members should continue their efforts to encourage Chinese economic growth, for if they do so, they will of course be creating opportunities for themselves. The opportunities for European companies in China are plentiful, for example demand for oil, gas, iron and other commodities continues to outstrip domestic supply. In financial services, Shanghai is now a financial centre, where most financial and professional services firms have a presence, and the insurance industry looks set to become a major area of growth as access rules are relaxed.

However, it is also important to note that, in spite of the far-reaching nature of China's WTO commitments, it would be wrong to regard their effect on China as just providing an opportunity for Europe or the US or Japan to grab business. Certainly, while China is now the second largest global investor in dollars after Japan, thanks to its hefty trade surplus with the US, China's overall trade is largely in balance thanks to imports of raw materials and Asian-made components and machinery. Since more than half of China's exports to the US are produced by foreign-invested factories, we can already see that liberalization is having the effect that it is intended to have, namely to help strengthen the Chinese economy as well as the global economy. Financial services are a good example. Foreign banks currently are able to conduct local currency business with domestic corporate customers and by next year will be able to do so with any Chinese customer. The phased implementation of this market opening has thus far protected the Chinese banks by limiting foreign ownership, but joint venture opportunities are being constantly developed, and are providing considerable management, technology and financial help to local banks. The WTO process, has, most important of all, led to major reform of the 'Big Four' state-owned banks.

For the Chinese leadership, opening up the economy was not a favour to the rest of the world, nor just a political gesture made in order to join the WTO. Rather it is a crucial part of the Chinese reform and modernization programme. The spur of foreign competition, with foreign entry into the market, not only in terms of trade but also in terms of investment, will help the Chinese economy to modernize. With the assistance of foreign investment, significant improvements have been made in many sectors that have had a direct and immediate effect on Chinese consumers – telecommunications, consumer goods, car and air transport to name but a few.

However, some areas of China's implementation of the market reform package remain a concern and much work needs to be done to ensure transparency and consistency, and thereby encourage foreign investment. Barriers to market entry, whether they be import licences, regional approvals or registrations are not always clear and identifiable – not least for smaller European companies wanting to develop a market presence. In this respect, creating an effective regulatory environment, the protection of intellectual property rights and the gradual evolution of the exchange rate policy will be key issues in China's full transition from a developing market to a free-market economy.

I am confident that China will conclude that further liberalization of the world economy is in its interests. Certainly so far, the net impact of China's presence in the WTO, has been a positive one. But it should be remembered that we are still in a transition phase and there are bound to be issues and disputes in the future. However, it is a mark of China's new-found economic maturity that these look set to be dealt with through the WTO's dispute mechanisms. Europe should seek to strengthen the already flourishing ties that exist with China, for if the pace of growth continues as it has done since the last edition of *Doing Business with China*, the next edition will, again, be reporting on a very different Chinese economic environment, and European business must continue to work hard to be an active part of it.

Foreword

Sir Digby Jones, Director General, Confederation of British Industry (CBI)

Everyone agrees that China is a very exciting market. It is big! The country accounts for a fifth of the world's population – the equivalent of all the people living in the European Union more than three times over. It is growing at a spectacular rate! Over the past 20 years, the average annual rate of growth has been 10 per cent or more. It is breaking all the records! More than US$1 million of foreign direct investment (FDI) arrives every week. Last year, in fact, China replaced the US as the world's largest recipient of FDI. It was also the world's fourth largest exporter of goods last year, producing 75 per cent of the world's toys, 58 per cent of the world's clothes and 29 per cent of the world's mobile phones. Its share of world trade had risen an amazing five per cent from one per cent when economic reform began.

As a potential market, China is massive. The low-cost base provided by the huge labour force is the primary attraction. That has brought a small revolution in the way business is being done. A recent poll done for the CBI showed that Asia was the most popular destination for British companies that move their operations overseas: and three in 10 British companies that have moved their operations overseas have moved them to China. Each time I go to China – and I went there three times in the last quarter of last year alone – I can see why so many companies want a share of this market.

The remarkable thing about China's growth is that it is not just about low-tech activity. China's business now encompasses a diverse range of activities. It is not just the workshop of the world for everything from garments to machinery, but increasingly for high-technology industries. And the many R&D centres are beginning to play a significant role in creating innovative capability. This trend will continue as China is producing over two million graduates a year – and 30 per cent of these are in science, engineering and technology-related disciplines.

One very positive factor underlines all this potential – it is that China's government continues to prioritize economic reforms and restructuring in order to modernize the economic and business environment. When I last met Commerce Minister, Bo Xilai, in October 2004, he reaffirmed that commitment.

Here is, therefore, the most tremendous opportunity, not to be overlooked. But this being China, things are not that straightforward. Scratch below the surface and it is clear the country's economic development is very irregular. The most developed industrial centres on the east coast are competing with developed countries for the range of goods and services and standard of living available, but that's not the case everywhere. Elsewhere, economic systems and transactions remain opaque, and laws and regulations are either inadequate, poorly implemented, or both.

More work needs to be done to restructure the state industrial sector and until that happens the efficiency of the private sector and the productivity of investments will continue to suffer.

More needs to be done to enable the orderly operation of the market and to ensure that local government activity and initiatives are consistent with those of central government.

Many companies find that the freedom to trade is actually diminished by discrimination or unjustified restrictions, compared with the way domestic firms are treated.

Inadequate or non-existent enforcement of basic legal principles in areas such as intellectual property protection is highly important to foreign investors too – it is the single most quoted barrier to foreign companies that are considering entering the market. So long as consistent local enforcement on the ground continues to be as patchy as it is, this will remain a barrier for foreign companies.

It is important to resolve these key issues if more business is going to be attracted to China and be persuaded that these things are not threats. It is especially important in attracting small and medium-sized enterprises (SMEs), which account for more than 90 per cent of all business in a functioning market economy.

SMEs are essential to an economy because they provide the energy and creativity that drives innovation.

I would like to encourage more businesses to look to China but how to convince them of the opportunity until it becomes clear that the issues I have outlined are being addressed? The prospects are promising but the promise still has to be fulfilled.

Sir Digby Jones is Director General of the CBI, which is Britain's premier business organization, comprising over 3,000 individual member companies and trade associations throughout the UK.

Foreword

Shen Jueren, Honorary Chairman, China Association of International Trade and Former Vice Minister of MOFTEC (now MOFCOM)

The publication of the fifth edition of *Doing Business with China* is worth celebrating, as it is, again, a book that will provide a lot of useful information for those who are doing or will do business with China.

What I feel particularly delighted about is that many chapters in the fifth edition of the book are contributed by writers from the European business community. This will not only add special characteristics to the book, but also give a feeling of affinity to readers.

It has been two years since the publication of the fourth edition of *Doing Business with China*, during which China has experienced new developments. China has diligently carried out its WTO commitments in terms of opening up the market, lowering the general tariff level, eliminating or reducing non-tariff barriers, strengthening the protection of intellectual property rights and improving the legal and regulatory environment, all of which have led to optimization of the investment climate, new developments in foreign trade and a sustained increase in foreign direct investments.

In 2004, China's foreign trade reached a total of US$1,154.7 billion, which is an increase of 35.7 per cent year on year. The rate of increase in exports was 35.4 per cent, hitting a record high of US$593.3 billion, while imports registered growth of 36 per cent, reaching a total of US$561.4 billion. While both exports and imports are increasing synchronically, import growth is slightly higher than export, which is a good sign for international business communities. Needless to say, China will continue to cooperate with the rest of the world and develop mutually beneficial trade relations.

2004 has also seen an increase in the actual utilization of foreign direct investments, which totalled US$60.6 billion – up 13.3 per cent year on year. While many multinational corporations expanded their investments in China, an increasing number of small to medium-sized companies are also coming to China to invest. At the same time, Chinese companies are also making further efforts to invest outside the country. Although the total size of China's external investment is relatively small, the trend is towards continuing growth.

The world economy is developing and I believe that concerted effort by all countries in the world will overcome unfavourable factors and secure brilliant future prospects.

I hope that the publication of this book will help people from other countries to enhance their understanding of China, promote economic and trade relations between China and other countries, and hence contribute to global prosperity and the well-being of all peoples.

Introduction

Jonathan Reuvid and Li Yong

China's entry to the World Trade Organization (WTO) just over three years ago was rightly perceived as a watershed in the evolution of the Chinese economy and its relationships with the rest of the world. WTO membership was followed swiftly by a smooth transfer of power to China's fourth generation leadership under the presidency of Mr Hu Jintao, with Mr Wen Jiabao as premier. In addition, it is now clear that the two events have also served as an accelerator to the widening impact of China on the world economy.

The onward march of the Chinese economy, at a GDP annual growth rate of around 9.5 per cent, has continued and, following the measures of restraint introduced during 2004, including the use of conventional monetary policy for the first time, it is widely acknowledged that any 'landing' in the next two years as the world economy slows is likely to be 'soft'.

This fifth edition of *Doing Business with China* focuses on developments in China's business and regulatory environment over the past three years and on the key industry sectors where China is already a global player or which offer major opportunities for well-researched foreign investment and trade.

Unlike previous editions, there are few contributions this time from Chinese government agencies and more from international professionals located in China and business people engaged currently in developing Chinese business. There are two reasons for this change in editorial policy. First, the regulations administered by Chinese government ministries and their forward plans are now more in the public domain and can be studied on the individual ministry websites (listed in Chapter 1.3). Second, the rule of commercial law has developed strongly since the end of 2001 and objective analysis by legal practitioners working in China has an increasing value to all companies seeking to establish business operations there.

In some ways, doing business with China has become more complex and the selection of partners and understanding of business relationships are, as ever, of crucial importance. Parts Five and Six remain the cornerstones of this book.

Foreign trade

Last December, China recorded a trade surplus of US$11 billion, a nine-year monthly high bringing the full-year balance to US$32 billion, the highest since 1998. The continuing surplus must be viewed against China's fulfilment of its WTO obligations to lower import tariffs over the period since 2001, with its general external tariff falling to 9.9 per cent in 2005. However, the removal of US and EU quotas restricting trade in garments and apparel this year is sure to boost Chinese exports of those products. Although export growth generally is expected to slacken in 2005 while imports remain stable, the surplus in trade with the US may not narrow unless America raises significantly the value of its exports of those technical products for which China has expressed a need.

Overall, China is estimated to have overtaken Japan in 2004 in terms of trade volume, becoming the world's third largest trading nation after the US and Germany. Asian trade is dominated by China and any significant fall in Chinese imports would seriously affect the economies of APEC countries and global demand. Some restraints on imports from China will remain so long as the EU and the US deny China classification as a 'market economy', but that seems no more than futile deferment of the inevitable.

China's continuing trade surpluses have refuelled pressures to revalue the RMB and remove its pegging to the US dollar. However, China is adamant that it will manage changes in both its currency regime and monetary policy in step with the domestic economy and, for reasons explained in the book, we see little likelihood of government policy change until restructuring of the banking system has been completed. The reorganization and strengthening of the 'Big Four' state-owned banks now underway is fundamental to this process and is, in any case, an urgent task in view of the further opening up of the industry to foreign banks in 2007.

Manufacturing

After many years of ostrich-like denial of the strengthening impact of Chinese manufacturing on the world's developed market economies, almost all of China's trading partners acknowledged in 2004 that the pattern of global manufacturing had shifted irrevocably and that the key question for manufacturers is how China is changing the world economy rather the converse. The competitive pressure that China's low-cost production exerts has proved startling, not just in light manufacturing but increasingly in products such as consumer durables and business equipment and even agriculture. As the capital equipment and technology that boosts China's imports is translated into production capacity, China's incremental exports are moving further up the value chain. Already, as Sir Digby Jones notes in his Foreword, some manufactured products have been lost forever to China and other Asian exporters.

However, in some industries the question of how long China will be able to maintain its cost advantage is beginning to be raised as China aligns the prices of many products to those of international markets.

Inward and outward investment

Strong inward investment has been at the heart of China's economic regeneration for the past 25 years. In 2004, inward investment had already exceeded the previous year's level by the end of October, at a total of US$52 billion and is unlikely to abate while key sectors of the market continue to open up to foreign investors and the currency is viewed as undervalued.

However, in 2004 the phenomenon of China as one of the biggest direct investors abroad emerged as a permanent fact of life. According to the United Nations Conference on Trade and Development (UNCTAD), 100-odd agencies world-wide now rate China as fifth in the league of countries from which investment is expected to come over the next two years after the US, Germany, the UK and France, and one place before Japan. In the most recent report of the International Institute for Management Development (IMD) on competitiveness, it is forecast that Chinese brands such as Haier, Konka, Midea and TCL will become international household names. This prediction was supplemented by the news in December 2004 of the purchase of IBM's personal computer business by Lenovo, China's top computer company, confirming that China is also in the market to acquire foreign brands. Other acquisitions of major foreign assets are already rumoured, such as a possible takeover bid for Unocal, the US oil company, by China National Offshore Oil Corporation (CNOOC). Such investments are an attractive way for China to deploy its mammoth US dollar reserves.

China's outward investment is being facilitated by its growing mastery of Stock Exchange listings outside the Chinese mainland, especially in Hong Kong. While China is allowing institutional investors to play a greater role in the pricing of domestic initial public offerings (IPOs), it is also encouraging major state-owned enterprises to introduce foreign investment through flotations on the Hong Kong stock exchange or further afield. As the investment group, City of London, said in a November 2004 report: 'China isn't last year's story; it is the next ten years' story'. These activities are covered in Part Seven and the two chapters on banking in Part Eight.

About the book

At first sight, readers familiar with past editions of *Doing Business with China,* may find the layout of this new edition little different. However, they will notice that it is considerably shorter, both as a result of the elimination of Chinese authors' texts that are now available online and because we decided not to include the lengthy economic data on Provinces, Autonomous Regions and Municipalites, also available online or from the annual *China Statistics Yearbook.* We felt that the last edition was hardly reader-friendly for business travellers. Otherwise we hope that readers will find most, if not all, of what they need to form sound judgements in planning their China strategies and entry to the Chinese market.

As always, we would like to thank all our contributors and to mention by name some of those without whom the book would not be possible. First among the professional firms is PricewaterhouseCoopers who have authored, for every edition, the taxation, audit and accountancy chapters now grouped together as Part Four. Once again Herbert Smith's Brussels and Shanghai offices have contributed the legal chapters relating to China's membership of the WTO (Parts One and Two) and chapters relating to foreign company investment in China (Part Three). This time, we welcome the international law firm, Adamas, as a major contributor, with new chapters on intellectual property and environmental protection (Part Three) and mergers and acquisitions (Part Seven).

We express particular appreciation on both our and the publisher's behalf to HSBC, the sponsor of our book, which has provided the first two authoritative chapters of Part Seven.

Other regular contributors who have authored new material are Professor Liu Baocheng of the University of International Business and Economics, Beijing, and Mark Norcliffe of the British Society of Motor Manufacturers and Traders. There are new contributions from Richard Hill of Rolls Royce, Humphrey Keenlyside of the China Britain Business Council and Jonsson Li, the last on China's emerging venture capital industry. We are also grateful to Snapshots International for the statistics they have provided, which have helped us to update many of the key sector reports. Our thanks, too, to our two editorial associates, Mr Shi Yonghai, Chairman of China Association of International Trade and Professor Liu Baocheng.

Finally, our appreciation for their support to Lord Brittan, the former EU commissioner, who has provided a Preface to every edition of this book and to the distinguished authors of the Forewords, Shen Jueren Honorary Chairman, China Association of International Trade, Former Vice Minister MOFTEC, now the Chinese Ministry of Commerce (MOFCOM) and Sir Digby Jones, Director General of the Confederation of British Industry (CBI).

Until the next edition

When we published the second edition of *Doing Business with China* in 1998, we were bold enough to forecast then that, in terms of absolute GDP, China would overtake Japan by 2020 and the US by mid-century. This opinion, reported in the publicity material for the book, was greeted with some derision. Towards the end of 2004, one of the leading global investment banks echoed that claim, although giving a few more years to Japan.

When announcing the acquisition of the IBM personal computer operation to the media, Lenovo's chairman referred to his company's growth and quoted the late Mr Deng Xiaoping's dictum: 'We had to cross the river by feeling for the stones'. That seems rather a good interim verdict on China's journey to becoming a leading world economic power.

Jonathan Reuvid, London
Li Yong, Beijing
February 2005

About the Editors

Jonathan Reuvid is Senior Editor for GMB Publishing and Consultant Editor to the Business and Reference division of Kogan Page. He has edited and co-authored more than 30 business titles, ranging from the Global Market Briefings series to handbooks and guides for the owners and directors of SMEs and the management of business start-ups.

An Oxford graduate, Jonathan specialized in joint venture development and technology transfers in China, after serving as Director of European Operations for Barnes Group, the Fortune 500 multinational, in the 1980s. Previously an oil industry economist, investment banker and financial consultant to SMEs, he took up a second career in business journals and book publishing in the 1990s but continues to consult on Chinese joint ventures.

Mr Li Yong is the Deputy Secretary General of China Association of International Trade, which is a national organization in China that advises governments on trade and investment policies and companies on corporate development strategies. He is also the assistant dean of the two leading Sino-foreign business schools – Sino–US School of International Management and Sino–French School of International Management – at the University of International Business and Economics. Most recently, he was elected council member of the Executive Council of the China International Cultural Exchange Centre, in recognition of his efforts to promote cultural understanding between China and the rest of the world.

Li Yong worked in Hong Kong for five years as the marketing services manager and later the assistant general manager in a research company that helped both Chinese and western companies with their marketing and entry strategies. Between 1993 and 2000, he was the managing director of the Centre for Market and Trade Development (CMTD), which is a leading business consulting function under the Ministry of Foreign Trade and Economic Cooperation (MOFTEC), which is now the Ministry of Commerce (MOFCOM).

In addition to his research and teaching responsibilities, Li Yong remains active in business consulting. He is the China director of PMC Consulting, which is a Hong Kong-based American company specializing in investment/business planning and strategy development in Asia. He has worked on many consulting projects for multinational companies and international institutions. He has extensive hands-on consulting experiences in a variety of industries and joint venture negotiations. He lectures extensively in and outside China on a variety of issues on doing business with China. He has also been invited by CCTV, China's national TV station, to speak on various international economic and trade issues.

Li Yong has been the co-editor and co-author for all the past four editions of *Doing Business with China*.

Editorial Associates

Mr Shi Yonghai, a distinguished senior researcher in the field of international trade in China, is now the Chairman of the China Association of International Trade. Previously, he was President of the Chinese Academy of International Trade and Economic Cooperation (CAITEC), the largest research organization under the Ministry of Foreign Trade and Economic Cooperation (MOFTEC). He was also the Minister Counsellor of the Economic and Commercial Section of the Chinese Embassy to Japan between 1990 and 1994.

Shi Yonghai has long been engaged in the research of international trade, particularly research and studies on the Japanese economy and issues regarding China's foreign trade and economic cooperation. He also participated as a leader in a number of important research projects, of which the latest included 'ISO 14000 and China's Foreign Trade', and environment- and trade-related issues in APEC countries. In addition, Shi Yonghai has been involved in researching key issues regarding China's effort to further open up and develop China's foreign trade and economic cooperation. Most recently, based on his research on the environment and trade issues, Shi Yonghai has initiated for the first time the concept of 'environmental competitiveness of products'. This concept has extended conventional theory on product competitiveness and has important implications both in theory and practice.

Liu Baocheng is an Associate Professor and Assistant Dean at the School of International Business Management of the University of International Business and Economics (UIBE), Beijing, China. He also serves as dean of the Sino-US School of International Management, which is a partnership between UIBE and the University of Maryland's Robert H Smith School of Business. At the same time, Liu Baocheng also holds a deanship at the Sino–French School of International Business Management. His area of research and teaching covers a variety of disciplines including marketing, cross-cultural negotiation and business law. His most recent publications include the translation of the *Blackwell Encyclopedia of Business Ethics and English for Business Negotiations*.

Besides his research and teaching experiences, Liu Baocheng has worked in the management of London Export Corporation, Union Merchant Overseas Corporation and Cathay Trading Ltd. He is still in active business executive positions with Unigene Laboraroty Inc., Herborium Inc. and Novark Consulting. His hands-on business experiences cover international trade, joint venture management and marketing research. He worked as senior research fellow for the Institute of International Business at Seton Hall University in the US for four years and served as an adjunct professor at Seton Hall and Montclair State University. He has been a speaker at various renowned academic and corporate institutions and in media. These include China Central Party University, China University of Central Administration, Citibank, BASF, OTIS, Schneider, Voice of America and China Central Television (CCTV).

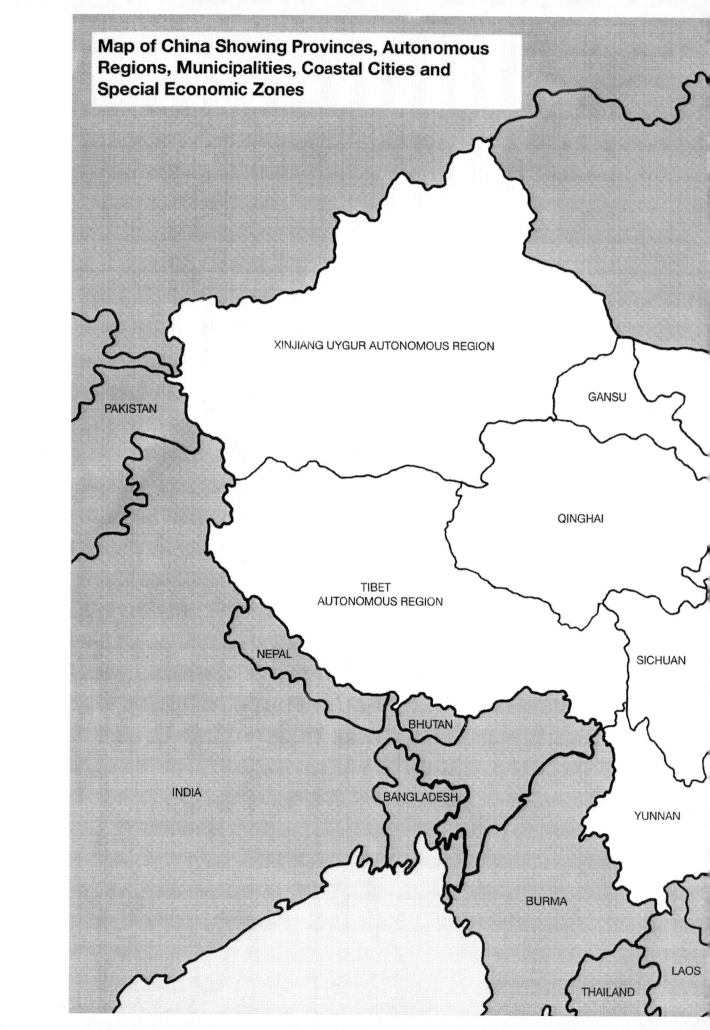

Map of China Showing Provinces, Autonomous Regions, Municipalities, Coastal Cities and Special Economic Zones

XINJIANG UYGUR AUTONOMOUS REGION

PAKISTAN

GANSU

QINGHAI

TIBET
AUTONOMOUS REGION

NEPAL

SICHUAN

BHUTAN

INDIA

BANGLADESH

YUNNAN

BURMA

LAOS

THAILAND

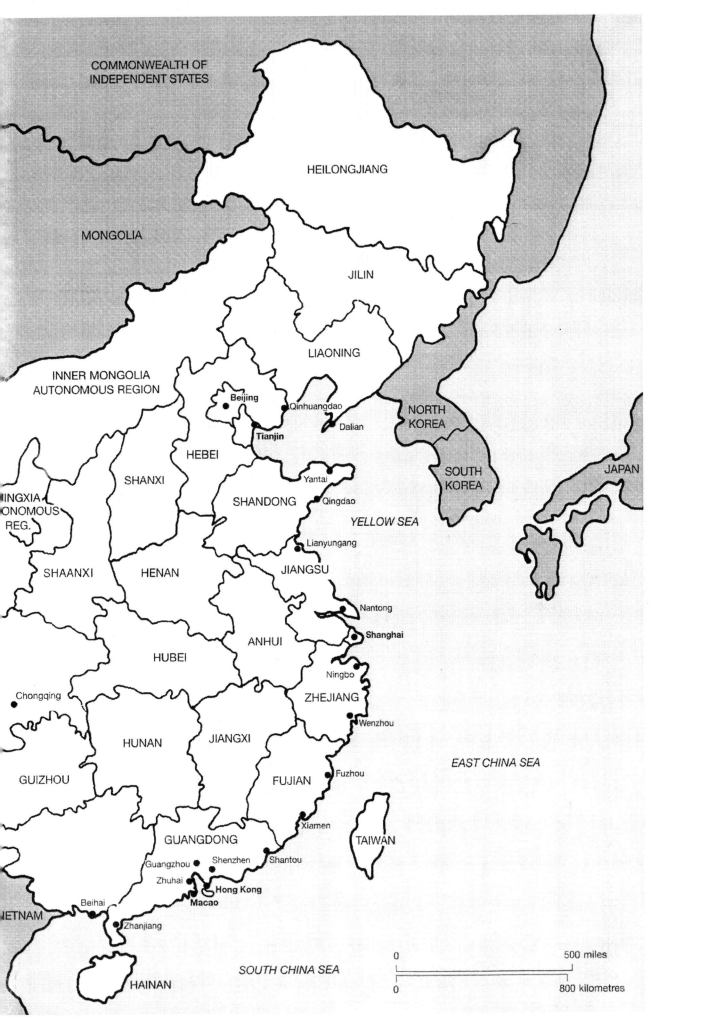

China Association of International Trade

Who are we?

Established in Beijing in July 1981, China Association of International Trade (CAIT) is the first national research organisation in the field of international trade in the wake of China's opening up and economic reform. Under the direct leadership of the Ministry of International Trade and Economic Cooperation, CAIT's mission is to research and explore solutions, both in terms of theory and practice, to issues regarding China's development of foreign trade and economic cooperation. CAIT has members all over China. They include both business entities and research organisations. CAIT has a pool of top-level well-known experts, government officials, scholars, entrepreneurs and ex-diplomats on its directorate.

What do we do?

In addition to its professional research oriented towards filling gaps between trade and investment theories and practices, CAIT is committed to studying issues that have important implications for China's trade and investment policies. CAIT also undertakes other activities involving both its member and non-member organisations, such as the organisation of various kinds of workshops, seminars and training courses, market research and consulting, international academic exchanges, provision of information and research findings for governments and enterprises, the publication of magazines and books and business referral services.

How can we help you?

CAIT has an extensive network of members and good working relationships with both government at all levels and the business community at large in China. We can help you in a number of different ways. We can be a point of contact for anything where you think you would need someone to help. Speak to us about what help you need and we will come up with a solution.

Contact:

China Association of International Trade
2, Dong Chang An Street
Beijing 100731, China

Tel: +86-10-65197955 Fax: +86-10-6525 5899 E-mail: caitmoftec@mail.china.com

Part One

China's Economy and Administration

China's Economic Performance and Outlook

Jonathan Reuvid

Economic performance: An overview

Until quite recently, it was fashionable among economic pundits world-wide to decry China's economic performance – in particular the published GDP growth statistics, which were said to be overstated. In 2003, many of the more prominent commentators changed their stance and started to contend that official Chinese growth statistics were very likely understated.

In the fourth quarter of 2004, there seemed to be a convergence of opinion between the international commentators and the China National Bureau of Statistics about current growth performance and outlook. Most opinion sources now expect a year-on-year (yoy) GDP growth outcome of 9.0 per cent for 2004, and forecast not less than 8.0 per cent for 2005.

Table 1.1.1 reproduces the current assessment by Coface, the leading European risk agency of China's major macro-economic indicators as at 8 March 2005.

Economic growth

By any standard, following its long period of sustained growth from 1979 to the millennium, China will have maintained remarkably consistent GDP growth in the more recent five-year period. For 2003, reported growth is estimated to have exceeded 9 per cent, but in the other four years it has varied narrowly between 7.5 and 8.5 per cent.

In the first quarter of 2004, the economy appeared to be galloping headlong towards serious overheating and economists returned to another of their favourite topics, debating whether the Chinese economy might

Table 1.1.1 Major macro-economic indicators

US$ billions	2000	2001	2002	2003 (e)	2004 (f)	2005 (f)
Economic growth (%)	8.0	7.5	8.0	9.3	9.0	8.0
Inflation (%)	0.4	0.7	−0.8	1.2	3.8	2.9
Public sector balance (% GDP)	−2.8	−2.6	−2.9	−2.5	−2.4	−2.7
Exports	249.1	266.1	325.7	438.3	571.0	764.0
Imports	214.7	232.1	281.5	393.6	543.0	729.0
Trade balance	34.5	34.0	44.2	44.7	28.0	35.0
Current account balance	20.5	17.4	35.4	45.9	37.0	34.0
Current account balance (% GDP)	1.9	1.5	2.7	3.3	2.3	1.9
Foreign debt	16.2	14.3	13.4	13.8	12.8	11.7
Debt service (% exports)	8.2	7.5	7.1	4.5	3.2	2.6
Currency reserves (import months)	7.3	8.6	9.9	10.4	10.1	9.4

(e) = estimate; (f) = forecast.
Source: Coface – www.trading-safely.com

suffer a 'hard landing' or whether a controlled 'soft landing' was more likely. Some predicted that investment would stall and that the boom in capital expenditure would collapse with a serious fallout on employment and family incomes. Others cited the action that the government was already taking to curtail domestic credit growth by increasing reserve requirements and shifting the focus of investment towards the neglected rural and inland provinces and on infrastructure, as evidence that a modulated slowdown would be achieved.

Encouragingly, at the end of January, the International Finance Corporation, the private sector arm of the World Bank, announced that it planned to increase its investment in China from the US$250 million invested in 2003 to the level of US$400 to US$500 million within two years.

By the end of the first quarter, international concern had hardened, with the International Energy Agency noting that oil production supply, now running at more than 6 million barrels a day compared with an average of 5.49 million barrels in 2003, could hardly keep up with demand from China. Serious shortages were being experienced in China of electricity, water, coal, coke and other raw materials. The official reported statistic for first quarter GDP growth was 9.7 per cent, with some suspicion that the actual rate of growth might have been as high as 11 or 12 per cent.

Particular concern was focused on runaway bank lending for questionable infrastructure and industrial projects. Officials recognized publicly that overpowerful local authorities had been exerting their influence on local banks to finance investments in steel, aluminium, cement and property investment, as well as infrastructure projects. Overall, fixed asset investment increased by 43 per cent yoy.

Macro-economic and monetary controls

As a modest counter-measure, The People's Bank of China raised the minimum level of deposits that banks must hold in reserve from 7 per cent to 7.5 per cent with effect from 25 April, thereby withdrawing about US$8.9 billion from the banking sector. At the time, this action was preferred to an interest rate rise that might draw in further 'hot money' inflows and increase pressures on domestic money supply and inflation. At the end of April total lending had risen 20.4 per cent yoy, a 0.3 per cent decline from March.

By June the focus of foreign observers' concern had shifted to inflation, which rose from 3.8 per cent in

April to 4.4 per cent yoy in May, while consumer prices in the year to May rose 9.5 per cent. However, the National Statistics Bureau released a batch of more promising results: industrial output in May increased 17.5 per cent yoy, compared with 19.1 per cent in April, while the growth of investment in fixed assets fell from 43.5 per cent yoy in March to 34.7 per cent in April and to 18.3 per cent in May.

In July, the State Council's Development Research Council expressed concern over the tighter money policy, declaring that the central bank's loan growth target of 17 per cent was below the level necessary to sustain China's investment-driven economy. In the meantime, China introduced new limits on foreign currency borrowing in the form of annual quotas on both foreign invested banks and Chinese banks that would depend on China's prevailing balance of payments situation, the funding requirements of Chinese companies and what the State Administration of Foreign Exchange (SAFE) characterized as the 'historical situation and business demand of foreign banks'. Total foreign debt at the end of 2003 had risen 13 per cent yoy to US$193.63 billion, of which short-term foreign debt accounted for US$77 billion, having grown 38.1 per cent since the end of 2002. Although foreign banks have dominated China's domestic trade in foreign currency with most lending directed to the foreign invested companies sector that has spearheaded China's spectacular export performance, SAFE foresaw market risk, interest rate risk or currency risk in excessive foreign currency lending domestically.

Western economic commentators have consistently underestimated the effectiveness of Chinese macro-economic controls, sometimes referred to as 'administrative measures'. As the market economy expands, the task becomes tougher, but for now China remains the last significant global economy where central government retains the ability to manage its economy by a combination of monetary policy and selective investment controls over industry.

By the beginning of the third quarter 2004, it seemed that the government's economic levers were proving effective and that a soft landing, at least in the short term, was predictable. The National Bureau of Statistics (NBS) reported second quarter GDP growth of 9.6 per cent yoy, down from 9.8 per cent in the first quarter and 9.9 per cent in the fourth quarter 2003. At the same time fixed asset investment growth fell sharply from more than 40 per cent in the first quarter, and registered 28.7 per cent for the first half overall.

Although the consumer price index climbed to 5 per cent in June – the level at which the central bank had previously indicated that it might raise interest rates – the CPI was clearly on a downward trend, with a month-on-month fall of 0.7 per cent in June from May. The slowdown in building investment was also helping to moderate the prices of aluminium, cement and steel. In terms of manufacturing activity, yoy industrial output growth eased in July for the fifth month in a row to 15.5 per cent compared with a peak of over 23 per cent in February.

Results for the first three quarters, 2004

Preliminary results for the first three quarters 2004 were announced towards the end of October, indicating that the orderly slowdown was continuing. GDP growth for the nine months is now estimated at 9.5 per cent yoy. The value added of primary industry was up 5.5 per cent; of secondary industry up 10.9 per cent; and of tertiary industry up 8.5 per cent.

There was welcome news in the agricultural sector, where 4.8 per cent growth in the summer grain harvest was followed by an increase of 8.8 per cent in the early rice crop. The autumn crop is expected to be equally strong, confirming that the sector is recovering from the depressed levels of recent years.

Over the nine-month period, the value added of industrial enterprises increased by 17 per cent yoy, with heavy industry registering growth of 18.5 per cent and light industry growth of 15.4 per cent. The NBS also calculates that the profits of the top 500 privately-owed companies increased 38.9 per cent over the same period in 2003 on sales revenues up 53 per cent.

Fixed asset investment appears to have stabilized. Although total investment over the first nine months of 2004 was 27.7 per cent up yoy, the growth rate was 15.3 per cent and 0.9 per cent below first quarter and first half levels. While urban investment was up 29.9 per cent yoy, investment in steel and cement dropped by 65.5 and 43.3 per cent respectively from first quarter levels. Investment in aluminium declined 6.5 per cent and even real estate investment fell 12.3 per cent compared with the first quarter.

Conversely, investment in agriculture, forestry, animal husbandry and the fishing industries grew 21.4 per cent in the three quarters yoy, which was also 21 per cent above the first quarter level. There is a growing consensus that investment in some sectors, in particular infrastructure projects, needs to be re-stimulated. The downside of the government's otherwise successful policies is that supplies of coal, electricity and oil could not match demand in 2004.

Credit restrictions appear not to have affected consumer demand too adversely although the impact on automobile sales has been marked (see Chapter 8.1). For the first nine months overall retail sales were 13 per cent over the same period in 2003 and real growth was 9.7 per cent after adjusting for price inflation. Compared with the period of negative price inflation in 2002/3, positive inflation has now returned to Chinese markets. In the first three quarters of 2004, food prices overall were 10 per cent up, including an increase in grain prices of 28.4 per cent. Housing prices rose 4.4 per cent, while consumer goods prices, including tobacco and alcohol, rose 1.3 per cent. In September, the month-on-month change in the CPI was 5.2 per cent, showing a modest 0.1 per cent decline on the August rate of change. The estimated CPI in Table 1.1.1 for the full year of 3.8 per cent is not an underestimate, and fears of continuing higher inflation have returned. A realistic outcome for 2005 may be more than the 2.9 per cent currently forecast.

Interest rates

On 28 October 2004, the Chinese government and the People's Bank of China surprised western financial markets with a 27 basis point rise in lending rates from 5.31 to 5.38 per cent and in deposit rates from 1.98 to 2.25 per cent, the first lending rate rise in nine years. At the same time banks were granted greater flexibility to increase interest rates further to higher risk customers.

The resort to conventional monetary policy, in addition to command economy-style 'administrative measures', addressed the threat from negative real interest rates to deposit account savings. (China's gross domestic savings rate of 43 per cent of GDP that underpins the Chinese economy, remains the highest in Asia and compares with a US savings rate of 14 per cent.) Negative interest rates were also a further threat of unwelcome distortions to the finance system. Some economists foresee that a second 25 basis point rise is likely in the near term.

Foreign trade

China's positive current account balance on foreign trade at the end of 2003 has been reported variously at between US$35 and US$45.9 billion. Imports expanded by an impressive 40 per cent in nominal dollars, while exports grew 35 per cent – remarkable levels of expansion for a country with such a high volume of trade.

According to WTO statistics, merchandise exports from Asia grew 17 per cent in 2003 while imports grew by 6 per cent, compared with growth in world trade of 16 per cent and 4 per cent respectively. As Table 1.1.2 shows, China's exports were less than 10 per cent below Japan's, while imports exceeded Japan by US$30 billion. China's trade values dominated those of all other individual Asian countries, while export and import growth rates dwarfed those of every other economy in the region, including Japan.

Over the first three quarters of 2004, total exports were US$416 billion, up 35 per cent, while total imports climbed by 38 per cent to above US$412 billion. For the full year, exports from China are forecast to exceed US$550 billion and imports to exceed US$520 billion. In the period January to August 2004, the EU headed the list of China's top 10 trading partners with US$112 billion, followed by the US, Japan, Hong Kong and the ASEAN countries combined. Therefore, any reduction in GDP growth leading to a contraction of imports across the board will have a serious adverse impact in the other Asia Pacific region economies, the EU and the US.

As noted in Chapter 1.2, China is engaged in a number of trade disputes following WTO entry, both with the US and the EU – as are the EU and the US with each other. In China's case, its WTO transition status carries the disadvantage that until it has been acknowledged as a 'market-based economy', it will have to defend itself against the anti-dumping measures of other countries on the basis of comparability with the prices of other emerging economies. By the end of May 2004, there were more than 200 anti-dumping cases in train against China.

The five main conditions for market economy status are: currency convertibility, openness to foreign investment, minimal government control of assets, sound corporate governance and no price controls. At the end of June 2004, the EU refused to recognize China as a market economy, having found that the economy suffered from too much state interference, weak rule of law and poor corporate governance. Until the EU has ruled that the five criteria have been met, it is improbable that the US will rule likewise.

Foreign direct investment

According to OECD statistics (June, 2004), China overtook the US in 2003 as the world's biggest recipient of foreign direct investment (FDI), having drawn in US$53 billion during the year compared with US$40 billion by the US.

In 2003, total contracted FDI into China increased sharply by 38 per cent to RMB1169 billion (US$141 billion), while utilized FDI was only marginally higher. MOFCOM's statistics in RMB for the period compared to 2002 are reproduced in Table 1.1.3.

The table shows that the contracted new investment from foreign-owned enterprises (FOEs) amounted to RMB816 billion (US$98 billion), up 43 per cent in respect of nearly 27,000 projects, 21 per cent more than in 2002. Equity and contractual joint ventures together (EJV and CJV) contributed a further RMB330 billion ($40 billion), up 34 per cent, resulting from 13,878 projects, respectively 20 per cent more and 3 per cent less than in the previous year.

Of course, the FDI totals include both further investment in established enterprises as well as investment in new enterprise. The strength of investment in FOEs and joint ventures is a reflection of their contribution of around 50 per cent to China's exports.

In the first three quarters of 2004, the total contracted value of FDI reached US$107 billion, a yoy increase of

Table 1.1.2 International trade values 2003 and recent growth rates (billion dollars and percentage)

	Exports				Imports			
	Value	Annual % change			Value	Annual % change		
	2003	1990-2000	2002	2003	2003	1990-2000	2002	2003
Japan	472	5	3	13	383	5	–3	14
China	438	15	22	35	413	15	25	40
India	55	9	14	11	70	8	12	20
Six Asian traders*	686	9	6	14	615	8	3	12
Asia	1,897	8	8	17	1,734	8	6	19
World	7,274	6	4	16	7,557	6	4	16

* Chinese Taipei, Hong Kong China, Rep. of Korea, Malaysia, Singapore and Thailand.
Source: WTO.

Table 1.1.3   Utilization of FDI in January to December 2003

Utilizing foreign investment	Number of projects			Approved foreign investment Contractual FDI value (RMB million)			Realized FDI value Period		
	2003	2002	+/– %	2003	2002	+/– %	2003	2002	+/– %
Total	41,081	34,171	20.22	1,169.01	847.51	37.94	561.40	550.11	2.05
Foreign direct investment	41,081	34,171	20.22	1,150.70	827.68	39.03	535.05	527.43	1.44
Equity joint venture	12,521	10,380	20.63	255.06	185.02	37.86	153.92	149.92	2.67
Contractual joint venture	1,547	1,595	–3.01	74.79	62.17	20.30	38.36	50.58	–24.14
Wholly foreign-owned enterprise	26,943	22,173	21.51	816.09	572.55	42.54	333.84	317.25	5.23

Source: Network Centre of MOFCOM

35.6 per cent, while utilized foreign investment was 21 per cent higher at nearly US$49 billion. By the end of September, China's foreign exchange reserves were approaching US$515 billion, an increase of US$111 billion from the beginning of the year.

Outlook

The smooth hand-over of power to China's new president, Hu Jintao, was the harbinger for a further period of economic prosperity and relatively low economic risk. Acknowledging that the economy was at risk of overheating, the President called for voluntary restraint in investment at the end of 2003. However, some local governments ignored the request for a cooling-off period and actually increased their spending in anticipation of a more mandatory clampdown. The President's response was to introduce the macro-economic controls discussed above, and it is unlikely in the short term that Mr Hu and his Premier, Mr Wen Jiabao, will loosen, except selectively, the controls, which include curbs on land sales, property development, investment in steel, cement and aluminium, as well as the restrictions on bank lending.

The fallout from the boom in property development, which caused too rapid a rise in property prices in many of the largest 35 cities, has driven the high demand for construction commodities and strained China's power generation and transport capacities. There has also been glut of uneconomic new steel mills that are likely to be closed down because they waste resources and threaten the country's infrastructure still further.

In September 2004, Mr Jiang Zemin stepped down as Chairman of the Party's Central Military Commission (CMC), the position occupied by Mr Deng Xiaoping during his period in semi-retirement as China's 'paramount leader', and Mr Hu was appointed in his place. Following this consolidation of power, Mr Hu and Mr Wen are freer to focus on macro-economic reform without impediment. They are expected to intensify efforts to build a stronger social security network, to narrow the gap between rich and poor and to crack down on corruption. Mr Hu has a reputation abroad as a reformer, but any prospect of a move towards tentative experiments in democracy is unlikely to be on the cards. Any political reform will be taken with extreme caution to avoid damage to the Party. Mr Hu's intentions were made clear in a speech on 25 September 2004, when he stated, 'History has proved that in China copying the model of western political systems is a dead-end road'.

On balance, this is good news for foreign investors in China. Deeper integration into the WTO is contributing to the continuing opening up of China. During the present catch-up phase, the public finances situation is unlikely to cause concern in the near term. The balance of public sector borrowing is no more than 2.5 per cent of GDP.

The most obvious threat is the slow progress in modernizing the public industrial and banking sectors. Continuing to prop up loss-making state-owned industries (SOEs) will maintain a flow of bad debts into the future, but that is a problem with which western European governments too are not unfamiliar.

The international impact of China's interest rates increase

The 28 October hike in interest rates provoked a disproportionate overnight reaction from bond markets world-wide. In particular, US Treasury bond yields rose instantly, but the markets settled quickly. There was also a short-term effect on metal commodities and crude oil prices, although any marked slowdown in Chinese demand seems unlikely within China's sustained growth scenario.

Towards a consumer society

The income of urban and rural residents continued to grow in the first three quarters of 2004. After adjusting for price inflation, the real rate of growth was 7 per cent, only a little lower than growth in 2003, while the per capita cash income of rural residents increased by 11.4 per cent. Both consumer confidence, up to 91.3 points, and the expectancy index reflecting the economic outlook revived in September. However, in terms of consumer wealth, although urban incomes have grown at an average 15 per cent per year, increasing fivefold since 1992, personal wealth still lags behind the regional and emerging country averages as Table 1.1.4 demonstrates.

The RMB exchange rate issue

At the beginning of 2004, pressure on China from G7 finance ministers, in particular the US and Japan, to adjust the RMB/US dollar exchange rate and to move away from the 'present peg' of RMB8.28 to US$1 – if not to revalue – intensified. As tighter controls on lending and open market operations started to soak up liquidity and Chinese companies were permitted to hold more foreign currency, pressure on the RMB abated and the demand for currency adjustment eased.

However, the exchange rate issue remains a topic of continuing debate. Following China's inclusion at a working dinner of the G7 finance ministers and central bank governors in October 2004, rhetoric between the US and Chinese governments softened. Although China has acknowledged its intention to introduce greater flexibility, no timetable was offered.

Some commentators have seen the more recent rise in interest rates as the prelude to a change in the dollar peg, but that may be wishful thinking. For China, whose foreign currency reserves now top US$600 billion, of which much is invested in US Treasury bonds, necessary preconditions would seem to be open capital account management (the system for conducting investment transactions) and completed reform of the state banks. Conservatively, this process could take five or six years, making 2010 a likely date for a fully-fledged floating currency.

Outward investment and competitiveness

In May 2004, the United Nations Conference on Trade and Development (UNCTAD) published a survey of more than 100 investment promotion agencies that ranked China fifth (after the US, Germany, the UK and France) among the countries from which they expected to receive investment over the next two years. Among many developing countries, particularly in Africa, China was ranked second after the US. Confirming China's pre-eminence in the Asia Pacific region, Japan was ranked sixth in the survey.

In another mid-year report on world competitiveness by the Lausanne-based Institute of Management Development (IMD), China and India were identified

Table 1.1.4 Indicators of personal wealth

Indicators	China	Regional average	Emerging countries average
GNP per capita (PPP dollars)	3,950	9,313	6,778
GNP per capita (US dollars)	890	5,650	3,568
Human development index	0.721	0.725	0.708
Wealthiest 10% share of national income (%)	30	32	33
Urban population percentage	37	49	60
Percentage under 15 years old	25	29	31
Number of telephones per 1,000 inhabitants	137	169	157
Number of computers per 1,000 inhabitants	19	107	66

Source: Coface – www.trading-safely.com

as the leaders among Asian economies in a profound shift in global competitiveness. The Chinese mainland improved five places in world rankings between 2003 and 2004, up to 24, while Hong Kong shifted four places, up to six. Within China, Zhejiang province rose from 38 to 19, while India climbed from 50 to 34.

Having become a global manufacturing centre and developed purchasing power, China is now in the third development stage of creating a middle-class market that will become a magnet for consumer goods and spur China's competitiveness further. According to recent predictions by Goldman Sachs, itself already a significant player in China's financial services industry, China will be the world's largest economy by 2050, followed by the US and India.

China as a WTO Member: Systemic Issues

Craig Pouncey and Lode van den Hende, Herbert Smith, Brussels

Introduction

On 11 December 2001 China became a WTO member, following a process of negotiation that took more than 15 years. Throughout the world this was considered a major achievement for China, for the WTO and for the global economy. China became the 15th country to accede to the WTO following its creation in 1995, with its accession negotiations and commitments more complex than any of its predecessors. Given the relative size of the economy this is not surprising. However, it is relatively surprising that so little has still been said about the precise meaning of China's accession, which is described in more than 800 pages of highly technical legal documentation.

The purpose of this chapter and Chapter 2.1 on WTO accession is twofold. In this chapter we explain what the WTO is, as well as the systemic consequences of China's WTO membership, both for China and for the WTO. Chapter 2.1 provides an overview of some of China's specific obligations in the area of 'market access', examining the extent to which China is obliged to allow foreign businesses, goods and services to trade or be traded in China, and an examination of how fully China has performed its obligations during its short period of membership.

What is the WTO?

The simplest way to describe the WTO is to compare it to the original European Economic Community (the predecessor of the European Union). The original EEC concentrated on opening markets via 'free movement' and non-discrimination disciplines that were legally enforceable on the Member States via a specialized international court. Those same principles underpin the WTO. In fact, some of the most important provisions of the EEC Treaty were inspired by provisions of the first General Agreement on Tariffs and Trade of 1947 (GATT 1947), the predecessor of the WTO.

Not direct reciprocity but 'most favoured nation' treatment

On the other hand, there are significant differences between the WTO and the EEC/EU, the most important being that whilst in the EEC/EU all Member States have the same obligations, this is not the case in the WTO. The obligations of a WTO member are to a large extent determined by the commitments and concessions made by the country concerned in a specific sector or for a specific product. These commitments and concessions are set out in detail in 'Schedules' that each WTO member has deposited with the WTO. It is important to note that once a WTO member makes a market access commitment, the benefit of that market access commitment extends to all other WTO members (and of course their companies). This is referred to as the 'Most Favoured Nation' (or MFN) principle.

However, it is important to note that the commitments made by WTO members are not necessarily parallel between members: the fact that country X gives access to services sector Y does not mean that country Z also does. This is fundamentally because of the way in which market access commitments are negotiated in the WTO (ie 'trade-offs' are made between market access 'offerings' across a wide range of services and products), with the result that access is not parallel across all sectors and products for all WTO members.

For instance, during the Olympic summer games in Australia in 2000, the EU-based press agency, Reuters, was denied access to certain areas of the stadiums where only Australian and US news agencies were allowed to bring their cameras. The European Commission successfully intervened on behalf of Reuters, pointing out that Australia had made relevant commitments in the relevant sector (ie the audio-visual sector). This is despite the fact that the EU itself had made no WTO commitments in that sector and that under WTO law, the EU could have lawfully applied such discriminatory measures against Australian press agencies.

This may seem awkward but the WTO should be looked at as a global deal, whereby every member country has accepted that the market access level offered by all other countries is sufficient. This functions like an entrance fee that is different for all members but once the other members have accepted the entrance fee, the acceding country can come in and enjoy all the rights and benefits of the club.

In addition, concessions are built into the system allowing for developing countries to gain access to developed markets quicker than might result from any negotiated 'trade-offs', and for transition periods for their own commitment implementations. However, China, along with the other acceding countries that have declared themselves as 'developing countries', has not been able to avail itself of these specific concessions, as delays to the implementation of various commitments are built into its specific accession documents.

An important consequence is that, whilst China's obligations in the WTO are determined by China's commitments and concessions in the WTO, China's rights as an exporter are largely determined by the commitments and concessions of the other WTO members. It is to be presumed that China undertook its obligations in full knowledge of the rights it obtains as a result of doing so.

Reduction of import tariffs, abolition of 'non-tariff' barriers and disciplines for agricultural subsidies

The core objective of the WTO in the area of trade in goods is to replace all 'non-tariff' barriers, such as quantitative import or export limits, with customs duties that are 'bound' at a maximum level the country cannot exceed. Tariffs are transparent and easily identifiable whereas non-tariff barriers tend, by definition, to be a more covert means of market protection. Through periodic negotiations, these maximum levels

are then reduced. The most recent started in November 2001 and are still ongoing. They are known as the 'Doha' Round, and seek the reduction of tariffs and other barriers to trade from all members, even including those newly acceded such as China.

The only exception to the rule that all quantitative restrictions (quotas) had to be removed was textiles, where under the Agreement on Textiles and Clothing, quantitative import restrictions can remain in place until 1 January 2005. After that date, quantitative restrictions need to be replaced by tariffs. This has caused considerable unrest with textile and clothing manufacturers in developed economies such as the EU and the US. China has been a vocal member of the grouping of developing countries seeking to ensure that the elimination of quotas in this area is carried out by 1 January 2005 and is not replaced by other forms of restrictions.

The Agreement on Technical Barriers to Trade and the Agreement on the Application of Sanitary and Phytosanitary (SPS) Measures aim to prevent technical product and testing rules being abused to frustrate imports. The Hormones dispute between the EU and the US is the best-known example of this, but there are also examples involving China. In early 2002, for instance, the EU banned the import of certain Chinese meat and seafood items said to be tainted with a banned antibiotic. In March 2002 the Chinese authorities reacted by prohibiting the sale of 177 items of perfume and cosmetics from Europe said to contain substances causing 'mad cow' disease.

Following accession, China was criticized for its slow notification of SPS measures, and while this seems to have now been resolved, China has continued to face criticism for undue quantitative restrictions on meat and poultry imports, such as the implementation of emergency measures including the temporary ban on all Canadian poultry in March 2004 to prevent the spread of Avian 'flu.

The Agreement of Agriculture obliges WTO members to reduce agriculture subsidies – both domestic support and export subsidies. China has agreed to abolish all export subsidies and to keep other trade-distorting internal support under 8.5 per cent of the total value of agricultural production (this threshold applies both to general support and to each specific product). This cap on agricultural subsidies appears to raise considerable concern in China because of the lack of competitiveness of its agricultural sector. It has been suggested, however, the WTO may also contribute to solving that competitiveness problem, which appears to be related to a poor distribution and warehousing infrastructure rather than to the farm gate prices (the price received by the farmers). This makes bulk commodities shipped from North or South America to processing plants on the Chinese coast cheaper at plant gate level than products grown in China. A liberalization of the distribution system, one of China's WTO obligations, could attract the necessary investment and foreign know-how to modernize the distribution system and, ultimately, improve the competitiveness of Chinese farm products at factory level. In this respect the Chinese authorities have been praised for circulating draft Regulations on Management of Foreign Investment in the Commercial Sector, but these have failed to offer detailed information on how Chinese distribution systems can be integrated into foreign business activity.

Trade defence instruments

Finally, a number of agreements regulate and restrict the use of trade defence instruments such as anti-dumping, anti-subsidy and safeguard measures. All these instruments involve the temporary introduction of restrictions on imports in specific circumstances:

- anti-dumping duties are applied when a country 'dumps' products on export markets at cheaper prices than the 'normal price' charged on the home market;
- anti-subsidy measures are applied when a product is sold on export markets below a normal market price due to subsidies received by the producer in his home country;
- safeguard measures are emergency measures aimed to prevent 'serious injury' to domestic industry caused by increasing imports.

Such trade defence measures are of course, *prima facie*, a breach of normal market WTO access commitments, and are highly regulated. Regulation of safeguard measures is particularly strict because, unlike anti-dumping and anti-subsidy measures, safeguard measures restrict imports that are not inherently 'unfair'. As a result the use of safeguard measures is relatively rare compared with the use of anti-subsidy and, in particular, anti-dumping measures.

China is one of the main targets of anti-dumping measures around the world and whilst it remained outside the WTO, it had no means of defending itself

against such anti-dumping measures. The situation is clearly different following WTO accession. Indeed, China has already launched its first WTO challenge against the safeguard measures imposed by the US in March 2002 against imports of steel from, among others, China. Initially, China sought to join a steel dispute procedure started by the EU as a third party, but after a delayed US response to this request, China requested its own consultations with the US under the WTO's Dispute Settlement Understanding (DSU) procedures. When this was not acknowledged it promptly established its own separate case.

A major issue for China with regard to the application of anti-dumping rules is the extent to which it is treated as a 'non-market' economy. The latter allows other WTO members much more discretion when imposing anti-dumping duties than they have with regard to a market economy country (a status that almost all WTO members have). As long as China is treated as a 'non-market' economy, a WTO member introducing anti-dumping duties can use data from another country, such as the US for instance, to calculate the 'fair' price. As costs in the US are normally much higher than those in China this can make it very easy to find 'dumping' when the Chinese export price is compared with a 'normal' US price. The terms of China's accession allow the application of this 'non-market' economy methodology for a period of 15 years.

It is possible, however, for individual companies to escape from that disadvantaged status if they can prove that their company operates in sector where 'market economy conditions prevail'. China's Protocol of Accession also provides for two specific safeguard clauses. A first one, which is unique to China, will be available for 12 years, and allows WTO members to take safeguard measures only with respect to imports from China that create market disruption (safeguard measures are normally against all imports irrespective of their origin). A second one, which will be available until the end of 2008, makes it easier than under the standard procedure to impose safeguard measures restricting imports of textiles in case of 'market disruptions' caused by Chinese exports. China is concerned that an overzealous implementation of this safeguard mechanism will restrict access to developed markets and prevent it exercising its considerable comparative advantage in the production of textiles and clothing.

While EU and US trade departments are being lobbied internally by domestic producers to protect their industry, they are also being asked by other developing countries to protect their export market in the face of Chinese dominance. The implementation of safeguard measures is not an easy issue to solve, and it may be one where the use of the WTO's dispute settlement mechanisms is required. On accession, China also agreed to allow specific WTO members various amounts of time to eliminate import restrictions on a range of specified products; however, the majority of these are due to expire in 2005.

Trade in services

The General Agreement on Trade in Services (GATS) regulates the way in which WTO members must open their services markets to each other. The real scope of a country's WTO obligations is determined, sector by sector, in its 'Schedule of Specific Commitments on Services' on the basis of four different 'modes of supply' of services:

- cross-border supply (for instance, via the internet);
- consumption abroad (for instance, Chinese tourists being able to 'consume' tourism services in France);
- commercial presence (for instance, an EU bank operating from a commercial location in China);
- presence of natural persons (for instance, EU building engineers providing their services 'on the spot' in China).

The scope of a country's GATS obligations depends entirely on the details of its schedule of commitments. It is perfectly possible, for example, for a WTO member to accept the supply of certain services via commercial presence whilst not accepting cross-border supply. Chapter 2.1 provides a more detailed overview of some of China's services commitments.

It is important to note that, in practice, the distinction between trade in goods and trade in services is not a rigorous one. For instance, a country's WTO obligations in the area of trade in goods may allow a WTO member to maintain a so-called Tariff Rate Quota for a specific product (ie it may allow the importation of a product up to a certain volume at a lower tariff, whilst imposing a considerably higher tariff on imports above that volume). If a country uses such instruments it also needs to decide which companies can import the 'in-quota' volumes at the lower customs duty rates. This is important because the companies that can make use of this quota can make a profit that is considerably higher than the profits that will be made by those importing out-of-quota volumes at the higher

duty rates. An unfair distribution of these import possibilities over Chinese and foreign companies can result in a violation of a WTO member's obligations in the field of distribution services. China was involved in such a debate with the US on the distribution of import licences for fertilizer, and is now involved in a related debate with the US over the VAT credit it gives domestic fertilizer producers.

Intellectual property

The Agreement on Trade Related Aspects of Intellectual Property Rights (TRIPS) obliges WTO members to guarantee a minimum level of protection for intellectual property rights such as copyright, trade marks and patents. To a large extent the TRIPS Agreement refers back to other international agreements in this area predating the WTO. However, this 'integration by reference' brings these pre-existing arrangements into the WTO system and gives them the same enforceability as other WTO obligations. Foreign companies have continually cited the abuse of intellectual property law by Chinese manufacturing companies as one of the key areas requiring advancement if China is to be fully integrated within the multilateral trading system. The situation does seem to have improved somewhat, with the authorities repeatedly promising to back protection for intellectual property rights and foreign companies having successfully argued their rights in front of domestic Chinese courts.

WTO dispute settlement and China as a litigant

The WTO has an internal dispute settlement system that has been described as the 'jewel in the crown' of the WTO. Many of the currently existing WTO rules on trade in goods already existed in the context of the GATT 1947. The rule of law, however, was much less prominently present in the GATT 1947, where a country that lost a dispute settlement procedure could prevent such a ruling from becoming binding by simply voting against it. This option was removed when the WTO entered into force in 1995. The WTO incorporates a legal enforcement system with real teeth and this is one of the main reasons why the WTO has become a much more prominent international organization than GATT 1947 ever was.

The dispute settlement system is used frequently. By 2003, the number of disputes taken to the WTO in its first nine years of existence exceeded the number taken under the old GATT regime in almost 50 years. It is important to note that these are all disputes between countries. The WTO dispute settlement system is only open to countries – not for private parties (although these will often ask their country of origin to start a procedure on their behalf and support their government in doing that). This frequent use of the dispute settlement system and a number of acrimonious disputes between the EU and the US have triggered criticism that the WTO is much too focused on litigation and that the EU and the US could eventually undermine the WTO by taking too many disputes to WTO dispute settlement rather than finding a mutually satisfactory solution.

It is important to put some of this criticism of WTO dispute settlement in a proper context. The WTO comprises a very large body of complex rules and 148 member countries. In this context divergent opinions are unavoidable and it is a strength of the WTO, not a weakness, that there is a neutral arbitrator that can decide the precise meaning of a text in a specific case. If that were not possible, the parties to the dispute would simply stand by their own interpretation and the practical effect of the agreements would remain limited (as is so often the case in international cooperation). Without the WTO, trade disputes would still exist without an effective means of resolution. Indeed, some of the disputes between the EU and the US (bananas, beef hormones, the FSC and aircraft subsidies) are considerably older than the WTO, and it is often only through WTO litigation that some real progress is made.

A much more legitimate question is how China, which has no western-style litigation tradition, functions in such a context. Most observers seemed to agree at the time of China's accession that it would be impossible for China to maintain a perfect implementation record, and that disputes over the correct implementation of China's WTO obligations were inevitable. Since accession, there have been relatively few full-blown disputes, with China being a respondent in only one request for consultations – that concerning the application of VAT on imports of semi-conductors.

The EU and the US seem to have adopted the position that it would be counterproductive to make extensive use of dispute settlement vis-à-vis China and, at least during this initial stage of its membership, will only do this as a measure of last resort. However, this does appear to be gradually changing and the apparent truce in the invocation of the WTO's dispute settlement procedures papers over the cracks of a flood of trade disputes related to China's WTO commitments that could be proceeded with.

While WTO members have thus far preferred to focus on the benefits of China's membership and, in many instances, have sought to change China's pattern of behaviour in relation to key areas such as intellectual property rights through the use of 'educational' and 'cooperation' projects. These also have the desired effect of pushing China into action before formal WTO dispute resolution procedures are taken. Current issues of concern to the EU and US are Chinese fertilizer subsidies, textile importation restrictions and domestic discrimination in the automotive and telecommunications markets and all could lead to formal WTO disputes if compromise negotiations break down.

This apparent reluctance to invoke formal WTO dispute settlement procedures is certainly also influenced by the behaviour of China as a complainant in dispute settlement procedures, and if China makes intensive use of dispute settlement it would seem that the EU and the US would become less reluctant to use it against China.

Conclusion

The importance of China's WTO accession is that it provides a legally binding roadmap to the full liberalization and modernization of the Chinese economy. This should not be interpreted as submission to an external power. On the contrary, China's WTO membership and the terms thereof are simply the next logical phase in its process of internal and external economic reform that was launched more than 25 years ago with the China's Open Door Policy, initially in agriculture. This reform is now progressing at pace, with China being invited to its first meeting of the G7 group of industrialized countries to discuss liberalization of its exchange rate mechanisms. People very close to the original accession negotiations have pointed out that all the changes that China has agreed to make in the framework of its WTO accession are changes that China wanted to make and would have been made in any event in the foreseeable future. Thus WTO accession has been a useful tool in keeping the internal free-market reform agenda on target rather than an externally imposed obligation. There will certainly be short-term conflicts about specific issues, and companies affected by these short-term conflicts may find that they need to work hard to minimize damage and ensure correct implementation of China's WTO obligations. In the long term, however, there should be no doubt that China is committed to fulfilling its WTO obligations, if only because these reflect China's own policy choices.

The Chinese Government Structure

Li Yong, Deputy Secretary General, China Association of International Trade

The presidency of the People's Republic of China

The President of the People's Republic of China is the Head of State, as well as the supreme representative of China both internally and externally. The state presidency is an independent state apparatus and a component part of China's state organization.

According to international practice, the Chinese president, like most heads of state in the world, has the power to promulgate statutes and holds supreme diplomatic and ceremonial rights. Under the current Constitution, the president has the power to:

- promulgate statutes adopted by the National People's Congress (NPC);
- appoint and remove members of the State Council;
- confer state medals and titles of honour, in line with the decisions of the NPC and its Standing Committee;
- issue orders for special pardons; proclaim martial law; declare a state of war and issue orders of mobilization;
- accept letters of credentials offered by foreign diplomatic representatives on behalf of the People's Republic of China;
- appoint and recall China's diplomatic envoys stationed abroad; and
- ratify and abrogate treaties and important agreements signed with foreign states.

China's system of head of state is a system of collective leadership. The president is subordinate to the NPC and directly receives instructions from this supreme organ of state power.

To date, six men have held the office of the president of the People's Republic of China: Mao Zedong, Liu Shaoqi, Li Xiannian, Yang Shangkun, Jiang Zemin and the current president, Hu Jintao (see Figure 1.3.1).

President: Vice-President:
Hu Jinta   Zeng Qinghong

Figure 1.3.1   Current president and vice-president

The central administrative system in the People's Republic of China includes the central administrative organs under the system of the NPC and the leadership of the central administrative organs over local administrative organs at various levels. The central administrative organ is the State Council of the People's Republic of China.

The National People's Congress (NPC)

The NPC is the highest organ of state power of the People's Republic of China. Its main functions and powers include formulation of laws, delegating authority, policy formulation and supervision of other governing organs.

Legislative power

The NPC has the right to enact and amend the Constitution of the People's Republic of China, and to enact and amend basic laws concerning criminal offenses, civil affairs, state organs and other matters.

Delegating authority

The power to delegate authority allows the Congress to select, empower and remove leadership and members of the highest state organs. The NPC has the right to select the members of the Standing Committee of the NPC; to elect the president and vice-president of the People's Republic of China; to appoint and approve premier, vice-premiers, state councillors, ministers in charge of ministries and commissions, auditor-general and secretary-general of the State Council; to elect the chairman of the Central Military Commission and decide other members of the Commission; and to elect the president of the Supreme People's Court and the procurator-general of the Supreme People's Procuratorate. The NPC has the right to remove any or all members it elects, and is therefore the final authority among all state organs.

Policy formulation

The NPC has the right to:

- examine and approve government reports;
- examine and approve the plan for national economic and social development and reports on its implementation;
- examine and approve the state budget and reports on its implementation;
- approve the establishment of provinces, autonomous regions and municipalities directly under the central government;
- decide on the establishment of special administrative regions and the systems to be instituted within these regions; and
- declare war and sign treaties of peace.

It also exercises other functions and powers as the supreme state power.

Supervision of governing organs

The NPC has the right to supervise the implementation of the Constitution. According to the Chinese Constitution, the State Council, the Supreme People's Court and the Supreme People's Procuratorate are all invested by the NPC, are responsible to it, and supervised by it. The NPC's exercise of its supervisory role is to oversee the actions of the government and other state organs on behalf of the people. This is an important guarantee for the normal and legal operation of the state apparatus.

Since 1954, the People's Republic of China has convened nine National People's Congresses listed in Table 1.3.1.

Table 1.3.1   National People's Congresses from 1954

No.	Month/Year	Chairman
1	September 1954	Liu Shaoqi
2	April 1959	Zhu De
3	December 1964	Zhu De
4	January 1975	Zhu De
5	March 1978	Ye Jianying
6	June 1983	Peng Zhen
7	March 1988	Wan Li
8	March 1993	Qiao Shi
9	March 1998	Li Peng
10	March 2003	Wu Bangguo

Under the current Constitution and related laws, the NPC holds a session on the first quarter of each year, convened by its Standing Committee. A single term of an NPC deputy is five years.

The NPC Standing Committee is the permanent supreme state organ of power and legislation. It exercises the highest state power and legislative power when the NPC is not in session. The Standing Committee is composed of 153 members, none of whom can assume an office in state administrative, judicial or procuratorial organs, so as to maintain a separation of powers and to better supervise these organs.

The NPC Standing Committee has the right to interpret the Constitution and supervises its implementation, enacts and amends laws (with the exception of laws relating to fields reserved for the NPC as a whole), partially supplements and amends laws enacted by the NPC when that body is not in session, and interprets laws. Since 1979, the NPC and its Standing Committee have enacted over 300 laws, and local people's congresses and their standing committees have drawn up more than 3,000 local rules and regulations.

Special committees are permanent organs representing the NPC. When the NPC is in session, the main work of these committees is to study, examine and draw up related motions. When the NPC is not in session, these committees work under the direction of the NPC Standing Committee. Currently, there are eight permanent special committees: the Ethnic Groups Committee; the Legal Committee; the

Finance and Economics Committee; the Education, Science, Culture and Public Health Committee; the Foreign Affairs Committee; the Overseas Chinese Committee; the Committee for Internal and Judicial Affairs; and the Committee on Environmental and Resource Protection.

The current leadership of the NPC is illustrated in Figure 1.3.2

The State Council, or the Central People's Government of the People's Republic of China, is the executive body of the highest organ of state power and the highest organ of state administration. It exercises unified leadership over local state administrative organs at various levels throughout the country, regulates the specific division of power and function of the state administrative organs at the central level and the provincial, autonomous regional and municipal level. The head of the State Council is Premier, who assumes overall responsibility for the work of the State Council and is responsible to the NPC and its Standing Committee on behalf of the State Council. The Premier is assisted by a Vice Premier and State Councillors. The Premier of the State Council is nominated by the president, reviewed by the NPC, and appointed and removed by the president. Other members of the State Council are nominated by the premier, reviewed by the NPC or its Standing Committee, and appointed and removed by the president. In the State Council, a single office is five years, and incumbents cannot be re-appointed after two successive terms. The Premier has the following powers of decision-making:

- the final decision-making power on all major issues in the work of the State Council;
- power to suggest to the NPC and its Standing Committee to appoint or remove the Vice Premiers, State Councillors, Ministers, the Auditor-general and Secretary-general;
- decisions, decrees and administrative rules and regulations promulgated by the State Council; bills and suggestions of appointments and removals submitted by the State Council to the NPC and its Standing Committee are legally valid only after the Premier has signed them.

Since 1998, the State Council has made a series of reforms to its organizational structure, which has been an attempt to streamline the government body, increase efficiency and advance the market-oriented economy. The new term of the State Council, as of March 2003, implemented further reforms on government structure, notably the consolidation of several functions that used to be under different commissions and ministries into the new Ministry of Commerce (MOFCOM), and the formation of a

Chairman

Wu Bangguo
Vice-chairmen

Wang Zhaoguo   Li Tieying   Ismail Amat   He Luli   Ding Shisun   Cheng Siwei   Xu Jiaiu   Jiang Zhenghua

Gu Xiulan   Raidi   Sheng Huaren   Lu Yongxiang   Uyunqimg   Han Qide   Fu Tieshan

Figure 1.3.2   Leadership of the NPC

commission for the supervision and administration of state-owned assets, which is called the State-owned Asset Supervision and Administration Commission (SASAC).

MOFCOM offers a unified access for foreign businesses and investors to China's regulatory activities in commerce and trade. SASAC is a move to further confine the government's role to the supervision of state-owned assets instead of participating in the management of state-owned enterprises.

To manage the banking industry effectively, the NPC also initiated, in March 2003, the establishment of a banking supervisory body, the China Banking Regulatory Commission, in addition to the central bank, the People's Bank of China.

The current leadership of the State Council is illustrated in Figure 1.3.3.

Main bodies of the State Council (since March 2003)

The State Council consists of ministries, commissions, the People's Bank of China and State Audit Office, who, under the unified leadership of the State Council, are in charge of directing and administering the administrative affairs in their respective areas and exercise prescribed state administrative powers.

These government departments are classified into categories by the nature of their functions (see Tables 1.3.2 to 1.3.5).

Premier

Wen Jiabao

Vice-premiers of the State Council:

Huang Ju   Wu Yi   Zeng Peiyan   Hui Liangyu

State councillors:

Zhou Yongkang   Cao Gangchuan   Tang Jiaxuan   Hua Jianmin   Chen Zhiji

Figure 1.3.3   Current leadership of the State Council

Table 1.3.2   Ministries (22)

Name of Ministry	Minister	Website address
Ministry of Agriculture	Du Qingling	http://www.agri.gov.cn
Ministry of Civil Affairs	Li Xueju	http://www.mca.gov.cn
Ministry of Commerce	Bo Xilai	http://www.mofcom.gov.cn
Ministry of Communications	Zhang Chunxian	http://www.moc.gov.cn
Ministry of Construction	Wang Guangtao	http://www.cin.gov.cn
Ministry of Culture	Sun Jiazheng	http://www.ccnt.gov.cn
Ministry of Education	Zhou Ji	http://www.moe.gov.cn
Ministry of Finance	Jin Renqing	http://www.mof.gov.cn
Ministry of Foreign Affairs	Li Zhaoxing	http://www.fmprc.gov.cn
Ministry of Health	Wu Yi	http://www.moh.gov.cn
Ministry of Information Industry	Wang Xudong	http://www.mii.gov.cn
Ministry of Justice	Zhang Fusen	http://www.legalinfo.gov.cn
Ministry of Labour and Social Security	Zheng Silin	http://www.molss.gov.cn
Ministry of Land and Resources	Sun Wensheng	http://www.mlr.gov.cn
Ministry of National Defense	Cao Gangchuan	n.a.
Ministry of Personnel	Zhang Bolin	http://www.mop.gov.cn
Ministry of Public Security	Zhou Yongkang	http://www.mps.gov.cn
Ministry of Railways	Liu Zhijun	http://www.chinamor.gov.cn
Ministry of Science and Technology	Xu Guanhua	http://www.most.gov.cn
Ministry of State Security	Xu Yongyue	n.a.
Ministry of Supervision	Li Zhilun	http://www.mos.gov.cn
Ministry of Water Resources	Wang Shucheng	http://www.mwr.gov.cn

Table 1.3.3   Commissions (4)

Name of Commission	Minister	Website address
State Development and Reform Commission	Ma Kai	http://www.sdpc.gov.cn
Commission of Science, Technology and Industry for National Defence	Zhang Yunchuan	http://www.costind.gov.cn
State Ethnic Affairs Commission	Li Dek Su	http://www.seac.gov.cn
State Population and Family Planning Commission	Zhang Weiqing	http://www.chinapop.gov.cn

Table 1.3.4   Especially set up directly under the State Council

Name	Head	Website address
State Owned Assets Supervision and Administration Commission	Li Rongrong	http://www.sasac.gov.cn

Table 1.3.5   Other constituents of the State Council

Name	Head	Website address
People's Bank of China	Zhou Xiaochuan	http://www.pbc.gov.cn
National Audit Office	Li Jinhua	http://www.audit.gov.cn

Other organs under the State Council

Apart from the above-mentioned organs that constitute the main body of the State Council, there are also other types of organization working under the State Council and under the Ministries and Commissions of the State Council (see Tables 1.3.6 to 1.3.9).

Table 1.3.6 Organs directly under the State Council (18)

Name	Head	Website address
General Administration of Customs	Mou Xinsheng	http://www.customs.gov.cn
State Administration of Taxation	Xie Xuren	http://www.chinatax.gov.cn
State Administration for Industry and Commerce	Wang Zhongfu	http://www.saic.gov.cn
State Environmental Protection Administration	Xie Zhenhua	http://www.zhb.gov.cn
General Administration of the Civil Aviation of China	Yang Yuanyuan	http://www.caac.gov.cn
State Administration of Radio, Film and Television	Xu Guangchun	http://www.sarft.gov.cn
State General Administration of Sports	Yuan Weimin	http://www.sport.gov.cn
National Bureau of Statistics	Li Deshui	http://www.stats.gov.cn
State Forestry Administration	Zhou Shengxian	http://www.forestry.gov.cn
State Drug Administration	Zheng Xiaoyu	http://www.sda.gov.cn
State Intellectual Property Office	Wang Jingchuan	http://www.sipo.gov.cn
National Tourism Administration	He Guangwei	http://www.cnta.gov.cn
State Administration of Religious Affairs	Ye Xiaowen	
Counselors' Office of the State Council	Cui Zhanfu	http://www.counsellor.gov.cn
Government Offices Administration of the State Council	Jiao Huancheng	http://www.ggj.gov.cn
State General Administration for Quality Supervision and Inspection and Quarantine	Li Changjiang	http://www.ciq.gov.cn
General Administration of Press and Publication	Shi Zongyuan	http://www.ppa. gov.cn
(National Copyright Administration)	Shi Zongyuan	http://www. ncac.gov.cn
State Administration for Work Safety (State Administration of Coal Mine Safety)	Wang Xianzheng	http://www.chinasafety.gov.cn

Table 1.3.7 Institutions directly under the State Council

Name	Head	Website address
Xinhua News Agency	Tian Congming	http://www.xinhua.org
Chinese Academy of Sciences	Lu Yongxiang	http://www.cashq.ac.cn
Chinese Academy of Social Sciences	Chen Kuiyuan	http://www.cass.net.cn
Chinese Academy of Engineering	Xu Kuangdi	http://www.cae.ac.cn
Development Research Center of the State Council	Wang Mengkui	http://www.drc.gov.cn
National School of Administration	Hua Jianmin (concurrent)	http://www.nsa.gov.cn
China Seismological Bureau	Song Ruixiang	http://www.seis.ac.cn
China Meteorological Administration	Qin Dahe	http://www.cma.gov.cn
China Securities Regulatory Commission	Shang Fulin	http://www.csrc.gov.cn
China Insurance Regulatory Commission	Wu Dingfu	http://www.circ.gov.cn
National Council for Social Security Fund	Xiang Huaicheng	n.a.
National Natural Science Foundation of China	Chen Yiyu	http://www.nsfc.gov.cn
State Electricity Regulatory Commission	Chai Songyue	http://www.serc.gov.cn
China Banking Regulatory Commission	Li Mingkang	http://www.cbrc.gov.cn

Table 1.3.8   Working organs of the State Council

Name	Head	Website address
Overseas Chinese Affairs Office of the State Council	Chen Yujie	n.a.
Hong Kong and Macao Affairs Office of the State Council	Liao Hui	http://www.hmo.gov.cn
Legislative Affairs Office of the State Council		http://www.chinalaw.gov.cn
Research Office of the State Council	Wei Liqun	n.a.
Taiwan Affairs Office of the State Council	Chen Yunlin	http://www.gwytb.govl.cn

Table 1.3.9   Administrations and Bureaux under the Ministries and Commissions of the State Council

Name	Head	Website address
State Bureau for Letters and Complaints	Wang Xuejun	n.a.
State Administration of Grain	Nie Zhenbang	http://www.grain.gov.cn
State Tobacco Monopoly Administration	Jiang Chengkang	http://www.tobacco.gov.cn
State Administration of Foreign Experts Affairs	Wan Xueyuan	http://www.safea.gov.cn
State Oceanic Administration	Wang Shuguang	http://www.nmemc.gov.cn
State Bureau of Surveying and Mapping	Chen Bangzhu	http://www.sbsm.gov.cn
State Post Bureau	Liu Andong	http://www.chinapost.gov.cn
State Administration of Cultural Heritage	Shan Jixiang	http://www.sach.gov.cn
State Administration of Traditional Chinese Medicine	She Jing	http://www.satcm.gov.cn
State Administration of Foreign Exchange	Guo Shuqing	http://www.safe.gov.cn
State Archives Bureau	Mao Fumin	http://www.saac.gov.cn

The government hierarchy

Typical structure of a ministry

The management body of a ministry usually consists of a minister, several vice-ministers and assistant ministers. Under the ministry there are departments, under which are divisions (see Figure 1.3.4). Normally, the divisions are the first point of contact with the ministry. Parallel with the departments, in some cases there are also industry associations and other institutions, such as information centres or research institutes, which are relatively independent in terms of operation, but organizationally affiliated in terms of nominations of key organizational heads.

Previously, ministries had under them business corporations and large state-owned enterprises, which are now independent as a result of government reform to separate government functions from enterprise management.

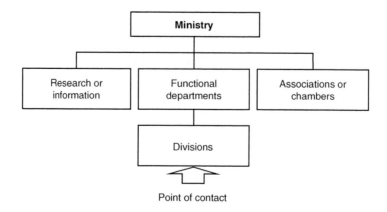

Figure 1.3.4   Typical organizational set-up of a government department

Local government

The local NPCs resemble the structure of the central NPC. There are also local people's congresses, which exercise functions and powers through their standing committees when the NPCs are not in session. As with the NPC, a local NPC standing committee is composed of a chairman, vice-chairmen and members.

The administrative arm of local people's congresses is the local government. The local governments are established at five levels, namely, provincial, municipal, district/city, county and township governments (see Figure 1.3.5). The local governments that are immediately under the central government are provincial-level governments. China now has, on its mainland, 22 provinces, five autonomous regions and four municipalities under state jurisdiction. All the governments in those 31 locations are provincial level governments. The heads of those provincial governments are ministerial level officials.

Provincial governments must accept the unified leadership of the State Council, which has the power to decide on the division of responsibilities between the Central Government and provincial administrative organs. The State Council also has the power to annul inappropriate decisions and orders of provincial governments. At the same time, provincial governments implement local laws, regulations and the decisions of the provincial people's congresses and their standing committees, and are responsible to and report on their work to the provincial people's congresses and their standing committees. Provincial people's congresses and their standing committees have the power to supervise the work of provincial governments, and change and annul inappropriate decisions of the provincial governments.

The structure of a provincial government resembles that of the central government. Under a provincial government, there are similar set-ups that correspond to the ministries and commissions at the central level. For example, there are provincial development planning commissions, bureaux of finance, bureaux of commerce, bureaux of education, drug administrations etc, that correspond to the State Development and Reform Commission, the Ministry of Finance, the Ministry of Commerce, the Ministry of Education, the State Drug Administration etc. The heads of the local bureaux, commissions, administrations etc, are appointed by the provincial governments and they are responsible to the provincial governments while at the same time, executing the policies made both by the provincial governments and the central ministries. A typical reporting structure is illustrated in Figure 1.3.6.

Lower level governments

Chinese cities vary not only in size, but also in official ranking. Some provincial capitals and cities of key economic importance have different administrative status and a certain level of independence from the provinces where they are located. There are 15 cities that are called 'separately planned cities', which means that they have independent administrative status and are singled out to enjoy quasi-provincial status in the national planning. In terms of reporting routes, the government functions such as bureaux, commissions and administration in these cities do not report to the corresponding provincial departments, but to those at the central level. The heads of those governments are

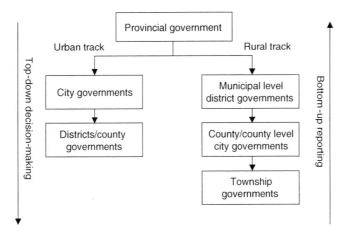

Figure 1.3.5 Local government structure

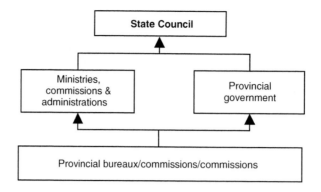

Figure 1.3.6   The reporting structure of provincial government

referred to as vice-ministerial officials. These cities are Shenyang, Dalian, Changchun, Harbin, Jinan, Qingdao, Nanjing, Ningbo, Hangzhou, Xiamen, Wuhan, Guangzhou, Shenzhen, Xian and Chengdu.

There are also municipal level districts (*di qu*) in parallel with municipal level cities. Most of the municipal level cities/districts are under the jurisdiction of the provincial government.

A municipal level district is not a district in a city, but an area that normally includes several counties. Administratively, these districts are at the same level as those larger cities, governing basically rural areas. There are, according to a report by *Economic Daily* in 2002, 31 provincial governments (including four municipalities under the direct jurisdiction of central government, namely, Beijing, Tianjin, Shanghai and Chongqing), about 333 municipal level district governments, 259 municipal level city governments and 400 county level governments. Municipal level district governments are largely present in most provinces and autonomous regions in China, with Hainan province as an exception, where the county governments report directly to the provincial governments. The set-up of the four municipalities under central government control varies from provinces and autonomous regions, as they are predominantly urban areas. At the very bottom of the administrative hierarchy are the administrative townships (*xiang*), and the same source indicated about 45,000 such governments in China.

In terms of official ranking, the head of a municipal level district/city is equivalent to the heads of provincial bureaux; the heads of commissions and administrations are all known as director-general level officials. The existing municipal level cities/districts are largely the heritage of the old administrative system

of China. It is not a rigid hierarchical ladder now, because county-level cities can be promoted to municipal level cities if all of the following criteria are met:

- over 500,000 total non-farming population, with the place of the government seat having over 200,000 of that population;
- total industrial and agricultural output value at 1990 constant price exceeding RMB3 billion, of which 80 per cent should be industrial output value;
- GDP over RMB2.5 billion;
- the share of the output value of tertiary industry reaching 35 per cent of the GDP and surpassing that of primary industry;
- annual budgetary fiscal revenue in excess of RMB200 million; and
- the city becoming a centre for the neighbouring areas.

Official ranking

Official ranking is an important part of China's administrative hierarchy. Although there is a saying that 'the person in charge is more helpful than the person who supervises', which means that the person with no official ranking can be very important in handling government relations, a better understanding of the official rankings may help understand the roles of the officials that you are dealing with and that they will play a part in the decision-making process. Figure 1.3.7 provides a comparison of the official rankings in different government structures.

As a result of the government's effort to separate government functions from enterprise management, the government, at all levels, are not supposed to be involved in business activities. The government reform

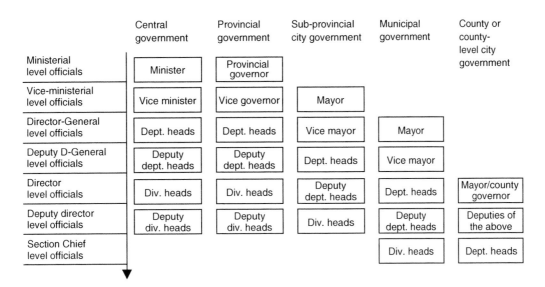

Figure 1.3.7 Official rankings in government

effort has also removed the official rankings associated with the management of state-owned enterprises. Enterprises mostly use corporate titles with no implications of official ranking.

China's Consumer Market

Li Yong, Deputy Secretary General, China Association of International Trade, and Liu Baocheng, Professor, University of International Business and Economics, with updates by Jonathan Reuvid

Introduction

When one thinks globally in terms of market expansion, China is a market that no business would ignore. One simple reason is that China is the largest single market that has yet to be developed. The population size, increasing consumer affluence and a strong momentum of economic growth make China an attractive marketplace in which many foreign companies have attempted to gain a foothold. In fact, many have. Most Fortune 500 companies have operations of one kind or another in the marketplace. Seventy per cent of the world's top 50 retailers are already active in China. These facts demonstrate that China is of significant strategic value for corporate growth and globalization. Indeed, manufacturing in China should mean reduced costs and increased competitiveness. Marketing in China should mean new sources of profit and additional gains in global market share.

Often, people tend to think of China in terms of a simplistic arithmetic calculation – if each of the 1.3 billion people spent one dollar or used a product once in a year, what enormous sales that would bring. It does not hurt to generalize on the market size with such a calculation, but to approach the market in such an arithmetic manner would satisfy only the desires of wishful thinking. In fact, no one should be so naive as to think of the market in these terms. It is true, however, that many marketers in China have overestimated market prospects by underestimating the complexity of the market. This introductory chapter on China's consumer market does not intend to provide solutions for market success, but aims to paint a picture of what the market looks like, particularly for those who have not yet stepped out of their national boundaries but are already planning international strategies that include China.

Consumer demographics

Population

Population is a factor in market size. For some products whose consumers are potentially every walking person, the total population represents the customer base and a percentage of the population would be the target of sales efforts. For other products, the population size would need to have a denominator before a company can assess the market. In other words, the size of the population does not determine a market that a company can address economically and realistically reach. It is an onion of which the outer skins need to be peeled off.

At the end of 2001, China registered a population of 1,276.7 million (excluding Hong Kong, Macao, Taiwan and other southern islands). Evidently China is now the most populous country in the world, while India is catching up. Some experts predict that India will replace China as the world's largest country. One underlying reason for this expectation is that China's population growth has slowed and the family planning policy has been effective in controlling the once explosive population. Table 1.4.1 depicts the trend of China's population growth over the last two decades or so and the slow growth trend is obvious. According to one estimate, by 2010 the population is expected to stay at 1.4 billion, and by the middle of this century the population growth will halt at a peak of 1.6 billion. Thereafter, the population is expected to decline.

Table 1.4.1   China's population changes
(1978–2001)

Year	Total population (000)	Natural growth rate (%)
1978	96,259	12.00
1979	97,542	11.61
1980	98,705	11.87
1981	1,000,720	14.55
1982	1,016,540	15.68
1983	1,030,080	13.29
1984	1,043,570	13.08
1985	1,058,510	14.26
1986	1,075,070	15.57
1987	1,093,000	16.61
1988	1,110,260	15.73
1989	1,127,040	15.04
1990	1,143,330	14.39
1991	1,158,230	12.98
1992	1,171,710	11.60
1993	1,185,170	11.45
1994	1,198,500	11.21
1995	1,211,210	10.55
1996	1,223,890	10.42
1997	1,236,260	10.06
1998	1,248,100	9.53
1999	1,259,090	8.77
2000	1,265,830	7.58
2001	1,276,270	6.95

Sources: China Statistical Yearbook 2001 and *China Statistical Abstract 2002*

Table 1.4.2   Population distribution by administrative divisions 2001

Region	Total population (000)	Natural growth rate (%)
Beijing	13,830	0.80
Tianjin	10,040	1.64
Hebei	66,990	4.98
Shanxi	32,720	7.16
Inner Mongolia	23,770	4.98
Liaoning	41,940	1.64
Jilin	26,910	3.38
Heilongjiang	38,110	2.99
Shanghai	16,140	–0.95
Jiangsu	73,550	2.41
Zhejiang	46,130	3.77
Anhui	63,280	6.61
Fujian	34,400	6.04
Jiangxi	41,860	9.38
Shandong	90,410	4.88
Henan	95,550	6.94
Hubei	59,750	2.44
Hunan	65,960	5.08
Guangdong	77,830	8.33
Guangxi	47,880	7.73
Hainan	7,960	9.47
Chongqing	30,970	2.80
Sichuan	86,400	4.37
Guizhou	37,990	11.30
Yunnan	42,870	10.94
Tibet	2,630	12.10
Shaanxi	36,590	4.16
Gansu	25,750	7.15
Qinghai	5,230	12.62
Ningxia	5,630	11.71
Xinjiang	18,760	11.13
National total	1,276,270	6.95

Source: China Statistical Abstract 2002

a) Military personnel were included in the national total population, but excluded from the regional total population

b) The national total population excluded the populations of Hong Kong, Macao and Taiwan

Population distribution by administrative divisions
Geographically, the Chinese population is distributed over 31 administrative regions, excluding Taiwan, Hong Kong and Macao. On its mainland, China has four provincial level municipalities under the direct jurisdiction of the central government (Beijing, Shanghai, Tianjin and Chongqing), five autonomous regions (Inner Mongolia, Guangxi, Tibet, Ningxia and Xinjiang) and 22 provinces.

The top ten most populous provinces are Henan, (95.55 million), Shandong (90.41 million), Sichuan (86.4 million), Jiangsu (73.55 million), Guangdong (77.83 million), Hebei (66.99 million), Hunan (65.96 million), Anhui (63.28 million), Hubei (59.75 million) and Guangxi (47.88 million). These ten most populous places account for 57 per cent of the total population (see Figure 1.4.1).

Urban and rural population distribution
China began to practise a residence control system in 1951. Migration from rural to urban residences has been under strict control, as a result of which the rural population has remained predominantly high. In 1978 the proportion of rural population was 82.08 per cent, against an urban population share of 17.92 per cent (see Table 1.4.3). With the

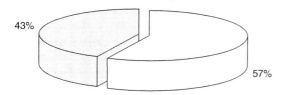

10 most populous provinces have
57% of the total population

43%

57%

Figure 1.4.1 Share of the ten most populous provinces

progress of urbanization, the share of urban population has increased to 37.65 per cent. This is a remarkable progress compared vertically with the past, but it is still quite low if compared horizontally with the world average of 47 per cent, not to mention a 70 per cent ratio of urban populations in developed countries.

Following China's accession to the WTO, agriculture is going to be one of the industries most impacted, and labour migration from rural to urban areas is expected to increase. At the same time, the urbanization process will quicken in order to absorb the

Table 1.4.3 Urban vs rural population

Year	Urban population (million)	% of total	Rural population (million)	% of total
1978	172.45	17.92	790.14	82.08
1980	191.40	19.39	795.65	80.61
1985	250.94	23.71	807.57	76.29
1987	276.74	25.32	816.26	74.68
1988	286.61	25.81	823.65	74.19
1989	295.40	26.21	831.64	73.79
1990	301.91	26.41	841.42	73.59
1991	305.43	26.37	852.80	73.63
1992	323.72	27.63	847.99	72.37
1993	333.51	28.14	851.66	71.86
1994	343.01	28.62	855.49	71.38
1995	351.74	29.04	859.47	70.96
1996	359.50	29.37	864.39	70.63
1997	369.89	29.92	866.37	70.08
1998	379.42	30.40	868.68	69.60
1999	388.92	30.89	870.17	69.11
2000	458.44	36.22	807.39	63.78
2001	480.64	37.65	795.63	62.34

Sources: China Statistical Yearbook 2001 and *China Statistical Abstract 2002*

surplus labour from rural areas. There are indications that policies regarding control over the migration of the rural population into urban areas have been relaxed and rural residents are expected to receive 'national treatment'. Undoubtedly, urbanization is going to be vitally important in narrowing the gap between rural areas and urban districts, boosting China's economic growth and creating more jobs. According to a report by *Guangming Daily* in July 2002, the number of people living in Chinese cities is expected to reach 1.12 billion by 2050, accounting for 70 per cent of the country's total population. More than 600 million Chinese people will shift from rural areas to urban districts in the next 50 years. The same report says that the Chinese mainland now has more than 660 cities and 19,000 towns, and by 2050, 80 per cent of towns will have grown into small or medium-sized cities. By then, China will have 50 ultra-large cities, each with an urban population of more than two million, 150 big cities, 500 medium-sized cities and 1,500 small cities.

Population breakdown by gender
As shown in Table 1.4.4, the male population as a percentage of the total population has been higher than that of females. The Chinese Constitution and legislation give equal rights to both male and female in terms of social status and employment opportunities, but the culture's preference for masculinity is considered to be the key reason for a greater male population. This is particularly true in the less developed rural areas. In 2001, the female population reached a historical low of 48.31 per cent over the period from 1988 to 2001. Although the imbalance between the male and female populations is not so significant as to cause problems with social and economic implications, experts have expressed concerns for social stability if this trend continues.

Age distribution
According to China's *Population Report*, over 30 per cent of the population were under 20 years of age. On the other hand, the population segment of the people aged over 60 accounted for over 10 per cent, and those above 65 reached 6.95 per cent in the 2000 census. Population ageing will become increasingly felt. By 2010, the people born in the baby boom period in the 1950s and 1960s will enter the elderly groupings and the elderly segment will experience the fastest growth. In the next 25 years the elderly population will be double today's count.

Table 1.4.4   Male vs female population

Year	Male		Female		Total population (million)
	Population (million)	% of total	Population (million)	% of total	
1988	572.01	51.52	538.25	48.48	1,110.26
1989	580.99	51.55	546.05	48.45	1,127.04
1990	589.04	51.52	554.29	48.48	1,143.33
1991	594.66	51.34	563.57	48.66	1,158.23
1992	598.11	51.05	573.60	48.95	1,171.71
1993	604.72	51.02	580.45	48.98	1,185.17
1994	612.46	51.10	586.04	48.90	1,198.50
1995	618.08	51.03	593.13	48.97	1,211.21
1996	622.00	50.82	601.89	49.18	1,223.89
1997	631.31	51.07	604.95	48.93	1,236.26
1998	636.29	50.98	611.81	49.02	1,248.10
1999	641.89	50.98	617.20	49.02	1,259.09
2000	653.55	51.63	612.28	48.37	1,265.83
2001	656.72	51.69	619.55	48.31	1,276.27

Sources: China Statistical Yearbook 2001 and *China Statistical Abstract 2002*

When studying the age distribution, marketers are invited to look into the two extremes of the population, one of which is the population of teenagers or what is called the 'little emperors' generation, and the other is the growing ageing population. Marketers have already invested efforts to address the needs of the pampered little emperors but little attention has been given to the elderly population.

The little emperors have enjoyed higher living standards and better education and training than previous generations in China. But they have also displayed distortions in behaviour. Research indicates that the little emperors do not only represent a group of consumers, but also have increasing influence over parents' purchase decision-making. Over time, there will be more 'only children' joining the workforce. They will have better education as a result of their parents' investment in only-child schooling. Considerable study effort is necessary to understand the behavioural characteristics of only children, as they will soon become the core of Chinese society.

Household structure

The average household size is getting smaller. In 2001 average household size in urban areas was 3.10 persons compared with 3.97 persons in 1990. One of the reasons for the decline in average family size is the low birth rate as a result of family planning. Social,

economic and cultural factors have also contributed to the reduction in the average family size. There is an increasing number of DINK (double income no kids) families in urban areas, particularly among those who have had higher education.

Urban households are characterized by high proportions of childless families, while rural households average four-person families. The average size of rural households was 4.15 persons. Experts have commented that the urban household structure resembles that of developed countries and will not change much in the foreseeable future. With the continued family planning effort, the average size of rural households is expected to reduce.

China's family planning policy, which was designed to reduce the population, encourages late marriage and late childbearing. Better and fewer births are strongly advocated and the single-child family is promoted as state policy. The basic principle of family planning policy is to integrate this state instruction with individual consent. While respecting and safeguarding the individual's basic rights, the policy calls for individual's social responsibility and obligations. Health care institutions throughout the country are providing various kinds of services for mothers, children and couples at the childbearing age. However, at the same time, from 2003, most young people of marriageable age in urban areas will be only children. The one-child policy is

Table 1.4.5   Age composition by region

Region	Population by age group (10,000)				% of total population		
	Age 0–14	Age 15–64	Age 65+	Total (10,000)	Age 0–14	Age 15–64	Age 65+
Beijing	188	1,078	116	1,382	13.60	78.04	8.36
Tianjin	168	750	83	1,001	16.75	74.93	8.33
Hebei	1,539	4,742	463	6,744	22.82	70.32	6.86
Shanxi	851	2,242	204	3,297	25.80	68.00	6.20
Inner Mongolia	506	1,743	127	2,376	21.28	73.37	5.35
Liaoning	749	3,157	332	4,238	17.68	74.49	7.83
Jilin	517	2,051	160	2,728	18.96	75.19	5.85
Heilongjiang	697	2,792	200	3,689	18.90	75.68	5.42
Shanghai	204	1,277	193	1,674	12.19	76.28	11.53
Jiangsu	1,462	5,325	651	7,438	19.65	71.59	8.76
Zhejiang	845	3,418	414	4,677	18.07	73.09	8.84
Anhui	1,528	4,012	446	5,986	25.52	67.03	7.45
Fujian	799	2,445	227	3,471	23.02	70.44	6.54
Jiangxi	1,076	2,811	253	4,140	25.99	67.90	6.11
Shandong	1,893	6,457	729	9,079	20.85	71.12	8.03
Henan	2,401	6,211	644	9,256	25.94	67.10	6.96
Hubei	1,379	4,269	380	6,028	22.87	70.82	6.31
Hunan	1,428	4,543	469	6,440	22.17	70.54	7.29
Guangdong	2,089	6,030	523	8,642	24.17	69.78	6.05
Guangxi	1,178	2,991	320	4,489	26.24	66.64	7.12
Hainan	216	519	52	787	27.47	65.95	6.58
Chongqing	678	2,168	244	3,090	21.93	70.17	7.90
Sichuan	1,887	5,822	620	8,329	22.65	69.90	7.45
Guizhou	1,068	2,253	204	3,525	30.29	63.92	5.79
Yunnan	1,116	2,915	257	4,288	26.02	67.98	6.00
Tibet	82	168	12	262	31.20	64.30	4.50
Shaanxi	902	2,490	214	3,605	25.01	69.06	5.93
Gansu	692	1,742	128	2,562	27.00	68.00	5.00
Qinghai	138	358	22	518	26.62	69.05	4.33
Ningxia	160	377	25	562	28.38	67.15	4.47
Xinjiang	526	1,312	87	1,925	27.30	68.17	4.53
National total	28,979	88,793	8,811	126,583	22.89	70.15	6.96

Notes: a) The national population total includes the number of service people in the Chinese People's Liberation Army, who are excluded from the regional population figures

b) Data in this table are preliminary results of the 5th national population census as of zero hour 1 November 2000

Source: China Statistical Yearbook 2001

expected to be relaxed – when two only children marry, they will be allowed to have more than one child.

Education

The proportion of illiteracy among adults has decreased from 182 million or 15.9 per cent of the population in 1990 to 84.81 million (6.7 per cent) in 2000. The government education fund in proportion to GDP has increased from the historical average of 2.4 per cent to 3.1 per cent. However, it is still below the world average of 4.8 per cent. As shown in Figure 1.4.2, 69.7 per cent of the population have received primary and junior high school education, while 11.1 per cent have had senior high school education. The percentage of the population that has received education at college level or above was only 3.6 per cent.

There still exists a marked disparity in the levels of education received by urban and rural populations. The segment of rural population aged 15 and above has a predominant share of primary education,

Table 1.4.6   Number and size of households

Year	Number of households (000)	Average household size
1990	288,300	3.97
1991	294,580	4.01
1992	300,390	3.95
1993	305,740	3.92
1994	311,040	3.89
1995	316,580	3.70
1996	321,680	3.70
1997	326,630	3.64
1998	341,190	3.63
1999	336,512	3.58
2000	348,370	3.13
2001	n.a.	3.10

Sources: China Populations Statistics Yearbook 1998, China Statistical Yearbook 2001 and China Statistical Abstract 2002

accounting for 43.29 per cent. The percentages of rural population having received junior high school, senior high school and college and above education were 28.2 per cent, 4.48 per cent and 0.27 per cent respectively. In contrast, a majority of the urban population has a higher level of education than the rural population.

The current education structure is such that urban education has shifted its focus to middle level education, while rural education is still concentrating on primary education.

Per capita disposable income

Since the economic reforms and open-door policy adopted in 1978, China has made remarkable progress in the improvement of the national standard of living. The pattern of growth is moving from the former, simple quantitative expansion to quality enhancement. As a result the quality of people's lives has been improved.

Although Chinese people, both urban and rural, have more income, the income disparity between urban and rural households has widened in absolute terms. In 1991, the gap between rural income and urban disposable income was RMB992, which rose to RMB4,493.2 in 2001. In the 10-year period from 1991 to 2001, the average growth of rural incomes was 12.82 per cent, while that of urban incomes was 14.97 per cent.

Urban household income

Apart from the disparity between rural and urban income, urban household income also varies among cities of different sizes. The per capita disposable income in extra-large cities is predominantly higher than all other cities of varying sizes. An interesting phenomenon is that the per capita disposable income in small cities is higher than both large and medium-sized cities.

Urban household incomes were unevenly distributed among different income groups and the gap between the highest income group and lowest income group has also widened. In 1997, for example, the gap between the lowest and highest income group was RMB9,758.09. In 2000, however, the disparity was RMB10,712.17.

Regional differences in urban per capita disposable income

Households in the relatively developed areas in eastern China have the highest income compared with middle and western China. Guangdong, Shanghai and Beijing were the top three provinces (municipalities) having the highest per capita disposable income, while Henan, Jilin and Gansu, Shanxi, Ningxia and Inner Mongolia stayed at the

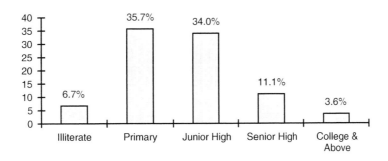

Source: State Statistical Yearbook 2001

Figure 1.4.2   Level of education by percentage of population in 2000

Table 1.4.7 Comparison of rural and urban incomes

Year	Per capita net income of rural residents (RMB)	Per capita disposable income of urban residents (RMB)
1978	133.6	343.4
1980	191.3	477.6
1985	397.6	739.1
1986	423.8	899.6
1987	462.6	1,002.2
1988	544.9	1,181.4
1989	601.5	1,375.7
1990	686.3	1,510.2
1991	708.6	1,700.6
1992	784.0	2,026.6
1993	921.6	2,577.4
1994	1,221.0	3,496.2
1995	1,577.7	4,283.0
1996	1,926.1	4,838.9
1997	2,090.1	5,160.3
1998	2,162.0	5,425.1
1999	2,210.3	5,854.0
2000	2,254.4	6,280.0
2001	2,366.4	6,859.6

Sources: China Statistical Yearbook 2000, 2001 and *China Statistical Abstract 2002*

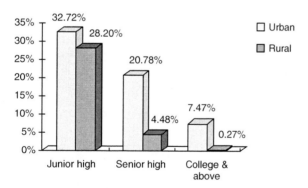

Source: State Statistical Bureau

Figure 1.4.3 Comparison of urban and rural education

bottom. Table 1.4.10 provides a picture of the regional differences in urban per capita disposable income and their changes between 1997 and 2001.

Rural household income and regional variations

With expansion of economic reform in the agricultural sector and the development of the agricultural economy, rural household income has been increasing.

Table 1.4.8 Per capita disposable income of urban households by city sizes

City size	Per capita disposable income (RMB)	
	1999	2000
All cities and county towns	5,854.02	6,279.98
Extra-large cities	7,667.78	8,371.66
Large cities	5,825.21	6,309.57
Medium-sized cities	5,449.25	5,860.92
Small cities	6,167.14	6,655.91
County towns	4,890.42	5,162.17

Sources: China Statistical Yearbook 2000, 2001

Table 1.4.9 Income distribution among different income groups in urban areas

Income group	Per capita disposable income (RMB)	
	1997	2000
Lowest income households	2,325.70	2,678.32
Low income households	3,492.27	3,658.53
Lower middle income households	4,363.78	4,651.72
Middle income households	5,512.12	5,930.82
Upper middle income households	6,904.96	7,524.98
High income households	8,631.94	9,484.67
Highest income households	12,083.79	13,390.49

Sources: China Statistical Yearbook 1998, 2001

In the period 1992–1997, per capita net income of rural households increased from RMB784 to RMB2,090 (about US$251.8), with an annual average rate of increase of 21.7 per cent. However, the rate of growth between 1997 and 2001 slowed down considerably to an average annual growth rate of 3.1 per cent.

The regional differences in rural incomes resemble the pattern of urban income. The per capita net income of rural households in the developed eastern areas of China is higher than in the middle and western areas. In 2001, the per capita net income of rural households in Shanghai was the highest of all other provinces and municipalities, being RMB5,870.87, followed by Beijing (RMB5,025.5), Zhejiang (RMB4,582.34), Tianjin (RMB3,947.72), Jiangsu (RMB3,784.71) and Guangdong (RMB3,769.79).

Tibet's rural per capita net income was the lowest, being RMB1,404.01, followed by Guizhou (RMB11,411.73), Shaanxi (RMB1,490.8), Gansu (RMB11,508.61) and Yunnan (RMB 1,533.74).

Table 1.4.10   Per capita disposable income (1997–2001) (RMB)

Region	1997	1998	1999	2000	2001
Beijing	7,813.2	8,472.0	9,182.8	10,394.7	11,577.8
Tianjin	6,608.4	7,110.5	7,649.8	8,140.5	8,958.7
Hebei	4,958.7	5,084.6	5,365.0	5,661.2	5,984.8
Shanxi	3,989.9	4,098.7	4,342.6	4,724.1	5,391.1
Inner Mongolia	3,944.7	4,353.0	4,770.5	5,129.1	5,535.9
Liaoning	4,518.1	4,617.2	4,898.6	5,357.8	5,797.0
Jilin	4,190.6	4,206.6	4,480.0	4,810.0	5,340.5
Heilongjiang	4,090.7	4,268.5	4,595.1	4,912.9	5,425.9
Shanghai	8,438.9	8,773.1	10,931.6	11,718.0	12,883.5
Jiangsu	5,765.2	6,017.9	6,538.2	6,800.2	7,375.1
Zhejiang	7,358.7	7,836.8	8,428.0	9,279.2	10,464.7
Anhui	4,599.3	4,770.5	5,064.6	5,293.6	5,668.8
Fujian	6,143.6	6,485.6	6,859.8	7,432.3	8,313.1
Jiangxi	4,071.3	4,251.4	4,720.6	5,103.6	5,506.0
Shandong	5,190.8	5,380.1	5,809.0	6,490.0	7,101.1
Henan	4,093.6	4,219.4	4,532.4	4,766.3	5,267.4
Hubei	4,673.2	4,826.4	5,212.8	5,524.5	5,856.0
Hunan	5,209.7	5,434.3	5,815.4	6,218.7	6,780.6
Guangdong	8,561.7	8,839.7	9,125.9	9,761.6	10,415.2
Guangxi	5,110.3	5,412.2	5,619.5	5,834.4	6,665.7
Hainan	4,849.9	4,852.9	5,338.3	5,358.3	5,838.8
Chongqing	5,322.7	5,466.6	5,896.0	6,276.0	6,721.1
Sichuan	4,763.3	5,127.1	5,477.9	5,894.3	6,360.5
Guizhou	4,441.9	4,565.4	4,934.0	5,122.2	5,451.9
Yunnan	5,5583	6,042.8	6,178.7	6,324.6	6,797.7
Tibet			6,908.7	7,426.3	7,869.2
Shaanxi	4,001.3	4,220.2	4,654.1	5,124.2	5,483.7
Gansu	3,592.4	4,009.6	4,475.2	4,916.3	5,382.9
Qinghai	3,999.4	4,240.1	4,703.4	51,700.0	5,853.7
Ningxia	3,836.5	4,112.4	4,472.9	4,912.4	5,544.2
Xinjiang	4,844.7	5,000.8	5,319.8	5,644.9	6,395.0
National average	5,160.3	5,425.1	5,854.0	6,280.0	6,859.6

Source: China Statistical Abstract 2002

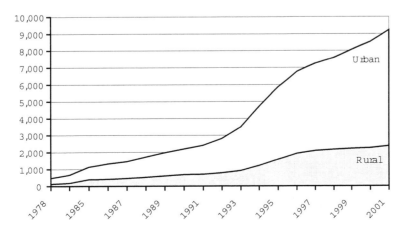

Sources: China Statistical Yearbook 2000, 2001 and China Statistical Abstract 2002

Figure 1.4.4   Income disparity among urban and rural residents – a widening gap

Savings

The rate of saving in China has surpassed all other countries in the world since the 1970s. In 1978, the first year of China's economic reform and opening up, the total urban and rural household savings were only RMB21.06 billion. Ten years later, the total household savings jumped to over RMB500 billion in 1989. Twenty years later, the savings by urban and rural households rocketed to RMB4,627.98 billion (about US$557.6 billion), with the rate of savings reaching over 30 per cent. By the end of 2001, the household savings further increased to RMB7.38 trillion (US$892.38 billion).

Although recently the saving rate has slowed down as a result of big-ticket consumption such as housing, the saving rate remains high. Although the government has introduced interest income tax, which has effectively reduced proceeds from bank savings, the rate of increase in savings is still rising. As shown in Figure 1.4.5, urban and rural household savings rose steeply from 1993, the first year after China's official adoption of the socialist market economy. The average annual rate of increase from 1991 to 2001 was 23.09 per cent.

Interestingly, however, the high savings rate is not motivated by the pursuit of monetary increments. The People's Bank of China (PBOC) conducted a survey on people's propensity to save, in 34 cities in May 1998. The survey results indicated that 53.4 per cent of the respondents stated that they would continue to save, when asked what they would do with their money if the interest rate remain unchanged. Nearly 70 per cent of the low and middle income residents interviewed stated that they are saving for long-term expenditures such as retirement, children's education, personal misfortunes and illnesses. The savings deposits tend to be mid-to-long term, and the interest earnings are regarded as an extra benefit. Even when the interest rate is low, the propensity to save would not be likely to change very much. *Economic Daily* explained that this unusually high propensity to save characterized the mentality of the Chinese people in the economic transition, which has increased uncertainty. Since the economic reform and opening up, factors of uncertainty have increased and people tend to choose to sacrifice today's consumption for the sake of future consumption. Housing, children's education, medical care and pension, which were covered by the government in the past, are now increasingly paid for by the Chinese people themselves. There are indications that even if inflation were to increase, the people's propensity to save would continue to rise, which is very different from the 'rules of the game' in western economies and it reflects the unique features of a socialist market economy with Chinese characteristics.

To sum up, the factors underlying such a persistently high savings rate are:

- household income has increased as a result of the sustained high GDP growth;
- consumer aspirations are dampened by the lack of new consumption lure;
- the expectation that future spending on housing, children's education and medical care will increase as a result of relevant reforms;
- an expectation of future uncertainties;
- cautious attitudes toward investment in financial products such as securities, bonds and funds.

According to the prediction of the State Information Centre, the savings rate will be about 12.2 per cent over the next five years.

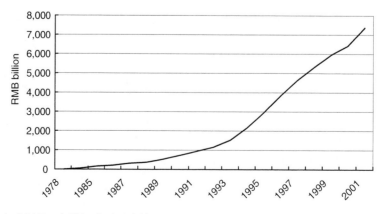

Sources: China Statistical Yearbook 2001 and *China Statistical Abstract 2002*

Figure 1.4.5   The growth of urban and rural household savings (1978–2001)

Consumption pattern

Chinese consumers have had increasingly more disposable income to satisfy their basic needs, as well as their aspirations for modern life styles. At the same time, the opening up and reforms have also benefited Chinese consumers with the material abundance that could not have been possible before. Consumer preferences, life styles and consumption patterns change over time, with the evolving of the consumer market.

Declining Engel's coefficient in urban areas

With the increase in disposable income, spending on food as a percentage of the total consumption expenditure has been declining, which indicates that the standard of living in China has been improving. As shown in the following figure, the Engel's coefficient was relatively high before 1980 at above 55 per cent. From 1982 to 1993, the coefficient was within the range of 50–55 per cent, although there were fluctuations. Starting in 1994, the Engel's coefficient has been below 50 per cent. By 2001, the Engel's coefficient had declined to 37.94 per cent compared with 39.18 per cent in 2000.

Continuously escalating consumer aspirations

With the declining Engel's coefficient, the Chinese people have more money to spend on non-staple items. The opening of the country to the outside world has also provided the Chinese people with an opportunity to realize their aspirations for what is called 'household modernization'. The changes are reflected in the durable items that the Chinese people hope to own. In the 1970s, it was a symbol of wealth for people to own a bicycle, a watch and a sewing machine. Such items were regarded as fashionable for the then newly-married couples. In the 1980s, the desired durable items became electrical household appliances, namely, television sets, washing machines, refrigerators and VCRs. Consumer aspirations continued to escalate in the 1990s, when people shifted to video cameras, audio systems, telephones, motorcycles and modern furniture. The Chinese people are now hoping to realize their dream of owning a personal computer, a private car, an apartment and modern home decor.

An average urban household now owns more than one bicycle and one television set. A majority of urban households have electrical household appliances such as washing machines, refrigerators and colour television sets. More and more households are acquiring air-conditioners, personal computers, cars and mobile phones (see Table 1.4.11). By the first quarter of 2002, the number of telephones subscribed reached 350 million, among which 161.5 million were mobile phones.

Changing life style

The life styles of the Chinese have also changed greatly since the economic reform and opening up. The green or blue uniforms have been replaced by modern fashion products and western suits. Western suits are accepted as formal clothing on formal occasions. Hosting friends at restaurants is no longer a luxury. The tradition of family gatherings at home is increasingly replaced by more opportunities to dine out together. Processed or semi-processed foods are becoming part of the Chinese people's life as a result of increased income and preferences for more leisure time. Unbranded generic products are losing their foothold in the market, as people are building their brand awareness in pursuit of better products.

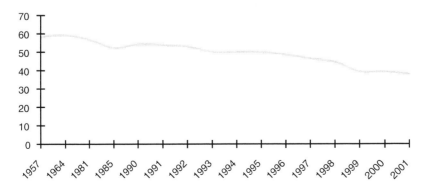

Sources: Engel's Coefficient, China Development Report (1998), Cheng Xuebin, page 258, China Statistical Abstract 2002

Figure 1.4.6   Engel's coefficient for urban residents is declining

Table 1.4.11 Average number of consumer durables owned per 100 Chinese urban households (1999 and 2001)

Description	1999	2001	Description	1999	2001
Motorcycle	15.12	20.4	Hi-fi system	19.66	23.8
Car	0.34	0.6	Video camera	1.06	1.6
Washing machine	91.44	92.2	Camera	38.11	39.8
Refrigerator	77.74	81.9	Microwave oven	12.15	22.3
Colour TV set	111.57	120.5	Air conditioner	24.48	35.8
VCD	24.71	42.6	Health equipment	3.83	4.0
VCR	21.73	19.9	Mobile phone	7.14	34.0
PC	5.91	13.3	Shower heater	45.49	52.0

Sources: China Statistical Yearbook 2000 and China Statistical Abstract 2002

Modern marketing has also contributed to the change in consumption habits. Supermarkets, chain convenience stores and membership club stores are attracting more customers, while direct mail and TV sales are gaining increasing acceptance. In addition, the decision-making processes of Chinese consumers are becoming more complex than formerly. The tradition of spending below earnings is now challenged by consumer credit.

It is not difficult now to see western influences in people's life style. The great tea-drinking nation has now given way to coffee drinking. Chocolate sales will go up on Valentine's Day. Cognac has invaded the territory of the traditional Chinese liquor, making China one of the largest cognac consumers in the world. Coca-Cola and Pepsi-Cola penetrated the market with their 'herbal medicine tastes'. Marco Polo's mistaken imitation of Chinese-style stuffed pie – pizza, with its stuffing on top rather than inside – has made a successful inroad into the country of great food culture. Completely western fast-food concepts such as McDonald's and Kentucky Fried Chicken are embraced by Chinese people, particularly the younger generation. Christmas is now celebrated unofficially by young non-Christian Chinese as a fashionable event. Interestingly, dogs and cats are now not only delicacies on dinner tables, but also loved and cared-for home pets. As a result, there are increasing numbers of pet hospitals in large urban centres of China. Pet foods are now advertised on the TV and other media.

Recent trends in the composition of consumer spending

Although consumer spending on food is steadily declining, food still remains at the top of average consumer spending, followed by recreational, educational and cultural services, housing, clothing, etc. (see Table 1.4.12).

However, the consumption of food is no longer seen as satisfying basic needs. The composition of food consumption is shifting toward more nutritious pursuits, which was reflected in the significant declines in spending on food grains. The consumption of non-staple foods, such as meat/poultry and their processed products, aquatic products, dried and fresh fruits, milk and dairy products, has been on the rise. The pursuit of healthier foods has also resulted in the decline in per capita consumption of fine grains and pork.

The second largest category of spending is spending on recreational, educational and cultural

Table 1.4.12 Composition of consumer spending in urban areas (%)

Description	1999	2000	2001
Consumption expenditure			
Food	42.78	39.18	37.94
Clothing	10.68	10.01	10.05
Home equipment, items and services	8.57	8.79	8.27
Medical and health care	5.32	6.36	6.47
Transportation and communications	6.73	7.90	8.61
Recreational, educational and cultural services	12.30	12.56	13.00
Housing	9.84	10.01	10.32
Miscellaneous commodities and services	4.96	5.17	5.35

Sources: China Statistical Yearbook 2000, 2001 and China Statistical Abstract 2002

Table 1.4.13 The food consumption pattern of urban households (per capita expenditure)

Item	1997	1998	1999	2000	2001
Grains	238.1	226.8	215.4	188.7	188.1
Oils and fats	70.7	75.3	73.7	66.5	58.9
Meat, poultry and their products	459.6	431.2	406.5	411.3	413.5
Aquatic products	141.0	142.5	144.0	143.5	152.0
Vegetables	203.9	197.0	194.6	192.3	194.3
Tobacco	92.2	93.6	94.8	100.9	103.8
Alcohol and drinks	91.0	91.6	95.3	103.2	103.9
Dried and fresh fruits	127.0	120.7	130.0	127.5	131.3
Dining out	203.4	227.0	249.6	287.8	314.2

Sources: China Statistical Yearbook 2000 and *China Statistical Abstract 2002*

services. The adoption of the 40-hour week and improved working conditions have given people more time for leisure activities and educational pursuits, and the related spending has been increasing. In 2001, 13 per cent of disposable income or RMB690 per capita was spent on such services. In 1997, the figure was only RMB448.4.

Housing reform has brought about increases in housing expenditure. The objective of the reform is to transform government-provided free housing into private housing ownership. Under such a scheme, apartments are sold to individuals or provided at cost. In 1997 the per capita spending on housing, including water, gas and electricity, was RMB358.6; by 2001 the figure had risen to RMB548, an increase of 52.82 per cent. Spending on housing is expected to continue to increase in the years to come.

Per capita spending on clothing also registered an increase in 2001, and is 6.63 per cent up on 2000 but only 2.47 per cent above 1997. In fact, spending dipped to RMB480.9 in 1998 from 1997's RMB520.9. In 2000, spending on clothing was still less than in 1997. In 2001, expenditure picked up and rose to RMB533.7.

With reform of the medical care system, medical expenses that used to be covered by the government are now increasingly paid by individuals. Per capita out-of-pocket expenditure on medical services and health care was RMB180 in 1997. In 2001, spending on this category had increased to 343.3 per capita. The expansion of medical care system reform will result in increased medical expenditure in the next few years.

Modern life demands convenient transportation and communications. Consumer spending on transportation and communications has been increasing at a high rate in the last few years. In 1997, per capita spending on transportation and communications was RMB233, an increase over the prior year of 17 per cent, while in 2001 the figure almost doubled to RMB457, an increase of 15.7 per cent over 2000. The key drivers of the increase are increased interest in travel as a result of the increase in income, and increased mobile telephone consumption.

The Chinese consumer market

Market dynamics

China's consumer market continues to expand at impressive speed. The State Development and Planning Commission has predicted that, in the tenth five-year plan (2001–2005) period, China will continue to maintain a relatively high economic growth. The average annual increase rate of GDP is expected to be 7–8 per cent with consumption raised to a higher level and urban and rural markets expanding further. By the end of 2001, total consumer spending, as reflected by total retail sales of consumer goods, reached RMB3,759.5 billion, which is 10.1 per cent higher than the previous year. In spite of the small proportion of the urban population, urban dwellers account for two-thirds of the purchasing power.

DRI-WEFA, an economics consulting firm in Lexington, Massachusetts, rated China among the three top emerging markets with fastest growth and expected its consumer spending to grow by 11 per cent in 2002. However, at the current level, the consumer market is still undergoing a stress test. The rate of increase in consumer spending had already dropped by 0.6 per cent in 2001. In July 2002, the State Statistics Bureau reported that total retail sales of consumer goods was

RMB309.66 billion. Though 8.6 per cent higher than the same month last year, the rate of increase was 1.2 per cent lower than the average annual rate in 2001. At the same time, the level of consumer spending dropped by 0.9 per cent for the same period. Market price remained stable for most of 2001 (see Table 1.4.14), but showed a clear sign of decline in the last quarter of the year.

While market prices continued to fall for the first nine months of 2002, the savings rate continued to rise. A fresh report by the People's Bank of China, the central bank, revealed that by the end of July aggregate bank deposits amounted to RMB8,300 billion, an increase of 7.5 per cent over 2001. This is characteristic of an emerging market where, on the one hand, there is a glut of goods and service of inferior quality, and on the other hand, consumers continue to save. The total balance of bank deposits by Chinese residents topped RMB7 trillion (US$853.6 billion), also a record high, earlier in 2002. When basic subsistence items like food, clothing and shelter are not in contention, quality products and services, as well as the support infrastructure become the major challenge to boost consumption levels. The consumption emphasis in the cities is placed on housing, private cars, education and personal communication. All of these, however, are curbed by the inadequate infrastructure in financial services and telecommunication networks.

In the short term, prices are expected to come under further pressure as some import tariff reductions begin to take effect, and increased competition from cheaper imports may spur more price wars within China.

On the retail side, consumers' favourites are changing over time. A survey of 100 large department stores in December 2001 provides some insight into changing consumer preferences and priority of spending.

Table 1.4.17 shows the results of a survey of 200 supermarkets identifying 30 top sellers, which again reflects the changing consumption pattern of urban dwellers.

Selected markets in China

Automotive market

Now the fastest growing market lies in the private sector. According to a sample survey by North-West Information News among 22,800 people in 57 Chinese cities, 12 per cent planned to buy a private car in 2002 and 29 per cent expressed their intentions to buy cars with bank loans. The State Development and Planning Commission expects private cars to account for 70 per cent of China's annual auto sales within the next 10 years. A detailed account of the expanding automobile market and opportunities for foreign companies to participate is given in Chapter 8.1.

Real estate market

Housing and home furnishing have become the top priority for Chinese people. At present, in China, the

Table 1.4.14 China's consumer price index in 2001 over 2000 as the base year

Items	Whole country	Cities	Countryside
Consumer Price Index	100.7	100.7	100.8
Food	100.0	100.1	99.8
Grain	99.3	99.2	99.7
Meat	101.6	101.7	101.4
Eggs	106.0	106.3	105.3
Aquatic products	97.1	96.9	97.8
Vegetables	101.4	101.4	100.9
Dining out	100.2	100.4	99.6
Cigarettes and liquor	99.7	99.7	99.6
Clothing	98.1	97.8	98.9
Household appliances and services	97.7	97.5	98.4
Health care products	100.0	99.3	101.1
Transportation and communication	99.0	99.1	98.7
Entertainment, education and entertainment	106.6	106.7	106.4
Housing	101.2	101.7	100.3

Source: Statistical Report on PRC National and Social Development, 2001 State Statistics Bureau

Table 1.4.15   Market price changes in 2001

Item	Percentage change over 2000
Food	
Grain	−0.7
Meat	1.6
Vegetables	1.4
Eggs	6.0
Household appliances	−2.3
Transportation and communication	1.0
Education and entertainment	6.6
Housing	1.2
Industrial goods	−1.3
Raw materials and energy	−0.2
Capital investment	0.4

Source: Statistical Report on PRC National and Social Development, 2001 State Statistical Bureau

average urban dwelling space is 9.6 square metres per person. This figure varies in different regions. In some cities it is below five square metres. Economic growth is the engine of real estate development, with demand geared-up for residences, office buildings and factory space. Huge market potential remains to be tapped as the real-estate industry accounts for only three per cent of China's GDP, compared with 10–20 per cent in developed countries. It is estimated that the annual expansion of the real-estate industry will exceed 10 percentage points. If China is aiming at a two-bedroom apartment for each family of three, it will mean the average dwelling space will be at least 10 square metres per person. By 2020, the urbanization level of China is expected to reach 51.4 per cent, which means that China's urban population will increase to 630 million. To meet this standard, China needs to build residential housing of 5.2 billion square metres within the next two decades.

Table 1.4.16   Growth rate of sales in December 2001

High Rollers		Slow climbers		Downhill walkers	
Articles	Growth rate (%)	Articles	Growth rate (%)	Articles	Growth rate (%)
Stationery	68.8	Footwear	14.0	Mini-metals and machine	
Electronic publications	55.3	Tobacco	10.5	tools	−40.1
Construction and home-		Athletic and recreational		Books and journals	−26.6
furnishing materials	54.5	products	10.3	Oil and petroleum products	−23.9
Caps	54.1	Liquor	8.6	Furniture	−14.6
Household electronics	45.2	Communication products	4.7	Audio-video equipment	−12.6

Source: China Economic Monitoring Centre 2002

Table 1.4.17   Top sellers in December 2001

TV sets above 64 cm	VCD/DVD players	Refrigerator
Household air-conditioner	Automatic washing machine	Cylinder washing machine
Gas burner	Cooking smoke disperser	Electric boiler
Electric rice cooker	Camera	Wrist watch
Vacuum cleaner	Leather shoes	Sports shoes
Men's suit	Men's shirt	Women's suit
Children's wear	Blue jeans	Leather clothes
Skin care products	Hair care products	Fruit juice
Grain wine	Grape wine	Beer
Lactic drinks	Carbonated drink	Bottled water

Source: China Economic Monitoring Centre 2002

The ratio of annual personal income to commercial house prices is 5.8:1. With the implementation of various state housing policies, and improvements in all kinds of housing systems such as low rent houses, economy dwellings, commercial housing, reforms policy houses, the ratio of personal incomes to house prices will drop down to 3:1. Since 1998 the sales revenue for commercial houses has been increasing at more than 20 per cent, while in 2001 it exceeded 30 per cent.

Credit card market

The consumer market is experiencing restraint in credit card use. For example, in Shanghai, the most financially developed city, the use of debit and credit cards accounted for only 2.7 per cent of all consumer spending in 2001 and only 3 per cent of retailers will accept them (*Far Eastern Economic Review*, Hong Kong, 14 February 2002).

In major cities, average spending through the use of credit cards is RMB1,779 per family, which is 5.7 per cent of total family expenditure. There are three likely reasons. First, the consumer may think that it is too difficult to obtain a credit card; second, the 'credit card' may actually be a debit card; third, many places do not accept credit cards and overdrawing on a debit card is simply impossible.

Communications market

In 2001, post and telecommunications registered total revenue of RMB437 billion, with 24 per cent increase over the previous year. Telecommunications is an area of exponential growth. The mother switchboards reached a total capacity of 200 million by the year-end. Of the 179 million handset users, 111 million were in the cities and 68 million in rural areas. In terms of mobile phones, China overtook the US and boasted the biggest market with 144.8 million users. These add up to present-day China having 26 phones per hundred people. The government continues to invest RMB84 million each year for the installation of optical fibres. Therefore, this momentum will be maintained for quite a long time to come as the potential is realized. Handset users in China are expected to exceed 260 million by 2005, and mobile phone users will grow at more than 20 per cent annually.

The internet is another nascent area of rapid growth. Internet users exceeded 30 million by the end of 2001. Internet application in business is surging. It is estimated by eMarketer, a firm specializing in internet and e-business research, that business-to-business e-commerce revenues in China will have grown from US$1.5 billion to US$21.8 billion by 2004.

In the telecoms equipment market, foreign-funded enterprises now account for over 70 per cent of the country's total production capacity. There are more than 20 Sino-foreign joint ventures, in the production of mobile phones, with Nokia, Motorola and Ericsson commanding more than 75 per cent of the Chinese market. The fibre-optic transmission equipment market is mainly dominated by joint ventures with investment from well-known foreign manufacturers. Satellite communications systems, facsimile machines and microwave communications equipment are mainly imported from abroad; very few joint ventures engage in the production of this equipment in China.

Cosmetics market

Being part of the fashion industry, the cosmetics market in China first took shape in the 1980s but its rapid development occurred in the 1990s, with growth at an annual rate of 35 per cent. There was a startling contrast: in 1980 people only spent RMB0.2 per capita on cosmetics, but in 1999, it had grown to RMB28. There are more than 3,000 factories and 600 organizations in the cosmetics market, employing more than six million people. At present, more than 1,000 kinds of cosmetics are displayed on shelves every week. The sale of cosmetics has reached more than RMB16 billion and continues to increase at the rate of 15 per cent every year. It is predicted that by 2010 total sales of this market will be RMB80 billion. The concentrated market segment for cosmetics is the 6,850,000 women in cities within the age range of 20 to 40. If each woman in China spends RMB50 per year on cosmetics, they can generate RMB13.3 billion to the market. China's cosmetics market still has plenty of room for growth since annual consumption of cosmetics is only 10 per cent of the world's average level. At the same time, purchasing power is concentrated in the cities. It is estimated that there are more than 1.1 million consumers in Beijing and Shanghai, and 0.4 million in Guangzhou. The consumption level in Chinese rural areas is only 10 per cent of the cities'.

Consumer confidence

Consumer confidence in the overall performance of the economy and their future income is very much an indicator of consumer willingness to spend. The

Report on Economic Performance in China 2001 offered the following observations.

Compared with 2000, in terms of the economic performance in 2001:

- 45 per cent of consumers felt that the year's economy was better;
- 46 per cent of consumers felt that it was basically the same;
- 9 per cent of consumers felt that it was worse.

Compared with 2000, in terms of family income in 2001:

- 32.5 per cent of consumers felt that their family income increased;
- 47.5 per cent of consumers felt that their family income remained basically the same;
- 19.9 per cent of consumers felt that their family income dropped;
- 0.1 per cent did not respond.

Globalization of the Chinese consumer market

Pushed by the wave of globalization, China is moving away from an economic system in which national markets are distinct entities, isolated from foreign markets by barriers of distance, time, culture and government intervention. Increasingly its national market is converging into an integral part of the global marketplace. One characteristic of this convergence is the increasing participation of foreign product and service providers in China.

China's accession to the WTO has accelerated the pace of market liberalization. As a result, international competition will internalize, exerting great pressure on domestic market players, and the pattern of competition is expected to change. Internationalization of domestic competition is bound to take place. Foreseeable results of this globalization are increased efficiency and enhanced consumer benefits.

China's WTO entry has also increased the possibilities of integrating the Chinese consumer market with the outside world. China is now regarded as a leading world manufacturing centre and Chinese producers are supplying not only the domestic market but also foreign markets. WTO rules are supposed to clear the obstacles that Chinese businesses used to have before China's accession. In this context, the consumer market is truly a global concept.

More recent developments – J Reuvid

The following notes are updates on the consumer markets referred to in this Chapter.

Private property

On the final day of the National People's Congress annual meeting in Beijing, the 1982 constitution was amended to recognize the ownership rights of private property owners. The wording of the resolution inserted was, simply, 'a citizen's lawful private property is inviolable'. Private property in China is now protected for the first time since 1949. The amendment is a response to sustained lobbying by entrepreneurs and businesspeople and should help to stop officials from requisitioning property and private possessions.

A unified land tax system and lower fees were foreshadowed in March 2004 by the State Administration of Taxes that would make home-buying more affordable for middle class families.

Credit cards

China has issued 714 million bank cards since 1985, on which some US$2.1 trillion worth of transactions were made in 2003. Of the cards issued, most are debit cards, with credit cards accounting for only about 4 per cent. As spending habits have changed, more than 300,000 retailers throughout China are now accepting bank cards. People with credit cards issued by foreign banks are now able to draw foreign currency directly from ATMs in China.

Communications

The number of subscribers to China Mobile, the world's biggest wireless communications carrier, increased by 20 per cent in 2003 as the company continued to buy provincial networks. A further 10 are planned for acquisition during 2004 to bring the total up to 29.

China is forecast to issue its first licences for high-speed mobile services in 2005 to boost competition for current operators China Mobile and China Telecom in the run-up to the 2008 Beijing Olympics.

A deal between the US chip giant Intel and the Chinese e-commerce company Alibaba will enable Chinese mobile users to trade on the Ailbaba platform. The first batch of phones will be released by Motorola and the Chinese phone maker, Dopoda.

Cosmetics

The cosmetics and toiletries market in China is worth US$5 billion, having grown at an average annual rate of 12.9 per cent from 1998 to 2002; it is expected to double *by 2010. A segmentation analysis by Snapshots International shows that skin care and colour cosmetics account for just over 30 per cent of the market in value and shampoo 20 per cent. Hair colourants and hair styling agents are at around 6.5 per cent of the market each followed by hair conditioners and sun protection products.*

The French cosmetics group, L'Oreal has purchased Yu-Sai, an up-market Chinese brand, previously owned by Coty of New York, adding nearly 25 per cent to its 2003 China sales of about €159 million.

In July, Avon Products, the world's largest direct seller of cosmetics, received verbal permission to run a pilot programme as a first step towards lifting the door-to-door selling ban imposed in 1998. Currently, Avon is permitted to sell its products only on counters in hyper-markets and through small beauty boutiques.

Updates on other consumer product industries are included in Part Eight.

Developing Statistics in China

Du Xishuang, Director, Senior Statistician, National Bureau of Statistics

Statistical work in China: origin and development

Efforts to initiate statistical activities and set up a statistical system in the new China started soon after the founding of the People's Republic. In October 1949, a Statistics Division was set up under the Commission of Finance and Economy of the central people's government. The National Bureau of Statistics was set up in August 1952. Subsequently, statistical structures and various statistical systems were established by localities, departments, enterprises and institutions across the country. During the 'Great Cultural Revolution' in the mid-and late-1960s, most statistical structures were either demolished or merged. Statistical work across the country suffered serious destruction, with statistical activities in many organizations plunged to a virtual standstill.

After China adopted the policy of reform and opening up in 1978, statistical work was soon resumed. By gradually being incorporated into the legal framework, statistical work has entered a new era of reform and development.

Since the 1980s, especially since the 1990s, with the deepening of economic restructuring and opening up, profound reforms have been carried out to China's statistical system. Significant changes have occurred in the following major respects:

- With regard to statistical service, the long-standing self-enclosure of statistical work has been gradually replaced by the opening up to society and to the rest of the world. More and more statistical information is regularly disseminated to the general public both at home and abroad. Exchanges with other countries and relevant international organizations have been expanded. Necessary statistical data are regularly provided to international organizations including the World Bank, IMF, UN Statistical Division, the Food and Agriculture Organization (FAO) etc. Major aspects of statistical methods have been brought in line with international organizations' norms and can be used directly in international comparison.

- With regard to the accounting system, the long-standing material production system (MPS) is gradually being replaced by the new national economics accounting system (SNA). This new system, which enables systematic accounting and description of the national economy through production accounts, input-output accounts, flow of funds accounts, balance of payments accounts, assets-liabilities accounts and economic circulation accounts, has brought national accounting in conformity with international accounting practices.

- With regard to statistical indicators and standards, the traditional system suitable for the planned economy has been gradually replaced by new ones in compliance with the market economy. This effort has expedited the pace of compliance with international practice and elevated the standardization of statistical work to a new level.

- With regard to statistical methods, the long-standing unitary method of statistical survey has been gradually replaced by a relatively scientific method system of statistical survey. A new survey system has been established, integrating censuses, sampling surveys, thorough surveys and other means.

- With regard to the building of a legal system, the long-standing situation of no applicable legislation has come to an end. Efforts have been made to bring statistical work within a legal framework. *The Statistics Law of the People's Republic of China* and the *Detailed Rules Concerning the Implementation of the Statistics Law* have been promulgated.

- With regard to statistical technology, the previous backward means of information transmission and processing has been transformed. A basic framework of statistics-related modern technology has taken shape. A nationwide statistical information network is basically built and in operation. A network links the National Bureau of Statistics and statistical agencies in all provinces, autonomous regions and municipalities directly under the central government, as well as those in some prefectures and cities. Online transmission of statistical information is now possible.

Functions of government statistics and the statistical system in China

Functions of government statistics

As an agency directly under the State Council, the National Bureau of Statistics is in charge of statistics and economic accounting in China. In accordance with the Statistics Law of the People's Republic of China and relevant regulations of the State Council, major functions of the National Bureau of Statistics include:

- To work out laws and regulations on statistical work; to formulate directive rules for statistical operation; to draw up plans for statistical modernization and nationwide statistical surveys; to organize and exercise leadership and supervision over statistical and economic accounting work in various localities and departments; and to supervise and inspect the enforcement of statistical laws and regulations.
- To set up and improve the national economic accounting system and statistical indicator system; to institute a unified basic statistical system for the whole country; to work out national statistical standards; to review and approve statistical standards by other government departments; to organize the administration of national statistical survey projects; to examine, approve and manage plans and schemes for statistical surveys by other departments.
- To organize the implementation of major censuses on the basic items relating to the state and strength of the country; to exercise unified administration over socio-economic surveys in various localities and departments; to collect, process and tabulate basic statistical information from across the country; to carry out analyses, forecasts and supervision from a statistical perspective on national economic and scientific progress and social development; to provide statistical information and relevant proposals for the State Council and government departments concerned.
- To act as the exclusive agency in verifying, approving, administering and publishing basic national statistical data and to disseminate regularly to the general public statistical information regarding national economic and social development.
- To build up and administer the national statistical information system and the national statistical database system; to formulate basic standards and operational rules for statistical database networks in various localities and departments.
- To exercise leadership over directly-affiliated surveying agencies in various localities; to exercise unified management over operating expenses of statistical activities for statistical agencies in local governments at and above county level; to assist in the management of directors and deputy directors of local statistical offices of provinces, autonomous regions and municipalities directly under the central government; to organize and administer qualification examinations and the evaluation of professional titles for statisticians across the country.

The statistical system in China

The official statistical system in China consists of the government statistical system and department statistical system.

The government statistical system

The institution of statistical agencies and employment of statisticians at all levels of the government constitute the government statistical system. The National Bureau of Statistics is established under the State Council, while independent statistical agencies are set up in local government at and above county level. At the township level, either statistical stations are instituted or full-time or part-time statisticians are employed. In addition, the National Bureau of Statistics has also established, under its direct leadership and administration, three survey-taking institutions, namely, Organization of Rural Socio-economic Surveys, Organization of Urban Socio-economic Surveys and Organization of Enterprise Surveys across the country.

The major functions of the overall government statistical system include: to work out plans for statistical surveys, making arrangements for and inspecting statistical work and economic accounting work at national or local level; to organize the implementation of national and local statistical surveys, to collect, process and provide statistical data for the whole country or a particular region; to conduct statistical analysis on economic and social development and to exercise statistical supervision; to administer and coordinate statistical survey questionnaires designed by various departments.

The statistical agencies of local governments not only collect and provide statistical data for government agencies at higher levels but also collect and provide statistical information and submit statistical analysis reports for local government.

Department statistical system
The institution of statistical agencies and employment of statisticians by various departments, both directly under the State Council and at local levels, constitute the department statistical system. Its major responsibilities include: to organize and coordinate statistical work of the department concerned, accomplish the tasks in national and local statistical surveys, work out and implement department statistical survey programmes, and to collect, process and provide statistical data; to make statistical analysis of and exercise statistical supervision over the development of the department and sector concerned; to organize and coordinate statistical work of enterprises and institutions within the jurisdiction of the department concerned and manage statistical questionnaires to be used by the department.

Statistical surveys organized and implemented by the National Bureau of Statistics

Regular census system

In accordance with the provisions of the Statistics Law of the People's Republic of China and requirements set by the State Council for the establishment of the national census system and reform of the statistical survey system, the National Bureau of Statistics officially initiated the regular census system in 1994. Census items include population, agriculture, industry, tertiary industry and basic units. A census on population, the tertiary industry, industry and agriculture is conducted every 10 years in years ending

with a zero, three, five and seven respectively. A census on basic units is held every five years in years ending with one or six. The first round of regular censuses, as legally required, has been completed, culminating in the ending of the first nationwide agricultural census.

Commencing the second round of regular censuses, the National Bureau of Statistics conducted the second nationwide census on basic units in 2001. Respondents to this census were all legal entities and affiliated active industrial units across the country (excluding Taiwan Province, Hong Kong and Macao). The standard date for this census was 31 December 2001. The surveying year of the census data was 2001. Major contents of the census encompassed four aspects: basic information of units' (code, name, address and communication numbers of the unit); major properties of the unit (industrial category, affiliation); basic economic activities of the unit (total employment, actual capital utilization, fixed assets and operating revenue); other information of the unit (type of accounting system, number of active industrial units).

The system of regular annual and monthly statistical surveys

Statistical Survey on Basic Units
Basic unit statistics are an annual survey carried out by provincial statistical agencies in non-census years under the instruction of the National Bureau of Statistics in order to obtain data on the total number of basic units across the country and their changes. This survey is the base of the regular survey system with which to ascertain the number of various units across the country and the distribution among various localities and economic sectors, and to prepare the framework for sampling surveys.

Statistical Survey on Population and Labour
The sample survey on population change is an annual event conducted between two population censuses to collect information on the yearly population change. Major contents of the survey include the number of births and deaths, education and employment of the population. Surveyors make visits to households to register information. The sample size is one per cent of the entire population. In years ending with a five, it is increased by one per cent and new contents are added.

The system of survey on labour includes the Urban Labour Survey and the General Statistics Reporting System on Labour. The system of the Urban Labour

Survey is a quarterly sample survey system launched by the National Bureau of Statistics in 1996. The survey covers urban populations across the country with respondents selected from the age group of persons aged 15 and over, taking households as the unit. The General Statistics Reporting System on Labour is a general requirement with regard to labour statistics set by the National Bureau of Statistics for provincial-level statistical agencies. Provincial-level statistical agencies, as required by the National Bureau of Statistics, instruct prefecture and county statistical officers to collect, process and report various labour statistical data, and submit the processed data to the National Bureau of Statistics.

Agriculture and Rural Statistical Surveys
The Agriculture and Rural Statistical Surveys include the Agriculture Production Sample Survey System, the Rural Community Basic Conditions Survey System and the General Statistics Reporting System on Agricultural, Forestry, Animal Husbandry and Fishery. Of these, the Agriculture Production Sample Survey is a quarterly survey, while others are annual surveys.

Statistical Survey on Industry and Transportation
The Statistical Survey System on Industry includes the Overall Statistics Reporting System, the Direct Reporting System of Key Industrial Enterprises and the Sample Survey System of Sub-scale Industrial Enterprises. Of these, the Overall Statistics Reporting System is a general requirement with regard to industrial and energy statistics set by the National Bureau of Statistics for provincial-level statistical agencies and relevant departments under the State Council. It covers all industrial enterprises with an individual annual revenue of and above RMB5 million and greater. The total number of respondent enterprises is 160,000. The major content of the survey includes production, input, output and sales. The Direct Reporting System of Key Industrial Enterprises was initiated by the National Bureau of Statistics in 2000, based on the existing data communications network within the statistical system. The selection of key enterprises is made by the National Bureau of Statistics with balanced consideration of their sale revenue, total assets and pre-tax profits. Selected enterprises report monthly data via the network in accordance with the format and other requirements set by the National Bureau of Statistics. The major content of the survey includes basic conditions of enterprises, major

economic indicators, production, marketing, inventory and ordering, investment in technological development and labour conditions. The Sample Survey System of Sub-scale Industrial Enterprises is conducted twice every year to obtain data for the January to September period and the whole year respectively. The sub-scale industrial enterprises are selected from those industrial enterprises with an annual sales revenue below RMB5 million.

The Overall Statistics Reporting System on Transportation, Post and Telecommunications is a general requirement with regard to transportation, post and telecommunications statistics set by the National Bureau of Statistics for provincial-level statistical agencies and relevant departments under the State Council. Provincial-level agencies are required to report annually the total number of civil vehicles in the area of their respective jurisdiction. Departments under the State Council are required to report data annually on the total business volume, finance and energy consumption for highways, water traffic, ports, railways, aviation, pipeline transportation, post and telecommunications. They are also required to report monthly headline data for these statistics.

Statistical Survey on the Construction Industry, Real Estate and Fixed Assets Investment
This survey system includes the Overall Statistics Reporting System on the Construction Industry, the Overall Statistics Reporting System on Fixed Assets Investment, the Direct Network Reporting System of 3000 Key Real Estate Enterprises and the Sample Survey on Rural Fixed Assets Investment.

Statistical Survey on the Wholesale and Retail Trading and Catering Industry
The survey includes the Overall Statistic Reporting System on Wholesale and Retail Trading and Catering Industry, the Sample Survey on Sub-benchmark Wholesale and Retail Trading and the Catering Industry, and the Direct Reporting System on Key Wholesale and Retail Trading Enterprises.

Household Survey
The Household Survey includes the Rural Household Survey and the Urban Household Survey. Respondents of the Rural Household Survey are permanent households in an area with a residence of longer than a year. The major content of the survey includes basic information, per capita income and net income, daily

consumption expenditure, the amount of major consumer goods consumption and the amount of durable goods. Taking the province as the universe, the method of multi-phase, random start and symmetrically equidistant sampling is applied. During the survey, sample households keep a record of their accounts and surveyors collect and report data monthly. The Urban Household Survey respondents are non-agricultural households in cities and county seats. The major content of the survey includes family members, employment details, cash income and expenditure, the amount of major goods purchased, housing conditions and the amount of durable goods. A total of 36,000 sample households are selected in 226 sample cities. During the survey, sample households keep a record of their accounts and surveyors collect and report data monthly.

Statistical Prices Survey

The Price Survey on Fixed Assets Investment, the Survey on Consumption Prices of Residents and the Survey on Prices of Industrial Goods together comprise the elements of the Prices Survey.

Besides these surveys, the National Bureau of Statistics also conducts other surveys, such as the Survey on Science and Technology, and the Enterprise Boom Cycle Survey, etc.

National Economic Accounting System

The National Economic Accounting System was formulated in conformity with the UN SNA.

The Gross Domestic Product Accounting System

China's gross domestic product and its components are calculated by the National Bureau of Statistics using different methods in light of characteristics and data sources in different departments. For some departments the accrued value is calculated using the production method. Some are calculated using the income method and obtained through aggregating the accruement of various departments. The gross domestic product accounting system is a general requirement with regard to GDP accounting set by the National Bureau of Statistics for provincial statistical agencies. It consists of annual and regular reports. The major content of annual reports includes total output, GDP at same-year prices, GDP at comparative prices, GDP calculated with expenditure methods, ultimate consumption and consumption level of residents. The regular report is the quarterly GDP.

Input-output Accounting System

The input-output survey is conducted every five years in China. National input-output sheets are compiled in years ending with a two and seven. The extended input-output sheets are compiled in years ending with a zero or five. In accordance with the requirements for the input-output survey and compilation plan, provincial-level statistical agencies and the National Bureau of Statistics compile their respective sheets in tandem. The input-output accounting system is a general requirement with regard to input-output accounting set by the National Bureau of Statistics and imposed on provincial-level statistical agencies. It consists of product sector input-output sheets, enterprises sector input (U tables) and enterprise sector output sheets (V tables). Provincial-level statistical agencies are only required to report product sector input-output sheets. The other two sheets are for reference.

The Funds Flow Accounting System

The National Bureau of Statistics and the Central Bank compile the funds flow table jointly. China's funds flow table is similar to internationally accepted forms. The table is divided into two parts. The upper part is goods transactions compiled by the National Bureau of Statistics; the lower part is financial transactions compiled by the Central Bank. The system is a general requirement for funds flow accounting set by the National Bureau of Statistics for provincial-level statistical agencies and the Central Bank. It includes funds flow tables (distribution of incomes) and funds flow tables (financial transactions), compiled respectively by provincial-level statistical agencies and provincial branches of the Central Bank. These data are reported annually.

Balance of Payments Accounting System

China started to establish its balance of payments system in 1980. The concept, principle and framework of the system derive from the *Balance of Payments Manual* compiled by the IMF. The State Administration of Foreign Exchange compiles the balance of payments sheet. Data needed for the compilation come mainly from business statistics and administrative records of relevant departments under the State Council.

The National Assets Accounting System

This system is a general requirement with regard to national assets accounting set by the National Bureau of Statistics and imposed on provincial-level statistical agencies. It consists of an assets-liabilities sheet and four sectors of assets-liabilities sheets for non-finance businesses, financial institutions, government departments and households. These data are reported annually.

The Economic Circulation Accounts System

This system is a general requirement with regard to economic circulation accounts set by the National Bureau of Statistics and required of provincial-level statistical agencies. It consists of 36 sheets in three categories, namely the overall economic account, sector accounts for institutions and comprehensive sector accounts for industries. These data are reported annually.

Publication and provision of statistical data

Chinese official statistical agencies provide information not only for governments and governmental organizations at various levels for decision-making purposes, but also for the public and international exchanges. They publish and provide statistical information in various forms to cater for the needs of customers with different interests on a monthly, quarterly and annual basis.

Printed statistical publications

Many kinds of statistical yearbooks are available to the public, such as the *China Statistical Yearbook*, all localities' statistics yearbooks at and above county level, and some special-subject year books (such as *China Industrial Statistics Yearbook*, *China Rural Statistics Yearbook*, etc.).

China Development Report

This is an illustrated version of the previous *China Statistical Yearbook*. It describes both the trajectory of China's reform and opening up and the forecasts made by experts from various fields. It is rich in content, including a review of the past year and prospects for the coming year. It also incorporates major documents and annuals of China's economic development.

Statistical newspapers and journals

Major newspapers and journals under the National Bureau of Statistics include: *China Information News* (published from Monday to Friday), *China Statistics* (monthly), *Statistical Research* (monthly), *China Economic Performance Monthly*, *China Conditions* (monthly). These newspaper and journals have comprehensive statistical information content.

China statistical information network servers

Websites are established to disseminate statistical information. On the website there are detailed data on the nation's economy and development, such as census data on the state and the strength of the country, survey reports and statistical data for 160 counties and regions. Using the links on the website, users can visit statistical agencies at all provincial levels.

Statistical bulletins and statistical service

The National Bureau of Statistics and district government statistical agencies at various levels release statistical bulletins on the national economy and the social development situation each year, and they hold press conferences regularly. During festivals or historical anniversaries, the government statistical organs make use of their statistical data and compile series reports on various topics.

Statistical information international exchange

Regular exchanges of statistical information are arranged with international organizations and many national statistical offices; partnerships have been set up between Chinese statistical offices and international, regional and foreign institutions.

Statistical analysis

Government statistical agencies also carry out extensive in-depth statistical analysis and provide more and more statistical analysis reports to the government, companies and the public. The government statistical offices at different levels submit many analysis reports each year. These reports are an important foundation for government at various levels to understand the current economic and social aspects, draw up policies and plans and supervise their implementation. Governments at various levels are paying more attention to the analysis and research reports of the government statistical offices. In recent years, the National Bureau of Statistics has submitted many important analyses and suggestions on the operation of the country's macro-economy and social development, and some have been adopted by the State Council. Government statistical offices are increasingly playing a significant role in the process of governmental decision-making.

Objectives of future reform

The overall objective of China's statistics is to establish a new statistical system that conforms to the requirements of the socialist market economy and current Chinese conditions, and to international practice. Priorities for this objective are the establishment of a scientific and efficient national statistical system, a rationally structured organizational management system with coordinated operation, a modern national statistical information network system, well-developed statistical legislation and a rationally structured contingent of competent statisticians equipped with modern knowledge and technology. In relation to this objective, much needs to be done. Further deepening of reforms is required. Practical experiences since the launch of China's reform and opening up policy will be adapted. In addition, exchanges and cooperation with other countries will be strengthened to learn from their successful practice and more advanced experiences.

Part Two

China Within the WTO

The Opening up of the Chinese Market as a WTO Member

Craig Pouncey and Lode van den Hende, Herbert Smith, Brussels

This chapter provides an overview of China's specific obligations in the area of 'market access' in the principal commercial sectors in which China has allowed foreign businesses, goods and services to trade or be traded in China. We have outlined the type of liberalization commitments that China has made and the type of legal issues that can arise. However, China's accession to the WTO is set out in more than 800 pages of detailed legal documentation and it is obviously not possible to provide a complete and accurate explanation of these issues in this short contribution. For fully accurate information it is necessary to consult the original documents or take appropriate advice.

At the outset, it is important to note that China has made two types of commitments:

- Like all WTO members, China has submitted schedules of commitments and concessions on trade in goods and services. Broadly speaking these determine the customs tariffs that China can apply to imported products and the extent to which China is obliged to allow foreign services companies to operate on its territory.
- China has also made a number of special concessions on its current and planned investment regime and on a number of specific issues such as trading rights. These 'special' commitments reflect the fact that China is an economy in transition from a state-based system to a market-based system. Thus, certain issues that arise in the Chinese context do not arise in the context of a 'normal market economy' and, for that reason, are not dealt with by traditional WTO rules. These special rules can be found in the Protocol of Accession and in the WTO Working Party Report on China's accession. As

China's transition towards a market economy progresses, the practical significance of these special rules will diminish accordingly.

Trading rights

Before China's accession, the right to import and export goods was available only to some 35,000 Chinese enterprises and, on a restricted basis, to some foreign-invested enterprises. All foreign-invested enterprises now have the right to import and export all goods throughout the customs territory of China. For a limited number of products (grain, vegetable oil, sugar, tobacco, cotton, oil and fertilizers) the right to import will remain reserved for state-trading enterprises. Importation of oil and fertilizers will gradually be opened to non-state importers. The right to export will also be liberalized, although exports of the following products will remain subject to state trading: tea, rice, corn, soy bean, certain minerals, coal, oil, cotton and silk (the silk export monopoly will be gradually opened up for competition).

Abolition of discriminatory measures and practices

China has explicitly agreed to eliminate all measures and practices that discriminate against foreign companies including:

- all taxes and dual pricing systems that discriminate against foreign or foreign-invested companies;
- restrictions on after sales services for imported products;
- special pricing rules and profit ceilings imposed on imported pharmaceuticals;

- special licensing rules for retail outlets selling imported cigarettes;
- special rules for the distribution and sale of imported spirits;
- special registration procedures for imported chemicals;
- differences in certification and inspection procedures for imported boilers and pressure vessels.

While in general it has been accepted that China has made substantial progress in the implementation of it commitments since acceding to the WTO's multilateral trading system, China has continued to face criticism of its use of non-transparent barriers to trade – particularly from US and EU business interests – in the agriculture and services sectors. These have been noted to include poor transparency in the application of tariff rate quotas, the continuance of provincial bureaucratic procedures and an over-reliance on high capitalization requirements for foreign investment in key sectors such as insurance and retailing. China has also been criticized, particularly in the US, over its sporadic implementation record.

Import tariff reductions and removal of quota restrictions

Like all WTO members, China has made commitments to remove or reduce 'border measures' such as import tariffs and import quotas. China's schedule for goods provides details for this on a product-by-product basis for thousands of products. Table 2.1.1 provides an overview of these reductions in a number of specific sectors (which will themselves sometimes contain very many individual sub-products, each with separate and different tariff rates). The figures mentioned are averages calculated by the European Commission and the US authorities and need to be approached with some care as it is not always clear how these averages have been calculated.

Furthermore, the use of averages can obscure important differences. When negotiating with China the other WTO members have concentrated on specific product categories that are of interest to their own exporters. For instance, at the request of the EU China has reduced its tariffs on five particular types of footwear from 25 per cent to 10 per cent. These five specific product categories account for more than 70 per cent of EU footwear exports to China. Thus, this reduction will have an important market opening effect for EU exporters, although the average tariff reduction for all footwear categories

may appear relatively limited. Table 2.1.1 nevertheless provides an indication of the scope of outstanding tariff reductions and highlights the sectors where the impact will be very significant, such as automobiles and alcoholic beverages.

Furthermore it is important to note that even for sectors where the reduction is limited, WTO accession provides an important advantage because it imposes a legal obligation on China to maintain (or 'bind') import tariffs at a specific and often low level. Indeed, in 2002, China's first full year of WTO membership, the overall average tariff rate fell from over 15 per cent to 12 per cent. Further tariff cuts are scheduled, with most of them taking place within five years of China's WTO accession. It will not be possible for China to increase these tariffs beyond that rate when importers become increasingly successful (China will only be able to do that using trade defence instruments, such as anti-dumping and safeguard measures, but these are subject to strict conditions and offer only temporary protection). Thus, WTO accession greatly increases legal certainty for importers.

Telecommunications

Basic telecommunication services (ie relay of voice or data)

Foreign service suppliers are permitted to establish joint ventures in accordance with the following conditions:

- For mobile services foreign investment in the joint venture can amount to a maximum of 25 per cent upon accession, 35 per cent after one year and 49 per cent after three years. For fixed-line services the foreign investment in joint ventures is opened only three years after China's accession, up to a maximum of 25 per cent. This is to be increased to 35 per cent after five years and 49 per cent after six years.
- Initially these joint ventures will be allowed to operate services in and between the cities of Shanghai, Guangzhou and Beijing. This would be expanded to include Chengdu, Chongqing, Dalian, Fuzhou, Hangzhou, Nanjing, Ningbo, Qingdao, Shenyang, Shenzen, Xiamen, Xian, Taiyuan and Wuhan.
- The commitment covers domestic and international voice and facsimile services, and packet-switched and circuit-switched data transmission services. It also extends to domestic leased circuit services.

Table 2.1.1   Target tariff rate reductions by sector

Products	Import tariffs and quota restrictions at the moment of WTO accession	Target reduction and target date
Automobiles	80–100% quotas in place	reduction to 25% by 1 July 2006 higher initial quota to be increased by 15% annually and phased out by 1 January 2005
Automobile parts	average of 17.4%	average of 9.5% by 1 July 2006
Beer	43%	completely eliminated by 1 January 2005
Chemicals	average of 8.8%	average of 6.9% by 1 January 2008
Cosmetics	average of 23.5%	average of 10.7% by 1 January 2008
Fish	average of 16.6%	average of 10.3%
Furniture	average of 13.9%	completely eliminated by 1 January 2005
Information technology products	average of 6.4%	tariffs on three-quarters of information technology products will be eliminated by 1 January 2003. All tariffs will be eliminated by 1 January 2005
Medical equipment	average of 6.5%	average of 3.9% by 1 January 2005
Paper	average of 15–25%	average of 5.4% by 1 January 2006
Spirits	average of 65%	average of 10% by 1 January 2005

Concerns have been continually raised by other WTO members that the high capitalization requirements for foreign joint venture investors is a measure that effectively bars foreign investment and inhibits the long-term growth and competitiveness of the Chinese telecoms market. The Chinese regulations effecting these capitalization requirements have been in place since the date of accession and remain in force despite continued EU and US criticism. Furthermore, the Chinese authorities are also looking to reduce the number of joint venture partners available by reducing the number of domestic telecom companies from seven to four large state companies. The WTO-compatibility of some of the manoeuvres of the Chinese authorities is doubtful.

Value-added telecommunications services

This covers electronic mail, voice mail, online information and database retrieval, electronic data interchange, enhanced/value-added facsimile services, code and protocol conversion, online information and/or data processing.

Foreign investment in a joint venture can amount to a maximum of 30 per cent. These joint ventures are allowed to operate services in all regions, as the original temporary geographic restrictions have been abolished. However, China's regulator, the Ministry of Information Industries (MII) recently reclassified

several international value-added services as basic services. This action had the effect of both delaying until December 2004 the ability of foreign entrants to offer these services, and of subjecting any would-be entrant to the high capitalization requirements placed on new basic services providers.

Specific rules concerning anti-competitive behaviour

China has also undertaken to respect the obligations contained in the so-called 'Reference Paper'. This WTO document defines a number of regulatory principles for the telecommunications sector and includes measures to prevent anti-competitive behaviour, such as cross-subsidization, and also sets out rules concerning licensing criteria, universal service and the independence of the regulator. China has been criticized for the poor implementation of this agreement, particularly on the basis that MII still occupies dual roles as protector of state enterprise operators and as industry regulator. Laws already drafted to effect a general liberalization of the telecoms sector have still not been brought into force.

Distribution services

Wholesale distribution services

There are commitments upon accession to allow foreign-owned enterprises distribution rights no later than 11 December 2002, with a later date of 11 December 2004 for books, newspapers, magazines, pharmaceutical products, pesticides and mulching film. For chemical fertilizers, processed oil and crude oil the date is set for 11 December 2006. The first 2002 deadline for implementation of its commitments was not met, but the Chinese authorities issued regulations in April 2004 on distribution rights separate from trading rights.

While the Chinese authorities have been praised for circulating the draft among foreign businesses for comment, the regulations have been criticized on the basis that they fail to address how existing foreign-invested companies in China can incorporate the new distribution rights into their existing trade patterns. A provision allowing the Chinese authorities to restrict foreign ownership in distribution companies on the basis that their investment plans fail to match regional development plans has caused controversy and would appear to be in breach of the Chinese commitment to implement its trade regime in a uniform and impartial way.

Retail services

As of 11 December 2004 there will be no geographic or quantitative restrictions or restrictions concerning equity or form of establishment. There are specific rules, however, for chain stores with more than 30 outlets. While the retail market was one of the sectors where the impact of WTO accession was expected to be greatest, the phasing in of this liberalization has been slow. Although joint venture retailing services are now permitted, restrictions on import and export volume, capital adequacy and market experience have reduced the number of potential market entrants. EU and US trade departments are understood to be pushing the Chinese to open this rapidly expanding domestic market in line with its WTO commitments.

Construction services

Upon accession it was possible to provide construction services via joint ventures with a foreign majority and, within three years, wholly foreign-owned enterprises were to be permitted to carry out foreign-financed projects (including projects funded by institutions such as the IMF and the World Bank) and Chinese-funded projects where Chinese construction firms can

justify the need for international assistance. This was implemented early and separate regulations on the administration of foreign investment in construction and engineering enterprises took effect on 1 December 2002. In April of 2003, the Chinese authorities issued implementing rules on the administration of the construction regulations. While these clarified many of the implementation questions raised by foreign businesses, they provided little comfort in respect of the high capitalization requirements for wholly foreign-owned enterprises and the continued limited scope of the projects for which they can apply.

Banking services

China gradually met its WTO commitments during the first year of membership and abolished most restrictions imposed on the operations of foreign banks in China. Foreign banks can now offer RMB banking services to Chinese corporations and will be allowed to offer to services to Chinese individuals on 11 December 2006. As from this date, China is also due to issue banking licences solely on the basis of prudential criteria, without quantitative limits on licences and restrictions on ownership, operation and juridical form of foreign banks.

There are no more geographic restrictions for foreign currency business, and geographic restrictions on local currency business will be phased out by 11 December 2006, on the basis of four new cities being opened up to local currency operations each year.

While in December 2001 revised regulations permitting foreign bank branches anywhere in China were introduced, and the capitalization requirements were reduced in December 2003, foreign banks still face serious stakeholding restrictions of 20 per cent in Chinese banks and of 33 per cent in joint venture managed funds.

Courier services

Foreign companies may provide courier services (except those reserved for the Chinese postal services) through joint and majority ownership. By 11 December 2005, foreign courier service suppliers may establish wholly foreign-owned subsidiaries. However, Chinese regulations introduced after WTO accession have sought to maintain the monopoly of China Post through the introduction of weight restrictions and bureaucratic licensing provisions.

Insurance

China has made significant efforts to implement laws affecting its commitments to increase transparency and strengthen insurance regulation. Laws phasing out geographic restrictions for foreign non-life insurers operating as wholly foreign-owned entities are still to be put in place by the implementation date of 11 December 2004. Currently 15 cities have been opened to foreign insurers.

A total of only around 50 foreign insurance companies currently operate in China, with 30 of those being by way of a joint venture with a domestic insurer. Less than 5 per cent of the national insurance market rests with foreign companies, and they have continually reported discriminatory treatment, such as high capitalization to obtain national licences and difficulties in receiving the necessary branch approvals concurrently.

Conclusion

As discussed in Chapter 1.2, China certainly has the political will to implement its obligations in a serious manner. At the same time, it is generally acknowledged that China has made ambitious commitments and that the short-term conflicts and difficulties it faces will continue to be eroded if this political will to liberalize market access is maintained.

It should be remembered that it has taken a number of EU Member States a long time to fulfil their EC obligations – for example to set up an independent telecommunications regulator that effectively safeguards competition and curtails the incumbent operators – and, clearly, one cannot expect such a process to run any smoother in China where the concept of pro-competitive regulation is entirely new.

The time it will take for China to implement its promises in full will also most certainly depend on the health of the Chinese economy. A continued blooming economy will give China the incentive to allow more foreign competition, whereas an economic downturn would probably encourage further protectionism.

Foreign Trade Activity and its Administration

Li Yong, Deputy Secretary General, China Association of International Trade

Trade environment

Until now, market access for new entrants to China's foreign trade activities has been strictly controlled. Significant changes have taken place in more than two decades of reform and the foreign trade administration system has gradually been liberalized. Liberalization of foreign trade is mainly manifested in the relaxation of restrictions on import and export trading rights and reduction of import and export licence control. In the past, only a small number of companies and enterprises had legitimate trading rights and a large number of commodities whose import and export were subject to licence control. These control measures created monopolistic advantages for those who had the privileges of trading rights, and barriers to the free flow of import and export.

Relaxation of trading rights

Alongside the progress of economic reform and the opening up drive, economic development has advanced to the point where the present limited trading rights will need to be expanded in order to meet increasing import and export needs. Reform of the foreign trade system has responded to these needs by loosening the reins on trading rights control. As a result, trading rights are no longer the privilege only of professional trading companies (ie companies that used to be under the jurisdiction of the foreign trade and investment authorities), but are also available to other types of companies, such as industrial trading companies, manufacturing enterprises, manufacturing joint ventures (who have automatic trading rights for their exports of own products and imports of necessary equipment and materials), research institutions, private entities and Sino–foreign joint venture trading companies, although the qualification requirements for some of these have been quite demanding. Even more encouraging is the fact that efforts to liberalize trading rights are ongoing, and lowering the threshold to an eventual registration of trading rights (instead of approval) has been set as the final objective of the reformation process. Reform has been accelerated by China's commitment under the WTO to further open up trading rights within a specified period of time. On joining the WTO, China agreed to grant full trading rights to joint venture enterprises with minority share foreign investment in 2002 and to majority share foreign-invested joint ventures in 2003. From 2005, all enterprises in China are granted full rights to trade.

Phase-out of non-tariff measures

At the same time, effort has also been made to reduce non-tariff measures such as the number of commodities that are subject to import and export licence controls. The reduction of non-tariff barriers was an ongoing process prior to WTO entry; by the end of 2001, for example, quotas and licensing requirements involved only 5 per cent of all imports compared with about 50 per cent little more than a decade ago. From 1 January 2002, the number of commodity categories further dropped from 33 to 12. China has pledged to eliminate the remaining import quota and licence restrictions by 2005.

Tariff reduction

In addition to non-tariff measures, China has also committed to reduce the import tariff level. In fact, by the time it entered the WTO in 2001, the general tariff level had already fallen to an average of 15 per cent. In

2002, the first year of China's WTO accession, the average tariff was further reduced to 12 per cent and by 2005 it will be reduced to 10 per cent (see Figure 2.2.1).

State trading

However, there are a number of products that are subject to state trading and designated trading. According to China's WTO protocol:

> …without prejudice to China's right to regulate trade in a manner consistent with the WTO Agreement, China shall progressively liberalize the availability and scope of the right to trade, so that within three years of accession, all enterprises in China shall have the right to trade in all goods throughout the customs territory of China, except for those goods listed in Annex 2A, which continue to be subject to state trading in accordance with this protocol.

In Annex 2A are two separate lists that specify the types of commodities falling into the scope of state trading: state importation and state exportation (see Tables 2.2.1 and 2.2.2). These commodities are considered essential goods with an important bearing on national security and social stability.

In addition to state trading products are products subject to designated trading, including natural rubber (four sub-categories), timber (28 sub-categories), plywood (three sub-categories), wool (nine sub-categories), acrylic (18 sub-categories) and steel (183 sub-categories).

Price controls

While China is committed to allowing prices for traded goods and services in every sector to be determined by market forces, and multi-tier pricing practices for such goods and services will be eliminated, China still maintains its control over the pricing of some categories of products and services.

Products that are subject to state pricing include tobacco (four sub-categories) salt (one category), natural gas (one category) and pharmaceuticals (40 sub-categories).

Public utilities subject to government prices are gas for civil use, tap water, electricity, heating power and water supplied by irrigation works.

Services subject to state pricing include postal and telecommunication services charges (including postal services charges, national and trans-provincial telecommunication services charges), entrance fees for tourist sites (significant historical relics and natural landscape under protection) and education services charges.

Apart from government priced products and services, there are also products and services to which government guideline pricing will apply. Products that are subject to such guideline pricing include grain (14 sub-categories), vegetable oil (four sub-categories), processed oil (seven sub-categories), chemical fertilizer (one category), silkworm cocoons (two sub-categories) and cotton (one category). The services that fall into this category are listed in Table 2.2.3.

Types of players in the field

The granting of full trading rights to all enterprises registered in China will take place over time, as described in Chapter 2.1. Within the three-year transitional period, companies that deal in import and

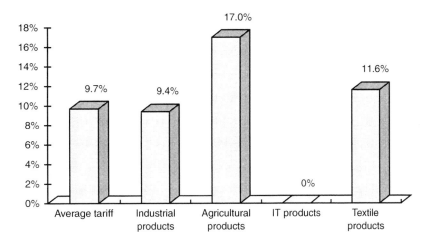

Figure 2.2.1 Average tariff by key categories of products by year 2005

Table 2.2.1   Products subject to state importation

Product	State Trading Enterprise
Vegetable oil (7 sub-categories)	1. China National Cereals, Oil & Foodstuff Import and Export Co.
	2. China National Native Products and Animal By-products Import & Export Co.
	3. China Resources Co.
	4. China Nam Kwong National Import & Export Co.
	5. China Liangfeng Cereals Import & Export Co.
	6. China Cereals, Oil & Foodstuff Co.(Group)
Sugar (6 sub-categories)	1. China National Cereals, Oil & Foodstuff Import and Export Co.
	2. China Export Commodities Base Construction Co.
	3. China Overseas Trade Co.
	4. China Sugar & Wine Co. (Group)
	5. China Commerce Foreign Trade Co.
Tobacco (6 sub-categories)	China National Tobacco Import & Export Co.
Crude oil (1 category)	1. China National Chemical Import & Export Co.
Processed oil (7 sub-categories)	2. China International United Petroleum & Chemicals Co.
	3. China National United Oil Co.
	4. Zhuhai Zhenrong Company
Fertilizer	1. China National Chemical Import & Export Co.
	2. China National Agricultural Means of Production Group Co.
Cotton (2 sub-categories)	1. China National Textiles Import & Export Co.
	2. Beijing Jiuda Textiles Group Co.
	3. Tianjing Textiles Industry Supply and Marketing Co.
	4. Shanghai Textiles Raw Materials Co.

Source: Ministry of Foreign Trade and Economic Cooperation, available in detail at www.moftec.gov.cn/table/wto/law05.doc

Table 2.2.2   Products subject to state exportation

Product	State Trading Enterprise
Tea (4 sub-categories)	China National Native Products and Animal By-Products Import & Export Co.
Rice (4 sub-categories)	China National Cereals Oil and Foodstuffs Import & Export Corp.
Corn (3 sub-categories)	
Soy bean (5 sub-categories)	Jilin Grain Import & Export Co. Ltd.
Tungsten ore (3 sub-categories)	1. China National Metals and Minerals Import & Export Co.
Ammonium paratungstates (2 sub-categories)	2. China National Non-ferrous Import & Export Co.
Tungstate products (8 sub-categories)	3. China Rare Earth and Metal Group Co.
	4. China National Chemical Import & Export Co.
Coal (5 sub-categories)	1. China National Coal Industry Import & Export Co.
	2. China National Metals and Minerals Import & Export Co.
	3. Shanxi Coal Import & Export Group Co.
	4. Shenhua Group Ltd.
Crude oil (1 category)	1. China National Chemical Import & Export Co.
Processed oil (13 sub-categories)	2. China International United Petroleum & Chemicals Co.
	3. China National United Oil Co.
Silk (13 sub-categories)	China National Silk Import & Export Co.
Unbleached silk (4 sub-categories)	
Cotton (2 sub-categories)	1. China National Textiles Import & Export Co.
Cotton yarn (44 sub-categories)	2. Qingdao Textiles United Import & Export Co.
Woven cotton fabrics (13 sub-categories)	3. Beijing No.2 Cotton Mill
	4. Beijing No.3 Cotton Mill
	5. Tianjin No.1 Cotton Mill
	6. Shanghai Shenda Co. Ltd

Table 2.2.2 (Contd)

Products	State Trading Enterprises
	7. Shanghai Huashen Textiles and Dying Co. (Group)
	8. Dalian Huanqiu Textiles Group Co.
	9. Shijiazhuang Changshan Textiles Group
	10. Luoyang Cotton Mill, Henan Province
	11. Songyue Textiles Industry Group, Henan Province
	12. Dezhou Cotton Mill
	13. Wuxi No.1 Cotton Mill
	14. Puxin Textiles Mill, Hubei Province
	15. Northwest No.1 Cotton Mill
	16. Chengdu Jiuxing Textiles Group Co.
	17. Suzhou Sulun Textiles Joint Company (Group)
	18. Northwest No.7 Cotton Mill
	19. Xiangmian Group Co., Hubei Province
	20. Handan Lihua Textiles Group Co.
	21. Xinjiang Textiles Industry Co. (Group)
	22. Anqing Textiles Mill
	23. Jinan No.2 Cotton Mill
	24. Tianjin No.2 Cotton Mill
	25. Jinhua Textiles Mill, Shanxi Province
	26. Jinwei Group Co., Zhejiang Province
	27. Northwest No.5 Cotton Mill
	28. Baoding No.1 Cotton Mill
	29. Liaoyang Textiles Mill
	30. Changchun Textiles Mill
	31. Huaxin Cotton Mill, Henan Province
	32. Baotou Textiles Mill
	33. Ninbo Hefeng Textiles Group Co.
	34. Northwest No.4 Cotton Mill
	35. Xinjiang Shihezi Bayi Cotton Mill
Antimony ores (2 sub-categories)	1. China National Metals and Minerals Import & Export Co.
Antimony oxide (1 category)	2. China National Non-ferrous Import & Export Co.
Antimony products (3 sub-categories)	3. China Rare Earth and Metal Group Co.
Silver (3 sub-categories)	1. China Banknote Printing and Minting Corporation
	2. China Copper Lead Zinc Group

Source: Ministry of Foreign Trade and Economic Cooperation, available in detail at www.moftec.gov.cn/table/wto/law06.doc

export still needed to have appropriate trading rights. Those who did not have rights to trade were not legally permitted to handle import or export contracts directly, although they could contract companies who had trading rights to carry out import or export on their behalf on a commission basis.

Developing an understanding of the various types of business structure in China is important to firms looking for import/export opportunities in this market, and can be critical to the success or otherwise of a foreign company's China business plan. The following seeks to outline the kinds of companies that foreign companies may encounter.

National foreign trade companies

National foreign trade companies are companies that are set up at the national level and were once affiliated with government departments. At the beginning of China's economic reform and opening up, foreign trade was virtually monopolized by 12 national foreign trade corporations under the then Ministry of Foreign Trade (now the Ministry of Commerce). With the deepening

Table 2.2.3 Services subject to government guideline pricing

Service	Notes
Transport services charges	Including rail transport of both passenger and freight, air transport of freight, port services and pipeline transport
Professional services charges	Including architectural and engineering services, legal services, assets assessment services, authentication, arbitration, notarization and inspection
Charges for commission agents' services	Including commission for trademarks, advertisement taxation and bidding agents
Charges for settlement, clearing and transmission services of banks	Including settlement, clearing and transmission services of the RMB, transaction fees and seat charges of national securities exchanges, as well as seat charges for China Foreign Exchange Centre
Selling price and renting fee of residential apartments	
Health related services	

Source: Ministry of Foreign Trade and Economic Cooperation, available in detail at www.moftec.gov.cn/table/wto/law09.doc

economic reform, other ministries governing different industries successively set up their own foreign trade functions, specializing in their particular product fields and known as 'industrial foreign trade companies'. Further government reform has resulted in separation of those national companies from their government affiliation and they have now become independent in their decision-making.

Being state-owned in nature, some have been publicly listed on the stock market. Although their role has been eroded by an increasing number of emerging companies that have acquired trading rights, they still enjoy the advantages of being close to central government decision-making and often act as the purchasing or selling agents of the government in the trade of products of national importance. Under the WTO arrangements, many of these companies are designated companies for products subject to state trading. On those non-state designated products (both import and export), they are now competing on most fronts with other forms of trading entities. Trading companies with 'China' or 'China National' in their business names are normally national (or state-level) foreign trade companies.

Provincial foreign trade companies

Provincial foreign trade companies were once subsidiaries of national foreign trade companies under the old foreign trade system. Even those companies set up by industrial ministries also had local representatives. Between 1988 and 1990, those provincial subsidiaries became independent of their national headquarters as part of government efforts to reform

the foreign trade system. These companies have since assumed a leading role in the development of foreign trade in their respective localities.

Foreign trade companies at lower administrative level

Also at the city level are foreign trade companies with rights to trade internationally. They undertake the tasks of generating export earnings and act as import agents for both local government purchase and orders by local enterprises. At the county level, the foreign trade companies more often perform the role of export suppliers than independent import or export operators.

Large industrial enterprises with trading rights

In the late 1980s, the Chinese government decided to grant large state-owned enterprises trading rights limited to the export of their own products and import of products needed for their production. Many of these large enterprises have now become conglomerates or group companies under which are the trading functions of separate corporate entities. Some of those trading functions are no longer limited to import and export related to production, but deal with a wider range of products in their import and export activities.

Foreign-invested enterprises

Foreign-invested enterprises include equity joint ventures, contractual joint ventures and wholly foreign-owned enterprises. These foreign-invested enterprises, previously allowed only to import what was needed for their production and to export what they produced, are now permitted to deal in other products.

Research institutions

To encourage the export of locally-developed technologies and development of local R&D capabilities, large research institutions that meet certain qualification requirements are permitted to have trading rights. Previously limited to their research-related imports and exports, they are now permitted to export products not of their own production.

Private enterprises

With the development of the private sector, many private enterprises have emerged as leading sources of export supply. In the late 1990s, the government decided to grant trading rights to private enterprises, again limited to imports and exports related to their production.

The impact of the WTO on China's foreign trade activities

The above categories of entities with various levels of trading rights constitute the body of China's exporting task force. Foreign-invested enterprises are becoming key contributors to China's export earnings and have held around a 50 per cent share in China's total export in recent years. Foreign trade companies, both at the national level and lower levels, are being disadvantaged by manufacturing enterprises with the trading rights beyond their own production capabilities.

The impact on patterns of foreign trade activities

With the situation described above, the advantages of traditional foreign trade companies are limited to the commodities and products that fall under the category of monopolistic trading. These products are characterized either by high levels of concentration, such as crude oil and petrochemicals, or extreme fragmentation such as textiles and light industrial products.

Recent trends have shown a weakening in the role of professional foreign trade companies. At the same time, foreign-invested enterprises have gained momentum with a share in the total trade volume of 49 per cent. The opening of trading rights to more companies has naturally led to increased competition for the export of products from highly fragmented industries, one consequence of which would be a reduction in the profitability of professional trading companies. Higher or stable profitability can only be achieved from the export of products of monopolistic trading. Obviously, such monopolistic trading rights are not available to

every foreign trade company. As a result, the larger foreign trade companies will be forced to move horizontally to invest in the production of products they have been exporting, and vertically engage in the manufacturing of what they perceive will have export potential. Those smaller foreign trade companies will have to shift their focus on general trading to differentiated product trading in order to survive. The role of foreign trade companies as intermediaries of trade between China and the outside world is diminishing.

Impact on the distribution of imported products

Together with the elimination of the restrictions on full trading rights, China has committed to opening up distribution rights to foreign participants. Before the WTO accession, foreign companies were not permitted to distribute their products (except those produced in China), nor were they allowed to own distribution establishments, wholesale channels or even warehousing networks. Imports had to be handled by foreign trade companies and the distribution was highly dependent on the importing foreign trade companies or distributor/wholesaler under separate arrangements. This considerably weakened the competitiveness of imported products and efficiency of distribution. China's commitments to the WTO on the opening up of the distribution sector is improving the situation. Foreign exporters are no longer 'air-locked' out of the Chinese market and import activities are more of an inherent part of distribution: under WTO commitments foreign exporters are now able to have hands-on control. Chinese foreign trade companies face the situation of once-high import profitability falling as a result of the lifting of restrictions on foreign participation in the distribution process. Large foreign trade companies may move down the supply chain to expand their own distribution capabilities. In the distribution sector, they will now meet competition from international distributors and retailers.

Impact on the flow of imports and exports

The impact of tariff reduction on China's foreign trade as a whole is twofold. On the import side, reductions in the average tariff level have contributed to the increased inflow of imports. Imports will put competitive pressure on those industries that are less efficient, less economical and technologically backward. The industries suffering the greatest impact will include agriculture, automobiles, petrochemicals, equipment manufacturing, pharmaceuticals and steel. For some imports, however, the effective rates of tariff were significantly lower than the official average rate of 15 per cent at the time of accession as a result of various tariff reductions, exemptions, rebates and evasions. In 1997, for example, the total tariff revenue was RMB35.14 billion, about US$4.28 billion. The total import value in the same year was US$142.36 billion. The effective tariff rate in 1997 was only 4 per cent. Therefore, the impact of tariff reductions on certain products is expected to be minimal. On the export side, the lowering of import tariffs will greatly improve the competitiveness of those export products that use imported materials. For example, the import tariff on chemical fibre will be reduced from the current 18 per cent to around 6 per cent by 2005. China's textile exports will benefit from the tariff reduction.

Conclusion

Following China's WTO accession, most of the non-tariff barriers that used to provide protective shelter for domestic industries and foreign trade companies are being removed. Also removed are the subsidies for the purpose of encouraging exports. China's market will be opened up for foreign participation to a much greater extent, thereby offering significant market possibilities for foreign businesses to do business with China.

Generally, the pattern of China's foreign trade will be reshuffled and foreign trade companies will need to reposition themselves under the regime of the WTO. In the battlefield of imports, foreign businesses will be engaged in head-on competition with the Chinese enterprises in China, and it is too early to conclude who will win.

In terms of exports, more Chinese companies will join the ranks of exporters, and the role played by foreign trade companies as intermediaries will weaken as a result. Horizontal or vertical integration is likely to take place as alternative strategic options for foreign trade companies. Participation of foreign players in the field of foreign trade will lead to competition for export resources and foreign markets.

China's Exchange Control System

Ma Shabo, Capital Account Administration Dept., State Administration of Foreign Exchange, and Li Yong,
Deputy Secretary General, China Association of International Trade

China's foreign exchange control regime

Foreign exchange control is an administration policy on foreign exchange expenditure and receipts, which a country adopts in a specific period of time for the purpose of maintaining the balance of international payments, stabilizing its currency value and sustaining the development of the national economy. Foreign exchange control is directly correlated with the level of a country's external economic exchanges, the degree of maturity of its financial market and the level and ability of its financial control and administration. It is also directly related to the state of a country's macro-economic development as well as its international finance and foreign exchange situations. However, with enhancement in the level of a country's economic development, foreign exchange control will be gradually relaxed.

Since the opening up in 1979, China's foreign exchange control regime has experienced quite a number of reforms with the expansion of economic reform, development of the national economy and gradual convergence with the world economy. Such reforms can be divided into the following periods.

The pre-1994 period

In this period, China's economy was under a planned regime, which was reflected accordingly in rigorous foreign exchange control regulation, characterized by the exercise of a principle of 'centralized administration and uniform operation'. All foreign exchange receipts, either by enterprises or an individual, had to be turned over to the state, while all foreign exchange expenditures had to be supplied by the state. The state controlled and adjusted foreign exchange receipts and expenditures through mandatory plans and directives.

Although the foreign exchange retention system and foreign exchange readjustment business were implemented in the period – an effort to gradually bring market mechanisms into the field of foreign exchange allocation – the foreign exchange control regime was still predominantly a function of the planned economy.

The period from 1994 to 1996

To match the systemic reforms that had taken place in the fields of foreign trade, taxation and finance, the State Administration of Foreign Exchange announced its major reform measures on 1 January 1994, which included the following key points:

- convergence of the exchange rates to implement a single market-based and managed floating exchange rate regime;
- abolition of foreign exchange retention and submission in favour of a system of selling foreign exchange through banks;
- establishment of a nationally uniform interbank foreign exchange market to improve the mechanism of exchange rate formation;
- elimination of mandatory plans and directives for foreign exchange receipts and payments and employment of economic and legal means to adjust the international balance of payments and foreign exchange revenue and expenditure;
- discontinuation of foreign exchange certificate issuance and the banning of foreign currency-denominated pricing and settlements.

As a result of these reforms, China lifted the exchange restrictions regarding trade and non-trade payments under commercial arrangements, thereby realizing conditional RMB convertibility under the current account.

Post-1996 period

Fruitful results had been achieved following the reforms to the foreign exchange regime in 1994. Foreign trade had grown rapidly, while utilization of foreign investment had drastically expanded. The international balance of payments was in equilibrium and the RMB exchange rate was steadily climbing. Under such circumstances another major reform was made to China's foreign exchange control regime, which involved:

- the inclusion of foreign-invested enterprises into the system of selling foreign exchange through the banks;
- the abolition of exchange restrictions on non-trade payments under non-commercial arrangements.

The above reform measure eliminated all exchange restrictions on current account payments, realizing the convertibility of the RMB under the current account. At the same time, China officially accepted Article 8 of the International Monetary Fund on 1 December 1996, promising a foreign exchange control regime with convertibility under current account and necessary control over capital account.

Trends of development in China's foreign exchange control regime

The ultimate goal of reform in China's foreign exchange control is to realize convertibility of the RMB under capital account and gradually achieve full RMB convertibility. Since 1996, although China has experienced the shock of the Asian financial crisis and now faces the challenges and opportunities of its WTO accession, China's goals for the reform of its foreign exchange control regime have not changed.

In July 1997, when the Asian financial crisis exploded from Thailand, China was considerably affected. In order to resist the impact of the Asian financial crisis and combat illegal business and financial activities within China, a series of interim measures were adopted. These measures were intended to reinforce, on the premise of convertibility under current account and regulation under capital account, verification of the authenticity of foreign exchange receipts and payments on current account, thereby plugging up the loopholes in currency management to prevent capital flight. After a period

of implementation, some adjustments were made in accordance with international practice and the level of impact made by such measures on the normal business activities of enterprises. Those measures that were in conformity with international practices and China's commitments and had not produced adverse effects on enterprise business activities were consolidated in the form of laws and regulations. Those that had generated significant negative impacts were adjusted or abolished in a timely manner. All these efforts ensured that China's foreign exchange control regime evolved on a normal track of development.

China has joined the WTO, as a result of which it will further reduce tariffs, phase out non-tariff barriers and further open up the market. Accordingly, entities having foreign exchange receipts and payments will increase in number, leading to drastic increases in the total volume of foreign exchange transactions. China's foreign exchange control regime is facing greater opportunities as well as challenges. To comply with WTO agreement and rules, China will rectify and amend laws and regulations to meet the WTO accession requirements.

At the same time, China will also push ahead gradually and prudently the convertibility of the capital account based on the improvement and development of China's macro-economic situation.

Control over the foreign exchange of foreign resident organizations

Administration of foreign exchange accounts

Resident organizations should file with the competent Administration of Foreign Exchange (AFE) by presenting the approval documents issued by relevant authorities and certificate of registration with the relevant Administration of Industry and Commerce. A Filing Form for Foreign Exchange Account by Foreign Resident Organization will be issued, against which the applicant can process the opening of the foreign exchange account at a designated bank.

The sources of foreign exchange receipt should be the remittance from outside China for operational outlays, and the expenditures should be expenses that are related to office operations.

Administration of foreign exchange payments

Foreign exchange received by foreign resident organizations can be deposited into their bank accounts or sold to the designated banks or remitted/carried out of China against valid proofs.

Legitimate RMB income earned by foreign resident organizations may be converted into foreign currency and remitted out of China at designated banks upon presentation of valid proofs and fee lists.

Should resident organizations and their personnel sell their personal items, equipment or appliances brought into China from abroad or purchased in China, they may convert the RMB proceeds into foreign currency and remit them out of the country through designated banks by presenting their business registration certificate (issued by the Administration of Industry and Commerce) and pertinent sales proofs.

Control over the foreign exchange of foreign-invested enterprises

Foreign exchange registration

1. Foreign-invested enterprises (FIEs) should, within 30 days after the issuance of the business licence, process foreign exchange registration with the competent AFE and obtain Certificate of Foreign Exchange Registration against presentation of the following documents: approval documents issued by examination and approval authorities, capital verification report, business licence and its copy and the approved contract and articles of association.

2. After foreign exchange registration, in the event of any changes in the name, address and scope of business, or ownership transfer, capital addition or merger, the FIEs should go to the pertinent Administration of Industry and Commerce to register the changes, after which the changes should be registered with the competent AFE in the foreign exchange register.

3. FIEs, upon expiry or accidental termination of the enterprise, should, with approval for dissolution from the original approval authorities, cancel the foreign exchange registration with the AFE within 30 days after liquidation.

4. Foreign exchange registration certificates will be reviewed on an annual basis by the relevant authorities. Fabrication, lending, transfer or selling of a registration certificate are strictly forbidden.

Control over foreign exchange accounts

Categories of accounts and scope of receipts and payment include:

- foreign exchange settlement account;
- special account for foreign exchange capital;
- temporary special account;
- special loan account;
- special debt service account;
- 'B' share account;
- special account for stocks.

The opening of foreign exchange accounts

FIEs can open foreign exchange accounts within and outside China and in different locations of China. In order to do so, they will have to meet the relevant requirements of exchange control.

The use of foreign exchange accounts

The AFE will review and ratify the highest limit for the foreign exchange account based on the paid-up capital and the cash flow needs under the current account of the FIE. Foreign exchange receipts within the limit are allowed to be retained but the part in excess of the limit will have to be sold to the designated banks.

Deposits by FIEs in foreign exchange control accounts can be converted into time deposits, but they are still subject to the control of a maximum limit.

The close of the account

The closure of a foreign exchange account by an FIE should be processed with the AFE within 10 days after the clearing of the account. The certificate of account closure by the opening bank and the certificate of foreign exchange registration should be presented for account closing procedures. After the foreign exchange bank account is closed, the amount belonging to the foreign investor can be transferred or remitted out of China, while the amount that goes to Chinese investors should be sold to the designated bank.

Control over foreign exchange receipts and payments

Control over exchange receipts and payments under current account

The exchange receipt on the current account of an FIE can be sold to the designated banks or retained in its foreign exchange account if the exchange receipts are within the ratified limit.

The exchange payments under the current account of an FIE can be made from its own foreign exchange account or the required amount for payments may be purchased from the designated banks.

Control over international commercial loans

FIEs can use international commercial loans without the approval of the AFE; however, they will need to go through the procedures of external debt registration. In addition, the cumulative amount of mid-term and long-term international borrowings by FIEs should not exceed the difference between the registered capital and the total investment.

Control over foreign currency bonds

The issuance of foreign currency bonds, convertible bonds, negotiable certificates of deposit and commercial documents by FIEs should be approved by the AFE and undergo external debt registration.

Control over foreign exchange borrowings from domestic financial institutions

The borrowing of foreign exchange loans by FIEs from domestic financial institutions does not require approval by the AFE, but FIEs will have to complete foreign exchange loan registration procedures.

Control over external guarantees

External guarantees within a period of less than a year provided by FIEs for domestic entities will need to be approved by the local administration of foreign exchange. The external guarantees for more than one year by FIEs for domestic or overseas entities will have to be approved by the State Administration of Foreign Exchange. External guarantees by wholly foreign-owned enterprises will not need approval by the AFE. An external pledge or hypothecation with the assets of an FIE as its security will not require approval from the AFE. However, all external guarantees will have to undergo registration procedures at the AFE.

Control over RMB borrowings from domestic Chinese-funded financial institutions against guarantees provided by external organizations

FIEs can use their own foreign exchange funds as pledges for their borrowing of RMB from domestic Chinese-funded financial institutions. FIEs can accept guarantees from their foreign shareholders, overseas banks or foreign banks within the territory of China for their borrowing of RMB loans from domestic Chinese-funded financial institutions. The RMB loans borrowed by FIEs can be used for the purpose of making up shortages in cash flow or long-term investments in fixed assets. The maximum term of such loans should not exceed five years.

Control over the payments under capital account

An FIE should present proof of external debt registration, external debt contract, and notice by creditors

for repayment of principal and interest to the AFE when applying for repayment of principal and interest. Upon approval by the AFE, the FIE may make payment through its foreign currency account or at designated banks against the approval documents.

For repayment of foreign exchange loan principal to domestic Chinese-funded financial institutions in China, the FIE will need to obtain approval from the AFE. No approval is needed, however, for the payment of interest.

Approval by the AFE will need to be obtained when FIEs perform the obligations of external guarantees.

Control over foreign exchange settlement and selling

The amount of current account foreign exchange receipts by FIEs in excess of the limit prescribed by the AFE will have to be settled.

- Foreign exchange capital, borrowed international commercial loans, the revenues from the issuance of 'B' shares and overseas public offerings can be settled. The settlement of borrowed foreign exchange loans by FIEs from domestic Chinese-funded financial institutions are not allowed.
- All selling and payments of foreign exchange should be processed against presentation of valid proofs and commercial documents, or by filing forms issued by the AFE, or through requisition of foreign exchange selling ratified by the AFE. All selling and payments of foreign exchange under capital account must be processed against the document of ratification issued by the AFE. Those who are unable to produce valid certificates as prescribed by the AFE and valid commercial documents will have to submit applications to the AFE for approval, against which selling and payments of foreign exchange can be processed. For the selling and payments of foreign exchange against the presentation of the filing document, the designated bank will examine and verify the authenticity of such document in accordance with relevant regulations. Such examination and verification will not be carried out by the designated banks if no approval documents issued by the AFE are presented. For the non-trade foreign exchange payments, the applicant needs to provide a taxation certificate in addition to other certificates and documents. Payments on capital account should be made with the applicant's own foreign exchange, and purchase of foreign exchange for payment purpose is only

allowed when the applicant's own foreign exchange falls short of the amount required.

- Control over the purchase of foreign exchange for payment purposes under trade arrangements governs the following realms of administration:
  - those who purchase foreign exchange for payments against prescribed valid certificates and valid commercial documents;
  - those who purchase foreign exchange for payments against foreign exchange filing forms;
  - those who purchase foreign exchange for payments against requisition of foreign exchange selling ratified and issued by the AFE; classification of customs declaration;
  - administration of foreign exchange purchases for payments by bonded warehouses;
  - administration of foreign exchange purchases for payments under the arrangements to transfer goods for additional processing.
- Control over foreign exchange purchases for payments under non-trade arrangements.
- Control over foreign exchange purchases for payments on capital account. Advance purchases of foreign exchange for repayment of loans is forbidden.

Control over the investment profits and investment capital

Administration over profits repatriation
The legitimate profit earned by an FIE can be remitted out of China. In doing so, the FIE needs to present the following documents:

- foreign exchange registration certificate;
- capital verification report by an independent accounting firm;
- Board resolution on profit distribution;
- tax payment certificate and tax declaration form;
- audit report on current-year profits by an accounting firm.

Upon approval, the FIE can expatriate the profit from its own account or purchase foreign exchange from designated banks for profit repatriation.

Administration over reinvestment
The foreign investors in FIEs are allowed, upon approval by the AFE, to make reinvestments with their after-tax profits or the funds available as a result of liquidation, equity transfer or anticipatory returns on

their investment. Against reinvestment certificates issued by the AFE, the FIEs can make foreign exchange payments from their foreign exchange accounts or purchase foreign exchange with the RMB they have earned to make the payments.

For reinvestment of profits, the following documents need to be examined and verified:

- foreign exchange registration certificate;
- capital verification report by a certified accounting firm;
- annual audit report;
- Board resolution on profit distribution;
- letter of confirmation on reinvestment by the foreign investors;
- tax payment certificate.

For reinvestment with the proceeds from a liquidation, an equity transfer and anticipatory returns on investment, the following criteria should be met. Foreign investors should be able to produce proof that:

- they have legitimately paid up capital in the original FIEs (for this purpose, documents such as the approval granted by the trade and investment authority, contract, articles of association and capital verification report will be examined and verified);
- they have proof that the funds for reinvestment are authentically from the proceeds of liquidation, equity transfer or anticipatory returns on investments and the procedures of such liquidation, equity transfer and anticipatory returns on investment are legal and in conformity with relevant regulations (documents regarding liquidation, equity transfer etc, will be examined and verified);
- the foreign investors making a reinvestment are, at the same time, a shareholder of the reinvested enterprise and have an obligation to make a capital contribution (such documents as the approval granted by competent trade and investment authorities for reinvestment, contract and articles of association will be examined and verified).

Administration over capital increases
With approval by the AFE, the foreign investors of FIEs can increase their capital contributions from their profit, development funds or reserve funds. Such capital increases can be processed with approval documents issued by the AFE.

Capital increase from profit

Examination and verification of the following documents will be required for a capital increase from profit:

- foreign exchange registration certificate;
- capital verification report by a certified accounting firm;
- annual audit report;
- Board resolution on profit distribution;
- letter of confirmation of capital increase by the foreign investors;
- approval documents by the original approving authority;
- tax payment certificate.

Capital increase with development funds and reserve funds

Examination and verification of the following documents will be required for capital increases with development funds and reserve funds:

- foreign exchange registration certificate;
- capital verification report by a certified accounting firm;
- approval documents by the original approving authority;
- Board resolution on capital increase;
- amended contract and articles of association;
- tax payment certificate.

Administration of equity transfers

After a transfer of equity by the foreign investor in an FIE, the proceeds from such a transfer, upon approval by the AFE, can be remitted out of China. The foreign investor can do so either from its foreign exchange account or by purchasing foreign exchange from the designated banks. However, the enterprise needs to submit an application to the AFE with the following documents:

- an application report;
- foreign exchange registration certificate;
- the agreement for equity transfer;
- approval documents regarding the change of equity structure issued by the competent trade and investment authority:
  - business licence after the equity changes, certificate of approval, approved and valid contract and articles of association;
  - the latest capital verification report and audit report (or valid asset valuation report);

- account statements of all the enterprise's foreign exchange accounts;
- tax payment certificate.

Administration of liquidation

When an FIE is legally liquidated, the portion of funds that belongs to foreign investors can be remitted out of China upon approval. The remittance can be made from the foreign exchange account of the FIEs or the foreign investor can purchase foreign exchange from the designated banks for the purpose of remittance. An application will have to be filed with the AFE with the following documents, and remittance can be processed against approval of the AFE:

- an application report;
- foreign exchange registration certificate;
- approval for liquidation and termination by competent trade and investment authority;
- resolution of the liquidation committee;
- capital verification report;
- liquidation report prepared by an accounting firm;
- advice of bank account;
- account statements of the foreign exchange accounts;
- cancellation certificate of Tax Registration.

Administration of the transfer of investment funds by investment holding companies

Investment holding companies need to obtain approvals from the AFE before they can transfer investment funds within the territory of China. To obtain approval, the following documents need to be provided together with an application to the AFE:

- capital verification report by a certified accounting firm;
- approval documents regarding the newly-invested enterprise and the business licence of industry and commerce, approved contract and articles of association;
- resolution regarding the investment project in China by the Board of the investment holding company;
- foreign exchange registration certificate.

China's foreign exchange regime after WTO accession

The impact of the WTO on China's foreign exchange control regime

As a part of China's effort to honour its commitments to the WTO, China's foreign exchange control regime will take an active stance in observing WTO rules. The State Administration of Foreign Exchange will gradually transform its functions in order to create favourable conditions for both foreign investors investing in China and Chinese enterprises doing business with the outside world. On the one hand, China has signed up to Article 8 of the IMF agreement, as a result of which the restrictions on convertibility of current accounts such as trade in goods and services have been removed. The RMB is currently convertible under current account and China's foreign exchange control regime is generally in line with the requirements of the WTO. Therefore, foreign exchange control was not a critical point in the WTO negotiations. In addition, unlike the issues of market access for service trade and tariff reduction, there have been no specific commitments regarding the timing and scope of the opening of foreign exchange control. On the other hand, although there are no requirements regarding the opening of foreign exchange control, the opening of the Chinese market, especially the opening up of the financial and service sectors, will inevitably bring profound influences to bear on China's foreign exchange control regime.

Joining the WTO does not require a country to give up its capital controls to realize full convertibility of its currency under capital account. In fact, many WTO members, developing or developed, are still maintaining control to varying degrees over their capital accounts. China has not made any commitment in relation to convertibility of the RMB under the capital account to the WTO, although the promotion of RMB convertibility under capital account and eventually full convertibility of the RMB are China's ultimate goal. In effect China's accession to the WTO will expedite the process.

In response to WTO accession, China's foreign exchange control authorities have voluntarily made adjustments to the laws and regulations regarding foreign exchange control. Reform efforts are aimed at improving the manner of exchange control by streamlining the examination and approval procedures, putting emphasis on ex-post supervision and inspection while reducing ex-ante administration. Since November 2002, a series of measures has been staged to adapt the control measures to the new situation under the circumstances of the WTO. These measures include:

- simplification of the examination and verification procedures for applications for foreign exchange by family-financed students going abroad to study.

The ceiling placed on the purchase of foreign exchange from the designated banks was raised from the previous US$2,000 to US$20,000. No approval from the AFE is needed for purchase of foreign exchange within the limit.

- implementation of trial reforms on the administration of domestic foreign exchange loans, aimed at reducing the examination and approval procedures. Six cities and provinces were chosen for the trial reform, where the requirements for case-by-case registration by debtors were replaced by requirements for regular registration by the creditors (ie the banks). When enterprises repay domestic foreign exchange loans with their own foreign exchange under a normal repayment schedule, the competent banks designated by the AFE will take the responsibility of reviewing the legitimacy and authenticity of the applications when processing the transactions, after which the banks are required to submit monthly statements to the AFE in their domiciles. The designated banks can independently open or cancel the special accounts of domestic foreign exchange loans.

- reduction of ex-ante examination and verification by giving trial authorization to banks in processing the settlement of foreign exchange capital funds of FIEs. The original responsibility of the AFE to examine and approve the settlements of foreign exchange capital funds under foreign investment projects was delegated to qualified state-designated banks. FIEs can go directly to the designated banks with relevant documents to process the settlements. Ex-ante examination and verification by the AFE is no longer needed. Eleven cities and provinces were chosen to carry out this experiment.

- adjustment of the administrative measures for the purchase of foreign exchange under some items of the capital account, and some restrictions have been lifted or relaxed. The background was that some interim measures were taken during the Asian financial crisis to restrict the purchase of foreign exchange in order to stabilize the foreign exchange market and prevent foreign exchange flight or arbitrage. The macro-economy has now been in healthy operation and the international balance of payment has fared well, all of which have enabled China to readjust those measures. The adjustments included a) the lifting of the restrictions on the purchase of foreign exchange for the repayment of overdue domestic loans, which now allows enterprises to submit exchange purchase application to the AFE for approval by stages and instalments, b) relaxation of the restrictions on the purchase of foreign exchange for advance repayment of domestic foreign exchange loans, the swap of external debts to loans and repayment of external debts and c) relaxation of the restrictions on the purchase of foreign exchange for the purpose of overseas investments.

- relaxation of the criteria for Chinese-funded enterprises to open foreign exchange settlement accounts in order to facilitate their production and business activities. This measure allows all Chinese-funded enterprises that have a) annual foreign exchange earnings equivalent to US$2 million or above, b) annual spending of foreign exchange equivalent to US$200,000 or above, c) trading rights to import and export, d) sound financial performance and e) no past record of violation of foreign exchange control regulations, to open foreign exchange settlement accounts and retain a certain amount of foreign exchange.

- the annulment of the validity period for the use of 'the paper for verification and cancellation of foreign exchange receipts on export'[1] and relaxation of the limit imposed on the numbers of issuance of such paper. This effort was intended to simplify the procedures of verification and cancellation to encourage the expansion of exports. According to this measure, enterprises that have been granted credit awards for outstanding export receipts and those that have fulfilled export receipt quotas are allowed to possess as many such papers as required for their export needs. At the same time, they are also allowed to process verifications and cancellations of their export exchange receipts on a monthly basis, while the AFE exercises memorandum examination on the balances.

New policy measures

In a continued effort to streamline the foreign exchange control system, the State Administration of Foreign Exchange announced a series of new policy measures in 2002. These new measures include the following:

- to continue to promote reform of the administration of foreign exchange accounts to support enterprises in their effort to develop foreign trade, while at the same time strengthening the monitoring of foreign exchange receipts and payments. Chinese-funded enterprises with the trading right of import and export are allowed, upon approval by the AFE to open foreign exchange settlement accounts.[2] Account ceilings will be determined as a proportion of the foreign exchange receipts under the current account of the enterprises and therefore can be adjusted. Experiments on the use of information management systems to monitor the foreign exchange accounts will be expanded in an effort to eventually achieve real-time monitoring of such accounts.

- to further streamline the verification and cancellation procedures for both imports and exports in order to facilitate the business operations of enterprises, while strengthening ex-post supervision. On the basis of last year's effort [which?] to implement various measures such as the introduction of a sub-system monitoring foreign exchange receipts on exports into the electronic law-enforcement system at ports of entry and exit and a memorandum examination system on foreign exchange receipt balances, new measures of verification and cancellation have been introduced which include:
  - relaxation of the time limit imposed on the filing of forward foreign exchange receipts with the AFE, extending the filing period from the previous 90 days to 180 days;
  - further streamlining of verification and cancellation procedures for those enterprises that have good records of verification and cancellation of foreign exchange receipts on export;
  - annulment of procedures for filing the registration of foreign exchange payments for some imports;

---

[1] Editor's note: Export foreign exchange verification and cancellation is an ex-post administrative measure designed to verify the foreign exchange receipts against the reported export value. The paper for verification and cancellation of foreign exchange receipts on export is a certificate produced and issued by the AFE bearing uniform serial numbers with a specified validity period. The paper is used for the following purposes: customs declaration, collecting the forex receipts on export from the designated bank, processing verification and cancellation of the forex receipts with the AFE, and applying to the tax authorities for export tax rebates. This paper is available to those Chinese companies that have import and export qualifications and all FIEs upon completion of certain procedures. – LY

[2] Editor's note: Prior to this, only FIEs and Chinese-funded enterprises that meet certain qualification standards could have such accounts.

- establishment of a memorandum examination mechanism regarding foreign exchange payments for imports;
- implementation of a classified handling approach for overdue verification and cancellation of import payments.

• to promote information management systems on personal purchases of foreign exchange in an effort to provide facilitation for normal use of foreign exchange by individuals and improve the means of supervising personal purchase of foreign exchange. The pilot operations of the information management system on personal purchase of foreign exchange are basically normal and have effectively prevented repeated purchases of foreign exchange by individuals. Such exercises will be adopted on a nationwide basis. The key consideration of such a move is to establish uniform procedures and criteria for market access, allowing qualified state-designated banks to open private foreign exchange banking business in order to provide better financial services to individuals, while at the same time encouraging fair competition among banks.

• to strengthen the exchange control over insurance businesses in an effort to normalize insurance operations involving foreign exchange and fill in the gaps in supervision and administration in the foreign insurance area. To adapt to the needs of rapidly developing insurance businesses after WTO accession, relevant regulations governing the exchange control of insurance businesses will be announced and implemented in the near future. Such regulations will exercise uniform control over foreign exchange transactions by both Chinese and foreign insurance agencies.

• to further promote the reform of the administration of capital fund settlements of FIEs and domestic foreign exchange loans. In this connection, examination and approval procedures will be reduced while emphasis will be placed on indirect administration.

On the basis of previous experiments, uniform implementation plans will be established in order to delegate control responsibilities regarding the examination and verification of capital fund settlements under foreign investment projects, domestic foreign exchange loans and repayment of foreign exchange loans with own foreign exchange to qualified state-designated banks. The AFE will exercise its control and regulation of foreign exchange receipts and payments activities through its supervision over banks' execution of relevant rules and regulations. Effective from 1 July 2002, FIEs can settle their capital accounts directly with the designated banks and foreign investors can complete all procedures at bank counters.

• to reinforce the work on the verification of capital contributions in FIEs in order to fully establish a registration system for the inflow of foreign investments. In compliance with the requirements of the *Notice on Further Strengthening the Work on the Verification of Capital Contributions of Foreign-invested Enterprises and Establishing a Complete Exchange Registration System for Foreign Investment*, certified public accounts are required, before the issuance of capital verification reports, to make validation enquiries to the AFE, which will check authenticity and legitimacy of capital contributions against its examination and verification records and through the import declaration network enquiry system, and at the same time register the actual inflow of foreign capital.

• to liquidate and gradually solve the problems of foreign exchange advances under banks' letters of credit in order to improve the quality of banking assets. The banks are allowed, with the approval of the AFE, to use RMB funds repaid by enterprises or recovered by legal means from enterprises or by realization of enterprise property to purchase foreign exchange to offset foreign exchange advances under letters of credit incurred before the stipulated time line.

Freight Forwarding in China

Liu Baocheng, Professor, University of International Business and Economics

The task of freight forwarding involves a facilitation service for the physical movement of goods. The customer of the freight forwarder is technically called the 'shipper' or 'consignor'. Broadly speaking, the facilitation service for the movement of goods can be broken down into three dimensions: transportation, communication and documentation. The freight forwarder does not have to transport the goods by itself using its own facilities, because this is primarily the function of the carrier that possesses seaborne vessels, railway wagons or airplanes. Frequently the freight forwarder offers short distance transportation, eg from the warehouse to the container yard or from the plant to the loading port with trucks. Briefly, the role of freight forwarding is to bridge the gap between the shipper and the carrier. The freight forwarder can act either as an agent for the shipper or as the receiver of the goods (see Figure 2.4.1).

Under the state economy, professional distribution options were scarce because provinces and organizations were supposed to be self-reliant. Firms had little choice but to rely on state distribution networks, which were organized along rigid, vertical command-control lines. Since China adopted the opening up policy at the end of 1978, transportation has been a burgeoning industry that has attracted the attention of both domestic and foreign freight forwarding firms. The underlying trend of the past 20 years is one of centrifugal force, as trading volume has expanded and infrastructure improved.

The government regiment over the administration of transport industries inclusive of the vehicles, terminals, routes and services, is divided into the different modes of operation. The Ministry of Communications (MOC) is in charge of water and highway transport; the Ministry of Railways (MOR) is in charge of railway transport; and the Civil Aviation Administration of China (CAAC) is in charge of air transport. The freight forwarding industry, particularly those parts related to import and export, is under the supervision of the Ministry of Commerce (MOFCOM).

Traditionally, foreign forwarding services were completely under the monopoly of the China National Foreign Trade Transportation Company (Sinotrans), itself under the administration of MOFCOM's predecessor, MOFTEC, since most of its direct clients are foreign trade corporations under MOFTEC's regime. The shipowner services were vested with China Ocean Shipping Agency (Penevico,

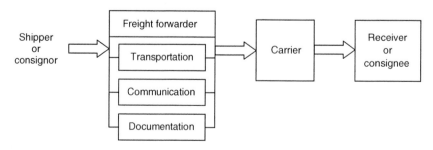

Figure 2.4.1 The position of a freight forwarder

an acronym derived from its former name – People's Navigation Company), with branches across Chinese coastal ports under MOC for the same reason. Since 1984, both Sinotrans and Penevico were given permission to step into each other's business. Soon the freight forwarding market was gradually liberalized for domestic companies. By the end of July 2002, according to the China International Freight Forwarders Association, the number of freight forwarders approved by MOFTEC that were eligible to conduct international business reached 3,216 (including subsidiaries) covering over 30 sectors of the national economy. Among them there is a 70:30 ratio, both in terms of ownership structure and geographic distribution – 70 per cent are state-owned and 30 per cent are joint ventures; 70 per cent are concentrated in the coastal regions and 30 per cent are spread out into the hinterland. At that time, nearly 300,000 people were employed in the freight forwarding industry.

In 1996, the State Council approved the establishment of the Shanghai Shipping Exchange under the auspices of the Ministry of Communications and Shanghai Municipal Government. The Exchange, being the first in China, was created to foster the development of China's shipping market and to help shape Shanghai into an international shipping centre. The Exchange has achieved great success in providing services to the shipping market, including organizing and procuring the filing of freight tariffs, coordinating freight rates, issuing shipping information, conducting research on shipping policies, publishing and issuing the Chinese freight rates index and establishing the Shanghai Shipping Service Centre.

Freight traffic

Transportation correlates with the trade pattern and the level of infrastructure sophistication. For example, the surge of highway transport in the early 1990s was the result of port congestion and the boom in domestic trade. As China's trade volume continues to expand rapidly, the strain on China's transportation infrastructure will become greater. Recognizing this, China's national and regional governments have been investing in improvements to physical infrastructure. In addition, freight forwarding and document processing are crucial elements to addressing this demand.

In the view of experts, in order to capitalize on the potential growth of the cargo market, China must improve its transportation infrastructure, open its

freight forwarding sector, improve service standards and streamline customs procedures.

Freight forwarding, in its professional sense, is still concentrated in the area of foreign trade, where 75 per cent of cargo volume is conducted via seaborne transport. In 2000, the leading ports in China registered an aggregate cargo throughput of 1.7 billion tonnes, an increase of 17.3 per cent year over year. Within the total foreign trade cargo, throughput amounted to 0.57 billion tonnes, up 33.2 per cent over 1999. Within the throughput of the leading ports, export cargo traffic was 46.5 per cent, and import cargo traffic was a little bit higher than export at 53.5 per cent.

Freight forwarding documentation

Documentation is an important part of the freight forwarding service. The most complex occurs with ocean shipping, which involves liner transport and charter transport. Typical documents include the following.

Booking note

This is the document filed by the freight forwarder on behalf of the shipper for reservation of shipping space with the carrier. Before issuing the booking note, the freight forwarder has to examine carefully the shipper's contract and letter of credit stipulations for compliance with the shipping terms therein.

Shipping order

This is the document issued by the carrier or its shipping agent to the shipper, often represented by the freight forwarder, confirming the agreement for the shipping service. Upon the issuance of the shipping order, a transportation contract is established between the carrier and the shipper. The freight forwarder will be able to clear the goods with customs on the strength of the shipping order.

Mate's receipt

After the goods are loaded on a vessel, for example, the chief mate of the carrier will issue the mate's receipt to the shipper represented by the freight forwarder to confirm receipt of the goods on board. The chief mate reserves the right to withhold this document if he finds discrepancies over the quantity and packaging of the goods.

Tally report

A tallyman is a third party notary who can be hired by either the carrier or the freight forwarder to ascertain the quantity of goods actually loaded on board.

Table 2.4.1 Total cargo transport: volumes, turnovers and growth rates of different transport modes (units: million tonnes/billion tonne-km)

Year	Waterways		Highways		Railways		Pipelines		Airways	
	Cargo volume	Turnover	Cargo volume	Turnover	Cargo volume	Turnover	Cargo volume	Turnover	Cargo volume	Turnover
1980	468	507.7	1,422	34.3	1,113	571.7	105	49.1	0.09	0.1
1985	633	772.9	5,381	190.3	1,307	812.6	137	60.3	0.20	0.4
1990	801	1,159.2	7,240	335.8	1,507	1,062.2	158	62.7	0.37	0.8
1995	1,132	1,755.2	9,404	469.5	1,659	1,287.0	153	59.0	1.01	2.2
1996	1,274	1,786.3	9,839	501.1	1,688	1,297.0	160	58.5	1.15	2.5
1997	1,134	1,923.5	9,765	527.2	1,697	1,309.7	160	57.9	1.25	2.9
1998	1,096	1,940.6	9,760	548.3	1,612	1,231.2	174	60.6	1.40	3.3
1999	1,146	2,126.3	9,904	572.4	1,569	1,261.6	202	62.8	2.00	4.2
2000	1,224	2,373.4	10,388	612.9	1,744	1,390.2	187	63.9	1.97	5.0
2000 growth (%)	6.8	11.6	4.9	7.1	11.2	10.2	−7.4	1.8	−1.5	19.0

Source: China Shipping Report 2001

Table 2.4.2 Throughputs and growth rates of the leading Chinese ports from 1990 to 2000

Year	1990	1991	1992	1993	1994	1995	1996	1997	1998	1999	2000
Throughput (million tonnes)	716	778	877	956	1,039	1,116	1,274	1,310	1,124	1,450	1,701
Growth (%)	−3.1	8.7	12.7	9.0	8.7	7.4	14.2	2.8	−14.2	29.0	17.3

Source: China Shipping Report 2001

Bill of lading

The bill of lading is the most important shipping document issued by the carrier. It serves as the official receipt of goods on board, substituting for the mate's receipt. More significantly it is regarded as a document of title to the goods.

Dangerous cargo list

If the goods are classified as dangerous cargoes, a separate dangerous cargo list must be tendered by the freight forwarder to the carrier. Loading and unloading a dangerous cargo have to be placed under strict supervision by the port superintendent to ensure conformity with the Port Dangerous Cargo Regulations.

Inspection certificates

Depending on the special nature of the goods and the sales contract requirements, the freight forwarder will help the shipper to obtain various types of inspection certificates such as quality certificates, sanitary certificates and quarantine certificates.

In addition, the weight list, packing list, General System of Preference (GSP) certificate and origin certificate are among the many further documents required to satisfy different modes of transport, contract stipulations and government regulations.

Large numbers of Chinese companies neither have strategic plans for freight forwarding arrangements nor maintain regular relations with a freight forwarder. Most of the foreign trading companies maintain their own freight forwarding department. To some firms, freight forwarding is a service readily available by phone call, and can be shopped around for in case of need. Some focus on low-cost providers and particularly those who are creative enough to be able to help bypass the bureaucracies of inspection and customs administrations.

The market entry barrier is noticeably low for local firms in the freight forwarding sector, which explains why the average gross profit for handling one container has dropped below US$50 from US$200 previously. Only 70 per cent of the freight forwarders

Table 2.4.3 Engagement with third party freight forwarding

Period of agreement	Percentage (%)	Number of freight forwarders used	Percentage (%)
Nil	35.85	Nil	0.00
Ad hoc	18.87	1	15.09
– 1 year	3.77	2	11.32
– 2 year	18.87	3	18.87
– 3 years	15.09	4	15.09
– 4 years	7.55	4	39.62

Source: China Freight Forwarding Gazette, August 2002

are able to earn a profit. The competitiveness of the freight forwarding business hinges heavily on the scale of operations. Most successful forwarders are those that are able to establish wholly-owned, full-service operations, with their own truck fleet, warehouses, container depot and connections with the various government agencies concerned.

Since transportation, particularly freight forwarding, is considered to be in the service sector, the Chinese government is cautious about opening this market to complete foreign competition. The concern is that many Chinese carriers and forwarders are likely to suffer because they lack the modern equipment and information technology that would allow them to keep up with foreign competitors. With entry into the WTO, China's liberalization process for foreign participation in various modes of transportation, warehousing, packing services and freight forwarding is finalized on a predictable timetable, albeit more slowly than in most other business sectors. In summary, the following specific commitments were made:

- China shall allow private freight forwarding entities to provide services and information for pre-shipment inspection commencing from the day of WTO entry.
- China shall allow foreign firms to enter into joint ventures with Chinese firms in liner shipping and tramp shipping. The equity share of the foreign firm shall not exceed 49 per cent. The chairman of the board and the general manager must be appointed by the Chinese party.

- While China imposes no restriction on the air transport services rendered by foreign firms, foreign firms are not permitted to operate independently in ocean-going freight forwarding, customs clearance or container depots in China unless they enter into joint ventures with a Chinese local counterpart, and the entire equity share of the foreign party shall not exceed 49 per cent.
- For highway transport, China permits majority equity ownership by foreign firms one year after its WTO entry and solely owned foreign entities are to be permitted three years after WTO entry.
- For railway transport, China will permit majority equity ownership by foreign firms three years after its WTO entry and solely owned foreign firms are to be permitted six years after WTO entry.
- For warehousing and other logistic services, China allows 49 per cent of the equity ownership by foreign firms. Majority ownership is permitted one year after WTO entry, and solely owned foreign entities are permitted three years after WTO entry.
- Freight forwarding firms who intend to set up joint ventures in China must show a minimum three-years' experience in this field and their equity share shall not exceed 50 per cent. One year after its WTO entry, China will permit the majority equity share to be held by the foreign party. Four years after its WTO entry, solely owned foreign operation shall be permitted in China.
- The registered capital of a freight forwarding joint venture shall be a minimum of US$1 million. Within four years of China's WTO entry, national treatment shall apply. The term of such a joint venture is limited to 20 years.
- A joint venture freight forwarding firm that has operated in China for over one year is permitted to open subsidiaries. For each subsidiary set up, the registered capital of the firm shall be increased by US$120,000. Two years after China's entry to the WTO, national treatment shall be applied to the registered capital requirement.
- A foreign freight forwarding firm that has entered into a joint venture for over five years in China is permitted to enter into a second joint venture with a Chinese partner. Two years after China's entry into the WTO, this requirement shall be reduced to two years.

Part Three

Legal Aspects of Foreign Company Operations in China

Foreign-Invested Enterprises and Alternative Business Structures

Gary Lock and Brinton M Scott, Herbert Smith, Shanghai

Introduction: Commercial and legal framework

The People's Republic of China (PRC) has undergone major economic reforms since adopting the Open Door Policy in 1978. Since that time, China has encouraged foreign direct investment (FDI) to stimulate the economy, modernize the country, build infrastructure and obtain advanced technology. As a part of this, China has made numerous economic changes, including decentralization of economic control from state management in certain sectors, the creation of special economic zones, and the relaxation of state-controlled production.

Development of the legal system

The Chinese government recognized early that a developed legal system would be necessary to support the planned economic reform. As a result, the National People's Congress (NPC) revived and institutionalized China's legal system in 1982 by radically amending the Constitution and, since then, rapidly developing a body of commercial law, including the 1993 *Company Law*, which unifies scores of regulations dealing with corporate governance.

Many of China's current laws are based on civil law systems, which are derived from general codes rather than judicial precedent as found in common law systems. Nevertheless, the PRC also emulates the concepts and models of other legal systems as well.

World Trade Organization

China acceded into the WTO on 11 December 2001. As a WTO member, China must further revise its legal system to meet the WTO's three main principles of non-discrimination, uniform treatment for all and a transparent legal system. China faces a six-year schedule, beginning in 2002, to formally integrate into the global trading system. As a lead up to its entry into the WTO, China repealed and amended dozens of investment-related laws and regulations. The difficulties facing WTO compliance, however, are compounded where provincial and local interests are involved. Thus, the process of modifying China's commercial legal framework is certain to be lengthy.

Foreign-invested enterprises: Common features

FDI in China most often takes the form of equity joint ventures (EJVs), wholly foreign-owned entities (WFOEs) or, less common than EJVs and WFOEs, cooperative joint ventures (CJVs) – collectively known as foreign-invested enterprises (FIEs). In addition to the more standard-form FIEs, other forms of foreign investment may include representative offices, compensation trade and specific agreements between foreign and domestic companies.

The two primary governmental bodies regulating, permitting and governing FIEs and other foreign business activities are the PRC Ministry of Commerce (MOFCOM)[1] and the State Administration for Industry and Commerce (SAIC) and their local branches, the Commission of Foreign Trade and Economic Cooperation (COFTEC) and Administration of Industry and Commerce (AIC) respectively.

---

[1] Formerly known as the Ministry of Foreign Trade and Economic Cooperation (MOFTEC), MOFCOM replaced MOFTEC in March 2003 by order of the National People's Congress under the Reform of State Council Organs Plan, which merged MOFTEC and the State Economic and Trade Commission (SETC) to form MOFCOM.

While there are differences among FIEs, they also share common characteristics and are often subject to the same or similar PRC legal requirements.

Legislation

FIEs are mainly governed by the following provisions and regulations:

- *PRC Company Law* (effective July 1994);
- *Investment within China by Foreign Investment Enterprises Tentative Provisions* (September 2000);
- *Foreign Investment Industrial Guidance Catalogue* (the Foreign Investment Guidelines, April 2002);
- *Issues Relevant to Strengthening the Administration of the Examination, Approval, Registration, Foreign Exchange Issues and Taxation of Foreign-invested Enterprises Circular* (January 2003);
- *PRC Foreign Trade Law* (revised, July 2004);
- *Administrative Measures on Foreign Investment in the Commercial Sector* (the Commercial Measures, effective June 2004).

Limitations on operations

Under the *Provisions for Guiding the Direction of Foreign Investment*, foreign investment projects are categorized as 'encouraged', 'permitted', 'restricted' or 'prohibited'. The *Foreign Investment Industrial Guidance Catalogue* (the Catalogue), implemented on 1 April 2002, lists specific types of foreign investment projects that fall into the following categories of 'encouraged,' 'restricted' and 'prohibited'. FDI projects not listed in the Catalogue are generally considered 'permitted' and do not require special approval.

Since China gained access to the WTO, the markets of many of its industries must be opened up for foreign investments pursuant to the WTO Agreement. The arrangements for the progressive opening up of the mainland markets are reflected in the Annex of the Catalogue. For example, the foreign equity ratio of mobile voice and data services industry will increase from no more than 35 per cent at present to no more than 49 per cent by 11 December 2004, and can ultimately be wholly foreign-owned by 11 December 2006.

Until recently, FIEs in China were prohibited or restricted from engaging in full-scale trading and distributing activities, but under the terms of its accession to the WTO, China agreed to progressively grant full trading and distribution rights to all types of FIEs, except for those goods subject to state trading or trade prohibitions. A first and significant step in this direction was taken by amending China's *Foreign Trade Law* and by issuing the *Administrative Measures for Foreign Investment in the Commercial Sector*. Under these provisions, since July 2004 trading rights are granted to domestic and foreign enterprises automatically upon completion of a routine filing process, provided that they are duly registered with the relevant AIC. Unlike before, there are no minimum capital requirements to be met. As far as distribution rights are concerned, foreign-invested joint ventures are already entitled to full distribution privileges, provided that they comply with the provisions set out in the Commercial Measures, and WFOEs will follow on 11 December 2004.

Consequently, unlike before, FIEs may now import products for sale purposes in China or provide services in respect of products they do not manufacture.

Capitalization

In the past, the aggregate foreign investment in an EJV or a CJV could not be less than 25 per cent of the registered capital of the EJV or CJV. Although this requirement has now been given up, the aggregate equity interest of a foreign investor in the registered capital of a joint venture must amount to 25 per cent or more in order for the joint venture to enjoy the preferential treatment generally available to FIEs, such as the reduction of import customs duties and taxes or the exemption thereof.

In this context registered capital refers to the total amount of capital contributed by the parties and registered with China authorities, while the total investment amount is the sum of registered capital and the company's potential/actual external borrowings.

Although there is not a nationally stated minimum registered capital requirement apart from those stipulated in the Company Law, FIEs must maintain certain debt to equity ratios based on a minimum level of registered capital (or equity), depending on the total amount of investment (ie debt plus equity) as detailed in Table 3.1.1.

Subject to certain limitations and verification procedures, the parties to an FIE may make their registered capital contributions in cash, tangible or intangible property (eg equipment, technology and intellectual property rights), land and buildings.

Save where special approval is obtained from the relevant examination and approval authority, the foreign party to an FIE is required to commit to making its capital contributions to the FIE within a

Table 3.1.1 Equity to debt ratios

Total investment	Minimum registered capital
below US$3 million	70% of total.
US$3–10 million	50% of total, unless total does not exceed US$4.2 million, then registered capital may not be less than US$2.1 million.
US$10–30 million	40% of total, unless total does not exceed US$12.5 million, then no less than US$5 million.
above US$30 million	33.33% of the total, unless total is less than US$36 million, then not less than US$12 million.

fixed time period from the date of issuance of the business licence of the FIE, depending on the size of its registered capital. Table 3.1.2 summarizes the position.

Approval authority

Approval authority for all FDI in China is ultimately vested in MOFCOM. MOFCOM delegates its approval authority to its local branches (Commissions of Foreign Trade and Economic Cooperation or COFTECs – also known as COFERTs and in some provinces renamed 'commerce bureaux' to be consistent with the new name of the Ministry) according to the amount and nature of the investment. As shown in Table 3.1.3, projects below certain investment amounts may be approved locally, whereas larger projects require central approval.

Local approval authorities, the Department-in-Charge (ie the entity charged with supervising the Chinese party and, ultimately, the FIE) and other relevant departments, such as the Labour Bureau, local planning commission and others, may also play roles in the approval process.

Table 3.1.2 Timing required for capital contributions

Registered capital	Timing
US$500,000 or less	Must be paid in full within 1 year from the date on which the business licence is issued.
US$500,000 to US$1 million	Must be paid in full within 1.5 years from the date on which the business licence is issued.
US$1–$3 million	Must be paid in full within 2 years from the date on which the business licence is issued.
US$3–10 million	Must be paid in full within 3 years from the date on which the business licence is issued.
above US$10 million	To be determined by relevant authorities; usually: Payment in lump-sum: must be paid in full within 6 months from the date on which the business licence is issued; Paid in instalments: first instalment of 15% of the registered capital must be paid within 3 months from the date on which the business licence is issued.

Table 3.1.3 Approval authorities for FDI in China

Investment amount	Approval authority
up to US$100 million	As of 16 July 2004, local branches of the State Development and Reform Commission (SDRC) approve application reports and local branches of MOFCOM approve joint venture contracts and articles of association; excluding 'restricted projects,' where the threshold is US$50 million.
US$100–500 million	SDRC and MOFCOM approval required; for restricted projects the threshold is US$50–100 million.
above US$500 million	SDRC, MOFCOM and the State Council; for restricted projects the threshold is above US$100 million.

Equity joint ventures (EJVs)

An EJV is an independent separate legal person with limited liability. In an EJV, the joint venture parties must subscribe to the registered capital of contributions to the joint venture. The capital contributions may be in cash or in kind; most commonly they consist of land use rights, buildings and/or equipment. Valuation of in-kind contributions to the joint venture is legally required so as to determine the joint venture parties' respective equity contributions. With respect to an in-kind contribution made by the foreign party, it is subject to an asset valuation by the local Commodity Inspection Bureau. State-owned assets are subject to asset valuation by the State Asset Valuation Bureau. Asset valuations are crucial in determining the equity contribution of each joint venture party. In particular, the parties to an EJV share profits and losses of the joint venture in accordance with the ratio of their respective contributions to the registered capital of the joint venture.

During the term of an EJV, which is typically between 15 and 30 years, the parties may not withdraw their contributions to the registered capital or transfer or assign their equity interests without prior governmental approval. Moreover, any transfer of equity interests is subject to the other joint venture party's consent. Equity transfers are also subject to the pre-emptive rights of the other investor(s). Upon termination and liquidation, the assets of an EJV are distributed in accordance with each party's equity stake in the venture.

Legislation

EJVs are primarily governed by the following laws and regulations:

- *PRC Sino-Foreign EJV Law* (2nd Revision, March 2001);
- *Detailed Rules for the Implementation of the Law of PRC on Sino-Foreign EJVs* (3rd Revision, July 2001);
- *Provisional Regulations on the Duration of Sino-Foreign EJVs* (October 1990);
- *Provisional Regulations of SAIC on the Ratio between the Registered Capital and Total Investment of Sino-Foreign EJVs* (March 1987);
- *Certain Regulations on the Subscription of Capital by the Parties to Sino-Foreign EJVs* (January 1988);
- *Supplementary Regulations on the Certain Regulations on the Subscription of Capital by the Parties to Sino-Foreign EJVs* (September 1997);
- *Contract Management Regulations for Sino-Foreign EJVs* (October 1990).

Establishing an EJV

The procedure of setting up an EJV often commences with the parties signing a letter of intent covering issues related to the project. Letters of intent should be sufficiently broad to allow a party to alter its position if necessary.

The next step is to prepare a joint feasibility study. The feasibility study is an important document, as it forms the basis for formal project approval by the relevant approval authorities. Therefore, care should be taken with regard to its contents. Feasibility studies generally include the business terms to be set forth in the joint venture contract, financial projections for the first five to ten years and a description of the planned business and operations.

Once completed, the parties must submit the feasibility study report, joint venture contract and articles of association, all of which must be in Chinese, to the relevant examination and approval authority. The approval authority must approve or reject the application within three months of its receipt. The approval authority may also request amendments to the documents if any terms therein are found to contravene Chinese law or policy. With the approval being granted, the EJV contract becomes effective.

Thereafter, the parties have 30 days to file the approval and other documentation with the SAIC or its local branch in order to obtain the EJV's business licence, which is usually issued within 30 days. Upon the issuance of the business licence the EJV is formally established as a legal person.

Within 30 days after the licence has been issued, the EJV must register with the relevant authorities in charge of foreign exchange, taxation administration, finance and customs.

Authorities of an EJV

The EJV's board of directors is its supreme authority, with the Chairman of the Board being the company's legal representative. The board of directors appoint the General Manager, who manages the company's day-to-day operations. The appointment of members of the Board is generally determined in proportion to each party's contribution to the joint venture, and decisions are usually rendered on a simple majority basis, except for the following decisions, for which

PRC law requires unanimous consent of all directors attending a meeting:

- any amendment to the articles of association;
- any increase or any transfer of registered capital and adjustment of each Party's capital contribution ratio;
- any merger or consolidation (by acquisition or otherwise) of the JV company with any other economic organization or any separation of significant assets (by way of transfer, assignment, sale, lease or other means of disposition) of the JV company; or
- the termination, dissolution or liquidation of the JV company.

Cooperative Joint Ventures (CJVs)

A Chinese–foreign CJV is a business organization formed by at least one Chinese cooperator and one foreign cooperator, such as a corporation, partnership or other organization, for the purpose of generating profit. A CJV can be an independent separate legal person with limited liability or an unincorporated joint venture.

The essential characteristic of a CJV is its flexibility, since the parties thereto may structure the organization in whatever way they think proper. The joint venture parties are free to fix between themselves their contributions to the joint venture.

The joint venture parties may provide cooperation conditions (eg provision of some forms of assistance or service to the joint venture) instead of injecting capital contributions into the joint venture. In a CJV, the parties may share the profits and losses of the joint venture according to a contractual formula that may or may not reflect their respective contributions to the registered capital of the joint venture. Moreover, the foreign party may recover its investment before the expiration of the term of the joint venture, provided that the joint venture contract contains a term that ownership of all fixed assets of the joint venture reverts to the Chinese party upon expiration of the joint venture term without compensation. Because of the flexibility of the CJV structure, CJVs are generally preferred for specific or fixed-life ventures, such as land developments or infrastructure projects.

As in the case of EJVs, any transfer of equity interests will require the consent of the relevant governmental body as well as of the other party. However, unlike an EJV, in a CJV pre-emptive rights are subject to contractual agreement between the parties.

Legislation

The following laws and regulations govern CJVs:

- *PRC Sino-Foreign CJV Law* (revised October 2000);
- *Detailed Implementing Regulations of China Law on Sino-Foreign CJVs* (September 1995);
- *Interpretation of the Implementation of Certain Articles of the Detailed Implementing Regulations of China Law on Sino-Foreign CJVs* (October 1996);
- *Certain Regulations on the Subscription of Capital by the Parties to Sino-Foreign EJVs* (January 1988);
- *Establishment of Sino-Foreign Foreign Trading Joint Ventures Tentative Procedures* (January 2002);
- *Foreign Investment Industries Guidance Catalogue* (April 2002).

Establishment and authorities of a CJV

The process of establishing a CJV follows nearly the same rules applying to EJVs. The managerial structure and its functions are also very similar to those of an EJV. The parties to a CJV, however, can decide to establish a management committee with a director and a deputy director, instead of establishing a board of directors with a chairman and a deputy chairman.

Wholly foreign-owned entities (WFOEs)

A WFOE is an independent legal person or company with limited liability. The equity interest in a WFOE is entirely owned by its foreign investor or investors. Initially, a WFOE could only be used as an investment vehicle if it either utilized advanced technology or exported a minimum of 50 per cent of its products. This requirement has now been relaxed to allow a foreign investor to establish a WFOE if it 'benefits the development of the Chinese national economy'.

The advantage of WFOEs over joint ventures lies in avoiding conflicting partner interests, corporate cultural differences and other control problems.

Currently WFOEs are still banned in certain business areas such as advertising, telecommunications and road and rail freight transportation. However, they will be largely permitted starting from December 2004 onwards, as set out in the *Annex to the Foreign Investment Guidelines*.

The establishment of commercial WFOEs engaging in retailing are currently subject to geographic restrictions, whereas those enterprises engaging in wholesaling are permitted in the whole of China. However, the geographic restrictions on retailing commercial WFOEs will likewise be lifted on 11 December 2004. Advertising WFOEs will be permitted as of December 2005.

Legislation

The following laws and regulations govern WFOEs:

- *PRC Law on Wholly Foreign-owned Enterprises* (revised October 2000);
- *Detailed Implementing Rules for China Law on Wholly Foreign-owned Enterprises* (December 1990);
- *Interpretation of Several Provisions of the Detailed Implementing Rules for China Law on Wholly Foreign-owned Enterprises* (December 1991).

The Establishment of a WFOE

The procedures for establishing wholly foreign-owned enterprises are similar to those for EJVs. However, before filing an application for the investment, the investor may be required to submit a project proposal to the local People's Government at or above the county level in the proposed place of establishment.

Representative offices

Representative offices are a popular, low cost, alternative to FIEs. Representative offices allow foreign entities to explore the PRC market, search for investment opportunities and introduce their products and services to China. Representative offices also offer certain advantages over FIEs. First, approvals are generally easier to obtain. Second, capital outlays are generally low. Finally, multiple offices may be established throughout China.

Legislation

The laws governing representative offices include:

- *PRC Interim Regulations Concerning the Control of Resident Representative Offices of Foreign Enterprises* (October 1980);
- *Circular Concerning the Registration of Resident Representative Offices of Foreign Enterprises* (May 1981);
- *Procedures of China State Administration for Industry and Commerce (SAIC) for the Registration and Administration of Resident Representative Offices of Foreign Enterprises* (March 1983);
- *Detailed Rules of the Ministry of Foreign Trade and Economic Cooperation (MOFTEC) for the Implementation of the Provisional Regulations Governing*

the Examination, Approval and Administration of Resident Representative Offices of Foreign Enterprises (February 1995);
- *Third Batch of Items in Respect of which Administrative Examination and Approval Requirements are Abolished Decision* (May 2004).

The application process

The establishment procedures for representative offices have recently been simplified for foreign companies in most industries. Previously a two-step application procedure was required. Now however, all that is necessary is a registration with the local Administration of Industry and Commerce (AIC). In addition, some cities no longer require that the applicant use an official sponsoring agency (as was the requirement in the past). To be sure, applicants will need to confirm on a case-by-case basis.

Scope of permitted activities

Although not allowed to engage in direct business operations, representative offices may:

- execute office and residential leases;
- obtain residence permits and multiple-entry visas for foreign staff;
- open foreign and local currency bank accounts in the company's name;
- display office signs and distribute business materials;
- employ local staff via government sanctioned employment agencies;
- liaise with contacts in China on the parent company's behalf;
- coordinate the parent company's PRC business activities; and
- conduct market surveys and research.

Although there is no clear guidance on what constitutes 'direct business activities', the following activities are generally considered outside the scope of a representative office's lawful operations:

- directly engaging in revenue generating activity;
- entering into commercial contracts in the parent company's name;
- buying property or importing production equipment;
- collecting or making payment in connection with sales and purchases; and
- providing services to entities other than the parent company.

Compensation trade

Compensation trade is a barter transaction whereby a Chinese party obtains foreign machinery, equipment or technology from a foreign party who receives the product the Chinese party produces with the imported machinery, equipment or technology as its compensation.

Legislation

No single comprehensive law governs this form of trade, although it is actively encouraged. Rather, the applicable laws are found in the unified *Contract Law of China* (the Contract Law), licensing regulations, including *China Measures for the Administration of Registration of Technology Import and Export Contracts* and *China Administration of Technology Import and Export Regulations*, and various tax and customs laws.

Other considerations

Compensation trade, popular between Hong Kong companies and Chinese enterprises in Guangdong and Fujian provinces, has rapidly developed in China in recent years. These arrangements usually involve fishery, agriculture, animal husbandry, natural resources, chemicals, light textiles and electronics.

Although product quality disputes are common, this form of trade is still frequently used. Incentives for using compensation trade include tax advantages, flexibility in structuring the agreement, and no involvement for the foreign party in labour issues.

Where possible, exporters will often obtain performance guarantees whereby a reliable financial institution will pay the purchase price if the importer fails to fulfil its obligations to deliver the products under the sales agreement. The Chinese party must be an enterprise or other economic organization with foreign trade authority (discussed in detail under Agency Relationships below) and cannot be an individual. This type of transaction does not produce a new or merged Chinese-foreign legal entity.

Processing and assembly agreements

Processing and assembly agreements exist where a Chinese party processes materials or assembles parts supplied by a foreign party. Usually, the foreign party also provides the manufacturing equipment. The Chinese party either earns a fee for services or retains a portion of the finished goods for on-sale as its compensation.

Whether the Chinese party retains the equipment at the end of the term is negotiable.

Legislation

There are regulations governing processing and assembly at national and local levels. The early regulations governed the activities of domestic and foreign entities separately. This approach has been gradually abandoned and most laws now apply uniformly to domestic and foreign entities. Some of the major laws in this area include the:

- *Regulations of the General Administration of PRC Customs on Administration of Importation of Materials and Parts for Fulfilling Product Export Contracts by FIEs* (issued 24 November 1986);
- *Administrative Measures of China Customs Governing Import and Export Commodities Involved in Import Processing* (issued 6 May 1999);
- *PRC Foreign Trade Law*, (revised, effective July 2004); and
- *Provisional Measures on Administration of Examination and Approval of Processing Trade* (June 1999).

Processing and assembly trade products are classified as prohibited (eg poisonous industrial garbage, seeds, used clothes), restricted (eg cotton, steel, sugar), or permitted. The *PRC Foreign Trade Law* details which products fall into which categories, including those that are prohibited.

Restrictions

The relevant department in charge of foreign economics and trade at the local level (COFTEC) has the right to approve all processing and assembly trade contracts. MOFCOM is responsible for nation-wide examination and approval.

After completing processing or assembly, the end products must be exported within a specified time limit. This is specified in the *Approval Certificate for Processing Trade Business* and is, in principle, the same term as the export contract, which is generally not more than one year. Further permission must be obtained to make domestic sales of imported parts and materials and the completed end products.

Management contracts

Foreign investors may cooperate with PRC enterprises through management contracts in certain locations and industries. Under such agreements, the foreign party generally provides day-to-day management and training for a PRC enterprise in return for a share of revenues. As Chinese enterprise is generally responsible for providing the business facilities, equipment and staff, this type of business arrangement allows the foreign party to invest in the PRC without making a substantial capital contribution.

Legislation

MOFTEC issued the *Contract Management Regulations for Sino-foreign Joint Equity Enterprises* on 15 October 1990, to govern foreign management contracts.

Joint ventures (JVs)

JVs may be contractually managed under certain conditions, such as when a JV is in financial trouble. The management contractor assumes all or part of the JV's operational and administrative rights and shares responsibility for the JV's risks and liabilities. The board of directors must unanimously consent to be administered and the JV must submit proof of this to its original approval authorities, together with other documentation such as the management contractor's legal and financial status. The term may not exceed five years. In order to provide management under such an agreement, the contractor must demonstrate that it conducts business in the same industry as the JV and has at least three years' of relevant management experience.

Agency relationships

A major cause of discontent for foreign entities seeking to sell to PRC consumers has been legal barriers, which have generally restricted or prohibited the importation and distribution of foreign manufactured goods. As a result, foreign entities unwilling to establish FIEs have been forced to enter China's market via other avenues, the most common of which are agency and distribution agreements.

Foreign entities often appoint Chinese enterprises as agents or distributors. The local enterprises handle issues related to domestic sales on the foreign principal's behalf and assist with procuring export goods or materials. One positive aspect of the principal–agent relationship is that, by using an agent's knowledge of PRC markets, business contacts and distribution channels, foreign enterprises may achieve a certain degree of market penetration.

Franchising

A number of foreign entities have considered franchising as alternative way to access China's market. However, the lack of a comprehensive and developed regulatory framework has limited the number of international franchise arrangements.

Legislation

China's laws governing franchising generally include:

- *The Rules for the Administration of Commercial Franchise Operations* (the Franchise Rules), issued on 17 November 1997 by the Ministry of Internal Trade;
- *The Circular Regarding the Response by the State Council to Questions Related to Foreign Investment in Domestic Trade,* issued by the State Council in 1992;
- *Foreign Investment Industries Guidance Catalogue* (the Foreign Investment Guidelines, April 2002);
- *The Measures for Pilot Projects for Commercial Enterprises with Foreign Investment,* issued by the SETC and MOFTEC in June 1999;
- *Administrative Measures on Foreign Investment in the Commercial Sector* (the Commercial Measures, effective June 2004).

Practical considerations

Under the terms of the Protocol that governed China's entry into the WTO, China agreed to open franchising to foreign investment by 1 January 2005. As of June 2004, foreign investment in franchising is supposed to be allowed under the Commercial Measures. However, in practice franchising is still restricted for foreign investors (except for qualified Hong Kong or Macao investors).

China has yet to publish a definitive set of franchising regulations, although the new regulations that are to replace the 1997 Franchise Rules are expected to be issued by MOFCOM at the end of 2004. In their draft form, the new regulations deal with administrative requirements, establish an approval authority, and cover legal liability, advertising requirements, publicity guidelines, disclosure of information and other issues. The new regulations also cover foreign companies and FIEs engaging in franchise activities.

Notwithstanding the lack of regulations addressing cross-border franchising, there already exist a number of multi-national franchisers operating in China today. These foreign franchisers generally rely on commercial legislation to engage in franchise-like transactions. For example, foreign investors sometimes break down their arrangements into a series of contracts that are more familiar within the PRC legal context (eg instead of a single franchise agreement, parties may conclude a trademark or know-how licence and agreements for management consulting services). This increases transaction costs, but phrases the transaction terms in concepts more familiar to MOFCOM and other approval authorities. It also avoids some of the pitfalls associated with painting the arrangement as something entirely new.

More recent information – B Scott

Since this chapter was first written, several new laws impacting foreign investment in China have been published. These laws include publication of the new Franchise Law and a new Foreign Investment Industrial Guidance Catalogue. Short summaries of each are provided below.

New Franchise Law

MOFCOM issued the new 'Administrative Measures on Commercial Franchise Operations' on 31 December 2004. Effective from 1 February 2005, the new measures provide specific guidelines for the establishment of a franchise operation in China and include a section on foreign-invested franchise operations. Under the new law, a franchiser may authorize a franchisee to use its trade-marks, tradename and business operation model, and charge a franchise royalty as a joining fee, a utilization fee or as other contracted expenses. The franchiser may grant a franchise directly to a franchisee, which will establish its own business, or the franchiser may grant an exclusive franchise right for a designated region. The new measures do not impose any minimal capital, asset or financial requirements. They do, however, provide that potential franchisers and franchisees must meet certain minimal qualification criteria. The minimum term of a franchise must be three years.

New Foreign Investment Industrial Guidance Catalogue

The National Development and Reform Commission and MOFCOM jointly enacted a new 'Foreign Investment Industrial Guidance Catalogue' in late November 2004. The new Catalogue makes a number of changes to the 2002 Catalogue. For example, some activities (eg movie production) that were prohibited under the 2002 Catalogue are now permitted. Also, some activities that were permitted under the 2002 Catalogue are now classified as restricted (eg in the category 'real estate industry', the development of large tracts of land is now restricted). In addition, the new Catalogue further implements and solidifies a number of China's WTO commitments. Investors will need to check the new Catalogue in detail before making any new investment plans.

4 March 2005

Employment Law for Chinese and Foreign Nationals

Gary Lock and Brinton M Scott, Herbert Smith, Shanghai

The Ministry of Labour and Social Security (the Ministry) formed in 1998 when China's Labour and Social Securities Ministries were merged. The Ministry is responsible for formulating national labour and social security policies. The labour and social security bureaux, which sit beneath the Ministry, are responsible for administering the national and local regulations.

Legislation

The PRC Labour Law (the Labour Law – effective from 1 January 1995) and the *PRC Trade Union Law* (issued on 28 June 1950 and revised on 3 April 1992 and 17 October 2001) are China's principal labour laws. The laws, which apply to all enterprises and economic organizations, address most employment issues, including recruitment, contracts, wages, work conditions, occupational health and safety, women in the workforce and dispute resolution.

The Labour Law requires all employers and employees to execute labour contracts that define the parties' rights and obligations and include the term and nature of the job, safety and working conditions, remuneration, discipline, and conditions for termination and breach of contract. Supplementary laws have also been issued for particular aspects of employment, including:

- *The Regulations on Labour Management in Foreign Investment Enterprises* (the Labour Management Regulations), adopted in 1994;
- *The Regulations of the State Council Governing Working Hours for Workers*, adopted in 1995;
- *The Provisional Administrative Measures on Wage Incomes of FIEs*, adopted in 1997;

- *Enterprise Pension Tentative Procedures* (May 2004);
- *Minimum Wages Provisions* (2004).

Labour practices also vary between regions as provincial and local labour departments have fairly wide discretion in handling local labour matters.

Recruitment

FIEs may recruit Chinese employees directly or through local employment service centres. Foreign nationals, however, require approval from the local labour bureau.

Wages

The Labour Law provides a minimum wage requirement, which is determined at a provincial level. The 2004 *Minimum Wages Provisions*, which supersede the 1993 *Regulations on Minimum Wages in Enterprises* (amended in October 1994), require all provinces, autonomous regions and directly administered municipalities to set minimum wage standards and report them to the Ministry. Employers that fail to meet these standards may be ordered to compensate employees for the difference, pay other compensation, or both. Employers must also deduct and withhold employee individual income tax, social security and related payments.

Subsidies

Employers must pay living subsidies and provide medical treatment allowances for all PRC employees. Employers and employees must also participate in the PRC social insurance system for unemployment, old age pension, medical treatment, work-related injuries and maternity care. In addition to the aforementioned mandatory subsidies, employers may also introduce incentive schemes such as bonuses or allowances. These schemes must be paid out of an employee bonus and welfare fund, which is created from the employer's after-tax profits.

Employment terms

The standard working week in China is five eight-hour days. Enterprises requiring different standards may, with approval from the local labour administration, adopt flexible work systems.

Overtime

Overtime may not exceed one hour a day and 36 hours a month, although under special circumstances and subject to agreement with trade unions and employees, this may be longer. Standard overtime wages are:

- 150 per cent of regular wage for overtime;
- 200 per cent of regular wage for work on rest days, where alternative rest days cannot be found; and
- 300 per cent of regular wage for work on statutory holidays.

Annual leave

Employees are only entitled to annual leave after one year's service with the same employer. The amount of annual leave varies according to work obligations, qualifications and other factors, but normally does not exceed two weeks a year. Employees are also entitled to home leave where they are required to live away from their spouse or parents. Employees visiting their spouse are entitled to 30 days home leave per year. Home leave to visit parents will be either 20 days per year or 20 days per four years, depending on whether or not the employee is married.

Other restrictions

Special laws protect various aspects of female employees, such as maternity benefits. 'Minor' employees between the ages of 16 and 18 years are also protected under special occupational health and safety measures, including special procedures for hiring minors. Hiring children less than 16 years old is strictly prohibited. Employers must also implement occupational health and safety programmes in the workplace, and conduct regular physical examinations for employees in hazardous occupations.

Termination

Employment law is complicated in China and employers should be especially wary when terminating employment relationships with employees.

Termination by the employer

Employers may dismiss employees without notice only when the employee:

- is dismissed during the statutory probation period;
- has seriously violated workplace rules;
- causes great losses to the employer due to serious dereliction of duty or embezzlement or another criminal offence; or
- is being investigated for a criminal offence.

Employers may otherwise dismiss employees, by first giving 30 day's notice only when the employee:

- is unable to take up his original or any new work upon returning from non-work-related medical treatment for illness or injury;
- is unqualified for his job and remains unqualified even after receiving training or an adjustment to another work post; and
- is unable to agree with the employer, after mutual consultation, to modify his labour contract when the purpose for which he was originally hired has significantly changed or no longer exists.

Employers may not dismiss employees when they:

- suffer from a work-related sickness or injury that has been medically confirmed as having completely or partially caused the employee to lose the ability to work;
- suffer from an illness or injury for which medical treatment within a specified period is allowed; or
- are pregnant, on maternity leave or within the specified period for nursing.

The Provisions Concerning Economic Redundancy in Enterprises (effective on 1 January 1995) allow employees to be laid-off or dismissed for economic reasons, such as when the employer:

- faces bankruptcy;
- undergoes statutory reorganization by Court order;
- undergoes a split or merger due to a group restructuring; or

- falls into 'serious operational difficulty' as defined by the local government.

However, employers must give priority to laid-off employees if they recruit again within six months after a layoff.

Termination by the employee

Employees may generally resign at will, but must normally give at least 30 days' notice. No notice is required if an employee resigns where:

- the employer has 'coerced' workers with violence, threats or illegal restrictions on personal freedom;
- where the employer fails to pay wages or provide working conditions as agreed to in the labour contract; or
- any time during his/her probation period.

Labour disputes

The PRC Regulations Concerning the Handling of Labour Disputes in Enterprises and the *Provisional Regulations on Handling of Personnel Disputes* establish the procedures for handling labour disputes. Under the dispute regulations, parties are encouraged to settle labour disputes by negotiation or mediation. If neither of these works, the parties must resort to compulsory arbitration before they may initiate legal proceedings.

Foreign employees

Foreign nationals may work in China only after obtaining Employment Permits and Residence Certificates, except where they:

- are a professional technician or management personnel employed directly by the Chinese government;

- hold a Foreign Expert Certificate issued by the Foreign Expert Bureau and are employed by state authorities or public institutions;
- have specialized skills working in offshore petroleum operations without the need to go ashore and hold a Work Permit for Foreign Personnel Engaged in Offshore Petroleum Operations in China; or
- engage in commercial activities with the approval of the Ministry of Culture and hold a permit to conduct temporary commercial activities.

Legislation

The Administrative Regulations on the Employment of Foreign Nationals in China (the Provisions), issued on 22 January 1996, govern the employment of foreign nationals in China (holders of Hong Kong, Taiwan and Macao travel documents are governed by separate regulations). The Provisions provide that an employer must prove that a 'special need' (defined as where there are requirements for a position for which there is a temporary shortage of suitable local candidates) exists before employing a foreign national.

Foreign nationals without residency rights seeking employment in China must:

- be at least 18 years of age and in good health;
- have no criminal record;
- have a confirmed prospective employer;
- hold a valid passport or other international travel document; and
- be qualified for the position for which a 'special need' exists.

Representative offices

Registered representative offices are subject to different regulations. All Chinese staff hired by representative offices must be employed from Chinese organizations authorized by the state to provide services to foreign enterprises. Direct private hiring is prohibited.

Intellectual Property Rights in China

Franck Desevedavy, Adamas, China

Introduction

In 1979, when the first law was enacted in China in order to accord protection to intellectual property (IP) rights, a trademark counterfeiter only faced a fine and a maximum of three years of imprisonment under the Criminal Code. Such a provision was the initial result of the 1979 Sino–US Trade Agreement that obligated China and the US to provide IP protection, and was the first sign of IP legislation development in China. Legislation was, in fact, initiated when China acceded to the Convention for the Establishment of World Intellectual Property Organizations (WIPOs) on 4 June 1980. Unlike other countries, where domestic legal frameworks are set up prior to acceding to international obligations, China has built a new set of laws and regulations relating to IP rights after, or while, entering into international treaties and conventions and, generally speaking, gradually opening up its market to foreign investors.

From 1992 to 2002, when China acceded to the WTO, a series of IP laws and regulations were published, including:

- *The Trade Mark Law* (adopted in 1982 and later amended in 2001);
- *The Patent Law* (adopted in 1982 and later amended in 2000);
- *The Copyright Law* (adopted in 1990 and later amended in 2001);
- *The Computer Software Protection Regulations* (adopted in 1991 and amended in 1992);
- *The Anti-Unfair Competition Law* (adopted in 1993);
- *The Criminal Code* (adopted in 1979 and amended in 1997).

In the meantime, China has adhered to all important treaties and conventions pertaining to IP, in addition to the Convention establishing the WIPO, including the following:

- 1985: *Paris Convention for the Protection of Industrial Property*;
- 1989: *Madrid Agreement Concerning the International Registration of Marks*;
- 1992: *Berne Convention for the Protection of Literary and Artistic Works*;
- 1994: *Patent Cooperation Agreement*;
- 1994: *Nice Agreement Concerning the International Classification of Goods and Services for the Purposes of the Registration of Marks*;
- 1995: *Budapest Treaty on the International Recognition of the Deposit of Micro-organisms for the Purposes of Patent Procedure*;
- 1996: *Locarno Agreement establishing an International Classification for Industrial Design*;
- 1997: *Strasbourg Agreement for the International Patent Classification*;
- 2001: *Agreement on Trade Related Aspects of Intellectual Property Rights (TRIPs)*.

China's accession to the WTO and to the TRIPs Agreement is almost the final step in the construction of a complete and modern legal framework relating to IP rights protection. China is now working on better implementation of these laws and regulations through its administrative and judicial bodies.

Enterprise names

Foreign investors in China first need to focus on the protection of the name of the new enterprise based in

China. They may try to expand a name that already exists abroad. Foreign companies (based abroad) are not permitted to register their names in China.

Representative office

Should a representative office be set up, the name used by such an office should be closely identified with that of the mother company based abroad. Therefore, the name that would be registered before the Ministry of Commerce (MOFCOM) will follow the following form: home jurisdiction + name of the parent company + location in China + 'Representative Office'.

The name of the representative office must be rendered in Chinese characters; however, if the name of a foreign company contains only letters from a foreign alphabet that are not easily translated, the letters can be included in the Chinese name provided that special permission is granted.

However, the protection gained from the Chinese registration procedure is vague due to the fact that such protection benefits only the Chinese translation of the foreign enterprise name. In order to avoid conflicts between similar registered names in Chinese, foreign investors should pay attention to the translation of the parent company's name or rely on the anti-unfair competition provisions of Chinese law.

Foreign invested enterprises

With regard to the naming of a Foreign Invested Enterprise (FIE), several regulations apply, such as the *Administrative Regulations Governing the Registration of Enterprise Names* (1991) and the *Implementing Measures on Enterprise Name Registration and Administration* (2000). The State Administration for Industry and Commerce (SAIC) and its local branches (AICs) are the authorities in charge of name approval and registration, respectively for names that start with, say, 'China', 'Chinese', 'National' or 'International', and for names that contain the name of an administrative region.

A procedure of pre-approval of the name is compulsory for any company to be set up in China (except for state-owned and collectively-owned enterprises). Application for the pre-approval of an intended FIE name should be made to the relevant administration before the approval of the joint venture contract (if any) and articles of association. Applicants are required to propose alternative names on the application form if the 'first choice' is barred because of an anteriority or similarity with an existing registered name.

The approved name is reserved for a period of six months and the investors should proceed with the full registration of the company before expiration of this period of time, since the current law does not provide for any renewal or extension.

The name should be created as follows: administrative region + trade name + line of business + legal form. Only the Chinese version of an enterprise name is registered, and only this name will appear on the business licence when delivered. Therefore, the protection afforded by such a registration is limited to the name in Chinese (a foreign name can be protected by the Trademark Law).

In case of disputes arising over enterprises names, the rule is that the first registered enterprise takes priority over the name. Any conflict can be referred to the SAIC (and its local offices) or a suit can be lodged before the People's Court. The registration of a new trademark shall not infringe upon prior rights of others, registered enterprise names included.

Industrial property rights: trademark, patent, utility model, design

Trademark, patent, utility model and design are protected by Chinese laws and regulations when in compliance with governing regimes and if duly registered before the relevant administration. Regulatory regimes for the above-mentioned IP rights are mostly similar to those existing in many countries, especially jurisdictions from continental Europe. However, some distinctive or important features deserve to be highlighted.

The responsible authorities are respectively: China Trade Mark Office (CTO) for trademark registration and the Patent Office of the State Intellectual Property Office (SIPO) for patent, utility model and design registration. Only registered rights are protected by the Trademark Law and/or the Patent Law, and China applies the 'first in takes priority' rule. Because China is party to most international treaties and conventions relating to IP rights, holders of rights from a jurisdiction that is also party to such conventions or treaties may apply for the benefit of a priority right (six-month period for a trademark, one-year period for a patent) in order to register their rights in China following a prior registration in their own jurisdiction.

Online searching for a trademark is not available in China and it is recommended that such a search be conducted at the CTO either directly or through a registered trademark agent. Any visible sign or combination of signs capable of distinguishing goods or services can be used as trademarks, including words, letters, graphics, numerals, three-dimensional symbols and combinations of colours, provided that the intended trademarks do not prejudice any prior rights.

Several signs cannot be used or registered as a trademark, such as:

- the name of a country;
- a national flag or emblem;
- identical signs to those of the Red Cross or the Red Crescent;
- any sign that is racially discriminatory, makes fraudulently exaggerated claims or claims harmful to socialist moral behaviour.

China brought collective and certification marks within the Trademark Law in 2001.

Once an application is accepted, the CTO conducts a preliminary examination of the application and decides whether to issue a first approval. If such an approval is granted, the intended trademark is published in the *Trademark Gazette* for a period of three months, after which, if no objection is lodged, the registration of the trademark, for a period of 10 years, is finally accepted. It takes about 18 or 20 months from the date an application is filed to the date of issue of a registration certificate, which is the time when the term of the registered trademark begins.

The 2001 amendment of the Trademark Law has demonstrated China's commitment to bringing its law in line with international practice, especially in granting protection to well-known trademarks, which can be recognized as such either by the administration or by the Courts.

Three categories of patents can be registered before the SIPO:

- an invention (a new technical solution relating to a product, a process or an improvement for the product or the process);
- a utility model (a new technical solution relating to the shape, structure, or their combination, or a product fit for practical use);
- a design (shape, pattern or their combination and the combination of colour and shape or design of a product, which creates an aesthetic effect and is fit for industrial application).

The condition of novelty is not limited to the territory of the PRC.

Foreign priority claims are admissible if the country in which the first application is submitted is a member of the Paris Convention (or has a special bilateral agreement with China); the period of time during which an application for priority can be lodged is 12 months for an invention, patent or a utility model and six months for a design.

The term for an invention patent is 20 years and the term of a utility model or design patent is 10 years, and the patent right for a utility model or a design can be extended by paying an annual fee, the whole law being in line with the TRIPs Agreement. Chinese law was amended in 2000 in order to eliminate the revocation procedure and to provide that the invalidation procedure is the only way to challenge the granting of a patent right.

Copyright

Surprisingly, a formal legal protection of copyright was non-existent until 1987, when among the 'General Principles of the Civil Law of the People's Republic of China' a right of authorship was enacted. From 1991 to the end of 2001, a copyright law was enacted and amended, subsequent regulations were promulgated and China became a member of the Berne Convention, in addition to its membership of the WTO.

The subject matter protected under the copyright law is similar to that usually encompassed: works of literature, art, natural sciences, social sciences, engineering and technology.

The condition required to be qualified for protection is that the work shall be original (ie created by the author), and two categories of rights are granted: moral rights, which are not alienable, and economic rights that enable the copyright owner to gain monetary reward through the exploitation of the work. Economic rights and some moral rights of disclosure enjoy a protection of 50 years following the creation of the work; some moral rights of disclosure have a term of 50 years following the death of the author; most moral rights (attribution, revision and integrity) have a perpetual term. The protection of software in China is secured by the copyright law and other regulations specially aimed at software protection.

Increasing the value of IP rights

All IP rights (economic rights only for copyright) in China can be licensed or assigned. Laws and regulations are very detailed on the definition of rights being licensed or assigned, on whether the licence is exclusive or non-exclusive, on the scope and duration of the licence, and on the payment terms and methods. Most of these agreements should be registered before the relevant administration, either because it is a compulsory obligation enacted by the law or because it is necessary to allow payment of a fixed price or royalty.

The owner of a technology, either patented or not patentable, may enter into a Technology Transfer Agreement with a Chinese counterpart governed by the Chinese Technology Transfer Law when the technologies have been or are in the process of being patented, or when the subject matter is considered as a technological secret. A transfer of technology will take the form of a Licence Agreement or an assignment of rights. Most of the difficulties arising from technology transfers relate to the valuation of the technology by the parties, by the Chinese administration and by the auditors, if any.

Trademarks and enterprise names can be registered as a domain name and enjoy the protection of Chinese laws and administrations when registered in China.

To increase the protection of IP rights, other laws and regulations include: *the Anti-Unfair Competition Law* (which covers 'passing-off' practices), *Trade Secrets Law, Internet Regulations,* and *Product Quality Law.*

Anti-counterfeiting procedures

The Chinese government is responding to calls from Chinese and foreign enterprises to enforce measures and to address the counterfeiting issue. Holders of rights have the choice between criminal, civil and administrative enforcement.

The police can be petitioned to investigate serious infringements when an IP owner files a complaint, or when a case is transferred from an administrative authority (such as AIC, Technical Supervision Bureau (TSB) or Customs). The police, under the supervision of Prosecutors, are the only body authorized to investigate, search and prosecute infringement cases under the Criminal Code. When the case is considered serious enough, counterfeiters are subject to Articles 140 to 149 and 213 to 215 of the Criminal Law and can be sentenced for a jail term of up to 15 years (or in some cases life imprisonment), fine and confiscation of property.

Civil courts can be used to obtain preliminary injunctions, statutory damages, compensation and cancellation of infringing rights.

Administrative bodies are widely used to confiscate infringing products and to apply for fines against counterfeiters. Foreign enterprises should increase their cooperation with Chinese Customs, who are empowered to confiscate products that violate registered IP rights and who use such powers to check goods regardless of whether they enter or exit Chinese territory.

In July 2001, the State Council introduced regulations intending to facilitate the transfer of more serious violations of various laws from administrative enforcement authorities to Chinese police, and to increase the power of prosecutors to supervise such transfers.

Trademark and Patent Application and Protection in China

Fan Weimin, Patent Attorney, CCPIT Patent & Trademark Law Office

In order to prepare for China's accession to the WTO and to improve intellectual property protection, China has revised its intellectual property laws and regulations in recent years. This chapter is intended to provide an overview of new trademark and patent application procedures and protection in China.

Trademark registration

Legislation

The Trademark Law of the PRC, which had come into force on 1 March 1983, was revised on 22 February 1993, and came into force on 1 July 1993. The Implementing Regulations of the Trademark Law of the PRC, which had come into force on 13 January 1988, were revised 28 July 1993 and again 15 May 1995. On 27 October 2001, the 24th Session of the Standing Committee of the 9th National People's Congress approved the second revision of the Trademark Law and the revised Law came into force on 1 December 2001. The Implementing Regulations of the Trademark Law of the PRC are currently being revised.

China has been a member of the World Intellectual Property Organization (WIPO) since 3 June 1980. On 19 March 1985, China acceded to the Paris Convention for the Protection of Industrial Property (Stockholm Act) and entered into the Madrid Agreement Concerning the International Registration of Marks on 4 October 1989. China also acceded to the Madrid Protocol on 1 December 1995.

Types of marks

Types of marks include trademarks, service marks, collective marks and certification marks.

Collective marks are defined as signs that are registered in the name of a group, an association or other organizations to be used by the members thereof in their commercial activities to indicate their membership of the organizations.

Certification marks describe the signs that are controlled by organizations capable of supervising certain goods or services and used by entities or individual persons outside the organization for their goods or services to certify the origin, material, mode of manufacture, quality or other characteristics of those goods or services.

Registrable marks

Registrable marks are any visually perceptible signs capable of distinguishing goods or services, including words, devices, letters of an alphabet, numerals, three-dimensional signs and combinations of colours as well as the combination of such signs. Registrable marks shall be so distinctive as to be distinguishable, and shall not conflict with any prior right acquired by another person or entity.

Well-known trademarks

The Trademark Office is responsible for the determination and administration of well-known trademarks. The following factors shall be considered in determining a well-known trademark:

- reputation of the trademark in the relevant sector of the public;
- duration of use of the trademark;
- duration, degree and geographical scope of any publicity for the trademark;

- history of protection of the trademark as a well-known trademark;
- other factors contributing to the reputation of the trademark.

A trademark shall not be registered and its use shall be prohibited where the trademark constitutes a reproduction, an imitation or a translation of a well-known trademark of another person not registered in China and is likely to:

- create confusion if the trademark is the subject of an application for registration regarding goods which are identical or similar to the goods to which the well-known trademark applies; or
- mislead the public and damage the interests of the owner of the registered well-known trademark, if the trademark is the subject of an application for registration regarding goods that are not identical or similar to the goods to which the well-known trademark applies.

Unregistrable marks

The following signs shall not be registered as trademarks:

- signs that consist exclusively of generic names, designs or models of the goods regarding which the trademark is used;
- signs that consist exclusively of direct indications of the quality, primary raw materials, functions, intended purposes, weight, quantity or other characteristics of the goods regarding which the trademark is used; or
- signs that are devoid of any distinctive character.

Signs mentioned in the preceding paragraphs may be registered as trademarks if they have acquired distinctive character through use and are capable of being readily identified and distinguished.

If a three-dimensional sign consists exclusively of the shape that results from the nature of the goods themselves, the shape of goods that is necessary to obtain a technical result, or the shape that gives substantial value to the goods, it shall not be registered as a trademark.

Other prohibited marks

The following signs shall not be used as trademarks:

- those identical with or similar to the name, national flag, national emblem, military flag, or decorations of the PRC, with names of the places where the central and state organs are located, or with the names and designs of landmark buildings;
- those identical with or similar to the names, national flags, national emblems or military flags of foreign countries, except where a foreign state's government agrees to their use;
- those identical with or similar to the names, flags or emblems, of international intergovernmental organizations, except where the organizations agree otherwise to their use or where it is not easy for their use to mislead the public;
- those identical with, or similar to, official signs and hallmarks, showing official control or warranty by them, except where their use is otherwise authorized;
- those identical, or similar to, the symbols or names of the Red Cross or the Red Crescent;
- those of a discriminatory nature against any nationality;
- those of an exaggerative and fraudulent nature in advertising goods;
- those detrimental to socialist morals or customs, or having other unhealthy influences.

The geographical name of an administrative division at or above the county level or a foreign geographical name well-known to the public shall not be used as a trademark, unless the geographical name has another meaning or the geographical name is used as a component part of a collective mark or a certification mark. Previously registered trademarks consisting of or containing geographical names shall continue to be valid.

Classification

China adopted, on 1 November 1988, the International Classification of Goods and Services formulated pursuant to the Nice Convention.

Conventional priority

Conventional priority may be claimed within six months from the date of filing outside China. Priority documents must be submitted to the Trademark Office within three months from the date of filing in China.

First-to-file rule

The Trademark Law adopts a strict first-to-file rule for obtaining trademark rights. The first applicant to file an application for registration of a mark will pre-empt all other later applications for the same mark in the same class. Where an application to register a mark has been rejected due to its identity or similarity to a previously registered mark, evidence of prior use will not be helpful for the purpose of challenging the registration, unless the mark is proved to be 'well-known' under the Paris Convention.

Filing requirement

It is important to note that each application shall cover only one trademark in one class and an official fee of about US$12 is levied for each item in excess of 10 in each class. Each application must include the following documents:

- application form;
- power of attorney, signed by the applicant (the notarization and legalization of the power of attorney is generally not required);
- five prints of the label, not exceeding 10 centimetres or being less than five centimetres in length and breadth. If the mark is in colour, one black and white label shall be submitted in addition to the five colour prints;
- priority document, if priority is claimed.

Examination

Applications are examined regarding the formality and substance. Examination regarding the formality will include the correctness of the document and classification. Examination regarding the substance will include the registrability of the mark and possible conflict with prior rights.

Amendment of application

Amendment is only possible when required by the Trademark Office. At the stage of examination in substance, amendment may lead to the deletion of a part of the mark or of the specification.

Failure to make an amendment required by the Trademark Office may lead to refusal of the application.

Provisional refusal

The Trademark Office may provisionally refuse an application if, after examination, it is found that the mark is devoid of distinctiveness or identical, or similar to, prior marks regarding identical or similar goods or services.

Publication

Applications that have passed examination will be published in the *Trademark Gazette*, which is published weekly for purposes of dispute.

Registration/duration/renewal

A mark will become registered if within the period of three months following its publication no opposition is filed against its registration, or the opposition filed is decided not to be justifiable.

A registration is valid for 10 years starting from the date of registration and can be renewed indefinitely for further 10-year periods each time.

Renewal applications shall be made within the six months before the expiry date or, subject to payment of an additional fee (official fee: about US$61), within the six months after the expiry date. Each renewal application shall include an application for renewal of trademark registration, a Power of Attorney and a copy of the Certificate of Trademark Registration.

Madrid registrations

An international registration in the PRC under the Madrid Agreement or Protocol can be effected by notifying the Madrid Union Office to add the PRC to the list of registration countries for a particular mark. Under the Madrid Agreement or Protocol, the Trademark Office has the right to reject trademarks not conforming with the trademark law.

Scope of protection

A registered mark is protected regarding the goods or services registered. In particular, any of the following acts shall be an infringement upon a registered mark:

- to use a trademark that is identical or similar to a registered trademark in relation to identical or similar goods without the authorization of the owner of the registered trademark;
- to knowingly sell goods that are in infringement of the exclusive right to use a registered trademark;
- to counterfeit or make, without authorization, representations of a registered trademark of another person or to sell such representations;
- to change a registered trademark and put goods bearing the changed trademark on the market without authorization of the owner of the registered trademark;
- to cause, in any other respect, prejudice to the exclusive right of another person to use a registered trademark.

Appeal

The provisional refusal of an application may be appealed against to the Trademark Review and

Adjudication Board (TRAB) within 15 days from the receipt of notification.

Opposition

Within three months from the date of publication anyone can oppose an accepted trademark. The Trademark Office shall make a written decision, which can be appealed against to the Trademark Review and Adjudication Board, if any party is not satisfied with the decision.

Cancellation or dispute

Where a registered trademark belongs to the category of unregistrable marks or other prohibited marks, or has been acquired by fraud or any other unfair means, any other organization or individual may request TRAB to make a judgement to cancel such a registered trademark.

Where a registered trademark:

- constitutes a reproduction, an imitation or a translation of a well-known trademark of another person not registered in China in respect of identical or similar goods, and is likely to create confusion;
- constitutes a reproduction, an imitation or a translation of a well-known trademark of another person already registered in China in respect of non-identical or dissimilar goods and is likely to mislead the public and damage the interests of the owner of the registered well-known trademark;
- has been acquired by the agent or representative of the original trademark owner without authorization, where the owner objects;
- consists of or contains a geographical indication regarding goods not originating in the region indicated to such an extent as to mislead the public (registrations made in good faith shall continue to be valid);
- infringes the existing earlier right of another person, with the intent of registering a trademark which is used by another person and enjoys a certain reputation;

the owner of the trademark or any interested party may, within five years from the date of registration, request TRAB to make a judgement to cancel the registered trademark. Where the registration has been made in bad faith the owner of a well-known trademark shall not be bound by the five-year time limit for filing a request.

In addition to the situations defined above, any person disputing a registered trademark may, within five years from the date of registration, apply to TRAB for adjudication.

Application for cancellation may be filed at any time where the registered trademark has ceased to be used for three consecutive years.

The power of the Board

Any party who is dissatisfied with the decision of TRAB may, within 30 days from receipt of the notification, institute legal proceedings with the People's Court.

Recording change of name/address/assignment/ licence

All changes in registration details including name and/or address shall be recorded with the Trademark Office.

When applying for the assignment of a registered trademark, both the assignor and assignee shall send jointly an Application for Assignment of Registered Trademark to the Trademark Office accompanied by the original Certificate of Trademark Registration. The assignee shall perform the formalities required in applying for the assignment of a registered trademark. An assignment is effective only when recorded with the Trademark Office.

A licence contract is to be recorded with the Trademark Office within three months following the execution of such a contract.

Use requirement

A registration is subject to cancellation if not in use for three consecutive years. Use of a trademark includes its use on goods, packaging or containers, or in trading documents, and use in advertising, exhibition or other business activities.

Marking

Marking is compulsory for a registered trademark; however, false marking will result in a fine of up to 20 per cent of the sales income of such falsely marked products.

Status of unregistered marks

An unregistered mark can be used; however, an unregistered trademark is not protected unless it is recognized as well known.

Registering the Chinese version for a Latin mark

Registering the Chinese version for a Latin mark is necessary if the Chinese version is to be used. Even if it is not to be used, registration of its Chinese version is also necessary if the Latin mark has *de facto* obtained its Chinese version that is well-accepted by consumers, especially when the mark was coined.

Representation

Any foreign nationals intending to apply for trademark registrations or to handle other trademark matters in China shall be represented by an agent licensed by the Chinese government.

Patent procurement

Legislation

On 1 April 1985 the Patent Law of the PRC and its Implementing Regulations came into effect. The Patent Law was revised on 4 September 1992 for the first time and became effective on 1 January 1993 together with its Implementing Regulations. On 25 August 2000, the 17th Session of the Standing Committee of the 9th National People's Congress approved the second revision of the Patent Law and the revised Law came into force on 1 July 2001.

China has been a member of the World Intellectual Property Organization (WIPO) since 3 June 1980. On 19 March 1985, China acceded to the Paris Convention for the Protection of Industrial Property (Stockholm Act). China became a member of the Patent Cooperation Treaty (PCT) on 1 January 1994 and has been a member of the Budapest Treaty for the Deposit of Micro-organisms since 1 July 1995. China entered into the Locarno Agreement Establishing an International Classification for Industrial Designs on 19 September 1996 and the Strasbourg Agreement Concerning International Patent Classification on 19 June 1997.

Language

All documents filed and formal communications with the State Intellectual Property Office of PRC (SIPO) and the Patent Re-examination Board must be in Chinese.

Types of patent

There are three types of patent: a patent for invention, a patent for a utility model and a patent for design.

Duration

The duration of a patent for invention is 20 years, and the duration of a patent for utility model or design is 10 years, and runs from the filing date in China.

Definition of invention, utility model and design

- 'Invention' means any new technical solution relating to a product, a process or improvement thereof.
- 'Utility model' means any new technical solution relating to the shape, the structure or their combination, of a product that is fit for practical use.
- 'Design' means any new design of the shape, the pattern or their combination, or the combination of the colour with shape or pattern of a product, which creates an aesthetic feeling and is fit for industrial application.

Unpatentable subject matters

No patent right shall be granted for any of the following:

- scientific discoveries;
- rules and methods for mental activities;
- methods for the diagnosis or the treatment of diseases;
- animal and plant varieties;
- substances obtained by means of nuclear transformation.

Patents may be granted for processes used in producing animal and plant varieties.

Biological material (micro-organisms)

Biological material *per se* is a patentable subject matter. Where an application for an invention concerns a new biological material that is not available and that cannot be described in the application in such a way as to enable the invention to be carried out by a person skilled in the art, the applicant shall deposit a sample of the biological material with an international depository authority (IDA) under the Budapest Treaty before the date of filing or, at the latest, on the date of filing (or the priority date where priority is claimed) and submit, at the time of filing or at the latest within four months from the filing date, a receipt of deposit and proof of viability from the depository authority.

Computer software

Computer software *per se* is not patentable. Computer software is protected, however, under the Copyright Law and can be protected under Patent Law if it falls within a technical field, resolves a technical problem and achieves a technical result.

New plant varieties

New plant varieties *per se* are not patentable; however, since 1 October 1997 new plant varieties may be protected under the Regulations on the Protection of New Plant Varieties. China has been a member state of the International Convention for the Protection of New Plant Varieties since 23 April 1999. The term of protection of new plant varieties runs from the date of grant thereof, and shall be 20 years for vines, forest trees, fruit trees and ornamental plants and 15 years for other plants, subject to the payment of annual fees.

Novelty

An invention or utility model is novel if before the filing date no identical invention or utility model has been disclosed in publications anywhere in the world, or has been publicly used or made known to the public by any other means in China. Novelty is destroyed by an application filed earlier by another person that describes an identical invention or utility mode and is published after the filing date of the said invention or utility model.

Similarly, a design is novel if it is not identical, or similar to, any design that before the filing date has been publicly disclosed in publications anywhere in the world or has been publicly used in China, and must not be in conflict with any prior right of any other person.

Inventiveness

An invention possesses inventiveness if, compared with the technical solutions existing before the filing date, the invention has prominent substantive features representing a notable progress.

Likewise, a utility model possesses inventiveness if it has substantive features and represents progress.

Conventional priority

Conventional priority for invention applications and utility model applications can be claimed within 12 months from the date of first filing outside China. Conventional priority for design applications can be claimed within six months from the date of first filing outside China. Priority documents must be submitted to the SIPO within three months from the date of filing in China.

Domestic priority

Domestic priority for invention applications and utility model applications can be claimed within 12 months from the date of first filing in China. A domestic parent application on which the domestic priority claim is based should not claim any conventional or domestic

priority, and the parent application will be deemed withdrawn when the new application claiming domestic priority is filed.

Late entry of PCT application

If an applicant under the PCT fails to go through the relevant formalities for entering the Chinese national phase within 20 or 30 months from the priority date, the applicant may, after paying a surcharge for the late entry (official fee: about US$121), go through these formalities before the expiration of the time limit of 22 months or 32 months, respectively, from the priority date.

First-to-file rule

The Patent Law, like the Trademark Law, adopts a first-to-file system.

Filing documents

Each application for an invention or utility model must include the following documents:

- power of attorney, signed by the applicant (without notarization);
- specification with claims and abstract drawings, if any (two sets of formal drawings);
- certified copy of the priority application if priority is claimed (translation of the full text is only necessary when required by the SIPO);
- assignment of priority right is required to be provided only if the applicant of the Chinese application differs from that of the priority application.

Each application for a design must include the following documents:

- power of attorney, signed by the applicant (without notarization);
- drawings or photographs of the design, in triplicate (minimum 3 × 8 centimetres, maximum 15 × 22 centimetres);
- certified copy of the priority application if priority is claimed.

Claim format

The 'European' claim format, which contains a preamble portion indicating the technical field and the technical features of the prior art and a characterizing portion stating the technical features of the invention, is highly recommended.

Publication

Patent applications for inventions are published promptly after the expiry of 18 months from the filing date or priority date, whichever is the earlier, after the preliminary examination.

Substantive examination

Patent applications for inventions are examined as to substance. In order to initiate the substantive examination procedure, applicants must submit a formal request within three years from the Chinese filing date or the priority date, whichever is earlier. Failure to do so will result in the application being deemed withdrawn.

Utility models and designs are not examined as to substance. Patents will be issued automatically after preliminary examination.

Duty of information disclosure

When the applicant of an invention application requests substantive examination, the applicant shall provide pre-filing date reference materials concerning the invention. The SIPO may ask the applicant to furnish any search reports and examination results issued by foreign patent authorities such as the European Patent Office (EPO), the United States Patent Treaty Organization (USPTO) and the Japanese Patent Office (JPO) during the examination of the corresponding foreign applications.

Unity requirement

An application for an invention or utility model shall be limited to one invention or utility model. Two or more inventions or utility models belonging to a single general inventive concept, which may be filed in one application, shall be technically interrelated and contain one or more identical or corresponding special technical features. The expression 'special technical features' shall mean those technical features that define a contribution, that each of those inventions, considered as a whole, makes over the prior art.

An application for designs shall be limited to one design incorporated in one product. Two or more designs that are incorporated in products belonging to the same class and are sold or used in sets, may be filed as one application. The expression 'the same class' means that the products incorporating the designs belong to the same sub-class in the classification of products for designs. The expression 'be sold or used in sets' means that the products incorporating the designs have the same design concept and are customarily sold or used at the same time.

Filing of divisional application

A divisional application shall be filed by an applicant before the expiry of two months from the date of receipt of the notification in which a patent right is granted for the parent application. Where an application for patent has been rejected, withdrawn or is deemed to have been withdrawn, no divisional application may be filed.

Multiple dependent claim

Any multiple dependent claim that refers to two or more claims shall refer to the preceding one in the alternative only, and shall not serve as a basis for any other multiple dependent claim.

Amendment of applications

Amendments of applications are allowed but may not go beyond the scope of original disclosure in the initial description and claims.

Applicants may amend their applications on their own initiative at the same time as the examination request is submitted, or within three months from the date of receipt of the notification from the SIPO informing the entry of the application into the examination stage.

For utility models and designs, amendments can be made within two months from the filing date. Applicants may amend the applications on their own initiative. Amendments should not change the essential elements of the designs.

Final rejections and appeals (re-examination)

If an application is found to be unacceptable by the SIPO and the applicant has been given an opportunity to make a response, a final rejection can be made.

Appeals against rejections may be made to the Patent Re-examination Board (the official term for an appeal to the Board is 're-examination').

Invalidation

Anyone may request the Patent Re-examination Board to declare a patent invalid from the date of announcement of the grant of the patent right.

The power of the Board

The Board's decisions on the allowability of invention, utility model and design applications on the validity of invention, utility model and design patents are not final, and therefore, can be further appealed against to the Court.

The scope of patent protection

The scope of patent protection for inventions and utility models is determined by the terms of the claims. The description and the appended drawings may be used to interpret the claims.

The scope of protection of designs is determined by the products incorporating the designs as shown in the drawings or photographs.

Patentees have the right to prevent others from making, using, offering to sell, selling or importing the patented products (or products incorporating patented designs), or using the patented processes, or offering to sell, selling or importing the products directly obtained by the patented processes, for production or business purposes.

Right of prior users

It is not an infringement if before the filing date of a patent application, a person has already made an identical product, used an identical process, or made necessary preparations for its manufacture or use, and this person continues to make or use it within its original scope only, after the patent is issued.

Maintenance fees and annuities

Maintenance fees are to be paid within two months from the date of receipt of the notification to grant the patent right. From the third year after the filing of a patent application and before the patent right is granted, an applicant is required to pay the maintenance fee for the application.

The annuities shall also be paid within two months from the date of receipt of the notification to grant the patent right.

There is a grace period for paying the annuities of six months.

Representation

Foreign entities and individuals having no permanent residence or business office in China must be represented by an authorized Chinese patent firm in patent prosecutions and other proceedings before the Chinese Patent Office and the Patent Re-examination Board.

Assignment and licence contracts

Assignment of patents to foreigners by Chinese entities or individuals must be approved by the competent departments of the State Council. Assignment contracts come into force after they are recorded with the SIPO. Any licence contract shall, within three months from the date of coming into force, be submitted to the Chinese Patent Office for recording.

Marking

Marking is not compulsory but recommended. The number of the patent application or patent should be indicated.

Enforcement

A unique feature of China's intellectual property enforcement mechanism is the so-called double track (litigation in court or administrative resolution) system. Under this system one may bring an action against the infringer directly in a court or request the relevant administrative authority to handle the dispute. It is important that administrative resolution need not necessarily be a procedure prior to judicial resolution.

Court system

The court system in China under the Organic Law of Courts consists of the following four levels:

- Supreme People's Court;
- higher courts: each province, autonomous region, as well as the municipalities directly under the central government, has one higher people's court;
- intermediate courts: each major city has one or two intermediate people's courts;
- basic courts: each county and each district of a major city has a basic people's court.

China has adopted a 'two instances' system for trial. At present a total of 43 intermediate people's courts are authorized as the first instance courts to deal with foreign-related trademark cases and patent cases.

Administrative authority for patent affairs

A distinct feature of the Chinese patent system is that administrative authorities for patent affairs are established as departments under the local governments in all the provinces, autonomous regions, municipalities directly under the central government, or cities that consist of districts. Each department has a large amount of patent administration work to attend to and the ability to deal with the matter. The function of the authorities is to administer patent affairs and handle patent disputes in the areas of their jurisdiction. The authorities are not branches of the Patent Office and do not accept patent applications.

Administration of Industry and Commerce (AIC)

AIC is established as administration departments under central and local governments. Its branches extend nationwide and reach the lowest level of a township. The function of AIC is of enterprise registration, market supervision, etc.

Trademark enforcement

Infringement

A person shall be liable for trademark infringement if he/she commits any of the following acts:

- uses a trademark that is identical with, or similar to, a registered trademark in relation to identical or similar goods without the authorization of the owner of the registered trademark;
- knowingly sells goods that are in infringement of the exclusive right to use a registered trademark;
- counterfeits, or makes without authorization, representations of a registered trademark of another person or sells such representations;
- changes a registered trademark and puts the goods bearing the changed trademark on the market without authorization of the owner of the registered trademark;
- in other respects causes prejudice to the exclusive right of another person to use a registered trademark.

Preliminary injunction

Where the owner of a registered trademark or an interested party has evidence indicating that another person is engaged in or will soon engage in an act of infringement of the owner's exclusive right to use his/her registered trademark and that, unless the act is stopped in a timely manner, irreparable injury will be caused to the owner's legitimate rights and interests, the owner may, before instituting legal proceedings, apply to the people's court for an injunction prohibiting the act and preserving the owner's assets.

Preservation of evidence

To stop an act of infringement where evidence may be destroyed or lost or become difficult to obtain in the future, the owner of a registered trademark or an interested party, before instituting legal proceedings, may apply to the people's court to have the evidence preserved.

The people's court shall make a decision within 48 hours from receipt of the application. Where the people's court decides to provide the preservative measures, the decision shall be executed immediately.

The people's court may order the applicant to provide security. Where no security is provided, the people's court shall reject the application.

Where the applicant fails to institute legal proceedings within 15 days from the day on which the people's court takes the preservative measures, the people's court shall revoke the measures.

Compensation for damage

The amount of damages for infringement of the exclusive right to use a registered trademark shall be the profit that the infringer has earned through the infringement during the period of the infringement, or the losses that the infringee has suffered through the infringement during the period of the infringement, including any reasonable expenses the infringee has incurred in an effort to stop the infringement.

Where the profit earned by the infringer or losses suffered by the infringee through such an infringement cannot be determined, the people's court shall grant compensation not exceeding RMB500,000 according to the circumstances of the act of infringement.

Where a party unknowingly offers for sale goods that are an infringement of the exclusive right of another person to use a registered trademark, but is able to prove that he/she has obtained the goods lawfully and identifies the supplier, such party shall not be held liable for damages.

Criminal sanction

Any person whose use, without the consent of the owner of a registered trademark, of a trademark that is identical to the registered trademark in relation to identical goods, commits a crime shall be prosecuted according to law for his/her criminal liabilities in addition to compensation for the damages that the infringee suffers.

Any person who counterfeits, or without authorization, makes representations of a registered trademark of another person, or offers for sale such representations, shall be prosecuted according to law for his/her criminal liabilities if such actions constitute a crime.

Any person who knowingly sells goods that bear a counterfeited registered trademark, thereby committing a crime, shall be prosecuted according to law for his/her criminal liabilities in addition to compensation for the damages that the infringee suffers.

In any of these cases the infringer may be subject to a maximum of seven years' imprisonment.

Administrative actions

A request for administrative actions may be filed with the AIC in the place of the infringement or the place of the infringer's residence. In trademark infringement cases, administrative actions through the AIC are the most effective and most frequently chosen approach. The AIC may take the following measures to halt the infringement:

- issue an order to stop immediately the sale of the goods;
- seize and destroy the representations of the trademark in question;
- issue an order to remove the infringing trademark from the remaining goods;
- seize such moulds, plates and any other tools of offence used directly and exclusively in the trademark infringement;
- issue an order to destroy the infringing articles, if it cannot stop sufficiently the infringing by taking the four previous measures, or if the infringing trademark and the goods involved cannot be separated from each other.

In comparison with court proceedings, the administrative proceedings are both efficient and cost-effective. If damages are sought, however, judicial proceedings are highly recommended.

Juridical actions

A trademark infringement can be brought before a court under whose jurisdiction the infringement takes place or where the infringer resides.

Statutory limitation

Administrative or court actions against trademark infringement must be brought within two years from the date that the trademark owner knows, or should have known, that the counterfeiting and/or infringing acts were taking place.

For successive infringement acts, however, courts may accept cases filed after the two-year time limit expires and order the infringer to cease infringing and compensate the infringee for the damage. Such damages may not include those suffered by the infringee more than two years prior to the date of the suit.

Burden of proof

The person who initiates proceedings bears the burden of proof. Without appropriate evidence the court or the AIC will not take any action.

Any denial of the charge of infringement or counter-claim must also be supported by evidence.

Appeal

A party may request reconsideration of the decision of an AIC by the AIC at a higher level. The decision of the higher AIC may be appealed against to the court having jurisdiction.

In court proceedings a party may appeal to the court of second instance if it is not satisfied with the decision of the court of first instance. The decision of the court of second instance is final and binding.

Patent enforcement

Infringement

A person will be liable for patent infringement and actions may be brought against him/her if, for business purposes and without authorization of a patentee, such person committed any of the following acts:

- making, using, offering for sale or selling the patented product;
- using the patented process;
- using, offering for sale or selling the product directly obtained by the patented process;
- importing the patented product; or
- importing the product directly obtained by the patented process.

Preliminary injunction

Where any patentee or interested party has evidence to prove that another person is infringing or will soon infringe his/her patent right and that, if such infringing act is not checked or prevented from occurring in time, it is likely to cause irreparable harm to such patentee, the latter may, before any legal proceedings are instituted, request the people's court to adopt measures for ordering the suspension of relevant acts and the preservation of property.

Compensation for damages

The amount of compensation for the damages caused by the infringement of the patent right shall be assessed on the basis of the losses suffered by the patentee or the profits that the infringer has earned through the infringement. If it is difficult to determine the losses or the profits, the amount may be assessed by reference to the appropriate multiple (from one to three times) of the amount of the exploitation fee of that patent under contractual licence.

Criminal sanction

Passing off the patent of another person will be a criminal offence if the circumstances are serious. The infringer will be subject to a penalty or detainment or up to three years' imprisonment.

Judicial or administrative actions

A patentee or an interested party may bring an action against an infringer in a court having jurisdiction, or seek to resolve the dispute through administrative action by making a request to the relevant administrative authority for patent affairs. The administrative authority is empowered to order the infringer to stop infringing acts and to mediate disputes on the claimed damages to the infringee. In cases of passing off, the administrative authority may order the confiscation of the illegal gains by the infringer, and impose on the infringer a penalty of up to three times the illegal gains, or RMB5,000 if there were no illegal gains.

A patent infringement should be brought before the court under whose jurisdiction the infringer is located or the infringement takes place, or the place where the infringing products are made or sold.

For administrative resolution the request should be filed with the administrative authority for patent affairs in the place where the infringement occurs.

Statutory limitation

An infringement suit must be initiated within two years from the date on which the patentee or any interested party obtains or should have obtained knowledge of the infringement act.

Burden of proof

The plaintiff has to submit evidence to prove his/her claim against infringement and to support his/her claim for damages. Any denial of the charge of infringement or counter-claim must be also supported by evidence.

The burden of proof will be borne by the defendant if the litigation concerns a process patent for the manufacture of a new product filed after 1 January 1993. In the case of such a charge, the defendant denying the charge should present evidence proving that his/her product is not manufactured using the patented process.

For a process patent filed before 1 January 1993, the burden of proof will be borne by the defendant regardless of whether the process is for the manufacture of a new

product. The court or administrative authority may ask for a search report to be made by the patent office.

Appeal

The decision of the court of first instance can be appealed against to the higher level court, whose decision is final and enforceable. The statutory time limit for an appeal is 15 days after the date on which the written judgement is served for domestic parties, or 30 days for foreign parties having no residence in China.

The decision of the administrative authority may be appealed against to the intermediate court having jurisdiction if a party is not satisfied with the decision. The judgement of the intermediate court may be appealed again to the higher level court.

Border enforcement by customs

The Regulations of the People's Republic of China on the Customs' Protection of Intellectual Property Rights were promulgated by the State Council 5 July 1995 and entered into effect 1 October 1995.

Scope of application

The Customs Regulations forbid the import or export of goods protected by Chinese laws and regulations including trademark, patent and copyright. The trademark or patent owners or their agents are first required to record their intellectual property (IP) rights with customs.

Record entry

IP rights owners must submit to the General Administration of Customs a written application including the following details:

- information about the applicant;
- information about the suspected infringing goods and the infringer (if possible);
- the Customs HS Code of suspected infringing products in the customs declaration;
- certificate of intellectual property rights: a copy of the Chinese trademark registration certificate, patent certificate or copyright certificate;
- a copy of the applicant's business licence or business registration certificate;
- clear colour photographs of the authentic or suspected infringing goods;
- a concise description of the features of the suspected infringing goods;

- a statement on disputes and documents for current litigation, cancellation and revocation actions, etc;
- a list of other parties using the IP rights in a legitimate way including the licencee and the trustees.

Customs shall notify the applicant whether the application is admitted for entry in the records within 30 days after receiving all the application documents.

Period of validity

The period of validity shall be seven years, counted from the day the record entry is admitted by the General Administration of Customs Office.

Subject to the validity of the IP, the IP owner may apply for a renewal of the record entry within six months before the period of validity of the record expires. The period of validity for each renewal of the record entry shall be seven years.

The record entry of the customs' protection shall expire when the period of validity of the registration for the trademark, patent or copyright recorded expires.

Application for protection measures

IP rights owners whose rights have been entered in the record of the Customs General, shall file an application with the customs located in the place of import or export of the suspected infringing products, to detain the goods and submit the guarantees equal to the CIF value of the imported goods or the FOB value of the exported goods when they consider it necessary.

Customs may detain the suspected infringing goods based on the request of the IP owner; it can also initiate *ex officio* action to detain suspected infringing goods and notify the IP owner in writing.

If the IP owner who applies to customs to take protection measures has not recorded his right with the Customs General, he shall undertake the formalities of recording the IP in accordance with the Regulation at the same time as he applies to the Customs General for protection measures.

Protection measures

If the consignee or consignor of the detained goods does not file an objection with customs on detention, customs has the power to:

- confiscate infringing goods;
- destroy the goods infringing a trademark, unless the infringing trademark can be removed from the goods;
- fine the infringer who imports or exports the infringing goods intentionally;
- transfer proceedings against the offender, whose act of importing or exporting goods infringing IP rights constitutes a crime, to the judicial authorities for investigation.

Rights of the suspected infringer and the IP rights owner

- The consignee or consignor of seized goods has seven days from the date of being served with a Customs Detaining Receipt to raise an objection to the customs seizure.
- The IP owner has 15 days from the date of being served a written notification from the Customs Department to apply to the appropriate authorities handling IP for remedies or to commence action in the people's court.
- A consignee or consignor of detained goods, who alleges that his goods do not infringe any IP rights, may apply for clearance of the goods. A bail bond in the amount equal to twice the CIF value of the imported goods or twice the FOB value of the exported goods shall be provided.

(Editor's note: Mr Fan Weimin can be contacted at the following address: 10/F, Ocean Plaza, 158 Fuxingmennei Street, Beijing 100031, China. Tel: 0086 10 6641 2345 Fax: 0086 10 6641 5678)

Environmental Due Diligence

Olivier Dubuis and Whui Min Chang, Attorney at Law, Adamas, China

China is adopting new and more stringent environmental legislation that places greater emphasis on preventive procedural controls for activities that have potential adverse environmental impact. Many of these new regulations meet or exceed the requirements of similar laws in western countries. The problem currently facing China is one of effective enforcement. As this aspect is rapidly changing, foreign investors should be aware of the risks related to environmental issues.

China already faces significant concerns over its air quality and provision of clean potable drinking water to large sections of the population. The level of treated wastewater remains very low, thus polluting water resources and river basins. It is likely that increasing pressure will be placed on those polluting industries, more specifically those large multinational organizations that can afford the costly expense of clean-up.

Many foreign organizations continue to invest in China without truly understanding the potential business risks associated with their investments.

What is environmental due diligence?

Environmental due diligence can be defined as the systematic identification of environmental risks and liabilities associated with an organization's properties and operations.

Who needs to perform environmental due diligence?

Prior to any significant investment decision (merger, acquisition, corporate restructuring or joint venture set-up), environmental due diligence is necessary.

There is an increasingly stringent movement of the regulatory framework in many developed countries towards the 'polluter pays' principle, with greater emphasis now being placed on environmental issues across all industries in order to manage potential risks associated with poor environmental performance or impact on the natural environment.

Environmental due diligence is conducted by sellers, buyers, investors and lenders in order to identify and to evaluate the environmental risks associated with the site or business operation under consideration.

For environmental issues, due diligence commonly involves legal and regulatory experts, as well as geotechnical and engineering experts, performing the full range of studies necessary to identify potential environmental liabilities associated with the acquisition or the partnership arrangement.

Why thorough due diligence is necessary before investing in China

While the majority of foreign organizations investing in China consider legal and financial risk as a crucial part of the due diligence process, only a very small proportion considers the full implications of environmental risk. The types of environmental issues typically uncovered during due diligence include the potential for past and present soil and groundwater contamination, inadequate abatement equipment, regulatory non-compliance, third-party impact and major reputation concerns.

By undertaking environmental due diligence in the transaction process, an organization is better placed to understand and to manage the type of risks and constraints likely to impact its current and future operations, and reduce the business risk of investment. It is prudent to undertake a thorough due diligence of the partner's past and present environmental performance in order to ascertain the level of legal compliance, the potential for soil and groundwater contamination, the technical level of existing effluent treatment facilities and the quantity of stored and non-treated hazardous solid wastes before entering a joint-venture partnership.

The unexpected financial obligations resulting from an environmental breach can be very costly and lead to upgrading facilities costs, penalties (mostly extremely onerous), prosecution and contaminated land clean-up or even plant closure. Furthermore, the representations and warranties that could have been agreed to by the seller are very difficult to negotiate and to enforce.

All issues of concern must be assessed in the light of local realities to estimate the actual degree of risk and the best approach to managing such risks.

When should the environmental due diligence be conducted?

Typically, environmental issues are considered in the closing stages of the due diligence process once many of the legal and financial concerns associated with the transaction have been finalized, with outstanding issues either incorporated into the indemnities or warranties or factored into the transaction agreement.

However, the preferred approach would be to conduct the environmental review in conjunction with legal and financial due diligence, allowing greater time to conduct a detailed investigation and to better evaluate the overall transaction. In fact, relevant information must be delivered early in a transaction process; otherwise meaningful evaluation and negotiating leverage may be lost, not to mention time if the new information is serious enough to cause one party to re-evaluate the transaction.

Typical issues commonly overlooked in a transaction

The absence of an air emission permit, the upcoming expiration of a fire certificate, the obsolescence or non-compliance of pre-treatment facilities, restrictions on the import, transportation or use of an essential raw material, the absence of dangerous goods storage or transportation licences, or the absence of an effluent discharges licence

could all give rise to potential issues that need to be addressed and solved before any transaction can occur.

The due diligence process focuses on:

- collecting relevant background information on the target company;
- obtaining all available environmental permits/records from the local Environmental Protection Bureau (EPB);
- reviewing the company's internal environmental records (if any);
- inspecting the company's facility;
- interviewing employees familiar with the company's processes and procedures;
- interviewing past employees familiar with the company's processes and procedures;
- interviewing local residents about facility conditions;
- comparing discharge standards and other relevant factors with Chinese environmental law, regulations and policies.

Potential liabilities for companies in China

Key liabilities are related to contaminated land. At present, Chinese law has yet to allocate responsibilities and liability associated with land clean-up.

Under current environmental protection laws, the responsible party can be sued for clean-up within three years of the date of acknowledgement of responsibility. New users of land could potentially be liable for pre-existing contamination; thus, it is important to conduct a thorough assessment of a site prior to acquisition.

In the future, the Chinese regulatory system is likely to continue to strengthen, placing greater emphasis on strict regulatory enforcement, resulting in an increase in the number and severity of penalties, prosecutions and imprisonments.

What are the usual steps of environmental due diligence?

Preparation

This could be a desk-based study, examining previous reports, historical maps and photos, and should include:

- an understanding of the business dynamics and EHS issues;
- coordination with legal and financial advisors;
- preparation of audit documentation and questionnaire.

Preliminary environmental site assessments (PESAs)

These involve:

- identifying and quantifying risks and liabilities;
- advising legal and financial teams on key issues during deal negotiation;
- preparing a due diligence report, highlighting key risks and liabilities, including:
  - permit requirements;
  - liability and management practices;
  - civil and criminal liability;
  - contaminated land liability;
  - storage;
  - air pollution control;
  - water pollution control;
  - water abstraction/use;
  - solid waste management (including packaging waste, transportation of waste);
  - hazardous materials management;
  - dangerous chemicals notification;
  - classification, packaging and labelling;
  - other facility-specific issues.

Intrusive inspections

These will include soil, surface water and ground water sampling analysis.

Remedial investigations

These will include conceptual and detailed remedial design and remediation cost analysis.

On-going operational matters

These would include:

- clean-up implementation and verification;
- planning long-term improvements in efficiency and risk management;
- implementation of annual EHS reviews, to ensure legal compliance and continual improvement.

The Law of the People's Republic of China on Environmental Impact Assessment

The Law, adopted by the Standing Committee of the National People's Congress on 28 October 2002, entered into effect on 1 September 2003. Even though the obligation principally affects domestic Chinese companies, the law is also relevant to foreign investment enterprises and foreign companies with construction-related activities in China.

The new law requires analysis, forecasting and assessment of possible environmental impacts caused by new governmental plans and private construction projects. Environmental assessments must describe measures and countermeasures to prevent or to mitigate adverse environmental impacts, as well as methods to follow up and to monitor the effectiveness of implementation. Under the law, project developers must retain consultants to prepare the required assessments.

The law requires the preparation of comprehensive assessment reports for projects that may cause a 'substantial environmental impact'. Developers must also conduct a public hearing (except where national security is implicated) or otherwise collect feedback from the general public and relevant experts before submitting construction applications for government approval. Government approval or disapproval must be issued within 60 days. A less comprehensive environmental impact statement may be prepared for projects that cause 'light environmental impact'. For projects with 'very small' environmental impact, it may only be necessary to complete an environmental impact registration form, for which government approval or disapproval can be issued within 15 days.

Environmental protection authorities under the State Council are responsible for examination and approval of certain major construction projects such as nuclear facilities, top-secret projects, construction projects of cross-province, autonomous regions or municipalities directly under the central government, or construction projects that are examined and approved by the State Council or by the relevant government agencies authorized by the State Council. Approval of other projects is given by the local government of the province, autonomous region or municipality directly under the central government (current status for Beijing, Tianjin, Shanghai and Chongqing municipalities).

If construction companies make any change in the nature, scale, location, production process or environmental protection methods proposed for the project, the company must apply for new approval of those changes.

The new law provides that if the construction project is not commenced within five years after the date of the approval of the construction work, the company is required to apply for a re-examination of the environmental assessment report. Furthermore, the competent environmental protection authorities will conduct follow-up inspections after the project is put into production or use. The authorities are also authorized to investigate and ascertain causes and liabilities for serious environmental pollution or ecological destruction.

If any company commences a construction project without the approval of a required environmental impact assessment, the relevant authorities may issue a cease and desist order and may impose penalties ranging from US$6,000 to US$24,000. In addition, individual managers directly responsible for the construction project may be subject to administrative penalties.

Commercial Dispute Resolution

Gary Lock and Brinton M Scott, Herbert Smith, Shanghai

Although no one commences transactions with the expectation that disputes will arise, foreign investors should consider various aspects of their investment or commercial activity in China in light of available dispute resolution options if the need arises.

Legislation

The legal framework generally governing dispute resolution in China consists of various laws including the:

- *New York Convention on the Recognition and Enforcement of Foreign Arbitral Awards* (the New York Convention);
- *PRC Civil Law*;
- *PRC Civil Procedure Law* (the Civil Procedure Law);
- *PRC Arbitration Law* (the Arbitration Law); and
- *PRC Contract Law*.

However, in specific cases other laws may also impact on the choice of law and available dispute resolution options. These laws include the *Labour Law*, the *PRC Law on Sino-foreign CJVs*, and the *PRC Law on Sino-foreign EJVs*.

There are four general methods that parties use to resolve commercial disputes arising in China: namely, negotiation (or 'friendly consultation'), mediation, arbitration and litigation.

Negotiation and mediation

Negotiation is often the first step in the PRC dispute resolution process. Foreign investors sometimes prefer negotiated settlements that are voluntarily accepted by their PRC counterparts in light of the difficulties associated with enforcing judgements in China.

Mediation can provide the first formal step in dispute resolution if the parties are unable to negotiate. There are a number of mediation forums available in China, ranging from the People's Conciliation Committees (grassroots bodies that are generally called upon to mediate private disputes) to highly-specialized commercial mediation centres. All mediation is voluntary, and agreements reached through mediation are binding. Further action may be taken in the People's Courts where parties refuse to participate, decline to accept a mediated solution, or where one party fails to adhere to the terms of a mediated settlement.

China International Chamber of Commerce Conciliation Centres

The China International Chamber of Commerce (CICC) and the China Council for the Promotion of International Trade (CCPIT) have established more than 30 permanent commercial mediation centres within China. CCPIT rules allow parties to appoint one or two mediators from a list of approved mediators with expertise in various fields, including international trade, finance, intellectual property, technology transfers, construction and law.

Mediators are allowed wide latitude to conduct mediation and may exercise discretion over the admission and handling of evidence. Parties to CCPIT mediation may not refer to any information provided or offers made during the mediation in any future litigation or arbitration.

Conciliation conducted by the People's Courts

The People's Courts also conduct mediation, either as preliminary proceedings prior to litigation or later in the course of litigation. The Civil Procedure Law requires the People's Courts to conduct mediation between parties before commencing final litigation, should mediation fail. If a mediated agreement is reached, it is signed by the judge, sealed by the Court and becomes enforceable upon execution by the opposing parties. Such a signed mediation agreement, formalized by the People's Court has the same legal effect as a final judgement and is subject to the same procedures for enforcement.

Arbitration

Arbitration is undoubtedly the most popular method of dispute resolution between Chinese and foreign parties, mostly because arbitrations may take place outside of China (popular venues include Hong Kong, Singapore, and Stockholm) and are still enforceable in China.

Arbitration outside China

In certain contexts, Chinese law allows the parties to a foreign-related transaction to agree to submit disputes to arbitral tribunals outside China. Such an agreement is usually done in the form of a dispute resolution clause that is included in any contractual documentation to which the parties are signatories.

China acceded to the New York Convention in 1987 with two formal reservations:

1. It only applies on the basis of reciprocity; and
2. It only applies to disputes deemed commercial under PRC law.

Arbitration in China

Although many disputes involving foreign parties are arbitrated offshore, if the parties have failed to provide for offshore arbitration in their agreement or PRC law forbids offshore resolution, it is also possible to arbitrate in China via PRC arbitral tribunals. The Arbitration Law establishes the standards for arbitrators and the requirements for PRC arbitration commissions and the arbitration proceedings they conduct.

The Arbitration Law requires parties to voluntarily agree to submit to arbitration either before or after a dispute arises. Where a party attempts to litigate a dispute covered by a valid agreement to arbitrate, the People's Courts must dismiss the suit and refer the parties to arbitration.

The viability of arbitration as a means of dispute resolution is augmented by the Civil Procedure Law and relevant arbitration centre rules that allow parties to seek orders to preserve property and evidence pending completion of an arbitration. The parties to the dispute may apply to the arbitration tribunal for such orders, which may then be given full legal effect by the People's Courts.

The Arbitration Law requires arbitration tribunals to conduct mediation before rendering final decisions. When mediation is unsuccessful, the award made by the arbitration tribunal is binding upon the parties. The losing party has six months to appeal a tribunal's decision. The Intermediate People's Courts retain powers to review and overturn awards where:

- there was no agreement to arbitrate;
- the issues arbitrated were not within the scope of the agreement to arbitrate;
- the dispute was outside the arbitration commission's jurisdiction;
- the composition of the arbitration tribunal or the arbitral proceedings did not conform to the tribunal's arbitration rules or other law;
- the arbitration decision was based upon fraudulent evidence;
- the arbitration tribunal clearly misapplied the law; or
- an arbitrator is guilty of misconduct, including the taking of bribes or otherwise acting out of self-interest.

Arbitration awards are also subject to cancellation by the Courts where they conflict with public policy.

The Arbitration Law contains special provisions for the arbitration of disputes that involve foreign investment and foreign trade (so-called Foreign Affairs). Such arbitration may be handled by special Foreign Affairs arbitration tribunals (including CIETAC, discussed below), whose awards are subject to narrower review by the People's Courts. The People's Courts may consider cancelling such an arbitration award where a party did not receive meaningful notice, and enforcement of the award would be contrary to public policy. However, awards are not subject to review due to the misapplication of law, insufficiency of evidence or misconduct by an arbitrator.

PRC Arbitration Tribunals

According to the Notice of the Office of the State Council on the *Clarification of Several Issues Concerning the Implementation of the Arbitration Law of China,* foreign-related disputes may be submitted to local arbitration tribunals where the parties have agreed. However, the parties may also select a Foreign Affairs arbitration forum.

The China International Economic and Trade Arbitration Commission

The most popular alternative to offshore arbitration is the China International Economic and Trade Arbitration Commission (CIETAC). Established in Beijing in 1956, the CIETAC also has commissions in Shanghai and Shenzhen. CIETAC tribunals have jurisdiction to arbitrate disputes between:

- international or foreign-related enterprises (including those from Hong Kong, Macao and Taiwan);
- separate FIEs; and
- FIEs and Chinese nationals.

CIETAC may also hear other types of disputes according to specific grants of jurisdiction pursuant to PRC law, such as internet domain name disputes.

CIETAC maintains a list of approved arbitrators that includes professionals and experts from fields such as law, international business and trade, and science and technology. Presently there are a total of 492 arbitrators, 158 of whom are foreign nationals or residents of Hong Kong.

The CIETAC Arbitration Rules were amended by CCPIT and CICC, effective on 1 October 2000. The Arbitration Rules lay out the administrative guidelines for CIETAC and procedural rules for conducting the arbitration. Parties may appoint agents, including foreign lawyers, to represent them at arbitration. Parties may also nominate the language in which arbitration is to be conducted.

Where the dispute is less than RMB500,000 or the parties otherwise agree, CIETAC can conduct streamlined summary arbitration proceedings. In summary proceedings, the arbitrators base their decisions on documentary evidence that the parties submit and must decide within 90 days of the formation of the tribunal when necessary. The tribunal may also conduct hearings to receive testimony. Where hearings are conducted, the tribunal must issue its decision within 30 days of the conclusion.

In respect of the monetary, capital, foreign exchange, gold and insurance markets the CIETAC has adopted new Arbitration Rules governing financial disputes (Financial Disputes Arbitration Rules, effective as of May 2003), which prevail over the general Arbitration Rules when there are discrepancies.

Enforcement of arbitral awards in PRC Courts

PRC Courts must enforce foreign arbitration awards pursuant to the requirements of the New York Convention, except in limited circumstances. The execution of New York Convention obligations is embodied in the Code of Civil Procedure. The PRC Code of Civil Procedure provides that a party may sue to enforce an arbitral award in the Intermediate People's Court where one party fails to comply with an award. An action may be brought where the adverse party or the property subject to execution is located. However, because local PRC Courts have a reputation of not always being impartial and above outside influences, they may sometimes refuse to enforce an arbitral award based on external considerations or law.

To counter this problem, the Supreme People's Court issued a directive to the local People's Courts instituting procedural safeguards to encourage the enforcement of awards made in foreign arbitral tribunals and by foreign affairs tribunals within China. The directive requires the Intermediate People's Courts to report their findings and reasoning to the Higher People's Courts where they refuse to enforce a foreign-related or foreign arbitral award. If the Higher People's Court affirms the lower Court's decision, they must in turn report their findings to the Supreme People's Court for final approval. Thus, no decision to bar enforcement of foreign or foreign affairs tribunal awards is final until the Supreme People's Court issues its approval. However, awards rendered by domestic PRC arbitration tribunals are not subject to the directive in cases that are not considered foreign-related under PRC law.

Hong Kong arbitral awards

Prior to Hong Kong's reunification with the mainland, PRC Courts were obligated to enforce arbitral awards issued by Hong Kong tribunals under the New York Convention. After Hong Kong's return however, such awards could no longer be considered foreign and therefore the New York Convention could not apply.

On 24 January 2000, China's Supreme People's Court issued the Arrangements of the Supreme People's Court on the Reciprocal Enforcement of Arbitral Awards by Mainland China and the Hong Kong SAR (the Arrangements) to solve this problem. The Arrangements require the Courts of the Hong Kong SAR (HKSAR) to enforce arbitral awards issued by mainland arbitration tribunals, subject to the Arbitration Law.

PRC Courts are similarly obligated to enforce arbitral awards issued by Hong Kong tribunals, pursuant to HKSAR law. When asked to enforce awards from the other jurisdiction, HKSAR and PRC Courts may refuse enforcement under circumstances very similar to those enumerated in the Arbitration Law and the New York Convention.

Litigation

Redress may also be sought in the People's Courts where mediation fails and the parties have not agreed to arbitrate their dispute. China grants the right to sue and be sued to all aliens, foreign enterprises and foreign organizations, based on reciprocity. PRC Courts will apply any restrictions placed on the rights of Chinese nationals when litigating in a foreign forum to the nationals of that forum.

In most civil claims, the People's Court where the defendant is domiciled will have jurisdiction. However, in contract and tort claims the People's Court in the jurisdiction where the contract was executed or tort was committed also has jurisdiction.

Appeals may be made to the appropriate Court of second instance, usually either the Intermediate or Higher People's Courts wherever a party objects to the ruling of the People's Courts. Courts of appeal must make their rulings within three months of the filing of the appeal, although extensions are granted in some cases. Rulings of the Courts of second instance are final and binding upon the parties.

Despite increased attempts at professionalism, PRC Courts are still susceptible to cronyism. Litigants are often subjected to prolonged delays even where Courts adhere to the letter of the law, especially when trying to enforce judgements. Nonetheless the Code of Civil Procedure requires that judgements be timely executed, and appeals to higher Courts allowed where execution is not rendered. In cases where property subject to execution is in the jurisdiction of another People's Court, that Court may be asked to execute the judgement within 15 days.

Part Four

Accounting, Auditing and Taxation in China

Accounting and Auditing Requirements and Practices

Yvonne Kam, PricewaterhouseCoopers

This chapter introduces the general framework governing the accounting and auditing requirements in the PRC. By looking at the characteristics and features of different types of enterprise set up since China opened its door, the accounting and auditing requirements as they developed over time are described below.

Background and development

The first comprehensive set of accounting regulations for foreign-invested enterprises (FIEs) was formulated in 1992. The latest wave of reform in accounting regulations took place in 2001. The trend of newly issued accounting standards is clearly steering towards International Financial Reporting Standards (IFRS).

With the founding of the PRC in 1949, all resources of production in the country came under state ownership and the main form of economic entity was the state-owned enterprise. The accounting rules and regulations, known as fund accounting, characterized by their rigidity and uniformity, were used primarily for establishing an information and reporting system for the implementation of state economic policies on the one hand and maintenance of administrative control over assets of the state on the other. To a greater extent, accounting rules also served as a tool to strengthen the financial discipline of an enterprise and to safeguard state property.

Since the promulgation of the Joint Venture Law in 1979 and the issuance of several interim accounting regulations, a comprehensive set of accounting regulations was formulated in 1992 to prescribe accounting treatments and the preparation of financial statements by FIEs. This was undoubtedly the first step away from the fund accounting concept, which applied to state-owned enterprises and is used mainly for the purpose of resource allocation in a planned economy.

Alongside economic reform and the open-door policy adopted since the early 1980s, foreign investors were allowed to set up enterprises and conduct business in China. A separate set of accounting regulations that was applicable to FIEs only was developed and implemented. Although these regulations or principles were somewhat in line with the IFRS (formerly known as International Accounting Standards or IAS), the requirements were subservient more to the purpose of ascertaining the amount of tax an enterprise should pay rather than to the purpose of ascertaining the 'fair presentation' of the financial statements.

Concurrently, China has undertaken a programme to restructure state-owned enterprises by transforming them into enterprises that issue shares and have limited liability (joint stock limited companies). Many enterprises will eventually go public. A third set of accounting regulations that catered specifically for joint stock limited companies were formulated in the early 1990s and revised in 1998.

The rapid growth of the economy, the demand for foreign investment, the gradual maturity of China's securities market and the accession into the WTO have highlighted the need for a sound, reliable and transparent accounting system more acceptable to foreign investors. The accounting regulations and system designed to cater for tax regulations and state ownership under the socialist system could no longer meet modern business management and funding requirements. To meet the demands of foreign investors and an increasing number of individual and institutional investors in the securities market, a series of regulations were issued. These include the Accounting Law, which was last revised in 1999, the Regulations on Financial Reporting of Enterprises issued in 2000 and, finally, the Accounting System for Business Enterprises (ASBE) issued in early 2001.

The ASBE, known to have been prepared after considering the accounting standards, guidelines and practices issued by the International Federation of Accountants (IFAC), International Accounting Standards Board (IASB) and other accounting bodies, is more in line with the IFRS. The ASBE sets out the fundamental framework for modern day accounting in China.

In 2001, the adoption of the ASBE was first made mandatory to the joint stock limited companies (including those offering shares to the public). The Accounting Regulations for Selected Joint Stock Limited Companies were then abolished.

In 2002, the adoption of the ASBE was made mandatory to the FIEs. The Accounting Regulations for Foreign Investment Enterprises of the PRC were then superceded. Although not yet mandatory, the adoption of these new rules by state-owned enterprises and other domestic enterprises is encouraged. In essence the ASBE will become the primary set of basic accounting regulations applicable to different types of enterprises.

In addition, since 1996, 33 new exposure drafts were issued to address specific accounting topics. As of today, 16 specific accounting standards have been issued and a list of them can be found in Table 4.1.1. The focus of these standards is clearly to steer the current system and standards towards IFRS and allow PRC accounting regulations to ultimately gain worldwide acceptance.

The hierarchy of the various laws and regulations governing accounting is depicted in Figure 4.1.1.

Setting accounting standards

In China, setting authoritative accounting standards is not the responsibility of the Accounting Society of China (ASC) or the Chinese Institute of Certified Public Accountants (CICPA). Instead, the Ministry of Finance (MOF) is responsible for formulating, promulgating and administering accounting regulations. Consequently, accounting standards are regulations and must be strictly adhered to.

With the introduction of the ASBE in 2001, a greater degree of judgement is given to companies when formulating their own accounting policies in certain areas to suit their specific circumstances. For example, companies can set their own fixed asset

Table 4.1.1 Accounting standards

Specific accounting standard	Applicable to	Effective date
Disclosures of related party relationship and related party transactions	Listed companies only	1 January 1997
Cash flow statements (revised)	All types of enterprises including FIEs	1 January 1998
Events occurring after the balance sheet date (revised)	Listed companies only	1 January 1998
Debt restructuring (revised)	All types of enterprises including FIEs	1 January 1999
Construction contracts	Listed companies only	1 January 1999
Investments (revised)[1]	Joint stock limited companies only	1 January 1999
Changes in accounting policies, estimates or fundamental errors (revised)	All types of enterprises including FIEs	1 January 1999
Revenue	Listed companies only	1 January 1999
Non-monetary transactions (revised)	All types of enterprises including FIEs	1 January 2000
Contingencies	All types of enterprises including FIEs	1 July 2000
Intangible assets[1]	Joint stock limited companies only	1 January 2001
Borrowing costs	All types of enterprises including FIEs	1 January 2001
Leases	All types of enterprises including FIEs	1 January 2001
Interim financial reporting	Listed companies only	1 January 2002
Fixed assets[1]	Joint stock limited companies only	1 January 2002
Inventories[1]	Joint stock limited companies only	1 January 2002

[1] These standards are mandatory to listed companies and/or joint stock limited companies and companies implementing the ASBE. However, all other types of companies, including non-listed companies and state-owned enterprises, are encouraged to adopt them.

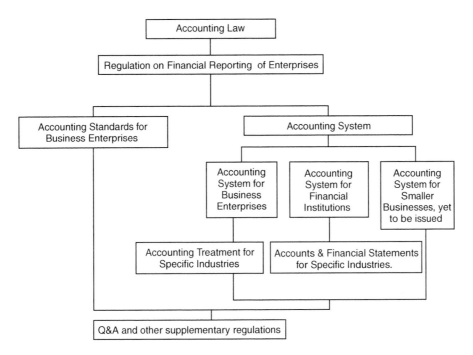

Figure 4.1.1 The hierarchy of laws and regulations governing accounting

depreciation policy to reflect the pattern in which the economic benefits of the assets are consumed by the company. As another example, companies can determine the amount of provision set against asset impairment. This will enable financial statements to be more meaningful and on which management can rely to make decisions and assess success of strategies.

Accounting concepts and bases

The quantitative characteristics employed in China's accounting regulations include accuracy, completeness, consistency, comparability, timeliness, materiality, accrual basis, matching, prudence, substance over form and going concern. The principles, by and large, mirror that of IFRS. Other major features of these regulations are as follows:

- Companies should adopt accounting policies in accordance with the relevant accounting regulations. Rather than generally accepted accounting standards (GAAP), which are issued by non-governmental bodies, PRC accounting regulations are legally enforceable. Substance over form should only be followed provided that the accounting regulations are not violated.
- The historical cost convention is prescribed. Assets are required to be recorded initially at actual cost

and subsequently adjusted for impairment, if any. Revaluations are generally not allowed.

- These regulations also require companies to use the calendar year, from 1 January to 31 December, as their financial year.
- Except as follows, transactions should be recorded using RMB (the lawful currency of the PRC). A foreign currency can be used as the recording currency if the company's transactions are mainly dominated in foreign currencies. However, the foreign currency books of accounts should be translated to RMB in preparing financial statements.
- The concept of fair market value on fixed and intangible assets, financial instruments, etc, is not commonly used due to the lack of an active market.
- Due to the infancy of the new system, certain footnote disclosures may not be as comprehensive as that acceptable elsewhere in the world. Yet, in certain areas, the Chinese standards are extremely stringent. This includes disclosing the corporate identity of related parties and commenting on the fairness of transactions conducted between related parties; preparing the cash flow statements using both the direct and indirect methods.

The old standards were neither broad nor flexible enough to allow discussion or manoeuvre on particular subjects. For the first time, in certain areas, ASBE gives management the authority to exercise judgement based on professional experience within a defined accounting framework.

Auditing requirements

Not only are the financial statements of all FIEs and companies offering shares to the public required to be audited, but those of most state-owned enterprises are also required to be audited nowadays.

In most countries, limited liability companies are subject to an annual audit carried out by independent external auditors, whose role is to express an objective opinion on the fair presentation of the financial statements. In China, in addition to fulfilling this primary objective, auditing has a secondary objective, which is to ascertain the accuracy and legality of the financial records of a business (whether the transactions conducted comply with relevant state laws and regulations). Auditors of state-owned enterprises in China are concerned with protecting the legal interests of the company as well as the interests of the state.

Auditing profession standards and forms of audit report

Although the auditing profession is still a relatively new profession, it is improving its sophistication and prominence. Only very recently has the impact of accountants or auditors on national economic activities become more apparent. By virtue of the PRC Accounting Law, promulgated in January 1985, the concept of accounting supervision was first established. Following the setting up of the Chinese Institute of Certified Public Accountants in 1988, the status of certified public accountants and professional accounting firms in society received a major boost. Subsequently, with the issuance of the Law on Certified Public Accountants, which became effective from 1 January 1994, the role of auditors carried out by certified public accountants was better defined.

In December 1988, the Ministry of Finance promulgated the Auditing and Certification Regulations (Provisional), which sets out the roles of certified public accountants, audit scope and procedures and the requirements for maintaining audit working papers. Between 1995 and 1996, four General Independent Auditing Standards – Basic Standards, Quality Control, Continuing Education and Ethics were issued. New specific auditing standards applicable from 1 January 1997 were also promulgated, which complete and clarify the provisional regulations and general standards. So far, 28 specific auditing standards, 10 practice bulletins and five practice guidelines have been issued. Together, they form the foundations of auditing standards in China, and these standards are very close to those of International Standards of Auditing (ISA).

The audit report normally contains an introductory paragraph, a scope paragraph and an opinion paragraph. The introductory paragraph identifies the financial statements being audited and sets out responsibilities of management and of the auditors. The scope paragraph sets out the principal audit work and procedures carried out. The opinion paragraph sets out whether the accounts have been prepared in accordance with the relevant accounting regulations. Any qualification should be expressed in the audit report.

In some instances, different government agencies may require additional items for certified public accountants to opine on. Sometimes, these additional requirements have not been agreed by the Ministry of Finance or the CICPA and fall beyond the expertise of what is normally expected of a certified public accountant. In some circumstances, these requirements issued by other government agencies have been retracted.

Conclusion

The Chinese economy is currently experiencing robust growth. In order to sustain this growth and ensure the long-term viability of the economy, integration with the broader global economy is imperative. In addition, to cope with modern business management and funding requirements, the internationalization of accounting standards is becoming more important, as it facilitates the provision of reliable and comparable information to both domestic and overseas investors.

In view of the rapid development of accounting reform in China, the above is only a representation of the latest information available at the time of writing and professional advice should be sought on the latest position before making any business commitments.

Taxation Issues

Kelvin Lee, PricewaterhouseCoopers

Corporate taxation in China

Introduction

This chapter discusses the existing income tax laws that affect foreign companies doing business in China. Since the Chinese taxation system is still in a developmental stage, attention should be paid to the interpretations and practice of the local tax authorities.

Currently, domestic enterprises, foreign enterprises (FEs) and foreign investment enterprises (FIEs) are governed by two different sets of Enterprise Income Tax Legislation. The legislation applies to foreign companies in production or with business operations, or which, although without establishments in China, have income from sources within China.

Establishments refer to management offices; business organizations; representative offices; factories; places where natural resources are exploited; places where contracted projects of construction, installation, assembly and exploration are operated; places where labour services are provided; and business agents.

FIEs are subject to income tax on their world-wide income, whereas the FEs are generally liable to income tax only in respect of their Chinese-sourced income.

Income tax on resident enterprises

Generally, the national income tax on FIEs and FEs with establishments is levied at 30 per cent, while local income tax is 3 per cent on the net taxable profit. FIEs are eligible for various tax holidays, other tax reductions and exemptions under the tax law, depending on their location and nature of operations.

The following are the preferential income tax rates for income derived from production and non-production operations carried on by FIEs and FEs located in various special tax regimes:

- Income from production or non-production businesses obtained by FIEs and FEs with establishments located in Special Economic Zones (SEZs) in Shenzhen, Zhuhai, Shantou, Xiamen and Hainan is subject to tax at 15 per cent.
- Income from production businesses obtained by FIEs located in the designated Economic and Technological Development Zones (ETDZs) is also subject to tax at 15 per cent.
- Income obtained by FIEs located in Coastal Economic Open Zones (CEOZs) and in the old urban districts of cities where the SEZs or ETDZs are located, and engaged in production operations, is subject to tax at 24 per cent.
- Income obtained by FIEs located in CEOZs and in the old urban districts of cities where the SEZs and ETDZs are located and are engaged in the following projects is subject to tax at 15 per cent:
  - technology-intensive or knowledge-intensive projects;
  - projects with a long investment return period with foreign investment of not less than US$30 million; and
  - energy, communications or port development projects.
- Income obtained by FIEs located in Shanghai Pudong New Area and engaged in productive operations, energy and transportation construction projects is subject to tax at 15 per cent.
- Financial institutions such as foreign bank branches and Sino-foreign joint venture banks established in SEZs and other areas approved by the State Council

are subject to tax at 15 per cent if the registered capital from the foreign investor or operating fund transferred from the foreign head office is over US$10 million and the operation period is longer than 10 years. This applies to foreign currency business only. For RMB currency business, the normal income tax rate will continue to apply.

- Enterprises located in certain free trade zones and export processing zones and certain western and central areas may also be subject to a 15 per cent reduced income tax rate.

Tax holidays and incentives

In addition to the preferential tax rates mentioned above, FIEs are entitled to the following tax holidays and incentives:

- Production FIEs scheduled to operate for a period of more than 10 years will be entitled to two years' tax exemption and three years' 50 per cent income tax rate reduction, commencing from the first profit-making year.
- After the expiry of the tax exemption and reduction period, a production FIE exporting 70 per cent or more of the value of its production output in a year may pay income tax at a 50 per cent reduction for that year subject to a minimum rate of 10 per cent.
- After the expiry of the tax exemption and reduction period, a 'technologically advanced FIE' may pay income tax at a 50 per cent reduction for a further three years subject, again, to a minimum rate of 10 per cent. The 'technologically advanced' status requires special certification from the local government.
- FIEs engaged in special projects, such as infrastructure projects with an operation period of 15 years or more, are entitled to five years' tax exemption followed by five years' 50 per cent income tax rate reduction.
- FIEs located in SEZs and engaged in service industries with foreign investment of more than US$5 million and an operation period of more than 10 years, with the approval of the SEZ tax bureau may enjoy one year's tax exemption followed by two years' 50 per cent income tax reduction commencing from the first profit-making year.
- Financial institutions such as foreign bank branches and Sino-foreign joint venture banks established in SEZs and other areas approved by the State Council

with registered capital from the foreign investor or operation fund transferred from the foreign head office of over US$10 million and an operation period of longer than 10 years may enjoy one year's tax exemption followed by two years' 50 per cent tax reduction, commencing from the first profit-making year. This tax holiday does not apply to RMB currency business.

- In order to induce reinvestment of profits by foreign investors, a 40 per cent tax refund is granted to the foreign investor that reinvests its share of distributed profits in the same or a new FIE for a period of more than five years. Profits reinvested by the foreign investor in the same or in a new export-orientated enterprise or technologically advanced enterprise for a period of more than five years may be granted a 100 per cent tax refund.
- On repatriation of after-tax profits, no income tax would be levied. In addition, dividend income received by FIEs in China is also tax exempt, though any relevant loss or expenses incurred are non-deductible.
- For FIEs engaged in encouraged projects that purchase China-made equipment within the total investment or FIEs that purchased China-made equipment beyond the total investment but for the purpose of technological upgrading or for producing high-technology products, 40 per cent of the costs of the domestic equipment can be used as a credit to offset the increment in the enterprise income tax liability in the year of equipment purchase, as compared with that of the previous year.
- If the expenditure on technology development of an FIE increases by 10 per cent or more over that of the previous year, the taxable income of that FIE for the current year will further be offset by 50 per cent of the actual amount of the spending on technology development.
- Newly-established software production enterprises will be eligible for two years of exemption and three years of 50 per cent reduction of Enterprise Income Tax (EIT) from the first year they make profits.
- Key software enterprises that fall within the state's planned arrangement that are not eligible for preferential tax exemption in a given year, will have EIT levied at the reduced rate of 10 per cent.
- FIEs in the central and western areas and under the encouraged category of the Investment Guidelines would enjoy an extension of the normal tax holiday for three years. That is, on top of the normal tax

holiday of two years' exemption and three years' 50 per cent reduction of EIT; the reduced EIT rate of 15 per cent will be applicable for another three years after this five-year normal tax holiday. An extended 15 per cent reduced EIT rate would be available provided that the projects will fall within the key encouraged projects category and satisfy other conditions.

- Separate tax holidays will be available on the increase portion for FIEs engaged in approved projects for the increase of new registered capital of US$60 million or more or increases by US$15 million that represents 50 per cent or more of the registered capital of the original FIE, subject to certain conditions and approval from the relevant tax authorities.

Local income tax

Local income tax is levied at 3 per cent of net taxable profit. Exemption or reduction in local income tax may be granted, at the discretion of the local tax authorities, to FIEs located in SEZs, in the ETDZs and in the old urban districts of cities where an SEZ is located.

Turnover taxes

Effective 1 January 1994, a turnover tax system that consists of value added tax (VAT), consumption tax (CT) and business tax (BT) was introduced by the Chinese authorities. VAT, CT and BT are indirect taxes charged on the gross turnover of businesses and enterprises operating in China.

Under the turnover tax system, FIEs will pay either VAT or BT, depending on the nature of their businesses. VAT is levied on the sales of tangible goods, provision of processing, repairs and replacement services, and the importation of goods within the PRC. The general value added tax rate is 17 per cent on products and imports, and a lower rate of 13 per cent is levied on certain specific products, mostly necessities. Export sales are exempted under VAT rules and an exporter who incurs input VAT on purchase or manufacture of goods should be able to claim a refund from the tax authorities. However, due to a reduction in the VAT export refund rates of some goods, exporters may bear part of the VAT they incurred in connection with the exported goods.

BT is applicable to enterprises in the service, transport and other non-production industries, as well as the transfer of intangible assets or immovable properties. Business tax rates range from 3 per cent to 20 per cent, depending on the category of business concerned.

CT is levied on the production in China of 11 categories of goods, including cigarettes, alcohol, cosmetics, jewellery, gasoline and motor vehicles. Importation of taxable goods is also subject to CT but export is exempt.

Turnover tax paid, except for VAT, is deductible for foreign enterprise income tax purposes, as both business tax and consumption tax are considered as costs to the business or enterprise concerned. VAT, however, is a tax that is borne by the end-user of taxable products and services and would not be deductible for income tax purposes.

The Chinese government has recently introduced the new consumption type of VAT policy in the three north-eastern provinces, namely Heilongjiang, Jilin and Liaoning (including Dalian). Under this new policy, it is feasible for enterprises within eight industries to claim credit for 'input VAT' incurred on the purchase of fixed assets against 'output VAT' realized on sales of their products.

Computation of taxable income for corporate income tax purpose

Capital gains

Gains arising from the disposal of an FIE's assets are generally included as part of the FIE's taxable income. The capital gain is the difference between the book value and the selling price of the asset.

Treatment of dividends received

Dividends received by FEs from any FIEs are exempt, while dividends received by FIEs in China can be regarded as non-taxable income, provided that no deduction claim is made for the relevant investment expenses.

Depreciation of fixed assets

Wear and tear allowances are granted on fixed assets and other capital assets used in the production of income. Except where especially approved, only the straight-line method of depreciation is allowed. In applying the straight-line depreciation method, a residual value of not less than 10 per cent of the original cost should be assumed. Depreciation in fixed assets should be computed starting from the month following that in which the fixed assets are put into use.

The minimum depreciation periods for different classes of fixed assets are as follows:

- premises, buildings and structures – 20 years;
- trains, ships, machinery and other production equipment – 10 years;
- means of transport (except for trains and ships), electronic facilities and equipment and other production-related tools, facilities, furniture etc – five years.

Amortization of intangible assets

Intangible assets should be amortized by the straight-line method over a period of not less than 10 years or the period as stipulated in an agreement relating to the said intangible asset.

Pre-operating expenses are to be amortized over a period of not less than five years.

Bad debts

FIEs engaged in the credit and leasing business may, after approval of the local tax authorities, provide for doubtful debts at not more than 3 per cent of the year-end balances of their loans (not including interbank loans) or of their accounts receivable, bills receivable and other receivables. Such provision is allowed as a deduction for income tax purposes.

Bad debts actually written off by an FIE should be reported to the local tax authorities for examination and confirmation.

Accounts receivable can be written off as bad under the following circumstances:

- bankruptcy of the debtor;
- death of the debtor; or
- the debt has been outstanding for over two years.

Entertainment expenses

Entertainment expenses incurred in relation to the production and business operation of an FIE have to be backed up by reliable records or vouchers, and are deductible within the following limits:

- For FIEs engaging in production and retailing, where the annual net sales are RMB15 million or less, the entertainment expenses allowed as a deduction shall not exceed 0.5 per cent of the net sales; for the portion above RMB15 million, the entertainment expenses allowed as deduction shall not exceed 0.3 per cent of the said portion.
- For FIEs engaging in service businesses, where the annual business income is RMB5 million or less,

the entertainment expenses allowed as deduction shall not exceed 1 per cent of the total business income; for the portion above RMB5 million, the entertainment expenses allowed as deduction shall not exceed 0.5 per cent of the said portion.

Wages, benefits and allowances

Wages, benefits and allowances paid to employees can be listed as expenses, except for foreign social insurance premiums paid for employees working inside China.

Fines

Fines and penalties paid are not allowed as deductible expenses.

Donations

Only donations to approved charitable organizations are allowed as deductible expenses.

Management fees

Management fees paid to related companies are not allowed as deductible expenses.

Loss carry-overs

In determining taxable income, losses incurred by an FIE in previous years may be off-set against future years' profits for a period not exceeding five years.

Other issues

Transactions between related parties

All FIEs are required to conduct revenue and capital transactions between related parties on an arm's length basis. Otherwise, the tax authorities have the right to disregard, vary or make adjustments to certain arrangements that are carried out for the purpose of tax avoidance and not for *bona fide* commercial reasons.

In September 2004, the China tax authorities released a set of procedures for application of an Advance Pricing Arrangement that gives taxpayers an additional tool to manage the uncertainty in related party transactions.

Consolidation of income

An FIE or FE that has two or more business establishments set up in China may elect one establishment for consolidated income tax filing and payment purposes. However, that establishment has to meet the following requirements:

- It shall assume supervisory and management responsibility over the business of other establishments; and

- It shall keep complete accounting records and vouchers that correctly reflect the income, expenses, profits and losses of other business establishments.

Tax periods

The tax year is the Gregorian calendar year starting from 1 January and ending on 31 December.

Currency

Income tax payable shall be computed in RMB. Income in foreign currency shall be converted into RMB according to the exchange rate quoted by the state exchange control authorities for purposes of tax payment.

Foreign tax reliefs

The Chinese taxation system provides for avoidance of double taxation and prevention of evasion for taxes incurred in territories outside China under tax treaties. Tax treaties or arrangements exist with 87 countries and regions, including Japan, the US, the UK, Belgium, France, Singapore, Malaysia, Norway, Denmark, Finland, Sweden, Canada, Thailand, Germany, New Zealand, Italy, Poland, Yugoslavia, Romania, Pakistan, Switzerland, Kuwait, the Netherlands, Korea, Vietnam, Mauritius, Hong Kong, Macao, etc.

Generally, FIEs are allowed to deduct from the amount of tax payable the foreign income tax already paid abroad in respect of the income derived from sources outside China. However, the deductible amount cannot exceed the amount of income tax otherwise payable in China in respect of the income derived from sources outside China.

Income tax on non-resident enterprises

Profit, dividend, interest, rental, royalty, gain from the disposal of buildings and structures and attached facilities located in China and gain from the assignment of land use rights within China and other China-sourced incomes as specified by the Ministry of Finance derived by foreign enterprises with no establishment in China are liable to a withholding tax (WHT) of 20 per cent on the gross income (or amount of gain in the case of disposal of buildings or assignment of land use rights) so derived. Starting from 1 January 2000, the WHT rate on interest, rental, royalty and other income was reduced to 10 per cent by concession. In addition, exemption may be granted under the following circumstances:

- After-tax profits distributed to foreign investors of FIEs are exempt from WHT.
- Interest earned by international lending agencies from loans extended to the Chinese Government and Chinese state banks shall be exempt from WHT.
- Interest earned by foreign banks from loans extended to Chinese state banks at preferential rates shall be exempt from WHT.
- Where the terms are favourable and the technology transferred is advanced, royalty income may be exempted from WHT.

Individual income tax (IIT) on foreign nationals

IIT in China is levied on wages, salaries and other income of foreign nationals, depending on the length of their residence in China and the source of the income.

The Chinese tax year runs from 1 January to 31 December. IIT returns are required to be filed and the corresponding taxes paid on a monthly basis.

A foreign national should pay IIT on income derived from sources within the territory of China. The income chargeable to individual income tax includes the following categories:

- wages and salaries;
- production or business income derived from private industrial or commercial enterprise;
- income from subcontract operations;
- royalties;
- interest, dividends and bonuses from investments;
- property rentals;
- income from transfer of property;
- incidental income; and
- other income specified as taxable by the Ministry of Finance.

Income taxes of foreign nationals and Chinese citizens are governed by one single income tax regime.

Foreign nationals who do not have PRC domicile are generally subject to PRC income tax only on those categories of income that are deemed to be China-sourced, unless the individual resides in China for over five years. For this purpose, residing for one full year is defined as living inside China for 365 days. Leaving China for fewer than 30 days at a time or cumulatively fewer than 90 days in a taxable year shall not be deemed as absence from China for the purpose of determining whether a person has resided in China for one full year.

Foreign nationals will be exempted from tax if their physical presence in the PRC, as calculated under relevant rules, is less than 90 days cumulatively within a calendar year and his/her remuneration is borne by a foreign employer that does not have a permanent establishment in China. This 90-day period is generally extended to 183 days if the individual is a tax resident of a country that has signed a tax treaty with China.

Monthly income from wages and salaries is taxed according to a progressive nine-scale rate, ranging from five per cent to 45 per cent. There is a set allowable deduction on income from wages and salaries of RMB800 per month. Due to cost of living allowance and foreign exchange adjustments, foreign nationals are entitled to an additional monthly deduction of RMB3,200. The monthly deduction amount for Chinese citizens varies from location to location and may be adjusted annually.

A taxpayer who has paid foreign income taxes on income from sources outside China, may apply for a tax credit against Chinese taxes provided that relevant supporting documentation is submitted. If an income tax treaty and domestic tax rules are both applicable to a transaction, then the income tax treaty provision will override the domestic tax rules where the income tax treaty confers more favourable treatment.

If an individual is treated as resident of another country by the tax authorities in that country, he may qualify for a measure of relief or exemption from Chinese tax under the tax treaty between that country and China. Most current agreements lay down various tests to determine in which of the two countries an individual is resident for tax purposes. Most current agreements also contain clauses that exempt a resident of one country from tax on employment income outside China and on employment income inside China if he is present in China for fewer than 183 days in the tax year.

Differences between the PRC Accounting Regulations and International Reporting Standards

Yvonne Kam, PricewaterhouseCoopers

In Chapter 4.1 we covered the current accounting and auditing requirements in China. We also highlighted the development and features of the PRC Accounting Standards and Regulations, which reflect the unique characteristics of the Chinese economy. In this chapter, we will discuss the significance of the International Financial Reporting Standards (IFRS) (formerly known as International Accounting Standards or IAS) and compare IFRS with PRC accounting regulations. IFRS has been chosen as the basis for comparison in this chapter because of its international acceptance and the similarities of its fundamental accounting concepts and principles with accounting standards published by other professional bodies. Therefore, the comparison will give us a picture of the major differences between PRC accounting regulations and other pronouncements, such as the US General Accepted Accounting Principles (GAAP).

IFRS (formerly known as IAS)

Although PRC accounting regulations are now significantly closer to IFRS, there are still differences.

The rapid growth of China's economy continues to attract an influx of foreign investment. Foreign investors, before committing to an investment project, would like to know how the financial statements of the target enterprise would look if the statements were prepared under accounting standards used in their own countries. Prior to the issuance of the Accounting System for Business Enterprises (ASBE) in 2001, and in the absence of a set of well-accepted accounting standards or practice in China, the IFRS played an important role in assisting foreign investors in making their investment decisions.

Our discussion in Chapter 4.1 highlighted that there is now a set of more uniform accounting regulations governing the preparation of financial statements by PRC enterprises and that these accounting regulations are significantly closer to IFRS. However, there are still a number of important areas in the PRC regulations that are not in line with the IFRS. We have summarized the major differences between the PRC accounting standards and the IFRS in Table 4.3.1, using the latest information available at the time of writing. Where necessary, the US GAAP requirements have also been included. While the table serves as an easy reference, we have also described below a few major differences for discussion:

- Fair value is generally not recognized under PRC regulations, due to the lack of open markets and the unavailability of fair values. In addition, financial assets and liabilities that are realizable beyond one year are not discounted to reflect the time value of money.
- Investments designated to be trading or available-for-sales are not carried at fair value but at lower of cost or market. The accounting for derivative instruments and hedge accounting are not addressed.
- The accounting for special purpose entities is not addressed. In addition, the method for accounting for business combinations and the scope of consolidation could be different.
- The PRC regulations provide for the use of deferred taxation on timing differences. However, in practice, the use of deferred tax is not common due to the complexity of implementation.
- Expenses incurred during the pre-operational period are capitalized onto the balance sheet until such time that the company enters into commercial operation.

The expense capitalized so far is expensed in the first month of commercial operation.

- Employer's accounting for post-retirement benefits other than defined contribution plans are not addressed. In addition, the accounting for equity compensation benefits is also not addressed.
- Common control transactions and the use of predecessor cost basis are not addressed.

Pitfalls when relying on audited financial statements of PRC companies

In addition to the GAAP differences identified above, there may be other pitfalls that potential investors should be aware of when reviewing financial statements of targets.

At a glance, it may appear that there are not too many material differences between the PRC accounting regulations and IFRS. However, due to the infancy of the modern accounting framework and system, there may not be an accounting standard to address every transaction. Also, the ability to exercise management judgement based on experience is a relatively new concept in PRC accounting regulations. Consequently, the rigor to which judgement is exercised may be very significant. In addition to the GAAP differences, a list of more common practical issues that foreign investors should be aware of when reviewing financial statements of listed companies or potential targets is listed below:

- Certain transactions may have been recorded based on their legal form rather than their economic substance. The 'substance over legal form' principle may not have been properly observed.
- Uncollectible receivables may not be adequately provided for.

- Trade receivables factored to banks with recourse and their related liabilities may have been improperly derecognized on the balance sheet.
- The net realizable value of inventory may not have been appropriately considered.
- Upon incorporation of the company, certain fixed assets may have been allowed a one-time step up in cost using revalued amounts. These revaluations may not have been performed using acceptable valuation principles internationally.
- Depreciation method (including residual value, estimated useful lives and depreciation method) of fixed assets may not reflect the pattern in which the asset's economic benefits are consumed by the company.
- Assets collateralized may not have been properly disclosed.
- Related party transactions may not have been conducted at arms-length or fully disclosed. Their pricing policies may not reflect the economic substance of the underlying transactions.
- Employee benefit costs, warranties, restructuring and redundancy costs, contingent liabilities or guarantees provided to third parties or related parties may not have been properly provided for or disclosed.
- Other off-balance-sheet items may not have been properly disclosed.

Conclusion

While the differences between the two sets of accounting standards may not appear significant, the infancy of the new accounting system, the rigor of implementation by various companies and the extent of management's capability to exercise fair judgement are practical challenges to surmount. Professional advice should be sought before relying on any published financial information.

Table 4.3.1 Summary of similarities and differences

Subject	IFRS	US GAAP	PRC Accounting Standards and Accounting System for Business Enterprises
Accounting framework			
Historical cost	Uses historical cost, but intangible assets, property plant and equipment (PPE) and investment property may be revalued. Derivatives, biological assets and most securities must be revalued.	No revaluations except for some securities and derivatives at fair value.	Except for certain restructuring of state-owned enterprises, in general, only historical costs are allowed.
Fair presentation override	In extremely rare cases, entities should override the standards where essential to give a fair presentation.	Conceptually similar to IFRS, but not used in practice.	Silent on 'fair presentation override'. In practice, accounting standards are regulations and are legally enforceable. Therefore, they are not to be overridden.
First-time adoption of accounting frameworks	Requires full retrospective application of all IFRSs effective at the reporting date for an entity's first IFRS financial statements, with some optional exemptions and limited mandatory exceptions.	First-time adoption of US GAAP requires retrospective application. In addition, particular standards specify treatment for first-time adoption of those standards.	First-time adoption of PRC accounting regulations requires retrospective application of all accounting regulations in effect.
Financial statements			
Components of financial statements	Two years' balance sheets, income statements, cash flow statements, changes in equity and accounting policies and notes.	Similar to IFRS, except three years required for public companies for all statements except balance sheet.	Two years' balance sheets, income and profit distribution statements, accounting policies and notes. Comparative cash flow statement not required except for interim reporting.
Balance sheet	Does not prescribe a particular format; an entity uses a liquidity presentation of assets and liabilities, instead of a current/non-current presentation, only when a liquidity presentation provides more relevant and reliable information. Certain items must be presented on the face of the balance sheet.	Entities may present either a classified or non-classified balance sheet. Items presented on the face of the balance sheet are generally presented in decreasing order of liquidity. Public companies must follow SEC guidelines regarding minimum disclosure requirements.	Balance sheets have prescribed formats and a current and non-current presentation is used.
Income statement format	Does not prescribe a standard format, although expenditure must be presented in one of two formats (function or nature). Certain items must be presented on the face of the income statement.	Present as either a single-step or multiple-step format. Expenditures must be presented by function.	Income statements have prescribed formats and expenditures must be presented by function.

Table 4.3.1 (Contd)

Subject	IFRS	US GAAP	PRC Accounting Standards and Accounting System for Business Enterprises
Exceptional items	Does not use the term, but requires separate disclosure of items that are of such size, incidence or nature that require separate disclosure to explain the performance of the entity.	Similar to IFRS, but individually significant items should be presented on the face of the income statement.	'Non-routine items', which is a specifically defined term, is used to calculate 'net profit excluding non-routine items', which is a note disclosure item and related EPS.
Extraordinary items	Prohibited.	Defined as being both infrequent and unusual, and are rare. Negative goodwill is presented as an extraordinary item.	Not used.
Statement of recognized gains and losses/other comprehensive income	Present the statement of recognized gains and losses either in notes or separately highlighted in primary statement of changes in shareholder equity.	Disclose total comprehensive income and accumulated other comprehensive income, either as a separate primary statement or combined with income statement, or with statement of changes in stockholders' equity.	Not used.
Statement of changes in shareholders' equity	Statement showing capital transactions with owners, the movement in accumulated profit and a reconciliation of all other components of equity. The statement must be presented as a primary statement.	Similar to IFRS. Securities and Exchange Commission (SEC) rules allow such information to be included in the notes.	The information is not presented as a primary statement but can be presented in the notes.
Cash flow statements – format and method	Standard headings, but limited flexibility of contents. Use direct or indirect method.	Similar headings to IFRS, but more specific guidance given for items included in each category. Use direct or indirect method.	Similar headings to IFRS, direct method together with a supporting note reconciling operating result to cash flows arising from operations must be presented.
Cash flow statements – definition of cash and cash equivalents	Cash includes overdrafts and cash equivalents with short-term maturities (less than three months).	Cash excludes overdrafts but includes cash equivalents with short-term maturities.	Cash equivalents include short-term highly liquid investments that are readily convertible to known amounts of cash and which are subject to an insignificant risk of changes in value. Time deposits are normally excluded from cash. Overdrafts not mentioned.
Cash flow statements – exemptions	No exemptions.	Limited exemptions for certain investment entities.	Similar to IFRS.

Table 4.3.1 (Contd)

Subject	IFRS	US GAAP	PRC Accounting Standards and Accounting System for Business Enterprises
Changes in accounting policies	Restate comparatives and prior-year opening retained earnings.	Generally include effect in current year income statement. Disclose pro-forma comparatives. Retrospective adjustments for specific items.	Similar to IFRS.
Correction of errors	Restate comparatives.	Similar to IFRS.	Similar to IFRS.
Changes in accounting estimates	Reported in income statement in the current period.	Similar to IFRS.	Similar to IFRS.

Consolidated financial statements

Subject	IFRS	US GAAP	PRC Accounting Standards and Accounting System for Business Enterprises
Preparation of consolidated financial statements	Consolidated financial statements should be prepared for entities with subsidiaries and special purposes entities (SPEs).	Similar to IFRS. In addition, those entities with variable interest entities (VIEs) should also prepare consolidated financial statements.	Only the following companies are required to prepare consolidated financial statements: • state-owned enterprises that have entrusted a third-party to be managed; • companies offering shares to the public; • companies engaging in import/export trade that must prepare consolidated financial statements; • other enterprises that are required to provide consolidated financial statements to third parties.
Definition of subsidiary	Based on voting control or power to govern. The existence of currently exercisable potential voting rights is also taken into consideration.	Controlling interest through majority ownership of voting shares or by contract. Also, VIEs in which a parent does not have voting control but absorbs the majority of losses or returns must be consolidated.	Based on voting control or power to govern. However, whether the existence of currently exercisable potential voting right would impact control is not addressed. In addition, control is presumed to exist when more than 50 per cent of the investee's voting right is held.
Special purposes entities (SPEs)	Consolidate where the substance of the relationship indicates control.	SPEs must be consolidated if consolidation requirements for VIEs are met. To avoid consolidation, the SPE must be a qualifying SPE.	Not addressed.

Table 4.3.1 (Contd)

Subject	IFRS	US GAAP	PRC Accounting Standards and Accounting System for Business Enterprises
Non-consolidation of subsidiaries	Dissimilar activities or temporary control are not a justification for non-consolidation.	Only if control does not rest with the majority owner and the owner is not the primary beneficiary of a VIE.	Subsidiaries that are insignificant (defined as less than 10 per cent in the aggregate in total assets, revenue and net profit or loss) need not be consolidated. Also, if the subsidiary is operating under severe long-term restrictions to remit cash to the parent, if the subsidiary is intended for sale or if the subsidiary is not of going concern assumption due to negative equity, they may be also be excluded from consolidation.
Definition of associate	Based on significant influence: presumed if 20 per cent interest or participation in entity's affairs.	Similar to IFRS.	Similar to IFRS.
Inter-company profit and loss	Unless costs cannot be recovered, all intragroup balances and transactions with subsidiaries are eliminated. All transactions with associates and joint ventures are not eliminated but any profits arising from intragroup transactions that are included in inventory or fixed assets should be eliminated to the extent of the entity's interest in the associate.	Similar to IFRS.	Only balances and transactions including the range of consolidation between the parent and its consolidated subsidiaries (excluding non-consolidated subsidiaries and associates) must be eliminated in full. There is no specific rule to eliminate unrealized profit in assets obtained from associates.
Presentation of associate results	Use equity method. Show share of post-tax result.	Similar to IFRS.	Similar to IFRS and is presented as part of investment income on the income statement.
Disclosures about significant associates	Give detailed information on significant associates' assets, liabilities, revenue and results.	Similar to IFRS.	Similar to IFRS except that the information should be presented for all associates.
Presentation of joint ventures	Both proportionate consolidation and equity method permitted.	Equity method is required except in specific circumstances.	Only proportionate consolidation permitted.

Table 4.3.1 (Contd)

Subject	IFRS	US GAAP	PRC Accounting Standards and Accounting System for Business Enterprises
Business combinations			
Types	All business combinations are acquisitions	Similar to IFRS.	No effective rules defining whether the uniting of interest (or pooling) method is prohibited or not. In practice, most business combinations are accounted for as acquisitions.
Purchase method – fair values on acquisition	Fair value the assets, liabilities and contingent liabilities of acquired entity. Only recognize liabilities for restructuring activities when the acquiree has at acquisition date an existing liability. Prohibited from recognizing liabilities for further losses or other costs expected to be incurred as a result of the business combinations.	Similar to IFRS, but specific rules for acquired in-process research and development (generally expensed) and contingent liabilities. Some restructuring liabilities relating solely to the acquired entity may be recognized in fair value exercise if specific criteria about restructuring plans are met.	Similar to IFRS only when the acquiree ceases to continue as a legal person or if 100 per cent of equity is acquired. Existing regulations do not address restructuring provisions in detail.
Purchase method – contingent consideration	Include in cost of combination at acquisition date if adjustment is probable and can be measured reliably.	Not recognized until the contingency is resolved or the amount is determinable.	Not addressed.
Purchase method – minority interests at acquisition	State at minority's proportion of the net fair value of acquired identifiable assets and liabilities.	Generally state at share of pre-acquisition carrying value of net assets.	The use of the economic entity approach vs. the parent company approach is not addressed. Only when the acquiree ceases to continue as a legal person or if 100 per cent equity is purchased would the assets and liabilities be fair valued.
Purchase method – goodwill and intangible assets with indefinite useful lives	Capitalize but do not amortize. Goodwill and indefinite-lived intangible assets should be reviewed for impairment at least annually at the cash generating unit level.	Similar to IFRS however impairment measurement model is different.	Goodwill and intangible assets are presumed to have finite lives and should be amortized over their investment period, if specified, and if not, a period not more than 10 years. Assessment for impairment should be performed periodically.

Table 4.3.1 (Contd)

Subject	IFRS	US GAAP	PRC Accounting Standards and Accounting System for Business Enterprises
Purchase method – subsequent adjustments to fair values	Fair values can be adjusted against goodwill within 12 months of the acquisition date. Record subsequent adjustments in income statement unless they are to correct an error.	Similar to IFRS. Once the fair value allocation is finalized, no further changes are permitted except for the resolution of known pre-acquisition contingencies. Adjustments made during the allocation period relating to data for which management was waiting to complete the allocation are recorded against goodwill.	Not addressed.
Purchase method – negative goodwill	Requires reassessment by acquirer of the identification and measurement of acquiree's identifiable assets, liabilities and contingent liabilities. Any excess remaining after that reassessment is recognized in income statement immediately.	Reduce proportionately the fair values assigned to non-current assets (with certain exceptions). Any excess is recognized in the income statement immediately as an extraordinary gain.	If the acquiree ceases to be a legal person and the cost of the acquisition is less than the fair value of identifiable assets and liabilities, the difference is amortized over a specified period. If the acquiree continues to exist as a legal person and the cost of the acquisition is less than the book value of the acquiree's assets and liabilities, the difference is recorded as 'capital surplus' immediately.
Purchase method – disclosure	Disclosures include names and descriptions of combining entities, date of acquisition, cost of combination, summary of fair values and pre-acquisition IFRS values of assets and liabilities acquired, and impact on results and financial position of acquirer.	Similar to IFRS, plus additional disclosures regarding the reasons for the acquisition, and details of allocations.	Similar to IFRS.
Uniting of interests method	Prohibited	Similar to IFRS.	No effective rules defining whether the uniting of interest (or pooling) method is prohibited or not. In practice, most business combinations are accounted for as acquisitions.

Revenue recognition

Revenue recognition	Based on several criteria, which require the recognition of revenue when risks and rewards have been transferred and the revenue can be measured reliably.	Four key criteria. In principle, similar to IFRS. Extensive detailed guidance exists for specific transactions.	Similar to IFRS.

Table 4.3.1 (Contd)

Subject	IFRS	US GAAP	PRC Accounting Standards and Accounting System for Business Enterprises
Construction contracts	Accounted for using the percentage of completion method. Completed contract method prohibited.	Percentage of completion method is preferable; however, completed contract method permitted in rare circumstances.	Similar to IFRS.
Expense recognition			
Interest expense	Interest expense recognized on an accrual basis. Effective yield method used to amortize non-cash finance charges.	Similar to IFRS.	Similar to IFRS except that the use of the effective yield method is not explicitly mentioned.
Employee benefits – pension costs – defined benefit plans	Must use projected unit credit method to determine benefit obligation.	Similar to IFRS conceptually, although several differences in detail.	Not addressed.
Employee share compensation	Recognize expense for services acquired. The corresponding amount will be recorded either as a liability or as an increase in equity, depending on whether the transaction is determined to be cash – or equity – settled. The amount to be recorded is measured at the fair value of the shares or share options *granted*.	Two alternative methods for determining cost: intrinsic value (market price at measurement date less any employee contribution or exercise price) or fair value at issue using option pricing model. Recognize cost of share awards or options over period of employee's performance.	Not addressed.
Employee benefits – other	Account for post-retirement benefits as pensions. Rules also given for termination benefits arising from redundancies and other post-employment and long-term employee benefits. Account for termination indemnity plans as pensions.	Similar to IFRS for post-retirement benefits. More detailed guidance given for termination benefits. Termination indemnity accounted for as pension plans and calculated as either the vested benefit obligation or the actuarial present value of the vested benefits.	Not addressed.
Assets			
Acquired intangible assets	Capitalize if recognition criteria are met; intangible assets must be amortized over useful life. Intangibles assigned an indefinite useful life must not be amortized but reviewed annually for impairment. Revaluations are permitted in rare circumstances.	Similar to IFRS. Revaluations are not permitted.	Capitalize if recognition criteria are met. Intangible assets are presumed to have finite lives and should be amortized over their expected useful lives, if specified, and if not, a period not more than 10 years. Periodic review for impairment is required.

Table 4.3.1   (Contd)

Subject	IFRS	US GAAP	PRC Accounting Standards and Accounting System for Business Enterprises
Internally generated intangible assets	Expense research costs as incurred. Capitalize and amortize development costs only if stringent criteria are met.	Expense both research and development costs as incurred. Some software and website development costs must be capitalized.	All research and development costs should be expensed as incurred.
Pre-operating costs	Expense as incurred.	Similar to IFRS.	All expenditures incurred prior to an enterprise entering into commercial operations are capitalized as 'pre-operating costs' and are expensed in the month when the enterprise enters commercial operation.
Property, plant and equipment	Use historical cost or revalued amounts. Frequent valuations of entire classes of assets are required when revaluation option is chosen.	Revaluations not permitted.	Revaluations not permitted.
Non-current assets held for sale	Non-current asset is classified as held for sale if its carrying amount will be recovered principally through a sale transaction rather than through continuing use. Measure a non-current asset classified as held for sale at the lower of its carrying amount and fair value less costs to sell.	Similar to IFRS.	Not addressed.
Leases – classification	It is a finance lease if substantially all risks and rewards of ownership are transferred. Substance rather than form is important.	Similar to IFRS, but considerably more extensive form-driven requirements.	Similar to IFRS.
Leases – lessor accounting	Record amounts due under finance leases as a receivable. Allocate gross earnings to give constant rate of return based on (pre-tax) net investment method.	Similar to IFRS, but specific rules for leveraged leases.	The effective interest method should be used. Other methods including the straight-line and the sum-of-the-digit methods may be used if the result is not significantly different from the effective interest method.

Table 4.3.1 (Contd)

Subject	IFRS	US GAAP	PRC Accounting Standards and Accounting System for Business Enterprises
Impairment of assets	If impairment indicated, write down assets to higher of fair value less costs to sell and value in use based on discounted cash flows. If no loss arises, reconsider useful lives of those assets. Reversals of losses permitted in certain circumstances.	For assets to be held and used, impairment is assessed on undiscounted cash flows. If less than carrying amount, measure impairment loss using market value or discounted cash flows. Reversals of losses prohibited. For assets held for disposal, impairment is based on lower of carrying amount and fair value less cost to sell.	Similar to IFRS. However, detailed guidance on calculation of value in use not yet issued.
Capitalization of borrowing costs	Permitted, but not required, for qualifying assets.	Required.	Required. However, only borrowing costs on project-specific borrowings should be capitalized as part of the cost of acquiring or constructing a tangible fixed asset.
Investment property	Measure at depreciated cost or fair value and recognize changes in fair value in the income statement.	Treat the same as for other properties (depreciated cost).	Not addressed. All properties, regardless of intention, are carried at cost less accumulated depreciation and impairment.
Inventories	Carry at lower of cost and net realizable value. Use FIFO or weighted average method to determine cost. LIFO prohibited. Reversal is required for subsequent increase in value of previous write-downs.	Similar to IFRS; however, use of LIFO permitted. Reversal of write-down is prohibited.	Similar to IFRS; however, use of LIFO permitted. Reversal is required for subsequent increase in value of previous write-downs.
Biological assets	Measured at fair value less estimated point-of-sale costs.	Not specified. Generally historical cost used.	Not addressed.

Table 4.3.1 (Contd)

Subject	IFRS	US GAAP	PRC Accounting Standards and Accounting System for Business Enterprises
Financial assets – measurement	Depends on classification of investment – if held to maturity or loan or receivable, then carry at amortized cost, otherwise at fair value. Unrealized gains/losses on fair value through profit or loss classification (including trading securities) recognized in the income statement and on available-for-sale investments recognized in equity.	Similar to IFRS. However, no ability to designate any financial asset or liability as at fair value through profit or loss.	Financial assets can generally be segregated into receivables and loans originated by the entity, short-term and long-term investments. Receivables and loans originated by the entity are carried at the lower of cost or recoverable amounts. It is generally not discounted to take into account the time value of money. Short-term investments are carried at the lower of cost or market. Long-term investments are carried at amortized costs less impairment. All changes in value are included in the profit and loss.
Derecognition of financial assets	Derecognize financial assets based on risks and rewards first; control is secondary test.	Derecognize based on control and requires legal isolation of assets even in bankruptcy.	On factoring of receivables, they are derecognized based on transfer of risks and rewards. On long-term investment, they are derecognized based on transfer of risks and rewards and cessation of control.
Liabilities			
Provisions – general	Record the provisions relating to present obligations from past events if outflow of resources is probable and can be reliably estimated.	Similar to IFRS, with rules for specific situations (employee termination costs, environmental liabilities, loss contingencies, etc).	Similar to IFRS except with the lack of specific rules governing employee benefit costs and restructuring costs associated with business combinations; generally, these costs are recognized on a pay-as-you-go basis.

Table 4.3.1   (Contd)

Subject	IFRS	US GAAP	PRC Accounting Standards and Accounting System for Business Enterprises
Provisions – restructuring	Recognize restructuring provisions if detailed formal plan announced or implementation effectively begun.	Recognition of a liability based solely on commitment to a plan is prohibited. Must meet the definition of a liability, including certain criteria regarding the likelihood that no changes will be made to the plan or that the plan will be withdrawn.	Broadly in line with the principles of IFRS but not addressed in detail.
Contingencies	Disclose unrecognized possible losses and probable gains.	Similar to IFRS.	Similar to IFRS. .
Deferred income taxes – general approach	Use full provision method (some exceptions) driven by balance sheet temporary differences. Recognize deferred tax assets if recovery is probable.	Similar to IFRS, but recognize all deferred tax assets and then provide valuation allowance if recovery is less than 50 per cent likely. A number of specific differences in application.	May choose tax payable method or tax effect accounting method. If the tax effect accounting method is used, either the deferral method or the liability method may be selected. Deferred taxation is calculated based on timing differences, rather than temporary differences.
Deferred income taxes – main exceptions	Non-deductible goodwill and temporary differences on initial recognition of assets and liabilities that do not impact on accounting or taxable profit.	Similar to IFRS regarding non-deductible goodwill. Initial recognition exemption does not exist.	Deferred taxation is calculated based on timing differences. If the deferred tax asset is not expected to be utilized within three years, it is generally not recognized.
Government grants	Recognize as deferred income and amortize. Entities may offset capital grants against asset values.	Similar to IFRS except long-lived asset contributions recorded as revenue.	In general, recognized as income upon receipt.
Leases – lessee accounting	Record finance leases as asset and obligation for future rentals. Normally depreciate over useful life of asset. Apportion rental payments to give constant interest rate on outstanding obligation. Generally charge operating lease rentals on straight-line basis.	Similar to IFRS. Specific rules must be met to record a finance or capital lease.	The asset is to be recognized at the lower of the present value of future minimum lease payments and the original carrying amount of the lessor. In addition, it may also be measured at the undiscounted amount of minimum lease payments if that undiscounted amount is not more than 30 per cent of total assets.

Table 4.3.1 (Contd)

Subject	IFRS	US GAAP	PRC Accounting Standards and Accounting System for Business Enterprises
Leases – lessee accounting – sale and leaseback transactions	For a finance lease, defer and amortize profit arising on sale and finance leaseback. If an operating lease arises then profit recognition depends on sale proceeds compared to fair value of the asset. Also need to consider substance/linkage of the transactions.	Timing of profit and loss recognition depends on whether seller relinquishes substantially all or a minor part of the use of the asset. Immediately recognize losses. Consider specific strict criteria if a property transaction.	For finance lease, defer and amortize profit arising on sale as an adjustment to depreciation. For an operating lease, defer and amortize profit on sale according to the proportion of the lease payments during the lease.
Financial liabilities – classification	Classify capital instruments depending on substance of the issuer's obligations. Mandatorily redeemable preference shares are classified as liabilities.	Generally where an instrument is not a share, classify as liability when obligation to transfer economic benefit exists. Similar to IFRS.	Generally where an instrument is not a share, classify as liability when obligation to transfer economic benefit exists. Financial liabilities existing beyond one year are not discounted. Accounting for redeemable preference shares not addressed.
Convertible debt	Account for convertible debt on split basis, allocating proceeds between equity and debt.	Convertible debt is usually recognized as a liability.	Similar to US GAAP.
Derecognition of financial liabilities	Derecognize liabilities when extinguished. The difference between the carrying amount and the amount paid is recognized in the income statement.	Similar to IFRS.	Similar to IFRS.

Equity instruments

Subject	IFRS	US GAAP	PRC Accounting Standards and Accounting System for Business Enterprises
Capital instruments – purchase of own shares	Show as deduction from equity.	Similar to IFRS.	Not addressed since PRC entities are not allowed to buy back their own shares.

Table 4.3.1 (Contd)

Subject	IFRS	US GAAP	PRC Accounting Standards and Accounting System for Business Enterprises
Derivatives and hedging			
Derivatives and other financial instruments – measurement of financial instruments and hedging activities	Measure derivatives and hedge instruments at fair value; recognize changes in fair value in income statement except for effective cash flow hedges, where the changes are deferred in equity until effect of the underlying transaction is recognized in the income statement. Gains/losses from hedge instruments that are used to hedge forecast transaction may be included in cost of non-financial asset/liability (basis adjustment).	Similar to IFRS, except no 'basis adjustment' on cash flow hedges of forecast transactions.	Not addressed.
Derivatives and other financial instruments – measurement of hedges of foreign entity investments	Gains/losses on hedges of foreign entity investments are recognized in equity, including hedge ineffectiveness on non-derivatives. For derivatives, record hedge ineffectiveness in the income statement. Gains/losses held in equity must be transferred to the income statement on disposal of investment.	Similar to IFRS, except all hedge ineffectiveness is recognized in the income statement.	Not addressed.
Other accounting and reporting topics			
Functional currency definition	Currency of the primary economic environment in which an entity operates.	Similar to IFRS.	Not defined.
Functional currency – determination	If the indicators are mixed and the functional currency is not obvious, management should use its judgement to determine the functional currency that most faithfully represents the economic results of the entity's operations by focusing on the currency of the economy that determines the pricing of transactions (not the currency in which transactions are denominated).	Similar to IFRS. However no specific hierarchy of factors to consider. Generally the currency in which the majority of revenues and expenses are settled.	In general, recorded using the RMB.

Table 4.3.1 (Contd)

Subject	IFRS	US GAAP	PRC Accounting Standards and Accounting System for Business Enterprises
Presentation currency	When financial statements are presented in a currency other than the functional currency, assets and liabilities are translated at the exchange rate at the balance sheet date. Income statement items are translated at the exchange rate at the dates of the transaction or use average rates if the rates do not fluctuate significantly.	Similar to IFRS.	Similar to IFRS. In addition to using the exchange rate at the dates of the transaction or the average rates to translate the income statement, the exchange rate at the balance sheet date may also be used.
Hyperinflationary economy – definition	Hyperinflation is indicated by characteristics of the economic environment of a country, which include the general population's attitude towards the local currency, prices linked to a price index; and the cumulative inflation rate over three years is approaching, or exceeds, 100 per cent.	A currency in a highly inflationary environment (three-year inflation rate of approximately 100 per cent or more).	Not addressed.
Hyperinflationary economy – measurement	It requires entities that have, as functional currency, the currency of a hyperinflationary economy to use it for measuring their transactions. However it requires re-measurement of the measurement unit at the balance sheet date.	Generally does not permit inflation-adjusted financial statements; instead requires the use of a more stable currency as the functional currency (usually the presentation currency). However SEC rules allow foreign issuers that use IFRS to omit quantification of any differences that would have resulted from the application of FAS 52.	Not addressed.
Earnings per share – diluted	Use weighted average potential dilutive shares as denominator for diluted EPS. Use 'treasury stock' method for share options/warrants.	Similar to IFRS.	Not addressed. Existing regulations only address calculation of basic EPS.
Related party transactions – definition	Determine by level of direct or indirect control, joint control and significant influence of one party over another or common control of both parties.	Similar to IFRS.	Similar to IFRS and, in addition, certain determination criteria are provided.

Table 4.3.1   (Contd)

Subject	IFRS	US GAAP	PRC Accounting Standards and Accounting System for Business Enterprises
Related party transactions – disclosures	Disclose name of related party and nature of relationship and types of transaction. For control relationships, give disclosures regardless of whether transactions occur. Some exemptions available for separate financial statements of subsidiaries.	Similar to IFRS. Exemptions are narrower than under IFRS.	The disclosure of control relationship is more stringent than IFRS. Detailed disclosures concerning the corporate identity of related parties are required. Accounting regulations further require disclosure of pricing policy of any related party transactions. State-owned enterprises are not regarded as related parties simply because they are controlled by the state.
Segment reporting – scope and basis of formats	Public entities: report primary and secondary (business and geographic) segments based on risks and returns and internal reporting structure.	Public entities: report based on operating segments and the way the chief operating decision-maker evaluates financial information for purposes of allocating resources and assessing performance.	Public entities: limited reporting on profit and loss by geographical and industry segments.
Segment reporting – accounting policies	Use group accounting policies.	Use internal financial reporting policies (even if accounting policies differ from group accounting policy).	Not addressed.
Segment reporting – disclosures	Disclosures for primary segment include revenues, results, capital expenditures, total assets and liabilities, and other items. For secondary segment, report revenues, total assets and capital expenditures.	Similar disclosures to IFRS (primary segment) except liabilities and geographical capital expenditures not required. Depreciation, amortization, tax, interest and exceptional/ extraordinary items disclosed if reported internally. Disclosure of factors used to identify segments is required.	Public entities: limited reporting on profit and loss by geographical and industry segments.
Discontinued operations – definition	Operations and cash flows that can be clearly distinguished for financial reporting and represent a separate major line of business or geographical area of operations, or is a subsidiary acquired exclusively with a view to resale.	Similar to IFRS. Component that is clearly distinguishable operationally and for financial reporting: reporting segment, operating segment, reporting unit, subsidiary or asset grouping.	Not addressed.

Table 4.3.1 (Contd)

Subject	IFRS	US GAAP	PRC Accounting Standards and Accounting System for Business Enterprises
Discontinued operations – measurement	Measured at the lower of carrying amount or fair value less costs to sell.	Similar to IFRS.	Not addressed.
Discontinued operations – presentation and main disclosures	Disclose at a minimum a single amount on the face of the income statement with analysis further disclosed in the notes for both current and prior periods. Assets and liabilities of a discontinued operation shall be presented separately from other assets and liabilities on the balance sheet.	Similar to IFRS. Report discontinued and held-for-sale operations as a separate line item on face of the income statement before extraordinary items and cumulative effect of accounting changes. Assets and liabilities of held-for-sale disposal groups segregated on balance sheet.	Not addressed.
Post-balance sheet events	Adjust financial statements for subsequent events, providing evidence of conditions at balance sheet date and materially affecting amounts in financial statements (adjusting events). Disclose non-adjusting events.	Similar to IFRS.	Similar to IFRS. The accounting treatment for post-balance sheet refinancing and waiver of breach of loan covenants are not specifically addressed but, in practice, are treated as adjusting events.
Interim financial reporting	Not mandatory to prepare interim statements but must use the standard if do prepare. Basis should be consistent with full-year statements and include comparatives.	If issued, the contents of interim statements are prescribed and the basis must be consistent with full-year statements. Quarterly reporting is required for SEC registrants (domestic US entities only).	Similar to IFRS. Interim reporting is mandatory for listed company only.
Insurance and reinsurance contracts – definition	Provides definition of insurance and reinsurance contracts.	Similar definition of insurance contract as IFRS but with stricter criteria for reinsurance.	Not addressed.

Table 4.3.1 (Contd)

Subject	IFRS	US GAAP	PRC Accounting Standards and Accounting System for Business Enterprises
Discretionary Participation Feature (DPF)	Provides a definition of a DPF and introduces certain requirements for financial instruments that contain such feature. Insurance contracts or financial instruments with DPF may have a compound nature and present an equity component. Consideration received for financial instruments with DPF may be recognized as revenue with an expense representing the increase in the liability.	DPF is not specifically covered in US GAAP other than implicitly in SOP 95–1 for insurance contracts only. Insurance contracts and financial instruments with DPF are measured under the existing GAAP and the resulting equity component is not separately disclosed. Financial instruments with DPF are always deposit accounted.	Not addressed.
Insurance and reinsurance contract – measurement	Subject to a few minimum requirements. The most important requirements are the tests on insurance liability adequacy and reinsurance asset impairment. Equalization and similar provisions are prohibited.	US GAAP has detailed measurement bases for the different types of insurance and reinsurance contracts. US GAAP also prescribes liability adequacy test, reinsurance impairment test and prohibits equalization provisions.	Not addressed.
Insurance and reinsurance contracts – deposit accounting and unbundling of deposit components	Deposit accounting is required when the measurement of the deposit component is reliable and the rights and obligations arising from it are not reflected in the balance sheet. Unbundling is permitted if the deposit is reliably measurable. If unbundling is not required, deposit components may be recognized as revenue.	Deposit accounting is covered by EITF 93–6 for a component of a contract. Reinsurance contracts that transfer only timing risk or only underwriting risk are deposit accounted. The concept of policyholders' account balance has been developed and detailed rules require deposit accounting (under FAS 97).	Not addressed.
Insurance and reinsurance contracts – embedded derivatives	Exemptions from separation and fair value are given for certain embedded derivatives. Persistency bonuses are considered embedded derivatives.	Embedded derivatives must be separated and fair valued unless they are clearly and closely related. Fixed dollar persistency bonuses are not embedded derivatives but rather a variation of interest rates.	Not addressed.

Table 4.3.1 (Contd)

Subject	IFRS	US GAAP	*PRC Accounting Standards and Accounting System for Business Enterprises*
Insurance and reinsurance contracts – disclosures	Extensive disclosure requirements focused on the accounting policies adopted, material amounts reported and factors that affect the uncertainty of the amounts and timing of insurance and reinsurance cash flows. Claims development tables are a required disclosure.	Disclosure requirements are less demanding. However, a number of disclosure items are covered in the MD&A and other non-audited sections of the annual report. Claims development tables are disclosed outside the financial statements.	Not addressed.
Separate accounts	No provision in IFRS giving guidance on assets or obligations in separate accounts presentation in the balance sheet and income statement.	FAS 60 and SOP 03–1 allow single line presentation in the balance sheet and offsetting of investment results with changes in policyholder liabilities in the income statement.	Not addressed.
Insurance contracts sold by an insurer to its owned defined benefit plan	Insurance contracts sold by an insurer to its own defined benefit plan are eliminated and not treated as plan assets in pension obligation accounting.	US GAAP has no specific guidance; however, practice is to treat such contracts as plan asset under FAS 87.	Not addressed.

Part Five

Market Entry and Business Development in China

Revisiting Chinese Cultural Roots

Liu Baocheng, Professor, University of International Business and Economics

China's foreign trade totalled US$509.77 billion in 2001. By the end of June 2002, total foreign investment in China amounted to US$419.8 billion, with investment from over 180 countries and regions. Nearly four-fifths of the top multinational companies have set up their subsidiaries here. As the frequency of business communication with China grows, cultural differences and clashes present some significant challenges. One must remain constantly alert, not only to different business behaviours, but also to their underlying values and their history, in order to prevent unnecessary mishaps.

Cultural traits

Effective cross-cultural communication requires knowledge, attitude and tactics. Chinese people eat with chopsticks; they always have good excuses for you to drink more at the dinner table; they are reluctant to say no even if a proposal is unacceptable; and so on. To present a long list of the differences in Chinese behaviour, one does not need to know an overwhelming amount about China. However, to understand and cope with these differences, it is necessary to go beyond this superficial level. As a matter of fact, behaviour is only the tip of the iceberg. Behind differences in behaviour lies attitude – attitudes towards oneself, time, the environment and the people around them. What is more profound and deeply embedded are different beliefs and values that are shaped by experience, history, tradition, family and society.

Table 5.1.1 is a broad summary of contrasting cultural traits between Chinese and westerners in terms of different business methods. While considering the diversity and ongoing changes in the cultures under discussion, the author does not attempt to avoid charges of stereotyping.

Cultural roots

Chinese people on the whole are not fervent adherents to any religion. Most have a practical mindset and are

Table 5.1.1   Summary of different cultural traits in Chinese and western business methods

Cultural trait	Chinese	Western
Religion	Basically atheist	Basically Christian
Business relations	Highly interpersonal	'Business is business'
Planning	Incremental	Objective driven
Decision-making	Collective	Individualistic
Negotiation style	Friendly	Aggressive
Expression	Contextual	Explicit
Communication	Infrequent	Frequent
Organizational structure	Hierarchical	Horizontal
Logical reasoning	Deductive	Inductive

more concerned with earthly happiness than any spiritual quest. However, with the long history of reverence for a supernatural power derived from early Chinese civilization, superstition and animism are still occasionally present and can cause social waves. A bewildering array and variety of gods – native, foreign, heroic and primitive – can be found in Chinese shrines. The Chinese have long been tolerant of all religions and customs, and religious wars and persecutions are rare in Chinese history.

Though officially atheist, Chinese people have been strongly influenced by two prominent schools of thought – Taoism and Confucianism – and by the religion of Buddhism. Taoism and Confucianism, particularly the latter, are more philosophical schools of thought than religions, and are devoted to social teachings. Buddhism and Islam are formal religions. The former is widespread across the country, whereas the latter is practised mostly in the north-western regions of the country.

As an officially atheist country, social customs are viewed more as part of the culture than as rigid rules of conduct and behaviour. The Chinese are known for their benevolence and tolerance. There are few taboos, and sensitive topics and 'deviant' behaviour by foreigners are generally tolerated, provided they are free from ill-intention. They are generally considerate when dealing with foreigners – there is a Chinese saying that 'ignorance is excusable'.

The influence of Taoism

Taoists believe that the world is constituted by the interplay of two interacting forces, *Yin* and *Yang*. The word *Tao* means 'the way' or 'the path'. Every object in the universe represents the process and outcome of interplay between these two forces, one passive, the other positive. These seemingly opposite forces can coexist, although one may prevail over the other at times. Moreover, even within *Yin*, there contains *Yang*, and vice versa. The state of *Yin* may, over time, shift to *Yang*.

Thanks to the Taoist influence, Chinese people are highly dialectical in their judgements. Expressions such as 'on the one hand... but on the other hand...' or 'yes... but...' are part of their daily language. For example, if goods are returned because of inferior quality, it is not surprising to hear a manager remark that 'this is a good thing, on the other hand, because it helps us to dig deep to the root cause of the problem'. Balance, coexistence and harmony with people, time

and environment, both within and outside oneself, are considered to be essential constituents of a good quality of life.

For some Chinese, the practice of *feng shui* (literally 'wind and water', which represent harmony with the physical environment) is popular when selecting building sites and arranging offices. Chinese people tend to be less enthusiastic to take initiative, be different or be confrontational. Drafting the contract or formulating the minutes of meetings is very likely to be the job of the foreign party. 'Let's meet halfway' is a typically proposed solution by the Chinese party during business negotiations.

The influence of Confucianism

Confucius was a pragmatic philosopher obsessed with defining specific personal relationships. Based on his central doctrine of *li* (proper conduct), Confucius expected every person strictly to observe his or her prescribed position in the different social strata, in order to maintain the 'perfect social order' into perpetuity. In Confucianism, ruler and subject, father and son, husband and wife, elder and younger brother and senior and junior are specifically assigned proper rules of conduct in relation to each other. With good character and personal virtue displayed by every member of society, penal laws became unnecessary, because acting contrary to *li* would result in the far graver moral and social sanction of shame. Without this sense of shame, however punitive the legislation may be, people would attempt to violate it.

Family is placed at the centre of society, and in Confucianism, to conceal the wrongdoings of family members is righteous behaviour. *Li* is also addressed in dealing with friends. 'What a joy to have friends from afar!' Confucius declared. The impact of Confucianism on the Chinese mode of thinking and way of life is profound. As one author put it, China may espouse Marxist socialism, but the bedrock beneath the socialist topsoil is almost pure Confucianism. A patriarchal organizational structure, *mianzi* (face), reverence to seniority, unquestionable loyalty to the ruler, nepotism, hospitality and humility are all familiar terms in the Confucian vocabulary.

Geert Hofstede attributed 'Confucian Dynamism' to 'a society's search for virtue' rather than a search for truth. This explains why China has been short of solid scientific foundations despite its rich civilization. Examinations for public offices were the only path for scholars to move into official rank, but these exams included no discipline of natural science; more attention was paid to conscience and social order. China maintained this tight superstructure throughout its history, but its foundations for natural science are weak.

In fact, the origin of Chinese scientific understanding largely lies in the Taoist alchemy – a superstitious pursuit of immortality – and the initial motivation for the grand overseas expeditions in the Ming Dynasty was neither adventure nor diplomacy but the search for the overthrown emperor who was thought to be hiding in exile. Missing out on the sweeping industrialization and renaissance in Europe, empiricism and scientific experimentation have been lacking, in favour of abstract thinking and relativism. Take traditional Chinese medicine, for example: most formulae involve a compound of herbal ingredients, validated by experience passed on through generations. Actual clinical studies, scientific processes, quality control and quality assurance are noticeably lacking.

The influence of Buddhism

Mahayana Buddhism was imported from India in the sixth century BC and soon became entwined with native faiths. The doctrine of *karma* denotes fate or destiny operating by the cyclical law of causation. The present life is the result of deeds in the past life and the future life is determined by actions in the present life. To many Chinese, the law of causation is interpreted in two ways, as with the tenets of native Chinese philosophies.

The passive interpretation conforms with the Taoist *wuwei* (let go, or do nothing); since every individual's destiny has been predetermined, and thereby all miseries, hardships and joys should be accepted as part of one's fate. Unlike Christianity, Buddhism calls on people to eradicate all desires and retreat from worldly affairs. The fact that Buddhist temples are secluded in high mountains and Christian churches are located in pre-eminent city areas is one manifestation of this contrast.

The positive interpretation is consistent with the Confucian insistence on active social service; good deeds in the present life will be rewarded in the next life. *Karma* is also used to supplement Confucianism, which is rendered futile if social forces fail to enforce conformity to the prescribed ethical standards. It is at least emotionally comforting for victims of wrongdoing to believe that these wrongdoers will eventually receive adequate retribution on the strength of karmic law, when they are unable or unwilling to take positive action against them.

The confluence of Buddhism and Taoism means the Chinese are more content with the state of being than of doing. Chinese people tend to enjoy indoor activities – playing poker games, mahjong, or simply spending hours cooking; they prefer to stay at home rather than travelling during their holidays. While none of these prevailing spiritual forces nurture entrepreneurship, they collectively breed impressive endurance during hardship or misfortune. Chinese people have experienced so many famines, disasters and military repressions over their history that they find their own path to survival in forbearance and endurance. Despite the low level of disposable income, the savings rate in China is among the highest in the world, and a large body of the elaborate national cuisine is actually a reflection of the people's capability to live through famines by using whatever materials they could lay their hands on. Apart from all kinds of plants and vegetables, as the saying goes, 'Chinese people eat anything with two legs but a man, anything with wings but a chopper, anything with four legs but a table'.

Cultural attitudes

Hospitality

In China, gift exchange is an indispensable part of relationship building. This practice extends even to the family of the recipient. The context of gift exchange is believed to generate an expansion of human sympathy. Foreigners are cautioned to avoid admiring the possessions of a Chinese friend during a house visit, as they will very likely be offered as gifts. Traditionally, it is impolite to unwrap gifts in front of the giver.

Wining and dining is an important part of business dealings. Obstruction at a negotiation table may well be solved after a couple of toasts at the dinner table. 'Going Dutch' is generally not acceptable. In paying the bill, initiative or even a friendly fight is expected. Splitting the bill may initially seem fair but Chinese people look at the long-term relationship: friends or business counterparts do not only meet once in a lifetime, so everyone has the opportunity to reciprocate. If only one party has to pay, the wealthier one, or one who will be reimbursed by his or her organization, is expected to take the initiative.

Face-saving

Actually, the real purpose of humility, modesty or self-depreciation is to save or gain face. 'I am not well prepared due to the short notice or personal incompetence...' is often heard at the beginning of a speech. 'Due to limited knowledge, the author begs for criticism of the mistakes in the book' is often found at the end of the preface to a book. A positive result is more likely if parties have been paying attention to face-saving. On the contrary, an outright 'no', pointing to the face or banging on the table will definitely lead to hostility. Chinese people have suffered a long history of foreign oppression and the imposition of 'unequal treaties', which render them more sensitive to perceived power games by foreigners. An American friend doing business with China won immediate applause when he said 'my grandfather was a member of the "Eight Foreign Troops" who looted Beijing, and now I am here to find a way to compensate within my limited capacity'.

Most business contracts start with the words 'through friendly negotiation, both parties unanimously agree to the following terms and conditions in the spirit of equality and mutual benefit'. Executives would do well to keep the stated objectives in mind so that they can structure proposals in a manner acceptable to their Chinese counterparts. Price negotiation is usually regarded as the highlight of a business deal. Scope must be allowed in the price quotation for strenuous bargaining. A 'take-it-or-leave-it' position, even when the price was structured at the bottom line is not perceived as sincere, because price reduction through bargaining is a necessary component of face-saving.

With regard to contract disputes, most contracts maintain a standard clause stipulating that amicable settlement through friendly negotiation or mutual consultation is a prerequisite before any other legal action, such as arbitration, takes place. One of the unique characteristics of Chinese arbitration is that before formal arbitration proceeds, disputants are, in the first place, referred to the Conciliation Centre for mediation. The goal of 'amicable settlement' – so different from the western norm of compromise through adversarial negotiations – reflects the Chinese insistence on peaceful coexistence and harmony in all human endeavour, including business. In conflict resolution, a losing party is far more likely to agree to end a struggle if a way out of the situation is suggested that is not too embarrassing. Excessively driving the other side to admit a loss is an unwise approach. The recent announcement by Philips to withdraw the lawsuit against the accused unauthorized use of DVD technology by Chinese companies ended with more gains

to Philips. If there is a creative way to frame the outcome of the dispute to the effect that all sides can claim at least some success, at least on the surface, it will make it much easier for the losing side to back down.

Forms of address and expressions

In addressing the elderly or senior, it is impolite to use the first name. It is advisable to include the job position of the senior person, for example 'Manager Wang', 'Teacher Liu' or 'Section Chief Zhao'. To the elderly with no senior position, one is advised to use *lao* (old), or *shifu* (master) (if he or she is a blue-collar worker) before the family name. To the younger, *xiao* (young) is often used before the family name to show cordiality. *Tongzhi* (comrade) is a legacy of the communist revolutionary usage, and the frequency of use has declined sharply except for some official occasions. There is a growing tendency to address white-collar workers with teacher before the family name. In the meantime, *xianshen* (Mr) and *xiaojie* (Miss) are increasingly popular in the cities. But while *taitai* (Mrs) is used behind the husband's family name, its popularity is limited, since most Chinese women are socially and economically independent and their maiden names are retained after marriage. Women hold half the sky! They appear in equal positions with men both in the business and entertainment scenes.

Chinese people are good and careful listeners. Ample time is given to their counterparts to spell out their intention, proposal and solution. Most Chinese are not adept at body language, but when they speak they demonstrate a clear line of logic. Exasperation or irritation is considered bad manners, however heated the discussion. A Minnesota magazine journalist, John Marshall, describes a businessman from a European company who had been pushed to his personal breaking point on the matter of price. The hot weather and the days of discussion over a fairly small price differential led him finally to rise from the table saying 'obviously, we are not going to get an agreement. You've had everything I can offer you except the shirt off my back, and you can have that now'. With that, he got up, unbuttoned his sweaty shirt, tossed it on the table, and walked out of the room. After the embarrassed silence that followed, the Chinese told the leader of the company's negotiation team that they would prefer the group not to return as its representative had shown such bad manners. (Source: Business strategy for the PRC, *Business International Asian Research Report*, 1980, p 296.)

Collectivism

It is not traditional for Chinese people to embrace individualism. For the greater part of its 2000-year history, China was ruled by an absolute monarchy. Unlike ancient Europe, where the basic unit of social production was the manor, the family was the basic unit of social production in traditional Chinese society. On this basis a series of ethical principles were developed that bound the Chinese tightly to their homes. In time, a mentality was formed among the Chinese, marked by heavy dependence on the collectives of family, clan and nation. This dependence inevitably produced inertia and a conservative attitude. People simply wanted to feel secure; they were afraid of change and lacked an enterprising spirit. Ironically, all such psychological needs were supposed to be met under the centralized system, in which everything from clothing to food, from housing to transportation, from cradle to grave was to be taken care of. People tended to look to the organization or the government for a secure life.

Managers of an organization are expected in some ways to assume the role of parents. Today, particularly in state-owned organizations, employees can be found pestering their managers for better housing or even for settlements of family disputes. Individualism is not a welcome quality where collective decisions and responsibility are the accepted way of the world. Excessive numbers of meetings are an important part of the work routine, either for ascertaining public opinion or broadcasting directives from senior staff. In spite of all its merits, collectivism is also, for the executives, a shield against uncertainty. They do not have to delegate their power, but neither do they have to shoulder individual responsibility if things go wrong. When security prevails over efficiency, mediocrity finds a rich soil. In virtually all Chinese organizations, clear job descriptions and professionalism are still in a lax condition. This lack of clear job descriptions and professional responsibility necessitates collective discussions and layers of approval. Paradoxically, under this type of collectivism, it is usually the top person who makes the final decision; collectivism is perfectly compatible with a hierarchical chain of command. It is not surprising that dozens of rubber stamps may be needed before a business licence can be obtained: it may take months to get contract approval and it would be foolish to expect decisions to be made on the spot.

Corruption

It may seem odd to relate contemporary corruption and abuse of power by government and corporate officials to the virtues advocated by Confucius. However, it not too far fetched to hold Confucius partly responsible for the prevailing corruption in China for the following reasons:

- his condemnation of legislation;
- his class distinction between the gentry and the petty;
- his proposition that it is righteous for the son to help conceal the wrongdoings of the father.

Believing in the essential and original goodness of man, Confucius held that strict laws were unnecessary and that virtue was the root of civilization. 'If the ruler is virtuous,' he said, 'the people will also be virtuous'. Therefore, power should not need to be checked. Confucius took such a partial stance in favour of the gentry class that he contrived defences for their misconduct: 'Mistakes of the gentry are like eclipses of the sun and moon: they will not keep them from shining', he proclaimed. Officials are part of the learned and the learned constitute the gentry's class. The Confucian *li* applied, in reality, only within this class stratum. He focused on the importance of moral teaching and establishing exemplary models, but to many, the temptation of economic interest was irresistible without the threat of penalty. Active concealment by family members, relatives and other barriers built up by corrupt officials add further complication to legal enforcement.

Guanxi

Guanxi (connection) may be seen as a web of strong personal connections where the connection's official position may be utilized to extend personal favours and commitments. For example, if a friend helped my daughter to find a better job, I would be more inclined to grant him an import licence within my authority. The culture of *guanxi* is based on binding social units: family, school, office or social networks. Though a controversial and subtle subject, *guanxi* is so widespread and pervasive in Chinese culture that it is a subject of study – Guanxiology. It does not aim at direct exchange or immediate gratification. Chinese culture holds it of paramount importance to reciprocate favours received. Even today, many families keep a record of the gifts from a wedding or funeral so that one day they will find a way to reciprocate.

Guanxi is a strategic reserve, which takes time to accumulate but can be cashed in in case of need and convenience. Some conclude that 'to get things done in China, it is not important to know what, but to know who'. It is particularly useful in tapping benefits from bureaucrats who possess freewheeling authority.

Excessive gift giving and extensive use of *guanxi* can be a subject of anti-corruption scrutiny, both along the Communist Party line and on the strength of public law. However, the importance of *guanxi* and the pervasiveness of corruption tend to be generally exaggerated to many westerners, to the point that it becomes misleading. Reform over the state-owned enterprises (SOEs) took the corporate management position out of the hands of former government officials and into those of business executives. The correlation between personal motivation and performance is being legitimized. While the burgeoning private enterprises are in no position to be bribed, they have the motivation to act as a source of corruption in dealing with government officials and corporate executives of SOEs, partly due to their flexibility when it comes to decision-making and distribution of cash.

Overall, the corruption situation in China is changing for the better. Incessant anti-corruption campaigning and legal changes have helped to restore bureaucratic reverence for, if not responsibility to, their duties. The ultimate driver lies in streamlined government functions, increased law enforcement, free market competition and free access to information. As China becomes an active member of the world community, especially by its entry into the WTO, wholesale changes have been taking place toward these objectives.

Today, the deep-rooted culture of *guanxi* still exists in China, but its importance is more restricted at the stage of 'knocking on the door'.

Tips for doing business with China

The three 'P's

Conventional terms like the three 'P's – patience, persistence and product – are still valid when doing business with China.

AT&T waited for eight years before being accepted as a partner in the telecoms business. Under Chinese law, foreign companies are required to have at least three years' history of maintaining representative offices in China before becoming eligible to enter into joint ventures with a Chinese counterpart in the service sector. The Chinese premier, Zhu Rongji, once said at a press conference to foreign companies lining up to join the Chinese market, 'your patience will be duly rewarded'. Once a strategy to enter into the Chinese market is validated, impatience is likely to end in disappointment.

After all, after 2,000 years of imperial dynasties, plus decades of isolation over the last century, China has only been open to the outside world for 26 years. Many things that are taken for granted in western countries are still new to the Chinese. They need time to catch up with the world. Two years ago, the author – representing a US firm – spent nearly an hour during a business negotiation with a Chinese partner explaining what NASDAQ and GAAP were. China has achieved remarkable success in its reform programmes. Compared with the Russian 'shock therapy', this incremental approach may proceed more slowly but has been effective. In the face of these realities, although power play can occasionally be effective, contempt and disgruntled attitudes can only lead to destructive confrontation.

The need for patience and persistence does not end when a business deal is signed. Patience and persistence are still necessary to ensure that the deal is implemented. Particularly in the case of technology transfer and other types of giant undertakings, such as a turnkey projects, more tutorial work and communication are needed to ensure the Chinese party really understands what is underway. Extra assistance is often required to pave the way for approval and foreign exchange allocation. Executive time and travel should be built into the initial phase of project budgeting. As competition grows and the experience of the Chinese party increases, patience and persistence become a crucial element to standing out among business rivals. Those who are able to endure a considerable period of delay to allow the Chinese parties time for collective decision-making, coordinating with different stakeholders, comparing different bidders, going through adjustment and readjustment of business policies, will be the likely winners in the end. During such a critical period, the frontline executives must be prepared for the toughest challenges communicating with their headquarters, while facing a black-box operation at the China end. However, perseverance despite these trials demonstrates the important quality of the will to succeed.

Finally, patience and persistence are not substitutes for high-quality products supported by sound technology and adequate service. Again, Chinese people are highly practical. Typically, their technical nego-tiators are very knowledgeable and often raise tough questions over materials, processes, patent validity, quality controls and assurances. The author once experienced a rather hard time putting to rest a request for the 'most advanced technology' through the addition of a number of conditional clauses such as 'at the time of delivery', 'to the best knowledge of the licensor' and 'by the standard set forth by the licensor' etc.

Self-reference criterion

As previously stated, effective cross-cultural communication requires knowledge, attitude and tactics. It is important to learn to shift positions to prevent cultural stereotyping and myopia. The self-reference criterion (SRC) (Lee, 1966) is a practical guide to getting along with Chinese culture. Summarized by Keegan in 1997, it is reflected in a four-step systematic framework:

1. Define the problem or goal in terms of home-country cultural traits, habits and norms.
2. Define the problem or goal in terms of host-country cultural traits, habits, and norms. Do not make value judgements.
3. Isolate the SRC influence and examine it carefully to see how it complicates the problem.

4. Redefine the problem without the SRC influence and solve for the host-country market situation.

Precautions

China is a vast country with over 1.3 billion people divided into 56 ethnic groups, speaking hundreds of different dialects. Although 5,000 years of history has resulted in substantial cultural homogeneity, diversity has always been the counter force to any attempt at generalization. Democratic movements and socialism, and the Great Cultural Revolution in particular, have overturned traditional Chinese values and beliefs. Opening to the outside world and domestic reforms over the last two decades have ushered in an unprecedented flow of western ideas – some soon evaporated, some remain foreign, and some have been distilled into the native value system. In a nutshell, today's China, like its marketplace, is a cultural kaleidoscope and no statement about Chinese culture should be taken at face value or have universal validity. Nonetheless, the practical value of this chapter rests on the presumption that the roots of a culture shaped by its long history are generally resistant to change. It is the author's hope that when readers are presented with the 'roots and soil', they will be able to identify or predict the fruit of the tree.

Cultural Differences and Clashes in Communication

Li Yong, Deputy Secretary General, China Association of International Trade, and Liu Baocheng, Professor, University of International Business and Economics

Games with familiar and unfamiliar rules

There is a story about a cross-cultural training session at a western company. The trainees were going to be expatriated to overseas positions. At one point in the training, the trainees were asked to take a break to play poker games. Very quickly, they agreed on the type of game they were going to play, and naturally they played one of the games they were familiar with, whose rules were clearly understood by all the players. After a while, the instructor interrupted their game and said, 'Now, you are not allowed to play the game with the familiar rules of your home country. Please continue the game'. The players' minds suddenly went blank. They looked at each other in silence with bewildered expressions on their faces, and with no idea how the game should continue. The instructor then broke the silence by saying, 'The country you guys are going to be assigned to is one that has no rules, or you will be completely ignorant of the rules there are. Are you ready for that?'

Indeed, it is easy to play a game with rules understood by all players, and it is fun to play games with players who understand the rules. However, it is not fun at all to play a game without a rule and with players who have different sets of rules for the same game. These cultural differences can cause different understandings of the same thing. When each of the players is trying to play the game according to the rules that they are familiar with, differences in the understanding of these rules will lead to cultural clashes. Of course, cultural differences have much more profound roots than a simple game, and solving cultural clashes is much more complicated than simply setting up uniform rules, as has been done in sports such as with the Olympic Games.

With the development of international trade and the world economy moving towards what is termed globalization, people's interactions against different cultural backgrounds have become increasingly frequent and inevitable. The world is now called a 'global village', and like it or not, it is true that we are living in a multicultural 'village'. In transnational economic operations, it is difficult, if not impossible, to establish rules, such as those of the Olympic Games, that people from all cultures will abide by. Historical concepts of the 'game' such as beliefs, ethical standards, religions, codes of practice, institutions and behavioural patterns, as well as factors of inter- and intra-competition, language, approaches to a particular objective, interactions of cultural traits, conflicts of value, legal framework and social structures all come into play, and make the pursuit of a uniform cultural rule under a bicultural or multicultural environment difficult and practically impossible to achieve. In addition to this, 'cultural' games are a dynamic process and there is no one single rule that can apply to all situations. There is only one rule to remember when it comes to cultural differences – people may look at the same thing but they all see it differently, regardless of whether they come from the same or a different culture. This rule goes some way to explaining the diversity of the world.

Returning to the training story, no information is given about how the trainees were instructed to deal with a situation in which there were no rules, or rules of which they were ignorant. One criticism of the instructor's first comment – that there are no rules in the country concerned – is that he was using self-reference criteria (see Chapter 5.1), one of the sources of cultural clashes. However, his second comment that there might be rules that the trainees were completely ignorant about offers a chance of cultural understanding, if the trainees were encouraged to learn more about the rules in a foreign country and make an effort to bridge the gap of cultural differences.

China as a member of the international community

Since China opened up to the outside world in 1978, it has made unremitting efforts toward integration into the global economy. Import and export as a percentage of GDP surged from 14 per cent in the early 1980s to 44 per cent in 2000. China's foreign trade volume in 2000 accounted for 3.2 per cent of world trade, an almost fourfold increase on 1978. According to the WTO, China ranked seventh in export volume and eighth in import volume in 2000. China has been the largest recipient of foreign direct investment (FDI) among developing countries since 1993. By the end of December 2001, the cumulative number of foreign-invested enterprises (FIEs) stood at 390,025, with a cumulative contracted investment of US$745.29 billion and an actual utilization of US$395.22 billion. About 80 per cent of Fortune 500 companies have so far made investments in China. The accession to the WTO will greatly facilitate China's participation in globalization.

The above facts and figures clearly demonstrate that China is already an active, participating member of the international business community. With increased foreign investment in China, an understanding of Chinese culture from the perspective of tactics for striking a deal in business negotiations is no longer enough when tackling clashes between Chinese culture and other cultures in economic alliances or joint ventures. Indeed, the opening up of China has ushered in not only foreign investments, technologies and management expertise, but also foreign cultures that challenge the traditional thinking processes and behavioural patterns of the Chinese people. Differences exist and clashes remain. Many joint ventures run into problems and cultural clashes are often a key factor. Culture-led failures of joint ventures, mergers or acquisitions are not unique phenomena in China. There has been a great deal of research in the west indicating a high percentage (from 50 per cent to as high as 75 per cent) of failures of joint ventures, mergers and acquisitions, and many of these failures are believed to have been caused by cultural conflicts.

Decisions to form joint ventures are usually made on economic grounds, as the pooling of the partners' resources are expected to be advantageous to both parties and lead to higher profitability. Stories of failures, however, have revealed a growing body of evidence that non-economic factors often set in and lead to poor joint venture performance. Because of the difficulties that exist in the effort to bridge cultural differences, there has been an increasing trend of solely-owned overseas operations: an attempt to avoid cultural clashes, at least at the management level. The same is true in China. Since 1997, an increasing number of solely foreign-owned enterprises has been established in China. In addition, many foreign investors holding minority shares in joint ventures have increased their capital input to become majority shareholders. All of these are efforts to gain management control and so reduce the chances of decision-making being held up by disagreements with local partners, but do not necessarily eliminate cultural differences and clashes, because the joint ventures are still operating in an environment dominated by Chinese culture and the need to deal with people who think different things, in different ways.

Some concluded that as globalization develops and national boundaries become increasingly blurred, interest in joint ventures would subside. However, in an era of great flux in the commercial world, strategic alliances work at all levels, and joint ventures are still a popular method of expanding businesses. The advantages of joint ventures are obvious. A joint venture can turn under-utilized resources into profit and create a new profit centre, help enter untapped markets quicker and at less cost than trying it alone, and minimize the risk of a large investment undertaking. There are a number of successful joint ventures in China but it takes sensitivity to a range of cultural differences over styles of communication, attitudes, value judgements and social and managerial behaviours to achieve this success.

Anecdotal analysis of the differences between Chinese and western cultures

Chinese cultural roots and traits, the underlying drivers of the Chinese mental and behavioural patterns, are discussed in Chapter 5.1. When examining cultural differences, note should also be taken of the fact that China is moving towards a more open society, and increased interaction of Chinese people with westerners has prepared the ground for acceptance of western management concepts and practices. Table 5.2.1 is a list of key differences in the business context between Chinese and western cultures.

Of course, this list is not exhaustive and many others can be added to it from different perspectives and experiences. The differences identified here are more relevant to the business environment than to personal traits. They are not only key variables of the Chinese 'collective mental programming' (Hofstede) process, but also the determinants of conflict management behaviour.

Power distance, one of Hofstede's measures of cultural difference, is one of the most prominent differences in Chinese culture compared with that of the west. The Confucian cultural and social traditions dictate a rigid social hierarchy – top-down control and distribution of power by rank, as a result of which bureaucracy is seldom challenged and reverence to rank and power is considered to be a virtue. The results of power distance are often manifested in a lack of efficient vertical communication, obedience in execution of the orders/instructions of the superior and avoidance of a direct challenge to power. The top-down control structure makes many Chinese organizations resemble the personal characteristics of the top leader.

In the context of a joint venture, power distance is also at play. Open argument with the management about, for example, corporate strategies, is rarely seen. Private, one-on-one meetings may encourage a Chinese manager to speak more freely about his opinion. Foreign managers should be careful with their mode of expression when challenging the ideas of Chinese managers who hold superior positions.

Power distance does not only exist within an organization. It is omnipresent in the web of the social hierarchy. The mental programming process in handling power distance is situational and involves complex considerations, among which 'face' is an important factor. Whether or not a person in an organization will challenge the ideas of another person depends on his judgement of the 'face' element as well as the other person's rank in the hierarchy. He is less likely to challenge his superiors and likely to challenge others of the same rank. Face is less of an element of consideration when dealing with underlings, but face-giving is also a lubricant of power distance in a bottom-up direction. For example, the Chinese have a tendency to credit the successes of corporate achievements to the supervising authority or government departments, a face-giving effort to minimize obstacles resulting from power distance. This, among other things, often causes 'culture shock' in foreigners. A German engineer, leading a group of technicians to install the equipment contributed by the German partner in China, was bewildered when he heard at the opening ceremony of the joint venture, that the successful commissioning and operation of the equipment was credited to 'the correct leadership' of the supervising authority, and his team's effort in making equipment run was not acknowledged. When he learned that it was a rhetorical formality to mention the supervising authority, he copied this exercise when the equipment failed and announced that the equipment went wrong due to the leadership of the supervising authority. Everyone present was taken aback.

Table 5.2.1 Key differences between Chinese and western cultures

Chinese culture	Western culture
Large power distance	Small power distance
Reverence to rank and power	Equality among people
Bureaucracy	Authority of law
Strong tendency of risk avoidance	Strong tendency of risk taking
Dominance of group interest and values	Dominance of individualistic interest
Doctrine of the mean and ambiguity	Clarity in expression
Resistance to change	Acceptance of change
Lack of original creativity	Pro-innovation
Pursuit of moral accomplishments	Pursuit of objective being
Cultivation of personal virtue	Knowledge and skill learning
Despise material gains	Recognition of material gains
'Face' is important	'Face' is unimportant
Connotation and tolerance	Candour and rigidity

The story of the German engineer reflects not only a lack of understanding of cultural context, but also the differences between Chinese and western culture in terms of the emphasis on group and individual contribution. China is generally a collectivist society. Individualism-collectivism, another of Hofstede's dimensions of culture, is an important parameter in measuring cultural variability, as it shows the norms and values that a culture attaches to social relationships and social exchanges. The Chinese people have a tendency to pursue collective goals rather than individual interests, and this is a fundamental characteristic of the Chinese culture governing the relationship between organization and individuals. Collectivism is still emphasized in China as a virtue and a citizen's social responsibility. In the official doctrine of collectivism, individualism is regarded as egoism or a source of selfish desire and is therefore suppressed for the common well-being. However, over the past 26 years since China opened up to the outside world, the collectivism tendency has been exposed to western individualism, and its influence is clear among the younger generation, who have a stronger sense of self-importance.

In a business environment, collective consensus is often sought in the decision-making process, although power distance may block different opinions. Managers often speak of collective interests to hold back individual desire, whereas the individual aspirations are often achieved in the name of collectivist pursuit. In addition to this, collectivism underlies egalitarianism in welfare and income distribution. An extreme example of this egalitarianism is a Chinese scholar who won a prize for his remarkable achievements but divided his prize money between not only his leaders and team members, but also people irrelevant to his work such as drivers and cooks. He attributed his success to the leaders at the top of the organization for their support and those at the bottom of the structure for their logistical support. Although this egalitarianism is weakening following Deng Xiaoping's advocacy of 'let some people get rich first', this inclination towards egalitarianism driven by collectivism should be taken into consideration in managing employee relations.

Where collectivism seems to correlate with the western management practice of teamwork is that people of a collectivist culture prefer to work in groups rather than individually. Although the Chinese characteristic of collectivism prepares the ground for team spirit in some ways, it still represents a departure from what teamwork requires. The lack of horizontal communication, tendency to work only with peers, reluctance to share knowledge and mistrust among co-workers arising from the lack of explicit expression, need to be carefully handled before teamwork and team spirit can be established.

To fit the Chinese culture into Hofstede's uncertainty avoidance dimension is difficult, because the tendency of uncertainty avoidance in Chinese culture is high in some cases and low in others, and so some researchers put China into the low category, others in the high. (The authors wish to avoid uncertainty by not making this judgement.) Typically, Chinese people have a tendency to avoid risks, resist change, tolerate contradictions, accept ambiguities, pursue cultivation of virtue rather than truth, observe informal rules (affective) and compromise on formal rules (instrumental). In a business context, the tendency of risk avoidance often leads to a different understanding of change, while tolerance of contradictions leads to different paths of conflict resolution. Ambiguity in expression as a typical feature of a high-context culture often makes cross-cultural communication ineffective. Ambiguity in Chinese culture comes from contextual and dialectical thinking, which contrasts with the westerners' linear thinking patterns.

Let us take a look at a case of cultural differences in a joint venture that will help the understanding of how some of Hofstede's culture dimensions are at play in a corporate environment.

Case study

The company is a joint venture between an overseas Chinese and western entrepreneur, operating in China with the Chinese holding the majority shares. After 10 years of development, the venture has become a multi-million dollar business and it is still growing. The company's marketing department consists of three teams. Interestingly, each team has the same function as the other, which is basically to solicit customers and provide 'tailor-made' services. To encourage teamwork, the company staged an incentive system that provides performance-related bonuses.

The outcome of the incentive system was both positive and negative. On the positive side, a competitive environment was established and sales increased. However, teams began to compete against each another for customers and hostility later arose among the teams. John, a marketing assistant, observed the development and communicated his concerns and observations to Robert, the company's western partner and vice-president with responsibility for marketing. This is a summary of his points:

- the three groups are competing against each another for clients and blocking client information;
- there is an unwillingness to cooperate and consult with each other among the teams;
- the teams undercut each other on prices in their fight for the same customer;
- there has been a lack of coordination, which has resulted in separate marketing promotions running at the same time and targeting the same customer categories, leading to a waste of corporate resources and time.

Robert decided to have a meeting with the Chinese marketing manager, Mr Zhang, and the team leaders to discuss these issues. During the meeting, Robert communicated his thoughts about the teamwork situation and invited the attendees to comment, in the hope that the issues could be solved at the meeting. Much to Robert's surprise however, John appeared to be the only one who was concerned about the situation. After the meeting, Robert had a private conversation with Mr Zhang, who said that the current situation was satisfactory and that the competition had increased the total sales of the company. Robert accepted it as a fact, but still expressed his opinion that Mr Zhang should improve the teams' coordination and cooperation.

A couple of months later, the Chinese partner, Mr Wang, had a discussion about John's sales performance. Mr Wang said that John had fallen behind all other marketing assistants and had not been able to get a contract for about two months. Wang then asked Robert if John should be relocated from his present position to the administrative department, where more people were needed as the business expanded. Robert was unhappy about Wang's suggestion and said that John had been a good member of staff and, unlike other Chinese staff, had been straightforward in communication, positive in his effort to develop corporate business, independent in his judgement and willing to speak out with his opinions and suggestions. Robert wanted to keep John in his marketing position as an independent source of understanding of what was really happening at the frontline of the corporate business. As Wang held management control as a majority shareholder, he insisted that Robert relocate John. Robert also heard from an informal source that Zhang had claimed that he would eliminate John from the scene because John had talked too much about his department's problems. John was removed from his marketing position. In this case, the points of differences are illustrated in Figures 5.2.1 to 5.2.3.

All these differences are attributed to a failure in effectively communicating the problems.

Sources of cultural clashes in communication

Increased exposure of one culture to another in the context of economic globalization is bound to lead to cultural clashes. It is unlikely that a person of one culture, entering a country of another culture, will completely forget his/her own culture and the familiar rules of his/her game, nor that he/she has a mission to achieve his/her corporate goals in the host country. It is impossible that he/she will be completely assimilated by the culture of the host country. The same is true for the people from the other culture. They cannot be expected completely to accept a foreign culture and to lose their own cultural identity. Given these cultural stances, the convenience of using self-reference criteria for people of both cultures will naturally come into play, and this is, in fact, the primary source of cultural clashes.

Cultural clashes can take many forms and it is impossible to produce an exhaustive list identifying all the sources of cultural clashes, because people interaction is a dynamic process. Table 5.2.2 summarizes the most common complaints by both westerners and the Chinese about the problems they face in cross-cultural communications.

Two things can be done to bridge the communication gap. One is to learn to understand the Chinese way of communication and the other is to educate Chinese counterparts to understand the rationale of the western way of doing things. Sometimes, an intermediary who understands both mindsets can be helpful in communicating the differences and achieving understanding.

Abrupt and forceful transplantation of western rules of management into a joint venture will only lead to conflict. In a Chinese-French joint venture, for example, the French brought, along with their equipment and technology, a complete set of French management rules, which were enforced without adaptation by the French managers who occupied all key managerial positions. Such an exercise aroused strong resentment from the workers and eventually

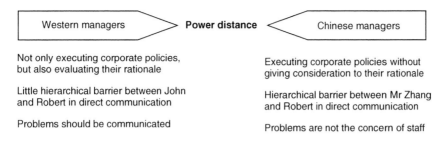

Figure 5.2.1 Power distance has determined different approaches in communication of problems

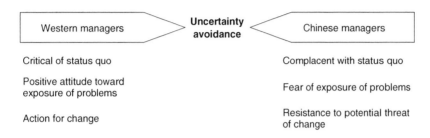

Figure 5.2.2 The varied degree of uncertainty avoidance

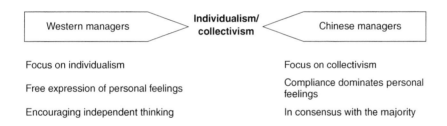

Figure 5.2.3 Collectivism-individualism predetermined behavioural differences in response to problems

Table 5.2.2 Cross-cultural communication problems

Complaints from western managers	*Complaints from Chinese managers*
Marathon negotiations and decision-making	Lack of understanding of the unique local environment
Decisions reached by discussion instead of voting	Over-rigid in handling business affairs and lack of flexibility
Indirect expression of opinions	Impersonality and rule-orientation without giving consideration to circumstances
Great importance is given to 'face'	Lack of thrift in the use of corporate money
Dependent on Guanxi and personal emotions in business dealings	Disregard for local management suggestions
Submissive nature and lack of creativity	Individualistic and arbitrary in decision-making
Ambiguity in policies, laws and regulations	Money-making is the top priority
Bureaucracy	Lack of respect and care for staff/employees
Excessive government intervention	Ignore the interests of Chinese partners
Complicated and closely-knit interpersonal relations	Arrogance and conceit

triggered a strike, which was finally resolved by the mediation of the Chinese government and the French Consulate General. A staff of the joint venture commented later: 'If the French-style management was executed by Chinese managers, it might perhaps be easier for us to accept. We just couldn't put up with the bullying and overbearing of the French'. This extreme case of cultural clash demonstrates the need for improved and effective communications to achieve mutual understanding and respect. Although the elements that should be taken into consideration for cross-cultural management are far more complicated than in a mono-cultural environment, readiness to understand and adapt to a foreign culture is certainly an effective means of improving efficiency.

In the same Chinese-French joint venture, the Chinese managers suggested restricted use of the copying machines, which, at that time, were not popular office equipment. The French did not listen, and placed the machines in the corridor for free use, as they did in France. The result was that the machines often went wrong because of incorrect operation, and some Chinese staff used the machine to copy personal documents, all of which led to an unnecessary increase in the cost of maintenance and paper. The French eventually adopted the Chinese suggestion and the cost related to the copying machines was brought under control. This example shows that people of different cultural backgrounds have different ways of thinking and behaving. The differences, if properly communicated, will complement one another as driving forces rather than barriers.

Education of the Chinese partners and workers at large is absolutely necessary. The objectives of education can be achieved through training, which should concentrate not only on skill improvements but also management understanding. A number of multinational companies have successfully implemented training programmes aimed at achieving trust and understanding. Hewlett Packard has successfully introduced its 'HP Way' into its China operations. Motorola has implemented training programmes, not only for its own staff, but also for its suppliers and customers. GE has established its core value of business ethics, honesty and credibility, by trying a number of different ways of communication, including the distribution of booklets of corporate ethics to its staff. Chinese workers at Lucent Technologies are motivated to produce better quality products than their counterparts in Atlanta.

Apart from the purely cultural, there are other differences, such as the attitude towards and ability to handle market changes, corporate development strategies, conception of business management and management style. In addition, educational background and professional experiences vary among Chinese and western managers. All of this will lead to clashes in the communication of corporate strategies, development plans and so on. One elevator joint venture was once in serious confrontation on issues of corporate development strategy. The foreign partner suggested that the joint venture should improve services and provide maintenance to customers, while the Chinese management, whose average age was 58, put the emphasis on improvement of production. On accounting issues, the foreign partner proposed that unrecoverable accounts should be written off as bad debts, while the Chinese side expressed concerns that the joint venture would suffer an accounting deficit.

Similar clashes as a result of differences in the conception of corporate development strategies were also seen in another joint venture, a Sino-US automobile manufacturing operation. In the early stages of the joint venture, the US partner suggested that the dividends should be reinvested into the joint venture to expand the scale of production. The response from the Chinese side was that the joint venture was comfortably well off, with annual sales of several hundred thousand cars, and the market demand was so strong that there was no need to invest in expansion, and to divide the annual profit of RMB200–300 million would be the practical choice. The US partner made a concession by offering a unilateral increase in their capital contribution; this was declined by the Chinese side, who calculated that the change in equity ratio would reduce their share of the dividend. By the mid-1990s, however, the market had begun to change and the old model quickly lost its market.

Managing cross-cultural differences for cross-cultural advantage

Culture is, in itself, a difference. Differences come from people. People can bridge differences. The effort to converge cultural differences can turn these differences into cross-cultural advantages. Let us take a look at how this is achieved at a Sino-US food company.

This is a 50/50 joint venture. The US partner sent just one manager to represent the parent company, a Chinese American who had obtained an MBA degree in the US and had a good understanding of Chinese culture and history. His position in the joint venture was general manager. He implemented a typical US model of management in terms of business strategy, marketing and accounting practices, while at the same time making efforts to minimize the cultural differences at both inter- and intra-cultural levels. Among many management measures adopted by this individual, the following have the distinctive features of cultural convergence.

Hierarchical management ladder to offset the negative side of power distance

He understood that too many deputy positions in a typical Chinese organization would often lead to a shirking of responsibilities, so he established a middle management team without deputies. The managers at each level were held responsible for their own performances, good or bad, with no room for excuses. They were also delegated independent decision-making rights, such as rewards and penalties for their subordinates, promotion and dismissal. Meanwhile, he made a strictly hierarchical reporting rule so that no one could circumvent their immediate supervisor. Management instructions were also required to follow through such a hierarchical ladder. This exercise incorporated the power distance characteristics of the Chinese culture, while assigning clearly defined responsibilities (job definition), decision-making (power definition) and reward (salary scheme according to positions held) to the managers.

Incentive system to encourage individualistic contributions without inflicting collectivist setbacks

To avoid the usual egalitarianism, a bonus system was established using a strict rating system. Bonuses were not part of the salary scheme as they are in other companies. The bonus amount was kept confidential in order to minimize the chances of negative impacts such as a loss of self-esteem, jealousy and comparison among the workers.

Requirements for teamwork expressed in a collectivist framework

The joint venture advocated team spirit in a slogan – 'Unity and Cooperation' – which has a typically collectivist feature. To encourage team cooperation and coordination, the general manager made a special rule that if one department failed to achieve its assigned targets, all other departments' rating scores would be reduced accordingly.

Respect for everyone to demonstrate US-style corporate culture

Inequality in the form of different treatment for people in different job positions is omnipresent and such inequality is tolerated by most Chinese people. To maintain order and management authority, such inequality is guarded by the hierarchical management ladder, but compensated for by equality in paid annual leave for non-management staff and workers.

Example set by the general manager in observing corporate rules

The general manager takes the lead in observing the rules he has established for the managers, staff and workers. A heart-warming scene was when the general manager was seen bending down to pick up a small piece of litter, which produced a strong psychological impact on the workers.

Informal communication with non-management staff and workers

To establish an effective channel of communication, the general manager uses his weekly breakfast meeting to interact informally with his staff and workers. This has shortened power distance.

Generosity only for the benefit of the joint venture

The general manager holds that the joint venture is a place of business operation, the ultimate goal of which is to profit from the market. Anything other than this will not be considered. He rejects the idea of an enterprise running redundant functions such as nurseries and schools. He refuses sponsorship requests that have nothing to do with the profit objectives, while being very generous in public events that increase corporate publicity and improve the corporate image. He also invests heavily in staff training, which has increased the sense of responsibility at all levels.

These approaches, together with other management measures, have turned a joint venture of cross-cultural differences into a harmonious enterprise of cross-cultural advantages. A year after the joint venture was put into operation, the Chinese side had recovered its investment with a marginal profit.

The above example illustrates the possibility of effectively managing cultural differences in the context of joint ventures. Analysis of this single success story is not intended to provide a universal reference point for all joint ventures in China, but it may provide insightful observations into how cultural differences can interact with each other to produce a positive rather than a negative result. One conclusion that can be drawn is that cultural differences are not written into the genes of human beings, be they from China or any other part of the world. A possible solution for cultural differences could come from the following:

- adapting to each other's culture;
- building shared values;
- adjusting decision-making references;
- forming a unique management style accommodating both cultures;
- establishing effective interpersonal communications that are free from prejudiced assumptions.

Networking Practice in China

Wei-ping Wu, BA, MA, DPhil, MIEX, Assistant Professor, Department of Marketing and International Business, Lingnan University, Hong Kong, and Li Yong, Deputy Secretary General, China Association of International Trade

In the study of Chinese business networks, a generally accepted conceptual framework that can give in-depth explanations to help understand the plentiful anecdotal evidence is still lacking. A sound approach should be able to analyze not only Chinese business networks in Mainland China but also those in other Chinese communities such as Hong Kong, Taiwan and south-east Asian countries. As recent phenomena indicate, Chinese business networks have gone beyond the geographical, political and social boundaries (Kao, 1993). The workings of such business networks may be recognized in the rapid economic development in southern China (East Asian Analytical Unit, 1995).

This chapter intends to combine transaction cost theory, network theories and the key Chinese cultural values of different Chinese communities, to present a new framework for analysing the Chinese business networks in Mainland China, Hong Kong, Taiwan and other Chinese communities, regardless of the different economic and social systems in which they operate. It also aims to provide foreign companies in China with some practical advice.

Business networks in China and overseas Chinese communities

One can often hear the word *guanxi* in any Chinese community, whether it is Mainland China (Bian, 1994; Wu, 1995a), Hong Kong (Wong, 1991), Singapore (Wong, 1995) or Taiwan (Kao, 1991; Numazaki, 1985), though there may be some slight differences in pronunciation as a result of the distinctive Chinese dialects spoken in those communities.

Guanxi has been regarded as a special relationship two persons have with each other (Alston, 1988), as a special kind of personal relationship in which long-term mutual benefit is more important than short-term individual gain (Zamet and Bovarnick, 1986), and as having the status and intensity of an ongoing relationship between two parties (Kirkbride et al, 1991). Bian (1994) states that *guanxi* has two meanings attached to it: the indirect relationship between two people and the direct relationship between two people and a contact person. For the purpose of this study, *guanxi* can be defined as a special personal relationship in which long-term mutual benefit is more important than short-term individual gain, and contains the key elements of indirect relationship between two people through proper introduction by a third party, and direct relationship between two people who trust each other and the contact person.

While *guanxi* operates on a dyadic level, *guanxiwang* (network)[1] certainly goes further than that. *Guanxiwang* refers to a network of exchanges or transactions between two parties and beyond. Goods and services, such as physical products or favours exchanged, can be anything of value and mutual benefit to the parties concerned, for example, raw materials, promotion, gifts, information, facilitation and so on. *Guanxiwang* is obtained when one set of separate, personal and total relationships between two individuals, A and B, and another set of such relationships between B and C are interlinked

---

[1] Network and *guanxiwang* are interchangeable throughout this chapter.

through the common agent, B, acting as a witness and facilitator (see Figure 5.3.1). As a result, the original 'total and personal relationship' (Alston, 1988) transforms into a complex network of social exchanges, with such interlinkage extended into other sets through numerous common agents like A, B and C. Therefore, it can be concluded that *guanxi* is not simply, as many believe, one of the key features of Chinese culture (Lockett, 1988) or one of the key 'themes' that depict core aspects of Chinese values (Kirkbride et al, 1991); it is the mother of all relationships.

Although there are various kinds of *guanxiwang* in China and overseas Chinese communities, they can be divided into two main groups: social networks and business networks. It is important to understand the relationship between a social network and a business network. A social network can be broadly defined as a web of social relationships established within the sphere of core family members, extended family members, friends, classmates, fellow townsmen and so on. According to Redding (1990), the Chinese social network consists of lineage, village or neighbourhood, clan or collection of lineage and special interest associations. Their main function is to protect and help each other and to have an ethnic and/or unique identity in a wider social context. A business network can be defined as a web of business organizations to create or internalize

a market for the purpose of profit maximization or cost minimization for all the members concerned.

There are four distinct types of such inter-firm networks:

1. ownership networks (firms linked though common ownership);
2. investment networks (firms linked by capital and investment);
3. production networks (firms linked by production sequences); and
4. distribution networks (firms linked by the distribution of commodities) (Hamilton et al, 1990).

While a social network is not a business network *per se*, the former can reinforce and overlap with the latter (Omohundro, 1983). It has been widely accepted that one needs a good personal relationship (*guanxi*) to do business successfully in the Chinese communities such as China, Taiwan and Singapore (Redding, 1990). It is common practice for the Chinese to do business with trusted friends. Johanson and Mattsson (1987) stress that it is individual actors that are the major players in an industrial or business network. Deglopper (1978) says: 'Business relations are always, to some degree, personal relations'. Consequently, sometimes the difference between the two can become very blurred.

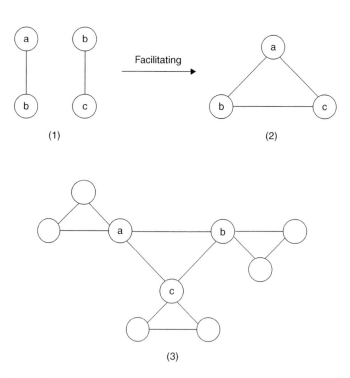

Figure 5.3.1 *Guanxi* and *guanxiwang*

There is an increasing body of research devoted to the study of the relationship between social/personal networks and business networks (Kao, 1991; Numazaki, 1985; Omohundro, 1983).

There is a bias in the study of Chinese business networks. Although there exists much corruption among overseas Chinese (Redding, 1990), very little has been mentioned in the study of overseas Chinese business networks. Yoshihara (1991) may be one of the few exceptions to echo indigenous peoples' view that Chinese businessmen in south-east Asia are not genuine entrepreneurs because they are basically successful by making the right political connections, favours and contracts. However, when it concerns Mainland China, *guanxiwang* is immediately branded as corruption (Agelasto, 1996; Li and Wu, 1993; *The Economist*, 1989). Many people often treat *guanxi* and *guanxiwang* as derogatory terms. *Guanxiwang* is regarded as an unhealthy social tendency. The truth is *guanxiwang, per se*, is purely a form of organizational governance – nothing more, nothing less. It has nothing to do with corruption when a transaction is legal and does not infringe any public interests, but simply takes place between members within a business network. *Guanxiwang* only becomes corrupt when the exchange or transaction taking place within a *guanxiwang* involves corrupt activities such as bribery. Because of the special characteristics of *guanxiwang* such as trust and bonding, corrupt deals are more likely to take place between members of a *guanxiwang*, particularly when an adequate and effective legal and disciplinary system is lacking.

Networks are essential to overseas Chinese success in China. They allow access to the right officials at the township or village level. Benefits flow both ways through the networks (East Asia Analytical Unit, 1995). Business networks existed throughout the history of the People's Republic of China (Bian, 1994). During the period of the Cultural Revolution, the classic market was not allowed to exist. For example, there were campaigns to cut 'the tail of capitalism' in the countryside. With the failure of bureaucratic governance and non-existence of market, an alternative, the network, played a major role in social and industrial exchanges and transactions in China. In recent empirical research on the relationship

between *guanxi* and the allocation of urban jobs in China, Bian (1994) found that *guanxi* accounted for a considerable proportion of jobs in all historical periods between 1949 and 1988. The operation of network was suppressed by a tight and rigid bureaucratic control before the economic reform. It has been revealed that with the loosening of state control, *guanxi* had been widely used to substitute for the imperfect market (Bian, 1994). Solinger (1989) discovered that the withdrawal of the planning system based on quotas and local government-directed input and output transactions gave rise to relational contracting, in which many of the former business relationships were maintained.

Therefore, it can be concluded that with the shared legacies of social history and the key Chinese cultural values, there is no significant difference between business networks in China and their counterparts in overseas Chinese communities. The difference, if any, is diminishing rapidly with the ever-increasing number of cross-border investments by overseas Chinese in China and the further deepening of Chinese economic reform.

The framework of Chinese business networks

However, to understand better the Chinese business network[2], a theoretical framework is necessary. This can be accomplished by extending existing transaction cost theory and network theories.

When both markets and hierarchies fail, an intermediate mode of governance can be used to facilitate a transaction (Williamson, 1979). Market failure can be caused by uncertainty and low volume conditions compounded by limited rationality and opportunism. Uncertainty can be greatly reduced within a network. For example, the volume uncertainty, where there are few suppliers and many buyers and raw materials are in short supply, should not pose any serious problem for those buyers who have good *guanxi* with suppliers, because they have a greater chance of getting supplies than those who are not a member of the network. Furthermore, low volume conditions can also be dealt with effectively within a network. The network relationship is usually established through introduction and facilitation and is also witnessed by a third party.

---

[2] Hereafter the term Chinese business network refers to the business networks in all Chinese communities.

Contracting parties are less likely to behave opportunistically as the culprit will be penalized by the network codes/rules. Contrary to the conventional belief that the Chinese system of networked transactions is uncodified (Boisot and Child, 1994), a network has its own rules and codes that are often 'invisible' but effective. An entrepreneur who behaves properly in honouring verbal promises, repaying loans on time and caring for his family can be drawn into a Chinese business network (Wong, 1995). It is fairly obvious that Chinese social networks such as clan associations, trade associations and dialect associations are established on the common values (codes) shared by members. For example, the foundation for a dialect association is the dialect that depicts shared values among members. Therefore, any opportunistic behaviour such as attempts to breach a contract or a 'gentleman's agreement' will be checked by potential penalties.

Another network mechanism is trust. Every single paper on the network will mention trust as the key element of a network relationship. Without trust, there will be no network. Trust is regarded as confidence in the continuation of a mutually satisfying relationship (Thorelli, 1986) or as 'glue' (Ouchi, 1980). Trust is established on the positive feelings built by interacting with one another for a reasonable period of time. Therefore, trust can greatly reduce the uncertainty that is usually faced by two contracting parties in a classic market. Networks can also provide other effective means to deal with hazards in a market situation. Under a network relationship, opportunistic behaviour will be checked by the prospect of future business transactions, the need for reciprocity, reputation and the prospect of ostracism among peers (Macaulay, 1963; Maitland et al, 1985; Williamson, 1983). These effects are in line with the key Chinese cultural values such as face, trust, reciprocity and so on. This is one of the main reasons why the business network has been ubiquitous in Chinese communities. As a result, therefore, with checked opportunistic behaviour and reduced uncertainty, the business network lowers transaction costs. As Williamson (1975) argues, it is not uncertainty or low volumes, individually or together, that result in market failure, it is the joining of these factors with limited rationality on the one hand and opportunism on the other that gives rise to exchange difficulties. Solinger (1989) discovered the advantages that business networks could provide in an economic environment where uncertainty persisted with regard to the honouring of

trading agreements, the assurance of quality in goods exchanged, the provision of working capital, and so forth. Chong (1994) argues that whether it is personal reputation or the firm's, reputation can often play an important role in reaching agreements in East Asia.

Nevertheless, existing discussions on whether to internalize an activity within a firm or to farm it out to other firms in a network (Walker and Weber, 1984) are rather limited in scope. The advantage of network is far beyond this 'make or buy' decision. By networking with potential partners in another industry or another consumer market, firms can support each other and share know-how and information. As a result, firms in a network relationship will become more competitive than their competitors outside the network. The firm is frequently faced with many limitations such as lack of finance, technology and the regulations of local government. Owing to the lack of information, there is sometimes no market to internalize in the first place. By networking with other enterprises, a firm can have better access to much needed information that is likely to flow between members within a network. Transactions require the production and exchange of information (Boisot and Child, 1988). Consequently, a market can be created with the availability of information within a network. Therefore, a network relationship can provide not only economies of scale (or whatever source of efficiency) (Jarillo, 1988) and synergy, but also help to create a new market that does not exist in the classic market. The benefit of a network is that it has the best of both worlds: markets and hierarchies. It provides the merits of a quasi internalization, such as reduced transaction costs and the creation of new markets, as well as the advantages of a classic market such as economies of scale, wider choice than total internalization and the flow of information. In conclusion, the network can provide three key advantages:

1. reduced transaction cost;
2. creation of a new market; and
3. synergy and economies of scale.

The network is not only efficient but also effective (Jarillo, 1988). It was found that those firms that relied solely on core family members were less successful than those that relied also on friends (Omohundro, 1983). This finding indicates that the limited sphere of family business is a liability rather than an asset to the success of a firm. It is the business network that can offer a wider sphere of interactions that resemble a classic market of more choice and an internalization that can protect firms from the hazards, such as uncertainty, attached to the classic market.

However, like other forms of transaction governance, business networks can fail (Thorelli, 1986). That is when the transaction costs of using a business network outweigh the benefits. For example, if the need for reciprocity disappears, either party may feel it is too costly to keep up the unnecessary relationship. As a result, the *guanxi* relation lapses (Alston, 1988). However, members of a business network may change, but the business network itself often survives and develops with the joining of new members. According to Johanson and Mattsson (1985, 1987), networks are stable and changing, with new relationships being established and old relationships dissolved. Therefore, the business network is a dynamic organization.

In real life, a firm may belong to dozens of business networks at the same time. Therefore, to many firms, network relationships are three-dimensional. A firm may have horizontal inter-organizational relationships as well as vertical business relationships, such as the relationship between the firm and local government offices. Sometimes these networks may overlap with each other. Therefore, to be a credited member, firms have to abide by the codes that are shared by other members. These 'invisible' codes and values are, more often than not, the substitution for an insufficient legal system.

Business networks and Chinese cultural values

Boisot and Child (1988), among others, stress that there is a potential interplay of cultural, economic and technological influences on transaction governance. Although *guanxiwang* is a transaction governance rather than a key feature of Chinese culture, it is inevitably influenced by Chinese cultural values such as trust, face, reciprocity, respect for age and authority, harmony and time. Most of these cultural values are interrelated; for example, making someone lose face will negatively affect a harmonious relationship. Hence, it is Chinese cultural values that make a major difference between *guanxiwang* and similar governance in western countries. The ubiquitous existence of business networks in China and overseas Chinese communities is determined by the fact that network codes overlap with the key Chinese cultural values (see Figure 5.3.2). Chinese business networks are sustained by Chinese cultural values and tradition. When these

values disappear, the networks will collapse (Wong, 1995). The following values have been identified as the key Chinese cultural values:

- trust (Redding, 1990; Wong, 1995);
- mistrust (Redding, 1990; Low, 1995; Wu, 1995a);
- reciprocity (Redding, 1990; Kirkbride et al, 1991);
- face (Yau, 1994; Lockett, 1988; Kirkbride et al, 1991; Redding, 1990)
- time (Yau, 1994; Kirkbride et al, 1991);
- harmony (Yau, 1988, 1994; Kirkbride et al, 1991);
- hierarchy;
- power distance (Kirkbride et al, 1991; Lockett, 1988; Yau, 1988, 1994); and
- long-term orientation (Bond, 1987).

These Chinese cultural values are the main representations of the seven core rituals of Confucianism: benevolence, harmony, midway, forbearance, filial piety, trust and cautious words (Li and Wu, 1993).

Trust/mistrust

In China, chronic suspicion prevails (Smith, 1894). The Chinese 'appear to be quite suspicious and cold towards strangers with whom relationships have not been established' (Yau, 1988). Nobody could be trusted except one's kinfolk in the form of the extended family (Hofstede, 1993). As the Chinese do not trust

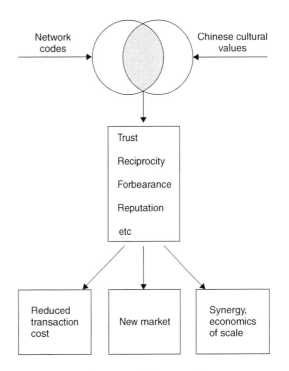

Figure 5.3.2   The research framework

outsiders, a social network consisting of family members, relatives, friends, classmates, colleagues etc is the immediate sphere on which trust can be established, reciprocated and developed. Such an obsession with trust is caused by another, often neglected, phenomenon in China – dishonesty. In business transactions, a great deal of adulteration of goods is practised, for example, weights and measures are juggled (Latourette, 1972). To protect one's interest and ensure that opportunistic behaviour such as cheating are kept to a minimum, trust must be established before any serious business relationship can be cemented. Trust-based *guanxiwang* is the alternative to the market, which is often driven by opportunistic behaviour.

Not coincidentally, for both transaction cost theory and network theory, trust has been also regarded as a critical component of the network (Jarillo, 1988; Thorelli, 1986; Williamson, 1983). Williamson advocates that exchange relationships based on personal trust will survive greater stress and display greater adaptability. Thorelli observes that trust in Oriental cultures may even take the place of contractual arrangements.

Face, hierarchy and power distance

Face is a concept of central importance because of its pervasive influence in interpersonal relations among the Chinese (Yau, 1988). According to Hu (1944), Chinese face can be classified into two types, *lian* and *mian-zi*. *Lian* 'represents the confidence of society in the integrity of the ego's moral character, loss of which makes it impossible for him to function properly within the community', while *mian-zi* 'stands for the kind of prestige that is emphasized... a reputation achieved through getting on in life, through success and ostentation'. When *lian* is lost, the person will feel that he/she can no longer live in the world.

Loss of *lian* within a *guanxiwang* as a consequence of opportunistic behaviour means that peers will no longer have confidence in the persons or firms concerned. As a result, their membership within a *guanxiwang* and in society will be untenable. Therefore, face can be another hostage that minimizes the possibility of opportunistic behaviour within a *guanxiwang*. This is another reason why *guanxiwang* cannot merely survive but can also develop in Mainland China and overseas Chinese communities.

Mian-zi can also be used to form new *guanxiwang*. One of Confucius' virtues is to respect authority and the elderly. Someone with authority, often elderly and with a good reputation, can ask favours of others. The person

may act as a common agent to start a new exchange relationship. Favours can also be asked between friends. It is an accepted norm that as 'old friends' one should give face to the other when favour is requested. Once again, it has been shown that the Chinese cultural values such as face, hierarchy and power distance are closely related to the creation and development of the business network.

Reciprocity

Guanxi cannot be sustained between two parties if there is no need of reciprocity. Like face, the principle of reciprocity is universal but, in the Chinese case, the concept has particular salience (Kirkbride et al, 1991). When internalized in both parties, the norm obliges the one who has first received a benefit to repay it at a later time. Consequently, there may be less hesitancy in being the first and a greater facility with which the exchange and the social relationship can get underway (Gouldner, 1960). For most Chinese, a transaction or exchange will only take place when there is mutual benefit for both parties involved. As indicated earlier, reciprocity is a 'hostage' that sustains a network relationship. Without reciprocity, established *guanxi* will elapse.

Time/long-term orientation

It was suggested in Yau (1994) that the time dimension for the Chinese has two orientations: past-time orientation and continuity. This implies that for the Chinese, once a relation is established it is hard to break and once a relation is broken, it is very difficult to re-establish (Yau, 1988).

Continuity indicates that Chinese people are long-term oriented. Once a *guanxi* is established, both parties will try their best to keep this relationship by reciprocating benefits. Compromise is found to be the preferred solution by the Chinese to an unsettled conflict (Kirkbride et al, 1991). Future business opportunities also act as hostages to a business relationship. The benefits of establishing a long-term supplier and buyer relationship have been regarded as one of the pillars of Japanese management style, which is now being enthusiastically followed by western firms (Imrie and Morris, 1992). Jarillo (1988) argues that an emphasis on long-term relationships is also essential to the development of trust, which is considered as a critical component of a network.

Harmony

The Confucian 'Doctrine of the Mean' urges individuals to avoid competition and conflict, and to maintain inner harmony (Hsu, 1947). It has been found that traditional Chinese cultural values and cognitive orientations have influenced the Chinese people to preserve overt harmony by avoiding confrontation and to adopt a non-assertive approach to conflict resolution (Kirkbride et al, 1991). *Guanxi* cannot survive without harmony between two parties in a relationship. Without harmonious relationships, trust cannot be established, face cannot be saved, reciprocity will not continue and no further *guanxi* can be established.

It is now evident that the key factors that help sustain and develop networks overlap with the key Chinese cultural values. This is why the network as a form of organizational governance is so widespread in both China and overseas Chinese communities.

Implications and recommendations

While an increasing number of western companies have entered the Chinese market, they are way behind firms from Hong Kong, Taiwan and south-east Asian countries. An estimated 80 per cent of all foreign investment came from overseas Chinese in Hong Kong, Taiwan and south-east Asian countries. The simple reason is that overseas Chinese share the common Chinese cultural values and they can either minimize or avoid problems by using their skills in understanding the Chinese cultural codes. In order to reduce these disadvantages, western firms are advised to pay attention to the following while operating in China.

Good personal relationship vs contract

As has been clearly demonstrated, the most important part of a business relationship is the building of personal relationships. Personal relationships often entwine with business relationships in China. Many foreign companies conduct business based on market situations without too much consideration of the personal feelings involved. They treat business impersonally, while the Chinese do the opposite. Foreigners tend to be contented with the signed contract, while the Chinese look beyond the contract for sincere commitment, as in a good personal relationship. This does not mean that the Chinese will not abide by the signed contract without a good personal relationship. It denotes the general tendency of Chinese people to do business with a long-term orientation. When a deal is closed, you can expect the Chinese to perform their part of it. With good personal relationships, you can always rely on your Chinese partner to find a better

solution when unexpected circumstances occur. In many cases, one can be better off with goodwill and friendship than one can be with a signed contract.

Guanxi and transaction costs

A well-established *guanxi*, however, can go beyond just business facilitation. In the Chinese business community, one can often hear people say, 'This is our old client, we should give them special terms' and 'We are old *guanxi*, therefore we can get better deals'. If someone chooses to ask why he or she is not treated on an equal footing, the answer is very likely, 'you are not our old client'. As a supplier, a good *guanxi* means that you can stay on the value chain of a manufacturer as long as you do not break the codes of *guanxi*, even if you have competition from other suppliers. As a buyer, an old client can get better terms of payment or take delivery of goods on credit, all of which would be impossible without maintaining a good *guanxi*. A well-established *guanxi* is built on the basis of mutual trust, giving face to one another, a good track record of exchanges of favours, long-term non-opportunistic intimacy, obligation or gratitude from past help, etc. It cannot be overused and the favours will have to be reciprocated in one way or another.

Guanxi and consumer/customer loyalty

In a business-to-business relationship, *guanxi* is usually with individuals who are often the representatives of firms. Apart from consistent quality, timely delivery, attractive price and good after-sales services, a good *guanxi* should also be built into the business relations. The obligation that a *guanxi* carries can be developed into a loyalty that ordinary business relations cannot achieve. Without *guanxi*, one can easily lose a customer simply because of an unavoidable human error. You will not even have recourse to remedy. With *guanxi*, you will be excused for future improvement and the business stays.

For a business that is serving the consumer market, *guanxi* or a relationship with the consumers shall be considered as an alternative perspective in approaching the objectives of brand image and brand loyalty. Many foreign companies are using a number of different ways to get publicity, secure more trials and create trust from consumers. Many of these efforts, although appealing and persuasive, still give people a feeling of distance, not being involved or directly related, and therefore cannot be translated into effective means of reinforcement. This also explains why people prefer, among many other means of promotion, discounts or give-aways. Obviously, price discount is not the best way to establish brand image and loyalty. But it will certainly help if you establish your image as a friend, communicate with the consumer on a friendly basis, provide favours to the consumer community, offer opportunities for consumer involvement and give consumers a privileged sense of belonging.

Reciprocity and long-term business relationship

In China, any business relationship should be considered from a long-term view. To maintain a long-term business relationship, one must reciprocate. One never knows when one will be in trouble and a friend in need is a friend indeed. This reflects the necessity of reciprocity. The experience of a joint venture in Beijing offers a typical example of reciprocity. In the early 1990s, one of the suppliers of cashmere in Inner Mongolia had funding problems when planning its technical transformation. The joint venture, a producer of cashmere knitwear, was approached for help. Considering the long-term relationship, the joint venture decided to provide funding for the supplier. In the mid-1990s, the market for cashmere knitwear heated up and the price of cashmere raw material rocketed and, as a consequence, many cashmere knitwear producers had difficulties in absorbing the price rise and had to reduce production. The joint venture faced the same problem. However, the supplier in Inner Mongolia did not forget the help that the joint venture had given and offered to supply cashmere raw material at below market price. The joint venture not only survived the price rise in raw material, but also captured the market that their competitors left because of the price rise. The implication of this joint venture's experience is that the commitment to a good and long-term business relationship and the obligations arising from such a relationship will survive market changes.

Maintain *guanxi* when terminating a business relationship

If a business is not meant to be long term, the way to end a business relationship should be properly selected. It is inappropriate to end a business relationship when a deal cannot be closed by complaining about the way the Chinese counterparts do things. This may not only cause loss of face by the Chinese counterpart, but also put an end to the *guanxi* that may otherwise have

continued. Some foreigners who know very little about China even threaten to report the business failure to the boss or the supervising authority. This conduct is despised as lacking in ethics and is detrimental to the business relationship not only with the Chinese counterparts but also with the other people in the network. As a result, many Chinese companies will avoid doing business with the foreign company.

Network codes and Chinese cultural values require that disputing parties solve problems through amicable means, ie solving the problem without damaging the harmonious business relations. This does not suggest that no litigation is used in settling problems through friendly discussions. It is advisable to exercise care and caution when taking court action. Litigation should be used as a last resort only, when the future course of the business relationship has become clearly unpredictable.

Midway and bureaucracy

The Confucian philosophy, 'Doctrine of the Mean', governs the behaviour and mental actions of the Chinese people. The general tendency that Chinese people do not give answers up-front, saying '*yanjiu yanjiu*' (we will study it), instead of yes or no is often regarded as a sign of bureaucracy by foreign business people. While bureaucracy does exist in China, in business, however, it may have other implications. In China, when people say *yanjiu yanjiu*, it might indicate that he or she is not sure, has limited authority, does not see your proposal as viable but does not want to disappoint you by saying no, or that he or she wants to have a collective decision rather than an individual one. What frustrates foreign business people is that the *yanjiu yanjiu* process could take a matter of weeks or months before they get an answer. If you can have a yes answer in a couple of weeks' time, it may imply that your proposal has been received positively. If it takes a couple of months to get a yes answer, there might have been a lot internal balancing and your proposal has cleared the way. Unfortunately, you will only have your assumptions to rely on when you cannot get either a positive or a negative answer, which may mean that your proposal is not going to work or it is not the right time to do it or there is internal disagreement that your Chinese partners do not want you to know of. To articulate your assumptions, it is recommended that foreigners enquire about the progress at appropriate and graceful intervals, which will help shape a reasonable answer.

Some foreigners who have had some experience in China might have found that negotiation may revert to things discussed and agreed. The reason, in many cases, is that the negotiator has received from his superiors instructions in principle, which often do not cover details that may be revealed in the course of discussion. This is, again, a reflection of the midway way of doing things and the in-built ambiguity of instructions in principle. This process can be easily observed if the superior happens to be present at the negotiation, during which the negotiator will be stopped, interrupted and corrected from time to time by the superior. The implication here may be that the subject brought up is likely to be something that has caused internal disagreements or is perceived to have operational difficulties from the higher level of the decision-maker's point of view. Sometimes, it may be more to the benefit of foreigners to help them out than to insist on things being agreed that the Chinese partners have, or perceive having, difficulties in executing.

Accessing business networks via recruiting contact persons

This aspect has a strong implication for foreign firms' recruitment policies. For those companies exploring the Chinese market, the advice is to recruit contacts, who can sometimes be life-saving. The contacts could be local residents having active business or social networks or immigrants with business-related work experiences or family background. The mistake is that, in many cases, foreign companies tend to employ the Chinese in their home country for their operations in China, simply because they look Chinese. Those Chinese may not have the understanding of the market that you would require for making a successful entry.

As has been argued already, operational issues such as volume uncertainty can be best dealt with within a network. It is a well-known fact that foreign firms are usually not sure who the Chinese decision-makers are. These contact persons could not only find the decision-makers without too much difficulty, but can also help build the trust between the Chinese decision-makers and western companies. They can not only save western companies time and money but also future business deals, because they have no trouble with cultural barriers and they are fully aware of the Chinese ritual codes and protocols. The implication here is that foreign companies, while recruiting contacts, can at the same time gain access to a network

in the Chinese market or become part of the existing network through the facilitation of those contacts.

However, although hiring a useful contact person is a good accomplishment as a start, retaining the contact person can sometimes be a daunting task. As the demand for contact persons or senior management is much higher than the market can supply, 'job hopping' is becoming more and more a practice in the Chinese job market. One of the reasons for this is the difference in approach between the Chinese and foreigners. As a business network is based on the linkage facilitated by trusted contact persons, this has determined that the way in which contact persons do things will have a distinctively different style from that of foreigners. In some cases, these different styles are not understood and supported by the foreign employers. Another reason could be a result of the general perception by foreigners that the average level of labour cost is low and that contact people are therefore not properly remunerated in terms of salary package. This issue has to be handled sensibly. Losing them to one's competitors means loss of money and future business contracts. The possible solution to this problem is diversification and development of the new contact person. However, proper training and reward packages may be another alternative. While the importance of contact people cannot be over-emphasized, the establishment of good business relationships with all important business clients, government offices and policy makers is a must for any business in the Chinese market to succeed.

Conclusion

To summarize, maintaining harmony is one of the key virtues of social behaviour. That is why in China, even if one is in the right, one should not treat the other party so harshly as to make him/her lose face. Important here is that in doing business in China, one should keep all relationships harmonious and long-term oriented whenever it is possible, as one does not know when a seemingly useless relationship will one day save one's commercial life or business. Western companies should also have a long-term commitment in the Chinese market. To succeed in the Chinese market, foreign firms are advised to use mentors (contact people) to start up a business relationship. Understanding the way things are done in China can be difficult for foreigners, but will be rewarding as well. Whenever possible, a harmonious relationship should be kept and favours must be reciprocated. A legal solution should be the last option for solving business problems. For readers who are interested in exploring how *guanxi* can be established and maintained, the chapter on effective public relations (Chapter 6.5) may provide some practical guidance.

It can be concluded that the Chinese business network is a 'dynamic organization', which has contributed a great deal to the recent economic transformation in China. This dynamism is embedded in the key Chinese cultural values, as network codes overlap with the key Chinese cultural values. Networks are not only efficient but also effective. They can internalize an existing market as well as create a non-existent market.

References and bibliography

Agelasto, Michael (1996) *Cellularism, Guanxiwang, and Corruption: a Microcosmic View from within a Chinese Educational Danwei*, paper given at the annual meeting of the Association of Asian Studies, April, Honolulu.

Alston, Jon (1988) 'Wa, Guanxi, and Inhwa: Managerial Principles in Japan, China and Korea', *Business Horizon*, March/April, 26–31.

Bian, Yanjie (1994) 'Guanxi and the Allocation of Urban Jobs in China', *The China Quarterly*, Vol. 4, 971–99.

Boisot, Max and Child, John (1988) 'The Iron Law of Fiefs: Bureaucratic Failure and the Problem of Governance in the Chinese Economic Reforms', *Administrative Science Quarterly*, 33: 507–27.

Boisot, Max and Child, John (1990) 'Efficiency, Ideology and Tradition in the Choice of Transactions Governance Structures: The Case of China as a Modernising Society', in Clegg, ST and Redding, Gordon S. (eds), *Capitalism in Contrasting Cultures*, Berlin: Walter de Gruyter.

Boisot, Max and Child, John (1994) 'China's Emerging Economic Order: Modernisation through "Weak" Markets and Quasi-Capitalism?', paper given to the conference on 'Management Issues for China in the 1990s', March 23–5, Cambridge.

Bond, Michael (1987) 'Chinese Values and the Search for Culture-Free Dimensions of Culture: The Chinese Culture Connection', *Journal of Cross-Cultural Psychology*, 18/2: 143–64.

Chong, Ju Choi (1994) 'Contract Enforcement across Cultures', *Organisation Studies*, 15/5: 673–82.

Deglopper, D.R. (1978) 'Doing Business in Lukang', in Wolf, A.P. (ed.), *Studies in Chinese Society*, Stanford: Stanford University Press.

East Asia Analytical Unit (1995) *Overseas Chinese Business Networks in Asia*, Department of Foreign Affairs and Trade, Australia: AGPS Press.

The Economist (1989) 'Free Markets for Free People'. 27 May: 62.

Gao, Gang (1994) 'The Fear of being Cheated: a Widespread Social Disease', *China News Digest*, an electronic Chinese magazine, No. 188.

Gouldner, Alvin W. (1960) 'The Norm of Reciprocity: A Preliminary Statement', *American Sociological Review*, 25/2: 161–78.

Granovetter, M. (1985) 'Economic Action and Social Structure: The Problem of Embeddedness', *American Journal of Sociology*, 91: 481–510.

Hamilton, Garry G., Zeile, William and Kim, Wan-Jin (1990) 'The Network Structures of East Asian Economics', in Clegg, ST and Redding, Gordon S. (eds), *Capitalism in Contrasting Cultures*, Berlin: Walter de Gruyter.

Hofstede, Geert (1993) 'Cultural Constraints in Management Theories', *Academy of Management Executive*, 7/1: 81–94.

Hsu, F.L.K. (1947) *Under the Ancestor's Shadow: Kingship, Personality, and Social Mobility in China*, Stanford: Stanford University Press.

Hu, H.C. (1944) 'Chinese Concept of Face', *American Anthropologist*, 46: 45–64.

Imrie, R. and Morris, J. (1992) 'A Review of Recent Changes in Buyer-Supplier Relations', *International Journal of Management Science*, 20, 5/6: 641–52.

Jarillo, Jose-Carlos (1988) 'On Strategic Networks', *Strategic Management Journal*, 9: 31–41.

Johanson, Jan and Mattsson, Lars-Gunnar (1985) 'Marketing Investments and Market Investments in Industrial Networks', *International Journal of Research in Marketing*, 2: 185–95.

Johanson, Jan and Mattsson, Lars-Gunnar (1987) 'Interorganisational Relations in Industrial Systems', *International Studies of Management and Organisation*, 17: 34–48.

Kao, Cheng-shu (1991) '"Personal Trust" in the Large Businesses in Taiwan: A Traditional Foundation for Contemporary Economic Activities', in Hamilton, G. (ed.), *Business Networks and Economic Development in East and Southeast Asia*, Centre for Asian Studies, University of Hong Kong.

Kao, John (1993) 'The World-wide Web of Chinese Business', *Harvard Business Review*. March/April: 24–36.

Kirkbride, Paul S. et al. (1991) 'Chinese Conflict Preferences and Negotiating Behaviour: Cultural and Psychological Influence', *Organisation Studies*, 12/3: 365–86.

Latourette, Kenneth Scott (1972) *The Chinese: their History and Culture*, London: Collier-Macmillan Limited.

Li, Xiandong and Wu, Qinghua (1993) Theoretical chapter on guanxinology, in Zheng, Liang, Wen, 'Control of Unhealthy Tendencies should be Tightened up not Loosened', *Democracy and Law*, 168: 2–3.

Lockett, Martin (1988) 'Culture and the Problems of Chinese Management', *Organisation Studies*, 9/4: 475–96.

Low, Linda (1995) 'The Overseas Chinese Connection: An ASEAN Perspective', *Journal of Southeast Asian Studies*, 89–117.

Macauley, Stewart (1963) 'Non-contractual Relations in Business: A Preliminary Study', *American Sociological Review*, 28: 55–69.

Maitland, Ian et al. (1985) 'Sociologists, Economists, and Opportunism', *Academy of Management Review*, 10/1: 59–65.

Numazaki, Ichiro (1985) 'The Role of Personal Networks in the Making of Taiwan's Guanxiquiye (Related Enterprises)', in Hamilton, G. (ed.), *Business Networks and Economic Development in East and Southeast Asia*, Centre for Asian Studies, University of Hong Kong, 1991.

Omohundro, John T. (1983) 'Social Networks and Business Success for the Philippine Chinese', in Lim, L. and Gosling, L.A. Peter (eds) *The Chinese in Southeast Asia*, Vol. 1, Ethnicity and Economic Activity, Singapore: Maruzen Asia.

Ouchi, William G. (1980) 'Markets, Bureaucracies and Clans', *Administrative Science Quarterly*, 25: 129–41.

People's Daily overseas edition (1996) 28 June: 6.

Redding, S. Gordon (1990) *The Spirit of Chinese Capitalism*, Berlin: Walter de Gruyter.

Redding, S. Gordon (1991) 'Weak Organisations and Strong Linkages: Managerial Ideology and Chinese Family Business Networks', in Hamilton, G.G. (ed.) *Business Networks and Economic Development in East and South East Asia*, Centre for Asian Studies, University of Hong Kong.

Redding, S. Gordon (1995) 'Overseas Chinese Networks: Understanding the Enigma', *Long Range Planning*, 28/1: 61–9.

Smith, Arthur H. (1894) *Chinese Characteristics*, London: Revell.

Solinger, D.J. (1989) 'Urban Reform and Relational Contracting in Post-Mao China. An Interpretation of the Transition from Plan to Market', *Studies in Comparative Communism*, 23: 171–85.

State Statistical Bureau, People's Republic of China (1995) *China Statistical Yearbook*, Beijing: China Statistical Publishing House.

Su Sijin (1994) *The Dynamics of Market-Oriented Growth of Chinese Firms in Post-Maoist China: An Institutional Approach*. Unpublished PhD thesis. Cornell University.

Thorelli, Hans B. (1986) 'Networks: Between Markets and Hierarchies', *Strategic Management Journal*, 7: 37–51.

Walker, Gordon, and Weber, David (1984) 'A Transaction Cost Approach to Make-or-Buy Decision', *Administrative Science Quarterly*, 29: 373–91.

Williamson, Oliver E. (1975) *Markets and Hierarchies*, New York: Free Press.

Williamson, Oliver E. (1979) 'Transaction Cost Economies: the Governance of Contractual Relations', *Journal of Law and Economics*, 22/2: 233–61.

Williamson, Oliver E. (1981) 'The Economics of Organisation', *American Journal of Sociology*, 87: 548–77.

Willamson, Oliver E. (1983) 'Credible Commitments: Using Hostages to Support Exchange', *American Economic Review*, 73: 519–40.

Wong, Gilbert (1991) 'Business Groups in a Dynamic Environment: Hong Kong 1976–1986', in Hamilton, G. (ed.) *Business Networks and Economic Development in East and South East Asia*, Centre for Asian Studies, University of Hong Kong.

Wong, Siu-lun (1995) 'Business Networks, Cultural Values and the State in Hong Kong and Singapore', in Brown, Rajeswary (ed.), *Chinese Business Enterprises in Asia*, New York: Routledge.

Wu, Wei-Ping (1995a) 'Towards a Definition of Guanxiwang (network) and its Significance in Business Transactions in China', *Proceedings of Academy of International Business Southeast Asia Regional Conference*, Perth, Australia: 129–34.

Wu, Wei-Ping (1995b) 'Barriers in the Path of Chinese Firms' Internationalisation Efforts', *Journal of Chinese Political Science*, 2: 109–26.

Yau, Oliver H.M. (1988) 'Chinese Cultural Values: their Dimensions and Marketing Implications', *European Journal of Marketing*, 22/5: 44–57.

Yau, Oliver H.M. (1994) *Consumer Behaviour in China: Customer Satisfaction and Cultural Values*, London: Routledge.

Yoshihara, Kunio (1991) *Ethnic Chinese and Ersatz Capitalism*, paper given to the International Conference on Southeast Asian Chinese: Culture, Economy and Society, organized by the Singapore Society of Asian Studies, the Association of Nanyang University Graduates and the Singapore Federation of Chinese Clans Association, 12–13 January, Singapore.

Zamet, M. Jonathan, and Bovarnick, Murray E. (1986) 'Employee Relations for Multinational Companies in China', *Columbia Journal of World Business*, Spring: 13–19.

Zhang, Jian Hau and Yu Lin (1995) *Xiang Zhen Qi Ye Di Jue Qi Yu Fa Zhan Mo Shi*, Wuhan: Hu Bei Jiao Yu Chu Ban She.

Due Diligence for Market Entrants

Li Yong, Deputy Secretary General, China Association of International Trade, and Jonathan Reuvid

Introduction

Interest in the China market arises from different causes, but is often not the result of serious study and informed discussion. Imagining the size of this market would excite any CEO and the simple maths of tapping into a tiny fraction of it may prompt a visit to China. It might be thought that such a visit can only be beneficial to both sides, but unfortunately this is not always the case. If the homework has not been done to prepare for the visit, and the mission is not supported by experienced and honest advisers, the stage may well be set not for the jump-start of a successful new project in China, but for a series of delays and disappointments based on false expectations and misunderstandings on both sides.

It is true that China presents many opportunities in terms of trade and investment. However, lack of understanding about the market is often the cause of failure and can thwart closely-calculated business plans. Thorough due diligence is of crucial importance in shortening the learning curve and minimizing possible risks. In this book, there are many chapters that focus on the complexity and intricacies of doing business in China and provide insightful comments on how a company should approach the market. This chapter intends to provide, for new market entrants, an additional and different perspective on what due diligence is needed. These may be over-used clichés, but an ounce of prevention is worth a pound of cure and a stitch in time does save nine. The point to emphasize is that due diligence is a much wider concept here than is generally realized. It is not a partner-specific investigation effort, but an endeavour to widen the scope of understanding about the market.

Where is the market?

This may seem an obvious question requiring no answer, as everybody knows that China has a population of 1.3 billion and that must be the market. However, the reality is not so simple. Only a few companies can really consider selling to 1.3 billion people, while most will be working on gaining a share of the market. Where this share of the market should come from is really a question of where the market is.

All too often, a foreign company would think first of large urban centres like Beijing, Shanghai and Guangzhou as points of entry, and many have been given advice by various kinds of advisers or consultants to attack these large urban markets because they have the most affluent consumers. It is true that these large urban centres are the most dynamic local economies where opportunities exist. However, they are crowded not only with domestic players but also with international competitors. The trend of internationalized competition is more pronounced in the large urban centres than in other areas. The benefits and costs of entering these markets need to be carefully weighed against other alternative entry strategies.

On China's mainland there are 31 administrative regions, each with its own development policy and plan, and each competing to develop its economy. Since the characteristics of all regions vary from the next, they can be regarded as separate markets. Due diligence investigation should concentrate on these regional differences and identify the most suitable entry market to attack. If a high level of competition exists in the market you are targeting, consider choosing a region that has a less high profile to establish your foothold in the market.

How to approach the market

Figure 5.4.1 shows a generalized situation in which a company can eventually reach its final market. There are a number of different routes for a foreign company to make its approach:

- through a local foreign trade corporation;
- through Hong Kong for an agent, distributor or partner;
- establishing a representative office;
- exhibiting at trade fairs;
- appointing a distributor or agent in China;
- direct marketing;
- advertising in industry-specific trade journals or magazines;
- opening your own distributorship or retail stores;
- negotiating a joint venture with a local company;
- bidding on projects.

China's accession to the WTO will improve the trade environment over the next five years. Tariff reductions and the dismantling of non-tariff barriers will greatly increase opportunities for export to China. China's commitment to opening up the service sector to foreign-owned distribution will allow greater levels of participation in the market. China's promise to grant full trading rights to all enterprises, without discrimination against foreign players, will offer a wider range of options for foreign businesses to tap into the development of the market. However, at the micro level, the possibility of failure still exists if the entry process is not carefully monitored. The alternative operating modes that are available now, and will be made available in the near future, have advantages and disadvantages, which are compared in Table 5.4.1.

Identifying your business partner

China has millions of companies and enterprises and there are many different reasons for a foreign business to find a Chinese business partner: export and import from China, investment in China, contract manufacturing and so on. It is an arduous job to search among such a vast number of companies and enterprises for the right partner to work with. Market research will help to generate a list of potential business partners. If you do not wish to employ a consulting firm, there are other alternatives for identifying business partners.

Contact the overseas offices of Chinese companies

Many large Chinese companies have set up their own overseas offices. These offices are responsible for the import and export of Chinese products. Working with these offices will save time, and communications with them are normally easier as they are run by people who understand the language of the host country. A list of such companies can be obtained from the Chinese embassies in the host country.

Approach the commercial section of the Chinese embassy in your location

Chinese embassies have a commercial function of responsibility for trade promotion. They normally maintain a database containing information on enterprises in different industries and this information is usually provided free of charge. In addition, they may also have information on important trade missions from China. Inviting Chinese trade missions to visit your company or production sites can be a convenient and cost-effective way of initiating contacts with potential business partners/buyers.

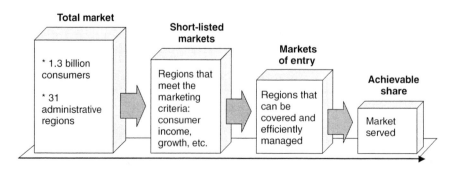

Figure 5.4.1   Roadmap to the market

Table 5.4.1 Alternative modes of operation for market entry

Mode of operation	Strengths	Weaknesses
Use of own staff	Full control of the process	Long learning curve, frequent travel, long lead time
Representative office in China	In the market, help of local staff and hands-on control	Very costly (minimum US$250,000/year for a basic establishment), limited functionality
Having an office in Hong Kong	Close to the market	Higher costs, frequent travel
Agents	Low cost, network advantages	Little control, dependence
Consultants	Expert experience, cost effective, inside track (local consultants)	Part-time service, no control
Joint venture	Have local partner, shared risk, understanding of local conditions	Limited to product/project, disagreement on corporate strategies and implementation
Wholly owned operation	Full control of the operation	Start-up difficulties due to limited understanding of the local conditions
Own distribution	Full control of the channels	Unfamiliarity with the channels, limited access at present

Visit industry associations or import and export chambers in China

If you are planning a trip to China, arrangements with relevant industry associations are a good way to gain an understanding of the industry in which you have a particular interest, and at the same time you can procure a list of referrals from them. Normally, it would useful to employ a local contact to arrange such visits. Most industry associations and all import and export chambers are located in Beijing.

Hold technical seminars or product introduction meetings

This type of activity should be designed as a targeted exercise and requires the help of a local company such as a consulting firm, a public relations company or the consulting function of an industry association to arrange for the appropriate audience. Such services are available on a fee basis.

Attend trade fairs and exhibitions

Numerous trade fairs and exhibitions are held in China and attended by an array of Chinese companies. Guangzhou Export Commodity Fair, for example, twice a year gathers together thousands of Chinese companies to demonstrate their products in sectioned areas of the exhibition compound. There are also professional trade industry-specific fairs or exhibitions in areas such as plastics, fine chemicals, automobiles, water treatment, electrical equipment and many more, held regularly or occasionally. These trade fairs and exhibitions are normally held in large cities such as

Beijing, Shanghai and Guangzhou. Information on major trade fairs can be obtained from the commercial section of Chinese embassies, overseas offices of the China Council for the Promotion of International Trade (CCPIT), industry associations, and import and export chambers.

Advertise in professional newspapers, magazines and journals

For industrial products, another possibility for establishing contacts is to advertise in professional newspapers, magazines and journals. There are thousands of trade press publications that target professional readers or industry specialists, who may contact you with specific business propositions.

Purchase mailing lists from database companies and launch direct mail advertising

There are now a number of companies offering database search services for a fee. Armed with a mailing list, companies who wish to test end-user interest can launch direct mail campaigns. Such an exercise will generate a shortlist of companies that have an interest in working with you.

Join the trade missions organized by your government or industry associations

Foreign governments and industry associations often maintain bilateral relations with their Chinese counterparts. They frequently organize trade missions to China, some of which are coordinated with state or official visits. In all cases, there will be scheduled arrangements for business interactions with Chinese companies. This exercise encourages government attention that will be beneficial in China, as Chinese companies tend to be very careful with projects that have a governmental background or support.

Internet search

Many Chinese enterprises have websites, thanks to the government's encouragement of information technology, and many are in English.

How to assess your business partner

Checking the credit history of Chinese companies can be challenging, if not impossible. Credit agencies claim that they have special contacts that will ensure accuracy in their reporting of the credit status of Chinese companies. However, it is always advisable to check with different sources and to crosscheck the results, if having a good and thorough understanding of your partner's financial situation is essential. In cases of exporting to China, the best proof of a company's credibility is whether or not the Chinese company is able to open a letter of credit from the bank. If so, you can save the effort of checking the company's financial standing because the opening bank will have done the job.

If you want to establish a business relationship that goes further than simply exporting to China, you may need to understand more than the financial situation. Other elements such as the vision the company has for the market, the management team and its possible terms of service, corporate background and relationships with suppliers and distributors. In many cases, observation of interpersonal relationships, the manufacturing site and the office area will give you a reasonable level of intelligence for judgemental evaluation. Talking to suppliers and distributors/agents, and even a customer or two, can be very useful for gaining an understanding of your partner.

In some places, there is a system of misconduct blacklists instituted for the purpose of establishing good business credibility. In Beijing, for example, the Beijing Administration of Industry and Commerce launched a Misconduct Record System in July 2001, blacklisting those who have been caught engaging in illegitimate economic activities or misconduct. Some banks also maintain a blacklist of companies or persons who fail to honour loan repayment contracts.

Key terms and conditions in an import contract

In China, importers tend to use standard form contracts in their import transactions. Foreign contracts are seldom accepted for fear of being trapped by contract stipulations with which they are not familiar. Adding special provisions to the contract form is normally acceptable. The key terms and conditions include the following.

Terms of price and shipment

In China's import businesses, many transactions are concluded at FOB prices in consideration for using Chinese shipping companies. C&F and CIF terms are accepted only if the freight is proved to be cost-effective.

Insurance

Commodities imported by China are normally in larger quantities and of a great many varieties. Some goods, due to transport reasons, need to be stored in foreign ports or wait for shipment or transhipment. It would be very complicated and troublesome to arrange insurance on a case by case basis. Therefore, companies that conduct frequent import businesses normally have 'open insurance' for their import cargoes, ie the importing companies submit their notifications of import cargo shipments and other relevant documents, which are acknowledged by the insurance company as insurance orders and against which the insurance premium will be settled with the insured.

Terms of payment

For most imports, payments are made by L/Cs (letters of credit). The opening of an L/C is based on the contract signed between the Chinese buyer and foreign seller. The L/Cs opened by Chinese banks, particularly reputable national banks, are accepted by foreign banks and there will be no problems of non-payment on the part of the Chinese banks if the requirements of the L/C are met. It should be noted, however, that the L/C, once effected by the bank, will become a contract independent of the purchase contract in the sense that the bank undertakes the responsibility of making payment provided that the documents submitted to it are in strict compliance with the stipulations of the L/C, regardless of the stipulations of the purchase contract. Conversely, if the documents submitted by the seller for negotiation of payment do not conform with the requirements of the L/C, the bank will reject payment regardless of the contract stipulations.

Therefore, it is always advisable for foreign exporters to check carefully the contents of the L/C against the terms agreed in the contract. If anything that is found in the L/C does not conform with the contract stipulations, the exporter should request amendments from the importer. As a matter of principle, Chinese importers and banks will not issue confirmed L/Cs.

Inspection

Certificates of quality and quantity or weight issued by manufacturers or public assessors are normally required as a part of the negotiating documents for payment under the relevant L/C. However, in cases where the quality, quantity or weight of the goods is found not to be in conformity with those stipulated in the contract after re-inspection by Chinese inspection authorities within the agreed period after arrival of the goods at the port of destination, the importer usually either returns the goods to the exporter or lodges claims against the seller for compensation of losses on the strength of inspection at the port of destination.

In the case of equipment imports, Chinese companies will often insert a clause in the contract withholding a portion of the payment, normally 5–10 per cent of the total contract value, which will be paid only when the equipment is installed and commissioned.

Dispute resolution

In cases of dispute, the formal contract has a provision that a solution must be sought through friendly consultation. If this does not produce a result, arbitration is then adopted to settle the disputes. Litigation is only a last resort.

How to manage sales and distribution effectively: selection of agents and distributors

As a starting point, companies should define an optimal mix of direct and wholesale accounts. The parameters should be first and foremost the cost-to-serve economics that determine optimal effectiveness in running one's own independent sales network versus alternative channels to market.

Markets can be divided into core and secondary by their level of importance to the company, location advantages and disadvantages and manageability. Generally, it is advisable to serve the core market with one's own sales force, while leaving secondary markets to agents and distributors.

To manage wholesalers properly, companies need to define their wholesaler selection criteria and performance measurement.

Selection criteria

Maturity
- company size;
- age (history);
- previous experience;
- technical capability (ability to lead technical personnel);
- management competence;
- financial stability.

Operating (serviced) area
- local operator (servicing only one market);
- regional operator (servicing several neighbouring/selected markets);
- national operator (servicing all key markets countrywide).

Terms and conditions
- payment terms;
- volume commitment;
- commitment to promotion and advertising.

Other
- transportation;
- feedback system;
- warehousing;
- after-sale service levels;
- required skills of salespeople.

When managing agent/distributor relationships, it is suggested that companies link performance with incentives and provide regular, scheduled training to the selected wholesalers in order to achieve optimal effectiveness.

How to source from China

Increased global competition requires marketers to lower their costs effectively in order to survive the competition. One of the options for achieving lower costs is to outsource parts, components or even the whole product. China is a low-cost outsourcing destination. There are basically two options when setting up your own production presence in China: direct import from China and/or contract manufacturing.

In both cases, two types of companies must be considered: export trading companies and manufacturing companies with export licences (licences are available to all enterprises within five years of China's accession to the WTO in November 2001). The advantages and disadvantages of both types are analysed in Table 5.4.2.

Caution must be exercised when choosing between the two types of vendor. The following provide some guidelines for foreign companies outsourcing in China.

Vendor maturity

Vendor maturity can be measured by several criteria including:

- company size (annual sales, total headcount, capacity);
- age (history);
- previous experience;
- export records;
- understanding of foreign customer concerns;
- financing capability for export sales;
- production capability (capacity to handle volume, equipment conditions, quality assurance system);
- management (professional backgrounds, understanding of export practices, language).

Factors to be considered if the vendor is a trading company:

- sourcing capabilities (financing, geographical coverage);
- experience (history, relationships with key suppliers and key ports, export records);

- staff (language proficiency, understanding of international trade practices, attitudes).

It is always worthwhile contacting several vendors to compare prices and quality before you decide with whom to contract. Even if you have chosen one that you think is satisfactory, start with a small order before you become totally dependent on the partner. It is also advisable to be aware that deliveries are often late because of infrastructure problems in some areas. Another factor that causes late delivery is over-commitment by producers to export orders. If you are to place an order, it is advisable to make time allowances for the expected delivery.

Dealing with language problems to achieve best possible communications

Apart from the differences of culture, history and politics, language is a significant barrier in business communications. It might be thought that the possibility of language problems would be high on the priority list of those entering the China market but evidence suggests that language difficulties are seldom given any serious thought.

Language problems in written communications

The work of organizing translations and the preparation of presentation materials are all too often delegated to a public relations department, which in turn passes the job on to someone whose experience they cannot judge. Worse still, foreign managers tend to

Table 5.4.2   Comparative strengths and weaknesses of importing channels from China

	Strengths	Weaknesses
Export trading company	Export-oriented	Lack of understanding about product
	Handling variety of products	Less control over quality
	More international exposure	Less control of production schedules
	Professional trade staff	Dependent on price mark-ups
	Sourcing from different areas (order consolidation)	Insufficient understanding of the manufacturers by the buyers
	Familiarity with trade practices	
Manufacturers	Understanding of product nature	Lack of understanding about trade practices
	Technically competent	Less international exposure
	Quality control	Operating in one area only
	Control over production schedules	Inability to consolidate orders
	No mark-up on product costs	Lack of experience in handling export-related matters
	Direct communication on product requirements	

take it for granted that the interpreter employed to do the job will carry it out. This may not be true. Frequently, mistakes in translations are made, even by large organizations that could easily afford to ensure that the bridge that they are trying to build into the China market gives them a good image as serious players, rather than making them a laughing stock. Smaller companies often use translation services in their home country or in Taiwan, Hong Kong and the mainland. Because of a lack of industry knowledge and reluctance to consult with industry people when translating, the poor quality of translation often results in non-professional language.

Despite the 20-odd years that have elapsed since China opened its doors to foreign trade and investment, some companies are still having their brochures translated by translators from Taiwan or Hong Kong, whose style of language and technical terminology are different from that of the mainland. Take the name of President Bush, for example: in each of these three locations the Chinese translation is different, although the name is transliterated in all cases. Differences in translating President Bush's name do not really cost anything, but variations in translations of technical terms and marketing concepts will be more likely to cause misunderstandings or costly clarification efforts. In addition, Hong Kong and other non-mainland printers are still to be found using archaic, complex characters, instead of the simplified characters that the younger generation on the mainland now learns in school; indeed, many have difficulty recognizing complex Chinese characters.

In business correspondence, poor translation may well lead to misunderstanding or disregarded communications between the two sides of a business relationship. In such cases, the translator often takes the easy option of using familiar words rather than going deeper to convey the meaning and feeling vested in the wording.

Language problems in oral communications

The problems in written communications are easily identified, since the evidence is on paper for all to see. But examples of interpretation problems in the spoken language are more difficult to document. It may be assumed, however, that the same people who are so ignorant and careless of written language are no less cavalier in their treatment of other aspects of the language problem. One of the authors of this chapter recently received a long-distance call from the manager of a joint venture, which he helped to establish several

years ago. They were having a board meeting to discuss the next steps in their marketing plan, but had problems understanding the foreign partner's proposition. He talked to the foreign manager for a while and found that it was in fact the interpreter who could not get the message across.

It is unfortunately true, broadly speaking, that the language barrier is seldom paid much attention by the business world and even if interpretation has been identified as a potential problem, sufficient resources may not be made available to find effective solutions.

The easygoing attitude that everything will be 'all right on the night' and that the Chinese side will provide an interpreter is not safe. If the interpreter, particularly one who has won the job on the basis of a language qualification from a university, finds him/herself out of his/her depth and there is no one to help, there is a serious danger that he/she will be too embarrassed to admit to the difficulty and ask for clarification. Worse still, to cover up his/her ignorance and embarrassment, the interpreter may be tempted to make something up. Such cover-ups may lead to the loss of some vital point, or to major misunderstandings.

It is certainly unwise to rely on the Chinese side to find someone from within their own organization who will perform effectively as an interpreter on behalf of both sides. In a non-negotiation environment, particularly in daily management communications in a joint venture, one of the problems, unconnected to language, is that the potential bias of the interpreter, conscious or otherwise, can easily lead to an interpretation that shades the meaning or to choosing 'doctored' language in order to please the audience.

It is also unrealistic to assume that any well-educated Chinese, who can speak understandable English, will be able to provide effective interpretation in complex negotiations. The foreigner's ignorance of the Chinese language will make it difficult to judge the quality of the interpretation; remember that there is a huge difference between the ability to conduct a reasonable dialogue in a private situation and the ability to interpret in public, particularly when faced with new subject matter which may be highly technical, and will certainly have a strange vocabulary, idiom, accents and personal idiosyncrasies. Even a practised, professional interpreter may have some difficulty with new specialist terms outside his/her general knowledge, or in understanding the idiosyncratic accents and idioms of strangers.

All these considerations apply whether the interpreter is from the Chinese or foreign side. The fundamental weakness is the same. It is perhaps surprising, in view of the number of occasions when this amateurish arrangement has been used, that so much business has eventually been negotiated. But the speed of negotiating could certainly have been much faster and many misunderstandings could have been avoided if proper arrangements for interpreting had been the rule, rather than the exception. We shall never know how many negotiations have failed and deals aborted because of failure to pay serious attention to overcoming the language barrier.

Advice for dealing with such language problems is:

- A glossary of technical terms should be prepared before the negotiation takes place. This will enable the interpreter to understand the technical side of the business and facilitate a smooth conduct of the technical discussions.
- Your own interpreter should be present. Whether or not he/she is going to play the role of interpreter, he/she should be assigned the additional role of picking up the points that have not been conveyed correctly in the process.
- Before you engage an outside interpreter, you should make sure that the interpreter is able to perform the job. Do not risk using an interpreter who speaks only 'understandable' English. He/she should be given sufficient briefing about the background of the business.
- The principal negotiator should be prepared to speak slowly with frequent pauses. In many cases, the principal negotiator will forget that he/she is talking to people who do not understand his/her language and keeps talking until he/she thinks he/she has finished his/her argument. But the interpreter may not be able to memorize your long speech. The longer you talk, the more likely you are to confuse your interpreter and the less you can put across effectively to your listeners.
- Debrief the interpreter after each session to ensure he/she is able to keep up with your style of speech.

Building an in-house China team

Undertaking proper market research to gain a better understanding of the market is one aspect of the effort to prepare for entry into China. Another is the development of an in-house China team to use this understanding to penetrate the market. All too often, a company does not deploy sufficient resources to build a China team within its organization. This is entirely understandable for those companies that are only testing the water, but those who have established a firm interest will need to set up an in-house, expert capability before launching themselves into a campaign to tackle the market. Unfortunately, few organizations attempt to do this, and in many cases such responsibility is delegated to a department handling the Asian region market in general.

Those who do attempt to set up their own China department naturally have some difficulty in deciding the best way to find and recruit staff who can offer the appropriate qualifications, including linguistic and general communication skills.

Recently graduated language students are one obvious pool of potential talent, but only a most exceptional recruit from the field is likely to meet more than a part of the job requirements. Even their linguistic skills are likely to be limited unless the student has spent years in China, not only while at university. Also, unless the students are much older than normal first degree graduates, their general business experience can hardly be very wide. All these considerations may make it difficult for new recruits, coming straight from university, to perform initially as anything other than a student interpreter. This is not to say that good recruits cannot be found from this pool of talent, but they will need time before their skills are likely to meet total requirements.

On the other hand, the pool of foreigners available who are both experienced in the China market and linguistically qualified, is likely to be severely limited. Most of those who might meet the requirements will either already be retired, or still be gainfully employed. If such an experienced person can be found to act in the liaison role, and recruited as a part of the company team planning its China entry strategy and tactics, this is certainly a good solution to the problem, but mature people with experience of the Chinese market and Chinese language qualification are more likely to be successfully in mid-career, rather than in the job market.

Fortunately, there is a third, growing source of suitable talent: the pool of Chinese with good English and an understanding of western culture, who have either worked in western countries for years or been educated in western schools. These second-generation Chinese, born, brought up and educated in western countries, are known as 'bananas'. When recruiting these, companies should be careful not to make judgements based only on their Chinese appearance. Their understanding of Chinese culture, business experiences with and/or in China are just as crucial as when you recruit your own fellow countrymen. There is an increasing number of young elite who, after several years of experience working in China, are now studying in western schools. Their business experience can be valuable in building your China team's capability.

If you intend to set up an office in China, it is possible to recruit local Chinese talents with business experience and essential communication skills. Although they may have less understanding of the foreign culture, many will have worked with foreign companies and gained a reasonable understanding of western business norms and practices. They will bring with them a much broader and deeper knowledge of the Chinese language, and should have a greater understanding of Chinese culture and systems. They can certainly make very good members of a foreign business team. However, although a decision to recruit from the mainland immediately broadens the scope of the search, such a solution may well not commend itself to a company that has no Chinese experience, and therefore no criteria by which to judge the suitability of the candidates. The use of a professional head-hunter may help to solve the problem. Following China's WTO accession, foreign head-hunting services in the form of joint ventures are now available.

Finally, since China is a country with a traditional respect for age, young graduates will have to overcome age prejudice, in addition to their lack of business and technical experience. Therefore, it is advisable to appoint a middle-aged manager to take charge of the China operation.

Using the services of advisers

Recruiting staff for an in-house China capability is difficult for companies that have decided to tackle the Chinese market and that, almost by definition, do not have any in-house expertise to enable them to judge the quality of outside advice, or the suitability of potential recruits on offer. Therefore, many companies entering the China market find themselves in uncharted waters and at the mercy of outside advisers and interpreters. The choice of reliable advisers and effective interpreters is crucial to the success of any initial operation, but there is no magic formula that can guarantee the right choice. The rule of thumb for businesses starting out in the China market is to take counsel from more than one adviser.

When seeking external advice, consulting firms can be valuable contacts, if they can provide a holistic evaluation of the market, knowledge about business practices and understanding of the cultural background based on their hands-on experience. In many cases, consulting firms claiming expertise on China do not even have Chinese staff in the team and rely second-hand on lessons that they learned from published literature. Being critical of everything Chinese, seems to be a convincing tool for some consulting firms. However, being critical is also an effective tool for screening consulting firms. Of course, there are a number of good consulting firms that can be of great assistance in designing your entry strategy. Nevertheless, the fact remains that the quality of specialist advice available to a company addressing the China market for the first time is variable.

Frequently, companies will encounter overseas Chinese offering various kinds of advisory services, and proclaiming their advantages of having 'close contact' with government or governmental organizations at certain levels. Sometimes they even produce some kind of a document – an agreement or Memorandum of Understanding (MOU) – to demonstrate their 'strong ties' with governmental organizations. Some of these claims are true, but many are not quite what they seem. The documents might have been obtained through cold contacts warmed up by the lure of offers of 'opportunities of cooperation' in exchange for cooperation agreements. It is all too easy for foreign businesspeople to be so impressed by the good English spoken by their new-found friend that they suspend their critical faculties. Such advisers will have a vested interest in maintaining the momentum of the China project; their instincts are likely to be to emphasize opportunity, not difficulty. The lesson from experience is that much damage has been caused by uncritical, careless acceptance by inexperienced foreign businesspeople of advice from golden-tongued, plausible overseas Chinese. Of course, there are good candidates to be found among overseas Chinese, but foreign companies should beware of too ready an acceptance of specious claims that racial origins and good connections can by themselves solve every business problem.

There are other types of advisers in China who can be extremely useful, but whom many companies have ignored in their effort to seek outside assistance. They can be any of the following:

- retired government officials;
- those who previously worked with the government but are now running private consulting practices or are freelance consultants;

- researchers in leading research institutions;
- university professors;
- journalists who specialize in covering the dynamics of a particular industry.

Such people have a considerable understanding of the China market and also many contacts that few, if any, foreign advisers might have in practice. They can be contracted under special arrangements to constitute part of your China team. Unfortunately, companies seldom take the time to seek out such local advisers.

Partner Selection and Negotiations

Jonathan Reuvid

Choosing a partner

Partner selection in China has never been easy. Following the continuing opening up of the Chinese market, in which accession to the WTO at the end of 2001 was a landmark, it might be expected that the process of finding and selecting a suitable partner would have become simpler. On the one hand, the steady deregulation of industry and service sectors, described in other chapters of this book, has provided the opportunity for western companies and entrepreneurs to access and invest in business activities from which they were previously excluded. On the other hand, the proliferation of new commercial laws and regulations has removed some of the uncertainties, although adding to the complexity of setting up business operations and participating in foreign-invested enterprises (FIEs). The Central Government is progressing towards a 'rule of law', but the process is far from complete. As discussed later in this chapter, foreign investors who might have decided previously to joint venture without the advice and input of a professional lawyer would be ill-advised to proceed without engaging one of the western law firms now well-established in China.

Availability of partners

In most sectors of business activity there is a wide choice of potential partners that can be identified quite easily, and it remains true that participation in a Sino-foreign joint venture (JV) is still a kind of 'Grail' for many Chinese companies. Other larger corporations that are already partners in one or more JVs are more blasé about JV engagement and, sometimes, foreign partners. With the dismantling of the state-owned agencies' monopoly of imports and exports, most Chinese manufacturers do not need the umbrella of a JV to export direct, and have learned quickly how to build channels to export markets. The corporation tax holidays enjoyed previously by equity JVs are being phased out (another by-product of WTO membership), so that the remaining major attraction of a JV is as a mechanism to draw in committed long-term foreign equity capital. Against that advantage, from some Chinese partners' viewpoint, is the certainty that a western partner will expect and probably insist on the introduction of alien International Financial Reporting Standards (IFRS) and corporate governance good practice that conflict with the Chinese partner's own management practices and business culture.

Within this new environment, although there is no shortage in most sectors of Chinese companies from which to select partners, it is by no means certain that the quality of available partners has improved. Western companies investing in China find the alternative of the wholly foreign-owned entity (WFOE) increasingly attractive. Larger corporations who have already set up and operated equity JVs are more likely to turn to the WFOE structure for further investment, except in those industries where the maximum equity holding by a foreign investors is restricted by law.

Partner selection among Chinese state-owned enterprises

There is a marked distinction between state-owned enterprises and their subsidiaries that have become a part of the 'New China' and those that remain firmly rooted in 'Old China' corporate culture.

New China companies are characterized by young (less than 45 years old) senior operations management, well educated, sometimes with western University degrees and often with western management experience through working abroad on assignment. Management reporting structures, operating systems, business planning, cost analysis and management (if not financial) accounting, production and quality control and cash flow management are akin to western practice. Their corporate brochures and approach to marketing are similar to western companies. In discussing JV relationships, top managers are interested in providing equity incentives for themselves (now widely permitted in China). Visiting foreign managers from the US or EU will feel immediately comfortable in a business environment that is not so unfamiliar.

By contrast, Old China companies pay 'lip service' to being part of the market economy and may have adopted international standards in quality assurance and production processes, but have made little progress in establishing line management responsibility and accountability or financial systems that correspond to international best practice. Such companies are generally recognizable from their corporate literature, which is strong on photographs of government leaders and other important officials visiting their factories and weak on product information, description of markets served and distribution channels. The hierarchical, bureaucratic style of management usually becomes apparent at the first meeting.

Bad combinations of old and new can be found in quite high profile state-owned enterprises (SOEs) that have developed a veneer of sophistication and adopted management incentives from what they perceive to be western practice within the same non-accountable bureaucratic hierarchy as before. One recent example is that of a leading manufacturer of high-value, commercial durables, which invited a well-respected American investment banker with longstanding Arab world family and business connections to visit Beijing to discuss an exclusive agency agreement to set up distributorships in leading Arab countries throughout the Middle East. Having secured the strong interest of market leaders in two of the most important country markets, the banker and his associate met with the Chinese company's Vice President of Sales, who was also Chairman of its import-export subsidiary, and laid out his plans country by country in good faith. Only at the end of the discussion did the President of the import-export company reveal that he had already signed an exclusive agreement with an importer in the larger of the two markets in exchange for a letter of credit for 100 units. The importer had neither sales nor distribution facilities. The Chairman claimed no knowledge of his subordinate's activities and appeared genuinely surprised.

To add insult to injury, a few days later the subordinate contacted the Beijing office of the Arab corporation that the banker had identified in the second market and tried to sell products to its General Manager who, having met with banker a few days before, assumed that the approach was made at his suggestion. In response, the import-export subsidiary President denied any acquaintance with or knowledge of the banker. Apparently, the President was paid commission on the value of the sale to the unsuitable distributor that he had appointed.

This highlights a not uncommon problem in big Chinese companies of top managers who abdicate rather than delegate. In this instance, the Group Vice President went into denial and did not apologise. It seems that it was too difficult for him in the culture of which he was a part to acknowledge the fault.

Similar stories of what western companies would consider unethical business practice are not uncommon in most developing countries, but China aspires to do better. Sadly, there are several leading business communities in both the Middle East and even Europe who will only transact business with Chinese exporters and importers on a letter of credit basis.

Of course, there are subsidiaries of Old China SOEs, with young and dynamic management in more competitive or high-tech sectors, who have transformed themselves into New China enterprises and are, in every respect except their parentage, attractive business partners. This quite common phenomenon is sometimes referred to as the 'mother-in-law' problem and emphasizes the need to carry out the general due diligence, as described by Li Yong in Chapter 5.4, prior to signature of any form of Letter of Intent or Heads of Agreement. The 'dead hand' of a bureaucratic parent company, who may have appointed the Chairman of a JV where the Chinese partner holds a majority shareholding, can prove fatal to successful business development.

These comments do not apply to successful, well-managed independent enterprises in the private sector, where more normal selection criteria apply. However, as a part of the initial due diligence of any potential private enterprise partner, it is important to review, the standing and relationship of the company with the local and provincial or municipal authorities. SOEs that, by definition, are owned by local or provincial governments, often have 'favourite son' status and are granted preferential treatment and, sometimes, financial support. Playing fields are seldom level, but it is important to establish that a private enterprise partner is not disadvantaged by being in contention with the authorities and has the support and encouragement of local government up to provincial level.

Selecting the jurisdiction

Another issue, which is touched on in several chapters in Part Three, is the disparity between the provinces in their interpretation of the laws and regulations of Central Government relating to FIEs. Now that approval and registration of FIEs, for all but the largest, has been delegated to authorities at provincial level (see Chapter 3.1), the relative efficiency and supportiveness of the provincial or municipal authorities should be taken into account. This is not just a matter of benevolence, for example, in terms of preferential electricity or water rates, but of how widely or narrowly the provincial authorities interpret the law.

Clearly, companies may wish to avoid provinces whose interpretation of, say, tax regulations is narrower than their advisers tell them is the intention of Beijing lawmakers. However, provinces that offer a more expansive interpretation than Beijing in granting business licences or interpreting the regulations also introduce an element of risk for FIEs who locate there and accept such dispensations. There is always the possibility that Beijing will rescind licences that they judge to be contrary to the Law, or claw back benefits that they consider illegal. As an example, several years ago a handful of western mobile telephone operators sought to bypass the restrictions on establishing FIEs in this industry sector by procuring business licences from compliant provincial authorities. Beijing stepped in and the licences were revoked.

Having alerted new entrants and those planning business investment in China to some of the pitfalls in partner selection and location, the second half of this chapter focuses on the negotiation process and procedures once a partner has been selected and the parties are ready to engage. The sequence of events and general conduct of formal negotiations has changed little in the last five years, but the approval process is greatly accelerated, particularly in those provinces or municipalities that have made a determined effort to expedite the development of projects, whether foreign or Chinese financed.

From MOU to JV agreement or draft contract

Initial discussions for a JV with a selected Chinese partner, if fruitful, will result in an MOU signed jointly. The MOU should contain a clear statement of intent to develop, together with a feasibility study for a JV, and to negotiate the terms of the joint venture to the mutual benefit of the parties. The MOU must be filed by the Chinese party, together with a 'pre-feasibility study' (in reality a checklist of the major parameters for the proposed JV), with the authorities to which it reports. More detailed negotiations cannot proceed until the reporting authorities have given a preliminary indication of approval to the project.

Formal MOUs in China, in a JV context, are not legally binding but are considered to be a commitment to continue discussions and to carry out a serious feasibility study. Therefore, it is considered to be a breach of good faith for a foreign company to enter into negotiations for the same project with another Chinese enterprise once a formal MOU has been signed, unless it is first terminated by the mutual consent of the two original parties. The same discipline should be expected of the Chinese partner. It follows that the initial choice of preferred partner is crucial. Signing an MOU in haste with an ill-chosen potential partner imposes a major impediment to further progress.

For this reason, it is important to carry out as much as possible of the commercial due diligence discussed in Chapter 5.4 before signing any MOU. If in doubt, the foreign company should confine itself to a simple minute that records that discussions have taken place, which will be reported to the boards of the two companies who will decide mutually, within an agreed period of time, whether or not to continue studying the project.

The pre-feasibility study

The pre-feasibility study usually takes the form of a standard checklist of the main parameters for the joint venture, some of which may be mentioned in the MOU but most of which are an expression of the initial 'ballpark' numbers that the parties may have discussed together. The checklist is not a joint declaration of the Chinese and foreign parties, but foreign partner input will certainly be requested. Key elements in the pre-feasibility checklist include:

- scope of business;
- total investment in the JV in US dollars;

- amount and shares of registered capital to be subscribed by the partners in US dollars;
- form of contribution for registered capital by each partner: cash, equipment, patented designs, technology, land use and buildings (proportions not usually quantified at this stage);
- nature of technology; must be to international standard, preferably advanced;
- planned production capacity (unit/volume output rather than value);
- proportion of output to be sold in export markets (normally not less than 20 per cent);
- surface area of facility and of covered factory space (existing or new building);
- in what proportions equipment is to be imported or sourced within China;
- workforce to be employed (provisional numbers);
- foreign partner's commitment to training and continuing technical support.

There is a 'chicken and egg' element in specifying these parameters at such an early stage, since most of this detail cannot be quantified with certainty in advance of a full-scale feasibility study. Indeed, it is advisable that the foreign party distances itself, as far as possible, from the pre-feasibility process so that responsibility for any major changes to the parameters that have to be identified to the authorities is limited.

The feasibility study

Assuming that the authorities' response to the pre-feasibility study and MOU is positive, the parties may now move forward jointly to a full-scale project feasibility study. It is quite possible that the authorities may reject one or more of the parameters in the pre-feasibility checklist – perhaps the form in which contributions to registered capital may be made, or a demand for a higher proportion of export sales. By this time, the relationship between the prospective partners should have advanced to the point where such obstacles are addressed together in the spirit of trying to find a solution that will satisfy the authorities and be acceptable to both sides.

The complexity of the feasibility study will be determined by the nature of the project, its technical content, procurement issues in respect of equipment, raw material and locally-sourced components, quality assurance standards and sales potential. It is recommended that all phases of the study be carried out by a joint team and that the data provided by either side

should have maximum transparency. In the course of the study, the Chinese members of the team will certainly want to visit the foreign partner's facilities and to inspect technology, equipment and manufacturing processes.

The amount of detail that the Chinese partner will require to complete the feasibility study for its purposes, and the scope of the study, will be broadly similar to the foreign partner's requirements. The Chinese side will focus particularly on the detailed specification and performance of any equipment and tooling to be imported and, if used equipment or tooling is involved, will need to satisfy itself fully as to condition and market value.

Market studies are a necessary part of the overall feasibility study to satisfy both partners that the products that the JV is targeted to manufacture are saleable in both export and domestic markets in the proportions and at the prices planned. In the early days of JVs in China, Chinese partners were often content to rely on a commitment by the foreign partner to take full responsibility for exports with the amounts to be exported in the early years specified in the JV contract. Chinese partners increasingly demand a fully-researched market study that demonstrates in which overseas markets and in what proportions the JV's products can be sold at the projected export sales price.

Conversely, foreign partners, seduced by the mirage of a billion-plus Chinese consumers, used to be content to rely upon government institutes' published statistics or projections and the Chinese partner's assurances of marketability. Increasingly today, prospective foreign JV partners demand studies of key regional markets in China by professional research organizations or western market research firms operating in China with appropriate fieldwork capabilities.

The business plan

The feasibility study should culminate in the preparation of a business plan by the two parties jointly. This is not a formal requirement by the authorities to whom the feasibility study must be submitted with the JV agreement or draft JV contract, although the Chinese partner needs to include an income and expenditure plan showing profit projections for the first three to five years of the JV's life.

However, from the foreign partner's perspective, the addition to the feasibility study of a business plan (in the western sense) and a draft budget for the period from company registration through start-up is strongly recommended. In particular, the business plan should include a cash-flow statement, as well as a profit and loss statement, and operating statements including analyses of fixed and variable expense and a manpower plan that specifies maximum staffing at each stage of development in the JV. In this way, the business plan becomes a financial blueprint, subject to review and amendment by the board of the JV after the company is formed, and a clear reference point for management discussion.

Until the early 1990s the concept of medium-term cash-flow planning (as opposed to income and expenditure projections) was foreign to most Chinese company managers, brought up in the traditions of command economy accounting. However, exposure to foreign investors and international accounting standards and procedures has effected considerable changes in Chinese corporate best practice, and the merits of 'market economy' business planning in the early stages of a JV are now well understood.

Negotiating the JV agreement, draft contract and articles of association

In the 1980s it was common for the designated JV partners to negotiate the detailed terms of the JV in the form of a non-binding joint venture agreement, which was then submitted to the local reporting authorities for approval, together with the Chinese version feasibility study.

Following approval, possibly with some amendment, the two sides would then reconvene, convert the JV agreement into a draft JV contract and, at the same time, draft the articles of association (or 'statutes' as they were sometimes called) for the JV company. As the incidence of JV negotiations multiplied and the pace of joint venturing quickened, many local authorities, notably the Commissions of Foreign Trade and Economic Cooperation (COFTECs) in major cities, relaxed the procedure and permitted the partners to proceed direct to the drafting of the JV contract and articles of association. Today, use of the preliminary JV agreement is generally limited to very complex or contentious projects, where some intermediary clarification is helpful or the parties prefer a more protracted negotiation. In the sections that follow, it is assumed that the parties proceed direct to the contract stage.

The use of advisers

At this point, the senior management of the foreign party entering into formal JV contract negotiations needs to select its negotiating and drafting team and decide how it will conduct the negotiations within the framework of standard Chinese practice. Normally, the principal Chinese party (always referred to as 'Party A' in the documents) will prepare a first draft of the JV contract and the articles of association, which it will submit, in advance of negotiation, to the principal foreign party (invariably referred to as 'Party B' in a bilateral agreement).

Perhaps the first issue to address is the force and practice of Joint Venture Law. The principal applicable law on equity JVs (and other forms of foreign investment also) is published in Chinese and in English in a single volume, entitled *Investment in China*, compiled jointly by the Foreign Investment Administration and China Economic and Trade Consultant Corporation of MOFCOM (see also the reference list of relevant laws in Chapter 3.1 'Foreign Invested Enterprises and Alternative Business Structures'). The laws set out clearly (and, generally, unambiguously) the content and principal clauses that must be included in both a JV contract and the articles of association. Many of the detailed clauses that appear in the first drafts submitted by Party A are culled direct from these laws, but the English language is usually not identical. One reason why the wording is often different is that copies of the laws with the official English translations are not generally in circulation among Chinese companies.

Variations of substance to the standard clauses of the Joint Venture Law, other than those dealing with the scope of the business, investment and registered capital contributions, scale of production, export content and the specific responsibilities of the parties, are not generally allowed by the authorities. Therefore, a commonsense approach to these secondary clauses is to incorporate them in the JV contract and articles of association as drafted, and translated, in the law unless either party has some major objection. Taking this approach to its logical conclusion, foreign companies negotiating a JV for the first time may be tempted to conduct the negotiations on a 'do it yourself' basis without external advisers, but such a course of action exposes the investor to unnecessary risk.

At the other extreme, the foreign investor may wish to both engage a law firm to advise on the legal documents and to participate in the negotiations. There are a number of leading international law firms with offices in China, with experienced foreign and Chinese staff authorized to practise law in China. However, involvement of western law firms in JV negotiating sessions can be counter-productive and an 'offstage' involvement may be preferable. In most JV negotiations the Chinese party will not involve an external Chinese lawyer, unless a western law firm is introduced. Mega-projects involving billion dollar investment, international financing or major infrastructure projects are a different matter, where the contractual documents are susceptible to western legal drafting, but the routine equity JV does not involve international law and the contracts are rigidly controlled by the standard Chinese framework.

JV contract negotiators are well advised to concentrate on substance rather than form. However forcefully they may seek to interpose tightly drafted clauses in western legal language, the final product will still contain wording through which the proverbial 'coach and horses' could be driven in a western court of law. Essentially, what matters is that the JV contract and articles of association are written in transparent business language, which is as unambiguous as possible to both parties.

The success of the JV will depend on a strong, enduring relationship between the partners. If mutual understanding and respect fail, the joint venturer should question what the remedies are. Chinese contracts always provide for 'the resolution of disputes through friendly consultation' and, if that fails, by arbitration. Arbitration in China has a good record with arbitrators often finding in favour of the foreign party (see Chapter 3.6 'Commercial Dispute Resolution'). Under a judicial system such as China's, where there are no formal case law precedents to which courts can refer, litigation is hazardous and an unattractive course of action. If the partnership relationship fails in China and becomes confrontational, the ultimate recourse is to walk away.

However, in the context of negotiating an acceptable JV contract and articles of association drafted in layman's language, the foreign partner can benefit from the services of external advisers in three respects:

- as noted at the initial discussion phase, competent translation both of the written word and through a skilled interpreter (to achieve unambiguity it is crucial that the Chinese and English versions have the same meaning, particularly since the contract will specify that 'in the event of any discrepancy between the two versions the Chinese version shall prevail');

- as a member of the negotiating team, an experienced consultant or staff member who has been through the whole process of a Chinese JV negotiation and the start-up of operations, and can input from experience what problems are likely to arise from contract omissions, loose wording or inadequate provisions for the management of the JV;

- as an adviser, an experienced China consultant, preferably Chinese, having good working relationships with, or connections to, the relevant departments of the approval authorities concerned, who can check out the key points that arise in negotiation on an ad hoc basis.

The third role cannot be performed in respect of sensitive issues without excellent connections. Foreign trade support groups having any foreign political association will not be effective in this field.

During the course of the negotiations, the foreign partner may also need to take advice on taxation or accountancy issues. The bigger international accountancy firms all have audit offices in China, mainly in Beijing and Shanghai, and their expert advice is readily available (see Chapter 4.1 'Accounting and Auditing Requirements and Practices' and Chapter 4.2 'Taxation Issues' for a general overview).

The negotiation process

JV contract negotiations are best conducted in the same city as the approval authorities to whom the draft contract and articles of association have to be submitted for preliminary approval. Therefore, if the Chinese partner is part of an SOE, the negotiations are better held in Beijing, where the relevant ministries are located so that informal opinion may be sought on the issues of substance. Whatever other ministry may be involved in the subsequent approval process, MOFCOM for the largest joint ventures or the appropriate local COFTEC will certainly be involved, since all foreign investment projects require ultimate MOFCOM endorsement.

Assuming that the foreign party has studied the draft contract and articles of association (and taken advice where appropriate) in advance of discussion, the actual negotiating sessions can take less than seven days. The negotiating procedures are well defined. As for the original set of meetings, the representatives of the two parties will be ranged either side of a meeting room table with up to 10 Chinese representatives present. The composition of the Chinese team may vary from day to day, but the same key members are likely to attend each session under the leadership of a designated chief negotiator.

In spite of the apparent formality, the climate of the discussions should be quite relaxed. If the parties have reached a high degree of unanimity on the structure and financing of the JV during the joint feasibility study through working together, there will be a presumption on both sides that the JV will go ahead. This does not mean to say that no serious differences of opinion will emerge in the course of formal negotiation, but a conducive atmosphere of mutual sincerity and flexibility will have been created. On many points of detailed drafting, the focus of discussion is more likely to be on satisfying the legal requirements and state policy guidelines or the requirements of the provincial government authorities, rather than resolving differences between the parties.

The work of amending the draft documents will be carried out methodically, beginning with the recitals and clause 1 of the JV contract and proceeding to the end of the contract before turning to the articles of association. Discussion of the articles is generally more straightforward than negotiation of the contract for two reasons:

- many of the articles are a repetition of clauses in the contract; and
- the contract is effectively a partnership agreement involving the relative detailed responsibilities of the parties, while the articles are concerned more with the ground rules and procedures for the management of the JV company.

There are practical points of Chinese negotiating style, of which foreign party negotiators should be aware. First, there is no merit in allowing discussions to stall on any single point at issue; it is quite acceptable for either party to say: 'let's come back to this subject tomorrow and go on now to the next point'. Provided that the foreign party has explained its point of view clearly and answered any questions on its stance, the delay is usually helpful. It gives both negotiating teams an opportunity to refer to their superiors for instruction or to develop an alternative to overcoming the obstacle. Where appropriate, it also allows time to take soundings from the relevant departmental authorities.

It is also perfectly acceptable for the foreign team, when faced with an unfamiliar point or doubt, to ask for an intermission in the discussions to caucus outside the meeting room. If this device is shown to be effective in removing roadblocks, it is possible that the Chinese team may employ the same expedient, although the 'common line' among the members of the Chinese negotiating group is likely to have been well rehearsed.

Understandably, the Chinese party will be concerned to broaden the scope and nature of Party B's responsibility, not only in terms of the export sales commitment but also in terms of training, continuing technical support and management expertise. As an argument for the provision of support at Party B's cost, Chinese negotiators are skilful at emphasizing the superior nature of the foreign partner's 'advanced technology' and expertise, which is always flattering and is usually effective in drawing out the maximum commitment that the foreign partner is prepared to make. The foreign negotiating team should take particular care to ensure that the scope of each responsibility is clearly defined in terms of quantifiable limits (eg maximum days, weeks, etc of management time in each specialized and general function).

As an important side issue, the foreign negotiating team should also be aware that the manager whom the Chinese partner intends to nominate as general manager of the JV, will probably be a member of the Chinese negotiating team, very possibly the chief negotiator. The right to nominate the general manager lies with the majority shareholder in any JV and, in the case of a 50/50 JV, it is normal for the general manager designate to be Chinese, even if there is a temporary foreign general manager at the outset. The contract negotiations are therefore a test for prospective general managers and a first opportunity for the foreign partner to assess candidates in action. Although the nomination of general manager is not usually made until after registration of the JV company and before the first board meeting, the foreign negotiating team should be at pains to identify the likely candidate during negotiations and, if it considers him/her unsuitable as a general manager, to find a way of making more senior Chinese management aware of its concern after the successful conclusion of negotiations.

The formal negotiations continue until the JV contract and the articles of association have been drafted in both languages, and are signed by both parties. Of course, these documents are not yet legally binding as they lack the formal approval of the authorities; they may also be signed by both parties subject to the ratification of the boards of directors of both companies. It is also wise to draft and sign a further memorandum, to which the draft contract and articles are appended, which records the closing position and sets out the actions that each partner will take in the interval before approval and signature of final binding contracts.

The senior foreign negotiator must have his company's authority to sign the draft documents on the spot, with the understanding that there will be no provision for further negotiation, except in respect of amendments that the approval authorities wish to be made.

Contents of the JV contract and articles of association

Expertise and guidance on interpretation of standard wording or drafting hints can be provided by an accredited JV consultant or professional adviser, as discussed earlier in this chapter.

Certain specific issues relating to the commitments and responsibilities of the partners to the JV company, rather than to each other, are normally incorporated in separate agreements, which are ratified by the JV's board of directors at the first board meeting. The substance of these agreements, if not the complete detail, is covered during the JV contract negotiations, and the parties may prefer to include the draft agreements in an appendix to the JV contract. There is not usually an absolute requirement by the approval authorities that the supplementary draft agreements are annexed to the main contract. However, in the interests of banishing ambiguity or uncertainty there is merit in inclusion.

The supplementary agreements that are most common are:

- export sales agreement between the JV and Party B; (a domestic market sales agreement between the JV and Party A is less common, as the JV is usually responsible for the sales of its own products/services in the home market);
- technology, patent or copyright licence between Party B and the JV;
- training agreement between Party B and the JV, covering training outside China and subsequent on-site training in China;
- lease from Party A to the JV in cases where Party A has the land use right and leases the land or an existing facility to the JV; and

- consultancy agreement between Party B and the JV to cover the continuing provision of foreign experts and/or management support.

For identification purposes, the joint venture contract may include schedules that provide technical process and product specifications and details of patent, copyright or other intellectual property registrations.

The joint venture articles of association are roughly similar to the memorandum and articles of association, which are standard under English company law, although provisions for the operating management of the company are more detailed in the Chinese version.

One innovation in Chinese articles of association is provision for the formation of a preparatory group or preparation committee, whose members are drawn from both parties and whose function is to carry out the necessary preparatory work for the start-up of the JV following receipt of the formal certificate of registration.

The approvals and registration process

As specified in the draft contract, it is the responsibility of the Chinese partner to submit the formal application documents to the relevant authorities and to lobby the departments involved within each reviewing body. This task is normally assigned to the Chinese chief negotiator personally.

The documents to be submitted to the approval authorities are listed in Detailed Rules for the Implementation of the Law of the People's Republic of China on Sino-foreign Equity Joint Ventures (promulgated on 20 September 1993 by the State Council and amended on 15 January 1986, 21 December 1987 and 22 July 2001), Article 9, and consist of the following:

- application for the establishment of an equity JV;
- the feasibility study report prepared by the parties to the venture;
- equity JV agreement (optional), contract and articles of association signed by representatives authorized by parties to the venture;
- list of candidates for chairman, deputy chairman and directors of the board appointed by parties to the venture; and
- written opinions of the department in charge and the people's government of the province, autonomous region or municipality directly under the central government where the equity JV is located with regard to the establishment of the equity JV.

All the documents submitted must be written in Chinese, but the second, third and fourth documents in this list may be written simultaneously in a foreign language agreed jointly by the parties.

The status of the Chinese partner, the nature and industrial classification of the project and the limits of authority of the municipality, province, autonomous region or city under whose jurisdiction the JV falls and the value of the total investment will together determine whether the authorities involved are at central government ministry level or at local level where ministry authority is entrusted to a local department, commission or bureau. At the appropriate level, the ministries involved will be the industry ministry to which the Chinese partner reports and, invariably, MOFCOM or its local COFTEC. In some cases, more than one industry ministry may be involved, and the approval process abounds with complexities (see Figure 1.3.4 in Chapter 1.3).

At central government level, each of the ministries involved has an effective right of veto over any JV application, but outright rejection is unlikely at this stage, particularly if a continuing dialogue with the authorities has been maintained during the negotiating phase.

However, even in the case of the largest, most carefully negotiated investment projects, where the highest central government authorities in Beijing were consulted throughout a negotiation process over a long period, conflict and confusion can still arise. At the beginning of July 2004, British American Tobacco (BAT) announced that it had been granted approval for a US$1.5 billion cigarette manufacturing plant by the State Council, China's cabinet. Within 24 hours, the State Tobacco Monopoly Administration (STMA), which controls the industry, denied that it had approved the BAT project, followed by a further denial by the State Development and Reform Commission, China's senior economic policy-making body (see Figure 1.3.5 in Chapter 1.3). Given that cigarettes are an especially sensitive political and economic issue, the BAT experience should not be regarded as typical, but rather as a cautionary tale. Nevertheless, it does illus-

trate that, even when provincial approval authorities only are involved, time spent on cultivating the support of all those government departments involved is never wasted.

Familiarity with the project and prior consultation will help to ease the approvals process, but it is likely that some amendments to the contract and articles will be demanded. Hopefully, these amendments will not be of substance and can be addressed by the parties between them at a distance. If not, then representatives of the parties will have to reconvene to determine whether an acceptable solution can be found. Reversals of ministry decisions are necessarily difficult to achieve, which underlines the value of consultation during the negotiation process.

Article 10 of the above law stipulates that the examination and approval authorities shall decide within three months whether or not to approve the documents submitted. If the documents are not approved, the authorities are obliged to demand any modifications, without which no approval shall be granted, within a limited period of time thereafter.

In practice, the decision and any modifications can often be completed within the specified three-month period. For smaller JVs, the approvals procedure can be much swifter. In Tianjin, for example, which has approval authority for projects up to US$30 million total investment, the municipality has located all of the relevant approvals departments in a single foreign investment service centre (FISC) under the leadership of Tianjin's COFTEC.

As noted earlier, the establishment of all equity JVs in China is subject to examination and approval by MOFCOM. On approval, the certificate of registration for the JV is issued by MOFCOM. Within one month after receipt, the Chinese partner shall register the certificate of registration with the administrative bureau for industry and commerce of the province, autonomous region or municipality directly under the central government where the JV is located. The date on which the bureau (referred to as the registration and administration office) shall then issue its business licence for the JV is regarded as the date of formal establishment of the equity JV.

Using Education and Training as a Strategic Marketing Tool in Winning International Business

Richard Hill, Rolls-Royce plc

There can be little doubt that the 1980s and 1990s saw a tremendous growth in the devotion by companies to quality and customer service in an attempt to gain the competitive edge in an increasingly competitive world. Competing on product and price characteristics alone is not only naïve and simplistic but has little chance of success as markets become increasingly sophisticated in the way they seek to influence customers. Irrespective of the sector in which companies operate, attention to the specific needs of the customer has proved consistently to be the most effective aspect of product or service differentiation in recent times.

This is a particularly important message for any company about to embark upon a period of internationalization, where marketing strategies and tactics are arguably more complex than those deployed in the domestic market. Appropriate strategies and tactics are important in any marketing context but particularly essential if a company is competing against a strong sitting tenant within the target country or if the international competition is particularly fierce. In these circumstances companies have to bring something new, extra or unique to the negotiating or tendering table in order to acquire the necessary commercial influence.

The ferocity of international competition and the need to exert commercial influence to win business are key features of the aerospace industry. This chapter demonstrates an increasingly important role played by education and training in developing relationships between companies and their customers with a view to creating a competitive advantage. The principles associated with the use of education and training as market access tools have been developed in Rolls-Royce over a number of years and will form the basis of this particular case study.

The high value of UK education and training programmes, as perceived by international customers, has led to a number of companies using them as a formal part of their marketing strategy for expanding commercial activity abroad. In this context, education and training are used to develop customers and potential customers, together with those who influence customers, thereby creating a relationship based on personal customer benefits. A relationship formed in this way can ultimately turn its focus more effectively to specific company products and services in due course, as a partnership of integrity and support has already been developed.

The use of education and training generally falls into one of two types of marketing support activity:

- The first of these is creating relationships through opening 'windows of opportunity' – that is, offering programmes of education and training as a means of demonstrating the willingness to work together in supporting the development needs of the target organization. Once the relationship is established, the resultant influence can be extended to broader commercial issues. This is fundamentally about positioning the company within the competitive arena. As discussed later, the window of opportunity may be found within a target customer organization or may lie with a third party, often an international governmental department that carries influence.

- The second broad activity is offering education and training as a 'sales concession' – that is, a commitment by the company to provide the customer with a given level of support stipulated in the sales contract. In very stark terms, a company may say 'if you buy this product from us, we will offer you training and education support to the value of US$X'. Clearly, a company offering this form of enhanced benefit will have undertaken research to identify areas of training need required by the customer, thereby making the differentiating carrot even more attractive.

One of the axioms of sustaining commercial success is that a company must create an association with a customer whereby the former features in the long-term plans of the latter. The experiences of a number of exporters have shown that a company's association with the training and development needs of customer employees leads to closer, long-term relationships that, in turn, bring a competitive advantage in the commercial arena.

Using education and training as a strategic marketing tool is essentially about the effective positioning of a company within a given market. The positioning activity of education and training operates at two levels and reflects the types of marketing activity identified above:

- at the micro level, where a company will be building a relationship with a customer directly with a view to commercial benefits;
- at the macro level, where a company will be enhancing integration with international institutions or government departments that might influence the target customers in the company's favour.

An effective business strategy will embrace activities that support a focus on both levels, allowing for parallel inter-action between the key stakeholders. This chapter will later describe the approach that Rolls-Royce takes in this regard as an illustration of this principle. In education and training terms, this means providing programmes direct to the customer or, alternatively, to international stakeholders who are capable and potentially willing to influence the buying decisions of the primary customer.

Positioning fundamentally gives a company a head start in anticipation of a potential market moving forward. In this context, therefore, the business advantage is gained from establishing relationships and creating influence through education and training as a precursor to, or an enhancement of, commercial enterprises.

Customer-related benefits

It is customary for sales and marketing executives to talk of 'benefits' in describing ancillary services to the customer, and education and training lends itself *de facto* to this descriptor. Generally speaking we can categorize customer-related benefits into three types. The first of these would be the benefit to the customer country as a whole. Education and training feature very highly on most political agendas around the world, but particularly in some of the developing countries. The need to develop the managerial and technical skills of a country's indigenous workforce has proved to be a strong political lever in recent years. This gives companies a key source of influence with ministries that have a vested interest in this arena. Notable among these, would be the ministries associated with education, trade and industry, reconstruction or long-term planning.

The second area of benefit activity relates directly to the target corporation. The provision of management programmes facilitates the development of corporate and functional thinking and enables a business to accelerate or enhance its business philosophy. It can also have the benefit of facilitating commercial activity as it effectively provides a common business language between companies when hitherto there were fundamental differences of approach. Some of the most notable examples of these benefits have been where companies have provided management education to companies that formerly operated in centrally planned economies and that have now moved to market economies. The fall of the Berlin Wall in 1989, for example, brought a rush of development needs from Eastern Europe, which also promised concomitant commercial advantages. Developing countries such as China have also created wide-ranging opportunities for companies to position themselves through the medium of management education and training.

The third area of benefit, quite obviously, is to any individual recipient of education and training provision. Rolls-Royce has found throughout the years that the personal impact on these programmes is one of the most effective aspects of relationship marketing. This personal impact can take a number of forms. It might, for example, be the knowledge or experience gained from formal courses or from a facilitated secondment. Equally, the benefit to the individual might come from a newly developed network resulting from the training programme. It has to be said, in honesty, that occasionally the real attraction may be simply a thinly disguised vacation. Whatever the objective, so long as the personal impact is perceived as good or beneficial, the position of the donor/sponsoring company is enhanced.

Having created the positional benefit, a key consideration for a company is how to sustain the relationship between the two parties. If a company has invested time and money in developing the relationship, it makes good sense to keep it warm and to make good use of it as appropriate. From experience, a key figure for the supplier company is the mentor or trainer of the target individual who holds the influence in the customer organization. Time and time again, we have seen very senior decision-makers far more receptive to their 'teacher' than any commercial or sales person. A personal bond has been established between 'teacher' and 'pupil' that is based on trust and integrity. Carefully handled, this can open commercial doors more quickly and more effectively than a conventional approach.

Company-related benefits

Without doubt, the principal benefit of providing training support is the influence it brings to bear on key stakeholders. The essence of this activity is to confer personal benefits, directly or indirectly, on those with decision-making influence so they will feel favourably disposed to you or what you represent. Direct benefits to the stakeholder will accrue where he/she is the direct recipient of support; indirect benefits occur where the supporting company facilitates the advancement of a wider political or commercial agenda associated with the stakeholder.

Education and training provision represents a high-value sales concession (measured in terms of customer worth) when offered as part of a commercial deal. The UK has long held a reputation for having a first-class education and training system. Access to such branded provision through a concessionary agreement carries a significant amount of influence when used as commercial differentiator. Hybrid programmes, which combine good practice in blue-chip organizations with respected educational inputs, are seen as particularly beneficial to international stakeholders. If, as part of the tender or contract, education and training can be offered in terms of market value as opposed to cost to the company, the value to the customer can be portrayed at a higher level. Having the option to position a service in terms of value rather than cost is clearly more beneficial commercially and far more preferable to a company having to offer a price concession on a product to win business.

There is little doubt that education and training programmes are a very effective vehicle for sustaining customer relationships over a long period of time. Such programmes are focused *prima facie* on conferring personal benefits as opposed to gaining overt commercial or corporate advantage. In this context, any discussion between the two parties takes place in an environment that is tailored for cordial discussion and becomes a fundamental part of any relationship marketing strategy.

The essence of good education and training is to create a mindset of continuous learning development and improvement, which is facilitated by frequent contact between teacher/mentor and student. Where the mentor is a company representative and the student a customer stakeholder, an obvious dual benefit will accrue. In all parts of the world, a student/delegate never forgets his or her teacher. On this basis, Rolls-Royce training consultants find they have ready access to very senior decision-makers, who have previously been exposed to training programmes or development events. It is noteworthy that in many cultures, particularly in the Far East, the position of 'teacher' is revered and seen as a source of knowledge, trust and shared confidence.

Types of international training activity

There are a number of ways in which training provision can support the broad commercial objectives of an organization. The first of these would be in the use of training as a commercial concession linked to a sale. In simple terms, a company would offer training support to the value of US$X if the tender or proposal were accepted. Sometimes the proposal might contain detailed proposals on training support or it might simply state a total value of training credit with the fine detail to be decided at a later stage. As intimated earlier, this can be a particularly effective tool if the supplier company has undertaken some form of reconnaissance on the customer that enables it to offer support that clearly addresses known issues.

Secondly, training can be used as a form of offset, which may be linked to, but separate from, a sales agreement. In this situation, a company will sign a contract with a major customer or with an influential ministry overseas but, in the event of any offset obligation by the supplier to the country, the obligation could be discharged by the supply of training or education. Often, the recipient of offset benefit lies outside the customer organization, as the rationale of offset is to benefit the greater economy of the customer country. Education and training, therefore, could be used very effectively as offset tools, as they represent a means of developing the country and can be seen to have a high investment value. If prior groundwork has been undertaken in an effective manner by the supplier, it may well be possible to direct training support to third parties with related influence in the customer country. In a number of countries, Rolls-Royce has won a major engine contract with national airlines but the recipients of subsequent training and education support have been in related activities such as civil aviation training centres or national technical institutes.

Thirdly, training can be used as part of a broad positioning strategy within a target country. At this level of activity, a company will work with an influential ministry in terms of providing management development programmes that will enhance the managerial or technical skills of a chosen sector or target population under government jurisdiction. Essentially the company is showing itself to be a 'good friend' of the country, effectively positioning the corporation inside the country and thereby creating a climate for a more successful commercial outcome.

The fourth area of training internationally is again related to enhancing the customer relationship base through joint-working approaches. In Rolls-Royce, for example, the International Training group has worked with a number of customers on projects that have been to mutual benefit. These projects might be where both companies have identified common development needs and have agreed a joint approach. (There is a powerful message of cooperation and effectiveness where the constituent parts of the supply chain are trained together.) Equally, it may be possible for both parties to collaborate on third-party projects that either attract external revenue or enhance joint positioning in parts of the world. For example, much of the development aid work funded by the European Commission relies on companies from different member countries working together to provide solutions. This creates significant opportunities for joint working, whereby both parties move towards a partnership arrangement and growing mutual dependence.

The Rolls-Royce approach

The Rolls-Royce approach to using education and training as a market access tool can be exemplified through its relationship with China. This relationship essentially is bilateral, working with both the direct customer and influencing government departments of that country.

With regards to the customer-related activity, Rolls-Royce has developed a strong partnership with the General Administration of the Civil Aviation of China (CAAC) and has run a number of training initiatives that have brought benefits to both technical and managerial employees within the industry.

Among these initiatives with CAAC, there are two that form the bedrock of a long-term training partnership. These are the establishment of the joint Training Centre in Tianjin and the development of a high-flyer programme for the aviation industry in China. The joint Training Centre was opened in 1997 and provides a range of short courses in both technical and managerial skills. It has a resident team of Chinese nationals, all of whom have had extensive training in, and by, Rolls-Royce. The training team in Tianjin is supported by visiting experts from Rolls-Royce who are able to supplement the skills of the resident team. Essentially, the joint Training Centre represents a physical demonstration of the company's long-term commitment to supporting China's civil aviation industry as a joint activity. It also exemplifies our partnership with CAAC and demonstrates our position as a world leader in management and technical development training. Within China, this has given Rolls-Royce the reputation of being the forerunner of customized training, providing tailored training for airline and airport representatives.

The other significant initiative with CAAC is a 'Senior Executive Development Programme', which provides an extensive six-month development initiative for China's identified cadre of high-potential employees. This is a particularly significant initiative in that it enables Rolls-Royce to work with the next generation of decision-makers, all of whom will have formed a strong personal relationship with the company. The programme is a truly integrated partnership in that Rolls-Royce works with the Civil Aviation Management Institute (CAMI) in developing the curriculum, where four and a half months are spent studying in Beijing followed by a six-week period of applied training in the UK. Such has been the success of this programme that the profile of Rolls-Royce has been significantly enhanced through national press and TV coverage.

Outside CAAC and its airlines, Rolls-Royce has also worked with other Chinese ministries or government departments on training and development programmes. Principal among these are relationships developed with the State Development Planning Commission (SDPC), the State Economic and Trade Commission (SETC) and the Central Committee of the CCP. The company had developed a strong relationship with SETC over many years. This culminated in Rolls-Royce establishing and leading a consortium of 18 major British companies to provide training and development support to a range of state-owned enterprises across most sectors in China. The nature of this support is broad and includes a 'Senior Executive Industrial Strategy Programme' (a three-week, UK-based initiative), consultancy, China-based seminars, company attachments and sponsored university education.

With regard to the SDPC, Rolls-Royce has worked with a number of British government departments and a range of Directorate-Generals within the European Commission. This company-government partnership has provided training support to senior executives within both central and provincial planning departments and has effectively become an inter-governmental initiative. This initiative is concerned with long-term strategic planning and gives insight into how this is put into effect at European, national, sectoral, corporate and business unit levels. Although there is no direct benefit to Rolls-Royce's position within any particular sector, it does effectively position the company as a 'good friend' of China and is instrumental in developing a relationship that is seen to have high integrity. The important message for companies trying to establish commercial activity in developing parts of the world is that the precursor for success is a relationship that is built on proven integrity.

British government endorsement for the approach

Exports of education and training from the UK are already worth in excess of US$12 billion a year. The increasing awareness by companies of the value of offering education or training as part of their export strategies will certainly result in an increase in this figure. The British government, through the Department of Trade and Industry, has pioneered a number of programmes to support industry across a wide variety of sectors:

- *China Britain Industrial Consortium.* Eighteen leading UK companies have taken part in a general management development scheme. They provided a five-year training and development programme to more than 1,000 senior managers in similar Chinese state-owned enterprises (SOEs).
- *Chevening Scholarships.* When the Prime Minister launched a campaign to attract more international students to the UK in June 1999, he also announced an expanded Chevening Scholarship programme and invited a greater involvement from UK industry.
- *British Overseas Industrial Placement Programme (BOND).* Sponsored by British Trade International and managed by the British Council, BOND enables young professionals from overseas firms involved in business in the UK to take attachments with British companies in certain sectors. The attachments are generally for 6–12 months.
- *Offset Programmes.* British Trade International, together with the Ministry of Defence's Defence Export Services Organization, have developed an internet-based service designed to help exporters with offset/industrial participation obligations.
- *Industry/non-government organization (NGO) partnerships.* In line with the current trend, NGO activity overseas is made up of an increasing amount of education and training in all its forms. Many developing countries now have a vast number of British trainers, advisers and volunteers with whom British companies can cooperate.
- *Multilateral development aid programmes.* The programmes of the multilateral development agencies such as the World Bank, European Commission and United Nations present considerable opportunities to providers of education and training services. Many projects funded by these organizations, even if they are not specifically targeted at the education sector, involve an industrial training element.

Within the UK, the government has established an advisory body, the Education and Training Export Group (ETEG), which comprises senior practitioners from all sectors. It has been largely responsible for promoting the use of training and education as a market access tool and, in March 2000, staged a high-level conference to this end entitled 'Profit through Knowledge'. In opening the conference, the Minister for Trade, Richard Caborn, talked about education and training as the 'best economic policy there is'. In terms of opening doors, sustaining long-term relationships and providing significant commercial differentiators, it is a policy that companies should automatically consider as part of their strategic approach to the international market.

Conclusion

This chapter has attempted to demonstrate the use of education and training as an effective form of relationship marketing. It has shown them to be a proven tool, working at national, corporate and, most importantly, at individual level. There is strong evidence to show that where individuals gain personal benefits from education and training, the donor or facilitator is held in high esteem and a continuing relationship between the two parties is easy to develop and sustain. Certainly, we have been made aware by our customers of the high value they ascribe to education and training in the UK generally and in Rolls-Royce specifically. There is little doubt that where an education/training partnership between customer and supplier can evolve as part of relationship strategy, the strength of this as a differentiator from other suppliers gives a tremendous competitive advantage.

© Richard Hill, Rolls-Royce plc

Employing Staff in China

Li Yong, Deputy Secretary General, China Association of International Trade

Since its economic reform and opening up, China's vast market potential and fast-growing economy have attracted the attention of foreign businesses. Having a presence in China is key to tapping into market opportunities. Foreign entry into the market takes a number of different forms such as representative offices, equity joint ventures, contractual joint ventures and wholly foreign-owned enterprises. Whatever the form of entry a business takes to establish its presence in China, employment of local staff is an unavoidable issue. However, not every kind of foreign establishment can legally employ Chinese staff on its own.

Employing staff in representative offices

Since the beginning of China's opening up to the outside world, representative offices have been frequently used and are the easiest and most convenient tool to explore the local market. A registration certificate must be obtained in order legally to employ Chinese nationals and this requires a series of formalities to be completed, such as opening a bank account for foreign exchange, applying for direct telecommunication lines and securing a multiple entry visa for expatriate managers. The business activities of the representative offices may only be within the range of business networking, product introduction, marketing, technology exchange and consulting services. They are not permitted to engage in direct profit-making activities.

Technically, representative offices do not have independent legal person status and they are not supposed to employ staff like joint ventures or wholly-owned operations can. According to the relevant laws and regulations governing the establishment and operation of foreign representative offices in China, they must take on staff through designated employment agencies that provide specialized services for foreign representative offices.

Employment service providers

In the early days of the opening up, when most foreign representative offices were concentrated in Beijing, the provision of Chinese nationals to work in foreign representative offices was monopolized by Beijing Foreign Enterprise Services Corporation (known as FESCO). Its services were designed to help foreign representative offices handle practical issues of human resource management, such as identification of qualified local staff, welfare, pensions, residency and mobility. This monopoly ended when other government sponsored 'foreign services' companies were established to compete with FESCO.

At present there are over 70 authorized foreign services companies, providing local staff to representative offices in 25 provinces and municipalities. The leading ones include:

- FESCO;
- China Star Corporation for International Economic and Technical Cooperation (China Star Corporation);
- China International Intellectech Corporation (CIIC);
- China International Enterprises Cooperation Co (CIECCO);
- China International Talents Development Centre (CITDC).

The key functions of foreign employment service providers in China include, but are not limited to, the following:

- providing assistance to customers setting up representative offices in China. This service is normally fee-based and designed to facilitate the process of application;
- identifying and recommending local staff to foreign representative offices. This service is provided on the basis of different fee arrangements, which vary from place to place and from organization to organization;
- manage as proxy labour relations of the staff assigned to foreign representative offices. Normally, foreign employment service companies maintain contractual relationships with foreign representative offices regarding staff deployment;
- providing welfare benefits to the deployed staff, depending on the terms and conditions agreed between the service companies and foreign representative offices, although the latter can deal with welfare benefits on its own;
- managing personnel logistics such as the management of personal archives (a record file containing information about staff education, career achievements, professional qualifications etc); transferring archives from previous employers; residence permits when staff come from other parts of the country; passport applications; visa applications for foreign travel; and subscriptions to social security where applicable;
- organizing job fairs and arrange job advertisements for foreign representative offices and other foreign-related organizations;
- head-hunting senior management staff according to customer requirements;
- offering various other services related to expatriate staff, such as obtaining multi-entry visas, work permits and residence permits.

How to recruit?

Normal procedure requires a foreign representative office to enter into an employment service contract with a government-authorized service agency. On the strength of this contract, the authorized employment service agency will recommend candidates to the representative office. The service agency will also sign contracts with candidates against its contract with the representative office.

Normally, staff will serve a probation period before official employment begins. According to the Labour Law of the People's Republic of China, the probation period should not exceed 15 days for a six-month contract, 30 days for a six- to twelve-month contract and 60 days for a one- to two-year contract. The maximum probation period should not exceed six months.

Relevant laws and regulations provide that the minimum ratio of Chinese staff in foreign representative offices is 1:1, which means that if you have one expatriate staff member in the office, there must be at least one local member of staff. If the recommended candidates do not meet requirements, the representative offices may look for suitable staff on their own. They can even agree on the terms and conditions regarding salaries, compensation packages and other benefits with the candidates they find by themselves. However, these staff must register with an authorized employment service agency before their employment is legal.

Dismissal of staff

Normally, there are two reasons for staff to leave the representative office. One is voluntary resignation and the other dismissal for reasons such as misconduct. In either case, 30 days advance notice is required from both the staff and the representative office. As the relationship between the staff and the representative office is based on an employment service contract between the representative office and the service agency, the service agency must be duly notified of the resignation or dismissal. In the case of voluntary resignation, the representative office is free of compensation obligations; in the case of dismissal these will have to be recognized. Normally, a staff member who is dismissed after less than six months' service will not receive any compensation. For members of staff who have worked for more than six months, there are varying degrees of compensation ranging from one month's to six months' pay.

It is illegal to dismiss an employee who is pregnant, nursing or on maternity leave, or any staff receiving prescribed treatment for illness or injury. In cases of misconduct by the Chinese staff, the dismissal should be accompanied with sufficient evidence of violation of Chinese laws and regulations or corporate regulations (which should be made known to the service agency). No compensation is required if the misconduct is recognized by the service agency.

Employment in joint ventures and wholly foreign-owned enterprises

Joint ventures and wholly foreign-owned enterprises have independent legal person status and therefore have much more autonomy in terms of employment.

The supervising authority for the employment of labour in these circumstances is the labour and social security department in the venture's place of domicile. The supervising authority exercises supervision of the labour contracts to make sure that the legitimate rights and interests of workers are well protected. Joint ventures and wholly foreign-owned enterprises have complete autonomy in terms of their employment decisions. The relationship between the supervising authority and the joint venture is that the joint ventures or wholly foreign-owned enterprise needs to file its recruitment plans with the local labour authority, which in turn will provide assistance with sourcing employees and processing necessary documents to validate the employment. The joint venture or wholly foreign-owned enterprise has freedom to determine what criteria to apply when screening qualified staff.

Labour contract

It is a requirement of the Labour Law that employers sign an employment contract with their employees. In some places, the labour authority will encourage employers to use their standardized labour contract, which is considered to be neutral and trustworthy. Employers can draft their own labour contract, but it must be strictly in compliance with the Labour Law. An employer may also enter into a collective labour contract with its employees. Terms and conditions are negotiated by the trade union or by elected representatives of the workers.

In a labour contract, the rights and obligations of both the employer and employees should be clearly defined. Clauses such as job description, labour remuneration, insurance and welfare, labour protection, safety conditions, disciplinary requirements, probation and validity period and conditions under which the contract can be terminated or changed should be included in the contract. Employers must file the standard labour contract with the governing labour authority. Although there is no explicit stipulation regarding what language a labour contract should use, it is advisable for the employer to use the Chinese language, or at least to produce a bilingual document. In any case, the labour authority requires a Chinese language contract (or translation). All contracts signed between the employer and the employees must be verified by the labour authority. Such verification is intended not only to ensure it is signed on the basis of equality and free will, but also to check the different language versions are consistent. There have been cases in which the stipulation of rights and obligations varies greatly between different language versions.

Some foreign-invested enterprises sign a probationary contract before they engage themselves in a formal labour contract, which is not correct practice. According to relevant laws and regulations, the probationary period is the precondition of a formal labour contract. A probationary contract does not free employers from their responsibilities and obligations. In cases of labour disputes, a probationary contract will be regarded as a formal contract. Employers may require a probation period, but it is not mandatory. The probation period should not exceed the statutory length, the maximum of which is six months depending on the length of contract term. During the probation period, either contracted party may terminate the contract without compensation from the employers. No prior notice is needed.

There are two important elements that the employer should take into account in the labour contract: confidentiality and non-competition covenant. A non-disclosure agreement will help protect employers' trade secrets and a non-competition commitment may prevent competitors from taking advantage of the staff's experience and knowledge about the company.

Termination of labour contract and labour disputes

According to the Labour Law, employers are required to provide 30 days' notice prior to dismissal of employees or termination of labour contracts. Under PRC Labour Law, an employer cannot dismiss an employee without cause.

The employer can terminate the labour contract by giving the employee 30 days' written notice if one of the following situations occurs:

1. If, after recovering from an illness or non-work-related injury, within a prescribed period of medical treatment, the employee is unable to perform the original duties or other alternative jobs arranged by the employer;
2. The employee is proved incapable of performing a job, even after receiving training or being transferred to another position;
3. Major changes in the circumstances on which the labour contract was based have led to the employer's inability to perform the original contract and agreement to amend the contract cannot be reached among parties of the contract.

However, employers cannot dismiss employees under the following circumstances:

1. employees who have been suffering from occupational diseases or work-related injuries and have been proved to have completely or partially lost the ability to work;
2. employees who have been suffering from illness or injuries but are still in the prescribed period of medical treatment;
3. employees who are pregnant, nursing or on maternity leave;
4. other circumstances as stipulated by pertinent laws and administrative regulations.

The employer has the right to terminate a labour contract with immediate effect if an employee:

1. fails to satisfy requirements during the probation period;
2. has seriously violated the disciplinary rules or regulations of the work place;
3. has committed a serious abuse of duties or engaged in practices, causing serious damages to the employer;
4. is charged with a criminal offence.

Once a dispute arises, the case must first go to arbitration with the labour arbitration committee. This procedure is required by law before a lawsuit can be filed. Application for arbitration must be filed within 60 days after the dispute. If either party is not satisfied with the arbitral award, they may file a lawsuit within 15 days of receipt of the award.

Foreign participation in China's job market

According to its WTO commitments, China will allow foreign human resource service enterprises to enter its talent market. The Ministry of Labour and Social Security and State Administration for Industry and Commerce jointly promulgated the *Provisional Regulation on the Establishment and Administration of Job Referral Agencies of Sino-Foreign Joint Ventures and Cooperatives*, which was implemented as of 1 December 2001. According to the regulation, foreign employment agencies can engage in the employment agency business in China through the establishment of equity or contractual joint ventures with qualified Chinese partners. The setting up of job referral agencies as Sino-foreign joint ventures and cooperatives must be approved by the provincial-level government labour and social security department and the provincial-level government foreign trade and economic cooperation department. The minimum capital requirement for such joint ventures is US$300,000. Wholly foreign-owned employment service companies are not allowed by the current regulation.

With the entry of foreign employment service companies, foreign-invested enterprises will receive services from local as well as foreign-invested employment service agencies. These latter will undoubtedly improve the overall quality of China's employment services industry.

Distribution in China

Liu Baocheng, Professor, University of International Business and Economics, with updates by Jonathan Reuvid

Introduction

Today, even in the domestic market, most manufacturers would choose not to sell their products directly to the end users – business users or consumers – not because they cannot, but because it is not cost-effective. Therefore, an effective distribution channel is vital to the success of manufacturers. To foreign manufacturers interested in the sales of products in the Chinese market, given the various market barriers and time-consuming learning curve, building and maintaining the right distribution channel utilizing local resources is often the right strategic approach.

Conceptually, a distribution channel consists of a set of interdependent organizations involved in the process of making a product or service available for use or consumption. En route between the manufacturers and the end users, there exist a number of intermediaries performing a variety of functions to bridge delivery of the right products to the right users or consumers. These intermediaries provide two primary services to the manufacturer: 1) to bring the products or services to the end user; 2) to feed the manufacturer the end user's response for improved marketing strategies. More specifically, a distribution channel is expected to perform the following:

- to represent the principal manufacturer and look after its interests in the target market;
- to gather information about the target market environment and customer needs;
- to develop and disseminate persuasive communications in the target market;
- to ensure logistics and successful delivery of the products and services to the target customers;

- to solicit and process orders for the principal manufacturer;
- to collect payment on behalf of the principal manufacturer;
- to communicate with customers and manage other local relationships;
- to deal with complaints and disputes.

Entry into the Chinese market

For foreign products to enter into the Chinese market, they must, in the first place, be imported. China, at present, maintains an import control system that requires a certified importer to take title to the products, although in most cases they are neither distributors nor end users. Their right to engage in the importation is conferred by the Ministry of Commerce (MOFCOM). At the same time, MOFCOM also retains an import control list over those products that are termed as 'strategic goods.' Products on the control list will have to be dealt with by a limited number of certified importers, who are granted separate licences. These licences are granted through a case-by-case review process. This means that a certified Chinese importer with the right type of import licence acts as a gatekeeper. Without their involvement, even if a foreign manufacturer has entered into a distribution agreement with a Chinese partner, the entry of these products will be denied at the Chinese customs house.

Samples with negligible value are permitted to go directly to the named receiver in China. However, they must be clearly marked with 'No Commercial Value.' The receiver has to present a whole set of documents such as business licence, customs registration number and the permit from relevant government authorities.

Foreign products as a donation in the name of a Chinese beneficiary are scrutinized carefully. Samples and donations that are suspected to be of higher value will be subject to arbitrary tariffs at the customs house. Foreign products prepared for participating in exhibitions or trade fairs to be held in China will be granted separate licences at the invitation and guarantee by the designated Chinese organizer, and they must be shipped out of the country within a stipulated timeframe. Duty-bonded warehouse and zones are available in big airports and seaports in China. Without paying customs tariff, foreign products can be stored or repacked in these warehouses or zones but are not allowed to enter into the local market. When the owners decide on market entry, they must pay the customs tariff and undergo the normal import procedures. In addition, foreign products of North American origin must be accompanied by a 'non-wooden package' declaration.

With the decentralization of foreign trading rights, competition among importers is on the rise. When an importer is unable or unwilling to distribute products in the Chinese market, foreign sellers will negotiate directly with a Chinese domestic distributor over the terms and conditions, and then, in order to conform to Chinese law, an importer is selected either by the foreign seller or by the distributor to handle the import contract and other import documentation. In this case, the importer merely acts as an agent and is remunerated on a commission basis. Depending on the value of an import licence and the size of the contract, the rate of commission may vary within the range of 3 per cent to 15 per cent of the contract value. This commission is calculated into the distribution agreement and usually paid by the distributor. However, by the letter of the law, the importer is regarded as an independent principal, and the agreement reached between the foreign seller and the domestic distributor is unenforceable. In reality, there are three contracts involved for foreign products to enter China: 1) an import contract between the foreign seller and the Chinese certified importer; 2) a distribution agreement between the foreign seller with a Chinese distributor; 3) an import agency agreement between the Chinese distributor and the certified importer. The relationships are illustrated in Figure 5.8.1.

This triangular contractual relationship is also compatible with the currency conversion requirement by Chinese government. By Chinese law on foreign exchange control, Chinese distributors have no direct access to foreign exchange. This arrangement will

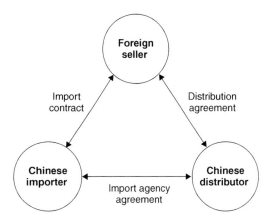

Figure 5.8.1 Contractual relations for foreign products entering the Chinese market

allow the distributor to pay local currency RMB to the Chinese importer, and the latter will utilize its foreign exchange account to pay for the imported products to the foreign seller.

Alternatively, the foreign manufacturer can sell directly to joint venture companies or wholly-owned foreign companies in China, because these companies are granted import rights within approval of their operations. The foreign manufacturer does not have to prove any equity involvement with these companies. Nonetheless, their companies are strictly confined to the specific products to be imported – they are only permitted to import products (equipment or raw materials) for their own use. In other words, they are not allowed to distribute the imported products in China.

Foreign invested enterprises (FIEs) in the form of joint ventures or wholly-owned operations are permitted to distribute the products of their own manufacture in the Chinese market. Their legitimacy is that they are registered as Chinese legal entities. The previous requirement for FIEs to commit a certain percentage of sales in overseas markets has been phased out. The ratio of domestic sales to overseas sales is left to commercial considerations between joint venture partners.

A common misconception by many foreign companies is that once they set up a representative office in China, they will be able to import directly through such an office to the Chinese market. In fact, under Chinese law, a foreign representative office is, by definition, a liaison function. It can engage in product promotion, information collection, customer relations, but it may not enter into direct transactions with either a foreign party or a Chinese party. Putting it into perspective, a foreign representative office is a cost centre rather than a profit centre; it merely acts as an extension and presence for the foreign company in China.

According to the market access commitment to the WTO, a foreign firm is permitted to send a sales representative to China for business negotiations; but such representative will not be allowed to conduct sales activities to the general public, and the maximum period for his or her stay in China is restricted to 90 days.

In order to circumvent market entry barriers, including high import tariffs, many foreign manufacturers have, in the past, opted to set up joint ventures and wholly-owned companies. With the timely alleviation or removal of these barriers as part of the WTO commitments, foreign firms are finding that market access is more relaxed. As direct import into China becomes easier and less costly, the incentives for foreign direct investment on these grounds are declining.

Forming joint venture foreign trade companies in China

If a foreign firm enters into a joint venture with a Chinese partner in the area of foreign trade, it will become eligible to engage in direct imports into, and exports from, China. Moreover, it will no longer be restricted to selling products of its own manufacture, as in the case of manufacturing-based joint ventures.

Nevertheless, China has been very prudent in opening up the service sector to foreign firm participation and particularly so in the area of foreign trade. The door opened a crack in 1996 when MOFTEC (the predecessor of MOFCOM) promulgated the *Interim Provisions for the Test Launch of Joint Venture Foreign Trade Companies in China*. The restrictions are rather severe and, in effect, shut the door for all small- and medium-sized firms. The conditions for the joint venture parties and the joint venture company are as follows:

- The joint venture foreign trade company is a liability limited Chinese entity, in which the foreign party must invest in not less than 25 per cent of the equity. Its legal representative must be appointed by the Chinese party.
- To be eligible as such a joint venture partner, a foreign party must satisfy the following criteria:
  - sales revenue in excess of US\$5 billion in the year prior to the application;

  - average annual trade value with China in excess of US\$50 million over the three years prior to the application;
  - the foreign party must have maintained a representative office in China for the past three years, or have invested over US\$30 million in China.
- To be eligible for such a joint venture partner, a Chinese party must satisfy the following criteria:
  - it must have obtained foreign trading rights;
  - annual average foreign trade value must exceed US\$200 million, of which the export value should be not less than \$100 million;
  - it has set up no less than three subsidiaries or joint ventures outside China, and the average annual overseas revenue should be no less than US\$10 million for the past three years.
- The joint venture foreign trade company to be formed must satisfy the following criteria:
  - registered capital should be no less than RMB100 million;
  - it has an independent business premises and an adequate number of qualified staff.

Choice of distribution channels in China

Decisions over the scope of distribution channels must be made in relation to both corporate resources and local conditions. The opportunities and threats presented by the macro-environment, patterns of competition, customer behaviour and the quality of prospective distributors are among the many elements to be considered in designing the distribution system.

Overall, it is advisable for a foreign company deliberating over a distribution channel system in China to examine carefully the following major elements:

- Chinese laws and regulations;
- Chinese customers' needs and expectations;
- corporate resources, including in-house expertise to extend into the target market;
- economy of scale – if the product range is sufficiently large, it may be more cost-efficient to extend the company's own distribution arm;
- the size of the market segment;
- knowledge and comfort level in the local market;
- level of short-term and long-term commitment to the Chinese market;
- characteristics of the products or services to be marketed in China;
- available alternatives for distributing in China;
- the level of expertise of prospective local distributors.

In spite of the continuous efforts of the open-door policy and government deregulation, the local distribution sector is among the last of the fortresses to be torn down in China. Many wholesaling and retailing channels are still monopolized by a limited number of state-owned enterprises (SOEs). This format, to a large extent, also applies to Chinese manufacturers. In certain industries, the monopolized distribution channels absorb most of the added value in the profit chain. Take the pharmaceutical market as an example: an average of 40–60 per cent of the end value of the product is eaten up by the various layers of distributors.

Customer's needs and expectations are closely related to the characteristics and price levels of the products as well as the depth of market penetration. For technology-intensive products with deeper market penetration, such as the current generation of personal computers in the Chinese market, the availability of professional service is instrumental in achieving market success. Recently, prior to the sale of its PC division (see Chapter 8.6), IBM vowed to develop more than 3,000 dealers in small and medium Chinese cities in the hope that the sales growth of PCs there would exceed that in larger cities.

Fresh participants with limited knowledge and expertise about the Chinese market are advised to be more patient and less ambitious. Existing local intermediaries are handy vehicles to test the water. Piggybacking on those firms who have accumulated considerable experience in China is also a sensible approach. Moving along the learning curve, foreign firms will find themselves arriving at an acceptable comfort level. After initial success, a foreign firm may find it appropriate to branch out in the market and more alternative channels of distribution will be discovered in different market segments.

When arriving at a certain stage of development, a foreign firm may take a helicopter view of the entire market and decide to shorten its distribution channel. The benefits of a shortened distribution channel are obvious:

- better control over the end market;
- closer participation in the profit chain; and
- quick flow of information.

The objective can be achieved by one of several alternative means: 1) partnership with powerful distributors; 2) exclusive franchising; 3) forward integration.

In summary, there are four types of distribution channels available in terms of different levels of market penetration.

- A two-stop channel. Along the route from a foreign firm (without considering the importer) to end customers, two intermediaries are involved, one being the wholesaler and the other being the retailer. The foreign firm can either leave everything to the wholesaler, help the wholesaler to identify retailers or, alternatively, draw up with the wholesaler the criteria and restrictions for selecting retailers.
- A one-stop retail channel. A foreign firm sells direct to the retailers. Typically, this type of firm has already stepped into regional markets in China and maintains distribution centres in each region.
- A one-stop franchise channel. A foreign firm enters into an exclusive sales agreement with a resourceful local partner and refrains from in-depth penetration in the local market.
- A non-stop channel. Foreign firms (after successful importation into China) conduct what is called direct marketing in China, ie selling directly to the end customers. For consumer products, they may organize their own frontline sales force to conduct personal selling, mail order, telemarketing, TV and internet selling. They may also sell through their own stores or rented booths in shopping malls. Vorwerk and Electrolux are very successful marketing their portable vacuum cleaners through door-to-door sales in China and their on-site demonstration is highly impressive and persuasive. Typically, the sales activities are supported by a coordinated logistical centre. For big-ticket items, such as industrial equipment, foreign firms may find it worth dispatching sales representatives to make presentations and negotiate with Chinese clients (see Figure 5.8.2).

Of course, the choice of distribution in China is not limited to the four types illustrated. Foreign firms may choose any combination compatible with their marketing strategies. As internet technology advances and China's market environment continues to liberalize, such choices will multiply.

Distribution streams

A manufacturer or its selected franchisee will form a national distribution headquarters. Such headquarters can be vested either in their home office (if it has an

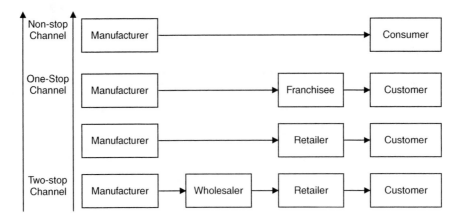

Figure 5.8.2 Types of distribution channels in China

entity in China) or in big cities that enjoy sound transportation and communication networks. A distribution system in China is typically designed along a vertical stream that follows the government administrative structure. Depending on the target market, products catering for urban consumption, particularly in big cities, will follow a three-tier structure, ie from cities to districts and then to communities, whereas products catering for rural consumption will move along from provinces to counties, then to communes and eventually to farmers in their villages, as illustrated in Figure 5.8.3.

On the other hand, for products that are targeted at both urban and rural residents, the distribution structure will first divide China into eight geographic regions. They comprise north-east China region, east China region, south China region, south-east China region, middle China region, north-west China region, south-west China region and north China region. Consumers in each region maintain their own distinctive characteristics in their language, social customs and income levels. For example, consumers in each east China region, including Shanghai, prefer seafood and vegetables, while consumers in the middle China region are more inclined to spicy food.

One big concern in managing distribution channels, particularly when they are lengthy and wide, is the problem of cross competition between different distributors. Distributors in certain regions often step out of their defined territories and solicit customers in the territories that are covered by other distributors. If this is unchecked, the interests of the manufacturer, the franchise and the wholesaler will be

damaged. To prevent such vicious competition, the following suggestions should be considered:

- to clearly define the distribution territory for each distributor;
- to limit the number of distributors in each region;
- to avoid the vague term of 'recommended price' and maintain a strict pricing policy between wholesaling and retailing;
- to enforce penalty clauses in the event of cross competition;

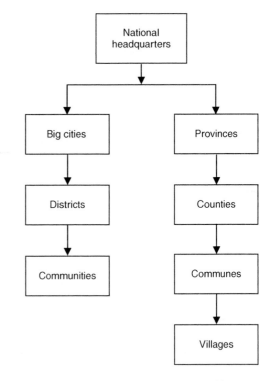

Figure 5.8.3 Distribution structure in China

- to attach territory labels to the products;
- to formulate a transfer pricing policy between distributors of different territories;
- to conduct routine surveillance against violations.

China's commitment to WTO entry

Since China officially became a member of the WTO as of December 2001, and as the implementation process to its WTO commitments steps up, distribution channels in the Chinese market are unleashing a remarkable prospect. The following is a reverse literal translation from a Chinese version of those commitments.

In the area of service provision and wholesale distribution, China will perform the following obligations:

- One year after China's WTO entry, foreign firms are permitted to set up joint ventures in China and engage in commissioned agency and wholesale business for all products except certain specified items.
- Three years after China's WTO entry, foreign firms are permitted to engage in the distribution of books, newspapers, journals, pharmaceuticals, pesticides and agricultural plastic film.
- Five years after China's WTO entry, foreign firms are permitted to engage in the distribution of chemical fertilizers, crude oils and refined oils.
- Two years after China's WTO entry, geographic and quantitative restrictions will be lifted for foreign service providers (except for chemical fertilizers, crude oils and refined oils, which call for a five-year phase-out period), and they are permitted to seize majority equity share in joint venture companies with Chinese partners.

In the area of retail distribution, China is more cautious in opening up the market for free foreign competition. China will perform the following obligations:

- China has made no commitment to distribution by mail order.
- Foreign firms are only permitted to engage in retail distribution within selected areas, which include the five Special Economic Zones (Shenzhen, Zhuhai, Shantou, Xiamen and Hainan) and six major cities (Beijing, Shanghai, Tianjin, Guangzhou, Dalian and Qingdao). In Beijing and Shanghai, no more than four joint venture retail firms are permitted, and no more than two are permitted in the each of the remaining cities. Two out of the four joint venture firms to be set up in Beijing are permitted to establish two branches in the same city.
- Immediately after its WTO entry, China would open Zhenzhou and Wuhan to joint venture retail distribution.
- Within two years after its WTO entry, China will permit foreign majority equity ownership within retail joint ventures, and all capital cities at provincial level, together with Chongqing and Ningbo, will be open to joint venture retail firms.
- Within one year after China's WTO entry, foreign firms will be permitted to engage in the retail of books, newspapers and journals.
- Within three years after China's WTO entry, foreign firms will be permitted to engage in the retail of pharmaceutical drugs, pesticides, agricultural plastic film and refined oils.
- Within five years after China's WTO entry, foreign firms will be permitted to engage in the retail of chemical fertilizers.
- Foreign chain store operators are permitted the freedom to engage with any local partner. They are permitted to engage in the retail of any products as specified in the timetable except automotives.
- Within three years after its WTO entry, China will remove all restrictions over foreign franchising as well as distribution without fixed premises.

Salt and tobacco are regarded as strategic goods, distribution of which is not open to foreign firms.

More recent information – J Reuvid

Freight transport market size

The following figures are based on rail, water and air freight. Road haulage is excluded:

- *Chinese freight tonnage increased by 11.6 per cent in volume in 2002. Total tonnage in 2002 was 4,672.4 million tonnes.*
- *Compound annual growth rate for the period 1998–2002 accelerated to 12 per cent (see Table 5.8.1).*
- *The strongest growth was in 2000, with a rate of 15.6 per cent.*

Freight transport segmentation

Water freight, representing 60 per cent of the market by volume, constituted the largest segment of the Chinese freight transport market in 2002 (see Table 5.8.2).

Table 5.8.1 Chinese freight transport volume 1998–2002 (million tonnes)

Year	Million tonnes	% growth
1998	2,967.0	
1999	3,230.7	8.9
2000	3,734.0	15.6
2001	4,188.7	12.2
2002	4,672.4	11.5
CAGR (1998–2002)		**12.0**

Source: Snapdata Research

Table 5.8.2 Chinese freight transport segmentation 2002 (volume: %)

Segment	% Share
Water freight	60.0
Rail freight	39.9
Freight airlines	0.1
Total	**100.0**

Source: Snapdata Research

Rail freight

At the beginning of the year an ambitious target of building 28,000 km of railway by the year 2020 was set by the State Council. In February 2004, the new Minister of Railways, Liu Zhijun, announced that the current railways in operation of 72,000 km would be extended to 100,000 km by that date and that the ratio of double-track railways and electrified lines would both reach 50 per cent.

In July 2004, the railway authority revealed that it was preparing new rules to attract foreign capital and to permit FIEs and domestic companies to invest in operating parts of the network. This shift in strategy reflects the chronic shortage of funds and transport bottlenecks, which magnified during the failed five-year term of the previous railways minister. Although much of China's rail freight is transported at fixed prices, lack of capacity, which Mr Liu has estimated at 40 per cent of rail shipment demand, has caused many transport operators to move cargo by road at greatly increased cost.

To achieve the new target China needs to spend more than US$12 billion each year, of which US$4.8 billion will be funded by the government but the remaining US$7.2 billion will have to come from investors, overseas listings or the Ministry itself.

Air freight

Under its accession commitments to the WTO, China is required to allow foreign companies majority ownership of freight transport companies by the end of 2004.

In the case of air freight, a landmark agreement signed in July 2004 between China and the US has opened up significant opportunities for international carriers, as 195 additional weekly flights between the US and China are to be added over the next six years, of which 111 are reserved for cargo carriers, representing a fivefold increase in total flights between the countries. The allocation of the 39 additional weekly slots available by March 2005 has been hotly contested.

Under this air services agreement, permission was granted for carriers such as FedEx to open cargo hubs from 2007 and to start constructing the logistics infrastructure that companies with local manufacturing operations require.

While FedEx is pursuing the possibility of opening a hub in Guangzhou and UPS and DHL both hope to establish facilities in Shanghai, DHL is pressing ahead with opening a US$100 million cargo terminal in Hong Kong.

Domestic express parcels market

However, access to the domestic express parcel market remains restricted as Beijing's State Postal Bureau, which also runs China Post, the national postal service and dominant parcel delivery service, clings to its near monopoly. China Post has already suffered a decline in it share of international express consignments to 30 per cent, largely as a result of competition from the major international carriers.

China Domestic, DHL's domestic express service and the first provided by a foreign company, only delivers packages weighing more than 2 kg. When it started its service, the Draft Law provided for foreign companies to deliver anything over 500 grams. The German-owned parcel carrier launched its service in May 2004 on the assumption that it had all the necessary government approvals. However, the State Postal Bureau declared that it had never sanctioned the venture.

A US-China Business Council study, published in September 2003, estimated that a de-restricted air express industry in China would generate US$84 billion in increased manufacturing output and US$3 billion of additional investment, and would create 800,000 jobs for export industries. The debate continues; however, the latest draft of the postal law permits foreign companies to deliver anything weighing more than 350 grams, which is taken as an encouraging sign.

How the CBBC Operates

Humphrey Keenlyside, China Britain Business Council

Introduction

The China Britain Business Council (CBBC) is the UK's leading agency helping British companies do business in China. It is a business-led partnership between government and industry, with a proven track record of developing British trade in China dating back to the 1950s. CBBC is recognized and respected at the highest level of both Chinese and British governments. It organizes many useful high-level business events with trade-related government ministers from both countries. It also delivers a range of practical assistance to British companies targetting the China market. This chapter explains how.

The year 2004 marked the 50th anniversary of the establishment of formal trade relations between the UK and the People's Republic of China. The year was also the first half-century for the China-Britain Business Council. In the sweep of Chinese history of 3,000 years, a mere 50 years is just a drop in the ocean. Nevertheless, that time period during which the UK and China have continued to develop trade and business, despite and during some turbulent times, indicates that most valued of attributes for doing business in China: long-term commitment.

CBBC has found itself playing a pivotal role during the past half century and, on occasion, an indispensable one. During the Cultural Revolution, for example, when China cut itself off from most of the world, official representatives from the British government were not recognized. It was only the Sino-British Trade Council (as CBBC was then known) that was allowed to wave the British flag and act as a point of contact between British and Chinese traders.

With the gradual emergence of a greater pragmatism towards the West, which culminated triumphantly with the launch of Deng Xiaoping's open door policy at the end of the 1970s, CBBC could concentrate on trade, rather than on difficult diplomacy. Every year since, as British trade, investment and commerce have picked up, so has the work of CBBC.

Today, CBBC is the UK's leading agency helping British companies do business in China. It has come to be respected and associated with British business in China at the very highest levels of Chinese society – a direct consequence of its long-standing commitment to developing business between the two countries.

It has now become the norm that whenever a top Chinese leader visits the UK, CBBC is tasked with organizing a major business event. Within the past six years, CBBC has organized business lunches, dinners or conferences for: Premier Zhu Rongji (1998); President Jiang Zemin (1999); Vice-President Hu Jintao (2002); and Premier Wen Jiabao (2004), as well as for visits by mayors of China's most important cities. It is often the case that CBBC will head a business delegation accompanying a British minister visiting China. These include two visits by Prime Minister Tony Blair (1998 and 2003).

How the CBBC helps British business in China

CBBC acts as a first port of call for any business contemplating an approach to the China market. The first step is gathering information. It is extremely important to be well informed and well briefed before making any decisions – even the most preliminary decisions, such as whether to visit the country. CBBC can provide background information about anything from the size of the market to the importance of appreciating cultural niceties. In partnership with trade associations, chambers of commerce, development agencies and other China-interested organizations, CBBC provides regular briefings on the Chinese market and business culture.

Advice

Initial advice from CBBC is free of charge. This can include:

- a one-to-one meeting with a CBBC member of staff;
- general background material on China, its economy and business environment;
- synopses on priority market sectors;
- fact sheets on various aspects of doing business in China;
- a signposting facility to translation, interpretation, legal and other advisory services.

There is also a wealth of information, including a full and valuable section called 'Market Intelligence', about the China business environment on the CBBC website (www.cbbc.org).

Research

The next step is to research the market. There are a number of schemes to assist would-be entrants to glean good information. Through CBBC, participants in the China market can secure market research for China, either through CBBC's own in-house research or via the government-sponsored Overseas Market Introduction Service (OMIS). Both schemes are open to all UK-registered companies.

CBBC can also help with a comprehensive online information service, available at its London head office. Information sources include, among others: directories of government, trade organizations and Chinese manufacturers; industrial sector yearbooks; business guides and handbooks on trading with and investing in China; and regularly updated sector information on a wide range of industries. For companies wishing to identify suppliers in China, the information department can also help with off-the-shelf lists of B2B websites covering the China market and tailored desk research to provide a list of potential suppliers

Visiting the market

Having established that there is potential for participation in the China market, the next stage is usually for the British company to visit the market. Here there are a number of options:

- attendance at a trade fair or exhibition;
- joining a trade mission;
- participating in a seminar or conference;
- going on a specially arranged personalized visit.

In each case, the primary objective will be to find out more information about the market, to learn more first hand about the particularities and peculiarities of the market and, probably just as important, to become enthused about the place. Too often, visiting businessmen and women on tight schedules miss out on the enjoyment there is to be had when visiting China. More information and recommendations can be found on CBBC's website.

In terms of missions, CBBC leads and arranges several missions to China each year with a particular focus on an activity (such as how to go about arranging production or manufacturing) or a sector (such as health care, financial services or education).

In all, CBBC has organized more than 200 trade missions and exhibitions to China and is responsible for the coordination of many of the UK Trade and Investment (UKTI)-sponsored missions and exhibitions. CBBC's contacts in China enables it arrange meetings with senior officials and leading Chinese enterprises.

The CBBC business meeting package

It also organizes individual missions for companies under the CBBC Business Meeting Package scheme, which comprises:

- a pre-visit consultation by phone or a one-to-one meeting at CBBC's London office;
- researching potential meeting contacts in China;
- arranging a programme of one-to-one business meetings;
- providing background information about the Chinese companies;
- appointing an interpreter;
- sending out an information pack with general information about China, business etiquette and tips on speaking through interpreters.

Seminar visits to China

CBBC has extensive experience of organizing UKTI-supported seminar visits to China. These seminars, all of which have a specific focus, have covered a wide range of sectors including financial services, environment, agriculture, aerospace, metros and light rail, and food processing.

An experienced Mandarin-speaking CBBC seminar manager advises and guides participants throughout the whole visit. This support ranges from an initial individual company consultation to discuss priorities and objectives, through practical assistance in arranging translation and production of presentation materials, to active support in China during the seminar. The manager, and CBBC staff in the relevant offices in China, work together to liaise with Chinese host organizations and relevant bodies to secure appropriate level support in China and to coordinate the practical logistics involved in setting up a seminar.

Establishing a presence

If the company then decides that it does wish to pursue an operation in China, the next step is deciding whether or not it is necessary to establish a presence. If the prospective business or company does decide that it wishes to establish a presence in China, the usual path is to set up a representative office. CBBC can help in this process.

However, an easier choice – which also has the advantage of enabling companies to decide whether the China market really is for them by providing an extra period in which to 'dip a toe in the water' – is to take advantage of the CBBC Launchpad scheme. This enables companies to set up a base in any of the CBBC China offices ahead of opening an individual office. Companies have a fully dedicated CBBC member of staff, office space and communications (a phone and access to a fax), advice and support and a message-taking service through a CBBC receptionist. Most companies go on to open a full representative office of their own, having used CBBC's Launchpad as a secure and risk-free way of establishing their business in China.

Launchpad is also helpful for those who have an office in one part of China but would like to extend market cover to other locations where CBBC has office facilities.

Continuing contact

Once a company is established in China, CBBC can continue to provide a useful role by acting as a continuing point of contact for all businesses in China. That is because it is important to develop a unified and coherent national commercial strategy towards China. That may seem odd. In no other country do businesses regard themselves as being part of a national collective, but Chinese people very often look at the company and the nationality of that company as being one and the same. Chinese leaders often draw comparisons between different countries and regions. They might say, for example, that the Germans are good at marketing, the Italians are creative, the French have a liking for big projects. These might be stereotypes, but they continue to be believed in many sectors of Chinese society.

Britain has gone to great lengths to challenge some of the stereotypical images. The Britain in China and Think UK campaigns have been designed specifically to present a modern, innovative and forward-thinking United Kingdom – and with considerable success.

Lobbying

CBBC acts to represent some of the collective strengths of British commerce and industry. This is particularly important when it comes to making the case on behalf of British business to Chinese leaders and is the final role where CBBC acts to work on behalf of British business in China – lobbying. The CBBC's excellent contacts at the very highest levels of Chinese government – developed over the past 50 years – give it a special position and influence.

Whilst use of CBBC's services is open to all, it is also a membership organization with some 400 British company members for which it provides a number of exclusive business services.

Sectoral expertise

Although CBBC is geared to providing general information about China, it also has expertise in certain sectors identified as being important in the future development of British business in China. In many cases, CBBC works in conjunction with other bodies to promote such sectoral expertise. The sectors upon which CBBC concentrates are identified in the box overleaf.

CBBC sectors of expertise

Financial Services

CBBC has a joint Financial Services China Committee with International Financial Services, London. This committee gathers members from the banking, law, accounting and insurance industries, as well as relevant government organizations.

Communication Technologies Forum (CTF)

CTF is an industry-led forum focused on helping UK companies access China's communication industries. The Forum, chaired by and representing business, is managed by CBBC and supported by UKTI, Communication Information Industries (CII) and the sector's two main trade associations, the Information Technology, Telecommunications and Electronics Association (Intellect) and the Telecommunication Industry Association (TIA). CTF acts as a focal point for China expertise and experience from within the UK communications and information technology industries. The Forum offers exclusive networking opportunities, round-table discussions with senior Chinese business leaders/officials, practical sector-focused seminars and industry-specific news and analysis.

Education

China, as one of the British government's key markets for education and training, continues to develop at an extremely fast pace. CBBC runs UK-based events in conjunction with the British Council to keep members informed of the latest market developments, as well as organizing tailor-made missions to China to explore potential opportunities and establish contacts. CBBC works closely with the British Council and UKTI in coordinating its China service for the education sector.

Agriculture

There are increasing opportunities in the food and agricultural sectors following China's accession to the WTO. CBBC plays an active role in the promotion of British food and agricultural investments in China. It runs an annual trade mission to China in partnership with the Department for Environment, Food and Rural Affairs (DEFRA) and has a dedicated staff member in Beijing working on the sector. Other activities include inward visits from China and seminars.

These are just some of the industry sectors that CBBC is promoting for China and priority sectors often change over time. Additionally, there are other CBBC initiatives to support SMEs and other industry sectors such as health care, environment, airports, automotive and sports/infrastructure (including opportunities arising from the Beijing 2008 Olympic Games).

Part Six

Marketing Issues in China

Industrial and Commercial Market Research

Li Yong, Deputy Secretary General, China Association of International Trade

China is a country with unique socio-economic features. A sound business strategy will have to be based on careful market research that will analyse the unique features of the marketplace and generate information for decision-making. There have been instances when foreign investors have failed to conduct effective market research after their entry into China; even worse, some companies do not appreciate the value of market research and simply believe that they have good products and so people in China will buy them. This has invariably led to varying degrees of failure.

When a company is established in China, continuing research efforts should be made in order to monitor the performance/position of the company in the changing marketplace against its competitors, changes in consumer/customer preferences and changes in market conditions likely to affect its sales volume or profitability.

Industrial market research

Is it possible to do industrial market research in China?

The intricacies of China's industrial operations and the complexities of its socio-economic environment have caused international market researchers to question whether it is possible to conduct industrial market research in China. Lack of familiarity with the information systems has also made them feel sceptical about the prospect of doing industrial market research in China to answer questions in relation to their business decisions, such as:

● what factories could make the product?
● what kind of demand is there for it?
● what are the channels of distribution like?

● what impact do prices have on demand in an economy that only recently adopted a market mechanism?
● how will the product be marketed?
● how will the market evolve over the next five or 10 years?
● what are the key market drivers?
● are there any entry restrictions?
● what are the unique characteristics of the local marketplace?

With the deepening of China's economic reform, private information has become increasingly public – a result of China's efforts to increase transparency. China's accession to the WTO will create a much more open environment for information sharing. Up-to-date, systematic and comprehensive secondary information can be found in the massive compendia published by Chinese organizations. Apart from the *China Statistical Yearbook,* published by the State Statistical Bureau, many Chinese ministries now publish yearbooks and almanacs containing information about the development of their respective sectors. There are also around 3,500 technical journals for professionals in many specialized fields. Such journals often contain technical descriptions of a technology, product or development trend of a particular sector. A careful observer of the Chinese market will also find an increasing number of professional newspapers featuring the dynamics of different industries.

However, collecting and studying secondary information, something many foreign companies are doing as part of their day-to-day research effort, may not be sufficient to support business decisions or delineate a complete picture of the market. Some of this information may have built-in discrepancies, such as incompleteness in ministry statistical releases, which may have excluded the industrial operations that fall outside its administrative jurisdiction, and inconsistencies in different statistical sources for the same industry because of the different statistical standards applied. Moreover, a legacy of the planned economy is that much of the secondary information depicts the picture on the production side and gives little insight into other critical information such as the demand dynamics of end-users and end-use segments, competitive environments, prevailing terms of sales and marketing practices, or the strengths and weaknesses of the existing distribution network.

The study of secondary information can achieve the following, from the standpoint of information users:

- obtain a macro picture of the business environment;
- identify market opportunities before commitment is made to more costly field research;
- pinpoint specific factors that need to be investigated further;
- locate the types of information to be collected through field research.

Given the insufficiencies and inadequacies of secondary information, it is necessary to carry out primary research in order to find first-hand information and remove the possible flaws that may exist in the secondary information. In some cases, primary data will have to be obtained, simply because no systematic statistics have ever existed, or the product in question has been grouped into a very broad statistical entry. Even if there is an abundance of secondary data, some of it will have to be screened and validated via field interviews.

General practices and methodologies in industrial market research

In China, understanding of industrial market research varies among research providers of different types and backgrounds and this determines the methodologies used to carry out research. Generally speaking, there are two schools of methodology in China. One school is represented by research providers who understand industrial market research as industrial market intelligence. They boast their close links with government officials, industry associations, key suppliers or access to sources of information not available from published sources. As a result, much of the research effort is devoted to 'ploughing' insider information or

statistics, and the research conclusions are constructed on the basis of documenting the findings of the 'ploughing' efforts. The advantages of such methodology are that the information documented can be systematic in terms of time sequences and official in terms of information sources. They can be of good value as a benchmark study, or for the understanding of less dynamic markets, but may not be good enough for an assessment of market opportunities.

The second school concentrates on an interactive and cross-checking approach and obtains research findings through systematically designed research planning. This does not exclude 'ploughing' secondary information from both published and unpublished sources, but also builds into the research process a series of interactive and cross-checking interviews along the value chain of a particular market. Secondary information is used as a benchmark for the truth-seeking efforts and validated in the process of interviews. The interviews not only focus on hard facts such as production, market size, terms of sales and logistical issues, but also on market dynamics such as general business mood, level of confidence in the future outlook, comments on development targets set forth by supervising authorities, the role of market specifiers in determining future market trends, the likely impact of inter-material competition and perceived market drivers. The interview process will demand highly skilled interviewers with sufficient understanding of the industry. Interview findings and conclusions drawn from them not only provide insights into the market, but also establish accountability in the assessment of market opportunities.

Consumer market research

Tools and techniques

Generally, the tools and techniques of consumer market research in China are much the same as for other countries. Although the application of the tools and techniques may vary a little, the basic principles of consumer market research do not change in the context of the Chinese market. The most frequently used techniques are:

- quantitative interviews;
  - face-to-face (in-home and central location intercept);
  - telephone;
  - mail;
  - diary;

- qualitative interviews (in-depth interviews);
  - face-to-face;
  - focus groups.

Other international market research techniques are employed to meet specific information needs. However, costly and highly sophisticated techniques are unusual.

Selection of nationally representative locations for consumer research

Target locations for research are usually Beijing, Shanghai and Guangzhou. These cities are thought to be representative of China in terms of distinctive consumer characteristics, and inferences on the population are established on the basis of findings there. These locations, however, may not be as representative as they are thought to be as they are the most developed areas in China and have the highest living standards compared with other cities in the country. In addition, the behavioural characteristics, purchasing motivations and decision-making processes are not necessarily shared by consumers in other areas of China. Of course, many studies do not intend to be representative of China and the three cities are only used for benchmarking purposes, or establishing benchmark parameters. Many other researchers also focus on these cities because they are seen as points of entry, or targets of penetration.

If a research project is intended to achieve a representative picture of China, it is recommended that other geographical locations are considered, such as Chengdu/Chongqing, Xian, Wuhan, Shenyang/Dalian.

Sampling practices

Probability and non-probability sampling are common in Chinese consumer research. Probability sampling is more often used in quantitative research and non-probability in qualitative research. Typical probability sampling methods are stratified sampling and cluster sampling. Applications of sampling methods vary from organization to organization. Statistical organizations (ie those within the system of the State Statistical Bureau, such as the Organization of Urban Socio-Economic Surveys and its local counterparts) claim that their sample bases are established by way of stratified sampling. Other research organizations tend to use cluster sampling methods, such as area sampling. A typical route to reach the households in the sampling process is described in Figure 6.1.1.

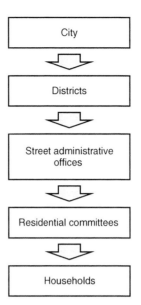

Figure 6.1.1 A typical route to reach the households in the sampling process

Normally, a city is divided into several districts. Under the district government, there are two levels of administrative bodies – street administrative offices and residential committees. A street administrative office usually exercises administrative responsibilities on behalf of the district government in a number of street blocks. Under each street administrative office are a varying number of residential committees. Residential committees are the basic elements of government administration.

Increasingly, however, many research organizations are using what is called street intercept – shopping centre or central location sampling – where samples are drawn by way of randomly intercepting people on the street, in shopping centres or in the central locations of a city. Although street intercept or shop intercept interviews have limitations, not least unrepresentative sampling, research organizations use this methodology to reduce costs and because it is increasingly difficult to carry out in-home face-to-face interviews.

Fieldwork practices

In fieldwork, street administrative offices and residential committees may be contacted to obtain information on residential committees/households in order to establish sampling frames. Fieldworkers can have easy access to households with the assistance of the residential committees.

In order to regulate market research activities, the statistical authority has promulgated a regulation requiring market research organizations to obtain approval from statistical authorities before gaining access to households. In reality, however, this regulation has not been effectively enforced.

As quantitative consumer research involves a relatively large sample size, most research organizations regularly employ university students to carry out field interviews. While proper training is important to ensure the quality of the interviews, an appropriate monitoring mechanism, such as random back-check, is even more important to ensure that the interviews are carried out in strict compliance with the designed methodology. Common problems with using student interviewers are questionnaires not being administered properly, sampling procedures not being strictly followed, interviewers faking questionnaires after repeated refusals or 'not-at-homes', and answers to open-ended questions not being properly probed and/or recorded.

The statistical organizations employ professional interviewers when carrying out field interviews. They are well trained and have routine contacts with residential committees, which will facilitate the interviews.

Differences in the research environment

Unfamiliarity with market differences often causes misunderstanding of the market and/or misinterpretation of the business environment, which may eventually lead to wrong decisions. It is important to note differences in the environment where the research is carried out. The following are generalizations of some of the major differences in the Chinese research environment. However, it is always advisable for researchers to analyze the research environment on a case-by-case basis before embarking on research planning and design.

Differences in the basic data

As is true in other countries, the statistical system in China has its own unique features. Some of the statistical information is collected and prepared in accordance with international standards, such as the Customs Statistics, which follow the Harmonious System (HS). Many other statistics still resemble the characteristics of the planned economy, although great efforts have been made by the statistical authority to improve the statistical system.

The State Statistical Bureau publishes a series of official statistics, including the most authoritative *China Statistical Yearbook*, but these tend to be more macro than micro compared with the statistics compiled by different ministries. In some instances, there are also discrepancies between the statistics of state statistical publications and ministerial releases. Even ministerial releases on industries can be incomplete because enterprises of the same or similar nature may fall under different ministries. In some cases, statistics on certain industries simply do not exist.

Differences in reporting systems

While the incompleteness of the statistical system can be attributed to problems such as outdated classification and obsolete collection methods, complicated reporting systems are also at fault. Normally, industrial statistics are reported in a bottom-up manner: ie enterprises or business entities report to their supervising departments at city/county levels, who will then report to higher level authorities such as provincial departments. The statistics will be relayed to central government departments, such as ministries. Departments in cities with separate planning from the central government are independent of the provincial departments and report directly to the corresponding departments at central levels. As government departments at different levels may have their own statistical requirements for reporting purposes, the statistics kept at different levels may also vary. For example, the central departments may only be interested in knowing the performances of the enterprises at county level and above, while a city or county level department will also collect information on lower level enterprises, such as village enterprises.

Differences in the social environment

The following are some some key differences:

- Market research organizations tend to group people/families into different social classes for particular research purposes. In China, the doctrine of equality among different professions has determined that there is no standardized classification of social class.
- Moreover, the socialist welfare system has also determined that employers provide housing for their employees. Although this is being reformed, the residents in a building tend to be the staff of the same work unit and may share some common characteristics.
- Increased security-consciousness and awareness of privacy have made in-home interviews more

difficult. Telephone owners still represent higher income households and direct mail questionnaires may not find their way to targeted respondents because personal details such as home addresses are not easily available.

- Reported household expenditure on some commodities, such as soft drinks, beer, staple food (ie rice or wheat flour), edible oil, and tea etc, may not reflect the actual consumption because some of these commodities are provided to employees of state-owned enterprises, government organizations and business corporations as a part of their welfare package and they are not counted as out-of-pocket expenditure.

Differences in reactions and length of interviews

The novelty of the structured questionnaire may arouse interest in the interviewee, but sophisticated and prolonged questioning may lead to a loss of interest or perfunctory answers. In most cases, respondents of a consumer study are open in their comments.

In industrial research, respondents tend to be very careful when giving comments. Respondents are easily alerted when being asked questions that they regard as probing into their commercial secrets. An offer to share the research findings at a later date is not regarded as recompense for giving out information.

In qualitative research, in-depth interviews with respondents in senior positions will normally take longer than planned. The expense of being polite and showing respect, which is essential when carrying out in-depth interviews in China, is to allow divergence. In interactive focus groups, people with dominant personalities tend to lead opinion and they should be carefully managed.

A local research organization tends to have a better understanding of the local market and will be able to adapt to their client's research requirements, particularly when the research organization has working experience with, and good understanding of, the information needs of foreign companies.

The research industry and research organizations in China

The market research industry emerged as a result of China's open-door policy. The entry of foreign capital in China created a demand for market research. In the early 1980s, the International Trade Research Institute was one of the few primary contacts for market research.

In 1984, a consultant arm of the Institute – the Centre for Market and Trade Development (CMTD) – was established to provide a specialist research service for foreign companies. In 1986, the Opinion Research Institute of the People's University was founded. Later in 1987, two doctors of sociology set up the first commercial market research company. There is now a large number of research organizations in China who are involved in one way or another in market/marketing research. There are over 300 registered marketing research organizations and large advertising companies that have market research functions. Professional research institutions and information centres also provide market research services of various kinds.

Foreign research organizations are also operating in China in different establishments. Gallup and AC Nielson are active in China. China's accession to the WTO will further open up the services industry and more foreign consulting and market research companies will establish their operations in China.

Recommendations for market research in China

To fully understand the Chinese market, it is necessary to consider the realities of the vast territorial and regional differences. Breaking China down into a multitude of smaller markets and prioritizing the research effort on the core market(s) would be a sensible strategy to begin with. In the planning stage of the research, it is important to understand the extremes of demography and geography. For consumer products, the key urban markets will be the natural place to start, while for industrial products, the layout of China's key industries will have to be taken into consideration. Market research should be able to find out, in addition to other critical information, where your core market is and what potential it can offer.

In choosing a research provider, it is important to test their understanding of the market and their understanding of how market research should be carried out to meet research objectives. Both within and outside of China, there are numerous research organizations and consulting firms that boast of their expertise and special connections in China, but their understanding of market research in China varies greatly. Some understand market research as market intelligence. They build their advantage on their claimed special connections with China or access to insider information or statistics that are not publicly available. As a result, much of the research effort is devoted to 'ploughing' this information, while neglecting changing dynamics. It is important to appreciate special connections or access to privately held information, but the capacity to be able to deploy an on-the-ground research force to explore first-hand information is even more important.

In designing the research, it is highly recommended that a company planning to carry out research in China takes the following into account:

- Objectives should be clearly defined to exclude any possible ambiguity. The statement of research requirements or terms of reference should not only include the scope and problems to which answers are needed, but also precise specifications of the meaning of all words and terms.
- The disparity between what the company wants to find out and what the research provider can realistically do under the proposed budget and schedule should be recognized, while the limitations of carrying out research in China should be frankly discussed.
- Protection of the ownership of the research results should be made clear in the form of a confidentiality agreement. There have been instances where research providers infringed on the ownership of the research findings by publishing them in newspapers.
- Sources of information need to be detailed to justify the validity and reliability of the research findings.

- A face-to-face meeting with key researchers upon completion of the research is important to pick up opinions and observations that might not be included in the report.

Why employ local research organizations?

Because of the complexity and sensitivity of industrial market research, foreign research organizations often remain in the wings, consigning the job to local research organizations. Apart from the language barrier, which can make communications difficult or impossible, there are other considerations when employing local research providers, such as concerns about disclosing identity, culture and tradition that may influence the general willingness to respond, and distortion may arise from language and/or cultural differences when it comes to understanding questions and answers.

The general practice of foreign research organizations in conducting industrial market research in China is that local research providers are commissioned to carry out fieldwork in a way that should follow international practice, and submit the findings to the foreign research organization for analysis and interpretation. The drawback of this practice is that the interpretation of the research findings without involvement of the local resident researchers may build distorted understanding into the analytical process and lead to misinterpreted conclusions.

Growing Consumerism Strategies for the China Market

*T S Chan and Wei-ping Wu, Department of Marketing and International Business,
Lingnan University, Hong Kong*

Summary

Since China's 'open door' policy began in 1978, Chinese consumers have experienced an unprecedented consumer revolution. However, due to historical, economic and other related reasons, regional differences exist in the development of consumerism in China. This chapter investigates three key dimensions of growing consumerism in China: health consciousness, environmental consciousness and confidence in business ethics, among the four major Chinese cities of Beijing, Guangzhou, Hangzhou and Xian. An ANOVA post hoc Scheffe test was employed for data analysis. Among the findings, it was revealed that consumers in Guangzhou were less environmentally conscious than their counterparts in the other three cities. It is concluded that firms should pay attention to existing regional differences in consumerism when formulating their marketing strategies for regional Chinese markets.

Introduction

With China's entry into the WTO, international firms are becoming excited about the lifting of the barriers to potentially the largest consumer market in the world. Since China's current economic reform was launched in 1978, foreign firms have shown tremendous enthusiasm about the emerging China market. Thousands of foreign investors have entered the market in the last two decades. In the meantime, a new Cultural Revolution has taken place in China (Pollay et al, 1990). Together with foreign investors, western goods, as well as marketing concepts and techniques, are flooding in. Consumers in China are quickly adopting new values and western ideas (Tai and Tam, 1997; Wei and Pan, 1999) because of their increased exposure to global media and western lifestyles (Batra, 1997). Consequently, a new wave of consumerism is sweeping the mainland (Tong, 1998).

For historical reasons, western China has been developing very slowly and the reason is thought to be the prevalent business philosophy (Sims and Schiff, 2000). People in western China are generally more traditional and conservative than those in the east and south. However, little is currently known about whether there are significant differences between eastern, western, northern and southern regions of China in terms of the development of consumerism. By providing a better understanding of the different development stages of consumerism across China, this chapter aims to provide some valuable insights for multi-national companies (MNCs) designing their marketing strategies for the different Chinese regional markets.

We will look specifically at three extremely important and widespread phenomena resulting from growing consumerism in today's China: health consciousness, environmental consciousness and business ethics consciousness. Along with ongoing economic development, most Chinese people have experienced a significant improvement in living standards and, as a result, are paying more and more attention to their own health. Health consciousness is seen as one of the 'megatrends' to impact on the China market (Tong, 1998) and Chinese women have been found to be more health conscious than their counterparts in Hong Kong and Taiwan (Tai and Tam, 1997). The 'open door' policy has also brought about Chinese people's growing awareness of the importance of environmental protection. They have demonstrated much stronger environmental concern than their US counterparts (Chan, 2000). Chinese female consumers were found to be more environmentally conscious than those in Hong Kong (Tai and Tam, 1997). At the same time, consumerism has both bridged and exposed gaps in trust among entrepreneurs, government bureaucrats and consumers (Veeck, 2000). Chinese consumers are becoming increasingly conscious of business ethics. A survey of business people in eastern China revealed that business ethics has become a new and popular topic and business leaders have begun to realize its importance (Wu, 1999). These three issues are important to an understanding of China's growing consumerism.

Method

Sampling

A random sampling method was applied. Four major Chinese cities – Beijing, Hangzhou, Guangzhou and Xian – were selected, representing northern, eastern, southern and western China respectively. Data were collected by research assistants in local cities, using personal interview methods in key local shopping districts. These research assistants were Mainland Chinese students recruited by referral and trained in the basic techniques of conducting personal interviews. Proper guidance and instruction were given before data collection started. Shopping centre intercepts were carried out between December 1999 and February 2000 with every fifth person until a target of 200 was reached. Finally, 200 usable questionnaires each were collected from Beijing, Hangzhou and Xian. Some questionnaires from the Guangzhou group had a significant number of missing values, resulting in only 196 usable cases. In the aggregate sample, there were 391 females and 402 males, so the sample was evenly distributed between males and females.

Overall, 40.2 per cent were aged 17 to 25, 24.8 per cent 26 to 35, 15.7 per cent 36 to 45, 15.9 per cent 46 to 55 and 3.4 per cent 56 to 68. These age groups represent those who are in active work and financially independent.

Measurement

After an extensive literature review, 10 items related to trust in business ethics, environmental consciousness and health consciousness were selected to measure lifestyle dimensions. The questionnaire was initially developed in English, translated into Chinese and translated back into English, following standard blind procedures to ensure the accuracy of translation. Finally, a Chinese version was used for data collection. A five-point Likert-type scale was used for both lifestyle and marketing mix statements on consumers' post purchase perceptions of product quality, service quality and price, ranging from (1) 'strongly agree' to (5) 'strongly disagree'.

To ensure that all the measurements have good internal consistency, a Cronbach alpha test was applied to the three derived scales: trust in business ethics (a=0.68), environmental consciousness (a=0.62) and health consciousness (a=0.55). While alphas for two out of three scales are reasonably acceptable, alpha for the health consciousness construct is slightly lower than the threshold of a=0.60. However, from an exploratory perspective, a slightly lower alpha is still acceptable (Nunnally, 1978). To confirm the existence of three dimensions, a factor analysis was conducted. A principle component analysis was used as the extraction method. The rotation converged on four iterations, using the varimax method. It can be observed from Table 6.2.1 that three factors (Eigenvalue >1) were derived, resulting in an accumulated explained variance of 58.67 per cent.

Results

Data from the four cities were compared using a one-way ANOVA post hoc Scheffe test (see Table 6.2.2). There is no difference in consumers' health consciousness across the four cities and with all the arithmetic means below 2.02 ('1' strongly agree and '5' strongly disagree), indicating that Chinese consumers in all four cities are very health conscious.

Consumers in Guangzhou have a lower confidence in business ethics than those in Hangzhou and Xian. While there is no significant difference in consumers' confidence in business ethics between Guangzhou and Beijing, consumers in the latter turn out to be less confident than those in Hangzhou.

Consumers in Guangzhou are less environmentally conscious than in the other three cities. Interestingly, there is no difference between these three cities. Nevertheless, all the respondents indicated a fairly good environmental consciousness, as all the arithmetic means are below 2.15.

Discussion and conclusion

Our goal was to explore the regional differences in China's growing consumerism. The results show that regional differences do exist.

Table 6.2.1 Factor analysis of lifestyle variables

	Factor 1	Factor 2	Factor 3
Trust in business ethics (a=0.69)			
You believe that product quality is improving	0.721	117	−7.339E-02
You believe that firms are beginning to pay attention to customers' complaints	0.721	4.763E	−6.228E-02
You believe that product trademarks start to follow rules and regulations	0.720	159	7.097E-02
You believe that the dangers arising from using products are decreasing	0.707	−9.076E-02	5.912E-02
Environmental consciousness (a=0.62)			
My country should invest in environmental protection	1.900E-02	0.820	3.729E-02
The possibility of an energy crisis still exists	2.112E-02	0.760	0.188
From the country's point of view, the one child policy is necessary	0.132	0.666	1.006E-02
Health consciousness (a=0.55)			
Drinking is a bad hobby	3.293E-02	−3.172E-02	0.865
Smoking can cause cancer	5.635E-02	0.249	0.768
Eigenvalue	2.081	1.805	1.394
Variance explained	23.126	20.057	15.491

Extraction Method: Principal Component Analysis
Rotation Method: Varimax with Kaiser Normalization
Rotation converged in 4 iterations

Table 6.2.2 One-way ANOVA post hoc Scheffe Test of differences in lifestyles among Guangzhou, Beijing, Hangzhou and Xian

	Guangzhou (1)			Beijing (2)			Hangzhou (3)			Xian (4)		
	SD[1]	N	Mean	SD	N	Mean	SD	N	Mean	SD	N	Mean
Health consciousness	186	1.946	0.930	198	1.980	0.714	199	2.020	0.763	198	1.846	0.846
Confidence in business ethics	185	2.635	0.607	195	2.542	0.545	196	2.297	0.515	196	2.431	0.551
Environmental consciousness	178	2.150	0.906	195	1.670	0.537	197	1.702	0.457	195	1.622	0.531

Scales range from (1) 'Strongly Agree' to (5) 'Strongly Disagree'. [1]Standard deviation

Health consciousness

It is very interesting that no significant regional differences in consumers' health consciousness were found. The arithmetic means of this variable for all four cities are smaller than 2.02, indicating that Chinese consumers in all four cities are reasonably health conscious. A possible explanation is that Chinese people are historically health conscious. For example, many health-enhancing practices such as Tai Chi and Chi Kong are still very popular in today's China. Tong (1998) observed that one of the attractions for visitors to China is the number of people doing exercises such as Tai Chi, Chi Kung, social dances, or Kung Fu in public places in the mornings. As China makes the transition from a subsistence society to a *Xiao Kang* (comfortable) society, increasing attention is being given to personal health (Tong, 1998). Chinese consumers are embracing a more casual and health conscious lifestyle (Geng et al, 1996).

Environmental consciousness

The findings reveal that consumers in Guangzhou are less environmentally conscious than their counterparts in the other three cities. But there was no difference in environmental consciousness among the other three. Guangzhou is known to be a more market-oriented city than the other three, which are mainly tourist cities. Over-emphasis on economic growth through commercialization may have somewhat dampened consumers' environmental concerns in Guangzhou. According to CNN's *Asia Now* (1999), the World Bank listed Guangzhou, capital of the fastest growing province, Guangdong, and seven other Chinese cities among the 10 most polluted cities in the world.

Consumers in Guangzhou may have been too preoccupied with making money to pay attention to environmental issues. Beijing's bid for the 2000 Olympic Games and current successful bid for the 2008 Olympic Games may have contributed towards the increasing environmental awareness of its residents.

Hangzhou is renowned for its natural beauty and is one of China's tourist cities, while Xian is not a tourist city but is less industrialized than coastal cities such as Guangzhou. Nevertheless, respondents from the four cities had a relatively high environmental consciousness, as the arithmetic means are below 2.15. This finding also lends further support to other studies that found Chinese consumers were more environmentally conscious than their western counterparts (Tai and Tam, 1997; Chan, 2000). However, what they do may not reflect what they say. Therefore, this finding should be treated with great caution.

Confidence in business ethics

Results show that consumers in Hangzhou and Beijing have less confidence in business ethics than those from Guangzhou and Xian. It is possible that with the increasing economic and commercial activities in Hangzhou, the number of illicit business practices is increasing. For example, in the Shenzhen Special Economic Zone, a model for China's economic reforms, one can buy cheaper Prada bags, pirated DVDs and even Louis Vuitton bags that are made in Guangdong (Perry, 2001). Furthermore, as the political, economic and cultural centre, Beijing is exposed to a greater number of media reports of illegal and ethical practices throughout China than either Hangzhou or Xian.

Managerial implications

This study reveals no significant difference in consumers' health consciousness across all four cities and finds that consumers are fairly health conscious. MNCs should therefore develop non-differentiated marketing strategies for China's growing health and health-related product market. As China prospers, people will live longer and be better taken care of. The traditional values of filial piety and respect for seniority will ensure that more resources are provided for health improvements and facilities for the aged. Therefore, there will be a substantial increase in consumption of health foods and health gadgets (Tong, 1998) and more health and health-related products will be needed

throughout China. Companies are advised to enter all four regional markets simultaneously.

For the green products market and 'green' consumers, MNCs should adopt a differentiated marketing strategy in China, as the respondents in Guangzhou were found to be less environmentally conscious than their counterparts from other cities. Greater efforts may have to be made for Guangzhou. However, as it is understood that it is not so easy to be 'green' after all, firms should calculate carefully the costs and potential gains from being 'green'. For tourist cities such as Hangzhou and Xian, 'green' products may be more appealing to the local consumers. MNCs can put more emphasis on 'green' aspects of their products in these regional markets. Nevertheless, since all respondents demonstrated a positive environmental consciousness and consumers are also becoming more inclined to purchase eco-friendly products than before (Chan, 2000), 'green' products will inevitably become more and more popular in China. MNCs should take advantage of being the first to produce and market products with an emphasis on 'green' features.

Respondents in Guangzhou were found to be less confident in business ethics than Hangzhou and Xian, while Beijing consumers have even less confidence than those in Xian. Therefore, MNCs should devote greater efforts to promoting consumers' confidence in their business operations in Guangzhou and Beijing. By promoting a positive corporate image throughout China, especially in cities such as Beijing, China's political, cultural and economic centre, MNCs can achieve a profound and far-reaching impact. Incidents of bad public relations by Toshiba and Mitsubishi Jeep seriously damaged both companies' images in China. Chinese consumers sued Toshiba for not compensating Chinese buyers (Smith, 2000), while the government banned the import of the Mitsubishi Jeep Pajero (Young, 2001). MNCs, if they do not control their product quality properly, may find their development strategies for the China market severely handicapped.

Limitations and future research directions

One of the limitations of the study is that the data were only collected from four cities. Other equally representative cities were not included in the survey because of budget constraints. For instance, if different minority ethnic groups had been surveyed, then the findings could have been more informative, possibly in terms of revealing more diversified consumerism resulting from regional differences in culture and ethnicity. Another limitation is that the reliability of the health consciousness scale is slightly lower than the threshold suggested by Nunnally (1978), even though the content validity seems reasonably high. Finally, the scope of the study is limited to the understanding of only three key dimensions of the growing consumerism in China.

Many more dimensions can be identified for future research. As Chinese consumers are maturing fast and the younger generation is becoming increasingly receptive to western products, ideas and lifestyles, it is necessary to identify new emerging dimensions of consumerism. Furthermore, with China's entry into the WTO, Chinese markets will become more accessible to MNCs. Future studies could cover much wider geographical areas, particularly other parts of western China with more diversified ethnic cultures and lifestyles.

Finally, as this study limited its scope to urban consumers, future studies could also look at the growing consumerism in rural areas and a comparison could be drawn between rural areas and urban cities. Although China is in the process of rapid industrialization, about 70 per cent of its population still live in the countryside. Although no difference was found in consumers' health consciousness in the four cities, samples from the countryside in different regions might reveal a different picture.

References and bibliography

Batra, Rajeev (1997), Marketing Issues and Challenges in Transitional Economies, *Journal of International Marketing*, 5 (4), pp 95–114.

Chan, Ricky R K (1999), Environmental Attitudes and Behaviour of Consumers in China: Survey Findings and Implications, *Journal of International Consumer Marketing*, 11 (4), pp 25–52.

Chan, Ricky Y K (2000), An Emerging Green Market in China: Myth or Reality? *Business Horizons*, March/April, pp 55–60.

Child, John and Sally Stewart (1997), Regional Differences in China and their Implications for Sino-Foreign Joint Ventures, *Journal of General Management*, 23 (2), pp 65–86.

CNN (1999), China's Industrial Growth Fuels Major Pollution Problems, *Asia Now*, 26 September.

Cosmas, S (1982), Lifestyles and Consumption Patterns, *Journal of Consumer Research*, 8 (4), pp 453–455.

Cui, Geng and Qiming Liu (2001), Emerging Market Segments in a Transitional Economy: A Study of Urban Consumers in China, *Journal of International Marketing*, 9 (1), pp 84–106.

Geng, Lizhong, Lockhart, B, Blakemore, C and Andrus, R (1996), Sports Marketing Strategy: A Consumer Behaviour Case Analysis in China, *Multinational Business Review*, Spring, pp 147–154.

Goldsmith, Ronald E, Freiden, Jon B. and Jacqueline C (1993), Social Values and Female Fashion Leadership: A Cross-cultural Study, *Psychology & Marketing*, 10 (5), pp 399–413.

Harnett, Michael (1998), Expectation is the Key to Pricing, *Discount Store News*, September, pp 16 and 21.

Hawkins, D, Best, R and Coney, K (1993), *Consumer Behaviour: Implications for Marketing Strategy*, Plano, TX: Business Publications.

Hui, Michael K. and David Tse (1996), What to Tell Consumers in Waits of Different Lengths: An Integrative Model of Service Evaluation, Journal of Marketing, 60 (April), pp 81–90

Lazer, W (1963), Lifestyle Concepts and Marketing, in *AMA Proceedings on Scientific Marketing*, Chicago: American Marketing Association.

Maslow, A (1968), Toward a Psychology of Being, New York: Van Nostrand Co.

McGowan, Karen M and Brenda J Sternquist (1998), Dimensions of Price as a Marketing Universal: A Comparison of Japanese and U.S. Consumers, *Journal of International Marketing*, 6 (4), 49–65.

Mitchell, A (1983), *The Nine American Lifestyles: Who We are and Where We Are Going*, New York: Warner Books.

Nunnally, Ian (1978), *Psychometric Theory*, McGraw Hill.

Perry, Alex (2001), Cross the Ling, Time, Asian Edition, 7 May, 18–21.

Shutte, Hellmut and Deannna Ciarlante (1998), *Consumer Behaviour in Asia*, London: Macmillan.

Sims, Thomas L and Jonathan James Schiff (2000), Your Investment, The China Business Review, November and December, 44–49

Smith, Graign S. (2000), Miffed Chinese Sue Japan Companies, *The New York Times*, 7 August, A.6.

Tai, Susan H C and Jackie L M Tam (1997), A Lifestyle Analysis of Female Consumers in Greater China, *Psychology & Marketing*, 14 (3), 287–307.

Thompson, Ann Marie and Peter F Kaminski (1993), Psychographic and Lifestyle Antecedents of Service Quality Expectations, *Journal of Services Marketing*, 7 (4), 53–61.

Tong, Louis (1998), Consumerism Sweeps the Mainland, *Marketing Management*, 6 (4), 32–3.

Tse, David K, N Zhou and Jonathan Zhu (1999), How They Spend their Money: An Empirical Investigation of Income Rise on Consumption Patterns for People's Republic of China Consumers, Working Paper, Chinese Management Centre, University of Hong Kong.

Wei, Ran (1997), Emerging Lifestyles in China and Consequences for Perception of Advertising, Buying Behaviour and Consumption Preferences, *International Journal of Advertising*, 16, 261–275.

Marketing Consumer Products in China

Li Yong, Deputy Secretary General, China Association of International Trade

The concept of marketing has only recently been introduced to China. Initially, it was as a university course, not as a tool in supporting sales efforts. As a result of economic reforms, the government has ended the closed distribution system and allowed free market forces to develop mechanisms that respond to true market needs instead of bureaucratic wants. However, the immaturity of the market economy has contributed to irrational product composition leading to over-supply of unmarketable commodities and piling up of inventories, while a buyer's market has eventually taken shape. In addition, the entry of foreign investment has further intensified the competition in the market. Marketers, both foreign and local, are racking their brains for marketing strategies that will attract more customers.

China has a booming consumer market. The gradual dispersion and decentralization of trading rights, which has replaced top-down leadership, central authority and monopolistic positions, have allowed marketers to compete on almost all fronts. The marketing tools commonly used in western countries are also employed by Chinese marketers, although they may not be as integrated and holistic as they could be.

Pricing practices

Most Chinese consumers are sensitive to price and will usually choose less expensive products. Price competition is the practice most frequently employed by enterprises to compete for market share. There have been 'price wars' on VCRs, microwave ovens, television sets and food products such as packaged milk. Many Chinese companies believe in the strategy of *bo li duo xiao*, which means low profit margin and volume sales. This belief has lead to a diverse range of pricing practices, including *shi dian li* (10 per cent profit), ex-factory price, zero wholesale mark-up, etc. All of these tactics are based on the assumption that lower price will increase the speed of turnover and eventually generate higher profit. This practice has led to vicious competition and culminated, for instance, in the price of packaged milk in Shanghai being lower than the cost.

While the low-price strategy is widely adopted, some marketers use a high-price strategy, taking advantage of the conventional wisdom that *pian yi wu hao huo* (cheap is no good) and *yi fen qian yi fen huo* (each additional cent paid is associated with additional value). This strategy is often associated with prestigious products or products that are intended to establish a prestigious reputation. Foreign branded products or imported products are generally high-priced and perceived as superior products.

Other pricing strategies common to developed markets are also used by Chinese marketers, including 'price lining', 'skim-the-oil' pricing, 'odd-even' pricing, 'was-is' pricing, 'special event' pricing and so on. It is interesting to observe the unique characteristics of psychological pricing practices in China, which go beyond the simple odd-even considerations. Some Chinese people have a superstitious belief in lucky numbers. Marketers price their products in such a way that the numbers denote good luck. For example, a piece of furniture may be priced at 1199 to indicate *chang chang jiu jiu* (long and lasting), or 4451 meaning *shi shi ru yi* (everything is as you wish). Other examples include: 518 (*wo yao fa*, meaning 'I will have a fortune'), 888 (*fa fa fa*, meaning 'fortune, fortune and fortune'), 1688 (*yi lu fa fa* – endless fortune down the road), etc.

Sales practices

The old days when products were produced and allocated according to government plans have gone. Companies have to rely on their own sales or marketing teams to get their products to the market. They now face multiple choices of ways to market their products, including direct and indirect marketing (see Figure 6.3.1).

Direct marketing can include such practices as soliciting direct orders from customers, setting up a retail outlet, door-to-door sales, telemarketing, TV sales, direct mail sales and internet marketing. Direct selling as a way of direct marketing used to be exercised by both domestic and foreign firms in China, the most notable being Amway and Avon. Unfortunately, criminals have also exploited direct selling systems and abuses such as price frauds, scams, sales of inferior/fake and smuggled products, seeking exorbitant wind-fall profits and tax evasions have been rife. All of these seriously impaired the interests of the consumers and derailed the normal economic order and so the Chinese government issued a ban on direct selling. Other direct marketing tools such as telemarketing, TV sales and internet marketing are relatively new to Chinese consumers and there have been reports that these tools have not been very successful.

Indirect marketing channels, as described in marketing textbooks, are all used in China for marketing consumer products. There are over 1.36 million wholesalers and nearly 14 million retailers of consumer products in China. Manufacturing enterprises are using diversified channels of distribution to get their products to the consumers. Many set up regional branches to perform the function of wholesaler or distributor. To establish direct communication with consumers, an increasing number of manufacturing enterprises rent sales counters at retail outlets such as department stores and employ their own sales clerks. It is not rare to see special counters in department stores that are promoted as a factory outlet.

As a part of the sales effort, the old rule of 'goods sold are non-returnable' no longer holds and many marketers offer goods on a returnable basis if not satisfied. Warranties are also offered for durable goods. It has become common for heavy items to be delivered to the consumer's home free of charge.

As the government is allowing consumer credit to play a role in stimulating the consumption of valuable items, many enterprises and retailers are offering consumer credit, either on its own or in cooperation with banks, to consumers. Some marketers have begun to offer interest-free credit packages. According to an estimate, 10 per cent of urban households can afford consumer credit of over RMB100,000, 30 per cent between RMB50,000 and RMB100,000 and 20 per cent below RMB50,000.

It is worth noting that an increasing number of supermarkets, hypermarkets and chain stores have emerged in recent years, challenging conventional modes of retailing. They offer greater channel reach for manufacturers of consumer products. However, getting into supermarket chains is a costly exercise (see Figure 6.3.2).

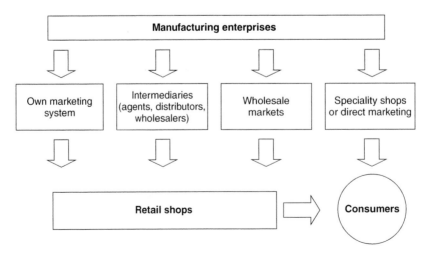

Figure 6.3.1 Typical marketing channels in China

Unconditional deduction:
45% of the total price of goods supplied for the first year, 24% for the second year
Consulting service fee:
Before 2001, 0.5% of the total price (including tax). Starting from 2002, 1% of the total price (including tax) to be deducted when settling payments in June, September and December
Unconditional discount:
3.5% of the total price (including tax) to be deducted from the payment on monthly basis
Conditional discounts:
0.5% of the total price (including tax) when the annual sales is ≥ RMB700k, 1% of the total price (including tax) when the annual sales is ≥ RMB1 million
Order charge:
3% per store
Entry fee:
RMB15,000 per store upon delivery of goods
Bar code fee:
RMB1000 per product category

Shelf fee for new arrivals:
RMB1,500 per store
Festival fee:
RMB1,000 per store/time on five occasions – New Year, Spring Festival, May Day, Mid-autumn Day and Christmas
Store anniversary fee:
RMB1,500 per store/time, for two anniversary occasions – international store anniversary and China store anniversary
POS poster fee:
RMB2,500 per store/time, once in a year
Promotional stacking fee:
RMB1,500 per store/time, three times in a year
Service charge for nationwide product recommendation:
1% of the total purchase price (including tax) to be deducted on a monthly basis
Store renovation fee:
RMB7,500 per store, to be charged at the location of the store
New store start-up fee:
RMB20,000 per store, to be charged at the location of the new store
Penalties:
a) all stores can only handle 5+1 categories as provided by the contract. Addition of products or change of a product category will result in termination of contract and a fine of RMB5,000.
b) delivery of products should be made in three days including the date of order. Suppliers are subject to a penalty of 0.3% of the contract value. A fine of RMB3,000 will be charged in case of failure to deliver.

Source: Beijing Evening Newspaper, 30 July 2002

Figure 6.3.2   The cost of entering the Carrefour chain

Advertising practices

Advertising is an important means of marketing. Many Chinese enterprises in one way or another believe that advertising will automatically generate sales. This belief has resulted in over-extended outlays on advertising and high prices. A recent example of exorbitant advertising expenditure is Qinchi Liquor, who spent RMB320 million (US$38.55 million) in the open bidding for prime time advertising on CCTV (China Central Television), the only national television network. The only reward seemed to be the title of 'king of the bid', rather than the expected sales increase.

Terms such as gross rating point (GRP) or cost per thousand (CPT) in advertising theory seem to be unknown to most advertising decision-makers. Consequently, few have given thought to an integrated and holistic approach to communication. Interestingly, however, those foreign joint ventures that have been successful in advertising their products are rarely seen on the seething bidding floor. None has gone so far as to chase the title of 'king of the bid'.

For many years, most advertising dollars have gone to television media, as they are seen as the most effective channels of communication to create product awareness among potential consumers in China.

Over 50 per cent of the media have agency agreements with advertising companies and nearly half their business is given to advertising agencies as a result of these agency agreements. Advertising agents normally receive 15 per cent commission on advertising sales. The majority of the media requires advance payment, while advertisers are left with little recourse if the advertisement is not aired or published at agreed times. The lack of reliable ratings data is another problem that makes it difficult for advertisers to make decisions and evaluate the effectiveness of their advertising efforts.

Comparison advertising is not permitted under the Advertising Law, nor is the use of superlatives. All advertising copy must be reviewed and approved by the regulatory authority, the State Industrial and Commercial Administration, before going into media. Claims such as 'No 1' or 'top selling' need to be supported by documentation, such as certificates issued by the relevant government agencies or authoritative survey organizations.

Higher prices used to be charged to foreign companies but this price discrimination has been removed and all companies, both foreign and local, now pay the same price. Advertising rates are reviewed and published on an annual basis.

Promotion practices

Both retailers and producers use consumer-oriented promotion techniques. These practices range from coupons, premiums and deals to prizes, lucky draws, contests and sweepstakes. The most common promotion methods are the following:

1. Buy one and get one or more free;
   open [the package] for a prize;
   more product for the same price;
   discount coupons or token money coupons.
2. Premiums;
   collecting labels or packages for prizes;
   numbered tickets for lucky draws;
   VIP discount card for purchases reaching a certain value;
   prize winning contests;
   live radio broadcast of contests;
   first-comer prize on live radio broadcast consulting on product attributes and usage;
   event-related price reduction or discount.
3. Free samples slip;
   on-site trials or demonstration;
   mail-back for lucky draw;
   turn in the old for a new one;
   membership privileges.
4. Free products against advertisement slip;
   quantity discount;
   life-time warranty;
   payment by instalments;
   consumer credit;
   shortage of one and compensation for ten.[1]
5. Self-penalty for under-delivered quality;[2]
   trial use on marginal cost;
   100 per cent refund if not satisfied.

The above list is not intended to be exhaustive. Obviously, these practices reflect the level of intensity in consumer market competition. When employing promotion techniques, either those listed above or others, it is important to develop appropriate consumer insights, which are extremely critical in a market that is large in territory, diverse in consumer preferences across regions and rapid in its pace of change. Some research results have indicated that consumers are pragmatic in their attitudes toward promotion exercises. Buy one and get one free, price reduction or discount, discount coupons and premiums seem to be favoured by consumers.

However, marketers need to be very careful when designing promotion strategies, and extreme situations should to be taken into consideration. The practice of free product offers against advertisement slips from newspapers has caused chaos in some instances when unexpected numbers of people besieged the site to claim free products that could not be supplied. The guarantee of 100 per cent refund for unsatisfied consumers needs to be carefully thought out to prevent exploitation of the guarantee. Amway has run into situations where false consumers came to claim a refund with discarded or reclaimed empty bottles.

---

[1] In China, some discredited factories do not deliver their promised products in terms of number or weight. To build consumer confidence, factories claim that they will compensate customers with ten times the amount of the shortage found.

[2] A similar practice, where manufacturers assure consumers that if the quality falls short of what is promised, they will penalize themselves to varying degrees.

Branding practices

The lack of well-known brands is considered to be one of the weaknesses of Chinese consumer product manufacturers. A 'famous brand strategy' has been advocated by the government in a bid to improve the brand images and marketability of locally produced products. Painstaking efforts by local marketers have yielded some results, with some brands having established national recognition. The majority, however, have not yet made much progress in breaking away from the images of a local brand. Worse still, many brands are still unknown to their intended consumers.

Local marketers have a tendency, as they do with numbers, to favour brand names that convey goodness, luck, happiness, longevity and prosperity. In some cases, brand names are associated with historical events. Few have tested their brand names before affixing them to their products. Because of the reputation of foreign products as of premium quality, many local marketers even go so far as to give brand names that read and sound foreign. Local brands are often unrelated to product content or attributes, and therefore brand communications tend to be weak. In fact until recently, little effort was invested in developing a name or product image using integrated and holistic approaches. Clever marketers skipped brand name testing by putting out advertisements inviting consumers to give names for their products, but whether the arbitrarily chosen ones are liked by consumers is still unknown.

While some local marketers are trying to use brand names that have a foreign touch, foreign marketers are struggling to find a proper Chinese name for their brands. Indeed, it is often very difficult to translate a western brand name into Chinese. The usual approach is either to take on a new name and create new meaning, or give a similarly-sounding phonetic name. For example, P&G's Rejoice shampoo had a completely new name, Piao Rou, whose pronunciation is totally different, meaning 'softly wave to and fro', while its Pantene shampoo was transliterated as Pan Ting, which is phonetically similar and does not carry a specific meaning. Ideally, a brand should both have phonetic similarity and good meaning. A classical example of this is Coca-Cola, which is phonetically translated as Ke Kou Ke Le with the meanings of 'deliciously enjoyable' and 'bringing about happy laughter'. Asics sportswear has a Chinese name, Ai Shi Ke Si, which is again pronounced very similarly, but the meaning of 'love the world and overcome selfishness (or ego)' does not seem to be particularly well associated with the product.

Some foreign marketers, recognizing the difficulties in translating their brand names into Chinese, avoided the effort of associating the name with any particular Chinese meaning. Brands such as Philips, Nokia, Motorola, Electrolux and Sony are all using their transliterated names, and all have established brand recognition.

There are also instances where brand names already in use in Hong Kong are transplanted to the mainland. Some of the brands were a result of transliteration into Cantonese and read differently in Mandarin. McDonald's, Pizza Hut and Del Monte are typical examples.

Whichever way you go in adapting your brands to the local conditions, it is important that the Chinese brand names should be easy to read and to remember, and not too long. Brand names longer than four Chinese characters will be difficult both to read and remember. The name chosen should consist of commonly used words. Strange words will cause difficulties in brand recognition. For example, the last word of the two-Chinese-word brand for Del Monte is difficult to find in a regular dictionary. Another factor that should be taken into consideration when adopting a Chinese brand name is the diverse dialects. A brand name that reads well in Mandarin may be read very differently in different dialects, meaning very different things. A normal exercise of brand name testing would cover at least three cities such as Guangzhou, Shanghai and Beijing to make sure that the name does not carry undesired meanings.

However, a good brand name does sell itself on the merit that it has a good meaning. Effective branding means more than Chinese labelling. A brand image manifests itself in many ways: in a memorable brand name and well-designed logo, attractive packaging, in the quality and services associated with the brand, and, importantly, in integrated marketing communications.

Brand Management and Publicity

Li Yong, Deputy Secretary General, China Association of International Trade

Brand management

Local brand vs foreign brand

Among many other things to consider in a venture investment in China, one key issue in the area of marketing is the branding of the product(s) that the venture will produce. In an equity joint venture with a Chinese partner, there is always a trade-off in terms of whose brand should be used in the marketing of the products. There are usually the following options:

Local brand

'Local brand' here refers to the brand(s) that have been used by the Chinese partner for marketing in China. In many cases the brand owned by the Chinese partner would be sold to the foreign partner as equity. Apart from the bargaining process, one key point of consideration would be whether a local brand has an advantage over other options such as the brand name owned by the foreign partner, or the creation of a new brand. The local brand may have the following attributes to attract it to the foreign partner:

- brand image already established;
- brand awareness, easy recognition and ready acceptance among customers/consumers;
- existing distribution network and market share.

However, a foreign partner may also have concerns about the pitfalls of using a local brand. These could include:

- poor brand image associated with poor quality products/services;

- low level of awareness, recognition and acceptance by customers/consumers;
- poor distribution and small market share.

It is a complicated process to find out whether or not a local brand has the necessary value. Careful market research is essential in determining whether a local brand should be adopted before commitment is made. Some joint ventures use a local brand to cash in on their expanded marketing efforts and improved product/service attributes. Some adopt local brands as part of their multi-branding strategy. All of these will have to be weighed against the cost and benefits of using a local brand.

Foreign brand

'Foreign brand' here refers to a brand that the foreign partner of a joint venture already owns and wants to introduce into the local market by way of investment. As a part of globalization, the introduction of foreign brands – particularly those that have been marketed internationally and gained world-wide recognition – is the preferred way of branding joint venture products. Using foreign brands is often perceived as a symbol of market presence and penetration.

However, promoting foreign brands in order to increase awareness and build a quality image will be a long-term engagement, resembling similar patterns of development as in the home country and entailing a strong financial commitment. The general perception by consumers in China that a foreign branded or a joint venture product is a synonym for good quality has encouraged many foreign companies entering into joint ventures in China to use their own brands. Chinese partners also welcome foreign brands in the conventional belief that a foreign brand will increase the marketability of the products. Increasingly, however, Chinese partners have learned from experience that there is a danger of losing their own established brand when they adopt a foreign brand from their foreign partner. Two examples are the microwave oven manufacturer and the colour film manufacturer who have refused a number of joint venture proposals because of the use of foreign brands.

Although some foreign manufacturers have been successful in using their own brands in China, others have experienced difficulties in keeping the quality image of the products and services that their brands represent. Factors associated with the brand image need to be considered and evaluated before a decision can be made to use your own brand. Among others, the following factors are considered to be critical:

- **Product quality.** When managing the brand in China, the brand owner will have be sure that the quality associated with the brand will be guaranteed in terms of raw materials and production. At the same time, the manufacturer's quality will have to be adapted to meet the standards set by local government. Otherwise, there may be quality problems subjecting the brand image to question.
- **Quality of services.** Service is an important part of the brand image. The brand owner will have to be sure that services will be provided to the consumer/customer in such a way that they satisfy the expectations of the brand. If quality services cannot be guaranteed, it will threaten the brand image.
- **Effectiveness of distribution.** The effectiveness of the joint venture's distribution network will have to be assessed. If the distribution is such that the foreign branded products cannot reach the consumers/customers in time and there is little that can be done to improve it in the short term, the strengths that the brand may have will only be a theoretical advantage.

The solution to these problems hinges on how much control the brand owner could have over the joint venture operations. This control is not just a matter of majority holding but it can be achieved through good contract negotiation. If the Chinese management shares the same marketing concepts as the foreign partners, the above disadvantages can be transformed into strengths. However, things do not always happen as expected. When the owner of a foreign brand cannot be sure whether the operations will be such that the chances of damaging the brand image as well as the corporate image are minimized, it might be safer to create a new brand.

New brand

A new brand can be the result of compromises from both sides of the joint venture, or similarities in strategic thinking. Whatever it might appear to be, a new brand is the product of the union between the Chinese and foreign partners. The advantages of having a completely new brand are that agreement between both sides can be easily reached and there will be a common objective in promoting the brand. The shared interests in the brand will provide incentives for both sides to cooperate. The disadvantages could be that there may not be ready recognition if part of the production is intended for export markets. If export is an essential part of the joint venture agreement, a separate brand arrangement might be necessary.

Joint branding

Another compromise, or a strategy to circumvent the deadlock of branding, is joint branding, where the identities of both partners can be maintained and reflected in the brand. In fact, this is not a bad strategy for foreign firms to adopt at the early stage of joint venturing, avoiding risking their own brand image if product quality and related services are unstable. A joint brand gives consumers/customers a clear message that the product is made by a joint venture, whose quality is generally believed to be higher than that of local products.

The advantages of such an exercise are:

- none of the partners of the joint venture need worry about losing their own brand identities;
- promotion of the joint brand will increase awareness of both brands;
- resources committed to promoting the joint brand will reflect the fair-deal principle;
- he image of foreign brands can be maintained as a separate brand;
- it is easy to create recognition in both domestic and overseas markets.

Selecting a good brand name

A good brand name may add value to the good quality and services associated with the brand. A bad brand name may already have given the consumer/customer an unpleasant impression, which may even have prevented them from trying the product. Goldlion, a brand for men's clothes and accessories, used to experience sluggish sales in Hong Kong, because the pronunciation of the literal translation of the brand in Cantonese was associated with the meaning 'willing loss', or 'lose always'. The Chinese translation was later changed to mean 'gold profit comes'; sales increased substantially and it has become a prestigious brand.

There are no hard and fast rules for picking a good brand name. When creating a new brand name or giving a foreign brand an appropriate Chinese name, it is advisable to consider the following principles:

- The brand name should use words that are within the vocabulary of most of the consumers. Unusual or difficult to pronounce words, or words that have more than one pronunciation should be avoided.
- The brand name should be short and easy to read, pronounce and remember. Most of the brand names in China are two or three words. Some, such as Coca-Cola and Pepsi-Cola, have four. There is hardly any brand that has five Chinese words.
- The pronunciation of the brand name should not carry any possible negative implications. The name of the beer brand 'Yunhu' (meaning cloud lake) also sounds like the words for 'dizzy' and 'muddle-headed' in Chinese.
- The brand name should carry positive implications with regard to the product's function, uses and features. Tylenol cold drug has a Chinese name – Tai Nuo – meaning 'safe' or 'peaceful promise'. The Chinese name of Signal toothpaste, Jie Nuo, means 'clean promise'.
- Naturally, a brand name should not have the potential to cause legal problems.

A good name might result from a brainstorming session among the marketing people of a company. In order to eliminate possible negative connotations, references or associations however, it will be safer to test the name or names among consumers/customers. China is a country of multiple dialects and so testing should be carried out in different places with different dialects. In practice, Beijing, Shanghai and Guangzhou are chosen to test brand names in order to make sure that the selected name does not have negative elements when pronounced in different dialects.

Brand protection

China has promulgated a series of laws and regulations to protect the rights of the owners of intellectual property. These are covered in more detail elsewhere in this book.

The government attaches great importance to its counterfeiting efforts and several campaigns are waged each year to fight against counterfeits. China's crackdown on counterfeits checks illegal activities from both the production and distribution sides. The production of counterfeits is illegal and sales of counterfeits are also illegal. If retailers are found to be selling counterfeits, they are subject to penalties and the buyer of the counterfeits is compensated at twice the price at which the counterfeits are sold. Apart from government efforts, there are also non-governmental organizations and individuals engaged in the crackdown on counterfeits. All these have enhanced consumer awareness to reject and fight against counterfeit products.

Brand owners should register the brand properly with relevant authorities in China in order to protect the brand from the legal point of view. The Great Hall of the People, the place where national conferences are held, has registered its name, 'Ren Min Da Hui Tang', with the State Administration of Industry and Commerce for 288 varieties in 22 categories. This was intended to prevent manufacturers from taking advantage of the trust that people have in the name. Wahaha Group, a manufacturer of baby health food, has registered not only the brand name 'Wahaha', but also other similar names, such as Hahawa, Wahawa, Hawaha and Hawawa. While a brand can be protected from the legal perspective, manufacturers can also take measures to prevent their products from being copied. One of these measures is to affix anti-fake labels to the products or the packages, or to use counter-faking devices. Some manufacturers have designed their distribution in such a way that the distributors take on some of the counterfeit monitoring in each of the regional markets. There are also manufacturers who publicly offer cash or material awards for those who report and help obtain evidence on counterfeit production.

Towards brand loyalty

Brand loyalty is considered to be the most desirable objective of marketing. China has moved from a shortage economy into an economy of relative abundance. Many consumer products are in excessive supply. Increased consumerism and 'buyers' markets' will make brand management a delicate job. While most Chinese enterprises are still using mass marketing techniques in an attempt to maintain their market shares, some, particularly joint ventures, have started to study marketing alternatives in order to establish brand loyalty.

It is important for brand managers as well as marketing managers to realize that a brand will not be as much of an asset or equity as in the past or present if there is no loyalty from consumers/customers. Brand loyalty is the core target of brand management and marketing. When a product is adopted or accepted, trust can be established by meeting consumer/customer expectations and providing satisfaction. However, trust will have to be reinforced to gain loyalty. Building brand loyalty involves a process that can go far beyond the products' physical attributes and their invisible merits. Brand loyalty is more of a psychological reinforcement process than a process of persuasion by different means of promotion. This is particularly true in China, where the legacy of 5,000 years of civilization governs a unique system of value judgement. When the marketing people are trying to formulate a strategy for brand loyalty marketing, Chinese cultural traits (see Chapters 5.1 and 5.2) should be exploited. To give consumers 'face' may result in consumer/customer loyalty. An appropriate use of the principle of reciprocity in personal relationships may create obligations/gratitude from the consumer/customer. Harmonious consumer/customer relations can be established by abiding by cultural codes.

Advertising

The advertising environment

Advertising is without doubt an effective means of communicating brand information to the consumer or customer. However, China is a very different country with distinctive features compared with the western world. Firms who either have a production presence in China, or who want to market their products directly in China, are advised to design their marketing campaign, or more specifically advertising campaign, very carefully. The first thing they should do is to study the advertising environment.

In general, insufficient demand and excessive supply have characterized the consumer market. Lack of motivation to consume has resulted in an accumulation of cash savings in the hands of consumers, which the lowered interest rate has failed to release. As a result, many advertisers are having sales problems and will have to reconsider their marketing strategies. Some have chosen to downsize their advertising input and increase sales efforts.

The conventional difficulty of a short supply of media seems to have been a problem. One of the reasons is that many media have expanded their resources to cash in on the fast-growing advertising market and competition for media has intensified. Apart from cross-medium competition, there is also inter-medium competition, typically the competition between terrestrial and cable television stations. As part of the effort to integrate television resources by the State Administration of Radio, Film and Television, most local terrestrial and cable television stations have undergone a merger process, bringing cable and terrestrial TV stations under one roof. It was reported that there are over 3,500 television channels, more than 1,000 newspapers and 7,000 plus magazines. By the end of 2000, there were over 70,000 advertising-related entities employing 0.64 million workers.

Fragmentation of the advertising industry has remained a problem, plaguing the growth of the industry. The trend of fragmentation seems to have continued over the last few years. The problems that come along with fragmentation are diseconomies of scale and fiercer competition. Fragmentation has also impeded the promotion of the advertising agency system, and the relationships between advertisers, advertising companies and media are distorted.

The government has enhanced its monitoring and control of the advertising industry, with the intention of disciplining the conduct and organization of the advertising industry and protecting the interests of consumers and advertisers. The first attempt to regulate the advertising industry was made in 1987 and further key legislation on advertising censorship was implemented in 1993. In 1995, the Advertising Law was officially promulgated. A newer version of the Advertising Law was drafted, reviewed and promulgated in the latter half of 2002.

Brand communication

There are many options when it comes to communicating brand information in China. But it is important to recognize that consumer attitudes have been changing fast over the past two decades. It is no longer possible for a company like Nestlé, one of the few pioneers of advertising in the early days of China opening up, to establish brand awareness virtually overnight. Consumers in China are more complex and sophisticated when receiving product and brand information. Increased consumerism has made consumers more critical of marketers' efforts to communicate product and brand information. The frequent use of celebrities in TV commercials, for example, has been criticized by consumers who question whether these celebrities are communicating the brand and product information for the sake of money or in the interests of consumers. De Beers' decades old slogan 'a diamond is forever' has faced challenges from Chinese consumers who have different judgements on what values diamonds suggest. The kind of values that can be associated with diamonds, such as being symbolic of long-lasting love, gifts of love and purity of love, were all interpreted quite differently. One cause of the different reactions is deep-rooted cultural values, which do not really recognize diamonds as an expression of love. In addition, the impact of western culture and associated changes in people's lifestyles has also had some influence on people's perception of love.

While taking cultural elements into consideration, marketers will also need to take a holistic approach in designing brand communications. Demographics are important in determining your target consumers and segmenting the market, but the complexities of the consumer world require more effort in the study of psychographics and geographics, which will help in establishing brand appeal. In a country as vast as China, people in different locations tend to have different consumption preferences. One example of this is that in north-eastern China, people tend to pursue common fashion values, while in southern China, for example Shanghai, consumers tend to be more individual and the emphasis is on personal taste.

Advertising congestion

Advertising congestion here does not mean that there are not enough media to carry advertisements, but rather refers to a phenomenon that almost all media are congested with advertisements to the extent that few could effectively catch the attention of viewers. Chinese firms seem to believe heavy advertising will help establish brand recognition and natural acceptance. There have been too many cases in which advertising created miracles, and almost all of them have ended up being closed down. However, people can still see enthusiastic advertisers lining up at CCTV's annual open bid and the top bidders are always Chinese companies. Very rarely, if ever, does one see any joint ventures or foreign firms among them.

In this situation, it is advisable for foreign brands to take an integrated marketing communications approach. As the cultural preferences, eating habits and dialect can be differ substantially from region to region within China, any attempt at national promotion in the early stages of market development will be a costly exercise. Combined use of different media at different times in different target markets can be more effective than an effort to cover the national market. PR events in priority markets can add a special twist to the advertising efforts.

One encouraging fact is that Chinese people are increasingly brand-conscious. When they purchase, they not only take products as products, they look to value at the same time. They make comparison by using knowledge and information about the product before they are willing pay for it. Therefore, the 'advertising' on the product packages is also an important means to communicate brand information.

Rampant branding

In the mid-1990s, Chinese enterprises were prompted by the continued influx of foreign branded products to come to realize the importance of branding. They found that branding as a marketing strategy would not only create additional value, but also maintain a group of loyal customers. Academics began to study the branding strategies of these international companies and came to the conclusion that for China to survive in the world market, it would need a large number of globally recognized brands. Therefore, a 'famous brand strategy' approach was incubated and created great enthusiasm among Chinese enterprises, which were eager to catch up with the lessons of branding strategy. This enthusiasm also found an echo in central government policies regarding improvement of product quality. At the central level was the China Council for the Promotion of Famous Brands, an organization that is responsible for 'uniform evaluation, management, publicity and cultivation' of brands. At the provincial level were 'leading groups' who drafted concrete plans to develop a certain number of 'national level famous brands' and 'provincial level famous brands'. The same process was copied at lower levels of government, all with plans to nurture their own famous brands.

Almost immediately, people found themselves besieged by brands, many of which had the label of 'famous brand' at county, city or provincial level. Some government departments were also involved in rating famous brands for enterprises that fell under their jurisdiction. Some foreign companies even found a way to milk the brand enthusiasm by offering foreign awards or accreditations to Chinese enterprises.

This desperate craving for famous brands has cooled down as a result of government efforts to stop various brand evaluation or rating exercises, which were regarded as misleading. But the sequel seems to be a rampant branding exercise. You can hardly buy a pair of shoes that do not bear a metal badge or an embroidered logo. The same is true with shirts: on the pocket of almost every shirt is an embroidered logo. You will be lucky if you can buy socks without an embroidered logo. Excessive branding has, in effect, caused problems for consumers, who are more prudent than before in selecting their preferred brands.

This chapter is intended to provide a portrait of the competitive situation in China in terms of branding awareness by Chinese enterprises. The truth is that some enterprises did succeed in building their brands in the process, which helped them win over their foreign rivals. This is particularly true in the consumer electronics industry. The message here is that Chinese consumers have become buried in an onslaught of brands, and winning their trust and loyalty is not the job of advertising alone.

Effective Public Relations

Li Yong, Deputy Secretary General, China Association of International Trade

Public relations in China shares some common characteristics with western concepts but has unique features, deeply ingrained as a legacy of its 5,000-year-old culture. An understanding of Chinese culture, related value judgements, codes and protocols is key to effective public relations. The business network discussed in Chapter 5.3 constitutes a part of this, but much of Chinese public relations is concerned with interpersonal relationships.

For the purposes of this chapter, the concept of public relations is divided into micro public relations, which involves interpersonal interactions, and macro public relations, which involves communication with the public on a collective basis.

Micro public relations

Micro public relations here refers to relations with your Chinese colleagues, business partners, investment partners, government officials and people of different social functions. The discussion below is not intended to provide a panacea for dealing with various types of relationships, but rather the general rules that foreign business people should pay attention to in order to get along with the Chinese.

Your business partners

First impressions

It is important in the initial meeting to establish a good 'first impression'. Showing respect for local customs and habits is a good start, but adopting some of them may 'shorten the distance' in the first meeting and win recognition from the Chinese partners. For example, using two hands to present and receive business cards is considered to be good manners.

Lightly knocking on the table with your forefinger and middle finger when you are served a cup of tea or drink will be taken as a sign of significant social experiences in southern coastal areas of China, particularly in the Guangdong area. Proposing or accepting a toast at a dinner table with one hand holding the cup and the other on the bottom of it is seen as respectful to the Chinese hosts. Neatly dressed and well-organized businesspeople will always leave a good impression on their Chinese partners.

Nurturing your image

Apart from social rituals, foreign firms should also establish an image of professionalism and authoritativeness in order to gain the trust of their Chinese partners. For example, as an importer of Chinese products, the capability of your distribution network should be discussed in as much detail as possible to ensure trust and to assure the Chinese partner of the advantages of using the network you have outside of China. A bank reference will help eliminate possible doubts about your credibility.

As an exporter, you are expected to understand the products and technology you are trying to promote in China. If you are to make a presentation about your company, visual aids and properly translated brochures are extremely useful for a better understanding by your Chinese counterparts. Some foreign companies have Chinese version brochures, but the translation is almost as difficult to understand as the foreign language. Some reference of export acceptability will be helpful in building up confidence in trading your products in China. Sales into China also often involve many technical exchanges between the foreign sellers and the Chinese buyers and an important part of this effort is endorsements from relevant technical authorities in China. The endorsements can be explicit and implicit. Explicit endorsement usually takes the form of technical certifications issued by relevant Chinese organizations, while implicit endorsements can be any type of public relations activity that you have had with well-known officials, technical experts or past projects in China. Evidence that your technology and products have gained endorsements and certifications elsewhere are also a plus. All of these should have a favourable impact on the decision-making of the Chinese partners.

Dealing with hidden relations

When you are sure you have given your Chinese partners a good impression in your initial contact and that they are also impressed by your technology and products, you may then advance to the stage of business negotiation. In a business negotiation, you may expect to deal only with negotiators. In fact there could be other unknown decision-makers, particularly when the business involves decisions made by other organizations that are not directly participating in the negotiation. For example, if you are selling power plant equipment, the organizations involved in the decision-making will include, among others, the State Power Corporation (previously the Ministry of Electric Power), the local power supply authority, the design institute, the environmental protection authority, banks providing the financing, and so on. These may not appear to be direct concerns in the negotiation but they are influencing the decision-making process and will have to be dealt with appropriately to facilitate this. It is recommended that foreign suppliers help the Chinese partners solve the problems arising from these hidden relations by giving understanding and patience to your counterpart in the first place and providing the necessary proof to alleviate possible concerns. At the same time, some lobbying of these organizations by the foreign partners may be helpful. For this purpose, informal meetings, technical seminars and entertainment can be organized through a contact who knows when and where these activities will be appropriate. These negotiations could be very delicate, and making inappropriate proposals could be even worse than doing nothing.

Keeping a good track record

Business relations are a long-term commitment in China. Keeping a good track record will not only improve your position in the market, but also enhance your corporate image from a public relations perspective. Good track records with previous customers in terms of product quality, technology reliability and after-sales technical support will save time in building trust in the products and technology with a new client. Even if you had not been able to gain publicity in the media, your good track record tends to generate good word-of-mouth publicity among the people in the industry. Good track records can accumulate into an impressive list of references, which will speak for itself in your promotional efforts.

Warm the threshold

Even if business with your Chinese partners is quite sporadic, keeping the relationship warm should be considered part of your long-term strategy. A Christmas/New Year card will remind them of your existence and tell them they are remembered. Occasional phone calls will give the relationship a personal touch. When you travel to China for unrelated business, having a chat over lunch/dinner would bring the relationship even closer. When the paths of your business do cross sometime in the future, you will still be treated as an old friend.

Your investment partner

Trust

Although in business you can have alternative partners, in an investment venture you could not possibly do so unless you wished to terminate the venture prematurely. You will have to stay with your investment partner for a considerable period of time: identification and selection of a good partner is very important, and is discussed in detail in Chapter 5.5. Once you have chosen your partner and the contract has been signed, success depends very much on how well you cooperate with your partners. Trust is the basic element of successful cooperation in a joint venture.

The rules for building trust here differ little from elsewhere. Cultural clashes can be a cause of mistrust. In addition however, the fact that you and your Chinese colleagues represent the interests of two different organizations can be an obstacle to building trust. In the absence of trust, the Chinese colleagues may read some hidden purpose into what you do and vice versa. This is particularly hazardous to the development of the joint venture and eventually your own interests. While keeping good personal relations with the Chinese management, it is advisable for foreign executives to do things under the umbrella of mutual interests. When there is a disagreement, it will never lead you anywhere if you try to convince your Chinese partners that this is the way things are done in your company. Blaming your Chinese counterparts to cause loss of face is especially detrimental to the working relations. It is better, for example, to say that there is an alternative that may work. Any material efforts that you make for the mutual benefit of the two parties will bring you closer to gaining trust from your Chinese partner.

Educating your partner

Dealing with your Chinese partner is a learning process on both sides. One of the general perceptions of Chinese enterprises when introducing foreign elements into a venture is to learn what is called 'advanced managerial expertise'. One side of this education could be a kind of demonstration by which your partner can learn your management style on site. The other side is the formal training that can be conducted both on the job at the location of the joint venture and off the job at the foreign partner's factory. The training can enhance understanding of the western management style and, at the same time, be conducive to gaining the support of local management. Once you have the understanding and support of the local partner, it will be much easier to carry out a business decision.

Communication with your partner

In an investment venture in China, communication between partners is a delicate matter. Mishandling communications may cause misunderstanding and eventually impede the efforts by both sides towards a harmonious relationship. Poor communications can lead to business failure. Establishing a good communications mechanism is a job for both partners. In many cases, foreign executives find that their Chinese colleagues remain silent at corporate meetings that are intended to solicit comments and suggestions from all managers; Chinese managers should be encouraged to talk openly about corporate decisions.

For the foreign partner, it is important to understand the reporting structure of the Chinese partner and the roles of the Chinese directors on the board. In the initial period of the joint venture, an appropriate channel of communication should be discussed with the Chinese partner in order to avoid possible misunderstanding in future communications. Routine meetings and internal circulation of corporate documents are means of communication that are familiar to Chinese executives.

Internal organizations

Treat trade unions as a means of communication with employees

According to relevant laws and regulations, a joint venture in China must have a trade union in order to protect the rights and interests of employees. Apart from its role as a spokesperson on behalf of the employees, if a harmonious relationship can be established a trade union can also serve as an effective channel of communication with employees. Any effort to turn a trade union into a mere cipher will not help eliminate possible conflicts with employees. On the contrary, to delegate some responsibilities to the trade union may help improve relationships between the employer and employees. In a Chinese organization, a trade union also has an employment relations and welfare function. In a joint venture, it is advisable to have the trade union assume a similar function. The union can be used to increase awareness by employees that their well-being is one of the primary interests of the venture. In furthering a better relationship with employees, the union can also be delegated the task of organizing employee activities, through which management can initiate closer, less formal and friendlier interactions with employees.

Party organizations are task forces

The Chinese communist party has over 60 million members, active in different sectors and industries in China. In each Chinese organization there is a party committee or branch responsible for the organization of the communist party. There are also some party organizations active in many Sino-foreign joint ventures. Because of ideological differences, the foreign management of a joint venture may have a certain degree of reluctance in accepting such organizations in the joint venture. In reality, however, many foreign managers have found that such organizations play an important role in the execution of decisions made by the board. Party members are supposed to be people of excellence and the elite at all levels of an organization. Party principles require members to take the lead in the face of difficulties and to set examples for non-members through their work. They can always be referred to for help in critical situations. In dealing with the party organizations, respect should be given to party members and they should be encouraged to take proactive roles at different levels of management. Appropriate time should also be allocated to these organizations for their own activities. As an offshoot of a good relationship with the party organizations, they can be used as task forces to help the management realize management objectives and enhance employee communications.

Employees

In internal public relations, a good image of the management team is of pivotal importance in establishing the trust of employees. Trust can be established through candid communication. The following list of rules is not exhaustive but should be taken into account when dealing with employees.

- The first meeting with employees is very important in terms of building trust. Employees should be clearly briefed on corporate objectives and their association with the well-being of employees.
- When introducing 'western advanced management', communications should be understandable and free of ambiguity. On points that are particularly 'foreign', there should be clarity. To play safe, implementation of management policy on a trial basis will allow adjustments at later stages.
- Communications with employees should be regular and ongoing. Employees should be informed of the progress that the company is making both in good and bad times.
- Employee participation in the management process should be encouraged. If possible, a platform should be provided for employees' suggestions and comments.
- A sense of employee pride should be developed by creating a unique corporate culture. Employee contributions should be recognized and appreciated in the form of both spiritual and material rewards.
- A ladder of promotion should be established in order to encourage employees to be career-motivated. Promotion schemes should be designed to meet different career needs, such as promotion to management positions and technical skills. Pay schemes should be linked to promotions.

Government officials

Because of the pervasive red-tape and bureaucracy in almost every government across the world, companies outside China tend to employ or engage professional lobbyists to deal with governments and government officials. In China, however, lobbying is not a professional trade. Although there is an increasing number of public relations companies who claim to have special connections with Chinese government officials, no such organizations could realistically offer the service of dealing with government officials on behalf of the client on a regular basis. Like anywhere else, government functionaries can be very influential over corporate decisions or in business deals, and therefore maintaining a good relationship with them is imperative for foreign firms doing business in China. The advantages of having a good relationship with government officials are as follows.

- **Advice on corporate decisions.** Government officials are involved in the policy-making process of the governments at different levels. They are also well informed with regard to trends and policy orientation. Their judgement on corporate decisions can be extremely valuable.
- **Gaining government understanding.** Contacts with government officials on a good relationship basis will help a company to deliver or communicate the messages of corporate strategies/actions and gain government understanding of the corporate position.
- **Facilitation of government procedures.** Advice by government officials on how to meet reporting requirements will save a lot of time and effort in gaining consent or approval from the government organizations.
- **Publicity for corporate image.** A formal meeting between the CEOs and high ranking officials such as ministers, provincial governors and city mayors, will receive a lot of publicity in the local media. A meeting with central level officials will be covered by TV and newspapers.
- *De facto* **recognition.** The comments made by government officials during formal meetings and a picture taken with them may appear to be an indication of *de facto* recognition of your company by government organizations.

To the uninitiated, the Chinese government can appear to be an incomprehensible labyrinth. The reporting structure and its associated requirements are even more so. You will be very lucky if your business partners have strong relations with government organizations at different levels. With the help of contact people, consultant organizations and public relations companies, contact with government organizations and officials can also be initiated. Once the contact is initiated, a reasonably good relationship with government officials can be maintained by employing appropriate personal and public relations skills.

Government officials can be invited to participate in ribbon-cutting ceremonies, news conferences, major corporate events, inspection tours, seminars, exhibitions and so on. Sponsoring government-initiated community projects and public affairs can also be a good way of cementing closer relationships with government officials and generating positive publicity.

People of different social functions

Apart from the types of people mentioned above, there are others that cannot be ignored in corporate public relations: industry experts, research professionals, personnel of industry and commerce bureaux, tax bureaux, customs offices and stars in the recreational industry. These are influential groups. They can be dealt with on a good personal basis with a view to creating external public relations effects. Of special significance are relations with journalists and reporters. Keeping a good relationship with them will always be useful.

Macro public relations

Macro public relations here refers to communications with the public on a collective basis. The target of macro public relations is to create, among the public, a favourable corporate or brand image that could not possibly be achieved on an interpersonal basis or by mere commercial advertising efforts.

Consumers

Consumers are the largest group with which a company deals. Increased consumerism has substantially improved consumers' awareness of their rights and made consumer relations more challenging to handle. The consumer no longer takes what is available and tolerates defective products, inadequate service or failures in quality and safety. The government has also invested significant effort in formulating laws and regulations to protect the rights of consumers, and consumer activists have emerged in recent years. Newspapers and TV stations are more interested in protecting the rights of consumers. They evaluate products under the supervision of a public notary and publicize the results in newspapers and on TV. There are also individual consumer activists, who fight against counterfeits by making volume purchases to claim multiple compensation. Consumers are becoming increasingly sceptical of advertising information, which in turn has made public relations practitioners more

consumer-oriented than before. The task of public relations is to establish effective channels of communications with consumers on a non-advertising basis.

The community

The community in which a company operates can mean the survival and development or otherwise of the company. A construction site may encounter resistance from the residents of neighbouring areas because of noise problems. An office building with a glazed exterior may be blamed for light pollution. A factory may be sabotaged by neighbouring farmers for suspected pollution. It is the task of public relations people to work towards gaining an understanding from the community, if not its support.

To convince the community that your company is a good citizen and part of the community, you should deliver the message that the company benefits and cares about the community in terms of providing employment opportunities, generating other community businesses and contributing to the communal well-being. At the same time, the company should build an image of visible safety and clean production in order to eliminate possible concerns. To gain community acceptance and approval, you should also provide support for community development, such as opening the service facilities to the community, offering assistance in maintaining public security, participating in social welfare activities, sponsoring community campaigns to clean up the environment and so on.

Media

A good working relationship with the media in China is imperative for successful public relations. The Chinese media are not only the mouthpiece of the government, but also opinion leaders. They now play an increasingly important role in shaping opinions, benchmarking values and disseminating information and knowledge. Public media in China are owned by the government and therefore have a special position in the minds of the Chinese people. Getting favourable publicity in the media signifies official acceptance and recognition.

Because of the special status of public media, maintaining good relationships with it is a common practice of public relations people in China. The 'competition' for good relationships resulted in the practice of paying for news reports. At one time, paid news reports were rampant, which jeopardized the impartiality of public media and subjected the public audience to questionable or misleading advocacy. As a result, the government reinforced its rules against paid news and journalists/reporters are likely to be expelled from the profession if they are found to have engaged in such deals. Therefore, public relations practitioners are advised not to attempt to influence the independence of public media. However, this does not preclude efforts to maintain a good working relationship with them. Of course, it always pays to build good personal relationships with journalists and reporters.

Maintaining a good working relationship requires much understanding of the media business, its unique feature of decision-making and its information needs. The need for news by public media often corresponds to the political, economic and social themes of the time. It will make good news if your story coincides with these current themes. Good public relations practitioners should be able to identify opportunities for corporate publicity and translate a corporate event into a story with news value. Being responsive and cooperative is the key to a good media relationship.

Government organizations

As discussed above, maintaining good personal relationships with government officials will help a company gain support and facilitation from government organizations on the basis of personal understanding. In practice, however, it would be impossible for any company to know all the government officials on an interpersonal basis, so good government relations should receive additional strategic consideration in macro public relations.

The Chinese government consists of a large number of national government agencies as well as provincial and local government units. Each has a distinctive set of responsibilities and is charged with a mission that gives it a level of policy making. The government regulates the macro economy and also disciplines corporate behaviour.

When dealing with government relations, the first step is to understand policies, laws and regulations to ensure that corporate operations are in line with government requirements. At the same time, companies should minimize, where possible, the likely conflicts with government organizations at different levels, if such conflicts cannot be avoided. Possible sources of conflict are unauthorized inspections and fines, illegitimate collection of fees, unjustified allocation of public spending funds and solicitation of sponsorships. Cooperation with government organizations is essential for harmonious government relations. Responding positively to government advocacy will not only result in appreciation from the government but also create positive public relations.

Issues management

Managing relations with the public is, in effect, an effort to minimize issues that may arise from possible conflicts. However, issues do arise. China has a unique political, economic and social system and issues management should be tailored to its unique features.

To avoid political issues, it is important for foreign companies to observe the rules of the political game in China – essentially to keep away from any political involvement. Corporate spokesmen should avoid commenting publicly on political issues. In business operations, foreign companies are advised to ensure there are no political associations in their products, brands and trade names. A Japanese computer software company, for example, ran into a political issue by marketing in China a war game package featuring Japanese war criminals.

Economic and social issues are more manageable than political issues. Common issues, among others, are environmental pollution, product quality, health concerns, safety problems, employment disputes, advertising claims, intellectual property and consumer complaints. The extent to which these issues affect an organization varies, depending on how they evolve in the process of corporate development in the context of China's economic and social environment. A company that does not have an issue now may well have one in the future. To manage issues that may arise in the future, a company should be able to anticipate emerging issues and plan their issues management. A tracking mechanism should be established to define and analyze existing and emerging issues. Possible sources of issues should be given priority tracking efforts.

Public media are one of the sources from which issues originate. For example, the media recently disclosed a research finding that air fresheners contain one kind of carcinogenic chemical. Soon after that, the media reported another research finding that dietary recipes marketed in China will not help to reduce weight and may be hazardous to health. All these reports will have a negative impact on companies producing these products. Identifying issues that may exist is important to prevent an issue from developing into a crisis.

Publicity techniques

Media publicity

Unlike advertising, media publicity is not in the hands of a company's management. Because of this, it has the kind of objectivity that advertising cannot possibly achieve. The Chinese media have developed very rapidly in recent years, particularly in technological terms. Transmission of news is as fast as in any other country. Avenues of publicity include televisions (terrestrial and cable), radio, newspapers, magazines and, increasingly, the internet.

Television

Television is now the most influential medium and the most important source of information in China. Getting publicity on television is considered to be the best result of a public relations effort. To achieve national publicity, China Central Television (CCTV) is the 'one and only' choice. The most influential news programme is the evening news between 7.00pm and 7.30pm each day. Other key news programmes include morning, noon and late night news.

Apart from CCTV, there are also local television stations. For publicity other than national coverage, provincial and provincial capitals and large cities' stations are the best media. Some provincial stations are also aired via satellite, which can be received by cable television subscribers in most parts of China.

It is the most challenging task for public relations people to get publicity on television. Practitioners are advised to make sure that the story you recommend will interest television people and that it has news value. An invitation should be sent to TV stations well in advance and be accompanied by an introduction of the story. Public relations people should prepare a copy of a news release for television editors. It should be clear and brief to suit the nature of television broadcasting. Supplementary materials should also be prepared in case the television editors need to understand more about the background to the story. You should also provide additional visual materials, if any, for the convenience of the editor to make a better visual presentation. Public relations people should always offer to provide transport for the camera crew, which will guarantee their punctual arrival on the scene.

Radio

Although the emergence of television as a key information disseminator has overwhelmed the role of radio, which was the key news medium 15 to 20 years ago, radio publicity still has characteristics that television cannot replace. For example, radio listening has less constraints in terms of time and place. People can listen to the radio even on the way to work, on bikes and in buses and taxies, from their personal stereos or radio receivers. Almost all cars are equipped with a radio receiver. Radio can reach an audience that television cannot.

The system of radio broadcasting resembles that of television. There is a Central People's Broadcast Station (CPBS), which broadcasts throughout the country. There are also local broadcast stations. Most stations use middle wave and FM to reach their audience.

Radio journalists are relatively more receptive to the story ideas of public relations people, although getting publicity can be also be challenging. For news releases, public relations practitioners should prepare a write-up in advance for the journalists to refer to when producing the programme. Always send formal letters of invitation before the event takes place. In many cases, a news report may not need to involve direct participation by radio journalists. Public relations should not take it for granted that radio journalists do not have to be invited. Inviting them will offer good opportunities for interpersonal relations.

Newspapers

Newspapers provide more diversity and depth of coverage than either television or radio. There are thousands of newspapers in China, which fall into the following basic categories: national daily, local daily, evening, morning, professional, weekend and feature newspapers.

National daily newspapers are normally institutional papers of the government, which target institutional readers. The same is true of local daily newspapers. All such dailies carry reports on government policies, economic achievements, progress of social development, etc. Newspapers that fall into the category of evening and morning papers cover local interests and tend to be aligned to general interests. Professional newspapers normally cover special areas of interests, such as industry information and developments. Weekend newspapers and feature newspapers are more entertainment-oriented.

Gaining publicity in newspapers is relatively easy compared with television and radio. One way to do so is to write to the newspaper in which you wish to have your stories covered. To make sure that your contribution receives personal attention, it is advisable to write to a specific editor rather than an editor in general. For some story coverage, it is better to invite journalists to come to the scene, in which case a prepared news release with some details should be provided. For stronger impact, public relations people normally invite journalists/reporters not only from television and radio, but also from several newspapers, to witness the event.

Magazines

Although there are thousands of magazines in China, they play a less important role in terms of creating corporate publicity. Most are published on a monthly or fortnightly basis; few are weekly. Magazines will not offer immediate publicity, but allow for more intense coverage of a corporate event. Publicity through magazines requires a different type of public relations strategy. Articles covering corporate stories should be structured with a featured style. Story-telling by independent writers can be a good strategy for objectivity.

Event publicity

This means publicizing a company or a brand by organizing an event that will catch public attention. Event publicity is also known as event marketing. Common events include the following.

- Sports events. Sports are gaining popularity in China. Sports events can create corporate publicity that cannot be achieved by merely advertising. Successful events include Philips Football Association Cup, Pepsi Cola Football League Competition, Motorola Badminton Tour Competition, Toupai (a Chinese liquor brand) International Wushu (kungfu) Competition, and others.
- Cultural events, such as film festivals, fashion shows, art festivals and music concerts can also be an avenue of publicity. For example, Samsung sponsored a music event featuring original student music composition.
- Social events designed to correspond to social concerns. Such events include nature conservation,

protection of endangered species, relief funding of disaster stricken areas, aid to poverty-stricken children to allow them to return to school, and sponsorship of tree planting in response to the government effort to reduce deforestation.
- Seminars/conferences that deal with issues of public concern, economic and social progress.

The above does not exhaust the possibilities of event publicity. All such events are intended to target the public at large. The purpose of organizing such events is to reinforce the image of a company as a corporate citizen, and hence the brand image of its products and services. For such events, public relations people are required to demonstrate their ability to capture points of public interest as well as their capabilities in planning and organizing the events. There are an increasing number of public relations companies providing such services in China.

The following tips might be useful for companies that intend to create publicity in China:

- The objective that the sponsoring organization wishes to achieve through the event should be clearly defined and justified.
- Understanding must be achieved between management and the public relations people that such an event will not bring immediate sales benefits.
- Understanding should also be achieved that event sponsoring should be a continuous effort. A one-off approach is not going to produce the expected publicity benefits.
- Careful planning for media coverage should be made well in advance with back-up plans for contingencies.
- The presence of government officials and celebrities can add special publicity impact.
- Excessive emphasis on the role of sponsor(s) should be avoided in order to prevent possible aversion by the public.
- Efforts should be made to create two-way communication with the public.
- Crisis prevention should be given due attention before the event.

Part Seven

Banking, Foreign Exchange Transactions and Corporate Finance

Banking Services for Foreign Invested Enterprises (FIEs)
HSBC

Overview of the Chinese banking sector

Since the 1970s, China's financial sector has gone through an unprecedented degree of structural transformation. Today, there are several layers to the Chinese banking system: the People's Bank of China (PBOC) serves as the central bank, providing overall regulatory guidance and governing macro-economic and monetary policy, and, since its establishment in 2003, the China Banking Regulatory Commission (CBRC) has taken over the regulatory responsibilities from the PBOC. The CBRC monitors the four majority-state-owned commercial banks,[1] and the 12 shareholding commercial banks. These banks were initially set up to provide specialized product niches. However, they have since evolved and now provide a full range of banking and other financial services.

At the local level, are more than 110 city commercial banks, around 700 urban credit cooperatives, and some 34,000 rural credit cooperatives that provide basic banking services. The Chinese government has also started giving its permission for the establishment of private banks.

Having built up their presence in China for over two decades, the foreign banks have now become an integral part of the Chinese financial sector. As of end-August 2004, 62 foreign banks from 19 countries had 199 operational branches and 216 representative offices in China. By the end of July 2004, the total assets of foreign banks in China were registered at US$64.3 billion (in comparison with US$29.9 billion in 1996 and US$34.2 billion in 1998), accounting for 1.82 per cent of the total banking assets in China. The outstanding balance of loans provided by foreign banks totalled US$30.1 billion, including US$23.8 billion of loans in foreign exchange, which accounted for 17.8 per cent of foreign exchange loans extended by banking institutions in China.

Regulatory structure and changing of regulations

The opening up of China's banking sector has been carried out in line with national economic reforms, generally starting from special economic zones then rolling out to coastal areas, inland capital cities and finally the whole country.

In a move to honour China's WTO commitments, the PBOC has announced a specific timetable for the opening of China's banking business to foreign banks. The major changes to the restrictions are scheduled to be completed by 2007, when foreign banks will be in a position to compete equally with their Chinese counterparts. In addition to the mainland's WTO liberalization measures, Hong Kong's banking sector is positioned to benefit further under CEPA (the Closer Economic Partnership Arrangement between Hong Kong and the mainland, in effect from 1 January 2004). For instance, Hong Kong banks will be allowed to open a branch on the mainland if they have total assets of US$6 billion or more, significantly lower than the entrance requirement under WTO commitments.

---

[1] Bank of China and Bank of Communications have issued, or are in the process of issuing, international share offerings for part of their capital. ICBC and Agricultural Bank will also partially list in due course.

Since 1 December 2003, subject to specific regulatory approval, foreign-funded banks in China have been allowed to deliver RMB business services to Chinese enterprises. So far, the Chinese cities that have been opened to allow the foreign-funded banks to conduct renminbi (RMB) business are:

- Shanghai;
- Shenzhen;
- Tianjin;
- Dalian;
- Guangzhou;
- Zhuhai;
- Qingdao;
- Nanjing;
- Wuhan;
- Jinan;
- Fuzhou;
- Chengdu; and
- Chongqing.

Up to end-June 2004, the total RMB assets and liabilities of foreign banks reached RMB84.4 billion and RMB72.1 billion respectively, while their total loans and deposits both reached RMB48.8 billion.

Foreign exchange business

Foreign banks were permitted to provide foreign exchange-related services in China without geographic and client restriction from 1 January 2002. As a result, foreign banks have been allowed to conduct foreign exchange business for Chinese enterprises and individuals in all locations within Mainland China.

RMB business

Conducting RMB business with foreign clients is permitted and has been expanded to include Chinese enterprise clients as detailed above and, by 2007, Chinese individuals. Initially, foreign financial institutions will be restricted to Shanghai, Shenzhen, Tianjin and Dalian for RMB business, with three to four cities added each year until all geographic restrictions are removed by 2007.

Looking ahead, a new phase of banking development in China is imminent, with competition intensifying in the wake of China's WTO entry. Hopefully, a more efficient industry will result from the competitive interaction among a growing number of domestic and foreign banks. This will benefit the economy in general and both foreign invested and domestic enterprises in particular.

Basic foreign currency bank accounts in China

Capital account

The capital account is set up for receiving injections of capital, overseas loans and other funds under capital account items. Given that the RMB is not yet fully convertible, restrictions apply to the exchange of capital account items involving foreign currency conversion.

The capital account is subject to State Administration of Foreign Exchange (SAFE) approval before it can be opened, and only one capital account is allowed per company. Generally, approval is given by the local office of SAFE for the capital account to be opened in the same city in which the venture is registered.

Since 1 July 2002, some items under the capital account can be settled directly with authorized banks via SAFE. Prior to the reform, each settlement transaction for capital accounts first had to be approved by SAFE before being submitted to banks. Now authorized banks are responsible for checking settlements and SAFE oversees bank operations.

Current account

The current account is used for remitting and receiving foreign currency trading payments as well as for service charges and fees and dividends to foreign shareholders.

For more details on banking accounts and payments, please see Chapter 7.2, 'A Practical Guide to China's Currency and Payments System'.

Trade services in China

A wide range of import and export services is offered by banks operating in Mainland China. The main import services offered include Documentary Credit Issuing and the provision of Shipping Guarantees and Clean Import Loans.

An extensive range of export services includes documentary collection, documentary credit confirmation and negotiation, as well as pre- and post-shipment finance. Export credit-backed facilities can be arranged through the various national export credit agencies to support the importation of capital goods into Mainland China.

Import services

DC issuing

A Documentary Credit (DC), also known as a Letter of Credit (L/C), is a written undertaking by a bank, issued on the instructions of the buyer in favour of the seller, to effect payment under stated conditions.

A DC gives the seller the comfort of knowing that he can look to the importer's bank for payment and that the buyer will only be able to gain access to the goods (via the necessary documents) once they have complied with all the terms of the DC. The buyer has the comfort of knowing that he will not be required to pay for the goods before he has control of the documents.

Shipping guarantee

Sometimes goods arrive before the documents. In such cases 'shipping guarantees' can be used. A shipping guarantee is an application from the bank to authorize the release of goods by a shipping company against an undertaking to deliver the original bill of lading in future. It is usually applicable under import DC transactions and allows prompt clearance of goods ahead of the arrival of documents. However, when taking the goods, protection against discrepant documents is lost.

Clean import loans

A working capital facility can be made available to pay for the goods imported under the DC. The finance will often be required to enable the buyer to turn the goods into manufactured items for onward sale. The advance will usually be made available for the manufacturing period on sight of original invoices and shipping documents only.

Export services

Documentary collection

Documentary collection is a dedicated export bill collection service offered by banks to follow up on bill payments as agents of the exporter.

Documents are received by the local branch of the exporter's bank. These documents are then forwarded to the collecting bank (for non-DC transactions) or the DC-issuing bank (for DC transactions), together with a collection order requesting payment.

DC confirmation

Documentary credit confirmation is a service offered by foreign banks to add an undertaking to pay in the event that the issuing bank is unable to, even though the documents submitted by the exporter are fully compliant.

An exporter's main concern is with receiving payment and it may be difficult to retrieve goods that have been shipped to the importer's country in the event that payment is not forthcoming, and so an exporter may choose to seek the reassurance of DC confirmation in situations where the issuing bank is not well known, or in financial difficulties itself, or if the administration of the importer's country presents risks – real or perceived – with which the exporter is uncomfortable.

DC negotiation

Documentary credit negotiation is a service offered by banks that involves checking and making a payment advance against the documents presented by the exporter, upon shipment of goods under an Export Documentary Credit.

The bank will check to ensure that the exporter's documents are in full compliance with the terms and conditions of the DC and, where possible, work with the exporter to make appropriate amendments to rectify any discrepancies. However, some discrepancies such as expired DCs or late shipment are not rectifiable.

Any discrepancy whatsoever could render the exporter's Export DC inoperative as an undertaking of payment from the issuing bank.

Pre-shipment finance

Pre-shipment finance provided by a bank is generally termed 'Loans against Exports'. Loans must be supported by original irrevocable DCs. Facilities may also allow advances to be made against confirmed orders by specified reputable buyers of international standing. Types of pre-shipment finance offered include packing credits, manufacturing advances and red clause credits.

Packing credits provide an exporter with finance after goods have been manufactured but before they are shipped. This helps to smooth the exporter's cash flow while the goods are being packed and waiting for shipment. The advance is repaid when the goods are shipped if the documents were negotiated with the exporter's bank.

Manufacturing advances are provided to exporters to meet manufacturing costs, such as the purchase of raw materials.

A red clause credit is a DC containing a clause from the issuing bank that authorizes the advising bank to grant an advance to the exporter before documents are presented. Facilities are not required for this type of pre-shipment finance as the advising bank is relying on the issuing bank for reimbursement rather than the customer.

Post-shipment finance

Post-shipment finance occurs when an exporter asks its bank to advance funds against a shipment that has already been made. The exporter can ease their cash flow by obtaining funds for their shipment without having to wait for the importer to pay.

Trade trends after WTO entry

China's WTO entry will change the way trade is conducted in the country in terms of levels of trade, types of goods being traded and associated financial and documentary arrangements.

The current trend of strongly growing imports into China is expected to continue. The growth in the import of primary and capital products has been particularly significant – the increase in primary goods being mainly due to the large jump in petroleum products, which will remain a major item for the foreseeable future. Imports of raw materials, including timber, pulp, minerals, chemicals and metals, have also risen strongly, while electrical, electronic and automotive products and instruments are rising significantly in line with China's economic restructuring and upgrading.

Payment terms

While the trade finance products available in China are largely generic, DCs remain prevalent in trade deals with foreign suppliers. However, there does appear to be an increasing number of requests to suppliers to offer open account terms, even for bulk commodities (raw materials).

On the export side, a greater percentage of transactions are on open account, and this number is growing. Estimates vary from 30–65 per cent, depending on the products involved and the location of the exporters. This growing trend will encourage trade banks to look at meeting the needs of the market quickly.

Cash management

Increased foreign investment in Mainland China has inevitably led to a greater focus on cash management. Historically, corporate growth in China has been a fragmented affair, resulting in numerous legal entities with completely separate operations and administration. Under local regulations, a subsidiary's scope of business is tightly defined by its 'business licence', and this makes it impossible to create centralized treasury or cash management operations under a holding company structure. However, the position improved significantly

in 1999 and 2001 when the Ministry of Commerce (MOFCOM), previously the Ministry of Foreign Trade and Economic Cooperation (MOFTEC) extended the business scope of holding companies. This enabled them (subject to certain conditions and approvals from MOFCOM) to:

- act as principal in selling their subsidiaries' products, thereby centralizing sales and invoicing;
- provide transporting and warehousing for their subsidiaries only; and
- house a research and development centre.

The payments infrastructure

A number of clearing systems and payment methods are commonly used in China. In-city payments are generally made by cheque, whereas cross-city RMB payments are generally made by telegraphic transfer or demand draft.

The most commonly used payment instrument for RMB transfers within the same city is the local transfer cheque. Whereas company-issued cheques would be sent directly to the beneficiary and then presented through local clearing, local transfer cheques are delivered directly to the payer's bank, which then clears them through the local clearing house. The advantage here is that local transfer cheques do not need to be stamped with the company's finance chop, and so the instruction can be sent electronically and the production of the local clearing cheque outsourced to the bank. An alternative payment method for in-city payments is the cashier's order, which, as a bank-issued payment instrument, can be credited to the beneficiary's account on sight.

Foreign companies operating in China face an additional challenge if their enterprise resource planning (ERP) systems do not produce Chinese language payments output files. This can result in significant manual intervention and re-keying to create payments files in Chinese. Banks can assist customers by building a link between the customer's ERP system and their electronic banking system if the latter has the ability to translate payment instructions into Chinese.

For cross-city payments, there are multiple channels, including the central bank-administered China National Automated Payments System (CNAPS), which spans 800 cities and provides access to cleared funds in one to two working days for the larger cities. However, the larger domestic commercial banks have developed efficient in-house clearing to clear between their own branches. For example, HSBC's strategic alliances with the 'big four' state commercial banks (Industrial and Commercial Bank of China, China Construction Bank, Bank of China and Agricultural Bank of China) give customers access to over 26,000 branches via partner banks' real-time internal clearing. As a result, telegraphic transfers can now, in some cases, be cleared within two to three hours.

Receivables management

Given the complex range of clearing mechanisms described above, receivables management can present a challenge, especially if remote locations are involved. However, various solutions are available. If the collecting entity is based in an area (such as Shanghai and Guangzhou) where foreign banks are allowed to provide RMB services, alliances with domestic banks can be used to improve collection times. Any items that come in through the domestic banks' branches will be concentrated through the domestic banks' electronic

systems and settled via a nostro account that the foreign bank maintains with a local bank.

Consolidated electronic reporting of these transactions is as important as the need to better manage the receivables cycle and this can be achieved via consolidated, timely electronic reporting of transactions via the foreign bank's electronic banking system. By assigning a unique transaction reference to each transaction and providing a file extract programme, banks can help customers to automate their reconciliation process within the customer's own ERP system.

Conclusion

Despite the market-specific requirements of cash management in China, significant opportunities exist for corporates to improve their payables and receivables and liquidity management practices. This is an area where extensive cooperation between foreign and domestic banks is likely to continue to develop services that meet the needs of multi-national clients with multiple subsidiaries operating in China.

A Practical Guide to China's Currency and Payments System

HSBC

This chapter provides answers to some frequently asked questions about currency and the payment system in China.

Currency issues

Is the renminbi (RMB) fully convertible?
No. Where you require conversion into RMB of foreign currency funds derived from capital account or current account transactions, or purchase of foreign currency with RMB funds or payment of foreign currency funds to settle capital account or current account transactions, you must present supporting documents and go through the verification procedures with the handling bank (for purchases or payments relating to current account transactions) or acquire the approval of the State Administrative Foreign Exchange (SAFE) (for purchases or payments relating to capital account transactions).

Can a local currency exposure be hedged to protect against changes in the RMB against other currencies?
Yes – both onshore and offshore hedging products are available. However, the onshore hedging market is still developing.

Can non-local currency exposure (eg USD) be hedged locally (in China) through forwards or non-deliverable forwards (NDFs)?
Yes, there are no restrictions on foreign currency to foreign currency (FCY/FCY) (eg EUR/USD, USD/JPY) hedging in China.

Can local accounts (in any currency) be included in a multilateral netting system run by a European Coordination Centre?
Cross-border netting is not possible at present in China.

Opening bank accounts

Can a non-resident entity, for example a regional treasury function, open an RMB account with a bank outside of China?
No – RMB is not a fully-convertible, international currency. RMB accounts can be opened onshore only. Representative offices, which are considered as resident entities but which are not permitted to undertake any operational business in China, are permitted to open a general RMB account only (see below for further information on general accounts).

What type of accounts would I need?

Foreign currency

There are various regulatory requirements applicable to the opening and operation of foreign currency accounts. Different types of foreign currency accounts are opened for different purposes, and the operation of these accounts is subject to regulatory restrictions in relation to these specific purposes.

There are a number of foreign currency account types:

- *Settlement Accounts* for current account items;
- *Capital Accounts* for capital account items – required for injecting or extracting equity;
- *Foreign Debt Special Accounts* for foreign debt principle;
- *Foreign Debt Principal Repayment and Interest Payment Accounts* for foreign debt repayment;
- *Foreign Currency Loan Account and Repayment Account* for local foreign currency borrowings and repayment.

The opening of foreign currency accounts requires prior approval from the local SAFE office, except for the last type of account shown above.

Approval for opening *settlement* accounts is often accompanied by a ceiling limit – these limits are determined by SAFE according to criteria such as, but not limited to:

- the size of business;
- trade turnover; and
- aid-up capital.

For existing companies, the ceiling limits are reviewed annually.

Funds received by settlement accounts in excess of this limit must be paid out or converted into RMB within a specified number of working days (currently seven).

Simple savings interest rates or tiered interest rates (according to the level of balances), and time deposits are available on settlement accounts and capital accounts. Interest rates for deposits (including current account and time deposits) below US$3 million or equivalent are regulated by the central bank. For deposits over US$3 million, or for non-resident customers, favourable interest rates may be negotiated between the customer and their bank.

Renminbi

There are several types of RMB accounts: the primary ones are the basic account and the general account. The main differences between the two types of accounts are:

- cash can only be withdrawn from the basic account;
- salary and bonus payments can only be effected from the basic account; and
- only one basic account can be opened by each company, irrespective of how many banks are used. Multiple general accounts can be opened.

RMB services being provided by foreign bank branches now include interest-bearing RMB checking accounts; statement savings accounts and time deposits; RMB lending and syndication; the issuance of RMB guarantees; and RMB payment settlement. RMB entrusted loans, bank acceptance discounting and pooling are also available. The major Chinese banks can provide all services in RMB, and in most cases, there is close cooperation between Chinese and foreign banks for more complex areas, such as payments and cash management systems.

Do I need an account with a domestic bank?

An account with a domestic bank may be a good solution if you:

- require a branch close to your offices, since the major Chinese banks have very extensive branch networks; or
- in those circumstances where a foreign bank cannot provide the required services – this may arise from the fact that your office lies outside the permitted catchment area of the branch of a foreign bank, as foreign banks are currently geographically limited in the scope of services that they can provide.

How do I open an account?

The following documents need to be provided to the branch of the bank in which you wish to open your account:

- Business Licence issued by the local office of the State Administration for Industry and Commerce;
- approval document issued by Chinese authorities for the establishment of the foreign-invested enterprise;
- Memorandum/Articles of Association and Amending Resolution (if any), and any relevant board resolutions;
- list of directors and copies of identity documents (passport or identity cards) for all signing directors and authorized signatories;
- completed account opening form, mandate and signature card; and
- letter of introduction (current/checking account only).

The following additional documents are required for foreign currency account opening:

- Account Opening Registration Certificate issued by the local office of SAFE;
- Foreign Exchange Certificate for a foreign-invested enterprise issued by the local office of SAFE.

Documents presented should be originals or certified true copies.

Making payments

What issues are most commonly faced by Corporate Treasurers?

Payments issues:

- fund delays and loss of interest, especially for cross-city, cross-bank remittances;
- incomplete transaction details/information;
- process of payments is highly manual;
- payments are predominantly paper based;
- information must be written in Chinese;
- paper forms must be manually signed and stamped by company chops.

Liquidity issues:

- difficulty in obtaining updated account information;
- overseas HQs often cannot have access to account information for accounts in China;
- limited investment options;
- low returns on RMB; and
- minimum period for placing time deposits is three months.

What regulatory restrictions are in place for foreign currency payments?

Where you require conversion into RMB of foreign currency funds derived from capital account or current account transactions, or purchase of foreign currency with RMB funds or payment of foreign currency funds to settle capital account or current account transactions, you must present supporting documents and go through the verification procedures with the handling bank (for purchases or payments relating to current account transactions) or acquire the approval of SAFE (for purchases or payments relating to capital account transactions).

Profits can be repatriated as current account payments – the documentation that is required is as follows:

- a board resolution agreeing to pay dividends for that year and specifying the amount to be paid;
- audited financials that show that a profit has been made;
- a tax receipt showing that profit tax has been paid – taxation certificate;

- an investment verification report by a PRC-registered auditor certifying that capital is paid up according to the capital injection schedule (per the original business approval presented to PRC authorities when the venture was formed);
- a letter from the foreign-invested enterprise instructing the bank to remit the funds abroad – a written application to the bank; and
- a Certificate of Foreign Exchange Registration of foreign-invested enterprises.

Profit repatriation is further subject to the following requirements:

- the company must be making a profit;
- prior to repatriation, the company is required to make up losses of previous years and make provisions to the Reserve Fund, Expansion Fund and Bonus and Welfare Fund.

Dividends distributed to foreign investors are exempt from PRC withholding income tax, but the repatriation of royalty, interest and technology transfer fees is subject to withholding income tax.

Decapitalization is also possible, subject to approval from the Ministry of Commerce and SAFE. It should be noted that cross-border movement of capital (ie into or out of Mainland China, including from the PRC to the Hong Kong SAR) remains highly regulated.

What is the regulatory framework for inter-company loans?[1]

- onshore-to-onshore inter-company loans denominated in RMB – direct company borrowings are not allowed but can be arranged through an intermediary bank (agent bank) using the 'entrusted loan' scheme, where the cash rich company can lend to the cash deficit company through an agent bank;
- onshore-to-onshore inter-company loans foreign currency – not undertaken under the present regulatory framework (see footnote);
- onshore-to-offshore inter-company loans denominated in foreign currency – not undertaken under the present regulatory framework (see footnote);

---

[1] At time of writing, new regulations governing foreign currency inter-company borrowings for multi-national corporations were in the process of being released by SAFE. These new regulations 'will provide a variety of solutions for multi-national companies to improve efficiency in the use of foreign exchange and reduce financing costs' (SAFE). A full analysis of the new regulations will be available by time of publication of this book.

- offshore-to-onshore inter-company loans denominated in foreign currency – allowed by way of a shareholders' loan, which has to be registered with SAFE (prior approval is not necessary). Any changes in the repayment schedule or terms and conditions of the loan have to be approved by SAFE.

In which currency are inter-company loans typically denominated?

In cases where both entities are onshore, RMB is the usual currency used. However, a bank (foreign or Chinese) must stand in between, using a structure known as an entrusted loan (see above). Loans directly from one onshore company to another affiliated company are not permitted. Foreign currency transactions have to be approved by SAFE on a case-by-case-basis. For offshore-to-onshore lending, only foreign currency is allowed, and withholding tax will be payable on the loan.[2]

Is there a need to register inter-company loans at either SAFE or PBOC

For offshore-to-onshore lending, you need to register with SAFE. For an onshore RMB entrusted loan, no approval or registration is required.

Is there a minimum maturity for inter-company loans? Is there a need for a specified maturity?

There are no such specific rules. A specific maturity has to be stipulated in the inter-company loan contract.

---

[2] Inter-company loans from offshore affiliated companies are subject to a 10 per cent withholding tax. No withholding tax will be applicable for local bank debt. For onshore entrusted loans, a 5 per cent business tax is applied to the credit interest income of the lender.

Import and Export Financing in China[1]

Export-Import Bank of China

China's import and export financing system

After more than two decades of reform and open-door policy, a complete trade system and finance system have basically taken shape. The two systems have been integrated into a reciprocal cycle – the trade system has expanded China's foreign trade, and the continuous increase of foreign trade in return has spurred the completion of the country's import and export finance system.

The major players of China's import and export financing

The major financial players in import and export finance comprise two segments in China: banking institutions and insurance institutions.

Banking institutions

In China, banks can devise various financial vehicles to provide many kinds of trade financing services to firms that meet their qualification standards. The major players in the banking industry comprise many banks with different functions. There are three policy banks, four solely state-owned banks, 10 small and mid-sized shareholding commercial banks, 100 small and mid-sized shareholding city commercial banks, and 191 foreign financial institutions. All of these are under the auspices of the central bank – the People's Bank of China. More specifically:

- The Export-Import Bank of China (Eximbank) is the only policy-oriented bank;

- Bank of China, Construction Bank of China and Agricultural Bank of China are solely state-owned;
- Bank of Communication, Everbright Bank, CITIC Enterprise Bank, Huaxia Bank, Minsheng Bank, Merchant Bank, Shenzhen Development Bank, Guangdong Development Bank, Shanghai Pudong Development Bank and Fujian Xingye Bank are shareholding commercial banks.

Insurance institutions

The major Chinese insurance institutions related to foreign trade are the Export Credit Insurance Company of China and the People's Insurance Company of China.

Financing tools in import and export

Banking services

Among the various foreign trade financing services available, the export credit funded by the government is provided by Eximbank, whereas general commercial loans are provided by commercial banks. Their businesses cover:

- export seller's credit, export buyer's credit, forfeiting, factoring, discounting, project financing, syndicated loans and offshore construction loans;
- issuance, acceptance, negotiation and confirmation of letters of credit, bank guarantees, export lending, packing credit, import lending, delivery guarantee, import credit line service and entrusted collection.

In addition, Eximbank also offers countermeasures against foreign exchange exposure, which include the

---

[1] This chapter was originally written in Chinese and translated by Liu Baocheng, Professor, University of International Business and Economics.

forward contracts and other derivatives like currency and rate options, hedging, swapping, etc.

Insurance services

The Export Credit Insurance Company of China and the People's Insurance Company of China provide insurance coverage over the following:

- short-term export credit;
- long- and mid-term export credit;
- political risk for Chinese overseas investment;
- political risk for foreign investment in China;
- import and export cargo transportation;
- sea-borne vessels;
- others.

Eximbank and China's foreign trade

Mission and organization of Eximbank

Eximbank was founded in 1994. It is an exclusively state-owned, policy-oriented bank under the direct leadership of the State Council. Its primary responsibility is to implement industrial, financial and trade policies set forth by the state. It provides policy-oriented financial support to the export of capital goods such as mechanical and electronic products, high-tech products and complete sets of equipment. It also offers other financial assistance to offshore engineering projects and overseas investment. It facilitates other types of international economic and technological cooperation and exchange.

Eximbank is headquartered in Beijing. In China it has two subsidiaries (in Beijing and Shanghai) and eight representative offices in major cities (Dalian, Qingdao, Xi'an, Nanjing, Chengdu, Wuhan, Fuzhou and Guangzhou). Outside China, Eximbank has one representative office in Ivory Coast and another one in South Africa. In 2002, it set up another subsidiary in Shenzhen and an additional office in Harbin.

Business development and the role of Eximbank

As a state policy-oriented financial institution dedicated to China's export promotion, Eximbank follows closely its articles of association approved by the State Council since its opening on 1 July 1994. It has steadily built up an extensive business portfolio to include export seller's credit, export credit insurance, overseas guarantee, export buyer's credit, etc. Since 1995, the bank has undertaken foreign government concessionary loans, foreign favourable loans and foreign trade development loans funded by the central government. Eximbank also provides other overseas investment support products, such as those in support of offshore contract manufacturing and overseas engineering projects, and has put together a relatively complete service package through its policy-oriented financial service network. At the end of 2001, the State Council decided to transfer the entire export credit insurance business to the newly established Export Credit Insurance Company of China.

By the end of June 2002, Eximbank had accumulated loans totalling close to RMB200 billion. Its export financing for mechanical, electronic, high-tech products and complete sets of equipment totalled over US$80 billion. Its market covers 31 provinces, cities and autonomous regions in China, and export markets supported by the bank extend to 85 countries globally. Hence Eximbank plays an increasingly important role in bolstering China's national economy in line with the 'stepping out' strategy.

The major lines of Eximbank

The business lines of Eximbank primarily include: export credit (seller's credit and buyer's credit), overseas guarantees, foreign favourable loans and foreign government concessionary loans.

Export seller's credit is the financial service provided to Chinese exporters that enables exporters to be in a position to accept deferred payment by foreign importers. This includes five different types of arrangement: project loans, short and mid-term credit lines, overseas engineering project loans, offshore contract manufacturing loans and overseas investment loans.

Export buyer's credit refers to the long- and mid-term loans in favour of foreign borrowers. Its purpose is to enable foreign importers to be in a position to offer upfront payment to Chinese exporters. This is an option in support of China's exports of goods and technology services.

Overseas guarantees denote the promise to pay offered to overseas creditors or beneficiaries in the form of a letter of guarantee. In the event that the debtor fails to honour its commitment to pay under contract stipulations, the bank will undertake the payment responsibility specified in the letter of guarantee. Such guarantees include such items as borrowing, tendering, contract performance and contract deposit. They cover areas such as the export of mechanical and electronic products, high-tech products and complete sets of equipment, offshore engineering projects, international tenders by domestic financial organizations and foreign government loans.

Foreign favourable loans are long- and mid-term low-interest loans offered to other developing countries by the Chinese government in the nature of foreign aid. Beneficiaries of this type of loan are Chinese and foreign firms who are able to construct production facilities in the designated countries. These facilities must demonstrate the prospect of economic return and the capability to pay back. Such loans can also be granted for the construction of infrastructures and social welfare projects that demonstrate the capability to pay back. Eximbank is the only bank to underwrite this type of loan.

Foreign government concessionary loans are those favourable loans and mixed loans offered by foreign governments to the Chinese government. Eximbank acts as an agent under the mandate of the Chinese Ministry of Finance to dispense these loans. Mixed loans are a combination of favourable loans offered by foreign governments and commercial loans offered by foreign banks. Eximbank is the primary concessionary bank for the loans offered by foreign governments.

Among all the business lines mentioned above, export financing constitutes the most important part of Eximbank's business. In practice it generally requires a 15 per cent down payment by the foreign importer, with the balance of 85 per cent being undertaken by Eximbank in the form of an export credit.

Sources of finance for Eximbank and its world credit rating

Renminbi business

According to its articles of association, besides its capital reserves, Eximbank raises credit capital through the issuance of financial bonds in China. In the event of a shortage of reserve funds, provisional loans can be applied for from the People's Bank of China, or short-term funds can be borrowed in the interbank market. By the end of June 2002, Eximbank had raised over RMB100 billion through 19 rounds of financial bonds. Long-term bonds were issued through interest rate difference bidding and short-term bonds were raised through a combination of interest rate difference bidding and price bidding. At present capital operations are also procured through interbank credit transfers, transactions of national bonds and national bonds buybacks.

Foreign exchange business

Except for the reserve fund the foreign exchange capital of Eximbank is primarily raised in the financial markets at home and abroad. In July 1996 and October 1999, the bank issued bushi bonds of 20 billion yen in Japan and US$200 million debenture bonds in the European financial market. In the meantime the bank also conducted interbank short-term capital financing. Its capital operations include interbank financing, foreign exchange transaction, bond sales and purchase as well as hedging and options.

In 2001, Eximbank's credit rating was rated BBB by US Standard & Poor's and A by Japan Rating and Investment Information, Inc., which is consistent with the sovereign rating standard.

China's import and export financing after WTO entry

China's entry into the WTO will drive China's import and export financing towards the improvement of financing services, the reduction of financing cost and further opening of the financial market to foreign financial institutions.

The WTO entry has built a more solid stage for Eximbank to exercise its role of policy orientation. The bank will be better able to integrate those successful experiences of foreign export financing institutions with Chinese realities and further deepen its reform and speed up its development. Under these new circumstances, effective measures must be taken at Eximbank to further promote China's foreign trade strategies. While the size of loans will be increased, Eximbank must also improve its lending structure, enhance its capability to weather financial exposures and upgrade the quality of lending. To meet the need for business development, Eximbank will improve its banking facilities and raise the quality level of financial services.

With regard to the treatment to foreign banks China has pledged, in the second article of Specific Concession List on Service Trade – List of Exemptions to Most Favoured Nations under Appendix 9 of the Entry Protocol of the People's Republic of China, to

- remove geographic restrictions on foreign exchange business after entry;
- phase out geographical restrictions over local currency according to the following timetable:
  - to eliminate all restrictions within five years after entry;

- to permit foreign financial institutions to provide services in China with no client restrictions;
- to allow foreign financial institutions to provide services to Chinese enterprises in local currency within two years of entry;
- to allow foreign financial institutions to provide services to all Chinese clients within five years of entry.

With the opening of financial markets, the service quality in foreign trade financing will be improved through competition, which in turn will benefit both Chinese and foreign companies in their import and export business.

Supplement to Chapter 7.3

Brief introduction to The Export-Import Bank of China

Approved by the State Council, The Export-Import Bank of China was founded on 26 April 1994 and officially opened for business on 1 July of the same year.

A policy-oriented financial institution under the direct leadership of the State Council, the Bank adheres to independent, break-even operating principles and strictly follows the guideline of carrying out management as a business entity.

The main mandate of the bank is to carry out state industrial policy, foreign trade policy and financial policy, to promote the export of Chinese mechanical and electronic products, complete sets of equipment and high- and new-tech products, and to enhance overseas economic and technological cooperation and exchanges by means of policy financial support.

The government of the People's Republic of China is the sole owner of the bank. The Ministry of Finance provided exclusively the bank's registered capital of RMB3.38 billion.

The bank mainly offers the following business services: export seller's credit, export buyer's credit, foreign exchange guarantees, Chinese government concessionary loans, the on-lending of foreign government loans, the issuing of financial bonds in domestic markets and debentures in overseas markets (excluding stocks).

As a state-owned policy bank mainly engaged in global business, the bank has developed broad business relations with international financial organizations and domestic and overseas banks. The Export-Import Bank of China is focused on establishing and strengthening mutual contacts with friends in financial and business circles both at home and abroad in order to develop business cooperation.

The Export-Import Bank of China

Articles of Association

CHAPTER I GENERAL PROVISIONS

Article 1

The legal name of the bank is 'The Export-Import Bank of China', abbreviated to 'China Eximbank'.

Article 2

The Export-Import Bank of China, under the direct leadership of the State Council, is a policy-oriented financial institution. It adopts the principles of independent, break-even operation and management as a business enterprise. Its financial business shall be subject to the direction and supervision of the Ministry of Finance, the Ministry of Foreign Trade and Economic Cooperation and the People's Bank of China.

Article 3

The Export-Import Bank of China mainly provides policy-oriented financial support for the export and import of capital goods such as mechanical and electronic products and complete sets of equipment.

Article 4

The head office of the Export-Import Bank of China is located in Beijing.

Article 5

The registered capital of the Export-Import Bank of China is RMB3.38 billion.

CHAPTER II SCOPE OF BUSINESS

Article 6

The main business of the Export-Import Bank of China is as follows:

1. providing export and import credit, including seller's credit and buyer's credit, for the export and import of capital goods such as mechanical and electronic products and complete sets of equipment;
2. on-lending foreign government loans, mixed credits, and export credits in connection with the export of mechanical and electronic products; extending government loans and mixed credits from the Chinese government to foreign countries;
3. engaging in international interbank loans, organizing and participating in domestic and international syndicated loans;
4. providing export credit insurance, export credit guarantees, import and export insurance and factoring service;
5. issuing financial bonds at home and negotiable securities abroad (excluding stocks);
6. undertaking foreign exchange business authorized by the relevant Chinese authorities;
7. representing China in international organizations of export and import banks, policy-oriented financial institutions and insurance providers;
8. providing advisory services in export and import business, project evaluation, and services in foreign economic and technological cooperation;
9. undertaking any other business approved and entrusted to by the relevant Chinese authorities.

CHAPTER III ORGANIZATION

Article 7

There shall be a Board of Directors of the Export-Import Bank of China. The President of the bank shall be responsible for its overall management under the leadership of the Board of Directors. The President of the bank shall be its legal representative.

Article 8

The Board of Directors of the Export-Import Bank of China shall be the bank's supreme decision-making body, and it shall be directly responsible to the State Council; the Board of Directors shall consist of a Chairman, two Vice-Chairmen and a number of Directors. The Chairman and Vice-Chairmen shall be appointed by the State Council, while Directors shall be nominated by the relevant ministries and commissions and approved by the State Council.

Article 9

The main functions of the Board of Directors are as follows:

1. to examine and determine the bank's long- and medium-term development programmes, operation policies and annual plans in accordance with the industrial policy and foreign trade policy of China;
2. to review and evaluate the President's reports on the bank's operations, and to supervise the bank's financial and accounting status and the efforts for maintaining and increasing the value of state-owned assets;
3. to examine and approve the bank's budget, financial statements and after-tax profit distribution scheme;
4. to discuss and decide on important issues concerning national policy for export credit, export credit guarantee and credit risks;
5. to consider and determine the establishment and removal of the bank's internal departments and the adjustment of their functions;
6. to examine and determine the important rules and regulations of financial management;
7. to examine the bank's policies and procedures with respect to personnel management and other important issues.

Article 10

Meetings of the Board of Directors of the Export-Import Bank of China shall be held regularly. Should any important issue arise, an interim meeting shall be convened. Board meetings shall be convened and presided over by the Chairman. Should the Chairman be absent from the meeting, he shall entrust one of the Vice-Chairmen to call and chair the meeting.

A Board meeting requires a quorum of over two-thirds of the directors. Resolutions of the Board meetings require adoption by over 50 per cent of the directors.

Article 11

There shall be a President and several Vice-Presidents of the Export-Import Bank of China, who shall be appointed by the State Council. Other personnel shall be appointed or dismissed according to the bank's rules and procedures.

Article 12

The President of the Export-Import Bank of China shall be responsible for the overall business management of the Bank. The Vice-Presidents shall assist the President in his duties according to division of responsibility. The specific functions of the functions of the President are as follows:

1. managing the overall operation of the bank;
2. implementing the resolutions of the Board of Directors;
3. reporting regularly to the Board of Directors on his work;
4. overseeing the formulation of the bank's development programme, management policies and annual business plan;
5. overseeing the formulation of the bank's budget, financial statements and after-tax profit distribution scheme;
6. overseeing the development of the bank's policies and procedures with respect to personnel management and financial management;
7. organizing and designing the bank's programmes for the establishment and discontinuation of its internal departments and adjustment of their functions;
8. other duties designated by the Board of Directors.

CHAPTER IV BUSINESS MANAGEMENT, FINANCIAL ACCOUNTING AND SUPERVISION

Article 13

The Export-Import Bank of China shall adopt the principles of independent accounting, and management as a business enterprise. It shall pay taxes in accordance with laws of China.

Article 14

The Export-Import Bank of China shall formulate the bank's detailed rules and regulations regarding its own financial management and accounting practices in accordance with the 'Accounting Law of the People's Republic of China', 'Standard Accounting Rules for Enterprises', 'General Provisions for Business Financing' and relevant financial and accounting rules of banking and insurance enterprises promulgated by the Ministry of Finance.

Article 15

The Export-Import Bank of China shall submit the bank's financial statements to the relevant government authorities, and subject itself to the supervision of the Ministry of Finance and the State Administration of Auditing.

Article 16

The Export-Import Bank of China shall establish an internal auditing system, which will govern the auditing of the bank's financial revenues and expenditures under the leadership of the bank's President.

Article 17

The Export-Import Bank of China shall be entitled to make decisions regarding the recruitment and dismissal of the bank's staff in accordance with relevant regulations and laws of China.

Article 18

The Export-Import Bank of China shall determine the compensation policies for its staff on the basis of the salary system for banking staff promulgated by the State Council, as well as in accordance with the relevant laws and policies of China.

CHAPTER V SUPPLEMENTARY ARTICLES

Article 19

The right to interpret these Articles of Association is vested in the Export-Import Bank of China.

Article 20

These Articles of Association shall come into force upon approval by the State Council.

Courtesy of the Export-Import Bank of China: www.eximbank. gov.cn/eximbank/english

China's Securities Market[1]

China Securities Regulatory Commission, with updates by Jonathan Reuvid

The current status of China's securities industry

China's securities market has evolved and developed gradually alongside the progress of China's opening up and economic reform. With the establishment of the Shanghai Stock Exchange in December 1990 and the Shenzhen Stock Exchange in June 1991, China's securities market has formally taken shape. In more than 10 years of development, the securities industry has experienced a process of transition from virtually nothing to its present scale, from decentralization to centralization, from manual operation to the adoption of modern technologies, from a regional to a national market and from a domestically oriented to an internationally integrated market. Remarkable progress has been achieved in both the size of the market and the trading technology. China's securities market is now the third largest in Asia after Tokyo and Hong Kong and has formed a market structure that comprises A-share, B-share, H-share and a multitude of other financing options, which have played a vitally important role in improving financing structures, optimizing resource allocations and propelling economic development.

By the end of June 2002, 1,188 companies were listed on the Shanghai and Shenzhen stock exchanges with a total market capitalization and float capitalization of RMB4.77 trillion and RMB1.56 trillion respectively. The number of investor accounts totalled RMB68.07 million. There were 51 close-ended contractual securities investment funds and five open-ended securities investment funds, with a total funding of about RMB100 billion. The futures market has reversed the continued downturn of the past few years and begun to gather momentum for growth. In terms of securities trading technology, paperless systems have been applied to the issuance and trading of shares and funds, and all securities trading agencies have started to implement uniform technical standards.

While the securities market is developing rapidly, the securities regulatory mechanism is also gradually being perfected. Initially, the regulation and supervision of the securities market was dispersed among a number of central government departments such as the State Planning Commission (now the State Development Planning Commission), the Ministry of Finance and State Commission for the Restructuring of the Economic Structure (now the Office for Restructuring the Economy), and local government. A dual regulatory system evolved later, with the Securities Commission of the State Council being responsible for macro control and the China Securities Regulatory Commission (CSRC) exercising specific regulatory functions. The promulgation of the Securities Law in December 1998 firmly established China's securities regulatory regime with centralized and unified regulation and supervision of the securities market in the country by CSRC at the core, supported by self-disciplinary regulation by the stock exchanges and Securities Industry Association.

CSRC is an agency directly affiliated with the State Council. Within it are 13 functional departments and three subordinate institutions. CSRC is also represented

---

[1] This chapter was originally written in Chinese and was translated by Li Yong.

regionally by nine securities regulatory offices, two offices directly affiliated with it and 25 special commissioner offices of securities regulation and supervision in key cities in China (see Figure 7.4.1). Self-regulating organizations in the industry include China Securities Industry Association, Shanghai and Shenzhen stock exchanges, China Association of Futures Industry and the commodity exchanges in Shanghai, Dalian and Zhengzhou. These organizations conduct self-regulation and supervision in accordance with relevant industry regulations. In a newly developing market such as China, the role of self-regulating organizations is still weak because of the immature market mechanism. With improvements in this and the levels of regulation and supervision, many regulatory and supervisory functions will gradually be transferred from the CSRC to self-regulating organizations.

The legal framework regarding the securities market is still in development. Under the principle of 'rule of law, regulation and supervision, self-discipline and standardization', a legal framework of laws and regulations governing the securities market has taken shape. The core of this is the Corporations Law and Securities Law, supplemented by administrative regulations, and the key body is the departmental regulations and normative circulars, rules established by the stock exchanges and the rules and regulations introduced by self-regulating organizations such as the Securities Industry Association.

The Corporations Law and Securities Law are the two basic laws governing China's securities market. The administrative regulations by the State Council either fill in the legislative blanks in related areas or provide specific details on related legal regimes. The departmental regulations and normative circulars issued by the CSRC in accordance with relevant laws and administrative regulations are to provide particulars and supplements on relevant laws and regulations, thereby constituting the important elements of China's legal system governing the securities market.

Following China's accession to the WTO, the CSRC has rectified and amended all regulations and administrative approval procedures in order to comply with the commitments China has made in relation to the securities industry. Some new rules have been promulgated, such as the Rules for the Establishment of Securities Companies with Foreign Equity Participation and the Rules for the Establishment of Fund Management Companies with Foreign Equity Participation. At the same time, both Shanghai and Shenzhen stock exchanges are revising their rules of management on memberships and on B-share trading seats, in compliance with China's WTO commitments.

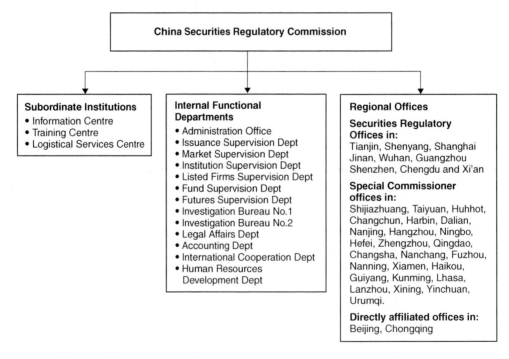

Figure 7.4.1 Breakdown of departments within the CSRC

New dynamics faced by China following WTO accession

On 11 December 2001, China officially joined the WTO. This marked a new phase in the opening up of the securities industry.

The main elements of China's opening up of the securities industry are the following:

1. Foreign securities institutions may engage directly (without a Chinese intermediary) in B-share business.
2. Upon accession, representative offices of foreign securities institutions in China may become Special Members of all Chinese stock exchanges.
3. Upon accession, foreign service suppliers will be permitted to establish joint ventures with foreign investment of up to 33 per cent participation to conduct domestic securities investment fund management business. Within three years of accession, the foreign investment participation limit will be increased to 49 per cent.
4. Within three years of accession, foreign securities institutions will be permitted to establish joint ventures, with foreign minority ownership not exceeding one third, to engage (without a Chinese intermediary) in underwriting A shares and in underwriting and trading of B and H shares as well as government and corporate debts and launching of funds.

Joining the WTO is necessary for the promotion of the sustained and healthy development of China's economy. It is an important milestone, marking China's entry into a new phase of opening up and has also offered an opportunity of historic significance for the long-term and normal development of China's securities industry and market. Firstly, following WTO accession, China's economy will be integrated into the world economic system; WTO membership will also provide new momentum for economic development, facilitating rapid economic growth, which will, in turn, yield a better development of China's securities industry. Secondly, the opening up of insurance and banking industries will attract foreign investors to China, as a result of which there will be expanded sources of market funds, and fund availability will be better than before. Thirdly, more intermediaries will come from mature markets to join China's securities industry. This will be conducive to adjusting the investor structure and elevating the professional level of securities agencies. Finally, participation in international competition will impel publicly listed companies to enhance the quality of their corporate performance and level of corporate governance.

While the securities industry has many opportunities, WTO accession has also brought great challenges. The first challenge is that the entry of foreign securities institutions will generate new tasks for China's securities regulation and supervision. International political and economic factors will have an increased impact on China's financial market, which will consequently increase the level of difficulty in regulating and supervising the securities market and therefore in handling possible crises.

The second challenge results from the great gap that has existed between Chinese securities institutions and their foreign counterparts in terms of size of capital, level of corporate governance and risk control. Although foreign securities institutions can only enter China's securities market in the form of joint ventures at present, their direct entry into the securities market will inevitably become a reality with the acceleration of the opening up process. If domestic securities institutions are not able to mature quickly, they will eventually be eliminated by the market.

The third challenge is that domestic listed companies will be subject to the ordeal of the law of the market – survival of the fittest – when competing with international giants on the same stage. The performances of the listed companies will polarize and there are likely to be large annual fluctuations. Last but not least, China's securities market needs to converge with international practices, which will require major reforms in an effort to improve market transparency and crack down on illegal conduct. The process of reform is in itself a great challenge for China's securities industry.

Future development trends

The sustained development of China's economy has motivated a demand for financing by a large number of enterprises. Such demand alone will require that the capital market continues to maintain its trend of rapid development. At the same time, China's savings rate has been high, and significant funds need to find diversified channels of investment. From the perspectives of both supply and demand, there will be greater development space for China's capital market, manifested specifically in the following:

1. There is still considerable room for the stock issuance market to develop. Stable growth of China's economy will increase enterprises' demands for financing, which will give impetus to the prosperity of the A-share market. With China's accelerating process of opening up and in order to meet the needs of foreign-invested enterprises (FIEs) for financing in China, CSRC has promulgated rules and regulations in relation to the financing of FIEs on the stock market in China. The issuance of shares and public listing of FIEs on the stock market has now entered the stage of actual operation, as a result of which China's securities market will quickly expand.

2. The general quality of publicly listed companies will improve. The CSRC will step up regulation and supervision of all publicly listed companies. This effort is, first, to improve the corporate governance structure of listed companies and guide them to establish modern enterprise systems. Second, the CSRC will push forward the improvement of accounting standards and information disclosure in order to make them converge gradually with international accounting standards and international practices. Third, China has implemented a classified system of regulation and supervision according to the quality of the publicly listed companies. The system has clarified the responsibilities of regulation and supervision, thereby forming a coordinating mechanism between the audit of share issuance and the regulation and supervision of listed companies. Finally, systems of appointing independent directors and delisting companies have been implemented. All these measures will help to improve the general quality and competitiveness of listed companies.

3. Institutional investors will increase. The outline tenth five-year plan for the national economy has expressly pointed out that active effort will be made between 2001 and 2005 to foster institutional investors such as securities investment funds, pension funds and insurance funds. At present, insurance funds can enter the securities market indirectly by purchasing securities investment funds. Pension funds, on the other hand, are taking on an increasingly important role and will in the future become the largest institutional investors in the capital market. At the same time, the entry of foreign institutional investors will play a positive role in terms of facilitating capital inflow, introducing technology and management expertise and

strengthening both cooperation and competition, all of which will be conducive to enhancing the level of maturity of China's securities market.

4. There will be diversified trading products available at the stock market. In recent years, China's funds and bonds markets have developed rapidly. T-bonds, corporate bonds and transferable bonds will expand further in terms of the size of issues, which will offer the investors more investment options. After WTO accession, the competitive advantages of foreign investors in the aspects of business competence, market experiences, risk management and fund size will correspondingly pose advance requirements for financial products on the securities market and prompt further diversity of trading products. With the increase in the depth and width of China's securities market, a pattern will develop characterized by domination of stock markets, rapid development of bonds and funds and further trials on financial derivatives.

5. Market transparency will increase further. With improvement of accounting rules and information disclosure standards, the authenticity and reliability of corporate financial and accounting information, as well as the transparency of corporate operations, will be further enhanced. The principle of transparency in WTO rules also requires that regulatory bodies change their conception of regulation and supervision, reduce the items subject to examination and approval and simplify examination and approval procedures so that the formulation and implementation of laws and regulations conforms with international practices and is transparent. All of these will help increase market transparency, enhance the predictability and procedural guarantee of policies and regulations, heighten public credibility and strengthen investor confidence.

Under the conditions of rapid and sustained development of China's macro economy and accompanied by enhancement of the level of securities regulation and supervision, gradual improvement of securities laws and regulations, the increasing importance given to the protection of investors' interests and the maturity of equity culture, China's securities industry will follow the liberalization, globalization and securitization trends of the international financial market. China's securities market will be more open, fair, efficient and orderly.

Recent developments in China's securities markets – J Reuvid

In a February 2004 announcement the State Council foreshadowed the strengthening of institutional investors through increasing financial channels for securities companies, which had suffered heavy losses during the period of falling investor confidence since mid-2001. The government pledged itself to attract new sources of funds into securities markets, not least the ailing stock and corporate bond markets.

The announcement reflected a consensus among Chinese policy makers that a fresh approach was needed to the intractable problem of how best to unload the state-owned shares in listed companies in a fully 'market-oriented manner' without distorting the country's bourses further.

Approximately two-thirds of the shares in listed companies were still held by the government or state entities, and the overhang of their potential sale into the public market had been the primary factor in the two and a half year slump in prices before the market began to move upwards in November 2003. The problem surfaced mid-year in 2001, when the government started to raise money for its national pension fund by selling state shares.

The announcement also suggested that individual state-owned enterprises (SOEs) could be allowed to negotiate agreements with the existing holders of publicly traded shares for the gradual disposal of their shares in individual companies. The document also supports, in the longer term, the establishment of a 'second board' for start-up companies and consent for approved Chinese investors to invest local funds into overseas stock markets.

Also in February, the Dutch bank Ing decided to forego half of its US$100 million allotment in the Chinese government QFII scheme to allow foreign investors access to China's capital markets, as a result of the poor demand for its China investment projects. Other foreign banks, such as UBS which had invested US$600 million through QFII, had been more successful.

In October 2004 the applications of three foreign investment institutions – UBS, Citigroup and Nikko Asset Management – for an additional quota of US$200 million each in the Chinese stock and debt markets were approved by the State Administration of Foreign Exchange, effectively an increase of almost 30 per cent in the amount of foreign cash that can be invested in Chinese markets.

Also in October, the State Council gave approval, in principle, to foreign banks to set up separate asset management arms that can consolidate money from investors to buy and sell stocks.

Equities

The problem of China's A shares appears intractable. By October 2004, both the Shanghai and Shenzhen stock markets had each lost 6 per cent in dollar terms, a worse performance than all Asia-Pacific markets except for Thailand. Compared with June 2001, the Shanghai market has since lost nearly 40 per cent of its value, while the Shenzhen exchange has fallen almost 50 per cent. The immediate cause for the decline in 2004 has been the government's clampdown on fixed asset investment and the selective allocation of credit in order to cool economic growth, but the A-share market remains disadvantaged by the endemic shortcoming of its structure. Since 1992, some 1,300 or so companies have been granted a domestic listing, but most of these have been industrial mega-enterprises. The better Chinese state-owned enterprises at the forefront of the economy, such as the telecoms and oil groups, have gained listings in New York and Hong Kong (where their equity is known as 'H' shares).

In the meantime, successful, dynamic private companies still find it sometimes impossible to gain approval to list domestically.

In March 2004, the CSRC revealed that it was studying a range of options on how to close the B-share markets in Shanghai and Shenzhen without damaging the interests of listed companies and investors. In practice, the B-share markets have become redundant following the introduction in 2003 of a scheme where selected foreign institutions can buy domestic RMB-denominated A shares. Most foreign investors have avoided the B-share market since the 1997 Asian financial crisis because of thin liquidity and the generally poor quality of the listed companies, preferring instead to invest in China by trading in overseas listed companies, primarily in Hong Kong, where the quality of the companies is judged superior.

Nor has the Hong Kong stock market remained immune to the slowdown in IPO activity in 2004, since the active final quarter of 2003. As in other Asian markets, since mid-June several large companies have been forced to defer their Hong Kong listings through a combination of a weak market and the poor performance of some offerings. Those affected include the IPO of China Power International, one of the country's top five electricity generators, and chipmaker CSMC Technologies, which scrapped its offering after a negative investor response.

By contrast, China Netcom, the country's second largest fixed-line telecoms provider, raised US$1.4 billion in November 2004 from an IPO in Hong Kong and New York. Others awaiting regulatory approval for IPOs over

US$500 million are Air China and Shinhua Coal. The landmark IPO of China Construction Bank (US$5–10 billion) is scheduled for 2005.

The successful launch of China Wonder, the holding company for Jinzhou Packing Machinery Company, which services the Chinese pharmaceutical market, on the London AIM market in October 2004 marks the first in a series of planned offerings by CYC Holdings, itself an AIM-listed company of four years' standing. Although a minor issue, with a small free float, this forerunner for the flotation on AIM of other dynamic private Chinese companies outside the traditional smokestack industries provided welcome news.

Brokerage houses

The Chinese brokerage houses have experienced a traumatic year, which highlights the problems in China's domestic financial sector. In January 2004, the government bailed out Southern Securities by a takeover for a reported RMB8.5 billion (approximately US$1 billion), revealing a web of questionable practices, including stock manipulation and possible insider dealing. Previously, in 2003, regulators closed down another firm, Dalian Securities, for 'severe irregularities'; other firms were put under the management of larger firms for similar reasons. Then at the end of June 2004, China Securities, the main rival to Southern Securities and one of China's four biggest brokerages, revealed severe losses resulting in the replacement of its chairman and president by the Beijing authorities.

Since then the CSRC has moved swiftly to increase its efforts to clean up the industry by merging or closing down the worst-performing securities houses. Following a survey in September, the CSRC is reported to have classified 63 out of China's 132 brokerages as 'risky' within the four risk categories that it has established. One house in the 'highly risky' category, MF Securities, is to be taken over by China Orient, a state asset management group. Another bail-out arranged by the government with funds from Goldman Sachs is that of Hainan Securities.

While announcing in October 2004 that it will extend its bail-out programme to most small, individual investors in troubled brokerages, the government has also introduced measures to help well-managed brokerages. Starting in November 2004, approved securities houses may now increase their funding channels by issuing short-term debt securities in Shanghai. Following a speech by Vice-Premier Huang Ju in Shenzen at the beginning of November, the government is believed to be considering the injection of US$7.2 billion new capital into China

Securities Depository and Settlement Corp (CSDC), an arm of the CSRC that sets aside money paid to it by brokerages to guarantee daily trades in Shanghai and Shenzhen.

The Goldman Sachs donation of RMB510 million (US$61 million) to pay out the depositors of Hainan Securities was a part of the process to win approval for its establishment of an investment bank (see Chapter 8.4).

Futures

In October 2004, ABN Amro announced that it was close to completing a deal with China Galaxy Securities, the country's largest broker, that would make the Dutch bank the first foreign company to access China's futures market. The partnership is expected to take the form of a joint venture to trade futures from 2005. At present, China's three futures exchanges are restricted to trades in commodity futures, but regulators are considering the introduction of equity futures. Chinese companies' growing dependence on imported commodities led to a significant rise in trading volumes during 2004. Between January and August, the three exchanges together traded 314.36 million contracts for a total of RMB10,700 billion (US$1.3 billion), representing a year-over-year rise of 27 per cent. The Shanghai Futures Exchange is already the world's third largest in volume terms, with the Dalian exchange ranking sixth.

Fund management and bonds

To date there are 15 Sino-foreign joint ventures (JVs) in fund management, of which only a third involve US partners, according to a recent survey conducted jointly by The Economist Corporate Network and KPMG. Under WTO rules, foreigners were limited to taking 33 per cent of any mainland fund JV, but the permitted level increased to 49 per cent from the end of 2004. The survey found that there was a preference among Chinese fund houses seeking JV partners for European over US firms because they are less concerned about management control.

At the end of the third quarter of 2003, there were reported to be 34 licensed fund management companies in China managing 96 investment funds, including 54 closed-end funds listed on either the Shanghai or Shenzhen stock exchanges. At US$20 billion, the amount under management is small compared with the total assets of the banking and insurance sectors; however, it has doubled since 2001.

Having issued a US$1.5 billion bond in October 2003, China's Ministry of Finance let it be known in July

2004 that it was working on a further bond issue worth more than US$1 billion, with separate tranches to be denominated in US dollars and euros. In the event, the Euro tranche offered in October was €1 billion of 10-year notes with a coupon of 4.25 per cent against a US dollar tranche limited to US$500 million of five-year notes with a coupon of 3.75 per cent. European pension funds and banks were reported to have subscribed for more than €4 billion of the euro tranche, with only 3.5 per cent of the orders coming from Chinese institutions. More than 40 per cent of the euro portion was said to have been taken up by investors that had never before bought Asian debt.

The independent research house, Matrix, has forecast that funds under management in China will increase tenfold by 2020, to more than US$1,600 billion, based on the transfer of retail and industrial liquidity from dormant pools of savings to actively managed funds. Life insurance funds are predicted to account for US$750 billion of the projected US$1,610 billion total with mutual funds and pensions accounting for US$500 billion and US$360 billion respectively. Matrix also forecasts that there will be a further US$400 billion of unregulated funds in circulation in 2010.

Supplement to Chapter 7.4

List of key laws and regulations concerning development of the securities and futures industry (December 1993 to June 2001)

Laws (three items of legislation)

1. *Company Law of the People's Republic of China*, adopted by the 5th Session of the Standing Committee of the 8th National People's Congress on 29 December 1993, amended in accordance with the Decision Concerning Amending The Company Law of the People's Republic of China by the 13th Session of the Standing Committee of the 9th National People's Congress on 25 December 1999, promulgated by Order No. 29 of the President of the People's Republic of China on 25 December 1999.

2. *Securities Law of the People's Republic of China*, adopted at the 6th Meeting of the Standing Committee of the 9th National People's Congress of the People's Republic of China on 29 December 1998, promulgated by Order No. 12 of the President of the People's Republic of China on 29 December 1998.

3. *Trust Law of the People's Republic of China*, adopted at the 21st Session of the Standing Committee of the 9th National People's Congress, promulgated by Order No. 50 of the President of the People's Republic of China on 28 April 2001.

Administrative regulations (18 sets)

1. *Notice of the State Council on Further Strengthening of the Macro Administration of the Securities Market*, promulgated on 17 December 1992. Guo Fa [1992] No. 68

2. *Provisional Regulations for Administration of the Issuance and Trading of Shares*, promulgated by Order No. 112 of the State Council of the People's Republic of China on 22 April 1993.

3. *Rules on the Administration of Enterprise Bonds*, promulgated by Order No. 121 of the State Council of the People's Republic of China on 2 August 1993.

4. *Interim Measures on the Prevention of Securities Frauds*, approved by the State Council on 15 August 1993 and promulgated by the State Council Securities Committee on 2 September 1993.

5. *Special Regulations on Overseas Offering and Listing of Companies Limited by Shares*, promulgated by Order No. 160 of the State Council of the People's Republic of China on 4 August 1994.

6. *State Council Regulations on Domestic Listing of Foreign Shares by Companies Limited by Shares*, adopted at the 37th Standing Conference of the State Council and promulgated by Order No. 189 of the State Council of the People's Republic of China on 25 December 1995.

7. *Interim Measures on the Administration of Convertible Corporate Bonds*, approved by the State Council and promulgated by the State Council Securities Committee on 25 March 1997.

8. *State Council Notice on Further Strengthening of the Administration of Overseas Shares Issuance and Public Offering*, promulgated on 20 June 1997, Gua Fa [1997] No. 21.

9. *Interim Measures on the Administration of Securities Investment Funds*, approved by the State Council on 5 November 1997 and promulgated by the State Council Securities Committee on 14 November 1997.

10. *Interim Measures on the Administration of Securities and Futures Investment Consultancy*, approved by the State Council on 30 November 1997 and promulgated by the State Council Securities Committee on 25 December 1997.

11. *Measures on Penalizing Illegal Financial Conducts*, promulgated by Order No. 260 of the State Council of the People's Republic of China on 22 February 1999.

12. *Provisional Rules on the Administration of Futures Trading*, promulgated by Order No. 267 of the State Council of the People's Republic of China on 2 June 1999.

13. *Rules of the Share Issuance Examination Committee of China Securities Regulatory Commission*, approved by the State Council on 19 August 1999 and promulgated by China Securities Regulatory Commission on 16 September 1999.

14. *Guidance for the Regulation, Supervision, Examination and Approval of the Applications by Domestic Enterprises for Listing on Hong Kong's Growth Enterprise Market*, approved by the State Council on 6 September 1999 and promulgated by China Securities Regulatory Commission on 21 September 1999.

15. *Interim Measures on the Administration of Venture Capital Funds of the Securities Exchanges*, approved by the State Council on 31 January 2000 and promulgated by China Securities Regulatory Commission and the Ministry of Finance on 4 April 2000.

16. *Interim Measures on the Administration of Securities Settlement of Venture Capital Funds*, approved by the State Council on 31 January 2000 and promulgated by China Securities Regulatory Commission and the Ministry of Finance on 4 April 2000.

17. *Procedures of Verification and Approval for Share Issuance*, approved by the State Council and promulgated by China Securities Regulatory Commission on 16 March 2000.

18. *Interim Measures on the Reduction of State-held Shares to Raise Social Security Funds*, promulgated on 6 June 2001, Guo Fa [2001] No. 22.

(Editor's note: The above list was provided by China Securities Regulatory Commission for Doing Business with China *(4th edition). There has been no official translation of the names of the laws and regulations, therefore they may vary in wording in other publications.)*

Mergers and Acquisitions: Acquiring a Business in China

Olivier Dubuis and Whui Min Chang, Attorney at Law, Adamas, China

The modernization of the Chinese legal system and the rapid integration of China in the global economy under the impulsion of the WTO agreements, the low level of industry concentration in China and the attractiveness of the Chinese market for multi-nationals as well as medium-size enterprises have contributed to create an environment favourable to the acquisition of domestic companies by foreign investors.

The legal regime

Company acquisitions are subject to different legal regimes, depending on the nature of the target – acquisition of equity interest in foreign-invested enterprises (FIEs); acquisition of equity interest in non-listed state-owned enterprises (SOEs); or acquisition of listed company shares.

Whereas the acquisition of equity interest in an FIE would be governed by the *'Changes in Equity Interest of Investors in FIEs Several Provisions'* promulgated by MOFTEC and SAIC on 28 May 1997 ('1997 Provisions'), acquisition of non-listed companies are regulated by the *'Tentative Provisions on Using Foreign Investment to Reorganize SO'* jointly promulgated by SETC, MOF, SAIC and SAFE on 8 November 2002 and effective as of 1 January 2003 ('2002 Provisions'), the *'Circular on Relevant Issues Regarding the Enhancement of Administration in the Examination and Approval, Registration, Foreign Exchange and Taxation of FIE'* jointly promulgated by MOFTEC, SAT, SAIC and SAFE on 30 December 2002 ('2002 Circular'), and the *'Provisional Regulations on Mergers and Acquisitions of Domestic Enterprises by Foreign Investors'* jointly promulgated by MOFTEC, SAT and SAFE on 7 March 2003 and effective as of 12 April 2003 ('2003 Regulations').

As for acquisitions in listed companies , they would be subject to the *'Measures for the Administration of Listed Companies Acquisition',* promulgated by CSRC on 28 September 2002 and effective as of 1 December 2002 ('2002 Measures'), and the *'Circular on State Shares and Legal Person Shares Transactions in Listed Companies with Foreign Investment',* promulgated by CSRC, MOF and SETC on 1 November 2002 ('2002 Circular').

Therefore, it is essential to first define the legal form of the target enterprise involved, its financial situation and the investment sector considered (encouraged, restricted, prohibited), as this will allow identification of the legal framework applicable to the acquisition project – FIE laws and regulations, SOE laws and regulations or listed companies laws and regulations, the approval process and authorities (MOFCOM (national level) or COFTEC (local level) and the possible involvement of other administrative authorities at local or central level.

Due diligence

Due diligence is the process of information gathering on a potential business acquisition. Good due diligence targets and evaluates the potential risks in an acquisition decision. In China, there are significant structural difficulties in information gathering, so it is crucial to work with a multi-disciplinary team, knowledgeable of the Chinese market and constraints specific to Chinese companies.

A thorough due diligence requires a complete understanding of the political, cultural and legal environment of the target, its industry and its environment. In addition to verifying the corporate ownership and financial documents, due diligence will address issues such as land and building use rights, labour and human resources, taxes, intellectual property and environmental compliance. (Chapter 7.6 examines the issues of due diligence in mergers and acquisitions in detail).

Structuring the deal

Mergers and acquisitions can be structured on an equity basis or an asset basis. Both these types of transactions can be conducted onshore (in China) or offshore (outside of China). The choice of structure and location affects the rights and liabilities transferred as well as the level of administrative approval and oversight required.

Equity versus asset basis

In an equity acquisition, the foreign investor purchases an equity stake in a non-foreign-invested enterprise in China (domestic company) by agreement, or subscribes to the capital increase of a domestic company, so as to convert and re-establish the domestic company as an FIE. The FIE established upon merger and acquisition shall succeed to the claims and debts of the target domestic company to the proportion of its equity holding.

In an asset acquisition, the FIE can either purchase the assets of an existing domestic enterprise with capital injected by the foreign investor and operate them in the name of the FIE, or the foreign investor can directly purchase the assets of the domestic enterprise and then invest these assets as registered capital in the FIE. The FIE established upon merger and acquisition shall succeed to assets purchased but not the claims and debts of the target domestic company. The main advantage is to be able to choose the assets to be acquired, but leaving those that are not essential to the operation of the business.

While the resulting net investment is the same, the second scenario can be structured to better protect against hidden liabilities and to minimize the foreign investor's total liquid assets contribution.

Onshore versus offshore transactions

Onshore

Purchasing a business onshore allows for the most direct, 'hands on' control of the acquired business. The business structure is more transparent. In addition, there are certain tax advantages for existing investors (refund on income taxes paid for profits from an existing FIE reinvested in another FIE). However, it is necessary to obtain approval from the authorities that originally approved the FIE, and this can be a time-consuming and costly process, adding more requirements (in the case of a state-owned assets acquisition) and variables – for example, unanimous approval of the board is required.

Offshore

When such a possibility exists, one of the simplest ways to structure a China acquisition is to do it offshore, that is, to acquire the shares of a company located outside of China (often Hong Kong, British Virgin Islands, etc) that holds a stake in an onshore company.

An offshore transaction has fewer Chinese approval requirements, and the resulting company can be easier to sell at a later date (a more lucrative exit strategy). Furthermore, under certain circumstances, the offshore company may also be listed offshore in order to use the shares as security.

It may also occur that an offshore company holds more than one company in its portfolio and, as such, it may be necessary to restructure the offshore company prior to acquisition or to acquire other companies held by the offshore vehicle, which may not contribute to the overall strategy of the acquiring company.

Valuation issues

In cases where state-owned assets are involved, a valuation process will be undertaken prior to the transaction. Such a procedure is applicable to any restructuring, assets transfer or equity transfer operation in relation to state-owned assets, and is conducted under specific rules and supervision of relevant administrative departments. However, the state-owned assets valuation procedures have been somewhat softened. The state-owned asset holder is not bound by the valuation results provided that he or she can explain (in writing) any difference between the valuation results and the final transaction price.

However, it must be noted that under the applicable valuation methods (actualized value of future income for equipment, replacement costs for the premises, market value for the land and liquidation value for the inventory), important differences may appear between the intended transaction price based on market value and the price retained pursuant to official valuation. It is therefore essential for the acquirer to closely follow and monitor the official valuation process.

Until the issuance of the 2003 Regulations, a transaction was not subject to any appraisal requirements when it did not involve state-owned assets. In fact, it was newly stated in the 2003 Regulations that the transaction prices of all acquisitions 'should be determined on the basis of the appraisal given by the asset appraisal institution'. This seems to provide a possibility for the approval authority to challenge the price of any acquisition that would not have gone through official appraisal procedure, regardless of whether state-owned assets are involved.

Taxes

A properly structured deal can offer tax advantages for both the buyer and the seller. Careful planning can allow the parties to maximize the net tax savings.

Among the seller's tax objectives are reduction of capital gains tax, making use of capital losses, and reduction of indirect taxation. For the buyer, the advantages include avoiding past tax liabilities, increasing depreciation value, use of tax loss carry forwards (five-year limit), reduction of withholding taxes on repatriation, reduction of capital gains tax upon exit.

If the purchase is paid for from the dividends paid to the buyer from another Chinese FIE, the buyer is entitled to a partial refund of up to half of the income taxes paid on the reinvested amount.

Share deal

A deal that takes place wholly offshore should not trigger any PRC tax liability. For onshore share deals, there is no appreciation of assets for depreciation purposes.

Payable
A Chinese seller pays enterprise income tax (generally 33 per cent) on capital gains. A foreign seller pays 10 per cent withholding tax on gross gain. Stamp duty of 0.05 per cent is payable; no business tax or VAT is due.

Holidays
If the foreign investor holds at least 25 per cent of the post-merger entity, it may enjoy preferential tax holidays available to FIEs.

Losses
A capital loss is only recognized if held by another Chinese company. The foreign seller loses any capital loss recognition. The buyer enjoys continuation of tax loss carry forwards.

Customs
No major customs issues are triggered.

Asset deal

Because asset transfers can be taxable in the PRC, the cost-benefits need to be closely scrutinized.

Payable
Gains or losses from transfer of assets must be realized in the taxable income of the seller. A Chinese seller will pay corporate income tax on profits (30 per cent) with the right to set off losses, stamp duty of 0.05 per cent on the transaction, land value appreciation tax on any gain (in practice, rarely levied). Business tax will be levied on the sale of real property and intangible assets; VAT will be levied on the sale of stock inventory. The buyer must pay the VAT on the transfer, but this 'input VAT' can be offset from 'output VAT' collected on the subsequent sale of the stock. There is no tax on the transfer of used equipment and machinery if there are no capital gains.

Holiday
There is a possibility of a fresh tax holiday.

Losses
Any tax loss carried forward disappears.

Customs
There is a claw-back (recapture) of import duty and import VAT if a disposal of tax/duty free imported equipment takes place within the five-year customs supervision period.

Approvals and consents

If the transaction is conducted offshore, the PRC authorities would have no jurisdiction over the transaction, except for the antitrust review as described hereafter. Approvals are therefore mainly required in the case of a direct onshore acquisition.

In the case of a direct onshore acquisition, the approval authority is the authority competent to approve newly established FIEs, depending on the level of investment and the category of investment. Usually, MOFCOM (Ministry of Commerce) and its relevant local branches and SAIC (State Industry of Industry and Commerce) and its local counterparts have jurisdiction for the approval and registration of FIEs established through the acquisition of domestic companies.

In the case of an equity acquisition, parties are required to submit an equity transfer agreement, new articles of association of the company, the joint venture contract or shareholder's agreement if a joint venture is formed, the unanimous board resolution of the target company and a valuation report in case of transactions involving state-owned assets.

Additional consents may be necessary for asset acquisition (for example, customs approvals) and special care should be taken in assessing all regulatory consents necessary to properly effectuate the transaction.

Apart from these necessary approvals, the acquirer needs to pay special attention to some consents that need to be obtained from the target company, such as consents and waivers (pre-emptive rights) from other shareholders of the target company, board approval, approval from employees (when a state-owned enterprise is involved, a social restructuring plan needs to be drafted and approved) and public announcements to creditors in cases of asset transfer.

Closing – payment for the approved purchase

If a foreign investor establishes an FIE upon acquisition of a domestic enterprise, the foreign investor shall, within three months of the date of issue of the business licence of the FIE, pay the full consideration to the shareholder that transfers his equity interest or the domestic enterprise that sells the assets. Earnings shall be distributed in accordance with the ratio of capital contribution actually paid up.

Equity acquisition

In an equity acquisition by foreign investors, if there is to be an increase in the capital of the FIE established upon merger and acquisition, the investors shall stipulate the time limit for capital contribution in the contract and the articles of association of the FIE established upon the conversion. If it is stipulated that the capital contribution shall be made in one lump sum, the investors shall pay capital contribution in full within six months of the date of issue of the business licence of the foreign-invested enterprise. If it is stipulated that the capital contribution shall be made in instalments, the first instalment of capital contribution of each investor may not be less than 15 per

cent of the amount to which it subscribes, and the contribution shall be paid in full within three months of the date of issue of the business licence of the FIE.

Asset acquisition

In an asset acquisition by foreign investors, the investors shall stipulate the time limit for capital contribution in the contract and the articles of association of the FIE to be established. If an FIE is established to purchase by agreement the assets of a domestic enterprise and to operate such assets, the investors shall pay the portion of the capital contribution that equals the amount of the consideration for such assets within the time limit for payment of consideration specified in the first paragraph of this section of the chapter, and the time limit for paying the rest of the capital contribution shall be agreed upon in the format specified in the second paragraph of this section.

Antitrust review

Scope of application

The Chinese texts are applicable to both equity and assets mergers and acquisitions, whether these transactions occur onshore or offshore.

Thresholds for notification

The thresholds for notification are relatively low compared with thresholds in the west. This causes a backlog of approval examinations with the competent authorities. The resulting time commitment and high investment costs can prove to be a serious impediment to a deal.

As under western law, the acquiring investor bears the responsibility of notifying the competent authorities when a potential transaction meets the relevant thresholds; however, the Chinese laws are silent on the consequences of non-notification.

Onshore thresholds
Where any party[1] to the offshore merger has:

- turnover in the Chinese market for the current year greater than RMB1.5 billion;
- current market share in China of 20 per cent or more;

---

[1] A party to the merger and acquisition referred to above includes the affiliated enterprises of foreign investors.

- post acquisition market share in China of party of 25 per cent or more;
- total number of enterprises merged and acquired within one year exceeding 10 in any relevant industry in China.

Where these criteria are not fulfilled, the foreign investor may still be required to provide a report if so requested by the competing domestic enterprises, the relevant functional departments or industry associations and, if in the opinion of MOFCOM or the SAIC a tremendous market share is involved in the merger and acquisition by foreign investors, or where other important factors exist such as serious effects on market competition or the national economy, people's livelihood and national economic security exist.

Procedure

Where a merger with and acquisition of a domestic enterprise by a foreign investor is considered by MOFCOM and the SAIC to result in potentially excessive concentration, obstruction to fair competition or harm to the interests of consumers, MOFCOM and the SAIC shall, within 90 days of the date of receipt of all the documents required, jointly or separately call a hearing to approve or disapprove the transaction according to law.

Offshore thresholds[2]

Where any party[3] to the offshore merger has:

- assets in China of more than RMB3 billion;
- turnover in the Chinese market for the current year greater than RMB1.5 billion;
- current market share in China of 20 per cent or more;
- post acquisition market share in China of the party reaches 25 per cent or more;

- total number of FIE exceeding 15 in any relevant industry in China where the party has an equity interest.

In theory, only if the threshold is met is notification required for an offshore transaction. In practice, if a change in ownership below this threshold comes to the attention of PRC authorities, a quasi-approval process or alterations to project documentation may be required.

Procedure

Where the threshold is met, the parties submit the proposal to MOFCOM and SAIC before the proposal is announced to the public or when it is submitted to the competent authority of the country where the parties are located. MOFCOM and the SAIC shall examine whether the merger and acquisition will result in excessive concentration in the domestic market, obstruction to fair competition in China or harm to the interests of domestic consumers, and shall decide whether or not to consent to the merger and acquisition. There is significant ambiguity as to due process and legal recourse 'in accordance with laws' and there are no quantified standards or specific provisions for a hearing.

Exceptions

Certain transactions that may enhance the fair competition conditions of the market, restructure failing enterprises and safeguard employment, introduce advanced technology and management personnel, enhance the competitiveness of the enterprise in the international market, or improve environmental conditions are exempt from substantive review. Any party to the merger or acquisition may apply to MOFCOM and SAIC for exemption of examination.

---

[2] For comparison: Thresholds in US and Europe
In the US:
Thresholds under the US H-S-R Act:
US$200 million of voting securities and/or assets of the acquired party to be held by the acquiring party after the transaction; or
US$50 million of voting securities and/or assets of the acquired to be held by the acquiring party after the transaction (the size-of-the-transaction test) and the sizes of the parties over US$100 million and US$10 million respectively (the size-of-the-person test).
Under the EU Merger Regulations:
Aggregate world-wide turnover of the parties over €5,000 million (US$6,100 million) and EU turnover of each party over €250 million (US$305 million), with exceptions.
[3] A party to the merger and acquisition referred to above includes the affiliated enterprises of foreign investors.

Mergers and Acquisitions Due Diligence

Olivier Dubuis and Whui Min Chang, Attorney at Law Adamas, China

China became the leading nation attracting the most foreign direct investment (FDI), surpassing the US in 2002 for the first time. While the vast majority of FDI flows into the creation of wholly owned foreign enterprises (WOFE) or joint ventures, mergers and acquisitions (M&A) account for an increasing minority of FDI in China.

In any M&A deal, whether a potential purchase is an asset acquisition or a share acquisition, it is necessary to take steps to ensure that the 'on paper' description of the target company corresponds to reality.

In an international deal, language and cultural barriers often complicate matters. As for China, it also presents a plethora of China-specific issues, often related to the sometimes totally foreign method of conducting business.

What is due diligence?

Due diligence is the discovery procedure before the buying decision. It is the process of information gathering on a potential business acquisition in order to analyze, as thoroughly as possible, issues that can be deal breakers.

Due diligence is far more comprehensive than a single audit. It looks not only at accuracy and validity of the documentation, but also defines past trends, future prospects and sustainability. Good due diligence targets and evaluates the potential risks in an acquisition decision. A thorough due diligence requires a comprehensive understanding of the political, cultural, and legal environment of the target, its industry, and its environment.

Whether the seller is a large state-owned corporation or a privately-held company, quality due diligence involves more than publicly available information. It goes behind the numbers presented in the financial statements to examine the core operations of the company, to see whether the big picture displayed in the financial statements and the legal documents, permits and licences appear to be true, and whether it is sustainable. Only by understanding social and markets factors of *how* the target reached its current position, can one begin to analyze *where* a target can go from there and how to monitor and control the investment.

Who does what?

The informed buyer will work with a multi-disciplinary team, knowledgeable on the Chinese market and constraints specific to the Chinese companies.

The internal buyer team is composed of key people from the finance, legal, commercial, technical and HR departments, as well as the individuals who will be in charge of post-acquisition integration or management.

The external team is comprised of outside specialists in the legal, financial, environmental and human resources fields. These individuals must have not only a thorough knowledge of the Chinese market, but the capacity and the experience of working together in multi-disciplinary teams.

While the specialties of the professionals may be diverse, in China their work must not be partitioned too precisely. In light of the difficulty in obtaining reliable information and specifics, good, frequent communication between the various participants is essential to gathering sufficient information and fact patterns to form a comprehensive evaluation of the target company.

China-specific due diligence issues

In China, the historical documents are often sketchy. Company documents may not reflect the current activities; for example, a certificate of approval or business licence issued to a former officer, corporate articles with outdated business scope or leases in the name of other entities. Furthermore, buyers are often presented with incomplete financial operational documents (tax returns, quarterly reports, tax filings, annual reports, balance sheets with off balance sheet transactions).

Information gathering is further complicated by the fact that interviews with regulatory resources often yield few tangible facts, especially when dealing with a state-owned enterprise. Third party database searches (Hoover's, Compass, Lexis, and the different credit ratings companies), as well as regulatory or agency files, often yield little or no information.

Faced with this lack of formal information, due diligence in China starts and ends on the physical premises. Given the difficulty of obtaining precise information, it is essential to obtain the participation of management of the target company and have them accept the concept of due diligence.

But the process of communicating with the Chinese company is complicated by the fact that technical or sensitive information must be obtained from various departments who may not even be aware of the proposed transaction. The complexity is further compounded by the fact that the majority of information that the buyer will seek to obtain could be regarded as 'secret' by the target company, especially for state-owned companies, where the information may even be classified as 'state secret'.

Therefore, it is important to explain the buyer's expectations to the Chinese company from the beginning, starting with the negotiation of the letter of intent. The Chinese company needs to understand:

- the importance of the due diligence process;
- the type of information that the buyer wishes to obtain;
- the need for a dedicated team within the target company to obtain and transmit to the buyer's advisers during the process of due diligence;
- the universal character of the due diligence process in the phases of acquisition;
- the limitation of the due diligence to the information necessary for the buyer to make a decision;

- the possible reciprocity of the mechanism (offering to the Chinese partner the opportunity to obtain some information on the buyer – this is seldom accepted);
- the obligations of confidentiality applicable to the information obtained during the due diligence process.

This preliminary negotiation stage can last from several weeks to several months. The foundations built during this stage will need to be strengthened through the due diligence process. When detailed lists of requested information are presented to the target company, it is advisable to explain this to the Chinese parties point by point. When the local managers do not understand what is expected of them, the potential buyer ends up translating and studying hundreds of irrelevant documents, thus wasting valuable resources.

Like a good roadmap, pre-due diligence groundwork and communication facilitate the process immensely. At every stage of the process, quality communication with the target company is an essential factor to future success.

Structural issues

The power of *guanxi*

In China, business decisions are often based more on long-standing ties than cold, hard economics. Most of these ties are unstated. The Chinese automatically operate within these parameters, and thus it is vital that these unwritten and unexplained parameters be factored into any investment decision.

Unreliable public records

From a corporate documents point of view, a small change in activity can trigger a necessary change in business scope, licences or registrations. These changes are not always recorded accurately in publicly available registries and documents. The situation is exacerbated in China by the disadvantage of legislation falling behind economic development, and lack of corporate governance within the Chinese companies.

Weak financial record keeping

Foreign investors tend to appoint international accounting firms to audit under international accounting standards, or use the Generally Accepted Accounting Procedures (GAAP) of their home country as a reference basis for revaluation and negotiation. Investors should be wary of automatically assuming audited accounts are prepared to an international standard.

Many Chinese companies under-invest in their financial reporting systems. Primitive handwritten manual ledgers are often kept and, typically, the financial controller has little or no formal training. The bookkeeping system can be error prone and labour intensive.

The importance of auditors/advisers being knowledgeable of a region cannot be overemphasized. These advisers are more in tune with particular business practices in the specific region and are thus better equipped to look for commonly occurring issues.

Comprehensive information gathering by the actual decision-makers increases the likelihood of uncovering undisclosed transactions and allows for a more accurate evaluation of whether to engage and at what cost.

Non-sustainable historical earnings

The buyer should be concerned as to whether the audited financial statement truly reflects the actual operations and financial state of the business. This concern can arise from a lack of familiarity with Chinese GAAP and sensitivity towards the credit image a company may create among the local professional community. Differences in accounting policies need to be taken into consideration. China's locally accepted accounting practices vary substantially from IAS (the International Accounting Standard) and from US GAAP, in particularly with regard to revenue recognition, capitalization and off balance sheet financing policies (see Chapter 4.3 for detailed analysis of the differences).

Poor quality forecasting

In China, forecasts are rarely prepared on a regular basis. Chinese companies, especially those that are collective owned, have a more 'reactive' than 'prospective' way of conducting business. This opportunistic attitude of management leads to assumptions that may be internally inconsistent and difficult to reconcile with past results. It is common to see a 'hockey stick' forecast, where a recent period of declining results is followed by a 'blue sky' forecast for the future. Forecasts often focus exclusively on earnings, without consideration for opening net assets position or cash flow required to support the projected earnings. Often forecasts are limited in usefulness. Watch out in particular for forecast earnings-based valuation models.

Less formal approach to business transactions and agreements, opaque group structures, related party transactions

Many businesses in China, especially large state-owned enterprises, are run in an informal conglomerate setting, and there is often a commingling of business and assets used across several business entities. In a situation where only a portion of a company is sold, it is common to find that certain infrastructure services, crucial to the continued operation of a company, have not been charged to the seller at all. It often occurs that there are assets without a business purpose on the books. More worryingly, certain assets used by the business may not show up at all on the books because they are held by the owner personally or by a third party. In addition to accounting for ownership and valuation of the key business assets, write-offs for aged receivables, obsolete inventory, idles assets, and inappropriate capitalized costs often need to be made.

Identifying all related party transactions in a business may not be simple, as it is not uncommon for key management to have undisclosed competing business interests. The importance of understanding the nature and scope of such transactions cannot be overemphasized. Commonly, such transactions are conducted under special pricing terms. It is often necessary to adjust these transactions to reflect normal commercial terms.

Land and buildings

Public records on legal title to properties are often unavailable or unreliable. Even where the documents are attainable, the person on the title and the company currently using the real property often appear to be unrelated.

Real property law in China varies from that of common law jurisdictions. Rather than the common law principle of fee simple, in China all land ownership is held by the government and, as such, land cannot be bought or sold. However, a land use right can be acquired.

The land use right is distinct from land ownership. While the land ownership remains at all times with the state, the corresponding land use right may be sold, transferred, leased or mortgaged, but only for a set period of time as set forth in the original rights grant documents.

A land use right may be acquired on the primary market (directly from the state) or on the secondary markets. Any acquirer of land in China must strictly adhere to the specific purpose outlined in the grant and may not arbitrarily develop the land outside the confines of the land use.

The State Land Administration Bureau has specific jurisdiction over land use in China. All land must be registered and recorded by it. The duration of the land use right depends upon the nature of the project to be undertaken.

There are three types of land use rights: collectively owned, allocated or granted. In each instance, it is necessary to verify the authority of the original grantor, the identity of the collective, allocator or grantor, and the stated purpose and scope of the transfer.

Labour/human resource issues

When performing due diligence on labour issues, it can be useful to speak to the Chinese Communist Party (CCP) representative within the company to find out their primary concerns.

Key questions to address include:

- Are labour practices in line with the law?
- Does the company abide by its overtime policy?
- Do all workers possess authorization to work?
- Have the necessary contributions been made to the required funds?
- Are there any cross-border issues (expatriates visa, income tax liabilities)?
- Have the appropriate severance payments for termination been made?
- Are all insurance policies carried and up to date (employment, asset, medical, etc)?

Taxes

The focus needs to be on both 'tax payment' and 'tax preferentials'.

Tax payment

Companies in China often use 'imaginative' ways to minimize tax liability that do not always follow tax regulations. There is a risk that pursuit by the relevant taxation authorities could result in substantial hidden liabilities, penalties and exposures.

Key points to check for include: taxes on imported machinery, import VAT and customs duties receipts, individual income tax, withholding tax, dual employment contracts and, under certain circumstances, customs taxes that may be declared due on royalty payments.

Tax preferentials

There is a plethora of tax preferentials granted to different businesses at the local, provincial, municipal and national levels. These advantages may be granted for encouraged industry sectors or locations.

The current status of these tax preferentials and their transferability can have a significant impact on the final valuation of a company. It is also important to keep in mind the issue of retroactive payment of taxes exempted under tax holidays, in an asset acquisition scenario.

When performing the due diligence, a thorough accounting to verify that the appropriate taxes and declarations have been provided to the tax authorities, is critical to avoid 'inheriting' these problems.

Intellectual property

Intellectual property (IP) rights in China are in a constant state of flux. In an acquisition, too often they are regarded as less crucial than real estate, equipment or employee matters.

The appropriate level of IP due diligence, in terms of both time and financial investment, depends on the overall value of the deal, the proportion of intangible assets and the parties' risk tolerance. It is necessary to assess only the IP actually useful to the conduct of the business and not all the IP theoretically possible for the target.

The growing importance of IP in China cannot be overemphasized. It is important to identify the IP used by the seller and verify whether the company actually owns the rights it has been exploiting. Addressing these issues before committing to the buying decision can save much headache later. If there is any ambiguity, this needs to be cleared up before a valuation or buying decision can be made. (IP issues are examined in more detail in Chapter 3.3.)

Environmental concerns

From an environmental point of view, it is important to evaluate the target's environmental history to ascertain the past level of legal compliance, the technical level of current protection facilities and equipment, and regulatory issues.

Frequently-seen environmental violations in China include the absence of an air emission permit, the upcoming expiration of a fire certificate, the obsolescence or non-compliance of pre-treatment facilities, restrictions on the import, transportation or use of an essential raw material, the absence of dangerous goods storage or transportation licences, the absence of an effluent discharges licence. (Environmental due diligence issues are discussed in Chapter 3.5.)

The financial burden of an environmental breach can be costly, leading to facilities upgrade costs, clean-up costs and even plant closure. Under current environmental protection laws, the responsible party can be sued for clean-up within three years of the date of acknowledgement of responsibility. New users of land could be potentially liable for pre-existing contamination.

'Must review' documentation

During the due diligence process all the following documentation should be reviewed carefully:

- all correspondence sent or received concerning land use or authorization, employee union concerns, administrative violations, tax payments or penalties and IP;
- all threatened or pending litigation and all settlement agreements and proposals;
- all tangible and non-tangible assets owned by the seller, including proprietary information owned by the seller and not protected by copyright, trademark or patent, including trade secrets, know-how and confidential information;
- seller's standard form agreements regarding marketing, distribution, employment confidentiality, non-disclosure, independent contracting and copyright;
- all seller policies and guidelines regarding copyright, trademark, patent and trade secrets;
- complete chain of title for all significant interests scheduled to be transferred;
- issuance and continuous validity of all licences and permits issued by national, provincial or other levels of government authorities.

Conclusion

To maximize the benefits of the due diligence process, the buyer should begin early and be persistent in following up on questions and inconsistencies. Issues raised early on are more likely to be resolved and less likely to become last minute deal breakers. Warranties in China provide the buyer with little protection. In the event of a successful warranty suit, the judgement is often very difficult to enforce. The only alternative is to do your homework. For a buyer willing to invest the time and effort involved for a thorough due diligence in China, the opportunities abound.

Venture Capital Investment in China

Jonsson Yinya Li, Research Fellow of VCRC, Renmin University of China

China's venture capital system

China's present venture capital (VC) system still relies heavily on funding from the government and its state-owned enterprises (SOEs); thus it needs to be transformed into a privately-driven investment sector. Historically, the motivating force behind the development of the VC industry has been the need of private equity capital to create a venture. To the venture capitalists, funds are being invested for profit, whilst to the entrepreneurs, the most needed support from venture capitalists is long-term equity funding and management support.

While many factors may hinder China's establishment of an effective VC system, there has been a misunderstanding as to how the Chinese define and understand 'venture capital'. In English, the word 'venture' is defined in a commercial context as taking risk in order to create a new business. However, in Chinese, the word 'venture' in venture capital is often translated as just 'risk'. Therefore in China, the term 'venture capital' is often understood as simply 'risk capital'. Consequently the full meaning of 'venture' (ie taking risk to create a new business) is often lost in the translation.

As high-tech industries currently induce high risks, VC is often being mistakenly thought of as capital invested in high-tech products or industries. Under the influence of China's past planned economy, most people understand neither the function nor the process of using venture capital to foster entrepreneurship and the building of private ventures. Many erroneously believe that the government can foster the development of VC investment simply through directing public funds to invest in high-tech industries. As such, growth of the VC industry has not, to date, been driven by market forces but by economic planning.

VC is also known as private equity investment in China, since the recipients of most VC investments are companies not listed on the stock exchanges. Most investments take the form of equity, and the financial instruments used are shares or loans convertible into shares at a predetermined price in the future. Investee enterprises can be high-risk companies, small companies specializing in the new and high technologies at early stages of development, or those companies that have just established a market. VC is a new phenomenon and has only become prominent in China since the mid-1990s. Traditionally, the four Chinese state-owned banks provided loans for technical updating and loans for capital construction to SOEs. Both types of loan resulted in an increased production capacity. One of the failures of this system was that these loans were not accessible to small and non-state-owned enterprises.

Therefore, in order to make good this shortcoming and to foster the development of small- and medium-sized enterprises (SMEs) – especially those associated in the fields of science and technology, resources, export, and community services – the government began to carry out the following policies and measures in the late 1990s:

- the establishment of government-controlled VC funds at national, provincial and local levels to give direct financial support to SMEs;
- the provision of government guarantee and interest payment subsidies would be made available for SMEs;
- the provision of incentives to encourage portfolio investment in SMEs;

- increased proportions of state bank loans to SMEs and the allocation of funding priorities to SMEs at city banks and cooperative financial institutions;
- permission for qualified SMEs to raise funds in bond markets;
- permission for second board listing of high-tech SMEs in the near future.

Venture capital activity

In 1999, 92 technology-oriented VC funding groups in China managed RMB4.3 billion (US$518 million), to which the Ministry of Science and Technology added RMB3 billion (US$361 million) in the form of an Innovation Fund for high-tech SMEs. The number of registered VC funds was estimated to have reached 100 in the first quarter of 2000; about 28 per cent of the total VC investment went into 'seed stage' projects, 54 per cent went into start-ups, and 18 per cent into expansion projects. It was also revealed that 89 per cent of VC investment projects were involved with the New & High Technology Industry Development Zone.

This outcome is largely the responsibility of provincial and municipal governments, who have been taking a very active investment role. A typical example of this was an injection of RMB100 million (US$12 million) from the Liaoning provincial government, to support small high-tech projects brought into the province by overseas Chinese scholars during Innovation Week in June 2001. According to the Hangzhou Science and Technology Commission, approximately 80 per cent of all the VC funds in China came from the government. To foster innovation, some special committees are drafting significant laws and regulations. The Chinese government promulgated the new *Regulations on the Administration of Foreign-invested Venture Investment Enterprises* (RFIVCIE) in January 2003. These new RFIVCIE regulations are put forward jointly by the Ministry of Foreign Trade and Economic Cooperation, the Ministry of Science and Technology, the State Administration for Industry and Commerce, the State Administration of Taxation and the State Administration of Foreign Exchange. This has certainly exerted a positive impact on VC investment in China.

Nevertheless a market does not suddenly become viable for all forms of VC investment. The environment evolves, becoming more supportive to certain types of investment rather than others. Investors can look to Europe where, although the issues of transparency, IP and legal protection and liquidity have

been addressed, there has not yet been a significant, entrepreneurial VC market by US standards. To be sure, there are pockets in the UK, southern Germany, southern France and Scandinavia, but nothing to compare with the US. This is a major reason why European investors who are interested in VC go to the US. It is where the 'action' is and where the expertise resides.

China excites investors for numerous reasons, such as the strong entrepreneurial culture, its strong record of technological innovation and engineering excellence, as well as a large domestic market. All of these elements are required for a successful technology-based VC community, but the situation for private equity will be different. Currently, some of the elements required to support an environment for a viable and sustainable technology VC investment environment, at least for very early-stage companies, are only beginning to emerge in China. Issues of law, transparency, intellectual property and liquidity are matters of tremendous concern to early-stage venture investors. As they are addressed and as investors build experience and confidence in working on a trans-Pacific basis, the level of investment will increase. Ultimately, investment decisions are based on 'perceived' risk and reward, all viewed through the lenses of an investor's 'comfort zone'. However, this process is not unique to China; in the past, the same process has occurred in varying degrees in Singapore, Israel and India.

Today, most investors are very excited about the opportunities in China, but, as with most things, change will not happen overnight. The question for an investor who is bullish about future opportunities should be: 'what can I do today to build up my understanding of risk and reward in venture capital?'. Five years ago, almost no one in the US venture community would have dreamed of investing in a company engaged in development work in China. Today, the climate of opinion has changed and there are notable examples of success. Hence, the level of investors' comfort has grown in line with levels of experience and success. This process will continue until investors move into the next phase of technological VC investment in China and make direct investments in Chinese companies. Again, some of this activity is happening today but, typically, within the context of larger start-ups and investors with direct VC experience, and having a physical presence, in China.

Nevertheless, Chinese VC development is still in its infancy compared with western countries, especially in technological and commercial applications, in relation to the demand for venture capital backing. The extent of this underdevelopment in the Chinese VC industry is apparent when reviewing the small scale of financing, low to average investments, low investment funds, and the few cases involved.

To date there have been four policy recommendations on the development of China's VC industry:

- to amend the Company and the Partnership Acts to provide a more flexible and effective operating environment for the VC industry. Currently, China has no law on regulations regarding limited partnerships. Some provisions in the Partnership Act even hinder the development of limited partnerships.
- to accelerate the enactment of an Investment Fund Act, as well as a Venture Capital Investment Management Act. Their aims should be to broaden the sources of capital available for the VC industry. VC companies in China currently face major restrictions on their funding sources; therefore China should learn from overseas experience and apply it by introducing the investment funds to provide a structure for VC organizations.
- to establish a multi-level securities market system to improve the exit mechanism for VC investment. Exit mechanisms are key to the VC market; and small capital markets and OTC markets, such as in Japan, can play an important role for the smooth exit of venture capital.
- to promote the use of stock options as a form of management incentive scheme for new ventures. China should speed up the enactment of Stock Option Management Regulations to regulate the issuance of stock options. At the same time, the Ministry of Finance should publish related policies on accounting and taxation treatments for stock options.

The sharp rise in activity

It could be said that the VC industry in China is developing in line with the global proliferation of the internet. After emerging from 2001's 'low tide' and the adjustment of 2002, the VC industry in China has finally gathered its senses. In 2003, the US$40 million from Softbank Asia Infrastructure Fund (SAIF) to Shanda, and the successful IPO of Ctrip Travel Online, not only revived expectations for the internet industry, but also gave a glimmer of hope to the outlook for the Chinese VC industry. As a result of much favourable information and many driving factors, the Chinese VC industry started to warm up. There was a significant rise in VC investment in the Asian and Pacific Region, whilst VC investment in the US and Europe was declining.

Against this encouraging backdrop, the total amount of VC investment in China climbed sharply to around US$990 million in 2003, which exceeded the total for 2001 and 2002, being 237 times more than 2001 and 137 times more than 2002. In more than 10 instances, companies attracted more than US$10 million – a reflection of the Chinese economy's continuing growth, as well as the attraction of international capital to the Chinese market. However, 2003 was not a rewarding year for most of the domestic Chinese VC firms, which received only about US$160 million for investments in some 100 projects, and accounting for 16 per cent of the total amount invested.

The first task was to survive and then to show their ability. In order to survive, domestic Chinese VC firms avoided direct competition with foreign VC firms that hold abundant capital and placed emphasis on biomedicine, new materials and traditional industry. Chinese VC firms showed their ability in numerous ways. They thought up 'brilliant' ideas in financing models, project management and exit channels in order to accumulate practical experience from the 'real' competition in the Chinese VC investment industry. Venture-backed enterprises that were preparing for IPOs received US$310 million, about 32 per cent of the total invested, while the US$780 million invested by foreign VC firms in 61 companies accounted for more than 80 per cent of total investment. Clearly the foreign VC firms dominate the VC industry in China at present and most successes are achieved by foreign VC firms because nearly all the big investments are provided by them.

The distribution of venture capital by sector and region

The main influence driving the increase in the Chinese VC industry is the global transfer of VC investment, demonstrated clearly by the fields and sectors to which it has been attracted. In 2003, ITC sectors still got the largest portion of investment. ITC manufacturing alone acquired huge internal investment which, at more than US$400 million, accounted for 40 per cent of the total amount. The telecoms industry also received about US$200 million in investment. Research reveals that the main reason for this concentration is that most of the internet enterprises into which investment has been made have matured and needed more capital.

Due to its favourable geographical location, Beijing has obtained the majority of investment and projects. However, the Yangtse River Region, focused on the core Shanghai area, has gained the lion's share in the distribution of capital totalling US$500 million against Beijing's US$180 million. The Guangdong (Canton) River Triangle Region attracted around US$75 million, whilst the Middle and Western Region took US$50 million and the North-east Region received US$10 million. The software enterprises based in Beijing and the telecom enterprises based in Shanghai respectively won the majority of the available investment.

Domestic and foreign VC firms

Even after the country's entry into WTO, China will still maintain greater control over other industries, including banking, financial services and insurance, than other members. However, China has finally opened the door to foreign VC investment and investors are challenged to prepare for this opportunity.

At the start of 2004, Zero2Ipo Corp short-listed companies for '2003 China Domestic Top 20 VC Investment Firm', as well as '2003 China Foreign Top 20 VC Investment Firm'. Many may ask why it did not just select the 20 strongest VC investment firms in China. The answer is, perhaps, that the Chinese domestic VC investment firms would be barely visible if the appraisal listed the 'Strongest 20 VC Investment in the China Market'. To focus on the strongest ranking would totally ignore the development history of the Chinese VC industry. Furthermore, it would be biased by the statistics and not represent the true state of affairs, thus making any forecasts insignificant.

NewMargin Corp appears in the ranking list three times. Although the management fund for NewMargin is not huge, they are keeping active in the field of China VC and have outstanding achievements among the domestic VC investment firms since their foundation. Two students from Stanford University conducted a Chinese VC investment market investigation for 2003 and reached the conclusion that there were three key factors for successful investment in the Chinese VC industry:

- local practice;
- international experience; and
- high level of management involvement.

Coincidentally, the researchers of MIT drew surprisingly similar results through a project that focused on NewMargin as a case study. NewMargin's success was a result of the above three factors. The partners include two Chinese and two Americans, who cherish the opportunities of participating in corporate management and try their best to improve the strength of their venture-backed enterprises. To date, all of their projects make money and none have failed.

Comparing local VC management firms with foreign VC management firms it becomes clear that local VC firms have not been financially strong. However, there are at least three advantages in cooperating with local VC management firms. First, it is easier to communicate with the project and to better comprehend the project's value because the local VC firms share the same culture and similar concepts. Secondly, they can identify rare investment opportunities through an intimate knowledge of the local market. Finally, they can use Chinese rather than English language expertise to their advantage.

Venture funds are mostly sourced from foreign capital – why is this? The reason is that China does not have a suitable political, social and economic environment for VC; thus investors are reluctant to hand over funds to Chinese VC management firms. All the social funds are embedded in investments outside the current Chinese VC situation. Society would like to invest in real estate, steel, cement and other sectors that belong to visible profit industries. The 'fresh' industries, in which VC firms are invested, find it difficult to be accepted, so domestic VC funds are fed on illusions. It will probably take at least five or six years for the scale of VC investment to increase.

Some researchers contend that domestic VC firms are now transferring their investments to traditional industries. The investment is transferred in particular to those industries in the medium and later stages of their development. The above two points have fuelled suspicion of the VC investment focus on start-up enterprises. Actually, the VC firms' investment focus has not departed from high-rising enterprises. Whatever an organization's stage of development, the industry or conditions, so long as Chinese enterprises have the ability to expand rapidly, VC investor firms would be as attracted to them as they are to enterprises in the US. The difference is that traditional industries in the US are declining steeply, whilst in China similar traditional industries have the space and opportunity to expand rapidly. At present one unique opportunity in China is the retreat of government funding and the advance of private sector capital. If the events of the past three years are anything to go by, there will be a climax for new start-up enterprises, which will compel foreign VC firms to pay more attention to China.

The high growth of the Chinese economy means there are more investment opportunities and VC is well placed at the right time in the Chinese market environment. VC firms will drive the opportunities for wealth, and spur the rising economic trends without hindering the economy's health. Experimentation, practice and development in the next three to five years will clarify the role of Chinese domestic VC.

VC's blessing for SME board

The main reason for making an investment is, of course, to realize a return – the bigger the better. VC investment is not the exception. Exit is the final stage of VC, achieved either through an IPO of the shares in a primary stock market or through an arranged sale to a financial or strategic buyer of the company. The western venture capitalists focus on exit through IPO. The successful timing of a venture-backed IPO provides significant benefits to venture capitalists in that taking companies public when equity values are high, minimizes the dilution of the venture investors' ownership stakes.

After 14 years' stock exchange market development in Mainland China, on 27 May 2004, the SME Board made its debut on Shenzhen Stock Exchange (SZSE). On 17 May 2004, with the approval of the State Council, the China Securities Regulatory Commission (CSRC) approved the SZSE, one of the country's two exchanges, to establish a SME Board under the Main Board, and endorsed the implementation plan. This development brought glad tidings to all venture capitalists, VC investment companies, and the long-shelved SMEs' listing plan for the establishment of the SME Board in Shenzhen. As the first region to develop

VC investment in Mainland China, Shenzhen leads the country in the number of investment institutions and the amount of capital for R&D and development of venture-backed SMEs and high-tech companies. Until November 2003, Shenzhen had registered 197 VC investment companies, which together accounted for one third of the investment nation-wide. Although the SME Board is not really a Chinese Second Board for VCs, many venture capitalists still applauded it warmly, since it gives VC companies a first ray of hope for an exit mechanism. Investment bankers have dreamt for years of establishing a NASDAQ-style Second Board in Mainland China. VC companies have undergone a tough period over the past five years, after the Chinese government decided to delay the creation of the Second Board in 2000.

After the world-wide low tide in VC, lots of high-tech projects have finished the seed, start-up and exploration stages to become profitable during their expansion phase in the last three years. Since the VC Board was not in place, the investors had lost a major channel to exit through IPO after cashing in on their projects, and the development of both the venture capitalists and venture-backed SMEs had therefore stagnated. The development of the VC industry is preconditioned upon the flourishing of start-up SMEs in the high-tech sectors. Chinese official statistics indicated that there are more than 1,500 SMEs eligible for listing on the SME Board, which is more than any overseas market in terms of flotation resources. The revitalization of listing shares on the SZSE has aroused Shenzhen's ambition to become a regional financial centre.

Milestones in China's venture capital industry

The development history of China's VC industry is charted in Table 7.7.1 but does not include the VC activities in Taiwan, Hong Kong and Macao.

Table 7.7.1 Chronological development of China's VC industry

Date	Development
1984	Science Technology Promotion R&D Centre of State Science and Technology Commission (SSTC, renamed as PRC Ministry of Science and Technology, MOST, on 10 March 1998) organized the research about the New Technology Resolution Revolution in Mainland China and brought forward the suggestion of building a VC system to promote the High Tech Development.
January 1985	*The Decision on Science Technology System Reform* was issued by the Central Committee of the Communist Party of China (CCCPC) and the State Council (SC), which proposed that 'VCs can be set up to support the rapid changing and risky high-tech development'. The concept and practice of VC was first introduced into Mainland China's sci-tech policy system.
1986	With the approval of the SC, and in order to support the implementation of the Torch Project, SSTC and the Ministry of Finance (MOF) co-funded the China New Technology Venture Capital Co. Ltd. (CNTVCC), which was the first share-holding limited company in Mainland China engaged in VC investment. SSTC and FOF respectively held 40% and 23% of the shares. CNTVCC provided services such as investment, loan, rental, financial guarantee and consultation, etc. (However, the company has now closed.)
1988	The Torch Fund was set up by the SSTC and listed in Singapore. With a fund at US$100 million, it was used for the development of China's new-tech enterprises. The Torch Fund is a typical VC fund.
1989	With the approval of SC and Ministry of Foreign Trade and Economic Cooperation (MOFTEC, renamed as the Ministry of Commerce, MOFCOM, on 10 March 2003), Hong Kong China Merchants Group (CMHK), SSTC and Commission of Science, Technology and Industry for National Defence (COSTIND) set up a joint venture, China Ke Zhao Hi-tech Co Ltd. The second VC company and first Sino-foreign VC investment company in Mainland China, it is mainly responsible for commercial transformation and industrialization of national high-tech achievements. The projects funded are mainly the projects for sci-tech promotion, such as Torch Project (35.7%), 863 Project (11.6%), Project of Promoting National Sci-tech Achievements (6.3%), Sparkle Project (10.4%), Project of Transformation from Military to Civil Use (1.5%).
1991	SC issued the *Temporary Stipulations for China's High-tech Industry Development Zones*, which proposed that a 'VC fund can be established in high-tech development zones for the establishment of high-risk, high-tech industry'.
1991	*The State Council Notice with Regard to Approve National High-tech Industry Development Zones and Other Policies Regulation* (1991 National No. 12) indicated the support of building VC funds in high-tech zones.
1991	SSTC, MOF and Industrial and Commercial Bank of China (ICBC) co-founded the National Science and Technology Venture Capital Development Centre (NSTVCDC).
1992	The first sci-tech VC fund was established in Shenyang.
May 1995	CCCPC and SC issued the *Decision on Speeding Up the Progress of Sci-tech*, 'to develop sci-tech VC industry and establish the mechanism of sci-tech VC'. The document further clarified the strategy of developing science and education in Mainland China.
1996	The SC issued the *Decision on Deepening the Sci-tech System Reform During the Ninth Five-year Project Period*, which emphasized the exploration and development of a high sci-tech VC system and the commercialization of sci-tech production.
June 1996	SC approved the State Economic and Trade Commission (SETC, renamed as PRC Ministry of Commerce, Ministry of Foreign Trade and Economic Cooperation, MOFCOM, on 10 March 2003) to implement 'technological VC projects', emphasizing that 'enterprises should play an important role in VC projects and commercializing the new technologies'.

Table 7.7.1 (Contd)

Date	Development
1996	National People's Congress (NPC) issued *PRC Law on Promoting Sci-tech Achievements to be Commercially Transformed*, stipulating that the state treasury fund for sci-tech transformation is used in guiding funds, discount loans, subsidiary funds and venture capital. In the third part of article 24, it stipulates 'National government encourages setting up the sci-tech transformation fund and VC fund. The fund source could be provided by national, regional, corporate or state-owned organizations. The fund should be used to support the commercial transformation of high-risk, high-devotion, high-output sectors and accelerate the industrialization of sci-tech results'. This is the first time the concept of VC has been put into a law clause.
November 1996	SSTC held the Province and City Sci-tech Finance Promotion Colloquium in Changsha, the capital of Hunan Province. There were many senior representatives from SSTC, the People's Bank of China (PBOC), Bank of China (BOC), ICBC, China Construction Bank (CCB), Agriculture Bank of China (ABC), and provincial and city STCs. All the participants wanted the SSTC to strengthen the R&D of VC systems.
1997	Dengnan, the deputy director of SSTC, was confirmed to be the head of the VC R&D Project. In cooperation with experts of Tsinghua University, SSCT brought forward four requirements in the Project: 1) clearly examine the VC system; 2) examine the relationship between the VC and capital market; 3) create the implementation of a blueprint of VC mechanisms; 4) suggest the policy regulation and law to achieve both breakthrough and performance.
October 1997	Mainland China's fund industry formally broke the ice with Wuhan Security Investment Fund and Shenzhen Nanshan Venture Capital Investment Fund.
November 1997	*After the Interim Regulations on Security Investment Fund Management* were promulgated, the Security Investment Fund developed rapidly. Open-end Funds and Closed-end Funds were expanding most quickly.
January 1998	Premier Li Peng presided over the fourth meeting of National Sci-tech Leaders Team. The meeting decided on what constituted the general blueprint of VC mechanisms for high-tech enterprises and began experimental units.
March 1998	During the Ninth National Committee of CPPCC, the China National Democratic Construction Association (CNDCA) Centre Committee brought forward the *Proposal of Using of Reference from Western Countries and Speed up the Mainland China's Venture Capital Industry*, which was known as the No.1 Proposal. Then the Proposal Committee of CPPCC held the Proposal Consultative Meeting and invited SSTC, SETC, MOF, PBOC and CSRC. Venture capital drew much attention from Chinese leaders and became a popular topic in the economic field.
September 1998	Deputy Minister of MOST met with Andrew Sheng, Chairman of the Hong Kong Stock Exchange (HKSE) and Peng Ruchuan, Director of China and International Development of HKSE, to discuss the VC system and Mainland China's high-tech enterprises' flotation in Hong Kong's Growth Enterprise Market (HKGEM).
October 1998	MOST advanced a new suggestion for CSRC solving the high-tech enterprises' IPO in A-share markets and formulating a policy for encouraging high-tech enterprises' overseas IPO.
October 1998	The Venture Capital Development Research Centre of Renmin University of China was set up and became the first formal VC research organization among the universities in Mainland China.
28 October 1998	The first company with the name *venture capital* was registered as *Beijing Sci-tech Venture Capital Co., Ltd.* with a registered capital of RMB500 million. The business scope covers the investment of high-efficient agriculture, bio-medicine, software systems, etc. It also operates a registered guarantee fund, which means it provides loan guarantees when registered capital of a newly set up company is not sufficient for a bank to make the loan.

Table 7.7.1 (Contd)

Date	Development
October 1998	Professor Mannie Manhong Liu's book, *Venture Capital: Innovation and Finance* (first edition), was published – an important tool for industry insiders.
November 1998	Vice-premier WEN Jiabao (current Chinese Premier since March 2003) wrote an official comment on the letter about VC written by Li Renjun, Member of the Standing Committee of the National Committee of the CPPCC and former vice-director of SPC, which mentioned the October suggestion for MOST's Deng Nan for reference. Vice-premier Li Lanqing also made the same comments.
December 1998	MOST report on the VC research work for the Education, Science, Culture and Health Committee of NPC (NPCESCHC) and the Financial and Economic Committee of NPC (NPCFEC).
December 1998	MOST officially sent the *Report on Establishment of China Sci-Tech Venture Capital Mechanism* to SC.
March 1999	Premier Zhu Rongji made an official comment on the MOST Report and the CSRC suggestion that sci-tech VC support of SMEs was needed, and asked MOST to do further research and hand in a new scheme and report to the SC. Vice-premier Li Lanqing also asked Zhu Lilan, the Minister of MOST, to do further research with other ministries and then wait for the examination and approval of SC.
March 1999	The Draft Lead Team and Advisors Team of NPCFEC's *PRC Law on Fund Investing in Securities* were set up. Drafting the *PRC Law Fund Investing in Securities* was initiated.
23 March 1999	Seven ministries including MOST, MOE, Ministry of Personnel (MOP), MOF, PBOC, SAT and the State Administration For Industry and Commerce (SAIC) issued *Several Stipulations on The Promotion of The Transformation of Sci-tech Achievements*, pointing out 12 measures and policies.
April 1999	SPC sent the *Interim Rules on Industrial Investment Fund Management (Draft)* to Legislative Affairs Office of the SC.
21 May 1999	The SC issued the *Temporary Stipulations On the Tech Venture Capital Fund of SMEs of Sci-tech Type* submitted by MOST and MOF. The SC decided to build up the SME Technical VC Fund with RMB3 billion and to have it administered by the SME VC Fund Administration Centre.
June 1999	Seven ministries, MOST, SPC, SETC, MOF, PBOC, SAT and CSRC united to report the *Instruction for Establishing China Sci-tech Venture Capital Mechanism*. Li Lanqing, Wen Jiabao and the SC leaders made the important comments, which were not only to schedule the establishment of a sci-tech VC system, but also to promote its recognition and practice.
16 June 1999	SETC issued *The Guiding Opinions on the Establishment of Pilot Schemes of SME Credit Guarantee* to promote the support for financing and venture capital of sci-tech SMEs.
20 June 1999	SC compiled the request of *Speeding Up the Construction of Zhongguancun High-tech Park* submitted by the Beijing Municipality and MOS. According to the plan, Zhongguancun would be built up into a top sci-tech park on an international level within 10 years.
20 August 1999	The Central Committee of the Communist Party of China (CCCPC) and the SC created the *Decision on Strengthening Tech Innovation, Developing the High-tech, and Realizing Industrialization*, a plan for the promotion of progress and the development of high-tech industries, fostering the capital market.
26 August 1999	Shenzhen Venture Capital Co., Ltd (SZVC, renamed as Shenzhen Capital Group Co., Ltd. (SCGC) in October 2002) was founded with RMB700 million as its first registered capital.
October 1999	The first session of the *Shenzhen High Tech Trade Fair* (SZHTTF) was inaugurated in Shenzhen.
December 1999	NPCFEC convened the International Pro-seminar to draft the Investment Fund Law.

Table 7.7.1 (Contd)

Date	Development
30 December 1999	With the SC leaders' approval, the General Office of the State Council transmitted and issued the National No. 105 Document, *Some Opinions on the Establishment of Venture Capital Mechanism*, which was presented by MOST, SPC, SETC, MOF, PBOC, SAT and CSRC.
July 2000	In line with the CSRC's *Regulation of Share Issue for Venture Backed Enterprises (draft)*, the Legislative Affairs Office of the SC solicited the opinions from MOST and other relative ministries.
11 October 2000	The first regulation on VC came into being in Mainland China. It was the *Temporary Stipulation of Shenzhen Venture Capital of High-tech Industry*, which was formally published in Shenzhen government's No. 96 document.
1 January 2000	*The Regulation of Zhongguangcun High-tech Park* was put in force. The regulation was the first regulation in the high-tech area that included the content of VC regulation.
14 February 2001	Kingdee Softward, a venture backed by IDG, was listed in the Hong Kong GEM and became Mainland China's first independent software venture in the international capital market.
2 March 2001	Beijing Municipality issued *Limited Partnership Management Measures (No. 69)*, which aims to accelerate the creation of standards for the development of VC investment companies in the form of limited partnerships.
14 August 2001	With RMB500 million, TianLu (Beijing) Venture Capital Investment Centre (TLVCIC) was set up by Xinjiang Tianye Co., Ltd., Xinjiang Shihezi Development Area Economy Development Co. Ltd and SinoTrust (Beijing) Management Consulting Ltd. The foundation of TLVCIC was Mainland China's first limited partnership VC corporation.
1 September 2001	*Interim Regulations on the Establishment of Foreign-invested Venture Investment Enterprises* (IREFVIE) were implemented in China by MOFTEC, MOST and SAIC.
March 2002	Originated by The Hong Kong Polytechnic University and China Venture Capital Co., Ltd, the *China Venture Capital Journal* was first published.
1 April 2002	*The Instruction Catalogue on Foreign Investment Industry* (revised edition) with its attachments was put into force, which was promulgated by SPC, SETC and MOFTEC on 4 March 2002. *The Instruction Catalogue on Foreign Investment Industry* which was approved by the SC on 29 December 1997 and promulgated by SPC, SETC and MOFTEC on 31 December 1997 was abolished at the same time as the revised edition was issued.
12 April 2002	Alcatel Shanghai Bell and NewMargin founded the Telecom Technology Fund, the first ever investment vehicle exclusively dedicated to China-origin telecom technology, with an initial investment of US18 million dollars.
19–20 April 2002	The first China Venture Capital Forum was held in Beijing.
June 2002	After less than one year, TianLu (Beijing) Venture Capital Investment Centre (TLVCIC), the first limited partnership VC firm, was disbanded. According to the requirements of CSRC, in its annual report, Xinjiang Tianye Co., Ltd. withdrew the investment capital and parted with SinoTrust. As the *Limited Partnership Management Measures* were issued by the Beijing Municipality in Zhongguangchun, Beijing, they were not enforceable nationallly. In its eighth clause, PRC Partner Company Law regulates that 'all the partners must assume unlimited liability with all the company's property'. Xinjiang Tianye's investment in TLVCIC exceeded the 50% of its net asset, which broke the regulations of CSRC. VC industry insiders called for amendments to Partner Company Law and Company Law.
19 June 2004	The China Venture Capital Association (CVCA) was incorporated in Hong Kong at the suggestion of Warburg Pincus.

Table 7.7.1   (Contd)

Date	Development
29 June 2002	NPC passed the *PRC Promotional Law for Small and Mid-Size Businesses*.
30 January 2003	The Chinese government promulgated the new *Regulations on the Administration of Foreign-invested Venture Investment Enterprise* (RFIVCIE), which was issued by MOFTEC, MOST, SAIC, SAT and SAFE and became effective on 1 March 2003; the IREFVIE, promulgated in 2001, was repealed on the same day.
March 2003	The China Venture Capital Research Institute (Hong Kong) Ltd was established. The institute is a joint venture between The Hong Kong Polytechnic University and China Venture Capital Co., Ltd. Headquartered in The Hong Kong Polytechnic University, it set up an operating institute in Shenzhen, which was registered as the Shenzhen Zhongtou Venture Capital Research Development Co., Ltd on 28 May 2003.
28 October 2003	The long-awaited *PRC Securities Investment Fund Law* was passed by China's standing Committee of NPC and would become effective on 1 June 2004. The passage of this law is the most comprehensive attempt by the Chinese government thus far to regulate the nascent investment fund business. Previously, the Chinese government had relied on a series of administrative regulations, most notably the *Provisional Measures on the Administration of Securities Investment Funds* promulgated about six years ago, to regulate this vibrant business.

This chapter is an excerpt form Jonsson Li's forthcoming book, *China's Emerging Venture Capital Industry* to be published by GMB Publishing in June 2005.

Part Eight

Key Sector Reports and Notes

China's Automotive Industry: Automobiles

Mark Norcliffe, Society of Motor Manufacturers and Traders (UK)

Market trends

In 2002, China's annual production and sale of passenger cars suddenly surged by over 40 per cent, breaching the symbolic barrier of one million units. Few industry analysts had predicted this break-through, and even fewer were prepared for the growth to continue. But that is exactly what happened. In 2003, cars sales rose a staggering 80 per cent to 2.1 million units and, with total vehicle production rising to 4.44 million units, China was catapulted into fourth place in the world table of automotive producing countries. However, in September 2004 the China National Bureau of Statistics (NBS) cut its 2004 full year forecast for production growth from 40 per cent to 18 per cent. Indeed, the month-over-month increase in September sales of 14 per cent was the first monthly rise since April, when Beijing's credit squeeze began to bite.

This rapid growth, coupled with a high profit level per unit, made China the top target for all the global vehicle manufacturers, leading to a host of new invest-ments and alliances. At the same time, a number of domestic Chinese companies (some with provincial government support) began to move into the sector. For the Chinese consumer, this meant a continuing downward spiral in prices and a huge increase in the range of available models.

Inevitably – and, in part, due to government spending restrictions – the market slowed in 2004, although car production was still expected to reach 2.4 million. This suggests that some car makers will struggle to recoup their current level of investment and will find themselves with excess production capacity. However, although there will be future losers in the automotive sector, China will remain firmly estab-lished as one of the world's leading countries for both the production and sales of motor vehicles.

Government policy

The Chinese government's long-awaited Auto Industry Development Policy was eventually published in June 2004. The document defines the automotive sector as a 'pillar industry', whilst clearly demonstrating the government's desire to concentrate growth on a small number of major industrial groups, and to boost China's indigenous research and devel-opment capabilities.

The policy foresees the major groups each holding approximately 15 per cent of the market (currently, only Volkswagen's partnerships with First Auto Works and Shanghai Automotive Industry Corporation, and the latter's joint venture with General Motors, have over 10 per cent market share). Foreign ownership within vehicle manufacturing joint ventures remains capped at 50 per cent, unless all production is destined for export. As a result of heavy lobbying by the interna-tional car makers, the original proposal that half of all vehicles produced by 2010 must come from local companies with full technology ownership has been quietly dropped.

Instead, the new policy focuses on restricting the number of domestic Chinese companies diversifying into car production. In future, new entrants will be required to make an initial investment of RMB2 billion, plus additional investments specifically in engine production and research facilities. Non-automotive companies will be prohibited from purchasing the business licences of bankrupt vehicle manufacturers.

The policy also includes measures to promote a reduction in average fuel consumption by 15 per cent before 2010, and to remove the ban on selling imported and domestically produced vehicles through a single marketing channel.

Location of the industry

In common with much of the nation's manufacturing capacity, the principal locations of China's auto industry have been determined by the political planning processes of the 1950s and 1960s. First Auto Works was centred on Changchun in Jilin Province, Second Auto Works, which subsequently became Dongfeng Motor Corporation, was based in Hebei Province, with the headquarters in the remote city of Shiyan. Only Shanghai Automotive Industry Corporation (SAIC) had a base close to its potential customers.

As the industry has evolved, its geographical footprint has changed, partly in recognition of the need to be closer to the end customer, partly as a result of the largest Chinese companies absorbing smaller provincial rivals, and partly through foreign partners seeking to diversify operations beyond their Chinese counterparts' traditional bases. At the same time, various provincial governments – eg Liaoning and Anhui – have sought to use investment in the automotive sector as a growth engine for their local economies.

Therefore, in contrast with the central government's wish for greater consolidation, China's new automotive map shows greater diversity and a wider geographical spread. Guangzhou has emerged as a substantial automotive centre, particularly favoured by Japanese investors; Tianjin, home to the new FAW/Toyota partnership, is a new challenger to Changchun; and Beijing itself, with new investments from Hyundai and DaimlerChrysler, is seeking to take a prominent position within the industry. Meanwhile, Dongfeng Motor Corporation has relocated operations to the more accessible city of Wuhan; and Zhejiang and Jiangsu Provinces have also acquired significant automotive manufacturing capacity, based on low labour and land costs.

The key players: their Chinese operations and strategies

The Americans

The 'Big Three' US vehicle manufacturers have experienced contrasting fortunes in China. Whilst Chrysler, who entered early, and Ford, who arrived late, have found progress difficult, General Motors are starting to reap a rich return from their substantial initial investment.

Chrysler

Chrysler Corporation was the first foreign vehicle manufacturer to establish a joint venture in China, when, in 1984, it entered into a 42/58 per cent agreement with Beijing Automotive Industry Corporation (BAIC). However, the partnership was undermined by a misunderstanding of the demands of the Chinese market and a poor choice of vehicles – the Jeep Cherokee and the military-style BJ2020 – and production slumped from 100,000 in 1995 to little more than 9,000 units in 2002.

Following the amalgamation between Chrysler and Daimler Benz of Germany, the Beijing-based operation became part of DaimlerChrysler *(q.v.)*

General Motors

General Motors (GM) won a hard-fought battle with Ford for the right to partner Shanghai Automotive Industry Corporation (SAIC) in a 50/50 venture – the so-called fifth and final automotive joint venture to win government backing. When production commenced in 1999, some commentators opined that the cost had been too high, and the launch model – the Buick Regal – was the wrong car.

However, GM had substantial plans for China, and has driven ahead with a rapid expansion of the model range, a series of deals with SAIC and other provincial manufacturers, and continued investment. Their reward has been a rapid rise in market share, to around 10 per cent, and second place in the league table behind long-time market leader Volkswagen. In the first five months of 2004, GM and its partners sold 219,888 vehicles. Profitability is also good, with an estimated average of over US$2,000 for each vehicle sold.

Although the rate of growth was reported as slackening at the end of June, an increase of 20–30 per cent for the full year is still projected.

Alongside the original Buick Regal, which has continued to sell much better than expected, GM have introduced further models from their own range and from Daewoo, the bankrupt Korean car maker whom they absorbed in 2001. These include the compact Sail (based on the Opel Corsa), the GL8 people-carrier, the Buick Excelle and the Chevrolet Spark (based on the Daewoo Lacetti and Matiz respectively). To raise production capacity, they have expanded the original

Shanghai plant to a three-shift operation, capable of turning out 200,000 vehicles per annum, and they have taken over an unused former Daewoo factory in Yantai, with the potential to produce an extra 100,000 vehicles. Plans announced in June 2004 foresee a further US$3 billion investment to double existing capacity. GM claim that this will be financed by profits earned in China. A further 20 new models, including the introduction of the Cadillac and Holden brands, are planned.

GM have also leveraged their relationship with cash-rich SAIC to finance investments in other car makers, both inside China and abroad. In southern China, GM and SAIC have taken a combined 84 per cent stake in Wuling Automobile Co, thus gaining access to the enormous mini-vehicle market. In Shenyang, where production of the Chevrolet Blazer SUV has only reached a disappointing 3,000 units per annum, the existing joint venture with Jinbei is being re-structured so that GM/SAIC will again have a controlling interest. SAIC took a minority shareholding in the deal, which gave GM control of Korea's Daewoo.

Within three years GM is planning to double capacity with SAIC and its other partners to 1.3 million units. GM has also announced that it will move its Asia Pacific headquarters from Singapore to Shanghai. In August 2004, GM became the first foreign automobile company to launch an auto finance venture in China, GMAC, in partnership with a subsidiary of SAIC.

Ford Motor Co

Having lost out to GM in the battle to forge a high-profile partnership with SAIC, Ford Motor Co was obliged to seek an alternative partner, through whom they could gain access to the Chinese market. Their choice was ChangAn Automobile Co, the Chongqing-based mini-vehicle manufacturer already in partnership with Suzuki.

Investment in the new plant – US$98 million – was modest compared with other late entrants to the market. Production commenced in early 2003, with an initial capacity of 50,000 units and the potential to increase to 150,000. However, sales of the compact Ikon (a Fiesta derivative) only totalled 17,000 in 2004. A second model – the Mondeo – was introduced in 2004, but the venture continues to be hampered by its location away from the booming provinces on China's eastern seaboard and by the limitations of the local supply chain. Significantly, Ford

has recently announced that its next model – the Volvo S40 – will be built in Nanjing.

The Europeans

European vehicle manufacturers were amongst the early entrants to the Chinese automotive market. Volkswagen, in particular, has derived a substantial financial return from that early investment. However, with the major Japanese and US corporations now pursuing aggressive and ambitious plans in China, the Europeans are having to revise their business strategies and raise their investment levels to defend their market share.

Volkswagen Group

Volkswagen (VW) has reaped a rich reward from its early investment in China. Its original (1985) joint venture with Shanghai Automotive Industry Corporation (SAIC) was complemented in a second 40/60 alliance with First Auto Works (FAW), and, in the early 1990s, the products of the two joint ventures – elderly Volkswagen models like the Santana and Jetta – accounted for 80 per cent of the passenger car market, and sold for premium prices.

That comfortable situation changed with the arrival of new global rivals, and the rapid expansion of the Chinese market. VW's market share has eroded rapidly, to less than 30 per cent by 2004. However, their overall sales actually rose, reflecting the overall market growth, and in 2003 totalled 697,000 – up a remarkable 36 per cent. And whilst the basic Santana model is now spurned by the middle-class buyers in Shanghai, Beijing and Guangzhou, it can still be sold for around RMB100,000 (US$12,000) in smaller provincial cities.

VW is responding to the challenge by making large new investments, including a brand new 300,000 capacity plant in Changchun and a similar expansion at existing plants in Shanghai. Overall, VW is committed to invest US$6.4 billion in China over the next five years and the company's Chinese manufacturing capacity will rise to 1.36 million units by 2007. Additionally, new engine factories will be built in Shanghai (with SAIC) and Dalian (with FAW). In a change of marketing strategy, VW has moved away from relying exclusively on old brands. Now the Chinese motorist has a choice of no less than 10 VW models, including the latest Polo, Audi A6, and the soon-to-be-introduced Touran. They have also instigated aggressive price-cutting, no doubt intended to slow the rate at which competitors can recoup the costs of their initial investments.

At the same time, the 'traditional' Santana brand has been retained, with a face-lifted '3000' version, and the Golf has been introduced from Brazil. These models are targeted at less affluent buyers who are entering the car market for the first time. However, faced with the challenge of new low-price offerings from indigenous vehicle makers, it is uncertain how successful VW will remain in this sector of the market.

In addition to its model strategy VW has pledged to cut costs by US$500 million at its China operations by the end of 2005. Meantime, operating profit from its Chinese joint ventures was €251 million pro rata for the first half of 2004 compared with €361 million in 2003.

VW will compete strongly to retain leadership in China – a market that they cannot afford to lose. They have an advantage over more recent arrivals, in that they can finance future growth out of past profits, and they are strongly positioned in established relationships with two of China's 'Big Three' automakers. However, those relationships bring their own problems – principally the difficulty of integrating the two independent supply chains and achieving economies of scale. Additionally, both FAW and SAIC now have other international partners.

PSA Peugeot Citroen

PSA Peugeot Citroen (PSA) was one of the first foreign car makers to enter China, However, their original 1985 venture – a minority shareholding with Guangzhou Auto Group Corporation – never prospered, and was abandoned in 1997. In the meantime, they formed a second partnership with Dongfeng Motor Industry Investment Co to build cars under the Citroen brand in Wuhan.

Initial production capacity was 150,000, but, by 2002, sales of the Fukang model (based on the Citroen ZX) and its locally-designed derivative, the 988, had only reached 85,000. The introduction of the Elysee, Picasso and Xsara models boosted the following year's sales over 100,000, still lagging beyond the overall growth in the market. However, PSA – perhaps conscious of the challenge posed by Dongfeng's new relationship with Nissan/Renault – has recently announced a further cash injection and the introduction, in the latter half of 2004, of the modern Peugeot 307 model.

DaimlerChrysler

When Daimler Benz, as a result of their merger with Chrysler, 'inherited' the US company's joint venture in Beijing, there must have been a strong temptation to close the enterprise. Relations with the Chinese partner were strained, sales had declined to less than 10 per cent of their peak, and the Jeep-based product range had long been overtaken by the more sophisticated and stylish offerings of competitors. However, with Chinese auto sales just beginning to blossom, DaimlerChrysler (DC) understood that they could not walk away from the market, and, after protracted negotiations, they committed themselves to a 30-year extension to the partnership with BAIC together with a further $1.1 billion joint venture to manufacture automobiles and trucks, including an annual 25,000 C-class and E-class Mercedes Benz by 2012. Unusually, the contract provides for DC to increase its 50 per cent holding up to 100 per cent, once the present investment regulations are relaxed.

Short-term revival was based upon the introduction of modern sports utility vehicles (SUVs) – a type of vehicle gaining popularity in China and in which Mitsubishi (37 per cent owned by DC) had particular expertise. Initially the strategy has proved successful: in the first quarter of 2004, sales rose threefold, with the Outlander model accounting for 52 per cent of the total and achieving the top SUV ranking in China. However, the subsequent decision of DaimlerChrysler to terminate their global partnership with Mitsubishi must create doubts about their future use of the Japanese company's models in China, and suggests that the planned increase in production capacity to 100,000 is unlikely to be achieved.

Whilst the original venture continues to struggle, DC have concluded a parallel agreement with BAIC to commence production of their C- and E-class saloons at a new Beijing plant by 2005. The initial sales target is 25,000 per annum. Imported Daimler saloons have long been popular with Chinese consumers, but it is significant that, of the current annual import total of 10,000, the majority are the luxury S-class model. The demand for locally produced, less luxurious products still has to be tested.

Fiat Auto

Fiat has a well-established relationship with Nanjing-based Yuejin Automobile Group Corporation, principally in the light commercial vehicle sector, where the Iveco Daily has sold strongly for many years. However, it has been slow to develop a presence in the passenger car market. Despite agreeing a 50/50 joint venture (Nanjing Fiat) in 1999, it was not until 2002 that the Palio, and, latterly, the Siena models were brought into production.

The Palio – Fiat's 'world car' – is a hatchback design, not well suited to Chinese tastes, whilst the Siena is perceived as smaller than its main competitors. As a result, sales have not matched expectations; the 2003 figure of 37,000 is less than 50 per cent of current plant capacity.

BMW

The BMW brand is well respected in China, with around 10,000 vehicles imported in 2002 and 2003. A large proportion of these were the top-of-the-range 7-series model, mirroring the trend noted with Daimler Benz – ie affluent Chinese consumers prefer the top models.

However, for local production, BMW has opted to introduce the 3- and 5-series models, through a 50/50 joint venture with Brilliance China Automotive Holdings, to be built at a new facility in Shenyang. Both the choice of model and partner represent something of a gamble. Brilliance is a relative newcomer to the Chinese auto industry, has achieved only limited sales of its own 'Zhonghua' saloon, and has been disrupted by the financial scandal surrounding its erstwhile chairman. Total BMW/Brilliance sales for 2003 are reported at 18,700.

The Japanese

Historical antipathy, the lack of a ready consumer market, and poor manufacturing standards, all contributed to the caution that Japanese vehicle manufacturers initially displayed to the Chinese market. Early links were built on licensing agreements and basic technology transfer; Honda's move into Guangzhou was very much the exception. Nevertheless, by 2001 this 'softly-softly' approach had given Japanese manufacturers 28 per cent of the passenger car market in China. Chinese consumers liked Japanese models, with their well-equipped interiors and thrifty engines, and Japanese producers liked to sell their cars in a high-margin market.

The sales boom of 2002 brought a dramatic change. The Japanese 'Big Three' – Toyota, Nissan and Honda – concluded that they should wait no longer, and all embarked on ambitious, but differing expansion strategies.

Toyota

Toyota's early forays into the Chinese market were confined to licensing agreements – with Tianjin Auto Industry Corporation (TAIC) to produce a derivative of the humble Daihatsu Charade, locally christened the Xiali, and with Shenyang Jinbei to produce the Hiace van.

In June 2002, they concluded a 50/50 joint venture with FAW, at an investment cost of US$1.3 billion. Political pressure may have swayed Toyota's choice of partner, and the joint management structure is in stark contrast to Toyota's normal global policy of taking 100 per cent control. As part of the deal, FAW effectively took over Toyota's existing partner TAIC – a move that reflected the government's wish to see consolidation within the auto industry. Although Toyota may have privately regarded the partnership as less than ideal, they have committed heavily to achieving success, with ambitious plans to build 400,000 vehicles a year by 2010. Already the modern Vios, Corolla and Crown models are in production, and new assembly plants have been opened in Tianjin. A new engine plant will also be built in Changchun.

Toyota and FAW have also agreed to assemble the eco-friendly petrol and electricity powered Prius from kits in Changchun. This smart move neatly deflects the age-old Chinese complaint about foreign partners not offering their latest technology. Indeed, hybrid cars might just take off faster in China than in western markets where we have all been conditioned by 100 years of the internal combustion engine. At the same time, Toyota is wary enough to retain the engineering technology in Japan.

Toyota has also followed a pattern increasingly common in the Chinese auto industry by forming a second 50/50 joint venture with a different partner – Guangzhou Automobile Group. Production of the Camry model will commence in 2005, with a target of 300,000 units by 2007. Another new engine plant is also under construction in Guangzhou. Planned investment is US$461 million.

Honda

Honda's early involvement in China was as a motorcycle maker. In 1998 they made a dramatic entry into passenger cars with the takeover of the failed Peugeot joint venture in Guangzhou. As a 'white knight', they were able effectively to sideline the local partner, Guangzhou Auto Industry Corporation (GAIC), and exercise a controlling influence from the outset. As a result, their Accord model achieved a high reputation for quality and strong sales with affluent Chinese buyers, and, in 2000, their Guangzhou plant was the only production facility in China operating above

70 per cent capacity. Honda has expanded the business cautiously, raising capacity to 240,000 in 2004 and expanding the model range with the Odyssey mini-van and the compact Fit.

Like Toyota, they have established a second partnership, developing a long-standing technical agreement with Dongfeng Motor Corporation into a full 50/50 joint venture. The new Dongfeng Honda Auto Co will produce the CR-V, a compact SUV in Wuhan at a rate of 30,000 per annum.

Honda made another bold move in 2004, with the announcement of a new plant in Guangzhou, which will build the compact Fit/Jazz model wholly for export. This is the first time that an international vehicle manufacturer has committed to using China as a major export base, and Honda's reward was government approval for an unprecedented 65 per cent majority shareholding in the new venture. The other partners are GAIC with 25 per cent and Dongfeng Motor with 10 per cent.

Nissan

The Nissan name was originally established in China through a series of technology agreements and a steady stream of imported models from Japan, which proved popular with Chinese consumers. Early manufacturing ventures were modest – a joint venture with Aeolus Automotive to build the Bluebird saloon and a minority shareholding in Zhengzhou Nissan Automobile Co, which concentrated on SUV production.

However, the market boom of 2002 propelled Nissan (along with their new European partner, Renault) into a new venture with Dongfeng Motor Corporation (DMC). In an unprecedented deal, Nissan/Renault was permitted to acquire 50 per cent of the state-owned DMC, for a payment of US$1 billion, whilst, at the same time, the partners created a new joint venture, under the title Dongfeng Motor Co, into which Aeolus Automotive was also integrated. This arrangement theoretically gives Nissan/Renault management control of the new venture, although it still has to be tested in practice.

The new Dongfeng Motor Co has set about an ambitious programme to raise production above 200,000 by 2006. They will also introduce a range of new models, including the Teana luxury saloon and the compact Micra, to complement the existing Bluebird and Sunny saloons, which are now perceived as dated by Chinese customers. Production will be centred on DMC's existing base in Wuhan and new assembly plants under construction in Guangzhou, where there will also be a new research and development centre.

Mitsubishi

Mitsubishi technology was first utilized in China, by First Auto Works, back in the 1980s, but it was not until 1996 that the Japanese vehicle manufacturer agreed two minority joint ventures with regional Chinese partners. Soueast (Fujian) Motor Corporation (itself half-owned by Taiwan-based China Motor Co, in whom Mitsubishi held a 20 per cent stake) commenced production of the Delica mini-van and Freeca SUV, and latterly the Lioncel saloon, whilst the Pajero SUV was built in partnership with Hunan Changfeng Motor Co.

Mitsubishi's image amongst Chinese customers was severely tarnished by a number of 'scandals' over vehicle recalls. Nevertheless, by 2003, total sales had grown to 151,000, and the company announced that China would be a key market in their plans for global revival. Eleven new models would be introduced, with targeted sales figures in excess of 300,000 by 2008. These projections were heavily dependent on the successful exploitation of Mitsubishi's expertise in sport utility vehicles to revive the fortunes of DaimlerChrysler's joint venture with Beijing Auto Industry Corporation *(q.v.)*. However, the recent unravelling of the broader partnership between Mitsubishi and DaimlerChrysler, and Mitsubishi's own lack of investment capital, must throw considerable doubts upon their long-term prospects in the Chinese market.

Suzuki

Throughout the 1980s and 1990s, Suzuki entered into a tangled web of licensing agreements with local Chinese partners, which has resulted in Suzuki technology appearing in a large range of basic mini-vehicles currently produced in China. In 1994, they opted for Chongqing-based ChangAn Automotive Corporation as their principal partner, and took a 35 per cent stake in a joint venture to build the Alto and Swift mini-cars. A second, minority venture was later concluded with Changhe Aircraft Group, again focusing on the production of mini-vehicles.

Although sales have risen above 100,000, Suzuki's position in the Chinese market is weakened by the lack of larger, up-market vehicles, which offer greater profit margins. At the same time, the arrival of domestic Chinese competitors such as Geely *(q.v.)* in the mini-car sector threatens a protracted price war.

Suzuki was further unsettled by the arrival of Ford Motor Co as a second partner for ChangAn – a feeling reflected in the sale of part of their shareholding in the original joint venture. In the medium term, Suzuki may concentrate more on India than China; their sales in India are currently double the level achieved in China.

Mazda

Although controlled by Ford Motor Co, Mazda has pursued an independent policy in China, in partnership with FAW-owned Hainan Motor Co. The joint venture's products have proved popular with private Chinese buyers, and sales – principally of the Premacy and 323 models, assembled from imported kits – have doubled since 2001. The Mazda 6 has now been added to the model range, and it is planned to raise production capacity from 50,000 to 150,000.

The Koreans

The Asian financial crisis of 1996–1997 precipitated a significant consolidation in the Korean automotive industry. Hyundai emerged as a clear winner, gaining control of one-time rival Kia, and securing a dominant share of the domestic Korean market. Meanwhile, bankrupt Daewoo was taken over by General Motors, and the fledgling Samsung automotive division was purchased by Renault.

From this strong domestic base, Hyundai embarked on a strategy to break into the top echelon of global vehicle manufacturers, with China marked as a key growth market.

Hyundai Group

In October 2002, Hyundai concluded a US$1.1 billion deal to create a 50/50 joint venture with Beijing Automotive Industry Corporation. Just two months later, with the new factory still under construction, the first Sonata saloon was produced. By the end of 2003, sales of this single model had exceeded 50,000, and Hyundai were targeting a total of 110,000 units for 2004, aided by the introduction of a high-specification version of the Elantra saloon.

Meanwhile, at Kia's existing plant near Nanjin (a 50/25/25 partnership with Jiangsu Yueda Motors and Dongfeng Motor Industry Investment Co), it is planned to raise capacity from 50,000 to 250,000, as the original Kia Pride is replaced by the Qianlima (a derivative of the Accent model specially developed for China) and the Carnival mini-van.

This rapid expansion has not been achieved without friction. In Beijing, Hyundai came into conflict with DaimlerChrysler, the existing partners of BAIC. As a result, DC disposed of their 10 per cent shareholding in Hyundai, and scaled back a number of joint development programmes. Relations with Yueda were also strained by disagreement about the location of a projected second manufacturing plant. A further proposal – that Hyundai should partner with privately-owned Huatai Automobile Co in Shandong Province to produce SUVs – is likely to fall foul of the government's wish to restrict foreign car makers to a maximum of two Chinese partners.

The Chinese

Although there are more than 120 registered vehicle makers in China, official policy has long recognized a 'Big Three' and a 'Smaller Five', who were to be encouraged to consolidate operations and to absorb the smaller producers. But as China's automotive market has expanded, the opposite trend has become apparent. New entrants have moved into car production and the only significant consolidation has been FAW's takeover of Tianjin Automotive Industry Corporation (TAIC).

The 'Big Three'

China's 'Big Three' – First Auto Works (FAW), Dongfeng Motor Corp (DMC) and Shanghai Automotive Industry Corp (SAIC) – between them accounted for 48 per cent of all vehicles produced in 2003. However, for passenger cars they are almost wholly dependent upon models provided by their joint venture partners. Only FAW, with their Audi-derived Hongqi (Red Flag) saloon, can claim an independent production capacity. However, the 'Big Three' do have substantial financial resources, and, with government encouragement, they are now moving to increase their independent research and development capabilities. The most active has been SAIC, which is currently bidding to take over Korean SUV maker, Ssangyong Motors, and is also seeking a technology partnership with Britain's MG Rover.

All of the 'Big Three' have also acquired at least two international partners – FAW have VW and Toyota; DMC are partnered by PSA and Nissan/Renault; and SAIC have VW and General Motors. They are, therefore, well placed to gain the major share of new automotive investments, and to manipulate the joint venture relationships to their maximum advantage.

The 'Smaller Five'

The Chinese automotive companies usually grouped together as the 'Smaller Five' are:

- Tianjin Automotive Industry Corporation (TAIC);
- Beijing Automotive Industry Corporation (BAIC);
- ChangAn Automobile Co;
- Guangzhou Automobile Industry Corporation (GAIC);
- Soueast (Fujian) Motor Corporation.

As with the 'Big Three', they rely heavily upon their foreign partners for technology, new models and investment. TAIC, lacking foreign input and relying on dated Daihatsu technology, were absorbed as part of the larger FAW/Toyota partnership, but the other second tier companies have generally prospered as the domestic market has expanded.

BAIC gained a major boost when DaimlerChrysler committed to a 30-year extension of the joint venture originally set up by the US corporation. The aggressive arrival of Hyundai as a second partner further strengthened Beijing's claim to be a significant automotive centre. ChangAn also gained a second international partner in Ford, with a consequent broadening of their model range and market appeal. Guangzhou emerged as a new southern hub of automotive manufacturing, with Honda, Toyota and Nissan all investing in new facilities. Soueast (Fujian) Motor Corporation's sales almost doubled, as partner Mitsubishi made a major push into the Chinese market.

The new entrants

One of the more surprising consequences of the rapid growth of vehicle sales in China has been the entry into the market of a number of indigenous Chinese companies, often with no previous experience of vehicle manufacturing. Some are privately owned enterprises, whose owners have made their fortunes in other industrial sectors. Others rely heavily for funding and political support on provincial governments keen to expand their local industrial bases.

Typically, these new arrivals have concentrated on producing low-priced vehicles aimed at provincial customers. They minimize production costs by locating in low cost areas, using existing components, conducting little research and development, and copying existing models – sometimes rather too closely for the liking of the major vehicle makers (GM, Honda and Nissan are currently engaged in intellectual property disputes). Their aggressive pricing policies have enabled them quickly to carve out a noticeable market share, and, whilst it unlikely that all the new entrants can succeed, it does appear that the independent vehicle manufacturer will remain part of the Chinese automotive scene.

Most prominent amongst the newcomers are:

- *Chery Automobile Co:* Based in Wuhu, and strongly backed by the Anhui provincial government, Chery originally made inroads into the market with a saloon car closely resembling the VW Jetta. Its second model – the QQ – was a close copy of the Chevrolet Spark, produced by General Motors. A third offering, the Qiyun, appeared in 2003. Although Chery's 'copycat' tactics have incurred the wrath – and legal challenge – of both VW and GM, they have nevertheless expanded sales to over 85,000 units in 2003.

- *Geely Automobile Holdings:* Privately owned by four brothers, who previously built successful businesses in construction and motorcycles, Zhejiang-based Geely is the fastest growing independent car maker. From a standing start in 2001, annual sales had grown to 80,000 by 2003, and the trend continues, with 40,000 vehicles sold in the first three months of 2004. Previously relying on Daihatsu derivatives, Geely plans to introduce a new Korean-designed model later in the year, and has further ambitions to produce China's first sports car. A new joint venture with Hong Kong financiers has reportedly pumped an extra $60 million into the company. Geely have also registered interest in Middle East markets, with plans to start vehicle production in Iran and appoint a distributor in Egypt, where penal import taxes on larger-engined automobiles may have opened a window of opportunity.

- *Shenyang Brilliance Jinbei Automotive Co:* Brilliance's early reputation as a good partner for foreign investors has been tarnished by alleged financial irregularities, disappointing sales of its 'Zhonghua' saloon, and reducing profitability in the Jinbei light commercial vehicle operation. Nevertheless, the company remains China's leading van producer, is supported (and part-owned) by the Liaoning provincial government, and now has BMW as a joint venture partner.

- *Harbin Hafei Motor Co:* Wholly controlled by Harbin Aircraft Industry Group, the northernmost of China's vehicle producers has introduced a range of cut-price models, including the Baili, Lobo and Saima, achieving sales of 30,000 units in 2003 – a threefold increase on the previous year.

Future developments in the Chinese auto market

Sales of cars in China have slowed markedly in the second half of 2004. In particular, the luxury end of the market has stagnated, reflecting a general tightening of the money supply, and perhaps a feeling amongst Chinese consumers that there are still more price cuts to come, as domestic competition increases and import tariffs reduce further. The comparatively strong market for economically priced cars will be of particular benefit to the independent Chinese manufacturers, who specialize in cheap and basic models.

It is important to recognize two significant factors in the rapid expansion of car sales. Firstly, the growth has been led principally by private buyers and, secondly, most purchases are not financed by credit. With an increasing number of Chinese attaining the income levels at which car ownership becomes an option, it seems likely that market will continue to grow – albeit at a more modest rate – reaching perhaps five million units by 2010.

At these levels of growth, vehicle manufacturers can enjoy a short-term bonanza, but, in the medium term, will face problems of over-capacity and a declining level of profitability per unit. The most successful vehicle manufacturers will be those who can maximize their production levels and, at the same time, drive down their costs-per-unit to those achieved in other countries.

China as an automotive exporter

The enormous growth in the Chinese automotive market since 2002 has been fuelled wholly by increasing domestic demand. This is somewhat at variance with other sectors of the Chinese economy, where growth has been driven principally by exports. During that period, the other main world automotive markets have either declined or seen only sluggish growth, thus encouraging the global car makers further to ramp up their investments and production levels in China. As the Chinese market starts to slow, it is clear that, if all the promised production targets are achieved, there will be considerable over-capacity within the industry.

These trends lead inevitably to the conclusion that China will, in the foreseeable future, become a net vehicle exporter. Already, Honda has committed to producing up to 60,000 compact cars for export from its new plant in Guangzhou, and VW has also stated that it expects to become a substantial exporter by 2007. At the same time, the Chinese vehicle manufacturers are beginning to explore export potential. Both FAW and Dongfeng already have some experience of selling commercial vehicles overseas, and, along with SAIC, are clearly keen to develop the skills to manufacture and sell passenger cars outside China. Chery is seeking to commence vehicle production in Iran.

It will be interesting to see whether, in the longer term, the flow of export vehicles from China remains part of the global manufacturing and distribution patterns of the established international vehicle manufacturers, or whether it comes under the control of Chinese companies.

Automotive Components

Liu Baocheng, Professor, University of International Business and Economics, and Che Yanhua, Volkswagen, China, with updates by Jonathan Reuvid

Market overview

China's automotive industry has enjoyed rapid development over the last two decades. Three large-scale automotive enterprises have been established: China First Automobile Group Corporation (FAW), Dongfeng Motor Corporation (DMC) and Shanghai Automotive Industry (Group) Corporation (SAIC). They accounted for 44 per cent of the country's total vehicle production and over 70 per cent of the total number of cars. According to the Chinese State Economic and Trade Commission (SETC), over the last three quarters of 2002, these three groups produced a total output value of RMB231.2 billion, an increase of 34.8 per cent. In the meantime, almost all the multi-national original vehicle manufacturers (OVMs) representative of the world '6+3' (ie, six groups: General Motors (GM), DaimlerChrysler, Ford, Toyota, Volkswagen and Renault; and three independent companies: Honda, BMW and Peugeot) have established their presence in China primarily in the form of joint ventures with Chinese partners. There are more than 600 foreign-invested automotive enterprises, involving 20 countries and regions. Total committed foreign investment in the automotive sector amounted to US$21 billion, with a total registered capital of US$10.6 billion and paid-up funds of US$4.5 billion. More than 300 original equipment (OE) and supplier technology projects are in place.

In 2000, total vehicle output reached 2.07 million with a value of RMB391.1 billion, an increase of 80 per cent on 1995. Chinese domestic manufacturers still have a dominant role, with over 95 per cent of the total market share. Car production rose by 86 per cent to 605,000 units,

while motorcycle production rose by 45 per cent to 11.53 million units over the same period. Demand for commercial vehicles >6t GVW exceeded 300,000 units, an increase of 14,000 units.

According to SETC's 2001 report, there were 2,391 automotive enterprises in China by the end of 1999, of which 118 were automobile manufacturers, 546 automotive converters, 136 motorcycle assemblers, 51 engine makers and 1,540 automotive/motorcycle parts and components companies.

Parts and components are the most crucial sector of the automotive industry. The major international suppliers, including Delphi, Alpine, Continental, Robert Bosch and Siemens, see China as one of their strategic target markets. Many have already found local partners in China in order to access local resources, and the industry anticipates huge demand in the years following the country's entry to the WTO.

Market structure

The business of the automotive parts industry can broadly be categorized into two levels: the original vehicle manufacture (OVM) market and the after market. The OVM market is where the part/component manufacturers provide their products directly to the original vehicle manufacturers. For instance, Delphi Automotive Systems is the OVM supplier for General Motors and Volkswagen. The after market is where the part/component manufacturers distribute their products to the specified channels and the end users. Many part/component manufacturers are involved in both markets.

The OVM market

This is a regular and stable market with the following characteristics:

- a B2B business model, where in most cases long-term contracts are maintained between the part/component suppliers and the OVMs;
- routine orders placement by the OVMs with the suppliers carrying a quantity of inventory for after-sales service. OVMs require the identification of their own brand names on the spare parts and their unique packaging to be distributed through their authorized service centres;
- transparent information flow between suppliers and clients, ie suppliers appoint account managers on the OVMs' sites to understand their real-time demands and requirements;
- the delivery system is shifting from the traditional single part delivery towards module delivery. Module suppliers are responsible for the whole process chain, from pre-development to the spare parts business;
- the prerequisites to be an original supplier of the big automakers are:
  - competence of quality;
  - correct ratio between price and performance;
  - security of delivery;
  - flexibility;
- the suppliers' performance review is based on:
  - client satisfaction;
  - flexibility and reactions to volume changes;
  - competitiveness;
  - reputation of delivery service;
  - client orientation;
  - innovative participation in the producer's R&D activities;
- massive investment in marketing is not needed. For example, there is no need to purchase a great deal of advertising space in auto magazines; most expenses are related to corporate image promotion.
- the most valuable market information for suppliers is the producers' production plan, which forms the basis of the suppliers' sales, marketing and integrated business plans.

The after market is quite different:

- the clients are distribution channels, business partners and end users and so the business model is much more dynamic and complex, and the products are considered consumer products. Therefore, the products need a unique brand identity and packaging, and the sellers have to segment their target markets and analyze consumer behaviour in order to establish a market differentiation strategy. For instance, some companies have developed a range of product portfolios with different prices, different brands and different packages to meet different markets;
- more resources in marketing activities are required in order to improve brand awareness, recognition, preference and loyalty. An integrated marketing communication plan is needed, ranging from participation in auto shows, solo shows, brand launch events, technical seminars, dealer conferences, print adverts, billboards, broadcasting, online promotion, POP etc;
- the PARC, age information and the typical ownership of the vehicle are the most valuable marketing data for suppliers. The PARC data shows the total market scale, the age information indicates the product's lifespan and the ownership information shows the different consumer behaviour with regard to taxis, business and households;
- the structure of the after market is more complex than for the OVMs and includes positions such as channel development manager; channel support manager; regional manager; brand manager; order processor; logistics manager and so on;
- the market players are not only parts/components manufacturers: some are also trading companies. For example, General Motors' Service Parts Organization International (SPOI) sometimes purchases parts and components internationally, brands them 'AC Delco' and then sells them to after market channels;
- many OVM suppliers are involved in the after market business. However, OVMs do not generally encourage their OVM suppliers to serve the after market independently and therefore most suppliers have the role of 'purifying' the market for the OVMs who are, after all, the 'authentic' parts providers;
- customer relations management (CRM) is increasingly important. The customer database is the backbone of the whole business operation, ranging from identifying ways of generating sales leads, qualifying sales prospects, segmenting sales leads, setting up dealer extranets, retaining existing customers and enticing competitors' customers to switch. Every detail of the whole value chain, from the supplier to the distribution channel and end users, calls for a specific strategy;

- the competition is much fiercer than in the OVM market. The players have to enhance their overall competitiveness, from product portfolio including packages and services, pricing policies and promotional mix to channel management.

The after market

Apart from imported products, three sectors currently serve the domestic automotive parts/components market in China. The first sector is the localized manufacturing facilities of global suppliers such as Delphi Automotive Systems, Bosch GmbH, Lucas Varity and SPOI, who are involved in both the OVM and after markets. The second sector comprises local suppliers such as Wangxiang Group, some of which have already been included in the world-wide purchasing systems of major multi-national OVMs. The last is the counterfeit and fake parts/components manufacturers. The three sectors' business behaviours are quite different and they apply different market strategies and market mixes. The first sector and part of the second have set up an entire distribution network, warehousing and logistics network, and have unique brand identities and packaging. The different distribution channel networks are illustrated in Figures 8.2.1 and 8.2.2

More and more suppliers are getting involved in the after market to extend their channel lengths. The after market potential is said to be worth around RMB50–60 billion (US$6–7.2 billion) and the PARC is RMB13–14 million, of which passenger cars account for a third.

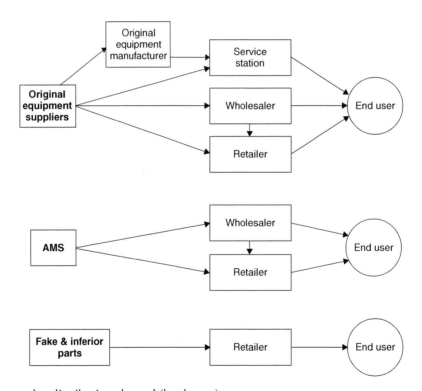

Figure 8.2.1 After market distribution channel (local parts)

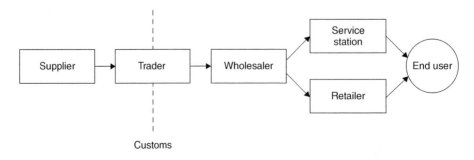

Figure 8.2.2 After market distribution channel (imported parts)

Business is evenly divided among the service stations and the after market. This is why so many multi-national automotive parts/components manufacturers and suppliers are involved in the after market business, especially in the car part sectors. The market is there, but how best to enter it and develop within it, and how to realize the profit diversification and leverage the existing business models? The first step is to identify problems and obstacles.

Many multi-national parts/components manufacturers are doing well in the OVM market, but it does not necessarily follow that they will be able to grab a sizeable share in the after market. The major OVMs are looking for new markets for growth and this is their reason for coming to China. They include Volkswagen, Audi, General Motors, Mitsubishi, Renault, Toyota, Volvo and BMW, amongst others. The OVM suppliers pay close attention to localization requirements. In the past, the OVM projects in China that met the localization rate of 40 per cent in the first year were able to obtain government approval and so the original suppliers of OVMs set up manufacturing facilities, sales offices or service centres in China.

Suppliers normally establish joint ventures to produce different parts. Table 8.2.1 shows how this can work, using Robert Bosch as an example.

OVM business is the focus of multi-national auto parts/components manufacturers and so their organizational behaviour and operations bear strong B2B characteristics, which eventually impact upon the after market.

1. Different marketable product portfolios and product re-engineering

Automotive parts and components include slow-moving and fast-moving products. Fast-moving products are marketable products in the after market, as are other consumer products, so companies that maintain wider product lines should select marketable products. For example, batteries, with a life span of around two years, fall into the fast-moving category, whereas steering columns are slow moving and are not usually after market marketable products. In addition, the OVM business prefers module and systems supplies, while the after market treats modules and systems as separate components and accessories. For example, when something goes wrong with the fuel pump in the fuel pump modules, the consumer demands replacement of the exact part and is reluctant to pay extra money for the whole module, which includes the fuel pump, racks and filters. If the consumer is using the fuel pump assembly branded Bosch, you must know whether your fuel pump is fit to replace the Bosch or not. So, on your product catalogue, you must state that your product number XXX is equivalent to Bosch product number XXX. The engineering process is more complicated and requires engineers' expertise not only in the whole module, but also in the separate parts. Unlike OVM supplies, the after market business requires the installation manual in the package.

2. Support from the whole organization

Given the differences between the OVM market and the after market, the OVM business is, in most cases, paid more attention by management. Most financial and manpower resources are traditionally allocated to the OVM business. However, once management decides to develop the after market and expects it to be a significant contributor to corporate revenue and profit diversification, the management must attach more importance to the after market. A complete and integrated team should be set up, which might range from four to 30, or even 60, people. Furthermore, marketing activities need considerable investment in order to improve brand awareness, to get brand recognition and build brand preference and loyalty. The after market needs support from every function, especially in the early stages when the business is small and

Table 8.2.1 Bosch joint ventures

Name of venture	Major customers	Major products	Bosch ownership (%)	Sales revenue (US$ million)	Total investment (US$ million)
Bosch Braking Systems	DCAC, BJ Jeep	Brakes	70	N/A	21
Nanjing Huade Spark Plugs	N/A	Spark plugs	51	1.2	35
Wuxi Euro-Asia Diesel Injection	N/A	Diesel injection	26	4	322
United Automotive Electronic	DCAC, SVW; FAW-VW	Engine management systems	50	48	322

low profile. It will take two or three years for the after market business to break even. So when the management conducts a performance review it must remember that in the early stages, profit alone is no indication of performance.

3. Differentiation strategy in terms of product, price and marketing activities is essential

In the OVM business, the same products are set at the same price and quality level but the after market business faces a dynamic environment and its customers cannot be treated as a homogenous group. Different sectors behave differently. Taxi drivers tend to buy the cheapest products; and are reluctant to pay a higher price. Private car owners are most concerned with the authenticity of the parts, and institutional car owners will pay even more. Marketing intelligence must make a detailed study to support the different product strategies with appropriate brand names and promotion plans.

4. Channel development and management experiences are crucial to the business success

The OVM business requires the ability to deal with business partners and car manufacturers. If the whole organization has very strong B2B experience, it will do well in dealing with business partners. After market products are sold through distribution channels, typically from the authorized exclusive distributors, authorized regional distributors, dealers and wholesalers to retailers. It is, therefore, of utmost important to understand how to develop and manage the distribution channel and how to impact the channel with the organization's culture, particularly in the current Chinese parts industry. The distributor selection procedures, price structures, warranty terms, channel support, distribution contracts and incentive programmes must be well established. Otherwise, the whole distribution channel will be in a mess. The distributor will fight for profits in the territory and will cut its price against others.

5. Brand building experience is valuable

OVM-oriented companies are typically engaged in corporate image building. While they promote their corporate identities through various marketing communications tools, they tend to ignore product brand promotion and so they need to learn the whole process of building product brand awareness, brand recognition, brand preference and brand loyalty. They will learn how to carry cross-promotion with their distribution channels. The pull and push strategies need to be applied simultaneously.

6. Quick response plays an important role in customer retention

The OVM business is comparably stable, since the business relationship between the OVM and its supplier is based on a long-term commitment, or the supplier carries over the OVM business from its overseas companies and so the suppliers are not worried about their business. In contrast, the after market is dynamic. In spite of the customer base available, if they are not treated properly (eg their purchase inquiry is not replied to), they will switch to competitors' brands; it is unlikely they will choose to wait. Meanwhile, even if customers are ready to buy, they can hardly be retained if the sellers cannot provide the right products or services in a timely fashion. Even worse, they will tell their friends and relations about their disappointment. Losing one customer can mean losing five or six business opportunities.

7. Internal records are different from that of OVM business

Normally, the marketing information system of OVM-oriented organizations is relatively simple. It usually includes the major customer books, macro-economic environment, government policies, competitor intelligence and automotive production information. Most information can be obtained from internal records and key accounts. In contrast, the marketing information systems for the after market will be much more complex and should cover a broader area. Apart from the content mentioned above, it should include information about the distribution network, the end user profile and consumer behaviour analyses, vehicle population and product life span, all of which are crucial to the after market business. The intelligence is not easy to obtain and cannot be found internally; it will require a third party to conduct the research, or the company might introduce successful marketing information systems from companies that manufacture or sell mass non-durable products.

Solving internal problems does not guarantee a bright future. The after market players must also understand what is going on within the industry and deal with the question of how to avoid the disadvantages, how to transcend the barriers and formulate their core competitiveness. The after market suppliers have to monitor closely the external environment.

Major issues in the auto-parts after market

The environment of the automotive parts/accessories after market in China is still currently in its infancy. A summary of the major problems follows.

Fragmented and complex distribution network

Using local distributors might in theory offer a cost advantage, but the distribution channels can be highly fragmented. Most foreign companies found that their Chinese joint venture partners have hundreds of direct distributors. For instance, a typical state-owned brewery in a large city has over 2,000 primary distributors, many of whom resell to hundreds of secondary wholesalers and thousand of independent 'street hawkers'. Many companies felt that their distributors were inadequate in terms of delivery, sales, merchandising, promotion and collection. Few had the most basic customer tracking, customer care and credit rating systems.

Unfortunately, a better distribution system is unlikely to emerge soon, again because of government restrictions on foreign investment. Currently, with a few exceptions, joint ventures are strictly limited to distributing goods that they manufacture themselves.

With regard to the channel characteristics of the automotive industry at present, although the number of dealers in automotive parts/accessories amounts to 220,000 nation-wide, few can achieve US$24 million sales revenue. Take Shanghai as an example, since it is the biggest OVM manufacturing site, with Shanghai

Volkswagen and Shanghai GM amongst others, and the biggest automotive parts/accessories warehouse. Many distributors from other regions order their products from Shanghai.

Figure 8.2.3 shows that it is not easy for after market suppliers to select the right distributors and manage the whole channel – vital to the success of the business.

Valuable after market-oriented information is hard to find

Information and intelligence for the OVM market are more complete and integrated than for the after market. Consulting companies can track monthly, quarterly and yearly production and sales by using their network around the country. While production and sales figures are not difficult to obtain through newspapers, automotive magazines and online services, there is not enough information for the after market that covers the vehicle population, vehicle utility purposes and vehicle age.

The process of segmenting the market and evaluating market potential involves many challenges. Not all official vehicle management organizations in China have computer-aided statistical systems and this is even more of a problem in remote areas. Furthermore, there is almost no way to assess the number of imported cars, because some cars are sold to China through illegal channels. Although there are some automotive consulting institutions who claim to have

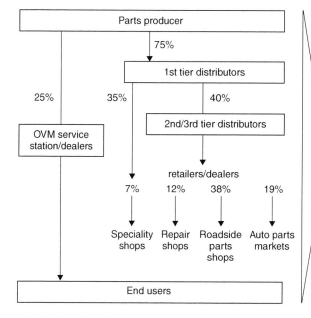

General characteristics

Fragmentation
– more than 220,000 auto maintenance and repair enterprises and numerous auto parts shops and roadside shops
– relatively unsophisticated

Difficult to control
– thousands of unauthorized enterprises selling parts
– quality problems with fake and inferior products

Figure 8.2.3 Shock absorber distribution map, volume flows

data to hand, they can only provide the vehicle population by general categories. These figures can only tell which car models have a larger market share, but not the car's life span, and so the replacement rate of different car models must be identified.

Companies might choose regional distributors in some specific areas according to their product lines and current market circumstances and so a multi-dimensional survey showing the car population by purpose, brand and region is essential. Annual sales revenues, financial standing, management skills and industry reputation are the basic assessment criteria when selecting distributors.

Strong domestic and international competition is imminent

The competition in after market business is much more intensive than for OVM. Figure 8.2.4 shows how fierce the competition is in the automotive parts/accessories after market field.

The major OVMs do not expect OVM suppliers to develop their distribution channel independently

OVMs have different attitudes towards the fact that their suppliers are developing their after market business independently. Major OVMs do not encourage their suppliers to develop their distribution network independently and to sell their parts/accessories outside OVM service stations. When OVMs place orders with suppliers, they will order extra products for their service stations. They put their brand names on their unique packaging, display the price tag including their mark-ups and distribute the

parts to the authorized service stations. Most OVMs have their own complete service network, and some have adopted '4S' policies, which integrate car selling, part supply, car repairing and information feedback into one system. For instance, Shanghai Volkswagen (SVW) suppliers have to follow the regulation that SVW supplier should provide service parts only to SVW. However, it has a dual supply system for each component purchase and the market is shared between two or three suppliers; sometimes the supplier is not satisfied with their OVM business share and looks elsewhere for markets to supply. Furthermore, SVW's prices for these parts are always higher, leading many suppliers to sell their cheaper parts via other channels. The suppliers have to promise that they will only supply parts to territories unoccupied by SVW, and that they will sell the parts at a higher price to the free market than to SVW. They state that their major function is to help the OVMs purify the market.

Accounts receivable is another problem after market suppliers need to consider seriously

Not all the multi-national players have enough experiences of dealing with accounts receivable. Products selling well or in huge volume does not necessarily mean the business has gained significant profit. After the products are sold, if the money cannot be collected, profit is lost.

As stated above, the distribution channel, consisting of authorized distributors, a dealer and wholesalers, is the mainstay of the after market. Whether the whole value chain is healthy or not will determine its business success. Therefore, selecting the distributors, financial status and credit must be the

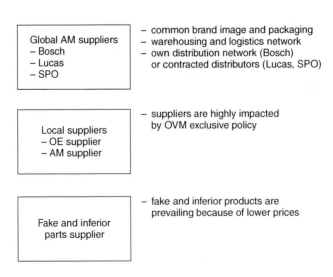

Figure 8.2.4 After market suppliers

priority. Only with these in mind can the supplier initiate a payment policy according to the channel structure and characteristics (see Figure 8.2.5).

However, at the beginning of the business, if you tell customers that you require them to accept the 'cash on delivery' payment term, your customers might switch to other brands and not come back again. So the suppliers are in a dilemma. They will certainly want to sell their products, but they must risk bad debts.

Fake and inferior products are prevailing in the markets

Apart from original equipment suppliers (OES), there are some small local producers in the market selling fake and inferior parts to the retailers and the end users. While family car and company car owners prefer authentic parts, many taxi drivers are willing to get their cars fixed at roadside shops, whose prices are cheaper because they source their products from the small producers who duplicate OES technology or put the OES brand name on the products they make themselves.

Why are some consumers willing to buy those products? There are two reasons. First, some drivers lack the knowledge to distinguish fake parts from authentic ones. Second, there is a significant price advantage against the original parts. Sometimes it is not only the roadside shops that sell the fake parts, but also a few authorized dealers. After the authorized dealers gain the title of 'brand authorized distributors', they actually stock both authentic and fake parts. They will sell the cheaper parts to their price-sensitive buyers and so jeopardize the OES' interests.

Faced with counterfeiting and arbitrary pricing, some companies are using counterfeit-proof packaging. By printing retail prices on packages and marking production runs differently by channel, counterfeits should be easier to identify. Nevertheless,

the sheer scale of these problems increases the level of complexity for managers in China.

Recommendations on market research and segmentation

The following are some recommendations:

- basic market analysis will draw a map of the major car brands in the market covering the car population (PARC) by brand, replacement rates by product and after market size by product, car brand and region. It will also determine component life span by mileage or time, market volume by product portfolio and cross-country analysis/cross check;
- geographic segmentation will segment the market by region and major metropolitan area and prioritize market penetration region by market size, growth and competitive intensity;
- end user segmentation will categorize the end user into different consumer groups and understand their distinctive characteristics, including expectations, preferences, drivers of product and channel choices. It will also uncover the best way to cater for the segmented targeted consumer groups;
- product analysis reveals the strength and weakness of the major products/brands in the market and match channels and end user preferences.

The above analyses must be based on facts, and the following sources and methodology can be applied to gather the relevant information:

- desk research: government statistics and reports, industry materials from newspapers/magazines/internet/other domestic and international media, data published by automotive research institutions (DRI, Boston Consulting); the annual reports of the OVMs and the OES;
- internal marketing information: the existing database or marketing information systems (MIS); the key account managers of major OVMs (remember, they always have good relations with OVM executives and are able to get first-hand information very quickly); the clipping and monitoring systems of the PR department;
- first hand interviews or surveys: to delegate a third party survey service institution to conduct a focus group interview, consisting of distributors, wholesalers, dealers, retailers and end users, or a specified

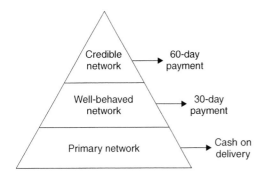

Figure 8.2.5 Payment terms

survey, will help the company get the first-hand materials. Nowadays, an online survey on the internet is another cost-effective way;

- industry events: while enjoying auto shows, trade fairs, technical shows and other customer occasions, remember to attend the seminars where famous market players, government officials and industry authorities deliver speeches and distribute market information.

Market entry

Winning in China has become a top priority for the multi-national automotive giants, many of which see the Chinese market as a once-in-a lifetime opportunity to catapult themselves into a position of global leadership. They make their mark on the Chinese market by setting up manufacturing facilities, transferring technologies and establishing service centres.

Tariffs and quotas

Currently, the country's import/export regulations are import tariff and VAT certificate.

Tariffs
The following tariffs apply:

- raw materials for manufacturing sites: approximately 5–15 per cent;
- spare parts or assemble parts using on whole vehicle: approximately 10–50 per cent;
- production machinery and test equipment: approximately 15–25 per cent.

VAT
The following VAT rates apply:

- most imported commodities: 17 per cent;
- some commodities (eg books): 13 per cent.

Tariff and VAT formulae
The following formulae apply:

- import tariff = CIF x tariff rate;
- VAT = (CIF tariff rate) x 17 per cent.

Following China's WTO entry, tariffs on whole vehicles as well as parts and components will be significantly lowered and import licences will gradually disappear. This will have various impacts on the automobile and supplier industry. For complete vehicles, the tariff will be gradually reduced from 70 per cent to 25 per cent by 2006 (from 50 per cent to 10 per cent for automotive components).

Of the different types of motor vehicle, the hardest hit will be passenger cars, high-tech engines, driving axles and key parts assemblies, with high-end, heavy-duty trucks next. The impact on mini-vehicles, medium-sized trucks and large and medium-sized buses will be relatively small and the motorcycle industry will be the least affected. The effect of increased import quotas prior to the final disappearance of the quota and licence scheme will be much greater than the reduction of tariffs. It will create tremendous pressures on domestic OE assemblers because once the import licence is phased out there will be a major increase in the number of cars and components imported at reduced tariff rates. For the after market suppliers, there will be new opportunities and challenges. The suppliers can import their products, manufactured globally at a lower cost into the China market, or they can purchase their products from international manufacturing facilities, brand them and import them into China. However, they will be faced with fierce competition.

The liberalization of the automobile service industry

At present, only the Chinese Trading Company, joint ventures and wholly-owned companies are licensed to handle goods import and export. However, joint ventures and wholly-owned companies can only import the raw material/parts for their production and export their own products.

Following WTO membership, China is opening up its service trade to overseas companies in the areas of vehicle and parts sales and distribution, automobile import and export, franchised dealership, shipping and transportation, automobile financing, car rental and leasing and financing for production. This will open up more channels for imports and seriously impact on China's market because the country lacks an established system of automobile service trade.

Competition

The after market business has vertical and horizontal distributors. The vertical distributors arrange their products by car models, for example Shanghai Longfeng Auto Parts Limited sells the various parts of Santana. The horizontal distributors arrange their goods by part categories, for example Liaoning Yejin

Auto Parts Company sells batteries of different brands. It depends on the company's capabilities and on the market situation and it can of course begin with vertical distributors, and then expand to horizontal channels.

Competition in the after market will originate from both local and international companies. International competitors can be divided into two categories; one being the manufacturers who are also involved in the trading business, for example, Delphi Automotive Systems and Bosch. The second group restricts itself to trading and buying products from manufacturers, putting their own brand names on them and selling on, for example NAPA. Many Chinese local manufacturers are beginning to realize that they must set up their own brand names and distribution network, and that they are enjoying a lower price due to lower costs. Some, such as Hangzhou Wanxiang Group, are becoming strong competition with multi-national companies in some market segments.

Recent developments – J Reuvid

In July 2004, Delphi opened a new US$50 million technical centre in Shanghai and forecast that its revenues from all operations in China would exceed US$1 billion for the full year representing an increase of 15–20 per cent on 2003.

In 2003, consolidated revenues from Delphi's majority-owned operations in China were US$630 million, a 50 per cent year-on-year increase on 2002. When revenues from the operations in which Delphi has minority shareholdings are included, the total for 2003 was about US$850 million.

Looking ahead, Delphi expects to source US$1 billion of products from China by 2007, reflecting its confidence in the global quality and cost standards of Chinese autoparts. Given the electronics complexity of modern automobiles, it is likely that some of the Chinese companies that sought to exploit the growing demand for parts but lack technology and systems experience may not remain competitive. World-class autoparts manufacturers in China who are global market leaders, such as Delphi and Visteon, will be the winners.

Table 8.2.2 Global tier-one companies with presence in China

Name	Locations	Activities
Bosch	Shanghai	Eight joint ventures – EMS; sparks, etc.
Delphi	Changchun	Fourteen joint ventures and wholly foreign-owned enterprises –
	Shanghai	electronics; chassis; harnesses;
	Wuhan	climate control
Valeo	Wuhan	Eight joint ventures and wholly foreign-owned enterprises –
		climate control; electrical products
Visteon	Changchun	Six joint ventures – interior;
	Shanghai	climate control;
	Wuhan	electronics
Allevard	Shanghai	
Brose	Shanghai	
Huchuson	Wuhan	
Magneti Marelli	Shanghai	
Pilkington	Changchun, Shanghai, Wuhan	
Sachs	Shanghai	
Siemens	Changchun, Shanghai	
ZF	Shanghai	

Source: ARA Research

China's Automotive Industry: Commercial Vehicles

Mark Norcliffe, Society of Motor Manufacturers and Traders (UK)

Market trends

In the early 1990s trucks accounted for 60 per cent of total vehicle production in China, buses represented a further 25 per cent, and passenger cars struggled to reach 15 per cent. By 2002, the market had moved into equilibrium, with each sector accounting for approximately 33 per cent of the production total. Thereafter, car production has raced ahead to become the largest single sector.

Whilst the growth trend in commercial vehicle (CV) manufacturing has been less spectacular, China nevertheless turned out more than 2.3 million CV units in 2003. This was made up of 1.19 million buses – a rise of 11 per cent over the previous year, which confirmed China's position as the top global bus market – and 1.22 million trucks – up 10 per cent on 2002. The demand for commercial vehicles is solidly underpinned by economic expansion, including greater mobility of goods and human resources, and a rapidly growing transport infrastructure. It therefore seems likely that, whilst the car market cools in 2004, the rise in CV production will continue.

Price remains the major consideration for Chinese commercial vehicle purchasers and, as a result, profits per unit are much lower than for passenger cars. Consequently, the major international car makers have been much slower to invest in China's CV sector, and the majority of the industry – and the models produced – remain in domestic ownership. The CV sector has also attracted less attention, and regulation, from central government. This has encouraged a number of new Chinese entrants, from differing industrial backgrounds, to enter the market.

For the same reason, imports of commercial vehicles remain very low – the 14,000 units imported in 2003 representing less than 1 per cent of the total Chinese market. This contrasts markedly with the car sector, where imports (mostly high-value luxury saloons) took 5 per cent of total sales.

The whole commercial vehicle industry has benefited from greatly increased mobility of both people and goods, and from the rapid expansion of China's transport network. However, a clear distinction can be seen between the development of the bus/coach and truck sectors. Customer demand for greater comfort and sophistication has driven an upgrading of products in the bus and coach sector, prompting a growth in foreign investment and joint venture partnerships. Trucks, whose drivers can be hired for a few dollars a day, remain mostly cheap and basic, and the market continues to be dominated by the two big domestic manufacturers – First Auto Works (FAW) and Dongfeng Motors (DFM).

Location and ownership of commercial vehicle builders

The mapping of China's commercial vehicle builders is complicated by official statistics, which do not draw a clear differentiation between those companies producing complete vehicles and those who build bodywork on to another manufacturer's chassis. Although there is a relatively small number of chassis makers, it is estimated that there may be up to 130 companies building bus bodies, and an astonishing 640 enterprises are recorded as constructors of 'special purpose goods vehicles' (of these, only 47 make in excess of 1,000 units per annum).

Geographically, the industry is widely scattered. The provinces of Jilin, Liaoning, Hubei, Shaanxi, Shandong, Sichuan, Jiangsu, Anhui and Guangxi all host commercial vehicle manufacturing plants. Ownership patterns are also diverse – ranging from state-owned giants like FAW and DMC, through provincially-supported enterprises (Shenyang Jinbei, Anhui Jianghuai Auto Co) to private consortia and companies. Part ownership by provincial or municipal government can be a substantial benefit to a commercial vehicle builder – the local authorities can offer not only advantageous manufacturing conditions but also an end-customer, through their control of local bus and truck fleets.

Central government has traditionally paid less attention to the regulation of CV production and sales than it has to passenger cars. Consequently, companies from outside the auto industry have found it comparatively easy to move into commercial vehicle building, usually by taking over an existing small manufacturer. Two recent examples of this trend are Chunlun, a leading domestic appliance maker, who has started production of light trucks in Jiangsu Province, and their competitor Midea, who has announced plans to develop a new bus plant in Kunming, Yunnan Province.

Foreign investment in China's commercial vehicle industry has lagged behind the levels committed to passenger car joint ventures. There have been some notably lengthy negotiations; Volvo, for example, talked with China National Heavy Duty Truck Group for nine years before striking a deal. The traditional low cost of commercial vehicles in China, the reluctance of purchasers to pay for greater sophistication, and the consequent small profit margins have all discouraged would-be investors. However, this pattern is now changing, driven principally by stricter emissions standards, improving infrastructure, greater mobility and a consumer demand for greater comfort. The major international players – Volvo, Mercedes Benz, MAN, Renault/Nissan, Mitsubishi, Hyundai, Hino and Iveco – are all pursuing closer relationships with Chinese partners.

The Chinese bus market

Classifications and market segmentation

The Chinese bus market is officially divided into four categories, whose specifications were changed in July 2002:

- large buses – over 9m in length (previously over 10m);
- medium buses – 6–9m in length (previously 7–10m);
- light buses – 3.5–6m in length (previously 3.5–7m);
- minibuses – less than 3.5m (unchanged).

Minibuses have traditionally held the largest market segment. Typically, they are simple, single-box vehicles, owned by private individuals or business groups, that are used for commercial hire. Their small (less than 1.0 litre) engines are often based on old Japanese technology, and do not meet modern emission standards. As a result, they are increasingly confined to medium and small-sized towns, and to the countryside. In 2003, mini vehicles still accounted for 57 per cent of Chinese bus production, but the year-on-year rate of growth was only 3.7 per cent.

The fastest growing market sector is light buses. In 2003 production reached 443,000 – an increase of 32.4 per cent. The most successful models are based on long-established Japanese designs; European-derived models have generally been less successful, perhaps because of the Chinese reluctance to embrace diesel technology. Light buses are bought in large numbers by taxi firms, and also by individual companies who have a statutory duty to transport their employees to and from the workplace.

In contrast, medium bus sales declined by 13 per cent in 2003, to just over 53,000. This reduction may be partially attributable to the SARS crisis, which caused a sharp fall in the demand for public transport. The sector is dominated by basic quality products, often poorly maintained, that have traditionally been used both for inner-city public transportation and for movement between urban centres. Increasingly, longer journeys are becoming the preserve of larger and more sophisticated buses that offer their passengers a greater degree of comfort.

Large buses still only account for around 2 per cent of the total Chinese market, but sales are growing at over 13 per cent. It is in this sector that international activity is most evident, with a number of manufacturing joint ventures now in operation. Improved body styling and levels of equipment have both boosted domestic sales and opened up the route to potential export sales.

Key players

Minibus production is dominated by three companies – ChangAn Automotive (28 per cent market share), Harbin Hafei Automotive Co (23 per cent) and SAIC-GM Wuling Automotive (19 per cent). The location of these enterprises, in the mid-west, far north and far south of China, mirrors the popularity of their products in rural areas, where the demand will continue to be for cheap, basic vehicles. However, the three market leaders, who all have access to more modern technology, may eventually decide to concentrate more efforts on higher value products, which offer better profit returns.

In the light bus sector, Jinbei Auto Holdings, based in Shenyang, have maintained their market leadership, manufacturing a derivative of the Toyota Hiace model. Sales in 2003 reached 78,000 (representing a 17 per cent market share), backed by an aggressive price-cutting campaign, which markedly reduced the company's overall profitability. A further eight domestic companies recorded annual sales in excess of 20,000, mostly with products based on Japanese technology. One notable recent feature in this sector has been the declining fortunes of European-based models. The Iveco Daily, manufactured in a long-standing joint venture with Nanjing Yuejin Auto Group, has continued to lose ground, whilst local production of both the Ford Transit and the Renault Trafic was terminated as the foreign partners concentrated on their new passenger car alliances.

It is in the medium and heavy bus sectors that the Chinese industry statistics are most confusing. Xiamen King Long United Automotive Industry Co is classified as a vehicle assembler rather than a manufacturer and therefore does not appear in the official listings. In fact, the company – a four-way domestic partnership – is reckoned to be China's largest producer, turning out 15,700 vehicles in 2003. This represents a tenfold increase since 1999 and, even if the projected growth in capacity to 150,000 can be regarded as optimistic, there is no doubting the company's ambition. Already active in a number of overseas markets, it has announced short-term plans to export coaches to the UK. Its international technology partners include Cummins, MAN, ZF, Hino and Mitsubishi.

Zhengzhou Yutong Coach Manufacturing Co also claimed to produce around 15,000 units in 2003. This private company has ambitious expansion plans, targeting a 25 per cent share of the domestic market and the acquisition of manufacturing sites throughout China. In 2003, a new joint venture was formed with MAN – called the Lion's Bus Co – to manufacture up to 6,000 bus chassis a year.

Changzhou Bus Company claims a place among the top five medium/heavy manufacturers, with a basic product range targeted at smaller cities. Unusually, it also manufactures most of its own chassis. The company gained useful 'free' technology when its US joint venture partner, Flexible, went into liquidation, and, more recently, a new joint venture has been concluded with Iveco, building a range of vehicles under the CBC-Iveco name.

A potentially powerful newcomer is Sunwin Bus, a 50/50 joint venture between Volvo Bus Corporation and Shanghai Automotive Industry Corporation (SAIC). Volvo already has another bus joint venture, in Xian, and SAIC has no previous experience in heavy commercial vehicles. However, the new venture does possess the significant advantage of a guaranteed major customer – the city of Shanghai, which has an immediate need for at least 1,000 new units a year. From this basis, the new partnership will be able to pursue sales in other municipalities, and determine whether the concept of combining a European chassis with Chinese bodywork will offer greater reliability and wider market appeal.

Joint ventures with foreign partners have not always succeeded in the heavy/medium segment of the market. Yaxing-Benz, formed in 1996 between Yangzhou Motor Coach Manufacturing and Mercedes Benz, saw sales decline by 46 per cent from 1999 to 2003, at which point the provincial government sold the majority of its shareholding to the private Green-Cool Group, an electronics manufacturer.

The Chinese truck market

Classifications and market segmentation

Around 80 per cent of China's trucks are powered by diesel engines. This contrasts markedly with the bus sector, where 85 per cent of vehicles have gasoline engines, and is a further indication that diesel is regarded in China as a second-rate fuel.

Trucks are also categorized under four headings, but based on vehicle weight rather than length:

- heavy trucks – over 14 tonnes gross weight (GW);
- medium trucks – 6–14 tonnes GW;
- light trucks – 1.8–6 tonnes GW;
- mini trucks – less than 1.8 tonnes GW.

Across the four market segments, bus and truck sales have followed roughly similar patterns. The production of mini trucks actually fell in 2003 to a total of 142,000, representing around 11 per cent of the total market. However, the rate of decline has been slower than commentators had predicted, demonstrating the continuing importance of these vehicles in more rural areas. The light truck sector, which includes the five tonne 'work-horse' popular with Chinese businesses, continues to grow – up almost 25 per cent in 2003 – and now accounts for 56 per cent of the new registrations.

Medium trucks have seen a continuation in the pattern of decline, which has been apparent, with only brief interruptions, since 1998. Their market share now hovers around 11 per cent. Heavy trucks continue to take an increasing share of production and sales, although growth in 2003 was a modest 4 per cent. They now account for 21 per cent of the market. Further growth in the heavy truck sector is likely to be stimulated by the growth of China's road network and increased activity by foreign investors.

Key players

Production of heavy and medium trucks continues to be dominated by the two state-owned giants – First Auto Works (FAW) and Dongfeng Motor Corporation (DMC) – who between them accounted for 73 per cent of new vehicles. However, these figures disguise a steady loss of market share in recent years. In contrast to their passenger car operations, the commercial vehicle divisions of both FAW and DMC have been slow to find foreign partners and to introduce new technologies. FAW, who plan a new 200,000-capacity truck plant in Changchun, have been in lengthy but unproductive negotiations with Mercedes Benz and MAN from Germany, and Japan's Mitsubishi. However, DMC's new alliance with Renault/Nissan offers the Wuhan-based company excellent access to modern technology, and commercial vehicles are a key part of the joint venture's ambitious growth plans.

Heavy vehicle producers who are already reaping the benefits of new foreign partnerships are China National Heavy Duty Truck Group (CNHTC) and Beijing Auto Industry Corporation (BAIC). CNHTC increased sales by 48 per cent in 2003 to almost 20,000 units. Most of these were sold under the 'Huanghe Wangzi' brand, based on Steyr technology and fitted with Euro-2 compliant engines. The Jinan-based company has also struck a deal with Volvo Trucks, after lengthy discussions, which foresees the additional production of 20,000 Volvo units each year. However, the growth in 2003 was also a reflection of the group's recovery under new top management from a relatively flat performance. Previously, CNHTC

reported direct to the central government but ownership was transferred to the jurisdiction of Shandong provincial government when the former president and all but one of the vice presidents were dismissed after irregularities were reported.

Meanwhile, BAIC – through its Beiqi Futian subsidiary – has developed a new 'Auman' brand of heavy vehicle, and stands to acquire more modern technology through its expanding partnership with DaimlerChrysler.

A new entrant into the Chinese market for large commercial vehicles is Hyundai. In partnership with Anhui Jianghuai Auto Co (JAC), the Korean auto maker has ambitious plans to introduce its full range of commercial vehicles to China, and is targeting combined truck and bus sales of 150,000 per annum.

The booming light truck sector continues to be dominated by domestic Chinese manufacturers. BAIC has a 32 per cent share of the market, but there are a further six companies – DMC, FAW, JAC, Jiangling Motors Group, Yuejin Motor Group and Qingling Motor Co — each producing in excess of 30,000 units per annum. Predominantly, their models are based upon Japanese technology, though in this sector too Korean-based products are starting to appear.

In mini-trucks, the clear leaders are SAIC-GM Wuling Automotive and ChangAn Automotive, who, in 2003, took 35 per cent and 31 per cent of the market respectively. Both companies have access to modern technology and new engines through their partnerships with General Motors and Suzuki, and therefore seem likely to maintain their dominant position, as rivals struggle to achieve improved emissions standards.

Emissions standards

China is moving to the imposition of Euro-2 emission standards for all newly registered commercial vehicles over 3.5 tonnes gross weight. Originally introduced in Beijing, Shanghai and other selected major cities during 2003, the standard is due to be applied nationwide by the end of 2004. However, with limited vehicle testing facilities, enforcement is likely to be patchy, and the continuing poor quality of local diesel fuel can cause even modern power units to struggle to meet the required emissions levels.

As a result, environmental legislation may be only partially effective in stimulating the modernization of China's commercial vehicle fleet. Particularly in rural and remote parts of the country, cheap and unsophisticated vehicles will continue to take the major market share.

Compressed natural gas (CNG) is gaining popularity as an alternative fuel, particularly for the urban bus and taxi fleets in major cities. This trend is likely to accelerate once a new pipeline is completed connecting the eastern cities to the gas fields in the west of the country.

Future developments

Countries with expanding economies normally require increasing numbers of commercial vehicles. China will be no exception; whilst growth in the passenger car market will fluctuate in response to private buyers' priorities and purchasing power, Chinese commercial vehicle production and sales can be expected to forge ahead at a steady rate. However, economic growth in China will not be equally distributed, and the richer provinces will continue to move further ahead of the more rural and remote regions. The supply of commercial vehicles will need to cater for both ends of the wealth spectrum, and it therefore seems likely that the fragmentation within the industry will persist, and indeed widen. In the medium term, the Chinese market will continue to support a large number of commercial vehicle builders, with a diverse range of products.

Central government policies will have some effect on the development of the commercial vehicle sector – in particular, legislation controlling emissions will drive up the level of engine technology. And, if China is to improve its poor road safety record, the government will also have to tackle issues of poorly maintained and badly loaded vehicles.

Currently, commercial vehicles in China have a legal life span of only eight years. Paradoxically, this regulation has impeded the raising of production standards, making it difficult for manufacturers to justify higher prices on the grounds of greater reliability and a longer working life. Cost will remain the key factor for Chinese CV buyers. It therefore seems probable that the most successful commercial vehicle makers will be those who can offer products specifically tailored to the demands of the local market but incorporating an appropriate element of global technology. A marketing strategy based on the introduction of the latest western models – successfully pursued by the international car makers – will be less likely to succeed in the commercial vehicle sector.

China as an exporter of commercial vehicles

Commercial vehicles make up the vast majority of China's current auto exports. In the first six months of 2003, 41,000 vehicles were exported, of which only 1,180 were passenger cars. Most exports are cheap and unsophisticated models, destined for markets in Africa, Asia and the Middle East. Technology limitations – particularly in meeting emissions standards – have barred Chinese manufacturers from the more lucrative western markets. However, that pattern is set to change.

Chinese truck makers with access to Euro-2 compliant engines are now starting to target export markets in Europe and even North America. One example is Fushian Engineering Corporation – a minor player within China – which is currently testing a truck designed specifically for export.

Technically, CNHTC, co-branding its premium trucks as Steyr, has an excellent opportunity to sell its products in Middle East markets where they satisfy Gulf and Saudi Arabian standards. However, poor market research and selection of unqualified exclusive distributors has deterred major local market distributors, who had expressed interest in adding keenly priced CNHTC trucks alongside their heavier European brands.

Chinese bus makers are further advanced. Xiamen King Long – a company wholly owned by Chinese partners – has recently added Malta to its list of global export markets, and has signed a joint venture agreement with JCBL of Chandrigarh to manufacture luxury coaches in India. Meanwhile, Zhengzhou Yutong Co and Anhui Ankal Automobile are poised to supply CNG-powered buses to the Philippines.

Banking: The Domestic Banks

Jonathan Reuvid

Background

Until 2003 banking was the area of Chinese government policy most criticized by international institutions and economists. The criticism was focused as much on the apparent lack of control exercised by the State Council and its management organ, The People's Bank of China (PBOC), over the lending policies of the four big state-owned banks as on banking regulations and management standards.

Throughout the 1980s and 1990s, the state banks had provided an apparently inexhaustible supply of borrowed funds to the monolithic state industries, through which much of the government's export-led drive to develop industry at a headlong pace was achieved. China is not unique among developing and developed countries in providing funds to support inefficient state-owned industries with scant regard to sound commercial criteria, but the scale of this activity in China was beyond international comparison. The management of state-owned enterprises (SOEs) appeared to be locked into the classic command economy principle of supplying the factors of production (capital, land and labour) necessary to achieve the state's output requirements without regard to efficiency or profit.

In a high growth economy such a lending policy could be sustained for many years at the expense of creating a mountain of non-performing loans (NPLs) that the state-owned banks were unable, or unwilling, to contain. However, the rapid growth of the private economy – a combination of privately-owned enterprises, companies with an ultimate parent company owned by provincial government but managed to international standards, and foreign-invested enterprises

(FIEs) – which has far outpaced the floundering state-owned giants in many sectors, increased the pressure on the government to address the problem of NPLs. Since WTO admission in 2001, the further opening of the market to foreign investors is ratcheting up competition generated by privately-owned companies in many of the key sectors reviewed in this book, even the banking sector itself. Official estimates at the beginning of 2004 suggested that some 20.32 per cent of the 'big four's' loan portfolios were non-performing.

International concern, fuelled by these developments, has always been driven by the recurring fear of a Chinese recession, particularly when western economies falter, and the likely consequences from the overhang of bad debts. NPLs that would be classified elsewhere as plain bad debt could render the big banks insolvent. So far, China's ability to macro-manage the economy has ensured that each slowdown in the economy has ended in a 'soft landing' and been of short duration, but the concern persists. Financial experts point to the Japanese experience of NPLs, still at US$330 billion in 2002, four years after its banks initiated their sell-off programme that had realized US$600 billion at that date.

The state banking sector

By the end of 2002, China's commercial bank assets had increased to RMB16,461 billion (US$1,975 billion), having grown at a compound annual growth rate of 5.3 per cent. The state-owned commercial banks represented 70.5 per cent of the market with national and provincially-owned commercial banks accounting for a further 21.8 per cent market share. At this point, the limited number of foreign commercial banks authorized to trade in China had achieved 7.7 per cent of the market (Source: Snapdata Research).

Banking policy

In the latter part of 2003, the government launched a reform programme for the governance of the 'big four' – China Construction Bank (CCB), Bank of China (BoC), Industrial and Commercial Bank of China (ICBC) and Agricultural Bank of China. In November, the Chairman of the China Banking Regulatory Commission (CBRC), Mr Liu Mingkang, unveiled 10-point guidelines to ensure that the biggest state banks, which were technically insolvent, would be turned around within three to five years. An international council of financial advisers, which included some of the most respected names in world finance, was assembled and the turnaround plan consisted of the appointment of foreign bankers as directors and senior managers, the sale of equity stakes to strategic investors, and some stock market issues in Shanghai or Hong Kong.

Recapitalization and the aftermath

The most immediate practical news was that Beijing would start to recapitalize 'one or two' of the big four banks in the form of capital injections, conditional upon each bank demonstrating its ability to reduce its NPLs through its own efforts and to improve its corporate governance. Flotation would be a further reward, for which CBC and BoC were designated the front-runners. Each of them received US$22.5 billion in interest-bearing loans on 31 December 2003. Following these injections, the capital adequacy ratios of both banks were considered to be comfortably above the 8 per cent minimum demanded under international rules.

The CBRC also indicated that all four banks might issue subordinated debt up to a total of RMB300 billion (US$37.5 billion) through bonds that could not be issued to retail investors but only to pension funds and insurance companies at coupon rates higher than for sovereign issues.

In January 2004, the government signalled a tougher stance on governance of the two banks that had received the US$45 billion capital boost, demonstrating that the injection of funds was in no way a 'free lunch'. The clampdown included the ending of life-long employment contracts, the removal of government titles from senior staff and the threat of resolute supervisory action if NPL

levels should rise again. The closure and merging of loss-making branches and businesses, together with staff redundancies, would be accelerated.

According to the CBRC plan, investment banks, insurance companies and international financial institutions will be eligible to become shareholders, as well as domestic and foreign commercial banks. Once CCB and BoC become shareholding banks, a stiffer supervisory regime will be applied. Should the capital base of either bank be eroded again by an accumulation of NPLs, it was declared that new lending would be restricted and management remuneration would be curtailed.

The following month, the ICBC, China's largest bank, announced that it had already requested regulatory approval for an issue of subordinated debt, the first in a planned programme to raise RMB100 billion (US$12 billion) over two to three years. The bank had already issued RMB3 billion (US$375 million) in December 2003. Inevitably, critics suggested that the cash infusions had outpaced improvements in corporate governance.

By March 2004, the CBRC was expressing impatience with the progress made by both CBC and BoC, while acknowledging the difficulty of dealing with their bad debt burdens. The two banks were targeted to achieve returns on equity of 11 per cent by 2005 and 13 per cent by 2007, with returns on assets in line with the average of the top 100 banks globally. The CBRC also expressed determination in removing those responsible for 'policy mistakes that caused losses'.

March also saw government action through the PBOC to curb bank lending to industries such as steel and property, where expansion was considered excessive. Overall bank lending in 2003 had been 20 per cent above 2002 and was seen as a cause of the economy's overheating. The action took the form of two permanent reforms by the PBOC. The first was an increase in the reserve requirement for some substandard financial institutions (excluding the big four banks and urban and rural credit cooperatives) from 7 per cent to 7.5 per cent from 25 April 2004. The PBOC also raised the upper limit on its interest rate charges to commercial banks, allowing the re-discount rate to float by up to 27 basis points over the benchmark 20-day rate of 2.97 per cent. This measure had two effects: it became more expensive for lower quality borrowers to obtain funds in the interbank market, and it also allowed PBOC to price bills at more attractive rates when necessary to reduce market liquidity.

In October, a further breakthrough reform was introduced when the PBoC moved to liberalize lending rates by authorizing banks to settle their lending rates freely and abolished the central bank's remit to set a fixed lending rate. A similar reform will eventually be applied to deposit rates but it is expected that an upper limit on rates will be maintained for some time.

Flotation plans

By August it had become clear that the overseas listings planned for CCB and BoC would be delayed until mid-2005 at the earliest. The complex financial restructuring of each bank, together with the programmes for reducing NPLs, updating software in the vast branch networks and auditing accounts, are demanding tasks that would take some months to carry out.

The two IPOs could raise up to US$14 billion, of which CCB is seeking US$10 billion, while BoC could sell US$4 billion of shares. Successful listings on international capital markets are crucial to maintaining foreign investors' positive view of China's commercial environment.

City banks

There are 112 city commercial banks in China, which have become attractive to foreign financial institutions seeking to invest in the financial sector. They are considered more manageable than banks with a nation-wide franchise, partly because their geographic focus may have insulated them somewhat from exposure to NPLs.

For example, in addition to the HSBC stake in the Bank of Shanghai and Citibank's shareholding in Pudong Development Bank, referred to below, the International Finance Corp, the private sector arm of the World Bank, has taken stakes in the Nanjing City and Xian City Commercial Banks, the Bank of Shanghai, the Industrial Bank and Minsheng Bank.

In February 2004, Beijing City Commercial Bank, one of the largest city banks, which is majority-owned by the Beijing Sate-owned Asset Management Corporation, a unit of the municipal government, announced its plans to sell from 15 per cent up to 34 per cent of its share capital to selected investors as a first step to seeking a stock market flotation.

Private banks

So far, there are only three private commercial banks in Mainland China: the Beijing-based Minsheng Bank,

established in 1996; Zheshang Bank, which opened for business in August 2004; and the recently approved Bohai Bank.

Zheshang Bank is based in the wealthy eastern province of Zhejiang, the heart of Chinese private enterprise, and was created from a former government-run commercial institution. After restructure, 13 of its 15 shareholders are now private enterprises, including Wanxiang Group, the leading vehicle parts manufacturer. Together, they hold 85.71 per cent of the registered share capital.

Towards the end of 2004, Bohai Bank, a Tianjin-based private lender was granted regulatory approval.

The creation of private banks is considered to be of growing importance, since the state banks have become increasingly unwilling or unable to lend to the booming but cash-starved private sector. Several former Rural Credit Cooperatives are also transforming themselves into private banks to serve rural clients.

Non-performing loans (NPLs)

NPL sales

A key plank in the government's policy platform for tackling NPLs was the transfer of packages of bad loans totalling RMB1,400 billion (US$169 billion) from the loan books of the big four banks into four specialist asset management companies (AMCs). The four AMCs set up in 1999 are: Cinda, Orient, Great Wall and Huarong Asset Management.

Early experience of selling off the packages was unpromising. An auction of 22 asset packages in December 2003, representing RMB25 billion of NPLs, found buyers for only three packages. The vendor, Huarong, hoped that post-auction negotiations with bidders would result in the sale of a further 14 packages. Reasons for the disappointing outcome were the relatively old age of many of the 12,000 overdue loans involved from 1,300 borrowers and their concentration in China's less developed western provinces, compounded by poor asset quality and documentation. A second auction by Huarong Asset Management was rather more successful.

Morgan Stanley pioneered an alternative approach for purchasing NPLs when it negotiated a direct deal with CCB to dispose of RMB4.3 billion in bad loans. However, approval of the deal was refused by the authorities in February 2004, mainly because the price offered was too low but also because there was a preference for using competitive auctions for the disposal of distressed assets.

However, CCB, in its drive to prepare for early overseas listing, came up with its own variation to the AMC solution. Instead of selling NPLs, the bank decided to first separate the collateral from loans and then to auction the collateral. The auction of 'settled assets' provided an innovative solution to the CBRC ban on banks selling NPLs at below face value. In its first offering by public auction, CCB set out to sell off about RMB5 billion (US$600 million) in settled assets, mainly along China's east coast. For investment banks making bids, the skill lay in deciding whether ownership titles to the assets were enforceable and how much the sale of each asset might realize.

This pioneering auction actually attracted 16 potential buyers and registered bidders, including Citigroup, Deutsche Bank, JP Morgan Chase, UBS, Shinsei Bank, Goldman Sachs, Merrill Lynch, Lehman Brothers, Morgan Stanley and General Electric. The sale involved three separate packages of assets ranging from shopping centres to residential complexes from Inner Mongolia to Southern Guangdong province.

In June 2004, the PBoC governor, Zhou Xiaochuan, while acknowledging that the success of the AMCs had been limited, confirmed that Beijing had given them additional powers for dealing with problem assets while introducing competition between them to encourage the adoption of market mechanisms to price the bad loans they hold. The shift to an auction approach in pricing the loans taken on from the big four banks, rather than accepting face value, makes it easier for the AMCs to sell on NPLs at realistic prices. In the same month, the new approach was put to the test in the largest auction to date of NPLs with a face value of RMB278.7 billion (US$28 billion) at which the four site-owned AMCs competed. The winner, China Cinda Asset Management won the right to deal with a mixed bag of NPLs from BoC and CCB.

A further auction of RMB150 billion (US$18 billion) of NPLs, open to both foreign and domestic investors, was launched by Great Wall Asset Management in November 2004, comprising packages of loans collected from its 30 regional offices. Completion of the sale process is scheduled for June 2005. Since September 2004, Great Wall has disposed of some 54 per cent of the NPLs that it had acquired from Agricultural Bank of China in 1999. Although the asset quality is considered to be poor, the present sale could almost clear the remaining portfolio.

NPL ratios

In March 2004, CCB and BoC reported improvements in their balance sheets, with BoC reducing its NPL ratio to under 16 per cent and CCB lowering its ratio to less than 12 per cent. The NPL ratio for the overall banking sector fell by 5.32 percentage points to 17.8 per cent.

However, the statistics were misleading since four of the five percentage points reduction was attributable to a rapid growth in new loans to fund over-investment in sectors such as the automotive and steel industries, raising the fear that the improvement could be only temporary if the new loans are relegated to NPL status later.

Nevertheless, in April after an exhaustive audit of BoC's portfolio of NPLs on a branch by branch basis, PricewaterhouseCoopers (PwC) concluded that the bank's NPL ratio was 15.64 per cent, only slightly more than the internal BoC estimate. In September, BoC announced that its NPL ratio had improved further to 7.9 per cent.

In November, the CBRC released statistics for the performance of the AMCs in the first three quarters of 2004 in their core NPL business. Accumulated disposal of the four AMCs was at the level of RMB575 billion, with RMB120 billion recovered in cash. The disposal ratio climbed to 47 per cent in the third quarter, while the asset recovery and cash recovery ratios were steady at around 27 per cent and 20 per cent respectively.

Transformation of the AMCs

The four AMCs were originally intended as one-off asset vehicles to be wound up after no more than 10 years. With the encouragement of the CBRC, they are now seeking to transform themselves into profit-driven financial institutions with powers to compete with investment banks in a wide range of services such as consultancy and underwriting. Already Huarong has expanded beyond its original mandate having been entrusted with management of the troubled D'Long corporate group, a privately-owned company with problem assets.

Transformation would certainly require refinancing because the AMCs have no hope of repaying the bonds that they issued to fund the purchase of banks' NPLs at face value in 1999. The AMCs are studying the possibility of inviting strategic investments by foreign companies and public listings.

Summary

Undoubtedly, 2004 was a year of considerable achievement in the reform of domestic Chinese banking and in the credit management of the four major state-owned banks. In spite of a shaky start, the credit spree, which had caused much of the foreign concern for the medium-term future of the economy, was successfully tempered and the industry overhaul proceeded apace.

Focusing on the improvement in banks' capital adequacy ratios (CAR) as a general yardstick of the financial sector's growing strength, Mr Lu Mingkang, chairman of CBRC, was able to forecast confidently in November that the number of banks able to reach the Basel I international standard of 8 per cent would rise by 11 to a total of 19. Credit growth for the year had been held steady below 14 per cent compared with the highs of 30–40 per cent of 2002–2003. Mr Liu predicted that the new requirements would ensure that credit expansion would remain in the 13–16 per cent band, a level that he characterized as comfortable.

Milestone changes during the year were the liberalization of lending rates in October, the authorization of banks to enter the fund management business, the encouragement of new private banks and a ground-breaking governance overhaul by one large state bank.

BoC is engaged in far-reaching management changes that will see each of 230,000 staff reapply for their jobs and the introduction of a performance-based pay system that will reward staff for prudent lending. In partnership with Cass Business School of the UK's City University, BoC has also developed an Executive MBA programme for its managers in Shanghai.

Banking: Foreign Bank Investment

Jonathan Reuvid

Commercial banking

In August 2004, China eased restrictions on the expansion of foreign banks in anticipation of the full opening of the market at the end of 2006. According to the rules posted on the China Banking Regulatory Commission's (CBRC) website, minimum capital requirements for banks wanting licences to do business with Chinese firms in RMB currency are reduced from RMB400 million (US$48 million) to RMB300 million (US$36 million). In parallel, the minimum capital requirement for foreign banks offering local currency services to Chinese individuals is cut from RMB600 million to RMB500 million.

The 64 foreign banks operating in China, with a total of about 200 branches, have seen their share of lending fall since 2002 as a result of the expansion of loans by local institutions, unrestricted until January 2004. The CBRC has now abolished the rule making foreign banks wait for the period of a year between the opening of each new branch, which makes organic growth easier.

However, one irksome restriction is the introduction in 2004 of new rules requiring foreign banks to apply for quotas for borrowing money offshore, which has made it more expensive for them to fund themselves.

The year ended with CBRC opening five new cities to foreign banks offering local currency services. As a part of the WTO accession agreement China had undertaken to permit foreign banks to do RMB business in three cities – Beijing, Kunming and Xiamen – by the end of 2004, but added Xi'an and Shenyang a year ahead of schedule to bring the total number of cities open up to 18. The acceleration towards full opening of the banking sector at the end of 2006 has been construed as evidence of the CBRC's positive view of the role for foreign banks in China, particularly in partnership with local institutions, as a force for improvement in governance. The CBRC reported that, at the end of October 2004, the assets of the 62 foreign banks in China amounted to RMB553 billion (US$66.8 billion) an increase of 41 per cent year-on-year. Nevertheless, restrictions on foreign banks' business and the challenges of the market have meant that foreign bank assets still account for only 1.8 per cent of the industry total.

CBRC chairman, Mr Liu Mingkang, is on record as recommending that all Chinese with extensive overseas operation should focus on adopting the more stringent Basel II international standards of banking practice. The Basel II rules in Chinese are now available publicly in China.

HSBC

For HSBC in China, 2004 was an exciting year of development in which it deepened its market penetration and consolidated its position as the leader in China among foreign commercial banks.

In February, the Shanghai branch of HSBC received permission to underwrite domestic Chinese government bonds, making it the first foreign bank to be admitted to the Ministry of Finance's bond underwriting group of 47 domestic members for the interbank market. In 2003, Beijing sold the equivalent of US$76 billion of bonds and is expected to have sold more than US$80 billion in 2004. HSBC Shanghai is empowered to underwrite and on-sell debt to about 1,000 Chinese financial institutions licensed by the Ministry of Finance to buy the bonds. The HSBC licence has placed the bank into the second tier of smaller underwriters but does not impose the minimum bidding requirements on the bank to which the larger first-tier institutions are subject.

Prior to 2004, HSBC had acquired an 8 per cent stake in Bank of Shanghai, which operates 200 branches in the city. Although the rules that govern foreign banks' expansion in China have been relaxed, the strict limits on the number of branches that a foreign bank may open up remained, and the only route to expansion was through the acquisition of shareholdings in established Chinese banks. In August, HSBC completed an agreement to purchase a 19.9 per cent shareholding in Bank of Communications (BoCom), China's fifth largest bank, just below the 20 per cent ceiling on foreign investment in Chinese banks. The cost of the link, after providing for the purchase of the shareholding in BoCom's newly increased capital, is US$1.75 billion.

The deal was approved by the CBRC as a part of a restructuring plan under which existing shareholders could inject up to RMB30 billion (US$3.6 billion) to raise the bank's capital adequacy ratio, which was below the international standard of 8 per cent. Prior to the HSBC investment, the top 20 shareholders owned 49.5 per cent of the bank, of which the Ministry of Finance was the largest with a stake of 28.8 per cent. In the event, China's Social Security fund has injected RMB10 billion into the bank, the Ministry of Finance RMB5 billion and the Central Huijin Investment Company, an arm of the Administration of Foreign Exchange, RMB3 billion. Other shareholders increased their shareholdings by RMB1.1 billion. BoCom was the first Chinese bank to achieve a share listing and is now planning an IPO in Hong Kong for the second half of 2005.

BoCom, which has operations in New York and Tokyo, is reported to have less of an NPL problem than the Big Four, with NPL of RMB10.8 billion (US$2.39 billion) accounting for only 3.3 per cent of its loan book at 30 June 2004. The bank is one of the 15 commercial banks authorized to operate throughout Mainland China, with 2,700 branches in 137 cities – one of the largest retail networks. It claims to have 20 million depositors and more than 50,000 corporate customers.

HSBC's lead over other foreign banks is likely to be maintained at least until the wider opening of the Chinese banking market in 2007.

Standard Chartered

In January 2004, Standard Chartered made US$36 million from the sale of its 0.4 per cent stake in Bank of China International (the state-owned bank's overseas subsidiary). The UK-based Standard Chartered also committed itself to incorporate its Hong Kong business in Hong Kong, to take advantage of new rules that allow companies incorporated in the Special Administrative Region (SAR) greater access to the mainland market.

At the beginning of the year Standard Chartered had confirmed that it was in discussions to acquire a stake in BoCom, which would have given it a foothold in the market and helped it to catch up with its international rivals. However, the talks failed when the Standard Chartered approach was pre-empted by HSBC (see above). Standard Chartered is continuing to look at possible partners in China including, it is thought, the commercial bank China Everbright. However, the failure to buy into BoCom was an undoubted setback.

Other foreign bank acquisitions

The foreign financial institutions that have already bought holdings in Chinese banks, in addition to HSBC include Citibank, Hang Seng Bank, the Bank of Nova Scotia, Newbridge Capital Corp, the Commonwealth Bank of Australia and the International Finance Corp. At 2004 year-end, nine additional foreign banks were awaiting approval to buy stakes in Chinese lenders other than BoC and China Construction Bank (CCB).

Asset and fund management

Following its merger with Crédit Lyonnais, the asset management business of Crédit Agricole has become the largest in France, and the bank announced in August 2004 that it was actively searching for a joint venture partner in China. Rivals Société Générale and BNP Paribas already have alliances in China.

To date, 15 overseas fund managers have set up joint ventures with local Chinese partners since the industry was liberalized in 2002. In whatever joint venture Crédit Agricole engages, the French bank will be limited to a 49 per cent stake from the end of 2004, under WTO agreements. Joint ventures are allowed to introduce new products but may not sell offshore funds to Chinese investors.

According to the research company, Morningstar Asia, total funds under management in China at the end of March 2004 stood at RMB158 billion (US$19 billion), an increase of 85 per cent from the 2003 year-end.

In November 2004, Beijing extended permission to local commercial banks to establish fund management ventures, signalling government willingness to attract foreign money managers into joint ventures. Banks were previously prohibited from directly owning securities companies. The reasons for this liberalization are twofold:

- to inject more funds into the stock market (at present banks account for more than 90 per cent of China's financial requirements);
- to reduce the reliance of Chinese banks on revenue from the difference between the loan and deposit rates by generating more income from fee-based operations.

Investment banking

Over the past decade, Morgan Stanley has led its competitors in China in the investment banking field with a 34 per cent holding in the domestic investment firm, China International Capital Corp, in which CCB is the majority shareholder.

Goldman Sachs

The news broke in July 2004 that Premier Wen Jiabao and the State Council had approved a groundbreaking joint venture between Goldman Sachs (Goldman), the US investment bank, and Fang Fenglei, a well connected local banker. At that stage the deal still needed to be ratified by the financial regulator, the China Securities Regulatory Commission (CSRC), but seemed to position Goldman as the first foreign firm capable of arranging equity and bond deals in China's fast-growing markets through a vehicle that it would effectively control.

The structure of the deal, since approved by CSRC, provides for Goldman to lend up to RMB800 million (US$97 million) to Fang Fenglei to set up a securities firm called Gao Hua, which translates as Goldman China. Gao Hua will own 67 per cent of the joint venture with Goldman holding the balance of 33 per cent. Gao Hua is to be fully owned by Mr Fang, other Chinese bankers and Lenovo, the leading Chinese computer maker. However, the terms of Goldman's loan to Mr Fang include an option to buy his controlling interest in Gao Hua whenever the rules allow.

The deal gives Goldman effective control of the joint venture without breaking China's securities laws. Unlike Sino-foreign investment banking ventures,

Gao Hua will be deemed a domestic firm and will be allowed to offer broking and trading products, as well as an equities advisory service. It also paves the way for Goldman to acquire a domestic securities house if the authorities lift the restrictions.

The entry price for Beijing's approval of the Goldman investment was the contribution of about RMB510 million (US$33 million) to rescue Hainan Securities, a bankrupt securities house in the form of a 'donation' to a fund set up to repay depositors. There is no other connection between Goldman and Hainan Securities. With Goldman committed to contribute some US$50 million of working capital for Gao, its total outlay will be less than US$200 million.

Other investment houses

Other Wall Street investment houses, including Credit Suisse First Boston (CSFB), Deutsche Bank, Merrill Lynch and UBS, had lobbied the Chinese authorities unsuccessfully against the Goldman joint venture throughout the previous year. Now the same firms are hoping that Beijing will allow them to have operational control of joint ventures with local brokerages as the government seeks further outside help to restore the shaky finances of many state-owned securities companies.

A recent study by CFSB has forecast that China's stock markets, with a present capitalization of US$500 billion, could become the world's second or third-largest by 2010, with market capitalization rising to US$2,000 billion.

Credit cards

In January 2004, Chinese regulators gave authorization to Citibank and HSBC to be the first two foreign banks to issue branded credit cards in cooperation with local partners. Citibank's partner is Shanghai Pudong Development Bank, and HSBC is in partnership with the Bank of Shanghai. Such alliances are seen as a means of harnessing foreign expertise to raise the credit risk assessment skills of Chinese banks.

Summary

While market penetration by foreign investors in both commercial and investment banking remained constrained, both HSBC in commercial banking and Goldman Sachs in investment banking have taken significant steps forward in growing their China business.

Computer Technology and IT

Jonathan Reuvid and Snapshots International

Market Size

Based on the sales of PCs, software, printers and servers, the growth of the computer technology market in china is charted in Table 8.6.1.

- Chinese computer technology sales increased by 30.8 per cent in value in 2002. Total sales for 2002 were RMB133.4 billion;
- compound annual growth rate (CAGR) for the period 1998–2002 was 22.2 per cent;
- the strongest growth was in 2002, with a rate of 30.8 per cent.

Table 8.6.1 Chinese computer technology value 1998–2002 (RMB billion)

Year	RMB billion	% growth
1998	59.8	
1999	70.2	17.3
2000	85.1	21.3
2001	102.0	19.8
2002	133.4	30.8
CAGR [1998–2002]		22.2%

Source: Snapdata Research

Market segmentation

PCs, representing 57.1 per cent of the market by value, constituted the largest segment of the Chinese computer technology market in 2002 (see Table 8.6.2).

The Ministry of Information Industry has predicted that laptop computer sales in 2004 will have increased from one million to around 8 million.

Table 8.6.2 Chinese computer technology segmentation 2002 (value %)

Segment	% share
PCs	57.1
Software	28.9
Printers	7.6
Servers	6.4
Total	**100.0**

Source: Snapdata Research

Growth in Chinese internet users has been spectacular, rising from less than one million in 1997 to more than 80 million in 2003, with a further 30 per cent growth forecast for 2004. According to China Internet Network Information Centre, the number of households with broadband has soared 160 per cent in 2004 to 17 million.

Manufacturing developments

BOE Technology

In February 2004, BOE Technology, a private Chinese electronics manufacturer, announced its intention to build China's biggest liquid crystal display (LCD) production unit in Beijing by 2007. The planned investment is in response to the booming global demand for flat screen monitors and televisions, and is based on the technology that BOE acquired in 2003 when it purchased Hydis, the flat screen production operation of Hynix Semiconductor, for US$380 million from its former South Korean parent group.

Hydis is said to be the world's ninth largest LCD manufacturer with a 4 per cent market share, and the investment marked one of China's biggest overseas investments at the time by a Chinese technology company. South Korea is currently the largest global LCD producing country with the two market leaders, LG Phillips LCD and Samsung Electronics reporting sales of US$5.12 billion and US$4.88 billion respectively for 2003.

The BOE acquisition has heightened Korean concerns of the increasing technology transfer to China as a threat to Korea's electronic and technology industries.

The fifth-generation production line investment of US$1.2 billion now underway is being part-funded by US$70 million Chinese bank loans, and BOE plans to add a sixth- or seventh-generation production line in 2007. Following construction of the thin film transistor (TFT)-LCD cluster, BOE aims to dominate the high growth potential Chinese market and become a leader in this East Asian industry sector.

Chip manufacture

In July 2004, the Japanese group Renesas announced its plans to triple production in China. Renesas was formed in 2003 as a result of the merger of the microcontroller operations of Mistubishi Electronic and Hitachi, and is now the world's third-largest computer-chip maker. Renesas has also established a Chinese subsidiary in Shanghai to manage its domestic distribution centres and supervise the operation of its manufacturing facilities.

The expansion, involving an investment of US$275 million in its two Chinese plants, will be carried out over three years and addresses Renesas' expectations for the development of a major local market for advanced semiconductors used in mobile phones and digital appliances. Renesas is targeting a 5 per cent share of the Chinese semiconductor market by 2008, when it expects its sales in China to have grown almost fourfold from US$720 million to US$2.7 billion.

Toshiba, the leading manufacturer of flash memory chips, forecasts that the greater Chinese market, including Hong Kong and Taiwan, will account for 40 per cent of world-wide semiconductor demand by 2010. Matushita, another major digital products manufacturer, is projecting sales of US$9 billion in China in 2005. The US Semiconductor Industry Association forecasts that investment in the Chinese chip industry will reach US$12 billion by the end of 2005 and could double by 2013, in spite of the continuing fear of high-tech piracy.

Philips

Philips, the Dutch electronics group, which numbers semiconductors among the electronics and traditional lighting products that it manufactures in China, generated US$2.5 billion in local revenues in 2003 and another US$4–5 billion in overseas sales of China-made products. It targeted to more than double its China revenues in the five years to 2007 and sees growing opportunities to supply electronic systems to the auto industry. It has already outsourced its product lines in significant amounts to the Chinese mainland; for example, 100 per cent of Philips audio products are now made in China.

Research

In April 2004, the Chinese government signed agreements with Microsoft and Hewlett Packard to build laboratories based on their competing operating systems, Windows and Linux, as a first step towards the creation of a national software and integrated circuits public service platform.

Computer games

In an attempt to reduce the dominance of imported computer games, accounting for 90 per cent of the online games in China, China has pledged to invest from RMB1 billion to RMB2 billion in a programme to develop some 100 high-quality games from 2004 to 2008.

There are now 14 million online game players in China. The Press and Publication Administration announced in April 2004 that there had been 6.4 million new players in 2003 alone and that the sector's sales had increased 46 per cent to RMB1.3 billion.

The China and US chip tax dispute

The first WTO case brought against China by the US concerning the preferential tax treatment for domestic Chinese semiconductor companies was resolved in July 2004, shortly before the US was to ask for a WTO panel to settle the dispute. China agreed to cease immediately the partial value added tax rebate that it had been giving to companies that design chips domestically, and by April 2005 will also remove its tax rebate for chips manufactured in China, calculated at 14 percentage points of the 17 per cent VAT levied on all chips.

US chip makers are the largest exporters to China, with sales of about US$2 billion, and believe that they can now win a significantly larger share of the

US$25 billion market, which is growing at a rate of some 25 per cent a year.

The acquisition of IBM's personal computer business

The year 2004 ended dramatically for the Chinese computer industry on 8 December when IBM announced the outright sale of its global personal computer (PC) business to Lenovo, China's largest computer supplier, for US$1.75 billion. Lenovo, which recently changed its name from the better known English-language brand name Legend, is paying US$650 million in cash and up to US$600 million in shares – giving IBM an 18.9 per cent shareholding – and assuming US$500 million of IBM debt. Lenovo shares are to be listed in New York within a year, in line with its new international status.

Apparently, the IBM business had been for sale for about three years and Lenovo's strongest competitor had been the US private equity fund, Texas Pacific Group, whose all-cash bid is understood to have been about US$100 million less.

The acquisition is the biggest overseas deal by a Chinese technology company to date and the largest Chinese international acquisition since the beginning of 2003. While marking IBM's exit from the PC market that it created in 1981, the deal will increase Lenovo's sales turnover fourfold to more than US$12 billion and allows it the use of the IBM brand under licence for five years with control of the 'Think' trademark of IBM's business laptops.

Lenovo itself was founded in 1984 but did not achieve success until 1994, when it was able to list in Hong Kong after its own-brand Legend PCs became its core business. By keeping costs and inventories down and designing products to local consumer demand, it became China's biggest supplier and accounted for more than 25 per cent of total PC sales (currently 27 per cent). More recently margins have been shrinking under stiff competition from Dell Computer and Hewlett Packard (HP) to less than 15 per cent so that the IBM PC business's gross margins of 20 per cent are part of its attraction.

IBM's competitors have been scornful of the deal, pointing out that the low price for a unit with sales of US$9 billion reflects its low profitability and suggesting that Lenovo will fail to manage a global business. However, Lenovo has moved rapidly to mitigate risks by transferring its head office to New York, maintaining IBM as preferred supplier of after-sales service outside China and appointing an IBM senior vice-president as chief executive. Lenovo's president has served notice on Dell and HP that 'we are not satisfied to be only number three'.

Developments in IT

In June 2004, Google announced that it had taken a stake in Baidu.com, its leading Chinese counterpart, as a prelude to cooperation between the two competitors. The size of the minority holding and investment cost were undisclosed. Google is one of eight companies that have invested in the most recent round of Baidu's fund-raising, all interested in the fast-growing Chinese market and in working with local partners.

Baidu was established less than five years ago and earned some 80 per cent of its revenues in 2003 from selling search-specific links, with the balance from advertising and corporate services. Already one of the strongest players in the market, Baidu claims over 48 per cent of searches by around 100 million Chinese internet users. Google is reckoned to be in second place with a share of slightly less than 30 per cent.

Immediate cooperation between Baidu and Google is in a combined drive to thwart 'spammers' and 'spy software' from accessing internet users' computers. Longer-term collaboration may take the form of Baidu granting Google access to its methods for handling Chinese text and its domestic marketing channels in exchange for Google sharing its search technology with Baidu.

In July 2004, Google entered into a further deal, this time with Netease, one of China's biggest internet portals, to provide web-page search services and to cooperate in online advertising under a strategic partnership. Netease, together with its competitors Sina.com and Sohu.com, is a US-listed company. Also at the beginning of July, Sina.com agreed to acquire Davidhill Capital Inc, the internet and mobile phone messaging technology company, for up to US$36 million.

The Google–Netease partnership strikes hard at Zhongsou.com, the local Chinese search technology company, which previously provided the search functions for all three of the leading Chinese portals. Its market share had already been eroded by the growing popularity of Baidu.

Consumables

Jonathan Reuvid and Snapshots International

This chapter is an overview of three selected consumable product markets of particular interest to international brand leaders investing in China, namely: non-alcoholic drinks, beer, cosmetics and toiletries.

Non-alcoholic drinks

Market size and segmentation

Chinese non-alcoholic drinks sales increased by 20.5 per cent in volume in 2002. Total sales for 2002 were 20,250 million litres (see Table 8.7.1).

Bottled water, representing 39.0 per cent of the market by volume, constituted the largest segment of the Chinese non-alcoholic drinks market in 2002.

Table 8.7.1 Chinese non-alcoholic drinks segmentation 2002 (volume %)

Segment	% share
Bottled water	39.0
Carbonated soft drinks	30.0
Fruit and vegetable juice	11.0
Tea drinks	7.0
Others	13.0
Total	100.0

Source: Snapdata Research

Coca Cola has been striving to extend its dominance of the soft drinks market in China. As China has grown from being Coca Cola's 15th to 6th biggest market over the decade since 1993, the marketing challenge has assumed a global dimension. Within another decade, Coca Cola expects China to be the biggest beverage market.

By the beginning of 2004, Coca Cola already had a 10 per cent share of the overall non-alcoholic drinks market segmented in Table 8.7.1, and as much as or more than 50 per cent of the carbonated drinks segment in most large cities – about double the share of Pepsi-Cola. However, expanding profitably beyond the wealthy urban districts into the less well-off suburbs, smaller towns and rural areas in such a way as to sell affordable drinks direct to the customer poses a different challenge.

Taking the province of Fujian with its 35 million population as an example, Coca Cola now claims 84 per cent of the carbonated soft drinks market in Xiamen, the province's wealthiest city. Throughout the province, sales rose 21 per cent year-on-year in 2002 and a further 24 per cent in 2003. In order to achieve this market penetration Coca Cola had to replace the province's eight wholesalers with 350 designated partners, each responsible for a designated area, supported by a Coca Cola sales representative who can track customers individually.

In March 2004, the Japanese IT giant, Itochu, and Asahi Breweries, Japan's leading beer maker formed a joint venture soft drinks company with Ting Yi, a leading Chinese food producer. The investment involving US$950 million makes this Japan's largest investment in China's food and soft drinks industries. Ting Yi is disposing of its 13 beverage units and the new joint holding company began operations in April 2004. It will start by focusing on existing products but is expected to diversify into new products, such as health drinks and coffee, later.

Beer wars

In February 2004, Scottish & Newcastle (S&N) announced that it had agreed to acquire a 19.5 per cent shareholding in the Shanghai-listed Chongqing Brewery for RMB525 million (US$63 million). S&N has had a relationship with Chongqing Beer Group (CBG), the parent company of Chongqing Brewery, which has been brewing S&N's McEwan's 1856 beer under licence for 10 years. CBG's key brands are Chongqing and Sancheng. It operates 16 breweries in the south-west of China and is claimed by S&N to be one of the most profitable brewers in China at the operating level. Under the terms of the deal, CBG will inject its unlisted brewery interests into the listed Chongqing Brewery giving S&N a connection to the combined businesses.

The summer months saw the arrival of takeover fever in the Chinese brewing industry, heralded by rumours of an increase in foreign investment in Guangdong Brewery. Earlier in the year, Heineken, the Dutch brewer, acquired a 21 per cent shareholding for US$71 million through the medium of a joint venture company, but the share price of Guangdong Brewery jumped 33 per cent on the Hong Kong stock exchange in July 2004. While the rumours of talks were denied by Guangdong, Heineken made it clear that it would consider an increase in its shareholding favourably if an additional stake became available.

But the real news was the saga of China's first contested takeover played out between Anheuser-Busch and SABMiller in June for control of Harbin Brewery. Until May, SABMiller, the South African brewery group listed in London, had an exclusive partnership with Harbin having acquired a 29 per cent stake in this brewery, the fourth largest in China. Through a joint venture with China Resources Breweries (CRB), Harbin's strongest local competitor, in which it owns 49 per cent, Miller had hoped to gain synergies by combining the operations of Harbin's 13 plants with the 11 of CRB.

Miller's offer of US$4.31 billion for Harbin sparked a counter-bid of US$5.58 billion from its US arch-rival Anheuser-Busch, the world's largest brewing group to which Miller ranks second. In China, Anheuser-Busch's partner is Tsingtao, the Chinese market leader. However, Tsingtao is weak in the north-east against Harbin, having only four breweries in the region. Like Miller, Anheuser-Busch already owned 29 per cent of Harbin purchased at a lower than bid price from an investment group that had previously acquired the holding from Harbin city government. The counter-bid price valued Harbin at 49 times the

previous year's earnings and was supported by Harbin's management who stood to secure options of up to HK$117 million. In the event, SABMiller blinked first and did not raise its bid, preferring to take a profit of US$211 million from the sale of its stake. As a result, Anheuser-Busch and its Budweiser brand have acquired a substantial market share in the north-east, which is the region with the highest beer consumption in China. The high price paid sends a signal to other prospective foreign investors that buying into Chinese brewers will be expensive.

In September, SABMiller struck back. CRB underlined its determination to expand its market share by acquiring three loss-making breweries from the Australian Lion Nathan group in Jiangsu Province, the Shanghai hinterland, for an investment of US$154 million. CRB had previously surprised analysts a month earlier by announcing plans to build a US$82 million new brewery in Guangdong province. CRB claims that, in 2004, it has expanded capacity by 'about 30 per cent through acquisitions at reasonable cost'.

Cosmetics and toiletries

Market size

Based on sales of sales of skin care, hair care, and sun care products, and colour cosmetics:

- Chinese cosmetics and toiletries sales increased by 15.5 per cent in value in 2002. Total sales for 2002 were RMB44.5 million ;
- compound annual growth rate for the period 1998–2002 was 12.9 per cent;
- the strongest growth was in 2002, with a rate of 15.5 per cent (see Table 8.7.2).

Table 8.7.2 Chinese cosmetics and toiletries value 1998–2002 (RMB billion)

Year	RMB billion	% growth
1998	27.4	
1999	30.1	9.9
2000	34.1	13.1
2001	38.5	13.1
2002	44.5	15.5
CAGR [1998–2002]		**12.9%**

Source: Snapdata Research

Segmentation

Skin care, representing 30.3 per cent of the market by value, constituted the largest segment of the Chinese cosmetics and toiletries market in 2002 (see Table 8.7.3).

The overall cosmetics and toiletries market is expected to double in size by the end of the decade.

Table 8.7.3 Chinese cosmetics and toiletries segmentation 2002 (value %)

Segment	% share
Skin care	30.3
Colour cosmetics	30.2
Shampoo	20.4
Hair colourants	6.5
Hair styling agents	6.3
Hair conditioners	3.4
Sun care	2.9
Total	**100.0**

Source: Snapdata Research

In March 2004, L'Oreal, the French cosmetics group, announced plans to double the size of its operations in China, with plans to acquire Yue-Sai, an up-market Chinese brand. L'Oreal's 2003 sales in China were reported as €159 million.

Energy

Jonathan Reuvid and Snapshots International

Power generation

The break-up of the China State Power Company's monopoly, in 2002, into five regional producers has resulted in uneven earnings for the three producers that are now listed in Hong Kong: Huaneng Power International, Huadian International Power and Datang International. The strong demand for energy in China might have been expected to boost profits significantly. However, the surge in coal prices impacted margins significantly and is reflected in results for the first six months of 2004. Huaneng's net profit rose a weaker than expected 8.6 per cent, while Huadian's net profit for the same period fell 1.9 per cent. Their major markets on the east coast and in Shandong Province respectively are far removed from their coal resources in the northern and far western provinces. Huadian suffered the worst because Shandong is one of the 10 Chinese provinces where there is still an overcapacity of power, and the company paid 14 per cent more for its fuel.

By contrast, Datang fared much better, helped by its proximity to the cheap coal supplies available from nearby Inner Mongolia, and reported a first half increase in profits of 42 per cent. Its good relationship with a handful of such coal suppliers has allowed Datang to lock in the cost of some 80 per cent of is coal supplies, while the concentration of its plant in northern China to serve its major Beijing and Tianjin markets has also helped.

Coal prices in China have risen 10–15 per cent in 2004 and Datang is likely to have maintained its advantage over the other two.

All three market leaders are working to reduce their reliance on coal. Huaneng is buying a major hydroelectric power plant in Sichuan Province from its parent company, which is expected to invest in a cluster of four thermal power plants, known as 'The Three Gorges' project in Anhui Province along the Jinsha River on the upper reaches of the Yangtze. It is also investing in a major coal producer and, together with Huadian and Datang, is exploring further investment opportunities in rail networks.

In the meantime, Datang has announced investment of US$1.9 billion in constructing the 1,750 megawatt (MW) Pengshui hydroelectric power station near Chongqing city and phase three of the Tuoketuo coal power plant in Inner Mongolia, which will have two 600 MW generating units. Both new power plants will begin operations in 2007.

As the demand for electricity continues to rise, the independent power producers led by the Hong Kong-listed China Resources Power, are gaining market share through aggressive acquisition strategies. Dozens of local power stations with a total of 35,000–37,000 MW went into production in 2004.

In July 2004, China Power International, another of the big five state-owned power generators, announced a delay in its planned US$500 million listing by at least two months as a result of rising coal prices. However, a dual listing in Hong Kong and New York was announced in October, based on faster expansion plans and healthy profits to raise up to US$330 million at a lower price/earnings multiple than other major power companies trading in Hong Kong. China Power owns three power plants, in Anhui, Henan and Jiangsu provinces, with total capacity of about 3,000 MW compared with Huaneng's capacity of 15,736 MW.

Market size

In terms of market size:

- Chinese energy generation increased by 4.3 per cent in volume in 2002. The total generated in 2002 was 1.48 billion tonnes standard coal equivalent (SCE);
- the compound annual growth rate for the period 1998–2002 was 2.7 per cent;
- the strongest growth was in 2001, with a rate of 6.4 per cent;
- the total output of electricity rose 15.5 per cent to 1.9 trillion kWh in 2003, according to official statistics.

Table 8.8.1 Chinese energy volume 1998–2002 ('000 tonnes (SCE))

Year	'000 tonnes (SCE)	% growth
1998	1,328,318.8	
1999	1,313,703.9	–1.1
2000	1,333,392.6	1.5
2001	1,419,048.0	6.4
2002	1,480,067.1	4.3
CAGR [1998–2002]		**2.7%**

Source: Snapdata Research

Energy segmentation

Coal

Energy generated from coal represents 67 per cent of the market by volume, and constituted the largest segment of the Chinese energy market in 2002 (see Table 8.8.2).

The output of coal rose 15 per cent in 2003 to 1.7 billion tonnes and continued to rise in 2004, in spite of several mining disasters that have highlighted the health and safety shortcomings of the industry in China.

In April 2004, a large coal field find was reported in Hami, Xinjiang, with massive reserves over 7.2 billion tonnes. Output is expected to reach 10 million tonnes a year and will account for more than one-third of Xinjiang's production.

Oil and gas

Oil and gas imports and production are reviewed separately in Chapter 8.11.

Hydroelectricity

In August 2004, the Gongboxia power station on the Yellow River in Qinghai Province, a major part

Table 8.8.2 Chinese energy segmentation in 2002 (% volume)

Segment	% share
Coal	67.0
Oil	23.6
Hydroelectricity	6.9
Natural gas	2.5
Total	**100.0**

Source: Snapdata Research

of the west-to-east power transmission project, began supplying power following a three-year construction period.

Nuclear energy

According to the World Nuclear Association (WNA), the potential for new nuclear reactor development is greatest in China. Currently, there are nine reactors in China with a combined capacity of 6,500 MW, supplying just under 2 per cent of electricity.

There are two 1,000 MW VER Russian reactors under construction at Tianwan on China's east coast and China is inviting tenders for four further reactors of about 1,000 MW capacity, costing approximately US$1.5 billion each. The government's long-term plan is to raise China's nuclear capacity to just under 40,000 MW, at a total investment cost of US$30 billion. The programme involves the construction of approximately two reactors a year, which the WNA describes as 'similar in scale to the large French nuclear construction programme undertaken in the 1980s'.

In March 2004, the Qinshan No. 2 Nuclear Power Plant generated power for the first time and, in June, started commercial operations feeding into the capacity-stretched East China grid. Qinshan is China's first self-designed and self-built national commercial power plant.

Likely bidders for the four new reactors going out to tender at Yangjiang in Guangdong Province and Sanmen in Zhejiang Province include Areva, the French nuclear developer, which has already supplied four reactors in Guangdong, and Atomic Energy of Canada (AECL), which has supplied Candu reactors at Qinshan. Other potential bidders include General Electric, Toshiba, Hitachi, Westinghouse (now owned by British Nuclear Fuels) and some South Korean constructors. China National Nuclear Corporation (CNNC), which operates the nation's reactors, has indicated that it may award US$8 billion to a single foreign bidder to build all four reactors, with work starting by 2007.

CNNC, which is the controlling investor in the Zhajiang Sanmen Nuclear Power Plant, has specified that the first phase of the plant will also contain two generating units of over 1,000 MW. The first phase was granted approval by the State Council in September 2004, together with approval for the second phase of the Guangdong Ling'ao nuclear power station. Ling'ao phase 2, wholly financed by the China Guangdong Nuclear Power Group, will also house two 1,000 MW generating units and is expected to become operational in 2011 or 2012.

8.9

China's Insurance Market

Liu Baocheng, University of International Business and Economics, with updates by Jonathan Reuvid

Overview

With a population base of over 1.3 billion, an economy of steady growth for over two decades, and now being a fresh member of WTO committed to opening its financial service market, China has every reason to stand out as the new 'El Dorado' for foreign insurance firms.

The growth rate of China's insurance industry has been exceptionally stunning – premium revenue topped US$47 billion in 2003 as compared with US$56 million in 1980 – an increase of over 840 times within a matter of 23 years, and the annual growth rate reached 27.1 per cent over the previous year. Most of the increase in absolute value took place during the latter half of the last decade (see Table 8.9.1.)

The total assets of China's insurance companies reached US$111.3 billion in 2003, an increase of 40.48 per cent over the previous year, in spite of the interruption of SARS. The industry churned US$47.3 billion in premiums, accounting for 3.3 per cent of the country's GDP (US$14,231 billion). It registered an increase of 27.1 per cent over the previous year's US$32.55 billion; 69 per cent of the total premium income was derived from life insurance, which marked a 28.7 per cent increase over 2002. Casualty insurance harvested US$4.16 billion in premiums, an increase of 69.7 per cent (see Table 8.9.2.). The reinsurance market registered total revenue of US$3.25 billion, of which 37 per cent was attributable to business reinsurance, showing a surge of 84.4 per cent over 2002.

John Coomber, CEO of Swiss Reinsurance, has forecast that China's insurance market will continue to experience double-digit growth over the next few years up to 2012, with life insurance at 12 per cent per annum and the non-life sector at 9.6 per cent.

Historical development

A brief historical account may help to explain such a capricious surge. Insurance, among all other industries in China, had been subject to rigid government manipulation under command economic policies. The Chinese domestic insurance industry was completely eradicated following a resolution by the National Finance Conference in 1958. Only the part relating to overseas insurance was retained. It was not until 1979 when the State Council approved the proposal filed by China's central bank – the People's Bank of China (PBOC) – that it gradually resumed operation. Before 1986, when the Xinjiang Farm Production Insurance Company was established, the entire Chinese insurance market was a state monopoly held by People's Insurance Company of China (PICC), acting as an affiliate to PBOC. Initially, no more than 30 products were offered. In 1988, the formation of Shenzhen Ping-An Insurance Company marked the emergence of the first shareholding firm operating in south-east coastal regions. The founding of China Pacific Insurance Company, financed by China's Communication Bank operating on a national level in 1991, symbolized the metamorphosis of China's insurance market from a monopoly into an oligopoly. In 1992, the first foreign insurance firm was permitted to open operations in China. In 1995, the passage of PRC Insurance Law provided the first across-the-board regulatory framework over the insurance market.

The positive feature contributing to the dramatic growth rate of the insurance sector is the liberalization process, although it has been slow, particularly in the eyes of foreign firms on the waiting list for approval to operate in China. In 1999, the State Council permitted

Table 8.9 1 The Annual Growth of China's Insurance Market

Exchange Rate: US$1= RMB 8.2

Year	GDP growth (%)	Revenue RMB billion	Revenue growth (%)	Insurance density (RMB/Person)	Insurance depth (%)
1980	7.8	0.5	–	0.47	0.10
1981	5.2	0.8	69.56	0.78	0.16
1982	10.9	1.0	32.05	1.01	0.20
1983	6.9	1.3	28.16	1.28	0.22
1984	15.2	2.0	51.52	1.92	0.29
1985	13.5	3.3	65.50	3.13	0.39
1986	8.8	4.6	38.37	4.26	0.65
1987	11.6	7.1	55.24	6.51	0.67
1988	11.3	10.9	54.01	9.86	0.72
1989	4.1	14.2	30.05	12.64	0.77
1990	3.8	17.8	24.93	15.56	0.85
1991	9.2	23.6	32.43	20.35	0.90
1992	14.2	36.8	56.15	31.39	1.00
1993	13.5	50.0	35.80	42.16	0.98
1994	12.6	60.0	20.09	49.00	0.97
1995	10.5	68.3	13.83	56.39	1.17
1996	9.6	77.7	13.78	63.49	1.15
1997	8.8	108.8	39.99	88.02	1.46
1998	7.8	126.2	15.97	101.12	1.61
1999	7.1	144.4	14.50	114.84	1.76
2000	8.0	160.0	10.74	126.21	1.79
2001	7.3	211.2	32.04	168.98	2.20
2002	8.0	305.3	44.59	237.64	2.98
2003	9.1	388.0	27.10	287.44	3.33

Sources: China Statistical Yearbook 2003 and *China Insurance Yearbook 2003*

Table 8.9.2 Market Revenue in 2003

Insurance type	Revenue (RMB billion)	Growth over 2002 (%)
Property	86.9	11.71
Life	266.9	28.7
Casualty	34.2	69.7
Total	**388.0**	**27.1**

Source: China Insurance Development and Reform Report, 2004

the expansion of insurance fund appropriation, ie to allow indirect participation in the stock market through financing security investment funds. 2001 saw the establishment of the first export credit insurance company. By the end of 2003, 61 insurance firms were in operation, of which 24 were domestic and 37 were owned by foreign firms; 24 are engaged in property insurance, 32 in life assurance and five in reinsurance.

Professional intermediaries consisted of 705 institutions with 507 insurance agents, 115 insurance brokers and 83 insurance surveyors. The number of insurance entities almost doubled in two years. Therefore, it can be said that by the turn of the century, the Chinese insurance market began to take sizeable shape, in spite of continual excessive government manipulation. More interestingly, as Table 8.9.3 shows, the number of foreign-invested insurance firms has exceeded the number of Chinese firms, although the major market shares are still in the hands of state-owned domestic firms. Firms specializing in insurance brokerage have emerged on the stage, with seven in operation and another seven under review. The number of insurance products offered exceeds the 1,000 level.

The number of professionals in the insurance industry became a bottleneck for its healthy growth. Before the open-door policy in 1978, the number of employees in the insurance sector was no more than 200. According to statistics for 2003, there were 1.5 million

Table 8.9.3 Comparison of the number of insurance firms in China (1999–2003)

Ownership year	Number of domestic firms	Number of foreign firms	Total
1999	13	15	28
2001	20	32	52
2003	24	37	61

people engaged in the insurance industry, with 100,000 in management positions and 1.4 million in frontline sales. Such a boom in staffing levels naturally resulted in a discounted qualification, particularly for people in frontline sales, both agency and brokerage. In 2003, for the third time, the China Insurance Regulatory Commission (CIRC) updated the certification requirement for executives in insurance firms, with emphasis on professional qualification. Similar certification programmes were also introduced for insurance brokerage and insurance survey. On the other hand, there remains a particular concern among the Chinese insurance companies that the aggressive entry of foreign companies will lure away their best employees.

Legal and regulatory framework

The PRC Property Insurance Contract Act (1983) and *Provisional Regulation on the Administration of Insurance Enterprises (1985)* (both abolished recently), were the first two pillar documents outlining the legal framework for the insurance market in China. *The Insurance Law of China* (consisting of eight chapters) was promulgated in May 1995 and took effect in October 1995. It is the most comprehensive legislation so far regulating the expanding insurance industry. The recently promulgated *Administrative Rules on Foreign Invested Insurance Companies (2001)* is the only legislation defining foreign invested insurance companies operating in China. However, the nature of this legislation is most likely to be transitional as more and more foreign companies push into the Chinese market and, over time, new problems begin to arise. For example, the current harsh restrictions over both domestic and foreign insurance firms is tending to ease. The following is a list of the major Chinese laws and regulations in connection with insurance:

- Insurance Law (1995);
- Contract Law (1999);
- Chapter 20 – Maritime Law (1993);
- Company Law (1994);
- Provisions on the Collection of Social Security Insurance Premium (1999);
- Provisions on Unemployment Insurance (1999);
- Administrative Rules on Insurance Companies (2000);
- Administrative Rules on Foreign-Invested Insurance Companies (2001);
- Administrative Rules on Insurance Brokerage Companies (2001);
- Administrative Rules on Insurance Agency (2001);
- Administrative Rules on Insurance Survey Institutions (2001);
- Provisions on Executive Review by China Insurance Regulative Commission (2001);
- Notice Against Unfair Competition within the Insurance Industry (2001);
- Provisional Rules on Intra-firm Insurance Agency 2001);
- Administrative Rules on Foreign-Invested Insurance Companies (2001).

Corporate Governance Guidelines for Insurance Firms are in the making by CIRC, with the aim of intervening in the internal corporate governance structure of insurance companies.

Because the insurance sector is still a nascent market in China, much of the legal framework remains to be consolidated. Old rules that cannot cope with the ongoing development are being phased out and a new wave of legislation has set in since the end of the last century. Most recently, a motion has been submitted to the People's National Congress, China's top legislature, to amend the Insurance Law. The proposed amendments include further liberalization of those areas such as insurance fund appropriation, corporate structure and regulatory process. News released to date revealed that it is highly likely that these amendments will be approved.

1998 witnessed two of the most dramatic restructuring events in the Chinese insurance industry. First, PICC, which held a dominant 80 per cent of the market, was split into four corporate entities with the parent holding company in the name of China Insurance Group (CIG). Second, the Chinese government decided to separate the three financial industries, namely, banking, security and insurance and, at the same time, to establish respective government arms for their regulation and supervision.

As a result, CIRC was established officially on 18 November 1998, the industry watchdog under the State Council vested with the following responsibilities to regulate and supervise the insurance industry in China:

- to formulate national strategies, policies, rules and regulations in the areas of the insurance industry;
- to conduct integrated supervision over the insurance market through its network spreading across the country;
- to examine and approve the establishment and reorganization of various insurance entities;
- to examine and approve the appointment of senior executives in various insurance entities;
- to formulate qualification criteria for various professional positions in the insurance industry;
- to formulate basic insurance terms and conditions as well as rate of premium for various lines of insurance operation, and ensure the conformance by various insurance entities;
- to formulate a financial accounting standard and ensure its conformance by various insurance entities;
- to supervise the financial operation and indemnity capability of insurance entities;
- to administer the indemnity and warranty fund deposited by insurance entities;
- to conduct risk assessment and market surveillance through systematic analysis, scanning and forecasting in the insurance market;
- to conduct statistics and news updates in the insurance industry;
- to be responsible for international exchanges and cooperation in the insurance industry;
- to handle complaints and disputes in the insurance industry;
- to administer industry associations and research institutions in the area of insurance;
- to execute other matters designated by the State Council.

The CIRC has 10 functional departments in Beijing and retains 31 representative offices in virtually all the capital cities of each province, autonomous region and centrally-administered metropolitan region. In 2002, CIRC became a member of the International Association of Insurance Supervisors (IAIS), which helps this organization to follow closely international standard practice in conducting supervision of the industry.

Market characteristics

Population size and income level are the two most important dimensions of a market. With a population size over 1.3 billion China offers the promise of becoming the world's largest insurance market. As of today, the greater part of the insurance market is concentrated in the cities with a population of around 460 million, in particular the coastal areas.

A helicopter view of China's insurance market reveals that a large market potential remains untapped. Of the total population, only 20 per cent has purchased life insurance and as few as 3 per cent of the labour force are covered under retirement insurance schemes. With regard to property insurance, 93 per cent of individuals and 85 per cent of business entities remain uncovered. Depth and density are the two most popular indices for measuring the sophistication of a country's effective insurance market demand and the status of insurance in the country's entire economy. The former refers to the ratio of total premium revenue over GDP, while the latter refers to per capita expenditure on insurance. Measured by the two indices, China ranks 66 and 78 respectively. In 2001, although its total insurance revenue reached 13 in the world and three in Asia, China was ranked 56 in the world by its insurance depth (at 2.2 per cent) and 73 by its insurance density (at US$20). Both of these rankings were far below the world average levels of 7.84 per cent and US$385.4 respectively. Insurance expenditure accounted for 2.3 per cent of household savings, which is well below the world average of 7 per cent, not to mention the 15 per cent average in developed countries. While total premium revenue reached 3.3 per cent of GDP in 2003, it still falls far behind the world average and indicates enormous scope for market expansion.

A Beijing-based firm – China Mainland Marketing Research Co – conducted a survey among the residents of Beijing, Shanghai and 20 other cities across China in connection with insurance. The result revealed that only 3 per cent held policies on personal property, and only 1.7 per cent held automobile insurance policies. But the survey also showed an encouraging trend: an impressive increase in the number of families in the low and average income brackets who hold insurance policies. Some 38 per cent of families with a monthly income below US$120.77 and 40 per cent of families with monthly incomes from US$120.89 to US$241.55 bought insurance, rising to 43 per cent of families with monthly incomes between US$241.67 and US$362.32, and 44 per cent of families with monthly incomes above US$362.32.

According to Mr Ma Mingzhe, Chairman and CEO of China PingAn Insurance Company, insurance will be the highest growth segment within the Chinese financial sector. The growth rate over the next five years will be maintained at 20–30 per cent. Other experts expect that by 2005, the total value of insurance premiums will reach US$33.82 billion, representing 2.3 per cent of total GDP value. The average premium per person will increase to US$27.78. Currently, China's insurance industry constitutes only a small fraction of the entire economy (2.2 per cent), contrasting with 11 per cent in Japan and 8 per cent in the US. From this base, Mr Ma further predicts that, by 2025, aggregate premium revenue in China will reach RMB5 trillion, an equivalent of US$610 billion. This figure will place China among the world's top five largest insurance markets.

Foreign insurance firms in China

There are three milestones in China's policy to open the insurance market for foreign companies. American International Group (AIG) was the first foreign insurance firm that was permitted to operate in China in 1992; and in 1996, Manulife-Sinochem, a joint venture between China National Foreign Trade Trust and Investment Company and the Canadian Manulife Financial, marked the beginning of China's permission for the formation of joint venture insurance companies. In October 2003, CIRC approved the first joint venture insurance brokerage firm between China National Cereals, Oils & Foodstuffs Import & Export Corporation and the Chicago-based Aon Corp. By the end of 2003, 37 foreign insurance companies had been granted permission to set up 62 business enterprises to offer insurance products in China, while 128 foreign firms from 19 countries have set up 192 representative offices, which are waiting for permission to establish their own insurance operations in China. Foreign insurers have a high level of interest in taking stakes in their Chinese partners. Morgan Stanley, Goldman Sachs and HSBC hold 23.74 per cent of the shares of PingAn Insurance, one of China's leading insurers listed in Hong Kong. New China Life Insurance, Taikang Life and Huatai all have overseas strategic investors holding 24.9 per cent, 25 per cent and 22.1 per cent of their shares respectively. So far, sizeable

foreign operations in the Chinese insurance market take the form of joint ventures with domestic companies while the equity percentage held by individual foreign partners is constrained, as Table 8.9.4 illustrates. The area of operation was formerly restricted to Shanghai and Guangzhou. Now, foreign-invested enterprises (FIEs) are permitted to spread across 15 coastal cities as far north as Dalian, and some are permitted to penetrate to inland cities such as Wuhan, Chongqing and Chengdu.

There is still a long way to go before the market becomes fully competitive. Three major state-owned companies occupy 92 per cent of the property insurance market and 86 per cent of the life insurance market. China Life, PingAn Group, Pacific Group and PICC hold an overriding 87.2 per cent majority of the US$111.3 billion total assets in the industry. As illustrated in Figure 8.9.1 foreign companies, including joint ventures, account for merely 2.17 per cent despite their apparently encouraging majority of the number of firms.

Despite the various restrictions, the business of foreign insurance firms has experienced rapid growth. In 2001, they registered revenue of US$0.4 billion. In Shanghai, they have already seized market shares of 14.4 per cent in life insurance and 6.7 per cent in property insurance. By the same measure, their market shares in Guangzhou are 11.8 per cent and 1.5 per cent respectively. Moreover in 2003, their revenue doubled that of 2001, having increased 45.5 per cent over 2002. The total market share in China achieved by foreign companies in 2003 was 1.73 per cent. Total assets held by foreign insurance companies were US$2.4 billion, up by 43.7 per cent.

China's insurance regulatory organization, in line with WTO rules, is stepping up rule-making and providing more transparent supervision and control in an effort to promote the insurance industry. Mr Wu Xiaoping, Vice Chairman of CIRC has said that foreign-funded insurance companies are an integral part of China's insurance system. In addition, Mr Wu has reiterated China's commitment to the WTO in the insurance sector, where geographic restrictions on foreign capital would be lifted as scheduled. Detailed directions on the implementation of rules governing foreign insurance companies will be promulgated to make sure that these companies enter into the market and run their operations in compliance with the law. Mr Wu has highlighted the roadmap for the development of China's insurance sector; China prefers foreign insurers to specialize now in policies covering

Table 8.9.4   Joint Venture Insurance Entities in China

Joint venture insurance firms	*Registered capital (RMB million)*	*Foreign partners*	*Country origin*	*Equity ratio by foreign partners (%)*
China Pacific Insurance Group	9,552.4	Morgan Stanley	US	6.87
		Goldman Sachs	US	6.87
		HSBC Life	Hong Kong	10.00
		Subtotal		23.74
New China (Life) Insurance	1,200	Zurich Insurance	Switzerland	10.00
		International Finance Corp.		6.00
		Meiji Life Insurance	Japan	4.50
		FMO Netherland	Holland	4.40
		Subtotal		24.90
TaiKang (Life) Insurance	600	Winterthur Life	Switzerland	10.00
		Government of Singapore Investment Corp.	Singapore	8.33
		Bank Leu	Luxembourg	5.67
		Softbank Corp.	Japan	1.00
		Subtotal		25.00
China Pacific (Property) Insurance Co.	1,300	ACE Tempest Re	US	10.00
		ACE INA	US	6.13
		ACE US Holdings	US	6.00
		Subtotal		22.13
Pacific (Life) Insurance	1,000	China Insurance International Holdings	Hong Kong	50.05
		Kimber International Investment Co.	US	12.45
		Fortis Insurance International NV.	Singapore	12.45
		Subtotal		74.95
Pacific Insurance	7,700	China Insurance International Holdings	Hong Kong	30.05
		China Bank (Asia) of Industry & Commerce	Hong Kong	24.99
		Subtotal		55.04

Source: adapted from *China Insurance Development and Reform Report*, 2004 and various corporate websites

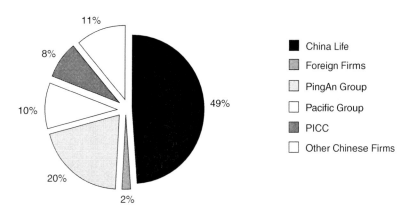

Figure 8.9.1   The share of total asset in the Chinese insurance market (2003)

health, pensions, agriculture and catastrophes. And foreign insurers are encouraged to engage in China's western areas and the old industrial base of the northeast. The outlook for the sector is that there will be a diversified insurance service system and insurance giants with international competitiveness. Mergers and acquisitions are possible among insurers to create corporations specializing in specific business, with subsidiaries complementary to one another.

According to the Administrative Rules on Foreign Invested Insurance Companies (2001), foreign insurance firms can apply to CIRC for setting up either joint ventures or wholly-owned entities in China. However, they must meet the following criteria:

- at least 30 years' history in the insurance market;
- a representative office in China for at least two years;
- minimum total assets of US$5 billion at the previous year-end before application;
- a complete regulatory system over the insurance industry in their own country;
- permission from their home country regulatory body.

The following documents must be filed with CIRC:

- application letter (to be countersigned by the Chinese partner in case of joint venture);
- business licence and certificate for indemnity capability issued by home country regulatory bodies;
- articles of association and annual reports for the past three years;
- application materials by the Chinese party in the case of joint venture;
- feasibility study and business plan;
- list of names and profiles of the persons responsible for the new entity;
- other materials as requested by CIRC.

CIRC shall notify the applicant within six months from the date of full application, after a due diligence review. Upon notification of initial approval, the applicant is given one year to prepare for the establishment of an insurance entity in China. Together with the completed standard application form, the applicant shall file the following documents with CIRC for approval:

- summary report;
- articles of association for the new entity;
- list of shareholders and intended capital contribution by each party;

- certificate of capital contribution by official organizations;
- power of attorney to nominated managers and introduction of their professional background;
- business plan for the following three years;
- intended insurance clauses, premium rates and statement of liability reserve fund;
- intended premises and facilities for business operation;
- guarantee letter against liabilities of the subsidiary from parent company;
- joint venture contract, in the case of a joint venture arrangement.

CIRC shall make a final decision within 60 days of the official application. If approved, a business licence to engage in insurance shall be issued. The business licence specifies the scope and geographical areas of business activities, together with the target market segments to be served by the insurance entity.

In addition, new insurance entities set up in China are subject to the following restrictions:

- They are required to have minimum actually paid up registered capital of RMB200 million or the equivalent amount of foreign currency. CIRC shall reserve the option to raise the bar for the requirement over the registered capital. After the entity is established, 20 per cent of the registered capital will be deposited into an escrow account in China designated by CIRC as a guarantee fund.
- They must arrange 30 per cent of their reinsurance business with designated Chinese insurance firms.
- A single entity is not permitted to engage in both property and life insurance.
- The currency unit of account shall be denominated in local Chinese renminbi.

In spite of the difficulties of obtaining approval, foreign insurance firms do enjoy certain preferential treatment in China. For example, while Chinese domestic firms have to pay an income tax rate at 33 per cent, foreign firms only pay 15 per cent income tax. In addition, foreign firms are permitted to engage in the purchase of stock market securities and corporate bonds.

According to an Agreement reached between China and the US, as well as its commitment as a member of WTO, China shall fully open its insurance market within five years. In the meantime, China attempts to take full advantage of the five years transitional period granted through the WTO negotiation to control the pace of market liberalization. According to a recent paper published in the Chinese government's official press, *The People's Daily*, China intends to restrain the market share occupied by foreign insurance firms to 5 per cent within the next five-year transitional period and to 10 per cent over the next 10 years.

Changes under the WTO commitments

In November 2001, China was officially admitted as a member of the WTO. Within the package deal in compliance with the General Agreement on Trade in Service (GATS), China has entered into wholesale commitments with regard to market access, national treatment, most favoured nations treatment and transparency. The restrictions over all types of insurance and related services for foreign insurance firms, which include geographic scope, equity limitation and business lines, will be alleviated pursuant to the specified timetable. They cover life, health and retirement pension insurances, non-life insurances and reinsurances. So far, reinsurance is now completely open, non-life insurance can be wholly foreign-owned within two years, and 50 per cent ownership of life insurance joint ventures is allowed. All geographic limitations will be phased out within three years. The following is a reverse summary translation of China's commitments under the WTO from the Chinese version. (The official wording is dependent on the original English version.)

1. China will permit foreign non-life insurance firms to set up subsidiaries in China and enter into joint venture with Chinese partners with an equity share up to 51 per cent. Within two years of WTO membership, foreign non-life insurance firms will be permitted to set up solely-owned operations in China, and the form of corporate entity will be left to the decision of business owners.

2. Immediately upon accession, the Chinese government would cease to dictate the terms and conditions of the joint venture between foreign insurance firms and Chinese partners, and the selection of the Chinese domestic partner would be the free decision of the foreign insurance firm.

3. Foreign firms engaged in insurance and reinsurance brokerage for carriage of goods by sea, air and land would be permitted to enter into joint ventures with domestic partners for no more than 50 per cent of the equity share, immediately upon

China's membership. Foreign equity participation can be increased up to 51 per cent within three years of China's WTO membership. These restrictions will be completely phased out within five years of China's WTO membership.

4. Foreign insurance firms operating in China will be gradually permitted to set up sub-branches, as geographic restrictions are removed.

5. Upon accession to the WTO, China would open Shanghai, Guangzhou, Dalian, Shenzhen and Foshan for foreign life and non-life insurers and brokers. Within two years of WTO membership, China will further open a dozen other cities. These include Beijing, Chengdu, Chongqing, Fuzhou, Suzhou, Xiamen, Ningbo, Shenyang, Wuhan and Tianjin. A year later, all geographic restrictions are to be lifted.

6. Upon accession to the WTO, China would permit foreign non-life insurance firms to offer all kinds of products and services to overseas clients, and to offer property, liability and credit insurance to foreign-invested enterprises (FIEs) in China. Within another two years, these restrictions will be removed and domestic Chinese enterprises will be open to foreign non-life insurers.

7. Upon accession to the WTO, foreign insurance firms are permitted to provide master policy insurance and large-scale commercial risk insurance nation-wide.

8. Upon accession to the WTO, China would permit foreign insurance firms to sell personal insurance to foreign and Chinese individual citizens, not groups. After another three years, they will be permitted to sell health and retirement pension to both individuals and groups.

9. Upon accession to the WTO, China would approve foreign insurance firms to operate in China to offer reinsurance, and no geographic or quantitative restrictions are imposed.

10. China will award licences for insurance business solely on the basis of prudence review, with no economic needs test or quantitative limits on the number of licences issued, as long as they meet the following standards:
    - the investor should have operated in a WTO member country for at least 30 years;
    - the investor should have had a representative office in China for at least two years;
    - the investor should have maintained US$5 billion of total assets at the year-end before the

application is filed (this restriction does not apply to brokerage firms);

- foreign brokerage firms, in order to qualify, should show a total asset of US$500 million. After two years of China's WTO membership, they should have total assets of US$400 million, and two years later, US$200 million.

Conclusion

The insurance market in China will undoubtedly continue to expand rapidly on the strength of:

- large unsatisfied demand;
- steady economic growth;
- enhanced consumer awareness;
- continuous enterprise reform;
- improving market order and increased competition;
- committed market access for foreign participation by the government.

Three years after WTO entry, the opening-up of China's insurance industry is far advanced. However, excessive optimism must be cautioned over the fact that the forces of market protectionism remain strong from political, business and academic arenas. Moreover, there are indications that China is utilizing the transitional period of up to five years to slow the process of market access to foreign competition.

More recent developments – J Reuvid

The China Life listing

In April 2004, the US Securities and Exchange Commission (SEC) began an informal inquiry into the December 2003 IPO of the state-owned China Life Insurance on the New York Stock Exchange and Hong Kong Stock Exchange. The offering which raised US$3.4 billion was the world's biggest in 2003 and was over-subscribed about 25 times.

The investigation arose when China's National Audit Office revealed alleged accounting irregularities involving RMB5.4 billion at the state-owned parent company, following a series of lawsuits alleging that it did not disclose the irregularities to investors. The irregularities uncovered by the state audit included the illegal use of insurance agents, the use of private accounts to buy assets for employees, the falsification of expenses in order to reduce taxes and the failure to pay various government imposts. The penalties imposed on the parent company amounted to US$8.4 million in back taxes and fines, less than expected in Hong Kong when announced.

In July 2004, China Life announced that the National Audit Office investigation would have no material impact on the listed company's operations, cash flow or financial position.

Carlyle investment in China Pacific

In July 2004, the US private equity group, Carlyle, announced the final stages of negotiation to purchase a stake of up to 25 per cent in China Pacific Life, the country's third largest assurer, for up to US$400 million. The deal awaits the approval of the Chinese regulators. Among the matters to be decided is whether ING, the longstanding insurance partner of China Pacific, or Prudential of the US should be Carlyle's partner in the consortium.

Increased investment scope for Chinese insurers

On 18 August 2004, CIRC announced landmark approval for insurers to buy US$8 billion of overseas debt, foreshadowing future permission to invest in overseas securities. The approval was a first step towards the authorities sanctioning the long-awaited qualified domestic institutional investor (QDII) scheme, which could allow hundreds of billions of dollars to be invested in overseas markets. Currently, CIRC has authorized insurers in China to purchase debt rated 'A' and above, overseas bonds issued by Chinese banks or firms, bank bills and other money market instruments, but not equities.

The Media Market

Jonathan Reuvid and Snapshots International

The rapid commercialization of the Chinese economy, in particular consumer products manufacturing, channels to market and retailing, have introduced international media marketing practices and techniques, albeit 'with Chinese characteristics'. Together with satellite and cable television and the revolutionary impact of the internet, these irresistible forces have eroded the government's levers of control over the media. Only news publications and most media organizations remain under the control of the state or the Communist Party, but many of those that are still nominally under their ownership are focusing more on generating profits rather than propaganda.

However, the State Administration of Radio, Film and Television (Sarft) recognizes that media incapable of competing for listeners and viewers will have little influence on public opinion, and understands that many state publications are financially onerous for the institutions that control them. Towards the end of 2003, the government instituted a review of more than 1,400 state and party newspapers and periodicals, closed almost half and ordered most of the rest to join commercial media groups or to take responsibility for their own finances. Publications that have been closed down by the reforms include *Beijing Tax*, a tax bureau periodical that depended on mandatory subscriptions from commercial and institutional taxpayers.

Market size

Recent growth in the value of the Chinese media is charted in Table 8.10.1, based on advertising sales, retail sales of books and newspaper subscriptions:

- Chinese media sales increased by 9.6 per cent in value in 2002. Total sales for 2002 were RMB250.1 billion.

- Compound annual growth rate (CAGR) for the period 1998–2002 was 10.6 per cent.
- The strongest growth was in 2000, with a rate of 13.2 per cent.

Table 8.10.1 Chinese media value 1998–2002 (RMB billion)

Year	RMB bn	% growth
1998	167.2	
1999	183.6	9.8
2000	207.9	13.2
2001	228.2	9.8
2002	250.1	9.6
CAGR [1998–2002]		**10.6%**

Source: Snapdata Research

In particular, China's television market is growing strongly, with advertising sales of approximately US$2.7 billion reported for 2003, up from from US$2.1 billion in 2002 and US$1.5 billion in 1998.

Media segmentation

As Table 8.10.2 demonstrates, newspapers, representing 46.8 per cent of the market by value, constituted the largest segment of the Chinese media market in 2002.

Recent developments

In February 2004, the restructuring of China Central Television (CCTV) was announced, with the spin-off of production units and non-broadcasting departments by

Table 8.10.2 Chinese media segmentation 2002 (value %)

Segment	% share
Newspapers	46.8
Advertising	36.5
Books	16.7
Total	**100.0**

Source: Snapdata Research

the state-owned broadcaster foreshadowed. Subsequent listings on overseas markets are envisaged. In 2003, CCTV generated revenues in excess of RMB8 billion (US$966.5 million) and the changes were intended to attract private and foreign funds and expertise into the television sector. Early targets for restructuring are the CCTV sports channel, which is a straightforward business with highly popular content, and the sports production operations, which could sell new programmes as a new company to its parent on a contract basis. The spin-off companies are to be supported financially by CCTV for about three years before being expected to achieve profitability and become self-funding.

The new policy drafted by Sarft provides for qualified foreign companies to apply for minority shareholding in the companies spun off from CCTV. 'Strong and influential' companies have become able to apply to hold minority stakes in Chinese production companies from the beginning of December 2004. Beijing hopes that a significant increase in private sector involvement through investment will enhance the quality and quantity of content produced for the China market. At the same time, local private companies will also be permitted to develop pay channels jointly, with the intention of attracting the investment needed to fund plans for the expansion of digital TV services and pay television in China.

Among the overseas companies expected to take rapid advantage of the new rules are Rupert Murdoch's News Corp, Viacom and Seven Network of Australia. Chinese companies must hold majority stakes in such joint ventures, each of which must have a unique logo so that they are not used to promote the brand of the foreign partner.

Hitherto, landing rights for channels run by overseas broadcasters such News Corp's Star TV and Viacom's music channel, MTV, have been restricted to hotels, approved housing compounds and restricted areas of Guangdong Province. In October 2004, Viacom announced its further expansion plans in China with a joint venture with Beijing Television and much wider coverage of the 24-hour MTV channel currently available in Guangdong Province. Viacom will produce Chinese language music and entertainment programmes for Beijing TV.

Earlier, in July 2004, the Hong Kong-based Star TV gained approval to launch China's first wholly foreign-owned advertising company, specifically to handle Star's advertising for its Chinese channels. The approval was granted by China as part of its 'Closer Economic Partnership Arrangement' (CEPA) with Hong Kong for which Star was able to qualify as a Hong Kong registered company.

Oil and Gas

Jonathan Reuvid

Overview

China's emergence as a global manufacturing centre and the world's largest steel maker has caused it to become both a net importer of coal and a major influence on the world oil market. In 2003, China overtook Japan as the world's second largest oil consumer after the US. The rapidly increasing Chinese demand for petroleum products and aviation fuels, as automotive consumption and air travel soar, have added to the upward pressure on prices during the period of less certain oil supplies following the Iraq war.

China's output of crude oil in 2003 was up 1.8 per cent year-on-year (yoy) at 170 million tonnes. Over the same period, imports of crude oil rose 31 per cent to 91 million tonnes and of oil products, by 39 per cent.

In the first six months of 2004, Chinese oil imports grew 40 per cent yoy, while China and India's combined oil consumption now accounts for 38 per cent of global consumption. The International Energy Agency (IEA) has almost doubled its forecast of Chinese oil demand for 2004 to six million barrels a day. In the period January to August, China imported a total of 79.9 million tonnes.

Structure of the industry

Exploration and production (E&O) of oil and gas in China is a state-owned industry, in the hands of three giant listed companies: PetroChina, Sinopec and the China National Offshore Oil Corporation (CNOOC). Hitherto, competition between the three has been limited since the activities of each have been concentrated on different sectors. While PetroChina has been focused on upstream gas and oil production,

Sinopec has refineries and chemical plants as well as onshore exploration and production operations, and CNOOC is the dominant E&O offshore company.

The relative size of the three Chinese majors can be measured in terms of their proved reserves, detailed in Table 8.11.1.

Table 8.11.1 Proved oil and gas reserves of China's 'big three'

	Crude oil (million barrels)	*Natural gas (billion cubic feet)*
PetroChina	8,884.8	13,373.7
Sinopec	3,257.0	2,887.6
CNOOC	1,436.1	4,154.4

Sources: Thomson Datastream; most recent annual reports

Recent allocations of exploration licences, such as the PetroChina licence for exploration and production in the South China Sea, suggested that the government was introducing a more competitive environment as the industry matures. However, although Sinopec has also been conducting exploration and production (E&P) offshore in the north-eastern Bohai Sea for years in direct competition with CNOOC, more than 90 per cent of its operating profit is derived from land-based upstream activities. In any case, the degree of competition between Sinopec and CNOOC in offshore E&P is limited by the rule that only CNOOC is permitted to do so with foreign partners.

Nevertheless, CNOOC Group has also been allowed to extend its activities into two new areas of operation with sound commercial prospects. First, in April 2004, CNOOC was granted permission for the first time to import crude oil, formerly the exclusive preserve of PetroChina and Sinopec. This oil will be used for CNOOC's growing downstream activities in areas that are traditionally Sinopec strongholds, such as a petrochemical plant with Royal Dutch/Shell in Guangdong Province. Second, CNOOC Group is also reported to be starting exploration in land-locked Mongolia within the oil-and gas-rich Ordos Basin, its first significant onshore E&P venture. At the same time CNOOC received government approval in August 2004 to build China's largest oil refinery with a capacity of 12 million tonnes in Guangdong Province. Construction is scheduled to begin at the end of 2005 and to be completed in the first half of 2008, at an investment cost of US$2 billion.

Overall, any major structural changes in the industry are likely to be gradual. The government will be wary of undermining the three companies' international stock market valuations, which are largely dependent on dominance in their respective sectors. In the long run, of course, if China's oil industry is to become globally competitive, its three main companies will need to become fully-integrated players.

The west–east gas pipeline

The gas pipeline of over 4,800 kilometres from the Siberian Kovykta field to the north-east provinces and Bohai Gulf area of China has been a cherished project for years, although final decisions were beset by disputes between the Russian and Chinese governments and, more recently, between oil majors. The US$18 billion pipeline would form the main artery for China's policy of economic development for the much poorer Chinese western provinces, crossing the Tarim basin in the far north-west of China and the western part of the Gobi desert, before feeding urban areas in the east around Shanghai.

By the end of 2006, the pipeline was expected to be running at about 1.2 billion cubic feet of natural gas per day, sufficient to supply six million homes. In February 2004, the UK engineering group, Rolls Royce, announced that it had won a US$150 million contract to supply compression equipment to the pipeline. The contract is for 20 packages of compressor equipment, of which 12 are to be built around gas turbines and the remainder around electric turbines.

However, the commercial arrangements for the project were thrown into disarray in August 2004 when PetroChina, China's largest oil producer, broke off negotiations with Royal Dutch/Shell, Exxon Mobil and Gazprom, the Russian gas monopoly, over their joint venture participation in the pipeline. Analysts commented that the talks had failed because PetroChina could not charge high enough gas prices for natural gas to consumers in Shanghai and other cities to satisfy the investment return requirement of the western potential partners of round 15 per cent. Throughout the negotiations China had also insisted on keeping the price of gas down for the project's main market of industrial users such as large petrochemical companies. Compounding the problem, government support for environmentally friendly gas is frustrated in some cities, where coal, and sometimes imported liquefied natural gas (LNG), remains much cheaper for local government and factories. Nevertheless, the main pipeline has been largely completed and has been delivering gas to Shanghai since January 2004. The failure of negotiations was no surprise to many observers, who noted that the talks had stalled since the retirement of Mr Zhu Rongji, China's former premier, who had been an enthusiastic protagonist for the introduction of foreign investment and expertise into the project. The project continues without foreign participation.

Exploration and production activity outside China

Until now, Sinopec Group has had just one major overseas gas project, having won exploration rights over an area of about 40,000 square kilometres in the Rub Al-khali Basin of Saudi Arabia.

In April 2004, Sinopec Group, the parent company of the listed Sinopec Corporation, announced discussions with the Iranian government on a purchase agreement for at least five million tonnes of LNG annually, representing 5 per cent of 2003 global production. As a part of the proposed deal, it was reported that Sinopec would be allowed access to a major Iranian oilfield. If the agreement is concluded, it would mark an important success for Iran in the present climate of US economic sanctions.

In 2003, China imported 8.3 million barrels of crude oil from Kazakhstan, an increase of 19 per cent yoy. However, these imports travel hundreds of kilometres by rail to Xinjiang and represent a tiny proportion of China's total annual imports of 636.8

million barrels. The signature of an agreement for the second section of a 3,000 kilometre pipeline deal between Kazakhstan and China, dating from 1997, was announced in May 2004, following the opening of the first 448 kilometre section in March. The link from Atasu in the Caspian oilfields to Xinjiang province is estimated to cost US$850 million.

In spite of this involvement, Sinopec was not allowed into a major exploration project in Kazakhstan, when western companies including Exxon and Eni exercised pre-emption rights.

PetroChina's domestic listing

In July 2004, PetroChina announced plans for a RMB30–40 billion domestic 'A' share listing to supplement the New York and Hong Kong listing of part of its operations in a US$9.2 billion offering in 2001. The offering is nearly three to four times the biggest initial public offering made in China so far. However, the timetable is uncertain.

The fund-raising plan is in response to the Chinese authorities' declared wish that PetroChina, Sinopec and CNOOC should also invest overseas to ensure that they have an interest in foreign resources, as part of the national 'energy security' policy.

Strategic petroleum reserve programme

In 2005, China will formally launch its strategic reserve programme. The first of four oil reserve bases with a capacity of five million cubic metres is already under construction in Zhanhai, Zhejiang Province. Further reserve bases, approved by the National Development and Reform Commission, will be located in Daishan (Zhejiang), Huangdao (Shandong) and Dalian (Laoning). All four bases are scheduled for completion by the end of 2008, providing a reserve equivalent to 10 days of crude oil imports. China will also hold 21 days of commercial oil reserves throughout China.

Investment activity

In July 2004, ExxonMobil was said to be planning a sale of its 19 per cent holding in Sinopec, following sales earlier in the year by BP and Royal Dutch/Shell of their stakes. This further sale will mark the end of the international groups' participation in Asia's largest oil refiner, taken in 2000 as a show of support for the Chinese oil industry at the time of Sinopec's overseas IPO.

Following the termination of talks by PetroChina in August over the participation of Royal Dutch/Shell, ExxonMobil and Gazprom in the west–east pipeline, Royal Dutch/Shell and Unocal of the US withdrew from the Xhu Trough development scheme in the East China Sea led by CNOOC and Sinopec. Shell remains committed to spending US$1 billion in China in its 2004 plan, mostly on a petrochemicals project.

In November 2004, Sinopec agreed an asset swap with its state-owned parent company, China Petrochemical Corporation (CPC), which has strengthened its focus on downstream activities. Sinopec is buying a number of petrochemical plants for US$326 million and a nation-wide network of petrol stations for US$227 million. At the same time, CPC is acquiring all of Sinopec's upstream operation assets for US$215 million, with the balance payable by Sinopec in cash.

The London-quoted Fortune Oil is one of the first private companies to invest in China's gas infrastructure trades in oil and operates a mooring point for oil tankers. In the six months to June 2004, volumes at its mooring facility increased by 25 per cent. However, Fortune's financial progress has been frustrated by delays in approval by the Assets Supervision and Administration Commission for the sale of its 24.5 per cent stake in Bluesky, a jet fuel company, to China Aviation Oil (CAO).

Following the revelations in December of the scandal surrounding the US$550 million losses in oil derivatives by CAO, a Singapore-listed company, an early resolution to Fortune Oil's problem seems less likely. Immediately following the debacle, it was considered likely by the banking community that China Aviation Holding Company, the Beijing parent of CAO, would come to the rescue of the western banks, which have suffered unhedged losses.

In the fall-out from the CAO embarrassment, it is possible that the opening up of the Chinese jet fuel market will be accelerated. Although China is committed through its WTO undertakings to open up its aviation fuel market, so far only BP has secured a foothold. The total jet fuel market in China is currently about six million tonnes per annum, about the size of London Heathrow's consumption, but is growing fast, probably at about 20 per cent yoy.

Natural gas fuelled power

In April 2004, a feasibility study was approved for the construction of a power plant fuelled by natural gas and steam in Lansou, Gansu Province, one of China's most heavily air-polluted cities. The project is a joint venture between Meiya (Lanzou) Power Co. and three foreign investors, including the Asian Infrastructure Fund. The power plant is scheduled to start commercial operations in 2007. The project will cost US$340 million, representing the biggest Sino-foreign joint venture investment to date.

The Petrochemical Industry

Li Yong, Deputy Secretary General, China Association of International Trade

After 50 years of development, China has become one of the world's largest crude oil producers. For 13 consecutive years, China's crude oil production has ranked fifth after the US, Saudi Arabia, Russia and Iran and, in 2001, its total output was 165 million tonnes. China has the largest refining capacity in Asia at 276 million tonnes, which makes it the third largest in the world after the US and Russia. China is also the third largest consumer of gasoline, diesel oil and kerosene after the US and Japan.

The petrochemical industry is basically dominated by three major groups – China National Petroleum Corporation (CNPC), China Petrochemical Corporation (Sinopec) and China National Offshore Oil Corporation – which was a result of the industry reshuffling in 1998. The total assets of the three groups amount to nearly RMB1 trillion, about 12 per cent of the total state-owned assets. Sinopec has the largest oil refining capacity in the country, accounting for 53 per cent of China's total refining capacity. CNPC takes the second position with 40 per cent, while the remaining 7 per cent is distributed among smaller local refineries. After years of effort to develop independent techno-logical capabilities, China's crude refining technology can now meet the refining requirements of the country.

China's ethylene capacity ranks fifth in the world; sixth in synthetic resins; fourth in synthetic rubber and first in synthetic fibre. With the deepening of economic reform and opening up of the market, China introduced a number of petrochemical processing technologies, which have enhanced local R&D capabilities in developing local technologies for downstream processing. The once import-dependent catalysts, for example, are now mostly produced by local producers and the rate of localized production of catalysts is well over 85 per cent. Some catalysts have reached international quality standards and are exported to foreign countries, reversing the one-way import situation of the past.

However, with the growth of China's economy, the gap between the development of the petrochemical industry and the increasing demand for petrochemical products has been widened. The main problems in the petrochemical industry are the low levels of industry concentration and an inability to supply the necessary products. There are over 130 crude refineries spread over most of the provinces, autonomous regions and municipalities. Eighteen ethylene plants are scattered over 15 cities. This contrasts sharply with the high concentration level of petrochemical operations in more developed countries. At the same time, the average plant size is also much smaller than the world average. Fragmentation and poor plant economics have led to a small market share of the petrochemical products being produced at home, such as synthetic resins, synthetic rubber, synthetic fibre and organic chemical raw material, which make up about 50 per cent of the market. The industry has also been troubled by the problem of fewer grade varieties, lower quality and smaller product ranges. The required grades and products of high enough quality have to be imported in great quantities from abroad each year. In addition, the insufficient supply of organic raw material at home has also hindered the development of downstream fine chemicals, leading to a lack of coordi-nation between the petrochemical and traditional chemical industries.

In the 1990s, the demand for ethylene in China grew at an average annual rate of 17 per cent, much higher than the average GDP growth in the same period. The growth in the production of ethylene in the period, however, averaged only 12 per cent per annum, leading to a widening gap between supply and demand. As a result, the importation of petrochemical products has been increasing at an average annual rate of 32 per cent. Importation of petrochemical raw materials, as expressed in its ethylene equivalent, accounts for about 50 per cent of China's total consumption of petrochemical products. For some petrochemical products, such as polystyrene (PS) and ABS, the rate of dependence on imports can be as high as 80 per cent.

As shown in Table 8.12.1, the self-sufficiency rates for synthetic fibre and rubber increased in 2001, while that for synthetic resins declined. This demonstrates the problem of a lagging supply of synthetic resins compared with rapid increasing demand.

The production pattern of China's petrochemical industry has the following characteristics:

- The production of ethylene, petrochemical raw materials and their products are largely concentrated in Sinopec and CNPC operations, whose total capacity now accounts for 90 per cent of the country's total. These two majors own 16 of China's 18 ethylene projects.
- State-owned enterprises at the local level, small- to medium-sized collectively-owned factories and private operators mainly operate in the downstream production of petrochemical products.
- Foreign-invested petrochemical enterprises produce those downstream products that are in short supply in China. Their products are typically concentrated in polymer and synthetic fibre categories and their production is based on imported feeds.

As shown in Table 8.12.2, Sinopec and CNPC have a dominant role in China's production of polyolefin resins. The two majors also own the majority of the production and capacity of synthetic rubber and synthetic fibre raw materials. In the case of PVC, production is dispersed among local operations, as a legacy of the historical distribution of production and diversification of raw material supplies. Styrenic resins such as PS and ABS are largely concentrated in joint venture operations. Synthetic fibres such as polyester, acrylic, polyamide and polypropylene fibres are produced by local enterprises.

China's ethylene industry will continue to develop over the next 10 years or so. The priority of development for domestic ethylene plants is on expansion of capacity to improve plant economics or increase economies of scale. Table 8.12.3 lists the 18 ethylene installations, their capacities and expansion plans.

According to the estimates in China's petrochemical industry's tenth Five-Year Plan, the demand for ethylene expressed in ethylene equivalent will grow at an annual rate of 8.5 per cent and reach 15 million tonnes of ethylene equivalent by 2005. To capture the growth, foreign investors have invested heavily in China's ethylene projects (see Table 8.12.4).

In the tenth Five-Year Plan period (2001–2005), China's economy is predicted to grow by between 7 and 8 per cent, which will drive the demand for ethylene downstream products, particularly the five major synthetic resins PE, PP, PVC, PS and ABS. According to estimates by China Packaging Technology Association, the market for the five major synthetic resins will develop at a rate of 6.1 per cent in this period. By 2005, the total demand will reach 24.45 million tonnes. Another estimate indicates that the demand for the five major synthetic resins will be between 25 and 27 million tonnes. However, it is important to observe the following trends in relation to the demand changes in the five major synthetic resins:

1. In the PE category, LLDPE will gradually gain greater market share over LDPE. As LLDPE technology improves, LLDPE will not only perform

Table 8.12.1 The gap between supply and demand of three major synthetic materials

| | Synthetic resins | | | Synthetic fibre | | | Synthetic rubber | | |
	1999	2000	2001	1999	2000	2001	1999	2000	2001
Production	8.417	10.80	12.03	5.487	6.15	7.599	0.684	0.836	1.045
Net imports	12.59	11.40	14.39	1.285	1.54	1.395	0.65	0.65	0.638
Apparent consumption	20.70	22.20	26.43	6.72	7.69	7.772	1.25	1.481	1.683
Rate of self-sufficiency (%)	39.2	48.6	46.0	81.0	80.0	82.0	48.0	56.5	62.0

Table 8.12.2   Distribution of petrochemical production by player

Products	Sinopec share (%)	CNPC share (%)	Others' share (%)
Ethylene	61	32	7
Polyethylene	63	32	5
Polypropylene	67	22	11
PVC	8	1	91
PS	43	7	50
ABS	0	89	11
BR	77	23	0
SBR	34	34	32
PET chip	35	10	55
PTA	78	11	11
Glycol	70	30	0
ACN	40	45	15
Hexanolactam	100	0	0
Terylene (polyester fibre)	17	3	80
Acrylic fibre	53	21	26
Polyamide fibre (nylon)	7	0	93
Polypropylene fibre	10	5	85

Source: Beijing Yigou Petrochemical Consulting

Table 8.12.3   China's ethylene capacity by plant and capacity expansion plans (thousand tonnes)

Company	Planned	Current	Expansion	Completion
Yanshan Petrochemical	300	660	660	2001
Shanghai Petrochemical Plant 1	300	400	700	2002
Shanghai Petrochemical Plant 2	110	145	145	
Yangtze Petrochemical	300	400	650	2002
Qilu Petrochemical	300	450	600	2003
Maoming Petrochemical	300	380	800	2004
Tianjin United Chemical	140	140	200	
Zhongyuan Ethylene	140	140	200	
Guangzhou Petrochemical	140	140	200	
Beijing Oriental Chemical Plant	140	140	200	
Daqing Petrochemical	300	480	600	2005
Jilin Petrochemical Plant 1	300	300	400	
Jilin Petrochemical Plant 2	115	145	145	
Fushun Petrochemical	124	144	144	
Liaoyang Chemical Fibre	88	88	88	
Lanzhou Petrochemical	80	160	160	
Dushanzi Petrochemical	140	140	220	2002
Panjin Ethylene	130	160	160	
Total	3,447	4,612	6,272	

Source: Beijing Yigou Petrochemical Consulting

Table 8.12.4 Key foreign-invested ethylene projects

Project	Planned capacity	Chinese investors (thousand tonnes)	Foreign investors
1. Huizhou Nanhai ethylene project	800	CNPC and Guangdong Province	Shell
2. BASF-YPC Integrated ethylene project	600	Sinopec and Yangtze Petrochemical	BASF
3. Shanghai BP ethylene project	900	Sinopec and Shanghai Petrochemical	BP
4. Fujian Ethylene project	600	Sinopec and Fujian Province	Exxon and Saudi
Total	2,900		Arabian Petroleum

better, which will expand its application areas, but will also become competitive on price against LDPE. The demand for LDPE will gradually reduce while that for LLDPE will pick up and the consumption of LLDPE will eventually surpass that of LDPE. In addition, LLDPE and LDPE applications in agricultural films will subside against the trend of demand for long-life, thinner, low unit usage and multi-functional agricultural films. The rate of growth in the demand of LLDPE/LDPE will slow in the next five years. However, the applications of LLDPE and LDPE will increase in other industries such as wires and cables, whose development is largely driven by the prospering telecommunications industry.

2. The consumption pattern of HDPE will change little by the year 2005. With the increase in the usage volume of materials in the packaging industry and the shift of packaging operations from Japan and Europe to China and other southeast Asian countries, this growth in demand for HDPE will be sustained. HDPE films will remain the largest area of HDPE application. With the development towards diversification of HDPE applications in hollow products, production of HDPE products such as multi-layer extruded tubes, plastic bottles in pharmaceutical and food applications and large- to medium-sized plastic containers will increase, leading to a moderate increase in the share of HDPE application in hollow plastic part manufacturing.

3. The usage of high value-added PP is growing. In some applications, high value-added PP, with its improved properties, has replaced engineering plastics, as a result of which the share of PP consumption in injection moulded products is expected to rise. At the same time, PP fibre will find an expanded area of application in the development of civil engineering materials. Rapid growth of PP application in the production of films for packaging purposes is also expected over the next five years, but the traditional application of PP in woven products will decline.

4. Driven by the development of so-called chemical construction materials, PVC has gained a strong momentum of growth over the past few years and will continue to be a key material for the production of door and window frames and pipes. Some large cities have formulated policies to encourage the use of plastic materials in property development projects, which will stimulate the growth of demand for rigid PVC products. PVC flexible products will face a mixed scenario, with increases of applications expected in the manufacturing of shoes and synthetic leather, while growth in film and cable applications will slow. PVC film will have to face the challenge posed by PE film.

5. Environmental concerns about white pollution have already had a negative impact on the demand for EPS in the applications of lunch boxes and fast-food containers, which has slowed in the last couple of years. Generally, the pattern of consumption for GPPS and HIPS will not see major changes and their applications will increase with the development of the end-use industries such as household electrical appliance and office automation. The negative impact of the ban on the use of EPS containers in the food service sector will be offset by the increase in the application of EPS in the building materials sector.

6. Under the pressure of increased application of PS in household electrical appliances, ABS consumption in large electrical appliance items is expected to decline, while its application in small household appliances will increase. More importantly, the development of China's automobile industry will be the key driving force for future growth of demand for ABS.

Table 8.12.5   Committed petrochemical tariff rates post WTO entry

Product description	Tariff rate 2002 (%)	Committed at the accession date (%)	Specific commitment Final committed rate (%)	Implementation
Organic chemicals				
Ethylene	2.8	3.5	2.0	2003
Propylene	2.8	3.5	2.0	2003
Butylene	2.8	3.5	2.0	2003
Butadiene	2.8	3.5	2.0	2003
Isopentene	2.8	3.5	2.0	2003
Benzene	4.0	4.7	2.0	2005
Toluene	5.0	6.0	2.0	2005
Ethylbenzene	5.5	6.7	2.0	2005
Paraxylene	5.0	6.0	2.0	2005
Alkylbenzene	5.5	6.7	2.0	2005
Phenol	5.5	7.0	5.5	2002
Acetone	5.5	5.5	5.5	
Glacial acetic acid	5.5	5.5	5.5	
Phthalic anhydride	6.6	8.3	6.5	2002
Synthetic fibre raw materials and polymers				
Glycol	8.8	10.5	5.5	2004
Acrylonitrile	6.5	6.5	6.5	
Hexanolactam	10.8	12.5	9.0	2003
PTA	12.8	13.9	6.5	2008
Polyester (other)	12.8	13.9	6.5	2008
Nylon 66 salt	6.5	6.5	6.5	
Synthetic resin				
LDPE	14.2	15.4	6.5	2008
HDPE	14.2	15.4	6.5	2008
Polypropylene	10.0	13.9	6.5	2008
PS	12.8	13.9	6.5	2008
ABS	12.8	13.9	6.5	2008
PVC	12.8	13.9	6.5	2008
Synthetic rubber				
SBR	7.5	7.5	7.5	
BR	7.5	7.5	7.5	
NBR	7.5	7.5	7.5	
IR	3.0	4.5	3.9	2002
EPR	7.5	7.5	7.5	
Synthetic fibre				
Polyester filament	11.4	14.6	5.0	2004
Polyester staple fibre	10.6	13.4	5.0	2004
Acrylic filament	8.3	10.0	5.0	2004
Acrylic staple fibre	8.3	10.0	5.0	2004
Acrylic top	8.3	10.0	5.0	2004
Nylon filament	9.8	12.2	5.0	2004
Nylon staple fibre	9.8	12.2	5.0	2004
PP staple fibre	9.8	12.2	5.0	2004

As predicted in the petrochemical industry's tenth Five-Year Plan, consumption of synthetic rubber between 2001 and 2005 is expected to grow at annual rate of 4 per cent to reach 1.1 million tonnes by 2005. Synthetic fibre, on the other hand, will experience a growth rate in the range of 5.4–8.3 per cent, with the total demand being between 10.8 and 12.6 million tonnes by 2005.

China's entry into the WTO will certainly impact, by varying degrees, on the development of its petrochemical industry. However, compared with other highly protected industries, the impact of the WTO will be less significant because protection has been gradually lifted since the 1980s and the majority of petrochemical products have been 'marketized', which means that the demand, production, purchase, sales and prices have been integrated with international market trends. However, it is speculated that the tariff reduction will stimulate the already large influx of imports, which will challenge the survival of low-efficiency petrochemical enterprises.

The expected increase in imports following China's accession to the WTO has caused concerns about further decline in the market share of domestically produced petrochemical products. The market share of imported synthetic resins rose from 33 per cent in 1990 to 52 per cent. The share of imported synthetic rubber has risen from only 9 per cent to the current 44 per cent and that of imported synthetic fibres is now 53 per cent. The increasing market share of imported petrochemical products puts a great deal of pressure on Chinese petrochemical enterprises in their competition with their foreign counterparts. The lifting of restrictions on trading rights and distribution within China will lead to head-on competition with foreign distributors of petrochemical products. Domestic companies will have to make further and greater efforts to reduce costs and enhance their ability to develop new products. As well as this, their marketing systems and adaptability to market changes will have to improve if they are to increase their chances of winning in the competition.

8.13

Promotional Advertising

Li Yong, Deputy Secretary General, China Association of International Trade

An overview

Advertising as an industry has developed in parallel with the opening up and economic reform in China since 1978. In the early stages of its development (1979–1981), advertising revenue totalled only RMB118 million. The increased awareness of modern marketing techniques and intensified competition in the domestic market have made advertisers spend increasing amounts on advertising, which has spurred the industry to develop at a dramatic pace. Over the last 20 years, the industry has been growing at an average annual rate of 38.49 per cent (see Table 8.13.1). By 2001, the total advertising spend had reached RMB79.5 billion, making China one of the 10 largest advertising markets in the world.

It is clear that the average annual growth rate in China's advertising industry has well surpassed that of the GDP and of many other industries. It is also easy

Table 8.13.1 China's advertising spend over the last two decades (RMB million)

Year	Total spend	Year	Total spend
1979–1981	118	1992	6,787
1982	150	1993	13,409
1983	234	1994	20,026
1984	365	1995	27,327
1985	605	1996	36,663
1986	845	1997	46,196
1987	1,112	1998	53,783
1988	1,493	1999	62,205
1989	1,999	2000	71,266
1990	2,502	2001	79,488
1991	3,509	Jan–Jun 2002	37,965

to see that such a high average growth rate is largely due to the development of the small denominator in the initial stage of the advertising industry. It is true that in the early 1990s the advertising industry hit a year-on-year growth rate as high as 97.57 per cent (1993), but it started to slow down from there. The advertising spend in 2001 was only an increase of 11.54 per cent on 2000; however, the net gain was RMB8.22 billion.

Although the growth rate has slowed, the increase in the advertising spend is still in double figures and has convinced more investors, particularly private investors, to enter the industry and cash in on this development. The number of advertising companies reached a total of 78,339 by 2001, an increase of 10.73 per cent. This increase was chiefly caused by the increase in the number of privately owned advertising agencies, which was 22.58 per cent up on 2000.

The advertising industry employed 709,076 people in 2001. With 78,339 advertising companies, the average staff size for each company was 11.59, a reflection of the fragmented nature of the industry (see Table 8.13.2).

The media

All media currently used to advertise in the developed world is also used in China. Traditional public media still play an important role in the transmission of advertising information. Television, radio, newspapers and magazines are considered to be the four pillars of the advertising media.

Television stations

Official statistics from the National Bureau of Statistics indicate that there were 362 television stations in China

Table 8.13.2 Year-on-year growth rate

Year	Advertising spend (RMB million)	Year-on-year growth
1991	3,509	
1992	6,787	93.42
1993	13,409	97.57
1994	20,026	49.35
1995	27,327	36.46
1996	36,663	34.16
1997	46,196	26.00
1998	53,783	16.42
1999	62,205	15.66
2000	71,266	14.57
2001	79,488	11.54

in 2001. This figure does not coincide with the number as given by the State Administration of Industry and Commerce, the supervising authority of China's advertising industry, whose statistics on advertising media shows that there were 3,076 television stations. The difference may come from the application of different standards, with the latter calculating the number of stations engaged in advertising activities, regardless of whether or not they come under one umbrella.

In the last few years, however, the television industry has undergone reshuffling and consolidation. Many independent cable and satellite television stations in key cities have merged with local stations such as municipal level or provincial level television stations and operate under one name. In Beijing, for example, the four cable channels have now become part of Beijing TV (BTV) channels. Reasons for these mergers include avoiding vicious competition for advertising revenue and optimizing channel resources.

In 2001, television coverage reached 94.2 per cent of the population. Cable television users in 2001 amounted to 90.91 million households. The increased coverage of television and its growing role as a key source of information and after-work leisure have made it a favourite medium for advertisers. In 2001, television stations received 22.57 per cent of total advertising revenue, which was RMB17.9 billion.

Radio

According to the same official statistics from the National Bureau of Statistics, there were a total of 300 radio stations in China. Again, this is contradicted by the State Administration of Industry and Commerce's

figure of 711. In 2001, advertising revenue from radio stations amounted to RMB1.83 billion, a little over 10 per cent of the television stations' revenue. Although radio coverage has been able to reach 92.9 per cent of the population, its role as a key source of information has been eroded by other competing media. Despite this, spending on radio advertising in 2001 grew by 2.3 per cent over 2000.

Newspapers

There were 2,007 newspapers by the end of 2000, according to official statistics. The figure from the State Administration of Industry and Commerce counted 2,182 in the year 2001. Advertising sales turnover stood at RMB15.8 billion in the same year. Unlike television and radio, which have a certain level of monopoly, newspapers are facing increasingly intense competition. Since many of the newspapers are of a local nature and carry information of local interest, many are used by advertisers to target consumers at a local level. National newspapers are often used to establish brand identity and image. In the battle for advertisers, newspapers still retain significant advantages, which explains their steady growth as a key medium of advertising – an impressive 19.84 per cent in 2001 as compared with 2000.

Magazines

Although there is a large number of magazines in China – a total of 8,725 in 2000 – advertising revenue was the smallest compared with other media. In 2001, the total advertising turnover was RMB1.19 billion, about 1.49 per cent of China's total advertising revenue. Interestingly, however, statistics by the State Administration of Industry and Commerce registered a total of 3,576 magazine publishing houses engaged in advertising sales. In the period from 1995 to 2000, there was a net increase of 1,142 magazines.

Advertising companies

These 'four pillars' of the public media attracted 46.13 per cent of the total advertising spend. The remainder went into the pockets of advertising companies. Reckoning in the advertising revenue by those advertising companies subordinate to non-advertising enterprises, the total share of the advertising companies would have been 52.1 per cent in 2001.

Clearly, advertising companies have played an important role in the advertising industry, as they should. What makes China's advertising industry different from other countries is that state-owned advertising companies have a dominant position in the industry and in 2001 accounted for only 22.67 per cent of the 78,339 advertising companies but took 54.94 per cent (RMB43.66 billion) of all advertising sales. However, a close look at the performance of those state-owned advertising companies reveals that the total number dropped by 2.4 per cent and the growth was a negative 8.3 per cent for state-owned advertising enterprises, against a moderate increase of 3.1 per cent. Their dominant position seems to have been eroded by companies owned by private and foreign-invested advertising bodies.

Private advertising companies dominated in terms of total number – 37,906 or 48.39 per cent of the total number of advertising establishments. Their sales reached RMB13.95 billion in 2001, 17.55 per cent of the total advertising spend in China and a 35.44 per cent increase on 2000. However, the average advertising sales for each private advertising company was quite small at only RMB0.37 million.

Foreign companies have been active in China's advertising industry. Familiar names such as Saatchi & Saatchi, J. Walter Thompson, Ogilvy & Mather, Dentsu and McCann Erickson have all entered the battlefield of China's advertising industry. According to the State Administration of Industry and Commerce, the total number of foreign-invested advertising agencies was 329 in 2001, a drop of 13.42 per cent. However, the growth in their total advertising sales was a remarkable 64.02 per cent in 2001

and their share in the country's total advertising spending was 9.35 per cent. The average advertising revenue for these foreign-invested advertising firms was RMB22.6 million, which clearly demonstrates the competitive advantages of foreign-invested advertising firms over local ones.

Most advertised products and services

In 2001, the most advertised products were pharmaceutical products, foods, real estate, electrical household appliances and cosmetics. These five categories constituted an aggregate share of 48.3 per cent, almost half of China's total advertising outlay in 2001 (see Table 8.13.3).

In terms of growth, advertising spend on alcoholic products, foods and pharmaceutical products experienced strong growth in 2001, with respective growth rates of 69, 30 and 29 per cent. However, it is probably affected by a host of factors such as industry slowdown and market competition – advertising spend by motor vehicles, electrical household appliances and medical apparatus declined by 46, 11 and 16 per cent respectively compared with 2000.

The emergence of internet advertising (e-advertising)

Development

When the first internet advertisement appeared in March 1997 on Chinabyte.com, China was already three years behind the US. However, this did mark the

Table 8.13.3 2001 advertising spend by products/services

Category	Spending (RMB billion)	% of 2000	Share in total spending (%)
Pharmaceuticals	9,669	128.99	12.16
Foods	8,995	129.91	11.32
Real estate	6,948	116.60	8.47
Electrical appliances	6,588	89.62	8.29
Cosmetics	6,334	133.43	7.97
Alcoholic products	4,120	169.34	5.18
Medical services	3,261	106.88	4.10
Garments and accessories	2,427	114.54	3.05
Motor vehicles	2,286	53.79	2.88
Medical apparatus	1,873	86.63	2.36
Tourism	1,583	122.62	1.99
Tobacco	910	105.94	1.14
Other	24,495	108.27	30.82

beginning of China's internet advertising industry and played a critical role in the development of its internet industry. From then on, internet advertising offered a new option in addition to conventional advertising modes for advertisers to establish a 'cyber communication' channel with their potential consumers/ customers. According to WiseCast, in 1998, advertisers spent a total of RMB30 million on internet advertising. In the following year, three times as much was spent, a total of RMB90 million. 2000 saw a dramatic increase of 289 per cent in internet advertising spend, a total of RMB350 million. Although the advertisers' enthusiasm was dampened by the downturn in the IT industry and the general slowdown of the world economy in 2001, internet advertising still managed a growth of 20 per cent to reach RMB420 million (see Figure 8.13.1).

Advertisers

Many advertisers still need time to recognize fully the role of internet advertising, and the popularity of the internet will also take time to develop before there is a sufficient 'internet population' to convince advertisers that advertising on the net will help them reach the target consumers/customers. According to a survey conducted by WiseCast, there was a total of 669 internet advertisers in 2000 and the number increased to 1,004 in 2001, an encouraging increase of 50 per cent. However, a closer look at the composition of the advertisers will reveal that the advertisers were basically 'patrons' of the internet or IT related businesses. In 2000, for example, the number of internet medium advertisers amounted to 220, 32.9 per cent of the total. There were also 101 advertisers of IT products and 23 from the telecommunications services sector.

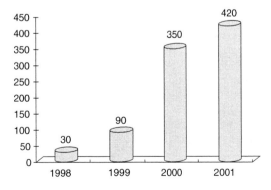

Source: WiseCast

Figure 8.13.1   Internet advertising spend in China (RMB million)

The same pattern continued in 2001, although the number of internet medium advertisers declined to 193. This decline was offset by the increase in the number of advertisers from the IT and telecommunications sectors, which totalled 155 and 45 respectively.

Advertisers that use conventional media are still sceptical of the reach that internet advertising can deliver. Few advertisers of fast-moving consumer products are using internet advertising. A good sign in 2001, however, was that there were 45 advertisers from medical services and the health-care sector posting their advertising on the internet, although their total spend ranked last after internet, IT products, real estate and home improvement products, financial services, consulting services for overseas students and emigration.

Internet users

On the other side of internet advertising is the audience, ie internet users. Since China began to build its internet infrastructure in 1994, the size of the internet population has been growing at a phenomenal speed. According to a survey conducted by China Internet Network Information Centre (CINIC) the number of internet users in China had reached 45.8 million by 30 June 2002, a net increase of 12.1 million (35.9 per cent) over the previous six months. This is an increase by a factor of 75 compared with 0.62 million internet users when CNNIC did the first survey in October 1997.

Internet users' attitudes to internet advertising is critical to the success of the advertisers, and for this reason, CNNIC conducted two surveys in January and June of 2001. The responses to this appeared to be quite encouraging (see Figure 8.13.2), provided the surveys are representative.

The survey results suggest that internet users are much happier to click on internet adverts than to receive e-mail advertisements, the latter being labelled junk mail and rejected by many foreign internet portals.

The regulatory environment

The advertising industry is closely regulated by the government, as it is in many other countries. The basic law that governs the advertising industry in China is the *Advertising Law of the People's Republic of China*. There are also other bylaws that regulate the advertisement of specific product lines such as tobacco, pharmaceutical products and medical equipment, amongst others. According to the Advertising Law, advertisements must not contain any of the following:

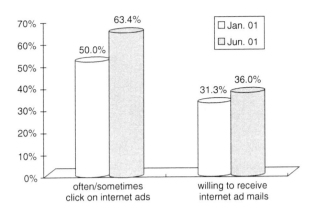

Source: China Internet Network Information Centre

Figure 8.13.2 Chinese internet users' attitudes towards Internet advertising

- the national flag, national emblem or national anthem of the People's Republic of China;
- the names of state organs or the names of staff of state organs;
- such words as 'state-level', 'highest-level' or 'best';
- matters hindering social stability or endangering the safety of life or property, or harming the public interest;
- matters hindering public order or violating good social customs;
- pornographic, superstitious, offensive, violent or unpleasant matters;
- discrimination on the grounds of ethnicity, race, religion or sex;
- matters hindering environmental and natural resources protection;
- matters that are prohibited by laws and administrative regulations.

In addition, the law prohibits the use of comparison between competing products and also requires advertisers to submit advertisements for approval, prior to publication, to the 'competent administrative departments' – the Administration of Industry and Commerce in the domicile of the advertising agent.

There are also regulations regarding the maximum amount of tax-free advertising outlay. The tax authority issued a regulation in May 2000 providing that the advertising outlay of an enterprise within the designated limit of 2 per cent of its total sales can be deducted from its income as non-taxable expenses. This regulation has partly affected the willingness of enterprises to spend on advertising. On 8 May 2001, the tax authority issued another regulation that relaxed the controls on tax-free advertising outlay for certain industries, such as pharmaceuticals, foods (including health-care products and drinks), household toiletries, electrical household appliances, telecommunications, software development, integrated circuits, property development, sports and cultural activities and shopping centres of furniture and building materials.

WTO commitments

In addition to the laws and regulations that govern advertising activities by businesses registered in China, there are also regulations regarding foreign entry into the advertising industry. Following China's accession to the WTO, the restrictions in terms of equity ownership will be gradually phased out. Upon accession, foreign advertising companies can only enter China's advertising industry in the form of joint ventures and the foreign equity share in the joint venture should not exceed 49 per cent. Within two years after accession, foreign majority ownership will be permitted and within four years wholly foreign-owned subsidiaries will be permitted. In terms of cross-border supply and consumption abroad, foreign advertising services can only be provided through advertising agents registered in China and having the appropriate right to do so.

Retailing

Li Yong, Deputy Secretary General, China Association of International Trade, and Chen Congcong, Guanghua Management School, Beijing University, with updates by Jonathan Reuvid

Introduction

Since China initiated its reform and opening up drive in 1978, the Chinese retail sector has undergone an enormous transformation. Between 1978 and 2000, the sector grew at an annual average rate of 13.5 per cent. Since the 1990s in particular, developments have been more remarkable. Store ownership has diversified considerably. Today, individuals, private businesses and foreign-invested ventures are active players in China's retail sector. The entry of foreign investment has injected new dynamics of competition, while at the same time speeding up the retail revolution process that has totally altered the retail structure and competitive landscape in China. China's retail market has begun to reach a much more advanced stage of maturity in recent years in the main urban areas. Almost all the new retail formats that have been developed in western economies have been introduced, including discount department stores, supermarkets, shopping centres/malls, franchise shops, factory outlets, warehouse stores/clubs and chain stores.

Market snapshots

Before China's accession to the WTO, the retail sector was sheltered by extreme protection, which is now being relaxed and the sector has been put on the 'fast track' of opening up. In three years' time, China will have to open up the retail sale sector across the board and eliminate the restrictions on region, amount and equity proportions of foreign wholesalers. Within five years, the country will open the wholesale sector. There will be an increase in the number of foreign retailers strategically entering the retail sector over the next few years.

Since the mid-1990s, total retail sales and consumption of consumer goods have been growing at a faster speed than that of the GDP. In 2001 for example, the rate of increase in the total retail sales of consumer goods was 10.1 per cent year on year, three percentage points higher than the rate of the GDP.

Driven by the fast-growing economy and increasing consumer affluence, China's retail market is expected to have great growth potential and should reach a total of RMB5.7 trillion by 2010.

The retail trade is highly fragmented and dominated by 'Mom-and-Pop' stores. According to a survey, the top 100 retailers in China have a share of less than 5 per cent of the retail market.

Retail formats have experienced great changes: chain stores have emerged as a significant force, growing at an annual rate of 48 per cent over the last few years. Correspondingly, sales by retail chains now account for more than 8 per cent of the total retail market. There is a trend for independent stores to evolve into chains. According to a survey conducted by the State Economic and Trade Commission and the National Statistical Bureau, there were 1,138 retail chains in China by the middle of 2001, with a total of 25,119 outlets. The total sales of these retail chains in the first half of 2001 was RMB102.41 billion.

The total retail sales of consumer goods as a percentage of GDP has been on the rise in recent years. By 2001, its share of GDP approached 40 per cent. Compared with developed countries such as the US, whose total retail sales accounts for over 60 per cent of its GDP, China's retail market still has considerable room for growth, and as a result, the rate of growth in the foreseeable future is expected to be higher than that of the GDP.

There has been a disparity in terms of the ratio of consumption between urban and rural residents. According to one estimate, over 60 per cent of retail sales come from urban areas. The rural market has yet to be developed.

The general oversupply of consumer goods has led to intense competition among retailers and profit margins for retailers are low. According to a survey by the Chinese Chain and Franchise Association of retail chains, with a total turnover exceeding RMB100 million, the average net profit is only 1.33 per cent while gross profit averages 12.4 per cent. The low profit margin is in effect one of the key driving forces for Chinese retail chains to develop towards expansion in scale to compete with foreign-invested retailers, who are competing on volume orders in addition to having other advantages.

The rate of contribution by the domestic market to the development of China's economy is increasing steadily. But the pattern of growth that had originally been investment- and production-driven has now begun to shift to consumption- and market-driven.

Key retail players

Although the total sales of the top 20 retail chains (see Table 8.14.1) as a percentage of total retail sales of consumer goods is relatively small at 2.6 per cent, the rate of growth was a phenomenal 43 per cent year on year, much higher than the 10.1 per cent increase in total retail sales of consumer goods. Equally impressive was the rate of increase in the expansion of retail outlets: 46.7 per cent over 2000.

Among the top 20 retail chains, four new chain store names made it into the top 20, while 16 remained in the top 20, albeit with different rankings. This ranking structure has led some analysts to believe that a group of retail chain enterprises with expanding scales, steady

Table 8.14.1   Top 20 retail chains, 2001

Rank	Company name	Turnover (RMB thousand)	Increase on 2000 (%)	No. of outlets	Increase on 2000 (%)	Rank in first half of 2001
1	Lianhua Supermarket Co Ltd	14,063,410	26.24	1,225	28.95	1
2	Hualian Supermarket Co Ltd	8,504,150	51.70	818	19.94	3
3	Beijing Hualian Comprehensive Supermarket Co Ltd	8,000,000	60.00	42	68.00	5
4	Shanghai Nonggongshang Supermarket Co Ltd	7,474,650	38.35	315	115.75	2
5	Sanlian Commercial Corp	7,026,000	32.28	177	98.87	2
6	Beijing Guomei Electrical Appliances Co Ltd	6,150,470	119.78	74	124.24	9
7	Suguo Supermarket Co Ltd	5,282,000	31.39	663	59.38	6
8	Yum! Brands China Investment Co Ltd (previously Tricon China Investment Co Ltd)	5,205,110	24.04	635	38.34	7
9	Shanghai Jinjiang Metro Co Ltd	4,949,220	32.20	15	87.50	8
10	China Resources Vanguard Co Ltd	4,647,660	34.94	344	42.15	13
11	Suning Electrical Appliances Chain Group Co Ltd	3,991,070	23.35	91	250.00	
12	Tianjin Home World Chain Commercial Group Co Ltd	3,266,680	47.76	28	40.00	11
13	Jiangsu Wenfengdashijie Chain Development Co Ltd	3,145,300	47.60	17	54.55	10
14	Jiangsu Five Star Appliances Co Ltd	2,546,000	74.38	66	26.92	12
15	Beijing Wumei Commercial Group Co Ltd	2,521,700	97.36	199	261.81	14
16	Beijing Jingkelong Commercial Mansion	1,893,310	33.94	57	5.56	15
17	Shenzhen Xinyijia Supermarket Co Ltd	1,890,000	148.36	16	128.57	
18	Shanghai Yongle Appliances Co Ltd	1,860,000	48.44	21	61.54	
19	Wuhan Zhongbai Group Co Ltd	1,784,010	41.55	84	1100.00	
20	Shanghai Jieqiang Tobacco Sugar and Wine (Group) Chain Co Ltd	1,717,570	19.88	240	20.00	17
Total		95,918,310	42.99	5,127	46.70	

Source: State Economic and Trade Commission

performance and some competitive advantages have started to emerge as a leading force in the retail market. However, there is a flaw in the ranking: some of the international retail chains operating in China, such as McDonald's and Carrefour, were not included because they registered under different company names in the process of joint venturing and could not be regarded as chain operators.

Geographically, seven of the top 20 are headquartered in Shanghai, four each in Beijing and Jiangsu Province, two in Guangdong Province and one each in Tianjin, Shandong Province and Hubei Province. None is located in western China. Such a pattern of geographical distribution is determined by the gap that exists in the economic development between eastern and western China and this pattern is not expected to change very much.

In terms of retail formats, 13 of the top 20 are supermarket chains specializing mainly in fast-moving consumer products, with the rest being food chains such as Yum! Brands' Kentucky Fried Chicken and electrical appliance speciality chains such as Beijing Guomei and Jiangsu Suning.

In parallel with the release of the above list, China Chain and Franchise Association also announced its ranking of China's top 100 retailers for the year 2001. The accredited retailers reflected a wider spectrum of the retail sector to include not only the fast expanding supermarket (69), food service (12) and electrical appliance (8) chains, but also department store (4), drug store (4) and other retail chains such as hotel (1) and speciality chains (2) (see Table 8.14.2).

Retail chains have been expanding quickly and are becoming a dominant force in the retail sector. According to the Association, the total sales of the top 100 retail chains in 2001 was RMB162 billion, an increase of 48 per cent over 2000. The share of the top 100 in China's total retail sales of consumer goods was 4.3 per cent in 2001, 1.4 percentage points higher than in 2000. The total number of retail outlets owned by the top 100 chains was 13,117, a rise of 56 per cent compared with 2000.

Over the last five years, the trend of retail outlet expansion and increase of sales turnover by the top 100 retail chains has been strong and persistent. In 1997, the average number of retail outlets of the top 100 retail chains was 24.4 and in 2001 the number jumped to 131.2 (see Figure 8.14.1).

Average sales of the top 100 retail chains have grown at an accelerated speed over the past few years. In 1997, for example, the average turnover of the 100 largest retail chains was only RMB240 million but leapt to RMB1.62 billion in 2001 (see Figure 8.14.2).

Table 8.14.2 Leading retail chains (excluding supermarket chains), 2001

Rank	Company name	2001 turnover (RMB thousand)	Increase over 2000 (%)	No. of outlets	Increase over 2000(%)
Department store chains					
10	Beijing Wangfujing Group Co Ltd	4,887,300	9	8	0
36	Shenzhen Maoye Commercial Masion Co Ltd	1,238,650	20	4	33
41	Beijing SCITEC Commercial Development Co Ltd	1,014,020	42	11	120
42	Shenzhen Tianhong Shopping Centre Co Ltd	1,008,080	16	3	0
Drug store chains					
61	Chongqing Heping Pharmacy Chain Co Ltd	567,070	23	518	73
90	Dalian Meluo Pharmacy Chain Co Ltd	320,760	n/a	105	n/a
96		295,000	217	203	233
97	Jianmin Pharmacy Chain of Guangzhou Pharmaceutical Corp	289,560	3	100	69
Hotel chains					
57	Dalian Friendship Group	630,000	15		
Specialty chains					
19	Lengend (Beijing) Co Ltd (computer retailing)	2,092,940	107	565	117
87	Giant (China) Co Ltd (bicycle retailing)	343,540	75	1,245	32

Source: China Chain and Franchise Association

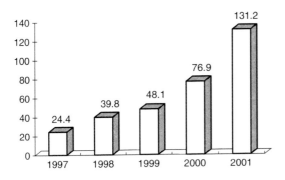

Source: China Chain and Franchise Association

Figure 8.14.1 Average number of retail outlets of the top 100 retail chains, 1997–2001

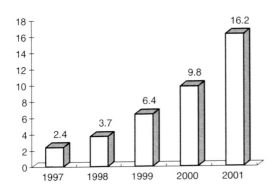

Source: China Chain and Franchise Association

Figure 8.14.2 Average turnover of the top 100 retail chains, 1997–2001 (RMB100 million)

Interestingly, however, the survey of the top 100 retail chains for 2001 again missed out some of the major foreign retail players such as Carrefour, Wal-mart, Pricesmart, Makro Jusco, 7-Eleven, Roson, Parkson and McDonald's. Such omissions, for whatever reasons, have limited the representative nature of both this and the other survey of the top 20 retail chains conducted by the State Economic and Trade Commission. However, these surveys at least provide a picture of the local retail leaders and how they have been doing in their competition for a share of the market.

Foreign entry

Regardless of the fact that some of the international retail chains have been excluded from the top 20 and top 100 retail chains in China, it is undeniable that many foreign retail magnates have already established a presence in China and achieved success there. At present, 70 per cent of the top 50 largest retail chains in the world have a presence in China. From the time

when China opened up the retail sector for foreign involvement on a trial basis in 1992 to the end of 2001, there were a total of 356 foreign-invested commercial enterprises operating in China, although only 40 of these were officially approved and the remaining 316 were operating without official licences.

Since the early 1990s, China's retail sector has been an international battlefield. The future competitive situation is expected to be even more aggressive as foreign retail chains start to penetrate deeper into the market.

Wal-mart, the magnate of the international retail community, entered China in 1996. Although it was relatively slow expanding its operations in the early stages, with only eight stores in the 4–5 years following its entry, it began a more aggressive expansion policy in 2001 and has now opened 20 stores in nine cities with plans to open 50 stores over the next three years. Its first Beijing shop was opened in 2002 and four more were planned over the next couple of years.

Carrefour, the first company to bring the huge retail store format to China in 1995, has spread all over the country, with 28 outlets in 15 big cities, making it the largest foreign retailer in China. It began to look at Chinese market opportunities in the early 1990s and opened its first premises in Beijing in a manner that circumvented the policy restrictions placed on the entry of foreign retailers to China. Along its road to expansion, Carrefour established some stores that did not have appropriate official approval and some that were virtually wholly-owned by Carrefour, which is against Chinese laws and regulations. It has been reported that Carrefour was requested to comply with government regulations by selling at least 35 per cent of its wholly-owned operations to local companies before its plan to open another 10 stores could be given the green light.

The German-based retail giant Metro has also been active in China. By 2000, it had established eight stores in the country. Since 2001, it has extended its operations to other parts of China, opening over 10 warehouse supermarkets in 11 cities, including Hangzhou, Wuhan, Chengdu and Chongqing.

COSCO, the twelfth largest retailer in world, has also made progress in China's retail market. It is said that COSCO has engaged one of the leading Chinese retail chains in its plan to open 10 large-scale warehouse supermarkets. New COSCO stores are expected to open in some of China's major urban centres.

Other international retail chains active in China include the Japan-based Ito-Yoado, Tesco, Auchan,

B&Q, OBI and Ikea who all have aggressive plans to expand in China.

Taiwanese retail chains are also attempting to take a slice of the market. Instead of the crowded larger cities, Taiwanese retail chains began with medium-sized cities with a more regional oriented strategy. Trust-mart, for example, is concentrating its retail operations in the Pearl Delta River area, and developing from there into the west of China, where it has opened seven stores. So far, Trust-mart has opened 26 retail outlets in China, second only to Carrefour in terms of the number of outlets. Another Taiwanese retail chain, RT-mart, has successfully avoided direct competition with international retail chains in key cities by moving into cities such as Nanjing, Wuxi, Changzhou, Yangzhou, Suzhou, Changshu, Kunshan, Nantong and Jiaxing, all of which are on the flank of Shanghai.

Opportunities as a result of China's WTO accession

The regulatory environment will improve after WTO accession. China's commitments to the WTO in relation to the opening of the retail sector will eventually remove some of the restrictions that still limit market access to foreign retailers. In response to the WTO rules and in an effort to honour China's WTO commitments, the State Development Planning Commission, the State Economic and Trade Commission and the Ministry of Foreign Trade and Economic Cooperation promulgated a new Catalogue of Industrial Guidance for Foreign Investment on 31 March 2002. This sets out the schedule for the opening of the retail sector in line with China's WTO commitments. According to the Catalogue, restrictions on foreign participation in China's retail sector will to be phased out as per the following schedule:

1. Foreign investment is permitted, except for books, newspapers, magazines, pharmaceuticals, pesticides, mulching films, fertilizers and processed oil.
2. A 50 per cent foreign equity share will be permitted and joint ventures will be permitted to deal in the retailing of books, newspapers and magazines no later than 11 December 2002.
3. Foreign majority ownership will be permitted no later than 11 December 2003.
4. Solely foreign-owned operations will be permitted and allowed to engage in the retailing of pharmaceuticals, pesticides, mulching film and processed oil no later than 11 December 2004.

5. Retailing of fertilizers by foreign-invested retailers will be permitted no later than 11 December 2006. Foreign majority ownership will not be permitted for those chain stores that engage in the following products and have over 30 outlets: motor vehicles (the restrictions on which will be removed no later than 11 December 2006), books, newspapers, magazines, pharmaceuticals, pesticides, mulching films, processed oil, fertilizers, grains, vegetable oils, sugar, tobacco and cotton.

The above schedule shows future opportunities for foreign investment in the retail sector. The macro opportunities are obvious – increasing consumer affluence in both urban and rural areas and the huge consumer base of 1.3 billion people. The micro opportunities are many – different options of entry such as joint venturing, merger, acquisition and wholly-owned subsidiary. A short-term option while the restrictions on wholly foreign-owned operations are still in force is to set up joint ventures in designated locations. This will offer immediate market access and incur minimal risk in terms of financial engagements. There are a number of Chinese retailers that have advantages such as retail sites, existing customer base, understanding of local conditions and brand recognition, while being disadvantaged by the lack of sufficient funding, management know-how, marketing expertise and retailing technology. These retailers can also be targets of mergers or acquisitions. For those who preferred to have a solely-owned operation, the only option was to wait until 2004.

Recent developments – J Reuvid

The supermarket and superstore scene

In food retailing the four big foreign-invested chains, following Tesco's recent acquisition described below, are Wal-Mart, Carrefour, Tesco's joint venture Hymall and Le Gou chains and Metro's Champion chain of stores. In terms of store numbers, the league table is shown in Table 8.14.3.

The highly fragmented local market is dominated by Chinese players, which often have larger networks and better store locations than their foreign competitors. The largest local Chinese competitor in Beijing is Wumart which has more than 20 per cent of the local market and had grown to become the 12th largest retailer in China by the end of 2004, with its 429 hypermarkets, supermarkets and convenience stores, expected to have risen by an additional 100 stores.

Table 8.14.3 Leading foreign invested food retail chains

| | No. of outlets | | |
| | | Forecast | |
	End-2003	End-2004	End-2005
Carrefour	41	56	68
Wal-Mart	34	43	53
Tesco/Hymall	–	30	40
Metro/Champion	18	23	33

Sources: Financial Times news items

Wumart raised HK$547.06 million (US$70 million) in an IPO in Hong Kong in 2003 and a further HK$248.2 million (US$32 million) through a subsequent placing in March 2004. Formed in 1994, Wumart has made a specialty of purchasing former state-owned chains and upgrading them. International Finance Corp, the private sector investment arm of the World Bank, holds a 3 per cent stake in the company.

Tesco

By April 2004, Tesco, the UK supermarket leader and Britain's biggest retailer, which had been studying the Chinese market and evaluating potential partners for more than two years, had identified Tsin Hing International as a preferred partner and was in negotiation to acquire a 50 per cent shareholding. Tsin Hing owns 25 hypermarkets in China, of which 10 are located in Shanghai, and trades under the Hymall and Le Gou brand names. The owners, four Taiwanese, were said to have been in negotiation with Tesco for some time.

In July 2004, the terms of the agreed investment were announced with a price of £140 million for the 50 per cent interest valuing Tsin Hing at more than 50 times 2003 earnings, an indication of the high valuations that investors are prepared to pay for strategic stakes in China. Under the terms of the deal, Tesco has the right to nominate the president of the joint venture, and Tsin Hing retains the chairman and chief executive appointments. The Tesco investment compares with the US$193 billion that Tsin Hing is reported to have invested since 1996 to claim second place in the league table.

Tsin Hing opened its first Hymall store in1998. The superstores are mainly located in the east, north and northeast of China, serving two million customers a week, and are targeted to have opened 10 more stores by the end of 2004 helping to increase current year sales to US$810 million. The Tsin Hing group has been established in

China since 1988 and is reported to have invested a total of US$1.2 billion. Its activities include making and selling cup noodles, an Asian fast-food staple product, and a well-known fried chicken chain.

The home improvement market

With the expansion of the Chinese private housing market, home improvement activity has burgeoned and DIY centres have sprung up in the major population centres, starting with Shanghai, Beijing and the wealthy coastal cities. With the government expecting 300–500 million people to move to the urban areas by 2020, continuing growth is assured.

The UK Kingfisher group's B&Q division is now the market leader in China with 20 superstores, which it plans to increase to almost 80 by 2008. The expansion plan will cost about US$135 million, excluding lease commitments and stock. In 2003, four years after opening its first store in China, B&Q reported its first profit on revenues of US$236 million, expected to rise by more than 10 per cent in 2004. Competition from both local and overseas companies is growing, with Home Depot, the US market leader expected to open its first DIY stores no later than 2006.

The government has now ordered that developers must sell most apartments furnished, compared with the concrete shells that they previously offered to exploit the high demand for housing. A quarter of B&Q's China sales are already made through its 'decorating service' in alliance with local developers.

Ikea, the Swedish home furnishing group, famous for its Scandinavian design and self-assembly flat packs, reported a 50 per cent year-on-year increase in sales in its two stores in Shanghai and Beijing in August 2004, up to US$120 million. It is now planning its expansion over the next six to eight years in the 15 biggest Chinese cities with populations over four million.

Publishing and book retailing

There are now 2,119 newspapers, 9,038 magazines and 568 publishing houses in Mainland China, following the end of the regulators' state funding and mandatory subscription schemes. Up to March 2004, 677 government and Party newspapers had been shut down, saving RMB1.8 billion in compulsory subscriptions. In the same period, 325 state-owned newspapers were transferred to commercial newspaper groups and 94 official journals became free distribution publications.

In August 2004, China promised to open fully its newspaper and book wholesale and retail sector to foreign

investors by the year-end, but overseas publishers continue to be barred from the publishing business in China. Under the terms of the WTO entry agreement, China was not required to permit full foreign ownership of book and newspaper retailers until 2006 but was obliged to lift restrictions on overseas investment in wholesalers by the end of 2004.

Bertelsmann, the German publishing giant, has the strongest foreign presence in the sector having established a joint venture bookstore chain in 2003, linked to its book club joint venture and an online bookstore.

In October, the state-owned Xinhua bookstore which now distributes about two-thirds of all books and magazines in China announced plans to sell up to 60 per cent of its shares to both private domestic and foreign investors, having incorporated itself as a joint-stock firm.

Steel Production and Core Minerals

Jonathan Reuvid

China's steel industry

China is now the largest steel making country in the world, accounting for 24.8 per cent of global production in June 2004 and producing more steel than the US and Japan combined. In descending order, the other major steel making regions are the rest of Asia/Oceania (21.8 per cent), the enlarged European Union (19.5 per cent), North America (12.5 per cent) and the CIS (11.0 per cent), leaving a balance of 10.4 per cent from other steel producing countries.

Steel production in 2004 is estimated to be between 250 and 260 million tonnes, about 40 million tonnes more than in 2003. This increased production has helped to reduce Chinese imports from the 2003 high of 37.2 million tonnes (US$19.9 billion). Even with this impressive rise in output, China is expected to have imported another 30 million tonnes in 2004 to meet demand. The tough credit squeeze imposed by central government might have been expected to slow down, if not curtail, demand, but production in July was reported to have been 22 million tonnes, the same level as the highest ever amount of 22.6 million tonnes recorded, in February, for a single month.

Baosteel production

The state-owned Baoshan Iron & Steel (Baosteel), China's largest steel maker, provides just under 10 per cent of China's steel output but has plans to raise its market share. Currently the world's sixth biggest steel maker, Baosteel is planning to increase its capacity within the next five years by 50 per cent. According to Chairwoman, Xie Qihua, the Shanghai-based company intends to invest US$6–7.2 billion to expand production from an expected 20 million tonnes in 2004

to 30 million tonnes in 2010. Looking further ahead, Ms Xie expressed an interest in opportunities for buying all or part of a US steel mill.

These plans set Baosteel apart from other large steel makers, which expect small production rises in the short term because of financial restraints or fear that strong demand might soon weaken.

China's increasing production capacity

However, Ms Xie stated that new capacity in China of a further 80 million tonnes is currently under construction, with most of this additional capacity targeted at construction materials that count for about 60 per cent of demand, rather than replacing imports. Moreover, in December 2004, Beijing confirmed approval for the construction of three large new steel mills in a breach of its policy to damp down investment growth but with the objective of eliminating dependence on imports within about three years.

The largest of the three is to be a 10 million tonnes-per-year facility in Zhanjiang city in Guangdong Province, followed by a five million tonnes-per-annum plant in Maanshan, Anhui Province, and a 1.5 million tonnes-per-annum stainless steel mill in Taiyuan, Shanxi Province. The high grade steel products that all three new plants will produce are intended to substitute for the steel currently imported by China's automotive and consumer electronic sectors.

The stainless steel production lines at Taiyuan are to be built by Voest-Alpine Industrieanlagenbau of Austria, and the steel coil mill by Demag, the German steel plant builder; both are scheduled for completion by the end of 2006. Investment in the expansion of the Zhanjiang capacity is in two phases (the first in plant to produce hot-rolled plates and coil, followed by cold-rolled galvanized and colour-coated sheets capacity) and is expected to cost about US$5 billion. Maanshan Iron and Steel plan to spend US$2.4 billion over three years on rolled coil capacity.

Baosteel share listing

In September 2004, and in response to minority shareholder demands, Baosteel adjusted its plans for a US$3.4 billion share issue downwards by reducing the offer from 50 per cent to 40 per cent of the five billion shares to be sold to existing public shareholders. The state-owned parent company, Shanghai Baosteel Group, that owns 85 per cent of Baosteel shares, has committed itself to buying 60 per cent of the stock on offer to ease fears of an overhang of shares undermining the share price, as with other recent flotations on the Shanghai stock market.

The minority shareholder influence set a precedent and was encouraged by China Securities Regulatory Commission (CSRC), which issued draft rules on its website requiring the approval of public shareholders in cases ranging from new share issues and bond sales, to large asset transfers and overseas listings of subsidiaries. The rules would also give investors greater access to corporate information, require listed companies to have independent directors and give board representation to minority shareholders.

Baosteel hopes to purchase a collection of diverse assets from the parent company, including a port facility on the Yangtze river, interests in iron ore mines in Australia and a computer software developer, as well as steel plants in China. These acquisitions, which would strengthen the listed company, are intended to make its shares more attractive to investors.

By October, thanks to its soaring earnings due to higher steel prices and demand, Baosteel was valued at about US$12 billion on the Shanghai Stock Exchange, rating it as the fifth-largest steel maker globally by market capitalization. Ms Xie Qihua indicated that the company was considering a New York listing in three to five years' time, but acknowledged that to make a flotation attractive to international investors, the Chinese government would have to reduce its stake significantly down to 78 per cent beyond the planned financial restructuring referred to above.

Foreign investment in Chinese steel production

At the beginning of 2004, the world's second-biggest steel maker by output, LSM, announced its investment of US$100 million in a new steel plant in China of 400,000 tonnes capacity, opening in 2006 or 2007. The venture will be wholly-owned by LSM, itself owned and managed by Lakshmi Mittal, the Indian entrepreneur – unlike Arcelor of Luxembourg and Thyssen-Krupp of Germany, which have already announced substantial investments through Chinese joint ventures. It is rumoured that LSM intends to introduce special coating processes that it has developed at its US site into its Yingkou site in northern China. It is also expected that LSM will import raw steel sheets from other LSM steel facilities in Kazakhstan and Romania, instead of purchasing similar materials from local steel producers.

In August, JFE Steel, the leading Japanese steel maker, announced that it was undertaking a feasibility study, with Guangzhou Iron and Steel, for an integrated steel mill in the Nansha development zone of Guangzhou. The venture would be the logical consequence of the evolution of Guangzhou as a hub for Japanese car makers and their suppliers. Honda has had a joint venture factory in the city since the late 1990s, Nissan opened a plant in Guangzhou in 2004 through its joint venture with Dongfeng, and Toyota has won approval for a joint venture plant in Nansha.

JFE and Guangzhou Iron and Steel are already building a factory jointly to produce hot-dip galvanized sheet steel, with an annual capacity of 400,000 tonnes, due to come on stream by early 2006. An integrated steel mill in China could reduce significantly China's need to export the base steel for the sheet required in automobile production.

Core metals

Aluminium

At the beginning of January 2004, Aluminium Corporation of China (Chalco), the largest producer of aluminium in China, raised HK$3.1 billion (US$400 million) by placing 550 million new shares equivalent to about 16 per cent of its issued capital on the Hong Kong Stock Exchange. The issue capitalized on Chalco's record high share price, with the shares offered at an 8 per cent discount. Alcoa, the US aluminium giant, bought 8 per cent of the offering to maintain its 8 per cent holding in Chalco. The proceeds of the placing are being used to buy smelters that process alumina, the raw material of aluminium, into the finished metal in its Shanxi plant.

Copper

In 2003, China emerged as the world's largest consumer of copper, driving international copper prices up to US$2,727 per tonne in February 2004. As with other commodity prices, the fall in the US dollar against other leading currencies contributed to the copper price escalation.

As a result of the government-driven slowdown in construction, copper prices in China had steadied at RMB24,800 (US$2,989) by mid-April. However, by the end of 2004 the international price, having resumed its upward movement, had stabilized at a new level around US$3,067 per tonne. Nickel and zinc prices, which also fell during April, according to Shanghai Non-Ferrous Metal Association statistics, also rose towards the end of the year, with zinc hitting a seven-year high of US$1,245 on 20 December 2004 and nickel steadying at US$14,650 per tonne.

Minmetals' acquisition of Noranda

In September 2004, Minmetals, one of the 53 state-owned enterprises administered direct from Beijing, announced its pending acquisition of Canada's mining giant, Noranda, for about US$5 billion.

The acquisition was funded from existing cash resources and loans provided by China Development Bank. With 2003 revenues of US$11.68 billion and assets of $5.3 billion, Minmetals is the 22nd largest company in China. Its interests extend from iron and steel to non-ferrous metals, raw materials and metal and electrical products.

The acquisition was supported financially by a consortium of other state-owned companies, including Baoshan Iron and Steel, Citic Investment Corporation, Jiangxi Copper and Taiyuan Iron and Steel.

The Noranda takeover was a departure from the normal pattern of Chinese overseas investment. Historically, Chinese companies have acquired assets rather than corporations, such as stakes in oilfields, gasfields and mineral reserves. The Minmetal acquisition demonstrates that China is ready to spend some of its massive US$480 billion foreign exchange reserves as FDI in western corporations.

Telecommunications

Jonathan Reuvid and Snapshots International

Fixed line telephone services

In China:

- the number of fixed telephone service subscribers increased by 17.9 per cent in 2002. The total number of subscribers in 2002 was 213.5 million;
- compound annual growth rate (CAGR) for the period 1998–2002 was 25.0 per cent;
- the strongest growth was in 2000, with a rate of 33.0 per cent (see Table 8.16.1).

Table 8.16.1 Chinese fixed telephone services volume 1998–2002 ('000 subscribers)

Year	('000) subscribers	% growth
1998	87,421.0	
1999	108,716.0	24.4
2000	144,609.5	33.0
2001	181,085.7	25.2
2002	213,500.0	17.9
CAGR [1998–2002]		**25.0%**

Source: Snapdata Research

Recent developments

In March 2004, Lenovo Group, China's leading personal computer company (known as 'Legend' until 2003) was the first Chinese company to enrol in the world-wide sponsorship programme for the 2008 Beijing Olympic Games, together with multinationals such as General Electric, Samsung and McDonald's. In August, Huawei Technologies and ZTE, the two leading Chinese telecommunications equipment manufacturers, were reported to be in discussions to join the ranks of sponsors. Both companies are based in Shenzhen.

ZTE provided broadband internet access to 16 stadiums at the 2004 Athens Olympic Games through OTE, the Greek telecoms operator. About 20 per cent of ZTE's US$1.9 billion sales are in exports and the company plans an IPO in Hong Kong in the first half of 2005. Huawei is more export oriented and forecasts US$2 billion in overseas sales for 2004, representing 40 per cent of its group US$5 billion sales target.

In September, China Telecom, the biggest fixed line operator, announced that it is to purchase data PC cards from Japan's Kyocera. The introduction of the cards, which slot into laptop computers, will enhance the appeal of China Telecom's personal access system wireless network (PAS) in competition with the leading Chinese wireless operators, China Mobile and China Unicom. PAS, marketed in China under the name *Xiaolingtong,* has been highly successful; networks using the technology are officially treated as fixed-line.

In November 2004, China Telecom and China Netcom, the two largest fixed-line operators, linked up their short messaging services. 'Little Smart' subscribers can now send short messages to counterparts in the 21 southern provinces dominated by China Telecom and in 10 northern provinces dominated by China Netcom.

Management reshuffle

At the beginning of November 2004, senior executives at China's three largest telecommunications groups, China Mobile, China Telecom and China Unicom, changed jobs with one another following the retirement of the presidents of both China Mobile and

China Telecom. All three companies are listed and publicly traded on the Hong Kong and New York stock exchanges; all three remain majority-controlled by the state.

Analysts puzzled over the logic behind the moves. The reshuffle could be seen as an attempt to rein in competition between the three market leaders, but caused unease among investors as a demonstration of what appears to be arbitrary state interference. Of course, changes in management have been dictated by the state in both banking and the oil industry but the rationale behind this round of 'musical chairs' is difficult to understand. The effects on investor confidence are considered likely to affect adversely the pending flotation of Netcom in Hong Kong and New York.

Mobile telephone services market

In China:

- the number of mobile phone service subscribers increased by 44.9 per cent in volume in 2002. The total number of subscribers in 2002 was 208.5 million;
- compound annual growth rate for the period 1998–2002 was 71.8 per cent;
- the strongest growth was in 2000, with a rate of 85.3 per cent (see Table 8.16.2)

Table 8.16.2 Chinese mobile phone services volume 1998–2002 ('000 subscribers)

Year	('000) subscribers	% growth
1998	23,931.5	
1999	43,295.5	80.9
2000	80,215.7	85.3
2001	143,852.5	79.3
2002	208,500.0	44.9
CAGR [1998–2002]		71.8%

Source: Snapdata Research

Recent developments

China Mobile, which reported 2003 profits up 9 per cent over 2002 at RMB35.6 billion, acquired 19 provincial networks in China over the past five years and is acquiring a further 10 in 2004. It is now the world's biggest wireless communications carrier by subscriber numbers.

Motorola is reported to be planning the launch of a mobile phone in China that will operate on most of the world's dominant wireless standards, in particular GSM and CDMA.

Sony Ericsson has increased its stake in its Beijing phone manufacturing joint venture, Sony Ericsson Putian Mobile Communications, from 10 per cent to 51 per cent and plans to use the company as a hub for research and development in China.

In 2005, China is forecast to issue its first licences for high-speed mobile services in order to boost competition for current operators China Mobile and China Unicom in advance of the 2008 Beijing Olympics.

Mobile phone users in China will soon be able to buy and sell, using their phones, as a result of an agreement between the giant US chipmaker Intel and Alibaba, the Chinese e-commerce company, to build China's first mobile commerce platform. The first batch of telephones with mobile modules will be released by Motorola and the Chinese phone maker Dopoda.

Handset manufacture

According to a GfK Asia market research report, the proportion of handsets sold of Chinese manufacture fell from 49 per cent to 46 per cent in the first half of 2004. Their proportion of sales value declined from 42 per cent to 37 per cent.

These findings appear to signal a resurgence in market share by the leading international mobile phone manufacturers, such as Motorola and Nokia, after the dramatic growth of local Chinese manufacturers from relative insignificance in 1999 to nearly half of handset sales by 2003. The resurgence of foreign brands is ascribed to the introduction of new handset designs with more advanced functions tailored to the Chinese market and an extension of their distribution systems beyond the largest Chinese cities where their sales staff was previously concentrated. The relative market shares of Nokia and Motorola are uncertain but they are believed to be running a close race.

GSM handsets now account for 57 per cent of sales compared with 49 per cent in 2003. The number of foreign brands on sale in China increased from 251 to 302 in the first six months of 2004, while local brands multiplied from 302 to 705. Although their rate of growth may have peaked, some leading Chinese brands such as Ningbo Bird and TCL Mobile Communications are expected to become major global handset manufacturers over the long term.

Travel and Tourism

Jonathan Reuvid and Snapshots International

Market size

In China:

- spending by tourists increased by 11.6 per cent in 2002. Total spend in 2002 was RMB558 billion;
- compound annual growth rate (CAGR) for the period 1998–2002 was 11.4 per cent;
- the strongest growth was in 2000, with a rate of 12.8 per cent (see Table 8.17.1).

Table 8.17.1 Chinese travel and tourism value 1998–2002 (RMB billion)

Year	RMB billion	% growth
1998	362.8	
1999	400.9	10.5
2000	452.2	12.8
2001	500.1	10.6
2002	558.0	11.6
CAGR [1998–2002]		**11.4%**

Source: Snapdata Research

According to an October 2004 survey by Visa International, China is now both the biggest source of tourists in the Asia-Pacific region and the most favoured tourist destination, with nearly 11.5 million visitors to China in 2003. Visitors spending on Visa cards alone reached RMB100 billion.

Market segmentation

Domestic tourists, representing 69.6 per cent of the market by value, constituted the largest segment of the Chinese travel and tourism market in 2002 (see Table 8.17.2).

Table 8.17.2 Chinese travel and tourism segmentation 2002 (% share)

Segment	% share
Domestic tourists	69.6
Overseas tourists	30.4
Total	100.0

Source: Snapdata Research

In 2004, an influx of 290,000 mainland tourists to Hong Kong was reported during the 'golden week' holiday period that started on National Day, 1 October. Unsurprisingly, favourite purchases included digital cameras, MP3 players and new varieties of mobile phones, as well as branded watches, fashion clothing, handbags and jewellery.

Air travel and aviation

For the period 1998–2002:

- the number of passengers carried by Chinese passenger airlines increased by 68.8 per cent in 2002. The total number of passengers carried in 2002 was 126.9 million;
- compound annual growth rate for the period was 21.8 per cent;
- the strongest growth was in 2002, with a rate of 68.8 per cent (see Table 8.17.3).

Table 8.17.3 Chinese passenger airlines volume 1998–2002 (million passengers)

Year	Million passengers	% growth
1998	57.6	
1999	60.9	5.8
2000	67.2	10.3
2001	75.2	11.9
2002	126.9	68.8
CAGR [1998–2002]		21.8%

Source: Snapdata Research

International airline services

In June 2004, Air France became the first European airline to offer regular flights to Guangzhou. The service from Paris is available five times a week and supplements its established daily flights to Beijing, Shanghai and Hong Kong.

By April, Scandinavian Airlines (SAS) had begun direct flights by Airbus-340 aircraft between Shanghai and Copenhagen three days a week with return flights the following day.

Lufthansa, which flies daily direct to Frankfurt from Beijing, Shanghai, Guangzhou and Hong Kong, has also increased its flights from Guangzhou to Munich via Shanghai to seven days a week. At the same time, KLM Royal Dutch Airlines has increased to daily its flights from Shanghai and Beijing to Amsterdam.

In the meantime, China Eastern Airlines now operates three flights weekly between Shanghai and London, while Air China provides a service twice a week between Yantai and Osaka, the shortest air route between China and Japan, taking only two hours and 15 minutes.

In October 2004, United Airlines expanded its four services from Chicago and San Francisco to Beijing and Shanghai by adding a second non-stop daily service from Shanghai to Chicago.

Air China, the national flagship carrier, ruled out a New York listing as the second offering for its US$500 million equity offering to supplement its Hong Kong listing. The decision was probably a result of the more stringent disclosure and financial requirements resulting from the Sarbanes-Oxley Act. Instead, Air China became listed on the London Stock Exchange from 15 December 2004.

At the beginning of October 2004, China National Aviation Company, the biggest shareholder of Hong Kong's Dragonair, announced that its own biggest shareholder, the unquoted Hong Kong holding company, CNACG, had transferred its 69 per cent stake in CNAC to Air China. The reshuffle will probably help Air China to achieve a higher valuation on flotation. For the time being, CNACG now holds 22.5 per cent of Air China while the remainder is owned by CNAH, the largest airline holding company in China, which is itself a wholly-owned subsidiary of CNACG.

In a further consolidation of airline interests in China and Hong Kong, Cathay Pacific, which owns 18 per cent of Dragonair, the regional airline of which CNAC is the controlling shareholder, has taken 9.9 per cent of Air China in anticipation of its flotation. Cathay Pacific, Air China and Dragonair now dominate Hong Kong's Chep Lak Kok airport and a three-way merger in the future is a likely outcome.

Domestic airline services

The new Baiyun International Airport at Guangzhou opened in August 2004 and is expected to handle 25 million passengers and one million tonnes of cargo a year up to 2010. Located 23 km north of the city, the airport is already planning a second phase and a third runway.

In September 2004, the mainland and Hong Kong agreed to allow the number of passenger flights between Hong Kong and the mainland to increase by 30 per cent to 1,600 per week, and the number of cargo flights to double to 84. However, Cathay Pacific, the dominant Hong Kong carrier, currently restricted to only three flights weekly to Beijing, cannot begin flying to Shanghai until October 2006.

Also in September, China Southern Airlines became the first Chinese airline to join a global alliance by entering SkyTeam, whose existing membership includes Air France, Delta Airlines and Korean Air.

In another kind of international expansion, Hainan Airlines, in which the financier George Soros is the major shareholder, entered a bid for Malev, the Hungarian airline, in August 2004.

Three Chinese private airlines are vying for approval by the Civil Aviation Administration of China (CAAC) to offer services to the public. The Okay Airlines Co. is expected to be the first and may be flying by the end of 2004, using six Boeing 737 aircraft. The two others are United Eagle Airlines and Air Spring.

Airport construction fee levies

Chinese airlines had been required to pay 5 per cent of domestic ticket revenues and 2 per cent of international ticket sales to an airport infrastructure construction fee fund. In 2002, China Eastern contributed about 4.4 per cent of its turnover amounting to RMB431 million to the fund, while China Southern paid RMB798 million, or about 3 per cent of its revenue.

At the beginning of 2004, hopes rose that Chinese airlines might gain a major boost to their profits from a halt to construction fees levied on them by Beijing. However CAAC indicated that the government might raise other tariffs to compensate for the resulting fall in its revenue.

Appendices

Contributor Contact Details

China

China Securities Regulatory Commission
Jin Yang Plaza
16 Jin Rong Street
Xi Cheng District
Beijing 100032
China
Tel: (86) 10 88061141
Fax: (86) 10 66210206
Website: www.csrc.gov.cn

Export-Import Bank of China
Jinyun Tower B
No.43A Xizhimenbei Street
Beijing 100044
China
Tel: (86) 10 62278899
Fax: (86) 10 62212024
Website: www.eximbank.gov.cn

Mr Ma Shabo
Capital Account Administration Dept
State Administration of Foreign Exchange
Hua Rong Building
18 Fu Cheng Lu
Haidian District
Beijing 100037
China

Mr Shi Yonghai
Chairman
China Association of International Trade
2 Dong Chang An Street
Beijing 100731
China
Tel: (86) 10 65197955
Fax: (86) 10 65245899

Mr Li Yong
Deputy Secretary General
China Association of International Trade
2 Dong Chang An Street
Beijing 100731
China
Tel: (86) 10 65197955
Mobile: (86) 13301 1298968
Fax: (86) 10 64295362
Email: liyongbeijing@126.com

Mr Fan Weimin
Patent Attorney
CCPIT Patent & Trademark Law Office
10/F Ocean Plaza
158 Fuxingmennei Street
Beijing 100031
China
Tel: (86) 10 6641 2345
Fax: (86) 10 6641 5678

Mr Liu Baocheng
Professor
Dean
Sino US School of International Management
University of International Business and Econonics
(UIBE)
Room 1401 Chengxin Building
Hu Xin Dong Jie
Chaoyang District
Beijing 100029
China
Tel: (86) 10 6449 4628
Fax: (86) 10 6449 4627
Email: simdean@uibe.edu.cn
Website: www.sim-gbs.org

Mr Du Xishuang
Director
Senior Statistician
National Bureau of Statistics
75 Yue Tan Nan Jie
San Li He
Beijing 100826
China
Tel: (86) 10 68573311 ext 80133
Fax: (86) 10 6857 6322

Wu Naiwen
Vice Chairman
China Customs Research Society
6 Jian Guo Men Nei Street
Beijing 100730
China
Tel: (86) 10 6519 5202
Fax: (86) 10 6519 5797

Chen Congcong
Guanghua Management School
Beijing University, China
Tel: (86) 10 6276 3162
Mobile: 13911 121 214

Professor T S Chan, Associate Vice President and
Academic Dean
Chair Professor in Marketing
Lingnan University
8 Castle Peak Road
Tuen Mun
Hong Kong
Tel (86) 852 26168302

Dr Wei-ping Wu
Department of Marketing and International Business
Lingnan University
8 Castle Peak Road
Tuen Mun
Hong Kong
Tel: (86) 852 26168236
Email: wpwu@ln.edu.hk

Others

Adamas
Beijing
Franck Desevedavy
Shenku Yard, Ritan Park
Chaoyang District
Beijing 100020, PRC
Tel: (86) 10 8563 1202
Fax: (86) 10 8561 2433
Email: desevedavy@adamas.com.cn

Shanghai
Chang Whui Min
Suite 607, 60 Dynasty Business Centre
No. 457, Urumqi Road North
Jing 'An District
Shanghai 20040, PRC
Tel: (86) 21 6249 0302
Fax: (86) 21 6249 0501
Email: chang@adamas.com.cn

China-Britain Business Council
Claire Urry
Abford House
15 Wilton Road
London SW1V 1LT, UK
Tel: (44) 20 7828 5176
Fax: (44) 20 7630 5780
Email: enquiries@cbbc.org
Website: www.cbbc.org

Confederation of British Industry (CBI)
Brian Cress
Centre Point
103 New Oxford Street
London WC1A 1DU, UK
Tel: (44) 20 7395 8121
Fax: (44) 20 7240 1578
Website: www.cbi.org.uk

Global Market Briefings
Jonathan Reuvid
Little Manor, Wroxton
Oxfordshire OX15 6QE, UK
Tel: (44) 1295 738070
Fax: (44) 1295 738090
Email: jrwroxton@aol.com

Herbert Smith
Beijing
Jeremy Xiao
14th Floor
Units 1410–1415
China World Tower 1
1 Jianguomenwai
Beijing 100004, PRC
Tel: (86) 10 6505 6512
Email: jeremy.xiao@herbertsmith.com

Shanghai
Brinton M Scott
38th Floor, Bund Center
222 Yan An Road East
Shanghai 200002, PRC
Tel: (86) 21 639 39115
Email: Brinton.Scott@herbertsmith.com

Brussels
Craig Pouncey
15 Rue Guimard
1040 Brussels, Belgium
Tel: (32) 2 511 7450
Email: craig.pouncey@herbertsmith.com

HSBC Holdings plc
Level 21, 8 Canada Square
London E14 5HQ, UK
Fax: 020 7992 4615
Contacts – China Affairs: Clare Hammond
Tel: (44) 20 7991 0283
Email: clarehammond@hsbcib.com

Daniel Sale
Tel: (44) 20 7991 3569 1183
Fax: (44) 20 7992 4615
Email: danielsale@hsbcib.com

Society of Motor Manufacturers and Traders (SMMT)
Mark Norcliffe
Forbes House
Halkin Street
London SW1X 7DS, UK
Tel: (44) 20 7235 9230
Fax: (44) 20 7344 1675
Email: mnorcliffe@smmt.co.uk

PricewaterhouseCoopers
Beijing
Eric Goujon
11th Floor China World Tower 1
1 Jian Guo Men Wai Avenue
Beijing 100004, PRC
Tel: (86) 10 6505 3333
Fax: (86) 10 8529 9000
Email: eric.goujon@cn.pwcglobal

Kerry Centre, 18th Floor
1 Guang Hua Lu, Chao Yang District
Beijing 100020, PRC
Tel: (86) 10 6561 2233
Fax: (86) 10 8529 9000

Chongqing
Room 1905, 19th Floor
Metropolitan Tower, 68 Zhou Rong Road
Chongqing 400010, PRC
Tel: (86) 23 6374 0008
Fax: (86) 23 6374 0990

Dalian
1705 Gold Name Tower
68 Renmin Lu, Zhongshan District
Dalian 116001, PRC
Tel: (86) 411 271 4468/78
Fax: (86) 411 271 4498

Guangzhou
Room 3312, 3308 Office Tower
CITIC Plaza, 233 Tianhe North Road
Guangzhou 510620, PRC
Tel: (86) 20 8363 3168
Fax: (86) 20 8363 4941

Hong Kong
21st Floor, Edinburgh Tower
The Landmark, 15 Queen's Road
Central, Hong Kong SAR, PRC
Tel: (852) 2289 8888
Fax: (852) 2577 2692

23rd Floor, Prince's Building
Central, Hong Kong SAR, PRC
Tel: (852) 2289 8888
Fax: (852) 2577 2692

Shanghai
12th & 19th Floor, Shanghai ShuiOn Plaza
333 Huai Hai Zhong Road
Shanghai 200020, PRC
Tel: (86) 21 6386 3388
Fax: (86) 21 6386 9000/3300

Shenzhen
Room 3706, Shun Hing Square
Di Wang Commercial Centre
5002 Shennan Road East
Shenzhen 518008, PRC
Tel: (86) 755 8246 1717
Fax: (86) 755 8246 1730

28/F Shenzhen International Financial Building
2022 Jianshe Road
Shenzhen 518001, PRC
Tel: (86) 755 8229 8288
Fax: (86) 755 8228 0044

Suzhou
11/F, International Building
#2 Su Hua Road
Suzhou Industrial Park
Jiangsu Province, Suzhou 215021, PRC
Tel: (86) 512 6288 6860
Fax: (86) 512 6288 6870

Tianjin
37th Floor, Golden Emperor Building
20, Nanjing Road
Hexi District
Tianjin 300041, PRC
Tel: (86) 22 2330 6789
Fax: (86) 22 2339 3662

Xian
Room 301, 3rd Floor
Zhong Da International, No.30 Nanda Street
Xian 710002, PRC
Tel: (86) 29 720 3336
Fax: (86) 29 720 3335

The United States-China Business Council
Washington
John Frisbie
1818 N Street NW
Suite 200
Washington DC 20036, USA
Tel: (1) 202 429 0340
Fax: (1) 202 775 2478
Email: jfrisbie@uschina.org

Beijing
CITIC Building
Suite 10–01
19 Jianguomenwai Dajie
Beijing 100004, PRC
Tel: (86) 10 6592 0727
Fax: (86) 10 6512 5854
Email: uscbc@eastneet.com.cn

Shanghai
Jinjiang Hotel
2312 West Building
59 Mar Ming Road
Shanghai 200020, PRC
Tel: (86) 21 6415 2579
Fax: (86) 21 6415 2584
Email: uscbc@uninet.com.cn

Rolls-Royce plc
Richard P Hill
PO Box 31
Derby DE24 88J, UK
Tel: (44) 1332 245044
Fax: (44) 1332 245092
Email: richard.hill@rolls-royce.com

Snapshots International
Debra Curtis
5 Dryden Street
London WC2E 9NB, UK
Tel: (44) 20 7829 8408
Fax: (44) 20 7829 84108
Email: debra.curtis@snapdata.com

Appendix II

Directory of Local Authorities of Commerce with Responsibilities for Foreign Trade and Economic Cooperation

1. Beijing Municipal Bureau of Commerce
No. 190 Chaonei Street, Dong Cheng District,
Beijing, China
Postcode 100010
Tel: 0086–010–65236688
Website:
http://www.bjfetc.gov.cn/fetc/fabu/english/index.jsp

2. Tianjin Municipal Commission of Commerce
80 Qufu Road, Heping District, Tianjin, China
Email: webmaster@goldentianjin.net.cn
Website: http://www.goldentianjin.net.cn/

3. Hebei Provincial Bureau of Commerce
184, Er Duan, Heping Xi Road, Shijiazhuang, Hebei
Province, China
Postcode: 050071
Tel: 0311–7044842; 0311–7029523
Fax: 0311–7041570
Website: http://www.hecom.gov.cn/

4. Shanxi Provincial Bureau of Commerce
15, Xin Jian Road, Taiyuan, Shanxi Province, China
Postcode: 030002
Tel: 0351–4041722
Fax: 0351–4081004
Email: sxdbc@ec.com.cn
Website: http://www.docsx.gov.cn/

5. Inner Mongolia Autonomous Region Bureau of Commerce
138, Zhong Shan Xi Lu, Huhhot, Inner Mongolia
Autonomous Region, China
Postcode: 010020
Tel: 0086–471–6964301
Fax: 0086–471–6962138
Email: nmgwjmt@public.hh.nm.cn;
nmgftec@mail.ec.com.cn
Website: http://www.nmgswt.gov.cn

6. Liaoning Provinical Foreign Trade and Economic Cooperation Bureau
45–1, Bei Ling Street, Huanggu District, Shenyang,
Liaoning Province, China
Postcode: 110032
Tel: 024–6892544; 024–6892225
Fax: 024–6893858
Website: http://china-liaoning.org

7. Jilin Provinical Department of Commerce
119, Ren Min Street, Changchun, Jilin Province,
China
Postcode: 130021
Tel: 0431–2644191; 0431–5626905
Fax: 0431–5624772
Website: http://www.jldofcom.gov.cn

8. Heilongjiang Provincial Department of Commerce
55, He Ping Lu, Dongli District, Harbin, Heilongjiang, China
Postcode: 150001
Tel: 0451–82643146
Fax: 0451–82642637
Website: http://www.hl-doftec.gov.cn

9. Shanghai Municipal Commission of Foreign Trade and Economic Cooperation
2104, #55 Lou Shan Guan Road, Shanghai, China
Postcode: 200335
Tel: 021–62756811, 62752200, 62751950
Fax: 021–62751159
Website: http://www.smert.gov.cn/

10. Zhejiang Provincial Foreign Trade and Economic Cooperation Bureau
18, Jiao Chang Road, Hangzhou, Zhejiang Province, China
Postcode: 310006
Tel: 0571–87706099
Fax: 0571–87706029
Website: http://www.zftec.gov.cn

11. Jiangsu Provincial Department of Foreign Trade and Economic Cooperation
50, Zhong Hua Road, Nanjing, Jiangsu Province, China
Postcode: 210008
Tel: 025–2254455, 2254466
Fax: 025–7712072
Website: http://www.jsmoftec.gov.cn/

12. Anhui Provinical Bureau of Commerce
85, Chang Jiang Road, Hefei, Anhui Province, China
Postcode: 230001
Tel: 0551–2831268; 0551–2831391
Website: http://www.ahbofcom.gov.cn

13. Fujian Provincial Department of Foreign Trade and Economic Cooperation
Floor 13–17, Shi Fa Building, 92 Liu Yi Bei Lu, Fuzhou, Fujian Province, China
Postcode: 350013
Tel: 0591–7841917; 0591–7853616
Fax: 0951–7856133
Website: http://www.fiet.gov.cn/

14. Jiangxi Provincial Foreign Trade and Economic Cooperation Bureau
60, Zhanqian Road, Nancang, Jiangxi Province, China
Postcode: 330002
Tel: 0791–6246326; 0791–6227281
Fax: 0791–6246307
Website: http://www.jxdoftec.gov.cn/

15. Shandong Provincial Commission of Foreign Trade and Economic Cooperation
121, Hei Hu Quan Xi Lu, Jinan, Shandong Province, China
Postcode: 250011
Tel: 0531–6917061; 0532–2870493; 531–6163333
Fax: 0531–6912793
Website: http://www.shandongbusiness.gov.cn

16. Hubei Provincial Department of Commerce
8, Jiang Han Bei Lu, Wuhan, Hubei Province, China
Postcode: 430022
Tel: 027–85773850; 85774233
Fax: 027–85773668
Website: http://www.hbdofcom.gov.cn

17. Henan Provincial Department of Commerce
115, Wen Hua Road, Zhengzhou, Henan Province, China
Postcode: 450003
Tel: 0371–3941359
Fax: 0371–3945422
Website: http://henan.mofcom.gov.cn/

18. Guangdong Provincial Department of Foreign Trade and Economic Cooperation
Fl. 8, Foreign Trade Tower, 351, Tian He Lu, Guangzhou, Guangdong Province, China
Postcode: 510620
Tel: 8620–38802165
Fax: 8620–38802219
Website: http://www.gddoftec.gov.cn/index.asp

19. Hunan Provincial Department of Commerce
80, Wu Yi Dong Lu, Changsha, Hunan Province, China
Postcode: 410001
Tel: 0731–2295145; 0731–2295060
Fax: 0731–2295160
Website: http://www3.hunan.gov.cn/wjt/

20. Guangxi Zhuang Autonomous Region Department of Commerce
137, Qi Xing Road, Nanning, Guangxi, China
Postcode: 530002
Tel: 0711–2813165; 0771–2800676
Fax: 0771–5851581
Website: http://www.gxdoftec.gov.cn/

21. Hainan Provincial Department of Commerce
Expert Building, Qiongyuan Hotel, Qiong Yuan Road, Haikou, Hainan Province, China
Postcode: 570203
Tel: 0898–5337135; 0898–5342896
Fax: 0898–5338762
Website: http://www.dofcom.gov.cn/

22. Sichuan Provincial Department of Commerce
4, Chenghua Road, Chengdu, Sichuan Province, China
Postcode: 610081
Tel: 028–83235033
Fax: 028–83226033/6708
Email: webmaster@scbg.org.cn
Website: http://www.scbg.org.cn/

23. Yunnan Provincial Department of Commerce
576, Beijing Road, Kunming, Yunnan Province, China
Postcode: 650011
Tel: 0871–3135001; 0871–3135371
Fax: 0871–3123541
Website: http://www.boftec.gov.cn/

24. Chongqing Municipal Commission of Foreign Trade and Economic Cooperation
65, Xi Jian Bei Lu, Chongqing, China
Postcode: 630020
Tel: 0811–67523525; 0811–67528098
Fax: 0811–67853458
Website: http://www.ft.cq.cn/

25. Sha'anxi Provincial Department of Commerce
Provincial Government Office Complex, Xi'an, Sha'anxi Province, China
Postcode: 710004
Tel: 029–7291591; 029–7291583
Fax: 029–7291618
Website: http://www.sx-trade.com/

26. Guizhou Provincial Department of Commerce
21, Beijing Road, Guiyang, Guizhou Province, China
Postcode: 550004
Tel: 0851–6822341
Fax: 0851–6826509
Website: http://www.gzec.com.cn/shangwu/index.jsp

27. Qinghai Provincial Department of Commerce
102, Shu Lin Xiang; Xining, Qinghai Province, China
Postcode: 810007
Tel: 0971–8174514; 0971–8176744
Fax: 0971–8176805

28. Tibet Autonomous Region Foreign Trade and Economic Cooperation Bureau
184, Beijing Zhong Road, Lhasa, Tibet Autonomous Region, China
Postcode: 850001
Tel: 0891–6339337; 0891–6322448
Fax: 0891–6335733
Website:
http://www.tardoftec.gov.cn/jieshao/jieshao.jsp

29. Xinjiang Uygur Autonomous Region Foreign Trade and Economic Cooperation Bureau
11, Tuanjie Road, Urumqi, Xinjiang Uygur Autonomous Region, China
Postcode: 830001
Tel: 0991–2877270; 0991–2860255
Fax: 0991–2860255
Website: http://www.xjftec.gov.cn

30. Gansu Provincial Department of Commerce
386, Ding Xi Road, Lanzhou, Gansu Province, China
Postcode: 730000
Tel: 0931–8619767
Fax: 0931–8618083; 8619394

31. Ningxia Hui Autonomous Region Department of Commerce
199, Jiefang Xi Road, Yinchuan, Ningxia Autonomous Region, China
Postcode: 750001
Tel: 0951–5044277; 0951–5044850
Fax: 0951–5044239
Website: http://www.nxdofcom.gov.cn/

Contact details of the foreign trade and economic cooperation authorities in key coastal cities

Beihai City Bureau of Commerce
4, Bei Bu Wan Dong Lu, Beihai, Guangxi, China
Postcode: 536000
Tel: 0779–3215778
Fax: 0779–2052748
Website: http://bh.gxec.com.cn/

Dalian City Foreign Trade and Economic Cooperation Bureau
219, Huang He Lu, Xigang District, Dalian, Liaoning Province, China
Postcode: 116011
Tel: 0411–83698000; 83686836
Fax: 0411–3686246
Website: http://wjw.china-dalian.com/

Fuzhou City City Foreign Trade and Economic Cooperation Commission
93, Wu Shan Lu, Fuzhou, Fujian Province, China
Postcode: 350001
Tel: 0591–555308
Fax: 0591–557232

Guangzhou City Foreign Trade and Economic Cooperation Commission
158, Dong Feng Xi Lu, Guangzhou, Guangdong Province, China
Postcode: 510049
Tel: 020–8886 6455
Fax: 020–81097902
Website: http://www.gzboftec.gov.cn/index.htm

Lianyungang City Foreign Trade and Economic Cooperation Bureau
9, Hai Lian Dong Lu, Lianyungang, Jiangsu Province, China
Postcode: 222006
Tel: 0518–5805793
Website: http://ftecb.lyg.gov.cn/

Nantong City Foreign Trade and Economic Cooperation Bureau
51, Gong Nong Lu, Nantong, Jiangsu Province, China
Tel: 0513 3562336
Website: http://www.wjmj.gov.cn/

Ningbo City Commission of Foreign Trade and Economic Cooperation
190, Ling Qiao Lu, Ningbo, Zhejiang Province, China
Postcode: 315000
Tel: 0574–87310963
Fax: 0574–87328288
Wesbite: http://www.nbfet.gov.cn/nbfet2004/

Qingdao City Foreign Trade and Economic Cooperation Bureau
Block A, Qingdao World Trade Centre, 6 Xiang Gang Zhong Lu, Shi Nan District, Qingdao, Shandong Province, China
Postcode: 266071
Tel: 0532–5918108
Fax: 0532–3836036
Email: qdfert@fert.qingdaochina.com
Website: http://www.qingdaochina.com/

Qinhuangdao City Bureau of Commerce
78, You Yi Lu, Harbour District, Qinghuangdao, Hebei Province, China
Postcode: 066002
Tel: 0335–3428988
Fax: 0335–3411560
Website: http://www.investnow.gov.cn/index.jsp

Wenzhou City Foreign Trade and Economic Cooperation Bureau
8, Li Ming Xi Lu, Wenzhou, Zhejiang Province, China
Postcode: 325000
Tel: +86–571–85156707
Fax: +86–571–85155825

Yantai City Foreign Trade and Economic Cooperation Bureau
71,Jian She Lu, Zhi Fu District, Yantai, Shandong, China
Postcode: 264000
Tel: 0535–6254375; 6245518
Website: http://www.yantai.gov.cn/cn/content/invest_yt/tzfw.jsp

Zhanjiang City Foreign Trade and Economic Cooperation Bureau
Xi Men, 31, Nan Fang Lu, Chi Kan, Zhanjiang, Guangdong Province, China
Postcode: 524038
Tel: 0759–3339742
Fax: 0759–3336897
Website: http://wjmj.zhanjiang.gov.cn/index.asp

Shenzhen City Foreign Trade and Economic Cooperation Bureau
8 Shang Bu Zhong Lu, Shenzhen, Guangdong Province, China
Postcode: 518006
Tel: 0755–82107310
Website: http://www.szboftec.gov.cn/

Shantou City Bureau of Trade and Industry
3, Da Hua Lu, Shantou, Guangdong Province, China
Postcode: 515031
Tel: 0754–8274257
Fax: 0754–8271037
Website: http://www.stfet.gov.cn/

Special Commissioner's offices of the Ministry of Foreign Trade and Economic Cooperaiton in 16 cities

Qingdao
12, Yan Er Dao Lu, Shi Nan District, Qingdao, Shandong Province, China
Postcode: 266071
Tel: 0532–5734278
Fax: 0532–5734682
Website: http://qdtb.mofcom.gov.cn/

Dalian
2, Zhong Shan Guang Chang, Zhong Shan District, Dalian, Liaoning Province, China
Postcode: 116002
Tel: 0411–82630778
Fax: 0411–82630213
Website: http://dltb.mofcom.gov.cn/

Tianjin
59, Nan Jing Road, Heping District, Tianjin, China
Postcode: 300042
Tel: 022–23317060; 23307724
Fax: 022-23308071
Website: http://tjtb.mofcom.gov.cn/

Shanghai
1, Yong Fu Lu, Xuhui District, Shanghai, China
Postcode: 200031
Tel: 021–64317212
Fax: 021–64335268
Website: http://shtb.mofcom.gov.cn/

Guangzhou
117, Liu Hua Lu, Guangzhou, Guangdong Province, China
Postcode: 510014
Tel: 020–26082508
Fax: 020–86677314
Website: http://gztb.mofcom.gov.cn/

Shenzhen
Fl. 4, Haian Centre, 229 Bin He Lu, Fu Tian District, Shenzhen, Guangdong Province, China
Postcode: 518032
Tel: 0755–83797220
Fax: 0755–83797143
Website: http://sztb.mofcom.gov.cn/

Haikou
Fl.7, Anhai Tower, Huahai Road, Kaikou, Hainan Province, China
Postcode: 570105
Tel: 0898–66776186
Fax: 0898–66776957
Website: http://hntb.mofcom.gov.cn/

Nanning
17, Yuan Hu Nan Lu, Nanning, Guangxi, China
Postcode: 530022
Tel: 0771–5867858
Fax: 0771–5867740
Website: http://nntb.mofcom.gov.cn/

Nanjing
Fl. 7, World Trade Tower, 50, Zhong Hua Lu, Nanjing, Jiangsu Province, China
Postcode: 210001
Tel: 025–57710291
Fax: 025–57710290
Email: njtb@moftec.gov.cn
Website: http://njtb.mofcom.gov.cn/

Wuhan
8, Jiang Han Bei Lu, Wuhan, Hubei Province, China
Postcode: 430021
Tel: 027–85774211
Fax: 027–85774298
Website: http://whtb.mofcom.gov.cn/

Zhenzhou
115, Wen Hua Lu, Zhengzhou, Henan Province,
China
Postcode: 450003
Tel: 0371–3576207; 0371–3576205; 0371–3576206
Fax: 0371–3942780
Website: http://zztb.mofcom.gov.cn/

Fuzhou
Fl. 9, Foreign Trade Tower, Wu Si Lu, Fuzhou, Fujian
Province, China
Postcode: 350001
Tel: 0591–87536473
Fax: 0591–87500312
Website: http://fztb.mofcom.gov.cn/

Xi'an
Fl. 5, 68, Huan Cheng Nan Lu Zhong Duan, Xi'an,
Sha'anxi Province, China
Postcode: 710054
Tel: 029–87861934
Fax: 029–87861932
Website: http://xatb.mofcom.gov.cn/

Chengdu
18, Fu Qing Xi Nan Jie, Xi San Duan, Yi Huan Lu,
Chengdu, Sichuan Province, China
Postcode: 610031
Tel: 028–87734181
Fax: 028–87781984
Website: http://cdtb.mofcom.gov.cn/

Hangzhou
18, Jiao Chang Lu, Xia Cheng District, Hangzhou,
Zhejiang Province, China
Postcode: 310006
Tel: 0571–87706098
Fax: 0571–87706019
Website: http://hztb.mofcom.gov.cn/

Kunming
B9, Wan Xing Garden, Guanshang, Kunming,
Yunnan Province, China
Postcode: 650200
Tel: 0871–7181299; 0871–7183566; 0871–7183508
Fax: 0871-7181396
Website: http://kmtb.mofcom.gov.cn/

Commercial Offices of PRC Embassies Worldwide

Afghanistan
Sardar Shah Mahmoud Ghazi Wai, Kabul,
Afghanistan
Tel: 0093–20446, 0093–25551, 0093–22340

Albania
Rruga Skenderbej Nr.57, Tirane, Albania
Tel: 00355–42–32077, 253505
Fax: 00355–42–32077
Email: cnemec@icc.al.eu.org
ekzet@adanet.net.al

Algeria
34, Bd, Des Martyrs, Alger, Algerie
Tel: 00213–21–693189, 00213–21–691865
Fax: 00213–21–692362
Email: dz@moftec.gov.cn; becchine@wissal.dz

Angola
Caixa Postal No.704, Rua Fernao Mendes Pinto
No. 26–28
Bairro Alvalade, Luanda, Angola
Tel: 002442–322803
Fax: 002442–322803
Email: luo.taiheng@netangola.com

Antigua and Barbuda
Mckinnons Way, St. John's, Antigua, W.I.
P. O. Box 1355
Tel: 001–809–4626414
Fax: 001–809–4620986

Argentina
La Pampa 3410, Buenos Aires, Argentina
Tel: 0054–1-5541258, 5542613
Fax: 0054–1-5538939
Email: ofeccocn@ba.net

Armenia
Nork-Marash, 9th Street, house 39, Yerevan,
Republic of Armenia 375048
Tel: 00374–1-655022, 651311, 653569
Fax: 00374–1-587898
Email: zzyswc@ns.r.am

Australia
15 Coronation Drive Yarralumla, ACT 2600
Canberra, Australia
Tel: 0061–2-62734785
Fax: 0061–2-62734987
Email: commerce@chinaembassy.org.au

Sydney, Australia
68 George Street, Redfern, New South Wales 2016,
Australia
Tel: 0061–2-6987788, 6987838
Fax: 0061–2-6987373
Email: eco@all.com.au

Melbourne, Australia
75–77 Irving Road, Toorak, Victoria 3142, Australia
Tel: 0061–3-95095547
Fax: 0061–3-98220320
Email: amjsch@netlink.com.au

Austria
A-1030 Wien, Metternichgasse 4, 1030 Vienna,
Austria
Tel: (00431) 7143149–19/20/21
Fax: (00431) 7143149–22
Email: handelsabtchina@aon.at

Azerbaijan
94 Str. T. Aliev, 370069, Azerbaijan, Baku
Tel: 99412–656214; 656215
Fax: 99412–988880
Mobile: 99450–2155718; 2155008
Email: zgswc@azeri.com, az@moftec.gov.cn

Bangladesh
Plot, 15, Park Road, Block-I, Baridhara, Dhaka,
Bangladesh
Tel: 00880–2-8823968, 8825272, 8823313
Fax: 00880–2-8823082
Email: checodhk@mail.citech-bd.com

The Bahamas
3rd Orchard Terrace Village Road, Nassau,
The Bahamas
P. O. Box SS6389
Tel: 1–242–3931960, 1–242–3931029
Fax: 1–242–3930733
Email: moftec_bahamas@sohu.com

Bahrain
Villa 928, Road 3118, Manama 331, State of Bahrain
Postal Address: P. O. BOX 5260, Manama, Bahrain
Tel: 973–233339
Fax: 973–272790
Email: chinacom@batelco.com.bh

Barbados
Maxwell Coast Road, Christ Church, Barbados, W. I.
P. O. Box 34A
Tel: 001–246–4283384
Fax: 001–246–4285860
Email: ecocom@sunbeach.net

Belarus
No.42, 22a Krasnoarmeiskaya Str, 220030 Minsk,
Belarus
Tel: 00375–17–2891413, 2292925, 2292928
Fax: 00375–17–2105841
Email: swchu@solo.by

Belgium
Boulevard General Jacques 19, 1050 Bruxelles,
Belgium
Tel: 0032–2-6404210
Fax: 0032–2-6403595
Email: comoffchnmsn@pophost.eunet.be

Benin
Route No. 2 De I'Aeroport Zone Des Ambassades,
Cotonou, Benin 08–0167 (or) 08–0462 Cotonou,
Benin
Tel: 00229–301909, 301097
Fax: 00229–301639

Bolivia
Calle H No. 100, Achumani, Sectors San Ramon,
La Paz, Bolivia
Tel: 00591–2-794567
Fax: 00591–2-797577

Bosnia and Herzegovina
Brace Begica 17, 71000 Sarajevo
Tel: 00387–215107
Fax: 00387–215108
Email: ecobh@bih.net.ba

Botswana
3097 North Ring Road, Gaborone, Botswana
P. O. Box 1031, Gaborone, Botswana
Tel: 00267–353270, 352209
Fax: 00267–300156

Brazil
SHIS QL 8, Conjunto 5, Casa 20, Lago Sul,
Brasilia-DF
CEP: 71620–255, Brasilia-DF, Brasil
Tel: 0055–61–2481446/2485205/2480776
Fax: 0055–61–2482139
Email: sanab843
ebmaster@chinaembaco.org.br

Sao Paulo, Brazil
Rua Estados Unidos, 170-Jardim America, CEP
01437, Sao Paulo-SP, Brazil
Tel: 0055–11–2829877, 8522663
Fax: 0055–11–30641813
Email: conchi@sti.com.br

Rio de Janeiro, Brazil
Rua Muniz Barretots Botafogo, Kio De Janeird, CEP
22251–090 Brazil
Tel: 0055–21–5514878
Fax: 0055–21–5515736, 5514533
Email: comeeco@uol.com.br

Brunei
Simpang 462 Lot 38868 KG Sungai Tilong Jalan
Muara Negara Brunei Darussalam
Tel: 006732–340891
Fax: 006732–335163 338277
Email: embcc@brunet.bn

Bulgaria
Sofia 3, 9, 'Pler Degelder' Str, 1113, Sofia, Bulgaria
Tel: 00359–2-724988, 9712032
Fax: 00359–2-9712416
Email: chinabiz@cn-bg.com

Burundi
Sur La Parcelle 675 a Vugizo, Bujumbura, Burundi
Tel: 00257–224246, 222558
Fax: 00257–221962
Telex: 5137 BCCHINE BDI
Email: conec@crinf.com

Cape Verde
C.P. No. 8, Praia; Achada De Santo Antonio Praia,
Republica De Cabo Verde
Tel: 00238–623029
Fax: 00238–623007
Email: cv@moftec.gov.cn

Cambodia
No. 156 BLC Mao Tsetung Phnom Penh, Cambodia
Tel: 00855–23–720923
Fax: 00855–23–720924

Cameroon
B.P. 11608 Yaounde Cameroun Ambassade De Chine
Tel: 00237–209522, 203191
Fax: 00237–210091

Douala, Cameroon
B.P. 2983, Douala, Cameroon
Tel: 00237–3425437
Fax: 00237–3422268
Email: consulchina@iccnet2000.com
douala@moftec.gov.cn

Canada
401 King Edward Avenue, Ontario, Canada K1N 9C9
Tel: 1–613–236–8828
Fax: 1–613–236–5078
Email: ecoffice@buildlink.com

Vancouver, Canada
3380 Granville Street, Vancouver BC, Canada
V6H 3K3
Tel: 001–604–7364021
Fax: 001–604–7364343
Telex: 04–54659
Email: ecomms@infoserve.net

Toronto, Canada
240 St. George Street, Toronto, Ontario, Canada,
M5R 2P4
Tel: 001–416–3246455, 3246454
Fax: 001–416–3246468

Calgary, Canada
Suite 100, 1011 6th Avenue SW, Calgary, Alberta,
Canada T2P 0W1
Tel: 001–403–264–3322
Fax: 001–403–264–6656

Central African Republic
Avenue des Martyrs Bangui, Central African Republic
Tel: 00236–614682
Fax: 00236–614358

Chile
Casilla 3417; Av. Pedro De Valdivia 1032,
Providencia, Santiago, Chile
Tel: 0056–2-2239988
Fax: 0056–2-2232465

Comores
B.P. 442 Moroni Comores
Tel: 00269–732937
Fax: 00269–732937
Email: jingsc@snpt.km

Congo, Democratic Republic of
466, Av. Colonel Lukusa, Kinshasa/Gombe,
Democratic Republic of Congo
Tel: 00243–12–26210, 83076, 46507
Fax: 001–212–3769255

Brazzaville, Congo
Avenue Monseigneur Augouard, Brazzaville, Congo
B.P. 2838, Brazzaville, Congo
Tel: 00242–830952
Fax: 00242–837702

Cote D'Ivoire
06 B.P. 206 Abidjan 06 Cote D'Ivoire
Tel: 00225–22420102
Fax: 00225- 22426373
Email: ci@moftec.gov.cn

Colombia
Cra.16 No.98–30, Bogota D.C,
Republica de Colombia
Tel: 00571–6222879 6223103
Fax: 00571–6223114
Email: ecocnco@hotmail.com
co@moftec.gov.cn

Croatia
Bukovacka 8A, 10000 Zagreb, Croatia
Tel: 00385–1-2421646, 2304546
Fax: 00385–1-2304484, 2421686
Email: e.c.office.chn@zg.tel.hr

Cuba
La, Calle 42, No. 313, 5 Avenid Miramar Playa,
Ciudad De La Habana, Cuba
Tel: 0053–7-332585
Fax: 0053–7-331021
Email: ecomochn@ip.etecsa.cu

Cyprus
P. O. Box 7088, No. 17 Agapinor Street, Nicosia,
Cyprus
Tel: 00357–2-375252
Fax: 00357–2-376699
Email: shangwu@cytanet.com.cy

Czech Republic
Velvyslsnectvi Cinske Li Dove, Republiky Obchodni
Oddeleni Pelleova 22 16000 Praha 6-Bubenec
Tel: 0042–2-24311324, 33028872
Fax: 0042–2- 33028876
Email: ec.embcn@cmail.cz

Denmark
Oeregaards Alle 12, DK – 2900 Hellerup,
Copenhagen, Denmark
Tel: 0045–39611013
Fax: 0045–39612913
Telex: 0045–19106 CHCOEM DK
Email: ecc@post7.tele.dk

Djibouti
Rue De Nairobi, Heron, Djibouti B.P. 4001 Djibouti
Tel: 00253–350575
Fax: 00253–354174

Dominican Republic
Calle Repoblacion Forestal No. 7, Edificio
Don Samudl, Los Millones, Apartado Postal 3513,
Santo Domingo, Republica Dominicana
Tel: 00566–2620, 7063, 8430, 567–3480
Fax: (1–809) 566–2620

Ecuador
Av. Atahualpa No. 349 Y Av. Amazonas Quito-Ecuador
Casilla 17–110–5143
Tel: 00593–2-2444362, 2433474
Fax: 00593–2-2433474
Email: ecocnec@hotmail.com

Egypt
22, Bahgat Aly Street, Zamalek, Cairo, Egypt
Tel: 00202–3404316, 3417423
Fax: 00202–7358728, 7362094
Email: ccechina@soficom.com.eg

Equatorial Guinea
Calle De Independencia 26-B-2 Consejero
Economico-Comercial De La Embajada De La
Republica Popular China En La Republica De Guinea
Ecuatorial
P. O. Box Malabo, No. 44
Tel: 00240–9-3440
Fax: 00240–9-3459

Eritrea
Eritrea Asmara Zone 4 Adm. 02 Street No. 702
Hause No. 74, P. O. Box 204
Tel: 002911–182273
Fax: 002911–182200

Estonia
Juhkentali 21, EE0001 Tallinn, Estonia
Tel: 00372–6607867, 6607868
Fax: 00372–6607818
Email: chincoff@online.ee

Ethiopia
High 24, Kebele 13, House, No. 729 Jimma Road,
Addis Ababa, Ethiopia
P. O. Box 5643
Tel: 002511–712266
Fax: 002511–710059, 713066

Fiji
147 Queen Elizabeth Drive, Private Mail Bag, Suva, Fiji
Tel: 00679–3304817 ext. 17
Fax: 00679–3304564

Finland
Vahanityntie 4, 00570 Helsinki 57, Finland
Tel: 00358–9-6848416, 6849641
Fax: 00358–9-6849595
Email: fin.shangwu@kolumbus.fi
Telex: 126055 CHINA SF

France
21, Rue De L'Amiral D'Estaing, 75016 Paris, France
Tel: 0033-1-53577000
Fax: 0033-1-47209471
Email: shangwu@amb-chine.fr, eccochn@sysium.com

Gabon
B.P. 3914 Libreville, Gabon
Tel: 00241–732873, 738839
Fax: 00241–738645, 738887

Georgia
52 Barnov Str., 380008 Tbilisi, Georgia
Tel: 0099532–983953
Fax: 0099532–931276
Email: gzj@access.sanet.ge

Germany
Selma-Lagerloef-Str. 11, 13189 Berlin, Germany
Tel 0049–30–47901910
Fax: 0049–30–4710230
Email: mail@trade-embassy-china.de
trade-embassy.china@snafu.de
Website: www.trade-embassy-china.de

Bonn, Germany
Friedrich-Ebert-Str. 59, 53177 Bonn Bad Godesberg,
Germany
Tel: 0049–228–955940
Fax: 0049–228–356781
Email: trade-bonn.cn@debitel.net

Hamburg, Germany
Elbchaussee 268, 22605 Hamburg, Germany
Tel: 0049–40–82276012, 82276016
Fax: 0049–40–82276021
Email: trade.consulate.cn.hh@t-online.de

Ghana
P. O. Box M344 Airport Residential Area, Accra,
Ghana
Tel: 00233–21–777462, 772541
Fax: 00233–21–777462, 772541
Email: jshchu@ghana.com

Greece
Diadochou Pavlou 7, P, Psychikon, 154, 52 Athens,
Greece
Tel: 0030–1-6723281
Fax: 0030–1-6741575
Telex: 226848 CPRC GR
Email: eccoprc@otenet.gr

Guinea
Bureau Du Conseiller Economique
Et Commercial Pres Ambassade De La Republique
Populaire De Chine En Republique De Guinee
B.P. 714 Conakry, Republic of Guinea
Tel: 001–224–464366
Fax: 001–212–4794818

Guinea-Bissau
Av. Francisco Joao Mendes, Bissau, Guineau-Bissau
Tel: 00245–203637
Fax: 00245–203590

Guyana
52, Brickdam, Georgetown, Cooperative Republic
Guyana
P. O. Box.101195
Tel: 00592–226-9965, 592–226-7428
Fax: 00592–226-4308
Email: guyecoc@networksgy.com
Website: www.guyana-in.com

Hungary
1068 Budapest, Benczur U. 17, Hungary
Tel: 0036–1-3225242
Fax: 0036–1-3229067
Email: shangwu@elender.hu

Iceland
Vidimelur 25, Reykjavik, Iceland
P. O. Box 7290 Reykjavik
Tel: 00354–1-5526322
Fax: 00354–1-5623922
Email: chinacom@chinacommercial.is

Indonesia
JL. Mega Kuningan, Barat 10, No. 2, Jakarta 12950,
Indonesia
Tel: 0062–21-5761047, 5761048, 5761049,
5761050
Fax: 0062–21-5761051
Email: cydcww@indosat.net.id, muxinh@indosat.net.id

India
No. 50, D-Shantipath Chanakyapuri, New Delhi
110021, India
Tel: 0091–11-4672687
Fax: 0091–11-6111099
Email: chinacom@del6.vsnl.net.in
chinacom@ndf.vsnl.net.in

Bombay, India
P. O. Box 189, GPO, Mumdai 400001, India
Tel: 0091–22-24915863
Fax: 0091–22-24924945

Iran
No.180, Farmanieh Ave, Tehran, Iran
Tel: 0098–21-2561567
Fax: 0098–21-2292283
Email: chinacom@neda.net, chinacom@dci.co.ir

Iraq
P. O. Box 15097, Al-Yarmuk, Baghdad, Iraq
Tel: 00964–1-5567897, 5562740
Telex: 2195 Chincom IK

Ireland
77, Allesbury Road, Dublin 4, Ireland
Tel: 00353–1-2600580
Fax: 00353–1-2696966
Telex: 91834 CODE EI
Email: chinacomm@tinet.ie

Israel
94, Derech Namir Road, Tel Aviv, 62337, Israel
Tel: 00972–3-5465922
Fax: 00972–3-5465926
Email: il@moftec.gov.cn

Italy
Via Della Camilluccia 613, 00135 Rome, Italy
Tel: 0039–6-36308534, 36303856
Fax: 0039–6-36308552
Telex: 622162 CINAC I
Email: gckli@tin.it/qigaoh@tin.it
Uffcomcina.uffcomcina@tin.it

Milan, Italy
Via Paleocapa, 4–2-21 Milan, Italy
Tel: 0039–2-72021905, 72021988
Fax: 0039–2-86452219

Kazakhstan
No.137, Furmanov Street, Almaty, Kazakhstan
Tel: 007–3272–533618
Email: ekcochina@asdc.kz

Korea, Democratic People's Republic of
Kinmaeuli Dong, Mao Lang Bong District,
Pyongyang, Democratic People's Republic of Korea
Tel: 00850–2-3813119, 3813120
Fax: 00850–2-3813425, 3813442

Korea, Republic of
Tel: 00822–22537521
Fax: 00822–22537524
Email: cninkr@thrunet.com

Pusan of the Republic of Korea
1418, U-2 Dong, Haeundae, Busan, Korea
Tel: 82–51-742-4991/2
Fax: 82–51-742-5446

Kuwait
Al-Shamiya, Block 8, Street 85, House No.4, Kuwait
Postal address: P. O. Box 25713
SAFAT, 13118 Safat, Kuwait
Tel: 00965–4822816, 4822817, 4817843
Fax: 00965–4822867, 4822873
Email: ecocom@qualitynet.net

Kyrghyzstan
Manac Ave.6 Bishkek 720017 Republic of Kyrgyz
Tel: 00996–312 665366, 224893, 224693, 224732, 660134
Fax: 00996–312 663148
Email: moftec@mail.elcat.kg

Jamaica
8, Seaview Ave, Kingston 10, Jamaica W.I.
Tel: 001–876–9276816
Fax: 001–876–9787780
Email: chinaemba@cwjamaica.com

Japan
5–8-16 Mono-Azabu, Minato-Ku, Tokyo, Japan
Tel: 0081–3-3440–2011
Fax: 0081–3-3446–8242
Email: cecj@ma.kcom.or.jp

Sapporo, Japan
5–1 Nishi 23-Chome Minam 13-J0 Chuo-Ku
Sapporo, Japan
Tel: 0081–11-5635563
Fax: 0081–11-5631818

Fukuoka, Japan
Fukuoka-Shi Chiuo-Ku Jigyohama 1–3-3, Japan
Tel: 0081–92–713–7532
Fax: 0081–92–781–8906

Osaka, Japan
Utsubohonmach1 3-Chome Osaka, Japan
Tel: 0081–6-4459471 0081–6-4459481
Fax: 0081–6-4459476

Jordan
No. 21, Zahran St. Southern Um Uthaina, Amman, Jordan
423 Um Essomaq & Khelda, Amman, 11821, Jordan
Postal Address: P. O. Box: 423, Amman 11821, Jordan
Tel: 00962–6-5516194
Fax: 00962–6-5537417
Email: jojsc@hotmail.com

Kenya
Ngong Road, Nairobi, Kenya
P. O. Box 48190, 47030, Nairobi
Tel: 00254–2-726180, 726179
Fax: 00254–2-713451, 726179
Email: chinakenya@yahoo.com
Website: www.chinakenya.com

Laos
Ruelle Vatnak Muong Sisattanak, Vientiane, Laos
Tel: 00856–21–253025, 253026
Mobile: 00856–020–513992
Fax: 00856–21–253024

Latvia
2 Darba Str. LV-1046 Riga, Latvia
Tel: 00371–7805475
Fax: 00371–7805470
Email: econ-ch@apollo.lv

Lebanon
71 Rue Nicolas Ibrahim Sursock, Ramlet El-Baida, Beirut, Lebanon
Postal address: P. O. Box 114–5098, Beirut
Tel: 00961–1-822493
Fax: 00961–1-826672
Email: becelb@hotmail.com
shixu_1999@hotmail.com

Lesotho
1st Floor, Block 2, 257 Oxford Road, Zuovo, Johannesburg
Tel: 011–8046311
Fax: 011–788–2428

Lithuania
Blindziu 34, LT-2004 Vilnius, Lithuania
Tel: 00370–2-722375, 722259, 722223
Fax: 00370–2-722161
Email: chinesecomoffice@tdd.lt

Libya
Near the petrol station No. 37, Kalkalish Street,
Tripoli, Libya
P. O. Box 6310 Andalus, Tripoli
Tel: 00218–21–4832237, 4831224, 4831234,
4838052
Fax: 00218–21–4831225, 4831877
Email: eccolibya@sina.com

Luxembourg
Boulevard General Jacques 19 1050 Bruxelles,
Belgique
Tel: 0032–0032–2-6404210
Fax: 0032–2-6403595
Email: comoffchnmsn@pophost.eunet.be

Malaysia
No. 39, Jalan Uiu Kelang, 68000 Ampang, Selangor
Darul Ehsan, Malaysia
Tel: 0060–3-4513226, 4513555
Fax: 0060–3-4513233
Email: comembmy@tm.net.my

Kuching, Malaysia
340 Fortune Garden, Lorong 5, Jalan Stampin Timur,
off Kuching by-pass, 93350
Kuching, Sarawak, Malaysia
Tel: 0060–82–461344
Fax: 0060–82–461424
Email: zhicun@tm.net.com

Malta
10, Oscar Testa Street, Attard BZN 02, Malta
Tel: 00–356–21433047, 21421891
Fax: 00–356–21421892
Email: eccochn@kemmunet.net.mt

Madagascar
Nanisana-Ambatobe, Antananarivo,
Republic of Madagascar
Tel: 261–20–2240856
Fax: 00261–20–2244529

Macedonia
St. Oslo 22-B 91000 Skopje, Republic of Macedonia
Tel: 00389 2 369658 369668
Fax: 00389 2 369688
Email: eco@mt.net.mk

Mali
B.P.1614, Bamako, Mali
Tel: 00223–223823
Fax: 00223–229019
Email: bcecmali@spider.toolnet.org

Mauritania
B.P. 5534, Nouakchott, R.I de Mauritanie
Tel: 0022–2-5251205/5252347
Fax: 0022–2-5258634
Email: bcecacm@opt.mr

Mauritius
Royal Road, Belle Rose, Rose Hill, Mauritius
Tel: 00230–4549113, 6755635
Fax: 00230–4540362, 6743523
Telex: 4829 CHINCOM IW
Email: ecocnemb@intnet.mu
mu@moftec.gov.cn

Mexico
Calle Platon No. 317, Col Polanco Mexico,
D.F.11560
Mexico, D.F.
Tel: 0052–5-2808592, 2802970
Fax: 0052–5-2804847, 2821646
Telex: 1763515 OCCHME
Email: ecocnmex@infoabc.com

Micronesia
P. O. Box 1836 Kolonia, Pohnpei
Federated States of Micronesia 96941
Tel: 00691–320–5072
Fax: 00691–320–7074

Moldova
Str. Anton Crihan Nr. 30 2009, Chisinau, Republic
of Moldova
Tel: 00373–2-213072, 222257, 225345
Fax: 00373–2-223335
Email: chnmd@chnmd.mld.net

Mongolia
No. 5 Friendship Street, Ulanbator, Mongolia
Tel: 009716–323940
Fax: 009716–311943

Morocco

2, Rue Mekki El-Bitaouri Souissi, Rabat, Morocco

Tel: 00212–7–752718, 754940

Fax: 00212–7–756966, 755769

Mozambique

Av. Do Zimbabwe N.1088 Maputo, Av. De Kim lL

Sung N.974

Maputo C.P.2545;C.P.1105

Tel: 00258–1–490306, 491879

Fax: 00258–1–490306, 491879

Email: coocai@teledata.mz

Myanmar

No. 53, Pyidaungsu Yeiktha Road, Yangon, Myanmar

Tel: 0095–2-35944

Fax: 0095–1-220386

Namibia

66 Gevers Street, Windhoek, Namibia

P. O. Box 21350

Tel: 00264–61–222702, 220210, 221460

Fax: 00264–61–221325

Email: nmbyjsc@iafrica.com.na

Nepal

Baluwater, Kathmandu, Nepal

Tel: 00977–1-434792

Email: ecco@info.com.np

The Netherlands

Groot Haesebroekseweg 2A 2243 EA Wassenaar,

The Netherlands

Tel: 0031-(0)70–5115559

Fax: 0031-(0)70–5111206

Email: coce@xs4all.nl

New Zealand

104a Korokoro Road, Lower Hutt, P. O. Box 12342,

Thorndon, Wellington, New Zealand

Tel: 00644–5870407

Fax: 00644–5870407

Email: chinaeco@paradise.net.nz

Website: www.chinaeco.org.nz

Niger

Boite Postale: 10777 Niamey, Republic of Niger

Tel: 00227–752859, 722126

Fax: 00227–752861, 722106

Email: ambbcec@intnet.ne

Nigeria

161A, Adeola Odeku Street, Victoria Island, Lagos,

Nigeria

P. O. Box 72697 V/I, Lagos

Tel: 00234–1-2612404, 2612414

Fax: 00234–1-2612414

Norway

Inkognitogaten 11, 0258 Oslo 2, Norway

Tel: 0047–22–560270, 438666, 449638

Fax: 0047–22–447230

Email: cnembn@online.no

zhouxinjian@moftec.gov.cn

Oman

Shati Al-Qurum, WAY3021, House No. 1784 3315

Ruwis Mascat, Sultanate of Oman

P. O. Box 3471 Ruwi, Post Code 112, Muscat,

Sultanate of Oman

Tel: 00968–697804

Fax: 00968–697482

Email: chinaceo@omantel.net.om

Pakistan

P. O. Box 2601, House No. 11, Street No. 19, F-8/2,

Islamabad, Pakistan

Tel: 0092–51–252426

Fax: 0092–51–256887

Email: ecco@comsats.net.pk

Karachi, Pakistan

43–6-B, Block 6, P.E.C.H.S. Karachi

Tel: 0092–21–4530523, 4530526

Fax: 0092–21–4530525

Panama

Edificio Torre Cosmos Campo Alegre, Calle Manuel

Maria Zcazabella Vista, Panama, Apartado 87–4631

Zona 7, Panama, Republic of Panama

Tel: 00507–654061, 654062

Fax: 00507–2654051, 2130265

Papua New Guinea

Sir John Guise Drive, Waigani, Papua New Guinea,

P. O. Box 1351, Boroko, Papua New Guinea

Tel: 00675–3251190

Fax: 675–3258247

Peru

Av. del Parque Norte 315, Corpac, San Isidro, Lima, Peru
P. O. Box 170140, Lima 17, Peru
Tel: 51–1-2261757, 2261728
Fax: 51-1-4750016
Email: ofcembch@amnet.com.pe
ofcechina@ofcechina.org.pe

The Philippines

No. 10, Flame Tree Road, South Forbes Park, Makati City 1200, Metro Manila, Philippines
Tel: 0063–2-8195991, 8195992, 8939067
Fax: 0063–2-8184553

Cebu, The Philippines

4th Fl. Eeurd Pacific Bldg, F. Gonzales Compound, Camputhaw St. Lahug Cebu City, 6000,
The Philippines
Tel: 006332–2316217, 2316218, 2316219
Fax: 006332–2315697
Tel: (During Holidays): 006332–2548727, 2548728
Email: wy-zh@hotmail.com

Poland

Str. Bonifraterska 1, 00–203 Warsaw, Poland
Tel: 0048–22-8313861, 8313836
Fax: 0048–22-6354211
Email: brhchiem@ipgate.pl
Telex: 813589 CHINA PL

Portugal

Rua Antonio De Saldanha, No 42, 1400, Lisbon, Portugal
Tel: 00351–21-3041266, 301 1947
Fax: 00351–21-3014950
Email: chinaembacom@mail.telepac.pt
Website: www.secom-china.com.pt

Qatar

No. 63, Al-Sham Street, West Bay Area, Doha
Postal Address: P. O. Box 17514, Doha, Qatar
Tel: 00974–4835680
Fax: 00974–4835184
Email: qcec@qatar.net.qa

Romania

Soseaua Nordului No.2, Bucharest, Romania
Tel: 0040–1-2321923
Fax: 0040–1-2307786
Telex: 11324 CHIAB R
Email: embchina@dial.kappa.ro

Russia

Tel: 007–095-9382111 1431544
Fax: 007–095-9382005
Email: shcach@dol.ru

Rwanda

B.P. 519 OU 182, Kigali, Rwanda
Tel: 00250–84965
Fax: 00250–84965
Email: becom@rwandal.com

Saudi Arabia

P. O. Box 99882 Riyadh 11625 Saudi Arabia
Tel: 00966–1-4655655, 4622485
Fax: 00966–1-4629617
00966–1-4629617
Email: comm-china@sol.net.sa

Jeddah, Saudi Arabia

Al-Andulous Road, Andulous Dist. (2)
P. O. Box 51373 Jeddah
21543 Jeddah, Kingdom of Saudi Arabia
Tel: 00966–2-6605430
Fax: 00966–2-6606546

Seychelles

P. O. Box 680 Victoria Mahe, Seychelles
Tel: 00248–266808
Fax: 00248–266866
Email: ecchina@seychelles.net

Sierra Leone

P. O. Box 778 B28, Kong Harman Road, Freetown, Sierra Leone
Tel: 00232–22-240075 (Economic Section), 240490 (Commercial Section), 240086
Fax: 00232–22-240086
Email: ecco@sierratel.sl

Singapore
150 Tanglin Road, Singapore 247969
Tel: 0065–67351716 64121900
Fax: 0065–67338590
Email: ecco@bizcn-sg.org.sg
jscsg@singnet.com.sg

Slovak Republic
Jeseneskeho 7, 811, 01, Bratislava, Slovenska Republika
Tel: 00421–2-52920154
Fax: 00421–2-52920153
Email: ekocn@ekocn.sk

Slovenia
Malci Beliceve 123 1000 Ljubljana, Republic of Slovenia
Tel: 00386–61–272759, 2005871/72/73
Fax: 00386–61–233838, 2005878
Email: ecco@china-embassy.si

South Africa
797 Park Street Clydesdale (Hatfiled) Pretoria 0083, South Africa
Tel: 0027–12–3440428, 0027–12–3441404
Fax: 0027–12–3440439
Email: commercial@chinese-embassy.co.za

Spain
Arturo Soria 142, Piso 2-A 28043 Madrid, Spain
Tel: 34–91–4132776/914135892/234 2244
Fax: 34–915194675
Email: prchina@es.dominios.net

Sri Lanka
120/3A Wijerama Mawatha, Colombo 07, Sri Lanka
Tel: 00941–684576–7
Fax: 00941–684578, 684579
Email: mhwtt@yahoo.com

Sudan
Manshia District, Khartoum, Sudan
P. O. Box 1425 Khartoum, Sudan
Tel: 00249–11–272274, 224816
Fax: 00249–11–272274

Suriname
4 Erosstraat, Paramaribo Suriname
P. O. Box 8116, Paramaribo, Suriname
Tel: 00597–451251/452352
Fax: 00597–452560
Email: ecco@sr.net

Sweden
Ringvagen 56 181 34 Lidingo, Sweden
Tel: 0046–8-7674083, 7679625, 7678740
Fax: 0046–8-7318404
Email: moftec.swe@swipnet.se

Switzerland
Widmannstr.7, 3074 Muri, Bern, Switzerland
Tel: 0041–31–9511401
Fax: 0041–31–9510575
Email: admin@sinoswiss.net

Syria
P. O. Box 2455, Damascus, Syria
Tel: 00963–11–6133008, 6133086
Fax: 00963–11–6133019
Telex: (0492) 413217 CHINEC SY
Email: eccoces@scs-net.org

Tajikistan
No. 143, Rudaki Street, Dushanbe, Republic of Tajikistan
Tel: 00992–372–244183, 242007
Fax: 00992–372–510024

Tanzania
No. 1390, Msasani Penisula Tanzania Plot No 3621, Msasani, Road Dar es Salaam (Economic), Tanzania
Tel: 00255–51–68198, 41288
Fax: 00255–51–66177

Thailand
57, Ratchadapisake Road, Bangkok 10310, Thailand
Tel: 0066–2-2457038, 2472122, 2474506
Fax: 0066–2-2472123
Email: clian@mozart.inst.cn.th

Songkhla, Thailand
9 Sadao Rood, Songkhla 9000, Thailand
Tel: 0066–74–322034, 325045
Fax: 0066–74–323772
Email: clian@mozart.inst.cn.th

Tonga
P. O. Box 877, Vuna Road, Nuku'alofa,
Kingdom of Tonga
Tel: 00676–24554 22899
Fax: 00676–22899 24595
Email: chinaton@kalianet.to

Togo
11, Rue Tevi-Benissan a Tokoin-Lycee B.P. 4714-
Lome-Togo
Tel: 00228–215470, 215243
Fax: 00228–218390, 215470
Email: sinoecom@cafe.lg

Trinidad and Tobago
40 Elizabeth Street, St. Clail Port of Spain, Trinidad,
W.I.
Tel: 001–809–6285556
Fax: 001–809–6288020

Tunis
Route De La Marsa KMG El Aouina 2405 Cite Taieb
M'Hiri, Tunis
Tel: 00216–1-845805
Fax: 00216–1-841996
Email: bcec.ambachine@email.ati.tn

Turkey
Horasan Sokak No.8, 06700 Gaziosmanpasa, Ankara,
Turkey
Tel: 0090–312–4377107
Fax: 0090–312–4466762
Email: tr@moftec.gov.cn

Istanbul, Turkey
The Economic and Commercial Section of the
Chinese Consulate in Istanbul Mecidiyekoy, Ortaklar
Cad. 14, Istanbul, Turkey
Tel: 0090–212–2666590
Fax: 0090–212–2992632
Telex: 26906 CCGT TR
Email: sws@netone.com.tr

Turkmenistan
744000 Turkmenistan Ashgabat Str. Sota Rustawely, 15
Tel: 00993–12 350269, 352308, 351928
Fax: 00993–12 510888
Email: ecchina@online.tm

Uganda
Plot 112–114–116, Luthuli Ave. Bugolobi
P. O. Box 8858, Kampala, Uganda
Tel: 00256–41–220572, 220578, 220570
Fax: 00256–41–220379
Email: cnecoug@infocom.co.ug

Ukraine
11, Lane Zemliancky, 252014, Kiev, Ukraine 01014
Tel: 380–44–2947710, 2948810
Fax: 380–44–2948040
Email: chinacom@ukrpack.net

United Arab Emirates
Al Falah Street, 1 th Lane, 35–1 Sector P. O. Box 25455
Abu Dhabi, UAE
Tel: 00971–2-6427073
Fax: 00971–2-764402
Email: Comchiem@emirates.net.ae

Dubai, UAE
P. O. Box 9374, Dubai, UAE
Tel: 00971–4–448032 00971–4–449445
Fax: 00971–4–448099
Email: moftec@emirates.net.ae

United Kingdom
Cleveland Court, 1–3 Leinster Gardens, London
W2 6DP, UK
Tel: 0044–207–2620253, 2623911, 7238923
Fax: 0044–207–7062777
Telex: 896440 CLEFSL G
Email: public@checo.demon.co.uk

United States of America
2133 Wisconsin Ave, NW, Washington DC 20007,
USA
Tel: 001–202–625–3380, 3360
Fax: 001–202–337–5864, 5845
Email: chinacom@erols.com

San Francisco, United States
1450 Laguna Street, San Francisco, CA 94115, USA
Tel: 001–415–5634858, 5634874
Fax: 001–415–5630494
Telex: 497021 CCSF

New York, United States
520 12 Avenue, New York, N.Y.10036, USA
Tel: 001–212–2123307404, 3307427, 3307428
Fax: 001–212–5020248

Los Angeles, United States
443 Shatto Place, Los Angeles, CA 90020, USA
Tel: 001–213–807–8016, 8017, 8026
Fax: 001–213–380–1961

Houston, United States
3417 Montrose Boulevard, Houston, Texas 77006,
USA
Tel: 001–713–5244064, 5240780, 5240778
Fax: 001–713–5243547
Email: moftec@wt.net

Chicago, United States
104 West Erie Street, Chicago, IL 60610, USA
Tel: 001–312–8030115
Fax: 001–312–8030114
Email: ccgc@ais.net

Uruguay
Calle Palma y Ombues No 6016, Montevideo,
Uruguay
Tel: 00598–2-6043899
Fax: 00598–2-6042637

Uzbekistan
No. 79, Akademik Yahyo G'Ulomoy Street, Tashkent
700047, Republic of Uzbekistan
Tel: 00–998–71–1206246

Vanuatu
Elluk Hill, Port Vila, Republic of Vanuatu
Postal Address: P. O. Box 210, Port Vila, Republic of
Vanuatu
Tel: 00678 28860
Fax: 00678 22730
Email: vu@moftec.gov.cn

Venezuela
Quinta La Orquidea Calle San Francisco Desviacion
San Pedro Urb. Prados Del Este Apartado 80520,
Zona Postal 1080-A, Caracas, Venezuela
Tel: 0058–2-9761678, 9762896

Vietnam
So Nha 46.52 Pho Hoang Dieu, Hanoi, Vietnam
Tel: 00966–2-6606546
Email: cscgc@dmp.net.sa

Ho Chi Minh City, Vietnam
So Nha 39 Ngnyen Thi Minh Khai, District 1,
Ho Chi Minh City, Vietnam
Tel: 00848–8292463
Fax: 00848–8231142

Western Samoa
Private Bag, Vailima, Apia, Western Samoa
Tel: 00685–20802
Fax: 00685–21115
Email: encco@samoa.net, encco@samoa.ws

Yemem
Al-Zubeiry Street, Sana'a, Yemen
Tel: 00967–1-275339, 275411
Fax: 00967–1-275339, 272298
Email: chinaeco-com@y.net.ye

Aden, Yemen
150# Andrus Street, Khormaksar, Aden, Republic of
Yemen
P. O. Box 6160 Khormaksay, Aden, Yemen
Tel: 00967–2-232630, 230968 71103966,
71103926;
00967–2-235599 ext. 121, 131, 132, 127, 123, 231,
125, 128
Fax: 00967–2-231377
Email: ecoccga@y.net.ye, liuchang@y.net.ye

Yugoslavia
Vasilija Gacese 5, 11000 Belgrad, Yugoslavia
Tel: 00381–11–651630, 651638
Fax: 00381–11–650726
Telex: 12492 CNCCO YU
Email: yu@moftec.gov.cn

Zambia
United Nations Avenue, Lusaka, Zambia
P. O. Box 31205 Lusaka, Zambia
Tel: 00260–1-253601, 262363, 264123
Fax: 00260–1-262363, 253001

Zanzibar

P. O. Box 1200 Zanzibar, Tanzania Chinese Consulate in Zanzibar
Tel: 0255–054–30816
Fax: 0255–054–32681

Zimbabwe

10, Cork Road, Avondale, Harare, Zimbabwe
P. O. Box 40 Harare, Zimbabwe; P .O. Box 1340, Harare, Zimbabwe
Tel: 00263–4-735194, 730516
Fax: 00263–4-700264, 735252
Email: eccoprc@samara.co.zw

The Permanent Mission of the People's Republic of China to the United Nations

West 66th Street, New York, NY 10023, USA
Tel: 001–212–6556100 001–212–6556152
Fax: 001–212–6556112
Email: fazhanzu@yahoo.com

The Permanent Mission of the People's Republic of China to the United Nations Industrial Development Organization

Untere Donaustrasse 41, 1020 Vienna, Austria
Tel: 00431–2163367, 2169380
Fax: 00431–2169389

The Permanent Mission of the People's Republic of China to the United Nations and Other International Organizations in Vienna

Poetzleinsdorfer Strasse 42, 1180 Vienna, Austria
Tel: 0043–0222–471364, 478338

The Permanent Mission of the People's Republic of China to the United Nations Office in Geneva and Other International Organizations in Switzerland

Chemin de Surville 11, 1213 Petit-Lancy, Geneva, Switzerland
Tel: 0041–22–7937013, 7933270
Fax: 0041–22–7937014
Email: eto.cn@ties.itu.int

Bureau du Sonseiller Economique et Commercial de la Mission de la Republique Populaire de China à la Communaute Europeenne

Boulevard General Jacques 19, 1050 Bruxelles, Belgique
Tel: 0032–2–6404210
Fax: 0032–2–6403595
Email: comoffchnmsn@pophost.eunet.be

Note: the above list of the commercial offices of the Chinese embassies and consulate generals is compiled with information available. Those not included herein are due to absence of relevant information.

Changes to the contact details of the Commercial Offices of PRC Embassies world-wide may be checked by visiting the MOFCOM website at http://english.mofcom.gov.cn/

Index

References in italic indicate figures or tables

A-share market 275
ABN Amro 276
accounting system 43, 47–48, 119–22, 129–30
  background 119–20, *121*
  concepts and bases 121–22
  due diligence problems 287
  international standards compared 129–30,
    131–48
  standards 120–21, *120*
Accounting System for Business Enterprises (ASBE)
    120
  comparison with international standards
    129–30, *131–48*
accounts, bank 256, 260–61
  exchange control 67
acquisitions *see* mergers and acquisitions
address and expressions, acceptable forms 154
Administration of Foreign Exchange (AFE) 66
Administration of Industry and Commerce (AIC)
    81–82, 105, 106
administrative regions
  household incomes 31–32, *33*
  population distribution 27, *27, 28*
advertising 235–36, 241–43, 365–69
  advertising companies 236, 366–67
  communicating brand information 241–43
  business partner searches 181
  growth rates *365, 366*
  internet 367–68, *368, 369*
  media 365–66
  most advertised products/services 367, *367*
advertising companies and agents 236, 366–67
advertising congestion 242
Advertising Law 368–69
advisers, using the services of 187–88, 193–94

AFE (Administration of Foreign Exchange) 66
after market, automotive components 312, 313–19,
    314, 315
  major issues 317–19, *317, 318, 319*
age distribution 28–29, *30*
agencies, employment 204–05, 207
agents and distributors 88, 183
Agreement of Agriculture 11–12
Agreement on the Application of Sanitary and
    Phytosanitary (SPS) Measures 11
Agreement on Technical Barriers to Trade 11
Agreement on Trade Related Aspects of Intellectual
    Property Rights (TRIPS) 13
Agricultural Bank of China 328
agricultural sector
  CBBC assistance 218
  subsidies 11–12
  2004 results 5
Agriculture and Rural Statistical Surveys 46
AIC *see* Administration of Industry and Commerce
air freight *214*, 214
air travel 382–84, *383*
airline services 383
airport construction fee levies 383–84
Aluminium Corporation of China (Chalco) 378
aluminium industry 378
AMCs (asset management companies) 329–30
Anheuser Busch 339
Anhui Ankal Automobile 326
Anhui Jianghuai Auto Co (JAC) 325
annual leave 91
annuities, patent fees 104
anti-competitive behaviour 55
anti-counterfeiting procedures 96, 240
anti-dumping measures 6, 12

anti-subsidy measures   12
antitrust review   283–84
appeals, IP applications   99–100, 103, 106, 107
approval authorities and processes
    FIEs   83, *83*
    JV contracts   196–97
arbitration   114–16, 207
    cultural attitudes   154
Arbitration Tribunals   114–15
articles of association   195, 196
Asahi Breweries   338
ASBE *see* Accounting System for Business Enterprises
asset acquisitions   281, 282, 283
asset and fund management, foreign banks   334
asset management companies (AMCs)   329–30
'assets treatment' accounting rules   *137–40*
auditing requirements   122
Auto Industry Development Policy   303
automotive components industry   312–21
    major after market issues   317–19, *317, 318,*
        319
    market entry   320–21, *321*
    market research   319–20
    market structure   312–16, *314, 315*
automotive industry   38, 303–11, 322–26
    commercial vehicles   322–26
    future developments   311
    government policy   303–04
    key players   304–11

B-shares   275
bad debts, taxation   126
BAIC *see* Beijing Automotive Industry Corporation
Baidu.com   337
balance of payments accounting system   47
'bananas'   186–87
Bank of China (BoC)   328, 329, 330, 331
Bank of Communications (BoCom)   333
banking services   255–59, 327–31, 332–34
    accounts   256, 260–61
    cash management   258
    city banks   329
    exchange-related services   256
    foreign bank investment   332–34
    foreign trade services   256–58, 264–65
    'market access' (WTO) obligations   56
    non-performing loans   329–30
    payments infrastructure   258–59
    private banks   329
    receivables management   259

regulatory structure   19, 255–56
    state sector   327–29
Baoshan Iron & Steel (Baosteel)   377–78
Basic Units Statistical Survey   45
beer market   338–39
Beijing
    consumerism survey   228, *229*, 230
    market research target   223
    venture capital activity   293
Beijing Administration of Industry and Commerce
    182
Beijing Automotive Industry Corporation (BAIC)
    304, 306, 309, 310, 325
Beijing City Commercial Bank   329
Beijing Foreign Enterprise Services Corporation
    (FESCO)   204
'Big Three'   309
bills of lading   76
biological material, patents for   101
BMW   307
BoC *see* Bank of China
BoCom (Bank of Communications)   333
BOE Technology   335–36
Bohai Bank   329
BOND (British Overseas Industrial Placement
    Programme)   202
bonds   274, 276–77
    exchange control   68
    Eximbank issues   266
book retailing market   375–76
booking notes, freight forwarding   75
border enforcement   107–08
borrowings, exchange controls   68
Bosch, after market joint ventures   315
bottled water market   338, *338*
branding practices   237, 238–43
    advertising   241–43
    brand loyalty   240–41
    brand protection   240
    local vs foreign   238–39
    selecting names   239–40
Brilliance China Automotive Holdings   307
British Overseas Industrial Placement Programme
    (BOND)   202
brokerage houses   276
Buddhism   153
bulletins, statistical   48
bureaucracy, 'midway' principle   174
bus market   323–24
business combinations *see* mergers and acquisitions

business ethics, consumerism survey   227, 228, *229*, 230

Business Meeting Package scheme, CBBC   216

business networks *see* networking practice

business norms *see* culture and cultural differences

business and investment partners   189–97
   approvals and registration   196–97
   assessing   182
   choosing   189–91
   identifying   180–82
   negotiating agreements   193–96
   reaching agreements   191–93
   relations with   244–46

business plans, drawing up JV agreements   192–93

business structures   81–89
   agencies   88
   common features   81–83, *83*
   compensation trade   87
   co-operative joint ventures   85
   equity joint ventures   84–85
   franchising   88–89
   joint ventures   88
   management contracts   87–88
   processing and assembly agreements   87
   representative offices   86
   wholly foreign-owned entities   85–86

business tax   125

buyer team, mergers and acquisitions   285

CAAC *see* Civil Aviation Administration of China

CAO (China Aviation Oil)   357

capital accounts   256, 261
   exchange controls on payments   68, 69–70

capital gains, taxation   125

capitalization requirements, FIEs   82–83, *83*

Carlyle Group   352

Carrefour   373, 374, *375*
   cost analysis for joining   235

cash-flow statements   193

cash management   258

Catalogue of Industrial Guidance for Foreign Investment   374

CBBC *see* China Britain Business Council

CBG (Chongqing Beer Group)   339

CBRC *see* China Banking Regulatory Commission

CCB *see* China Construction Bank

CCPIT (China Council for the Promotion of International Trade)   113

CCTV *see* China Central Television

census system   45

Central Military Commission (CMC)   7

Central People's Broadcast Station (CPBS)   250

Centre for Market and Trade Development (CMTD)   225

CEOZs (Coastal Economic Open Zones)   123

CAPA (Closer Economic Partnership Arrangement)   255

Chalco (Aluminium Corporation of China)   378

ChangAn Automotive Corporation   308–09, 310, 323, 325

Changshou Bus Company   324

Chery Automobile Co   310

Chevening Scholarship Programme   202

China Association of Futures Industry   272

China Aviation Oil (CAO)   357

China Banking Regulatory Commission (CBRC)   19, 255, 328, 330, 333

China Britain Business Council (CBBC)   215–18
   assistance to British business   215–17
   sectors of expertise   217, 218

China Britain Industrial Consortium   202

China Central Television (CCTV)   250, 353–54

China Construction Bank (CCB)   276, 328, 329, 330

China Council for the Promotion of International Trade (CCPIT)   113

China Development Report   48

China Domestic   214

China Galaxy Securities   276

China Insurance Regulatory Commission (CIRC)   346, 347, 350

China Insurance Group (CIG)   346

China International Chamber of Commerce (CICC)   113

China International Economic and Trade Arbitration Commission (CIETAC)   115

China Internet Network Information Centre (CNNIC)   368

China Life   348, 352

China Mainland Marketing Research Co survey   347–48

China Mobile   41, 380–81

China National Automated Payments System (CNAPS)   258

China National Foreign Trade Transportation Company (Sinotrans)   74, 75

China National Heavy Duty Truck Group (CNHTC)   325, 326

China National Nuclear Corporation (CNNC)   342–43

China National Offshore Oil Corporation (CNOOC)   355–56, *355*, 359

China National Petroleum Corporation (CNPC)   359

China Netcom   275, 380

China Ocean Shipping Agency (Penevico)   74–75

China Pacific Insurance Company   344

China Pacific Life   352

China Petrochemical Corporation (CPC) (Sinopec)   355, *355*, 356–57, 359

China Post   214

China Power International   341

China Resources Breweries (CRB)   339

China Securities Depository and Settlement Corp (CSDC)   276

China Securities Industry Association   272

China Securities Regulatory Commission (CSRC)   271–72, *272*, 274, 276, 334, 378

China Telecom   380–81

China Trade Mark Office (CTO)   94

China Unicom   380–81

China Wonder   276

Chinese vehicle manufacturers   309–11

chip manufacture (computer industry)   336

Chongqing Beer Group (CBG)   339

Chrysler Corporation   304

Chunlun   323

Cinda   329

CICC (China International Chamber of Commerce)   113

CIETAC (China International Economic and Trade Arbitration Commission)   115

CIG (China Insurance Group)   346

CIRC *see* China Insurance Regulatory Commission

Citibank   334

cities, government of   23–24, *25*

city banks   329

Civil Aviation Administration of China (CAAC)   74, 201

CJVs (cooperative joint ventures)   85

clean import loans   257

Closer Economic Partnership Arrangement (CEPA)   255

clothing, consumer spending on   37

CMC (Central Military Commission)   7

CMTD (Centre for Market and Trade Development)   225

CNAPS (China National Automated Payments System)   258

CNHTC (China National Heavy Duty Truck Group)   325, 326

CNNC (China National Nuclear Corporation)   342–43

CNNIC (China Internet Network Information Centre)   368

CNOOC *see* China National Offshore Oil Corporation

CNPC (China National Petroleum Corporation)   359

coal industry   342, *342*

Coastal Economic Open Zones (CEOZs)   123

Coca Cola   338

COFTEC *see* Commission of Foreign Trade and Economic Cooperation

'collectivism' aspect of culture   155, 161, *163,* 165

Commerce Bureaux, Commissions and Departments, contact details   391–96

commercial dispute resolution   113–16

Commercial Offices of PRC Embassies, contact details   397–410

commercial vehicle (CV) industry   322–26
   bus market   323–24
   location and ownership   322–23
   truck market   324–26

Commission of Foreign Trade and Economic Cooperation (COFTEC)   81, 83

commissions, government   *20*

commodity exchanges   272, 276

communication clashes *see* culture and cultural differences

Communication Technologies Forum (CTF)   218

communications market *see* telecommunications sector

community public relations   248

compensation trade   87

competition issues, automotive component industry   318, 320–21

computer games   336

computer technology industry   335–37
   IBM PC business acquisition   337
   manufacturing developments   335–37
   market size   335, *335*
   market segmentation   335, *335*
   protection of software   101

conciliation   113–14

Confucianism   152–53, 171

construction industry
   'market access' (WTO) obligations   56
   real estate and fixed assets investments survey   46

consulting firms   187

consumable product markets   338–40, *338, 339, 340*

consumer credit   234
consumer durable ownership   35, *36*
consumer loyalty, and *guanxi*   173–74
consumer market   26–42
  consumer confidence   40–41
  education   30–31, *31, 32*
  globalization   41
  household structure   29–30, *31*
  income levels   31–32, *32, 33*
  market dynamics   37–38, *38, 39*
  patterns of consumption   35–37, *35, 36, 37*
  population   26–29, *27, 28, 29, 30*
  public relations   248
  recent developments   41–42
  regional differences survey   227–32
  research   222–24, *223*
  savings   34, *34*
  selected markets   38–40
  2004 statistics   5, 8, *8*
consumer price index   *38*
consumer spending trends   36–37, *36*
consumerism, regional differences survey   227–32
  discussion and conclusion   228–31, *229*
  methods   228
consumption tax (CT)   125
contact persons, accessing networks via   175
contract negotiation   193–96
contracts of employment   206
contributor contact details   387–90
conventional priority, patent procurement   102
cooperative joint ventures (CJVs)   85
copper industry   379
copyright   95
corporate taxation   123–27
  computation of taxable income   125–26
Corporations Law   272
corruption
  business networks   169
  cultural roots   155
COSCO   373
cosmetics market   40, 41–42, 339–40, *339, 340*
counterfeiting
  automotive component industry   319
  procedures to counter   96, 240
courier services
  'market access' (WTO) obligations   56
court system   104
CPBS (Central People's Broadcast Station)   250
CPC *see* China Petrochemical Corporation
CRB (China Resources Breweries)   339

Crédit Agricole   333
credit card market   40, 41, 334
credit histories of Chinese companies   182
credit rating, Eximbank   266
CSDC (China Securities Depository and Settlement Corp)   276
CSRC *see* China Securities Regulatory Commission
CT (consumption tax)   125
CTF (Communication Technologies Forum)   218
CTO (China Trade Mark Office)   94
culture and cultural differences   151–57, 158–66
  attitudes   153–56
  business networks   171–73, *171*
  case study   161–62, *163*
  managing differences   164–66
  roots   151–53
  sources of communication clashes   162–64, *163*, 246
  tips for doing business   156–57
  traits   151, *151*
  western culture compared   159–61, *160*
currency   260
  accounting rules comparison   *143–44*
  exchange rate issues   8, 66
  foreign business involving RMBs   256
  foreign currency accounts   260–61
  foreign currency bonds   68
  restrictions on foreign   262
  taxation   127
current accounts   256, 260–61
customs regulations
  intellectual property   107–08
  mergers and acquisitions   282
  products   208–09
CV *see* commercial vehicle industry
CYC Holdings   276

DaimlerChrysler (DC)   306, 309
damages, IP rights infringements   105, 106–07
dangerous cargo lists   76
Datang International   341
DC *see* DaimlerChrysler; documentary credits
Delphi   321
depreciation of fixed assets, taxation   125–26
derivatives and hedging, international comparison *143*
designs, patents for   94, 101–05, 106–08
direct marketing tools   234
'discontinued operations' accounting rules   *145–46*
Discretionary Participation Feature (DPF) rules   *147*

dismissal of staff   91
   from JVs/WFOEs   206–07
   from representative offices   205
dispute resolution, commercial   113–16
   arbitration   114–16
   conciliation   113–14
   import contracts   183
   litigation   116
   negotiation and mediation   113
   WTO system   13–14
distribution   208–14
   automotive parts   317
   choice of channels   210–11, *212*
   entry into market   208–10, *209*
   forming JVs   210
   freight forwarding   74–77, *74, 76, 77*
   'market access' (WTO) obligations   55–56, 213
   structure   211–13, *212*
distributors and agents   183
dividends, taxation   125, 262
DMC *see* Dongfeng Motor Corporation
Document Collection service   257
documentary credit confirmation service   257
documentary credit negotiation service   257
documentary credits (DCs) (letters of credit)
   182–83, 257, 258
domestic airline services   383
domestic bank accounts   261
domestic express parcels market   214
domestic priority, patent procurement   102
donations, taxation on   126
Dongfeng Motor Corporation (DMC)   308, 309
   commercial vehicles   322, 325
double taxation avoidance   127
DPF (Discretionary Participation Feature) rules   *147*
due diligence *see* market entrants, essential advice;
   mergers and acquisitions: due diligence

'earnings per share' accounting rules   *144*
Economic and Technological Development Zones
   (ETDZs), taxation   123, 125
Economic Circulation Accounts System   48
economic performance and outlook   3–9, *3, 6, 7, 8*
education   30–31, *31, 32*
   investment partners   246
   see also training as a strategic marketing tool
Education and Training Export Group (ETEG)   202
egalitarianism aspect to Chinese culture   161, 165
EIT (Enterprise Income Tax)   124
EJVs (equity joint ventures)   84–85

electricity *see* energy industry
embassies, Chinese   180
   contact details   397–410
emissions standards   325–26
employees, relations with   247
employment and employment law   90–92, 204–07
   foreign participation in job market   92, 207
   in JVs and WFOEs   205–07
   in representative offices   204–05
   termination or employment   91–92
   terms of employment   91
employment permits   92
employment service providers   204–05, 207
energy industry   341–43
   market size   342, *342*
   oil and gas   355–58, *355*
   segmentation   342–43, *342*
Engel's coefficient   35
Enterprise Income Tax (EIT)   124
enterprise names, protection of   93–94
enterprise resource planning (ERP) systems   258
entertainment expenses, taxation   126
environmental consciousness, consumerism survey
   227–28, *229*, 229–30
environmental due diligence   109–12
   definition   109
   legislation   111–12
   mergers and acquisitions   288–89
   procedure for assessment   110–11
Environmental Impact Assessment Law   111–12
equities market *see* securities market
'equity instrument' accounting rules   *142*
equity joint ventures (EJVs)   84–85
equity (share) acquisitions   281, 282, 283
equity transfers, exchange controls   70
ERP (enterprise resource planning) systems   258
ETEG (Education and Training Export Group)   202
ETDZs *see* Economic and Technological
   Development Zones
ethylene production   359–60, *360, 361, 363*
European vehicle manufacturers   305–07
event publicity/marketing   251
exchange control system   65–73
   banking sector   256
   development   65–66
   distribution agreements   209
   foreign exchange accounts   67
   foreign resident organizations   66–70
   impact of WTO accession ..   70–72
exchange rates   8

exhibitions   181, 216
Eximbank *see* Export-Import Bank of China
'expense recognition' accounting rules   *137*
export buyer's credit   265
Export Credit Insurance Company   264, 265
Export-Import Bank of China (Eximbank)   264,
    265–66, 268
    articles of association   268–70
    major lines   265–66
    sources of finance and credit rating   266
export seller's credit   265
exports *see* foreign trade
express parcels market   214
expressions and forms of address   154
external guarantees, exchange controls   68

'face-saving' cultural values   153–54, 160
    in business networks   171, 172
'famous brands'   242–43
Fang Fenglei   334
FAW *see* First Auto Works
FCY payments, regulatory restrictions   262
FDI *see* foreign direct investment
feasibility studies, JV agreements   192
FESCO (Beijing Foreign Enterprise Services
    Corporation)   204
Fiat Auto   306–07
fieldwork practices, consumer market research   223–24
FIEs *see* foreign invested enterprises
financial record keeping, due diligence problems
    286–87
Financial Services China Committee, CBBC   218
financial statement accountancy rules   *131–34*
fines, taxation on   126
First Auto Works (FAW)   307, 308, 309
    commercial vehicles   322, 325
'first impressions'   244
first-to-file rule, trademark registration   98–99, 102
fixed line telephone services   380–81, *380*
food consumption   36, *36, 37*
food retailing   374–75, *375*
Ford Motor Co   305
forecasting quality issues, due diligence   287
foreign banks   332–34
    asset and fund management   333–34
    commercial   332–33
    credit cards   334
    investment banking   334
foreign currency accounts   260–61
foreign currency bonds, exchange controls   68

foreign direct investment (FDI)   6–7, *7*
foreign employees   92
foreign exchange *see* exchange control system
foreign favourable loans, Eximbank   266
foreign government concessionary loans   266
foreign invested enterprises (FIEs)   62
    approval authority   83, *83*
    capitalization   82–83, *83*
    distribution rights   209
    exchange control   67–70
    limitations on operations   82
    name registration   94
    taxation   123–27
    see also business structures
foreign investment
    oil and gas industries   357
    steel industry   378
foreign resident organizations, exchange control
    66–70
foreign trade   5–6, *6*, 58–62, 264–70
    bank services   256–58
    Eximbank   265–66, 268–70
    financing system   264–65
    outsourcing   183–84
    trade environment   58–59, *59, 60–61, 62*
    types of players   59–63
    vehicle export   311, 326
    WTO membership implications   11–13, 53–54,
        63–64, 266–67
foreign trade companies, national   61–62
Fortune Oil   357
franchising   88–89
    distribution channels   211
freight forwarding   74–77
    documentation   75–77
    traffic   75, *74, 76, 77*
freight transport, market size and segmentation
    213–14, *214*
fund management   276–77
funds flow accounting system   47
futures market   276

GAAP *see* General Accepted Accounting Principle*s*
GAIC *see* Guanzghou Automobile Industry
    Corporation
Gao Hua   334
gas industry   342, *342,* 355–58, *355*
GATS *see* General Agreement on Trade in Services
GDP growth statistics   3–4, *3,* 5
Geely Automobile Holdings   310

gender, population distribution by 28, *29*

General Accepted Accounting Principles (GAAP) 129, *131–48*

General Administration of Customs 107–08

General Administration of the Civil Aviation of China (CAAC) 74, 201

General Agreement on Trade in Services (GATS) 13, 351

General Motors (GM) 304–05

'gift exchange' norms 153

globalization of consumer market 41

GM (General Motors) 304–05

Goldman Sachs 276, 334

Google 337

government structure 16–25

    hierarchy 22–24, *22, 23, 24*

    National People's Congress 16–19, *17, 18*

    official ranking 24–25, *25*

    presidency 16, *16*

    State Council 18–21, *19, 20, 21, 22*

    relations with officials 247–48

    relations with organizations 249

    statistical system 44–45

Great Wall Asset Management 329, 330

gross domestic product accounting system 47

Guangdong Brewery 339

Guangdong River Triangle Region 293

Guangzhou

    consumerism survey 228, *229*, 229–30

    market research target 223

Guangzhou Automobile Group 307

Guanzghou Automobile Industry Corporation (GAIC) 307, 310

Guangzhou Iron & Steel 378

guanxi (connection) 155–56

    business networks 167, *168*, 169, 173–74

    mergers and acquisitions 286

    terminating business relationships 174

guanxiwang (network) 167–68, *168*, 169

    see also networking practice

Guangzhou Automobile Group 307

Hainan Motor Co 309

handset manufacture, telecoms industry 381

Hangzhou, consumerism survey 228, *229*, 230

Harbin Brewery 339

Harbin Hafei Motor Co 310–11, 323

'harmony' cultural value 171, 172–73

health consciousness, consumerism survey 227, *229*, 229, 230

heavy truck market 325

hedging and derivatives *143*, 260

Heineken 339

'hidden' decision-makers, relations with 245

'hierarchy' cultural value 171, 172

Hofstede's dimensions of culture 160, 161

holidays 91

home improvements market 375

Honda 307–08

Hong Kong arbitral awards 115–16

Hong Kong banks 255

hospitality norms 153

household structure 29–30, *31*

Household Survey 46–47

housing, consumer spending on 37

HSBC 332–33, 334

Hu Jintao 7, 16, *16*

Huadian International Power 341

Huaneng Power International 341

Huarong Asset Management 329

Huawei Technologies 380

human resource issues, mergers and acquisitions 288

Hunan Changefeng Motor Co 308

Hydis 335–36

hydro electricity 342, *342*

Hyundai Group 309

IAS *see* International Financial Reporting Standards

IBM sale 337

ICBC (Industrial and Commercial Bank of China) 328

IFRS *see* International Financial Reporting Standards

IIT (individual income tax) 127–28

image, projecting the right 244–45

import agency agreements 209, *209*

import and export chambers 181

import contracts 208–09, *209*

    key terms and conditions 182

import control system, MOFCOM 208

import services, banks 257

import tariffs

    automotive components 320

    reductions 54, *55*, 58–59, *59*

imports *see* foreign trade

income consolidation, taxation 126–27

income levels 31–32, *32, 33*

income tax 123–28

    corporate 123–27

individual   127–28
indirect marketing tools   234
individual income tax (IIT)   127–28
Industrial and Commercial Bank of China (ICBC)   328
industrial market research   221–22
industry and transportation statistical survey   46
industry associations   181
industry sector results (2004)   5
informal approach to business transactions, due diligence problems   287
information technology sector   337
    venture capital activity   292
in-house China teams, building up   186–87
injunctions, IP rights   105, 106
input-output accounting system   47
inspection certificates, booking notes, freight forwarding   76
inspection requirements, import contracts   183
institutional investors, increase in numbers   274, 275
insurance   344–52
    accounting rules comparisons   *146–48*
    foreign firms   348–51, *349*
    foreign trade related   264, 265
    historical development   344–46, *345, 346*
    import contract term   182
    legal and regulatory framework   346–47
    'market access' (WTO) obligations   57, 351–52
    market characteristics   347–48
    recent developments   352
intangible assets, taxation   126
intellectual property (IP) rights   93–96, 97–108
    border enforcement by customs   107–08
    anti-counterfeiting procedures   96
    copyright   95
    enterprise names   93–94
    increasing value   95–96
    industrial property rights   94–95
        patents   101–05, 106–07
        trademarks   97–101, 105–06
    mergers and acquisitions   288
    WTO obligations   13, 93
inter-company loans   262–63
interest rates   5, 8
internal organizations, relations with   246–47
international airline services   383
International Accounting Standards (IAS) *see* International Financial Reporting Standards
International Finance Corps   329

International Financial Reporting Standards (IFRS)   119, 120, 129–30
    comparison with PRC accounting regulations   *313–48*
International Trade Research Institute   225
internet
    advertising   367–68, *368, 369*
    search for business partners   182
    use   40
interpreters, problems with   185–86
interviews, market research   222–23, 225
inventions, patents for   94–95, 101–05, 106–08
investment   8–9
    levels (2004)   5
    see also foreign direct investment
investment banking, foreign banks   334
investment holding companies, exchange controls   70
investment partners *see* business and investment partners
investment profits and capital, exchange controls   69–70
IP *see* intellectual property rights
issues management, public relations   249
IT sector *see* information technology sector
Itochu   338

JAC (Anhui Jianghuai Auto Co)   325
Japanese vehicle manufacturers   307–09
JFE Steel   378
Jiang Zemin   7
Jinbei Auto Holdings   324
Joint Venture Law   193
joint ventures (JVs)   84–85, 88, 191–97
    approvals and registration   196–97
    business partners   189
    cultural issues   159, 161–66, *163*
    employment of staff   205–07
    foreign trade companies   210
    insurance entities   *349*
    negotiating contracts   193–96

Korean vehicle manufacturers   309

labour contracts   206
labour disputes   92
labour issues, mergers and acquisitions   288
Labour Law   90
land and buildings, due diligence issues   287–88
land use rights   287–88

language problems   184–86
large bus market   323, 324
large industrial enterprises with trading rights   62
Latin marks, registering Chinese versions   100–01
Launchpad scheme, CBBC   217
L/C (letters of credit) *see* documentary credits
leave, annual   91
Lenovo Group   337, 380
letters of credit (L/C) *see* documentary credits
'liability treatment' accountancy rules   *140–42*
life insurance   347
life styles, changes in   35–36
light bus market   323, 324
light truck market   325
liquidation administration, exchange controls   70
litigation, dispute resolution   116
living subsidies   90–91
loans, inter-company   262–63
'Loans against Exports'   257
lobbying role, CBBC   217
local authorities of commerce, contact details
    391–96
local government   23, *23, 24, 25*
local income tax   125
local research organizations, pros and cons of using
    226
local transfer cheques   258
location selection market research   223
'long-term orientation' cultural value   171, 172, 174
L'Oreal   340
loss carry-overs, taxation   126
LSM, steel industry investment   378

macro-economic controls   4–5
macro-economic indicators   3, *3*
macro-public relations   248–51
Madrid Agreement or Protocol   99
magazines
    advertising   366
    publicity   251
maintenance fees, patents   104
management contracts   87–88
management fees, taxation on   126
M&As *see* mergers and acquisitions
manufacturing advances   257
'market access' issues, China's WTO membership
    53–57
market economy, China as   6
market entrants, essential advice for   179–88
    agents and distributors   183

approaching market   180, *180, 181*
assessing business partners ..   182
automotive component industry   320
building in-house team   186–87
identifying business partners   180–82
key terms and conditions   182–83
language problems   184–86
location of ,market   179
sourcing from China   183–84, 184
using advisers   187–88
market intelligence, research compared   222,
    225–26
market research   221–26
    automotive component industry   317–18,
        319–20
    CBBC assistance   216
    consumer   222–24, *223*
    consumerism regional differences survey   227–32
    differences in environment   224–25
    industrial   221–22
    recommendations   225–26
market visits, CBBC   216
marketing of consumer products   233–37
    advertising   235–36
    branding   237
    pricing   233
    promotion   236
    sales practices   234, *234, 235*
mate's receipts, freight forwarding   75
Matushita   336
Mazda   309
media market   353–54, *353, 354*
    advertising   365–66
    public relations with   248–49
mediation and negotiation   113
medical care, consumer spending on   37
medical treatment allowances   90–91
medium bus market   323, 324
medium truck market   325
Memoranda of Understanding (MOUs)   191
mergers and acquisitions (M&As)   280–89
    accounting rules comparison   *135–36*
    antitrust review   283–84
    approvals and consents   282–83
    closing the deal   283
    due diligence   280–81, 285–89
    environmental concerns   288–89
    intellectual property   288
    land and buildings   287–88
    legal regime   280

structural issues 286–87
structuring the deal 281–82
taxes 282, 288
metal industry 377–79
Metro 373, 374, *375*
MFN ('most favoured nation') principle 10
micro public relations 244–48
Middle and Western Region 293
Midea 323
'midway' principle and bureaucracy 174–75
mini-bus market 323
ministries *20*
typical structure 22, *22*
Ministry of Commerce (MOFCOM) 19, 81, 83
acquisition approvals 282–83, 284
freight forwarding services 74
import control system 208
JV approval 197
Ministry of Communications (MOC) 74
Ministry of Finance (MOF), accounting regulations
120
Ministry of Foreign Trade and Economic
Cooperation (MOFTEC) 74, 75
Ministry of Labour and Social Security 90
Ministry of Railways (MOR) 74
mini-truck market 324, 325
Minmetals 379
Minsheng Bank 329
Mitsubishi 308
mobile phone services 381, *381*
MOC (Ministry of Communications) 74
MOF (Ministry of finance) 120
MOFCOM *see* Ministry of Commerce
MOFTEC *see* Ministry of Foreign Trade and
Economic Cooperation
monetary controls 4–5
MOR (Ministry of Railways) 74
Morgan Stanley 329–30, 334
'most favoured nation' (MFN) principle 10
Motorola 381
MOUs (Memoranda of Understanding) 191
multilateral development aid programmes 202
municipal level districts 24, *25*
'must review' documentation, due diligence processes
289

names
registration of business 93–94
selection of brand names 239–40
national assets accounting system 47–48

National Audit Office 19, *20*
National Bureau of Statistics (NBS) 4, 44, 45–48
National Economic Accounting System (SNA) 43,
47–48
national foreign trade companies 61–62
National People's Congress (NPC) 16–18, *17, 18*
local 23, *23, 24*
natural gas fuelled power 357–58
NBS *see* National Bureau of Statistics
negotiation and mediation 113
setting up JV agreements 193–96
Netease 337
networking practice 167–78, *168*
accessing business networks 175
effect of cultural values 171–73, *171*
implications and recommendations 173–76
references and bibliography 176–78
social networks compared 168–69
theoretical framework 169–71
New China companies 189–90
new plant varieties, patentability 101–02
NewMargin Corp 293
newspapers and journals 353, *354*
advertising 366
advertising for business partners 181
publicity 250–51
statistical 48
NGOs *see* non-governmental organizations
Nissan 308
Nokia 381
non-alcoholic drinks market 338, *338*
non-competition agreements 206
non-disclosure agreements 206
non-governmental organizations (NGOs), training
partnerships with industry 202
'non-market' economy, WTO treatment of China as
12
non-performing loans (NPLs) 327, 329–30
non-probability sampling 223
non-resident enterprises, taxation 127
non-stop distribution channels 211, *212*
'non-tariff' barriers *see* quotas
Noranda takeover 379
North East Region 293
NPC *see* National People's Congress
NPLs *see* non-performing loans
nuclear energy 342–43

Office for Restructuring the Economy 271
official rankings 24–25, *25*

offset programmes   202
offshore acquisition transactions   281, 283–84
oil industry   342, *342*, 355–58, *355*
Old China companies   190
OMIS (Overseas Market Introduction Service)   216
one-stop distribution channels   211, *212*
onshore acquisition transactions   281, 283–84
operations limitations, FIEs   82
Opinion Research Institute   225
oral communications, language problems   185–86
Orient asset management company   329
original vehicle manufacturer (OVM) market   312, 313, 315–16
outsourcing   183–84
overseas guarantees, Eximbank   265–66
overseas Chinese business networks   169
Overseas Market Introduction Service (OMIS)   216
overseas offices of Chinese companies   180
OVM *see* original vehicle manufacturer market
overtime   91

Pacific Group   348
packing credits   257
partners *see* business and investment partners
party organizations, relations with   246–47
Patent Re-examination Board   101, 103
patents   94–95, 101–05, 106–08
  enforcement   106–08
  procurement   101–05
'patience, persistence and product' (three Ps)   156–57
payments systems   258–59, 262–63
  automotive components industry   318–19, *319*
  trade finance   182–83, 258
PBOC *see* People's Bank of China
Penevico (China Ocean Shipping Agency)   74–75
People's Bank of China (PBOC)   19, *20*, 255, 327, 344
People's Insurance Company of China (PICC)   264, 265, 344, 346, 348
People's (PRC) Courts, dispute resolution   113–14, 115, 116
personal relationships, importance of   173
  see also guanxi
PESAs (preliminary environmental site assessments)   111
petrochemical industry   359–64, *360, 361, 362, 363*
PetroChina   355, *355*, 356, 357
Philips   336
PICC *see* People's Insurance Company of China
PingAn Group   348
pipeline project   356

plant varieties, patentability   101–02
population   26–29, *27, 28, 29, 30*
Population and Labour Statistical Survey   45–46
post-shipment finance   258
'power distance' cultural differences   160, 161, *163,* 165
  in business networking   172
pre-feasibility studies, JV agreements   191–92
preliminary environmental site assessments (PESAs)   111
preliminary injunctions, IP rights   105, 106
pre-shipment finance   257
presidency   7, 16, *16*
price controls   59, *62*
Prices Survey   47
pricing practices, consumer products   233
private banks   329
private enterprises   63
private property   41
probability sampling   223
probation periods, employment   205, 206
probationary contracts of employment   206
processing and assembly agreements   87
product introduction meetings   181
profit repatriation requirements   262
profits, exchange control   69–70
promotion practices, consumer products   236
promotional advertising *see* advertising
property insurance   347
provincial foreign trade companies   62
provincial government   23, *23, 24, 25*
  importance when choosing business partners   191
PSA Peugeot Citroen   306
public relations   244–51
  macro   248–51
  micro   244–48
publicity techniques   250–51
publishing sector   375–76

QDII (qualified domestic institutional investor) scheme   352
Qinshan No 2 Nuclear Power Plant 342
qualified domestic institutional investor (QDII) scheme   352
quota restrictions (non-tariff barriers)   11, 54, *55,* 58

radio
  advertising   366
  publicity   250

rail freight   *214*,   214
real estate market   38–40
receipts and payments, exchange controls   67–68
receivables management   259
'reciprocity' cultural value   171, 172, 174
record keeping, due diligence issues   286–87
recreational, educational and cultural services,
    consumer spending on   36–37, *36*
recruitment   90
red clause credits   257
redundancy   91–92
'Reference Paper'   55
regional differences
    automotive industry locations   304, 323–24
    consumerism survey   227–32, *229*
registration process, JV contracts   196
'related party' rules, international comparisons
    144–45
religion   151–53
Renesas   336
reporting differences, market research statistics   224
representative offices   86, 92
    CBBC assistance   217
    employment of staff   204–05
    lack of distribution rights   209–10
    name registration   94
research
    CBBC   216
    computer technology   336
    see also market research
research institutions   63, 225
residence certificates   92
resident enterprises, taxation   123–27
retailing   370–76
    distribution channels   211, 213
    effect of WTO entry   56, 374
    foreign entry   373–74
    key players   371–73   *371, 372, 373*
    recent developments   374–76, *375*
'revenue recognition' accounting rules   *136–37*
'risk/uncertainty avoidance' aspect to Chinese culture
    161, *163*
RMB *see* currency
RMB accounts   260, 261
Rolls-Royce, education and training example
    201–02
RT-mart   374
rural–urban differences
    household income   31–32, *32, 33*
    population distribution   27–28, *28*

SAB Miller   339
SAFE *see* State Administration of Foreign Exchange
safeguard measures, WTO   12
SAIC *see* Shanghai Automotive Industry Corporation;
    State Administration for
    Industry and Commerce
sales practices, consumer products   234, *234, 235*
sample products, import requirements   208–09
sampling practices, market research   223, *223*
Sarft *see* State Administration of Radio, Film and
    Television
SASAC *see* State-owned Asset Supervision and
    Administration Commission
savings levels   34, *34*
Scottish & Newcastle   338–39
SDPC *see* State Development Planning Commission
secondary market research information   221–22
Securities Law   272
securities market   271–79, 294
    current status   271–72, *272*
    future development trends   273–74
    key laws and regulations   278–79
    recent developments   275–77
    WTO accession   273
'segment reporting' accounting rules   *145*
self-reference criterion (SRC)   157
seminar visits   216–17
Senior Executive Development Programme, Rolls-
    Royce/CAAC   201
services sector, GATS obligations   13
SETC *see* State Economic and Trade Commission
settlement accounts   261
settlement and selling of foreign exchange   68–69
SEZs *see* Special Economic Zones
Shanghai, as market research target   223
Shanghai Automotive Industry Corporation (SAIC)
    304–05, 309, 324
Shanghai Pudong New Area   123
Shanghai Shipping Exchange   75
Shenyang Brilliance Jinbei Automotive Co   310
Shenzhen Stock Exchange (SZSE)   294
shipping guarantees   257
shipping orders, freight forwarding   75
shop intercept interviews, market research   223
Sina.com   337
Sinopec (China Petrochemical Corporation) group
    355, *355,* 356–57, 359
Sinotrans *see* China National Foreign Trade
    Transportation Company
SIPO *see* State Intellectual Property Office

'Smaller Five' 310
SME Board 294
SNA *see* National Economic Accounting System
social environment differences, statistical reporting
    224–25
social insurance system 90–91
social networks, business networks compared
    168–69
SOEs *see* state-owned enterprises
Sony Ericsson 381
Soueast (Fujian) Motor Corporation 308, 310
special committees, National People's Congress
    17–18
Special Economic Zones (SEZs), taxation 123, 124,
    125
SPS (Agreement on the Application of Sanitary and
    Phytosanitary Measures) 11
SRC (self-reference criterion) 157
Standard Chartered 333
Standing Committee, National People's Congress
    17
Star TV 354
State Administration for Industry and Commerce
    (SAIC) 81, 282, 284
State Administration of Foreign Exchange (SAFE)
    4, 65, 71, 72
    approval of foreign currency accounts 256,
        260–61
State Administration of Radio, Film and Television
    (Sarft) 353, 354
state banking sector 327–29
State Development Planning Commission (SDPC)
    202, 271
State Economic and Trade Commission (SETC)
    202, 312
State Intellectual Property Office (SIPO) 94, 101,
    103
State-owned Asset Supervision and Administration
    Commission (SASAC) 19, *20*
state-owned enterprises (SOEs) 62
    as business partners 189–91
State Postal Bureau, Beijing 214
State Statistical Bureau 224
state trading products 59, *60–61*
statistical work 43–49, 221
    analysis 48
    differences 224
    functions of government statistics 44
    National Bureau of Statistics surveys 45–47
    National Economic Accounting System 47–48

    origins and development 43–44
    publication and provision of data 48
steel industry 377–79
stock market *see* securities market
strategic petroleum reserve programme 357
street intercept interviews, market research 223
subsidies, employers to employees 90–91
Sunwin Bus 324
supermarkets/hypermarkets 234, *235*
surveys, annual and monthly statistical 45–47
Suzuki 308–09
synthetic materials production 360–64, *360, 361,*
    363
SZSE (Shenzhen Stock Exchange) 294

TAIC *see* Tianjin Auto Industry Corporation
tally reports, freight forwarding 75
Taoism 152
tariff rate reductions 54, *55*, 58–59, *59*
tax holidays and incentives 124–25, 282
tax periods 127
tax preferentials 288
taxable income, computation of 125–26
taxation 123–28
    corporate 123–27
    individual 127–28
    mergers and acquisitions 282, 288
technical certification 245
technical seminars 181
telecommunications sector 40, 41, 380–81
    fixed line 380–81, *380*
    handset manufacture 381
    'market access' (WTO) obligations 54–55
    mobile 381, *381*
    venture capital activity 292–93
television 353–54
    advertising 365–66
    publicity techniques 250
termination of employment 91–92
    JVs and WFOEs 206–07
    representative offices 205
Tesco 374, *375, 375*
textile industry, import restrictions 11
Tianjin Auto Industry Corporation (TAIC) 307,
    310
Tianjin Training Centre 201
'time' cultural value 171, 172
Ting Yi 338
toiletries market *see* cosmetics market
Toshiba 336

tourism   382–84, *382, 383*
Toyota   307
TRAB *see* Trademark Review and Adjudication
   Board
track record, importance in PR   245
trade defence instruments, regulation of   12–13
   see also anti-dumping
trade fairs   181
trade missions   181–82, 216
trade unions, relations with   246
Trademark Office   97, 99, 100
Trademark Review and Adjudication Board (TRAB)
   99–100
trademarks   94–95, 97–101, 105–06
   enforcement   105–06
   registration   97–101
training as strategic marketing tool   198–203
   British government endorsement   202–03
   CBBC role   218
   company-related benefits   200
   customer-related benefits   199–200
   Rolls-Royce approach   201–02
   types of activity   200–01
Training Centre, Tianjin   201
transparency principle   274
transportation and communications
   consumer spending   37
   freight forwarding   74–77, *74, 76, 77*
travel and tourism   382–84, *382, 383*
TRIPS (Agreement on Trade Related Aspects of
   Intellectual Property Rights)   13
truck market   324–26
Trust-mart   374
trust/mistrust values
   business networks   170, 171–72
   investment partners   245–46
Tsin-Hing group   375
turnover taxes   125
two-stop distribution channels   211, *212*

'uncertainty/risk avoidance' dimension   161, *163*
urban–rural differences
   household income   31–32, *32, 33*
   population distribution   27–28, *28*
US vehicle manufacturers   304–05
utility models, patents for   94–95, 101–05, 106–08

valuation issues, mergers and acquisitions   281–82
value added tax (VAT)   125
   automotive components   320

VAT *see* value added tax
VC *see* venture capital investment
venture capital (VC) investment   290–99
   activity   291–94
   chronological development   294, *295–99*
   SME Board   294
Viacom   354
visits to China   216–17
Volkswagen Group   305–06
Volvo   324

wages   90
   taxation of benefits and allowances   126
Wahawa Group   240
Wal-mart   373
water freight   213, *214*
wealth, personal   8, *8*
websites, statistical information   48
'well-known' trademarks   97–98
Wen Jiabao   7
western culture, Chinese culture compared   159–61,
   160
WFOEs *see* wholly foreign-owned entities
Wholesale and Retail trading and Catering Industry
   Statistical Survey   46
wholesale distribution services, WTO obligations
   55–56
wholly foreign-owned entities (WFOEs)   85–86,
   189
   distribution rights   209
   employment of staff   205–07
work permits, foreign employees   92
World Trade Organization (WTO) membership
   10–11, 81
   advertising activities   369
   automotive component industry   320
   banking sector   255, 258, 332
   distribution channels   213
   exchange rate controls   66, 70–73
   foreign trade   11–12, 63–64, 266–67
   freight forwarding   77
   insurance sector   351–52
   market access issues   10, 53–57, 58
   most favoured nation treatment   10–11
   petrochemical industry   364
   retail sector   374
   securities market   273
written communications, language problems
   184–85
WTO *see* World Trade Organization

Wuling Automotive   323–24, 325
Wumart   374–75

Xiamen King Long United Automotive Industry Co
    324, 326
Xian, consumerism survey results   228, *229*, 230

Yangtse River Region   293
Yuejin Automobile Group Corporation   306

Zeng Qinghong   16
Zero2Ipo Corp   293
Zhengzhou Yutong Coach Manufacturing Co   324,
    326
Zheshang Bank   329
Zhongsou.com   337
ZTE   380